CREATED EQUAL

CREATED EQUAL

A SOCIAL AND POLITICAL HISTORY OF THE UNITED STATES

BRIEF SECOND EDITION
VOLUME II ■ FROM 1865

Jacqueline Jones
Brandeis University

Peter H. Wood
Duke University

Thomas Borstelmann
University of Nebraska

Elaine Tyler May
University of Minnesota

Vicki L. Ruiz
University of California, Irvine

PEARSON
Longman

New York San Francisco Boston
London Toronto Sydney Tokyo Singapore Madrid
Mexico City Munich Paris Cape Town Hong Kong Montreal

Executive Editor: Michael Boezi
Development Editor: Marion B. Castellucci
Assistant Development Manager: David Kear
Executive Marketing Manager: Sue Westmoreland
Supplements Editor: Brian Belardi
Production Manager: Ellen MacElree
Project Coordination, Text Design, and Electronic Page Makeup: Electronic Publishing Services Inc., NYC
Cover Design Manager: Wendy Ann Fredericks
Cover Designer: Base Art Co., Ltd.
Cover and frontispiece photos: Courtesy of The Library of Congress
Photo Researcher: Photosearch, Inc.
Manufacturing Buyer: Lucy Hebard
Printer and Binder: Courier/Kendallville
Cover Printer: Coral Graphics

Credits for literary selections, selected maps and figures, and photos not credited on page appear on pages C-1 to C-2.

Library of Congress Cataloging-in-Publication Data

Created equal : a social and political history of the United States / Jacqueline Jones ... [et al.]. -- Brief 2nd ed.
   p. cm.
 Includes bibliographical references and index.
 ISBN-13: 978-0-321-42980-3 (Complete Edition)
 ISBN-10:   0-321-42980-X
 1. United States—History. 2. United States—Social conditions. 3. United States—Politics and government. 4. Pluralism (Social sciences)—United States—History. 5. Minorities—United States—History. 6. Pluralism (Social sciences)—United States—History—Sources. 7. Minorities—United States—History—Sources.
 E178.C86 2007
 973--dc22

                    2006101651

Please visit our website at http://www.ablongman.com

ISBN-13: 978-0-321-42980-3 (Complete Edition)
ISBN-10:   0-321-42980-X
ISBN-13: 978-0-321-42981-0 (Volume I: To 1877)
ISBN-10:   0-321-42981-8
ISBN-13: 978-0-321-42979-7 (Volume II: From 1865)
ISBN-10:   0-321-42979-6

ISBN-13: 978-0-205-77152-3 (Complete Edition
ISBN-10:   0-205-77152-1   Ala Carte)
ISBN-13: 978-0-205-77153-0 (Volume I: To 1877
ISBN-10:   0-205-77153-X   Ala Carte Edition)
ISBN-13: 978-0-205-77154-7 (Volume II: From 1865
ISBN-10:   0-205-77154-8   Ala Carte Edition)

6 7 8 9 10–CRK–10

1 2 3 4 5 6 7 8 9 10–CRK–15 14 13 12 11 10

To our own teachers, who helped set us on the historian's path, and to our students, who help keep us there. You have touched our intellects, our hearts, and our lives.

A nuestros propios maestros, quienes nos ayudaron a seguir en el sendero de historiador, y a nuestros estudiantes que ayudan a mantenernos alli. Usted ha tocado nuestros intelectos, nuestros corazones, y nuestras vidas.

Brief Contents

Detailed Contents

Maps

Figures and Tables

Figures

Tables

Preface

> *"We hold these truths to be self-evident: That all men are created equal; that they are endowed by their Creator with certain unalienable rights; that among these are life, liberty, and the pursuit of happiness. . . . "*

Ever since the Continental Congress approved the Declaration of Independence on July 4, 1776, the noble sentiments expressed in the document have inspired people in the United States and around the world. The Founding Fathers conceived of the new nation in what we today would consider narrow terms—as a political community of white men of property. Gradually, as the generations unfolded, diverse racial and ethnic groups, as well as women of all backgrounds, cited the Declaration in their struggle to achieve a more inclusive definition of American citizenship. American history is the story of various groups of men and women, all "created equal" in their common humanity, claiming an American identity for themselves.

In fact, American history consists of many stories—the story of territorial growth and expansion, the story of the rise of the middle class, the story of technological innovation and economic development, and the story of U.S. engagement with the wider world. *Created Equal* incorporates these traditional narratives into a new and fresh interpretation of American history, one that includes the stories of diverse groups of people and explores expanding notions of American identity. Not surprisingly, when we first published our overview, it took us more than a thousand pages to tell this dramatic story. But even as the first full-length edition of *Created Equal* rolled off the press, we knew that we wanted to tackle a shorter version. Our aim was not merely to lighten students' backpacks. Instead, we hoped to make this rich saga more accessible to a broad audience, so we published a brief edition several years ago. Since then we have revised the full edition, and we have now taken time to craft a second brief edition as well.

The Second Edition

This second brief edition of *Created Equal* retains and strengthens the basic structure of the original brief text—its organization, themes, and style. This edition covers key events during both administrations of President George W. Bush, adding new material in sections titled "The President and the War on Terrorism," "Security and Politics at Home," "The War in Iraq," and "The Election of 2004 and After." The second edition also includes substantial revisions that reflect the suggestions of the many instructors who used the first edition in their classrooms.

First-time users of the book told us that they appreciated the elements that make *Created Equal* unique. These elements include a strong chronological narrative emphasizing significant political developments throughout American history, the stories of individuals that enliven the narrative, and the intertwining of four themes: our rich social diversity, the changing natural environment, class and power relations, and ongoing globalization: the vital intersection of foreign and domestic affairs. We added new material related to all of these themes.

Several new features enhance the book's accessibility for students. At the request of instructors we have included an "Interpreting History" primary document feature in each chapter, and the new topics covered by these primary materials vary widely. For the eighteenth century, documents include a brochure recruiting German immigrants to Carolina (Chapter 5), a surprising Proclamation of Independence from 1776 (Chapter 7), and a candid discussion of demobilization by a Revolutionary War soldier (Chapter 8). Among the new texts for the nineteenth century are documents describing opportunities for sheep farming in New Mexico (Chapter 11), a Southern labor contract during Reconstruction (Chapter 15), and Congressional testimony regarding conduct of the 1898 War in the Philippines (Chapter 18). The new "Interpreting History" features for the twentieth century include songs of the Great Depression (Chapter 22), a provocative sermon by Martin Luther King Jr. concerning the Vietnam War (Chapter 26), and the views of two ministers on religion and politics in the 1980s (Chapter 28). We have added study questions with each document to encourage students to hone their critical thinking skills. Also, a glossary at the back of the book defines terms that are highlighted in the body of the text, providing a handy reference for students as they read.

Perhaps most important of all—since historical interpretation never stands still, and new research calls for deeper discussion—we have enlivened the narrative with fresh material in many chapters. Chapter 2, for example, concludes with a new section on dramatic changes in the early Chesapeake economy entitled "Tobacco Becomes a Way of Life," and Chapter 10 contains a new section on "The Market Revolution" of the early nineteenth century. The next five chapters (11-14) incorporate new material on such varied topics as the Erie Canal, the treatment of the insane, the role of immigrants in the Confederacy, and General Custer's defeat at the Little Big Horn. New opening vignettes concern industrialist Andrew Carnegie (Chapter 16) and the attacks of September 11, 2001 (Chapter 30).

Four Themes

We have chosen to highlight four significant themes that run throughout American history.

- **Diversity.** In considering the theme of diversity, we acknowledge that the formation of social identity is a central element of the American story. We examine how individual Americans have understood and identified themselves by gender, religion, region, income, race, and ethnicity, among other factors. Native Americans, African Americans, Spanish-speaking inhabitants of the Southwest, Chinese immigrants, members of the laboring classes, women of all groups—all of these people have played a major role in defining what it means to be an American. At the same time, diverse forms of identity are by no means fixed or static. For example, in the early twentieth century, a Russian immigrant garment worker on New York's Lower East Side might think of herself in any number of ways—as a Jew, an employee, a union member, a single woman, a resident of a thriving city—and these forms of identity might change over time, depending on the woman's circumstances.

- **Class and systems of power.** Socioeconomic class and power systems have shaped American society in profound ways, and an understanding of them is fundamental to understanding events in American history. Class and power structures take many forms. The institution of slavery denied people of African descent basic human freedoms. Class differences based on income and formal education mocked broader ideals of social equality. Some groups used the law to deny other groups the right to participate in the political system. Popular ideas related to alleged social differences and innate inferiority served to justify the treatment of certain groups as second-class citizens. U.S. military leaders launched military campaigns against vulnerable peoples within and outside the nation's borders. By the end of the nineteenth century, the United States boasted the largest and most comfortable middle class in the world—and yet the most substantial political and economic power was distributed among a relatively small contingent of white men. During the twentieth century, Americans dismantled the legal system of inequality that reduced blacks, women, and other groups to second-class citizenship. Nevertheless, a growing gap between the rich and poor continued to mock the notion of true equality.

- **Globalization.** The globalization of the United States' economy and society increased in recent decades. But as an immigrant nation and the modern world's superpower,

America has long been engaged with the rest of the world. Since the earliest days of colonial settlement, Americans have traded goods, cultural practices, and ideas with peoples outside their borders. America's foreign and domestic relations have always been intertwined. After World War II, Americans' fears of communism and the Soviet Union exerted a profound effect upon the country's politics and society. In the wake of the terrorist attacks of September 11, 2001, all Americans were forced to confront the role of the United States in the larger world, with all the opportunities and dangers that role entailed.

- **Environment.** The role of the environment in American history has been significant. The physical landscape has profoundly shaped American society, and has in turn been shaped by it. The theme of the environment is key to understanding cultural, political, and economic developments. Many Native American groups shared a sense of oneness with the land; for them, the material and spiritual worlds were intimately related. In contrast, many European Americans saw the land as a means of making a living or making money, or as the source of valuable raw materials—in other words, as a thing to be bought, sold, and used. The vast richness of the American landscape has provoked violent conflict over the years, even as it has formed a key component in American wealth and power. We examine regional differences in all geographical areas—not just the eastern seaboard.

These four themes serve as the lenses through which we view the traditional narrative framework of American history. Readers of *Created Equal* will understand the major political developments that shaped the country's past, as well as the role of diverse groups in initiating and reacting to those developments. Chapter 13, for example, which focuses on the 1850s, includes a detailed account of the effects of the slavery crisis on Congress and the political party system, as well as a discussion of shifting group identities affecting Indians, Latinos, northern women, and enslaved and free blacks. Chapter 18, focusing on the 1890s, covers the rise of the Populist party and stirrings of American imperialism, as well as a discussion of barriers to a U.S. workers' political party and challenges to traditional gender roles. Thus, *Created Equal* builds upon the basic history that forms the foundation of most major textbooks and offers a rich and comprehensive look at the past by including the stories of all Americans.

Chronological Organization

One of the challenges in writing *Created Equal* has been to emphasize the way in which the four major themes come together and influence each other, affecting specific generations of Americans. Thus, the text is organized into ten parts, most of these covering a generation. Many textbooks organize discussions of immigrants, cities, the West, and foreign diplomacy (to name a few topics) into separate chapters that cover large time periods. In contrast, *Created Equal* integrates material related to a variety of topics within individual chapters. Although the text adheres to a chronological organization, it stresses coherent discussions of specific topics within that framework. This provides students with a richer understanding of events. Chapter 15, for example, which covers the dozen or so years after the end of the Civil War, deals with Reconstruction in the South, Indian wars on the High Plains, and the rise of the women's and labor movements, stressing the relationships among all these developments. To cite another example: many texts devote a chapter exclusively to America's post–World War II rise to global power; *Created Equal* integrates material related to that development in a series of six chapters that cover the period of 1945 to 2006. Each of these chapters illustrates the effects of dramatic world developments on American social relations and domestic policy on a decade-by-decade basis. This approach allows readers to appreciate the rich complexity of any particular time period and to understand that major events occur not in a vacuum, but in a larger social context.

Special Features

The book includes a number of features designed to make American history clear and engaging to the reader, and to encourage students to "do" history on their own. These features include:

- **Parts and timelines.** *Created Equal* consists of ten parts covering three chapters each. An opening section that lays out the basic themes of the period introduces each part. Each part opener also includes an illustrated timeline highlighting major events covered in the three chapters that follow.

- **Chapter introductory vignettes and conclusions.** Each chapter begins with a story that introduces the reader to groups and individuals representative of the themes developed in the chapter. Among the chapter introductory vignettes are the stories of a Norwegian immigrant woman in Wisconsin (Chapter 12), a group of runaway slaves accused of treason by Confederate authorities in wartime (Chapter 14), Spanish-speaking inhabitants of northern New Mexico struggling to retain their culture in the face of an onslaught of European American settlers (Chapter 17), and a Sioux Indian boy at a government boarding school (Chapter 18). At the end of each chapter, a concluding section sums up the chapter's themes and points the reader toward the next chapter.

- **Maps, charts, pullout quotes, and artifacts.** Illustrations—photographs, tables, pictures of objects from the time period, and figures—enhance the narrative. Large maps offer geographical detail and invite students to see the relationship between geography and history. Highlighted quotes help the reader grasp the chapter's major themes.

- **"Interpreting History."** Every chapter includes a boxed feature entitled "Interpreting History." Each full-page box consists of an intriguing primary document on a topic relevant to the chapter's themes. Through these documents, we hear the voices of a variety of Americans, such as an eighteenth-century Virginia slave, a council of Cherokee women, industrial titan Andrew Carnegie, and environmental activist Rachel Carson. We have added a brief introduction before each original text, and we have placed several questions at the end of the feature in order to guide study and prompt further discussion.

- **"Sites to Visit" and "For Further Reading."** At the end of each chapter is a list of "Sites to Visit," identifying sites on the World Wide Web relevant to the chapter and occasionally listing the location of important historical sites and landmarks as well. There is also a list of suggested works related to each section of the chapter. These features encourage students to follow up on major topics on their own—either on the computer or in the library.

- *New!* **MyHistoryLab Icons** Icons in the margins throughout the book identify additional materials on MyHistoryLab.com, Longman's premium Web site for U.S. history. Each icon indicates the type of resource—document, image, map, video, or audio—and is placed in context to relate directly to the chapter contents and themes.

- **Glossary.** The second edition includes a glossary of terms culled from the text and defined at the back of the book. Sample terms (out of several hundred) include pocket veto, aqueduct, canal locks, sit-down strike, antebellum, carpetbaggers, scalawags, vigilantes, and fatigue work. Glossary terms are highlighted in **boldface type** in the chapter text.

Combining Social and Political History

In designing this book, we have built upon a strong chronological foundation, emphasizing change over time. After all, it is important to understand events in their full contemporary context as they unfold. Within this logical and familiar chronological framework, the text offers a unique combination of social and political perspectives. *Created Equal* introduces students to recent scholarship in social history as well as providing a firm grounding in the traditional political narrative. In each period, from the distant past to the present day, we have interwoven the important political developments with the social and economic changes taking place throughout the country.

Along the way, we incorporate numerous groups and individuals who impelled, and experienced, the nation's most significant changes. Their stories, both familiar and unfamiliar, enliven the narrative and help to provide a more accurate, thorough, and compelling view of the American past. We hope that readers will gain an understanding of our country's social diversity but also learn about the power relations that have shaped our past—which groups have had influence and how they have maintained and wielded that influence. *Created Equal* tells the evolving saga of America in all its complexity. It is the story of a diverse and idealistic people—"created equal," yet struggling through generations to achieve true equality.

The Authors

Supplements For Qualified College Adopters

Instructor Supplements

• *Instructor Resource Center* This instructor-only resource allows you to browse and download book-specific instructor resources (see below) and to receive immediate access and instructions on installing course management content to your campus server. If you already have access to CourseCompass, you can log in to the IRC immediately using your existing login and password. Otherwise, please visit the Instructor Resource Center at **www.ablongman.com/irc** to register for access today.

• *Instructor's Manual* This book-specific supplement offers suggestions on how to generate lively class discussion and involve students in active learning, as well as a file of exam questions and lists of resources, including films, slides, photo collections, records, and audio cassettes. It was prepared by Yvonne Johnson of Central Missouri University and Nancy Zens of Central Oregon Community College. ISBN: 0-205-56251-5.

• *Test Bank* Prepared by David Rice of the University of Florida, this test bank contains more than 3,500 objective, conceptual, and essay questions. All questions are keyed to specific pages in *Created Equal*, Brief Edition. ISBN: 0-205-56248-5.

• *TestGen-EQ Computerized Testing System* This flexible, easy-to-master computerized test bank includes all of the items in the printed test bank. The software allows instructors to edit existing questions and to add their own items. Tests can be printed in several different formats and can include features such as graphs and tables. ISBN: 0-205-53007-9.

• *Text-Specific Transparency Set* A set of full-color transparencies showing maps from the comprehensive edition of *Created Equal*. The transparencies are available for download at **www.ablongman.com/irc**.

• *PowerPoint Presentations* These presentations prepared to accompany the comprehensive version of *Created Equal* may include key points and terms for a lecture on the chapter, as well as full-color slides of selected important maps, graphs, and charts within a particular chapter. The presentations are available for download at **www.ablongman.com/irc**.

• *History Digital Media Archive CD-ROM* This resource contains electronic images, interactive and static maps, and video clips. ISBN: 0-321-14976-9.

• *Visual Archives of American History, Updated Edition* Available on two CD-ROMs, this encyclopedic collection of instructor resources contains dozens of narrated vignettes and videos, as well as hundreds of photos and illustrations. ISBN: 0-321-18694-X.

• *Discovering American History Through Maps and Views Transparencies* This set of 140 full-color acetates contains an introduction to teaching history through maps and a detailed commentary on each transparency. Prepared by Gerald Danzer of the University of Illinois at Chicago, the collection includes pictorial maps, views, photos, urban plans, building diagrams, and works of art. The transparencies are available for download at www.ablongman.com/irc.

• *History Video Program* Qualified adopters are granted access to our list of over 250 videos for classroom use. Adopters can choose 1 video per 100 books that are ordered each semester (maximum of 3 for each adopter). Videos are available for virtually every topic of United States history.

• *Readers and Biographies—Available at Half Price!* Qualified adopters can choose from more than 100 half-priced options to supplement *Created Equal*, Brief Second Edition. From comprehensive readers and brief biographies to discounted Penguin books, Longman has a wide selection of products to broaden your students' history experience beyond the textbook. To learn more about this special offer, visit us at www.ablongman.com/historyvaluepacks.

Student Supplements

• *Voices of* **Created Equal** This collection of primary sources, tied to the table of contents of *Created Equal*, includes both classic and lesser-known documents describing the rich mosaic of American life from the pre-contact era to the present day. Ranging from letters, diary excerpts, stories, and novels, to speeches, court cases, and government reports, these sources tell the story of American history in the words of those who lived it. These titles are available at no additional cost when bundled with a *Created Equal* text. Volume I ISBN: 0-321-39591-3; Volume II ISBN: 0-321-39599-9.

• *Study Guide* Created by William Pelz of De Paul University, each volume includes chapter outlines, significant themes and highlights, a glossary, learning enrichment ideas, sample test questions, exercises for identification and interpretation, and geography exercises based on maps in the brief version of *Created Equal*. Volume I ISBN: 0-205-56249-3; Volume II ISBN: 0-205-56250-7.

• *Study Card for American History* Students are given a chronological context to understand important political, diplomatic, social, economical, cultural, and technological events in American history on this study card. This study card is available at no additional cost when valuepacked with a new book. ISBN: 0-321-29232-4.

• *Research Navigator™ Guide* This guidebook includes exercises and tips on how to use the Internet to further your study of American history. It also includes an access code for Research Navigator™—the easiest way for students to start a research assignment or research paper. Research Navigator™ is composed of three exclusive databases of credible and reliable source material including EBSCO's ContentSelect™ Academic Journal Database, *New York Times* Search by Subject Archive, and "Best of the Web" Link Library. This comprehensive site also includes a detailed help section. Also available on MyHistoryLab. ISBN: 0-205-40838-9.

• *Longman American History Atlas* A full-color reference tool and visual guide to American history that includes almost 100 maps and covers the full scope of history. The Atlas is $3.00 when bundled with a new book. ISBN: 0-321-00486-8.

• *Mapping American History,* **Third Edition** This two-volume workbook, written by Sharon Bollinger of El Paso Community College, presents the basic geography of the United States, helping students place the history of the United States into perspective. Available at no additional cost to qualified college adopters when bundled with a new book. Volume I ISBN: 0-321-47559-3; Volume II ISBN: 0-321-47560-7.

Supplements for Students and Instructors

• *MyHistoryLab* MyHistory Lab is a comprehensive collection of Longman's online multimedia resources. Instructive, intuitive, and interactive, MyHistoryLab allows both students and professors to be a few clicks away from a host of materials that support your American history survey course: primary sources; maps and illustrations; quizzes and review materials; and an electronic version of the textbook itself. MyHistoryLab gives students dozens of different avenues in which to learn, explore, and analyze the material outside of the classroom, no matter what type of learner they are. One-Semester Student Access Code Card ISBN: 0-205-53961-0; Two-Semester Student Access Code Card ISBN: 0-205-53956-4; Course Compass Student Access Code Card ISBN: 0-205-53960-2; BlackBoard WEB CT Student Access Code Card ISBN: 0-205-55039-8. Available for purchase at **www.myhistorylab.com**, or packaged at no additional charge with your textbook.

• *MyHistoryKit* MyHistoryKit for American history contains a sampling of Longman's premium history content from MHL. This Web site includes practice tests to challenge students' knowledge, learning objectives and chapter summaries introducing the major American history topics, flashcards for help with studying and remembering terms and events, Web links to assist in the research process, media and primary source activities (documents, maps, video and audio clips, and more), and Research Navigator™. Available for purchase at **www.myhistorykit.com** or packaged at no additional cost with your textbook.

• *American History Study Site* The American History Study Site is an open-access Web site that is designed to support all of Longman's American history survey titles. Organized by topic, this Web site includes practice tests to challenge students' knowledge, flashcards for help with studying and remembering terms and events, and Web links to assist in the research process.

Meet the Authors

Jacqueline Jones teaches American history at Brandeis University, where she is Harry S. Truman Professor. She was born in Christiana, Delaware, a small town of 400 people in the northern part of the state. The local public school was desegregated in 1955, when she was a third grader. That event, combined with the peculiar social etiquette of relations between blacks and whites in the town, sparked her interest in American history. She attended the University of Delaware in nearby Newark and went on to graduate school at the University of Wisconsin, Madison, where she received her Ph.D. in history. Her scholarly interests have evolved over time, focusing on American labor, and women's, African American, and southern history. In 1999 she received a MacArthur Fellowship. One of her biggest challenges has been to balance her responsibilities as teacher, historian, wife, and mother (of two daughters). She is currently working on a history of Savannah, Georgia, during the Civil War era (1854–1872). She is the author of several books, including *Soldiers of Light and Love: Northern Teachers and Georgia Blacks* (1980); *Labor of Love, Labor of Sorrow: Black Women, Work, and Family Since Slavery* (1985), which won the Bancroft Prize and was a finalist for a Pulitzer Prize; *The Dispossessed: America's Underclasses Since the Civil War* (1992); and *American Work: Four Centuries of Black and White Labor* (1998). In 2001 she completed a memoir that recounts her childhood in *Christiana: Creek Walking: Growing Up in Delaware in the 1950s*.

Peter H. Wood was born in St. Louis (before the famous arch was built). He recalls seeing Jackie Robinson play against the Cardinals, visiting the courthouse where the *Dred Scott* case originated, and traveling up the Mississippi to Hannibal, birthplace of Mark Twain. Summer work on the northern Great Lakes aroused his interest in Native American cultures, past and present. He studied at Harvard (B.A., 1964; Ph.D., 1972) and at Oxford, where he was a Rhodes Scholar (1964–1966). His pioneering book *Black Majority* (1974), concerning slavery in colonial South Carolina, won the Beveridge Prize of the American Historical Association. Since 1975 he has taught early American history at Duke University, where he also coached the women's lacrosse club for three years. The topics of his articles range from the French explorer LaSalle to Gerald Ford's pardon of Richard Nixon. In 1989 he coedited *Powhatan's Mantle: Indians in the Colonial Southeast*. His demographic essay in that volume (now in a new edition) provided the first clear picture of population change in the eighteenth-century South. His most recent books are *Strange New Land: Africans in Colonial America* (2003) and *Weathering the Storm: Inside Winslow Homer's "Gulf Stream"* (2004). Dr. Wood has served on the boards of the Highlander Center, Harvard University, Houston's Rothko Chapel, the Menil Foundation, and the Institute of Early American History and Culture in Williamsburg. He is married to colonial historian Elizabeth Fenn; his varied interests include archaeology, documentary film, and growing gourds. He keeps a baseball bat used by Ted Williams beside his desk.

Thomas ("Tim") Borstelmann, the son of a university psychologist, taught and coached at the elementary and high school levels in Washington state and Colorado before returning to graduate school. From 1991 to 2003, he taught American history at Cornell University while living in Syracuse, New York, before becoming the Elwood N. and Katherine Thompson Distinguished Professor of Modern World History at the University of Nebraska–Lincoln. He lives with his wife, a health care administrator, and two sons in Lincoln. An avid bicyclist, runner, swimmer, and cross-country skier, he earned his B.A. from Stanford University in 1980 and Ph.D. from Duke University in 1990. He became a historian to figure out the Cold War and American race relations, in part because he had grown up in the South. His first book, concerning American relations with southern Africa in the mid-twentieth century, won the Stuart L. Bernath Book Prize of the Society for Historians of Foreign Relations. His second book, *The Cold War and the Color Line,* appeared in 2001. His commitment to the classroom earned him a major teaching award at Cornell, the Robert and Helen Appel Fellowship. He found writing *Created Equal* a natural complement to what he does in the classroom, trying to provide both telling details of the American past and the broad picture of how the United States has developed as it has. A specialist in U.S. foreign relations and modern world history, he is equally fascinated with domestic American politics and social change. He is currently working on a book about the United States and the world in the 1970s.

Elaine Tyler May grew up in the shadow of Hollywood, performing in neighborhood circuses with her friends. She went to high school before girls could play on sports teams, so she spent her after-school hours as a cheerleader and her summer days as a bodysurfing beach bum. Her passion for American history developed in college when she spent her junior year in Japan. The year was 1968. The Vietnam War was raging, along with turmoil at home. As an American in Asia, often called on to explain her nation's actions, she yearned for a deeper understanding of America's past and its place in the world. She returned home to study history at UCLA, where she earned her B.A., M.A., and Ph.D. She has taught at Princeton and Harvard Universities and since 1978 at the University of Minnesota. She has written four books examining the relationship between politics, public policy, and private life. Her widely acclaimed *Homeward Bound: American Families in the Cold War Era* was the first study to link the baby boom and suburbia to the politics of the Cold War. The *Chronicle of Higher Education* featured *Barren in the Promised Land: Childless Americans and the Pursuit of Happiness* as a pioneering study of the history of reproduction. *Lingua Franca* named her coedited volume *Here, There, and Everywhere: The Foreign Politics of American Popular Culture* a "Breakthrough Book." She served as president of the American Studies Association in 1996 and as Distinguished Fulbright Professor of American History in Dublin, Ireland, in 1997. She is married to historian Lary May and has three children, who have inherited their parents' passion for history.

Vicki L. Ruiz is a professor of history and Chicano/Latino studies at the University of California, Irvine. She is currently chair of the department of history. For her, history remains a grand adventure, one that she began at the kitchen table, listening to the stories of her mother and grandmother, and continued with the help of the local bookmobile. She read constantly as she sat on the dock, catching small fish ("grunts") to be used as bait on her father's fishing boat. As she grew older, she was promoted to working with her mother, selling tickets for the *Blue Sea II.* The first in her family to receive an advanced degree, she graduated from Gulf Coast Community College and Florida State University, then went on to earn a Ph.D. in history at Stanford in 1982, the fourth Mexican American woman to receive a doctorate in history. Her first book, *Cannery Women, Cannery Lives,* received an award from the National Women's Political Caucus, and her second, *From Out of the Shadows: Mexican Women in 20th-Century America,* was named a *Choice* Outstanding Academic Book of 1998 by the American Library Association. She is coeditor with Ellen Carol Dubois of *Unequal Sisters: A Multicultural Reader in U.S. Women's History.* She and Virginia Sánchez Korrol have also edited the three-volume *Latinas in the United States: A Historical Encyclopedia* and a recent anthology *Latina Legacies.* Ruiz and Sánchez Korrol were recognized by *Latina Magazine* as Latinas of the Year in Education for 2000 and in 2005 they received a "21 Leaders for the 21st Century" award by women's e-news network. In addition, she and Donna Gabaccia have completed the anthology *American Dreaming, Global Realities: Re-Thinking U.S. Immigration History.* Active in student mentorship projects, summer institutes for teachers, and public humanities programs, Dr. Ruiz served as an appointee to the National Council of the Humanities. A fellow in the Society of American Historians, she was elected to the national governing bodies of the American Historical Association, the Organization of American Historians, and the American Studies Association. Currently, she is immediate past president of both the Berkshire Conference of Women Historians and the Organization of American Historians. She is also the president-elect of the American Studies Association. The mother of two grown sons, she is married to Victor Becerra, urban planner and gourmet cook extraordinaire.

Acknowledgments

As authors, we could not have completed this project without the loving support of our families. We wish to thank Jeffrey Abramson, Lil Fenn, Lynn Borstelmann, Lary May, and Victor Becerra for their interest, forbearance, and encouragement over the course of several editions. Our own children have been a source of inspiration, as have our many students, past and present. We are grateful to scores of colleagues and friends who have helped shape this book, both directly and indirectly, in more ways than they know. Along the way, Matt Basso, Chad Cover, Eben Miller, Andrea Sachs, Mary Strunk, and Melissa Williams provided useful research and administrative assistance; their help was invaluable. Louis Balizet provided careful reading of several chapter drafts.

Our friends at Longman have continued their generous support and assistance for our efforts. We thank all the creative people associated with Longman (and there are many) who have had a hand in bringing this book to life. We are especially grateful to Michael Boezi and Marion Castellucci for their care and encouragement in bringing this edition to life. Former Development Manager Betty Slack improved the text in lasting ways; Executive Marketing Manager Sue Westmoreland and her great sales force have embraced the book with enthusiasm. We also acknowledge with gratitude the contributions of Managing Editor Val Zaborski, Production Manager Ellen MacElree, and Production Editor Scott Hitchcock and the staff at Electronic Publishing Services Inc. who put the finishing touches on this brief second edition and deftly guided it through the many phases of production.

Finally, we wish to express our deep gratitude to the following individuals who read and commented on the first brief edition. Their thoughtful criticism, advice, and suggestions have all helped improve the book: S. Carol Berg, *College of St. Benedict;* Roger Bromert, *Southwestern Oklahoma State University;* Charlotte Brooks, *State University of New York—Albany;* Eduardo Canedo, *Columbia University;* Nancy Carnevale, *Montclair State University;* John A. Collins, *Freed-Hardeman University;* Cole P. Dawson, *Warner Pacific College;* Barbara C. Fertig, *Armstrong Atlantic State University;* Van Forsyth, *Clark College;* Martin Hershock, *University of Michigan, Dearborn;* Richard Hughes, *Eastern Oregon University;* Kimberly Jensen, *Western Oregon University;* Cynthia M. Kennedy, *Clarion University of Pennsylvania;* Annette Laing, *Georgia Southern University;* Michael Lansing, *Augsburg College;* Carolyn J. Lawes, *Old Dominion University;* Sandy Moats, *University of Wisconsin—Parkside ;* Earl F. Mulderink, *Southern Utah University;* C. Samuel Nelson II, *Ridgewater College;* Jason C. Newman, *Cosumnes River College;* David R. Novak, *Purdue University;* Melissa Soto-Schwartz, *Cuyahoga Community College;* Deborah Syrdal, *Humboldt State University;* Michael M. Topp, *University of Texas, El Paso;* Sylvia Tyson, *Texas Lutheran University;* Mark D. Van Ells, *Queenborough Community College, CUNY;* David Voelker, *University of Wisconsin—Green Bay;* Charles Westmoreland, *University of Mississippi;* Julie Winch, *University of Massachusetts, Boston;* David Wolcott, *Miami University;* and Jason Young, *State University of New York, Buffalo*

This brief edition owes much to the many conscientious historians who reviewed the full-length edition of the textbook. For their insights and constructive critiques, we are indebted to the following reviewers.

Ken Adderley
Upper Iowa University
Leslie Alexander
Ohio State University
Marynita Anderson
Nassau Community College

John Andrew
Franklin and Marshall College
Abel Bartley
University of Akron
Donald Scott Barton
Central Carolina Technical College

Mia Bay
Rutgers University
Chris Bierwith
Treasure Valley Community College
Charles Bolton
University of Arkansas at Little Rock

Susan Burch
Gallaudet University

Tommy Bynum
Georgia Perimeter College

Robert B. Carey
Empire State College–SUNY

Todd Carney
Southern Oregon University

Kathleen Carter
Highpoint University

Jonathan Chu
University of Massachusetts

Barak Cook
University of Missouri

Amy E. Davis
University of California–Los Angeles

Judy DeMark
Northern Michigan University

James A. Denton
University of Colorado

Joseph A. Devine
Stephen F. Austin University

Margaret Dwight
North Carolina Agricultural and Technical University

Nancy Gabin
Purdue University

Lori Ginzberg
Pennsylvania State University

Gregory Goodwin
Bakersfield College

Amy S. Greenberg
Pennsylvania State University

Charlotte Haller
Worcester State College

Nadine Isitani Hata
El Camino College

James Hedtke
Cabrini College

Traci Hodgson
Chemeketa Community College

Rose Holz
University of Nebraska–Lincoln

Fred Hoxie
University of Illinois

Tera Hunter
Carnegie Mellon University

Creed Hyatt
Lehigh Carbon Community College

David Jaffe
City College of New York

Jeremy Johnson
Northwest College

Yvonne Johnson
Central Missouri State University

Kurt Keichtle
University of Wisconsin

Anne Klejment
University of St. Thomas

Dennis Kortheuer
California State University–Long Beach

Joel Kunze
Upper Iowa University

Joseph Laythe
Edinboro College of Pennsylvania

Chana Kai Lee
Indiana University

Dan Letwin
Pennsylvania State University

Gaylen Lewis
Bakersfield College

Kenneth Lipartito
Florida International University

Kyle Longley
Arizona State University

Edith L. Macdonald
University of Central Florida

Lorie Maltby
Henderson Community College

Sandra Mathews-Lamb
Nebraska Wesleyan University

Constance M. McGovern
Frostburg State University

Henry McKiven
University of South Alabama

James H. Merrell
Vassar College

Carl Moneyhan
University of Arkansas–Little Rock

Earl Mulderink
Southern Utah State University

Jason C. Newman
Consumnes River College

Steven Noll
University of Florida

Jim Norris
North Dakota State University

Elsa Nystrom
Kennesaw State University

Keith Pacholl
California State University–Fullerton

William Pelz
Elgin Community College

Melanie Perrault
University of Central Arkansas

Delores D. Petersen
Foothill College

Robert Pierce
Foothill College

Louis Potts
University of Missouri–Kansas City

Sarah Purcell
Central Michigan University

Niler Pyeatt
Wayland Baptist University

Steven Reschly
Truman State University

Arthur Robinson
Santa Rosa Junior College

Robert E. Rook
Fort Hays State University

Thomas J. Rowland
University of Wisconsin–Oshkosh

Steven Ruggles
University of Minnesota

Leonard J. Sadosky
Iowa State University

Rebecca Shoemaker
Indiana State University

Howard Shore
Columbia River High School

James Sidbury
University of Texas

Arwin D. Smallwood
Bradley University

Margaret Spratt
California University of Pennsylvania

Rachel Standish
Foothill College

Jon Stauff
St. Ambrose University

David Steigerwald
Ohio State University–Marion

Kay Stockbridge
Central Carolina Technical College

Daniel Thorp
Virginia Tech University

Michael M. Topp
University of Texas–El Paso

Clifford Trafzer
University of California–Riverside

Deborah Gray White
Rutgers University

Scott Wong
Williams College

Bill Woodward
Seattle Pacific University

Nancy Zens
Central Oregon Community College

David Zonderman
North Carolina State University

CREATED EQUAL

Consolidating a Triumphant Union, 1865–1877

I N SAVANNAH, GEORGIA, IN MID-DECEMBER 1864, AFRICAN AMERICAN MEN, WOMEN, AND children rejoiced when the troops of Union General William Tecumseh Sherman liberated the city: the day of jubilee had come at last! The city's black community immediately formed its own school system under the sponsorship of a new group, the Savannah Education Association (SEA). The association owed its creation to the desire of freedpeople of all ages to learn to read and write. A committee of nine black clergy began by hiring fifteen black teachers and acquiring buildings (including the Old Bryan Slave Mart) for use as schools. By January 1, 1865, Savannah blacks had raised $800 to pay teachers' salaries, enabling several hundred black children to attend classes free of charge.

Following hard on the heels of the Union army, a group of northern white missionaries arrived in Savannah to seek black converts for two Protestant denominations, the Presbyterians and the Congregationalists. On the first day of school, in January 1865, these northern newcomers watched a grand procession of children wend its way through the streets of Savannah. The missionaries expressed amazement that the SEA was an entirely black-run organization. These whites had believed the former slaves incapable of creating such an impressive educational system.

In March 1865, the federal government, under the auspices of the newly formed Bureau of Refugees, Freedmen, and Abandoned Lands (Freedmen's Bureau), agreed to work with missionaries in opening schools for black children throughout the former Confederate states. In Georgia, missionaries and government officials soon became alarmed that black leaders were willing to accept financial aid from them but

Courtesy of the Georgia Historical Society, William Wilson Collection

■ In Savannah, African American Sunday school pupils pose for photographer William Wilson in 1890. After the Civil War, many southern black communities created, or enlarged and solidified, their own institutions, including schools and churches.

not willing to relinquish control of SEA schools to the whites in return. The Northerners were also distressed by the militancy of certain local black leaders. One of these leaders was Aaron Bradley, who, armed with a pistol and bowie knife, was urging other black men to vote as a bloc in all elections.

In an effort to wrest control of the SEA from Savannah blacks, northern missionaries and agents of the Freedmen's Bureau decided to withhold funds from the association. By March 1866, these efforts had paid off: the city's black community, swollen by a refugee population, was no longer able to support its own schools. Northern whites took over SEA operations, and the association ceased to exist.

Postwar political interest in the South unleashed a major conflict between supporters of African American rights and supporters of southern white privilege. Republican congressmen hoped to *reconstruct* the South by enabling African Americans to own land and to become full citizens. Southern freedpeople sought to free themselves from white employers, landlords, and clergy and to establish control over their own workplaces, families, and churches. In contrast, President Andrew Johnson appeared bent on *restoring* the antebellum power relations that made southern black people field laborers dependent on white landowners. For their part, many southern whites were determined to prevent black people from becoming truly free. Most former rebels remained embittered about the outcome of the war and vengeful toward the freedpeople.

After the war, western economic development presented new challenges for men who had fought for the Union. In order to open the West to European American miners and homesteaders, the U.S. army clashed repeatedly with Native Americans. On the Plains and in the Northwest, Indians resisted white efforts to force them to abandon their nomadic way of life and take up sedentary farming. William Tecumseh Sherman, Philip H. Sheridan, and George Custer were among the U.S. military officers who had commanded troops in the Civil War and now attempted to subdue the Plains Indians and further white settlement. Sherman declared, "We must act with vindictive earnestness against the Sioux, even to their extermination, men, women and children." The former head of the Freedmen's Bureau, General Oliver O. Howard, oversaw the expulsion of Chief Joseph and his people, the Nez Perce, from their homeland in southeast Washington's Walla Walla Valley in 1877.

The Civil War hardened the positions of the two major political parties. The Republicans remained in favor of a strong national government, one that promoted economic growth. The Democrats tended to support states' efforts to manage their own affairs, which included regulating relations between employers and employees, whites and blacks. The railroad industry represented a robust, Republican-sponsored partnership between private enterprise and the federal government. Between 1862 and 1872, the government gave the industry subsidies that included millions of dollars in cash and more than 100 million acres of land. During the postwar period, federal government officials attempted to complete the political process that the military defeat of the South had only begun: the consolidation of the Union, North and South, East and West. This process encompassed the nation as a whole.

The Struggle over the South

The Civil War had a devastating impact on the South in physical, social, and economic terms. The region had lost an estimated $2 billion in investments in slaves; modest homesteads and grand plantations alike lay in ruins; and gardens, orchards, and cotton fields were barren. More than 3 million former slaves eagerly embraced freedom, but the vast majority lacked the land, cash, and credit necessary to build family homesteads for themselves. Hoping to achieve social and economic self-determination, African American men and women traveled great distances, usually on foot, in efforts to locate loved ones and reunite families that had been separated during slavery. At the same time, landowning whites considered black people primarily as a source of agricultural labor; these whites resisted the idea that the freedpeople should be granted citizenship rights.

In the North, Republican lawmakers disagreed among themselves how best to punish the defeated but defiant rebels. President Abraham Lincoln had indicated early that after the war the government should bring the South back into the Union quickly and painlessly. His successor wanted to see members of the southern planter elite humiliated, but resisted the notion that freedpeople should become independent of white landowners. In Congress, moderate and radical Republicans argued about how far the government should go in ensuring the former slaves' freedom.

Wartime Preludes to Postwar Policies

Wartime experiments with African American free labor in Union-occupied areas foreshadowed bitter postwar debates. As early as November 1861, Union forces had occupied the Sea Islands off Port Royal Sound in South Carolina. In response, wealthy cotton planters fled to the mainland. Over the next few months, three groups of northern civilians landed on the Sea Islands with the intention of guiding blacks in the transition from slave to free labor. Teachers arrived intent on creating schools, and missionaries hoped to start churches. A third group, representing Boston investors, had also settled on the Sea Islands to assess economic opportunities; by early 1862, they decided to institute a system of wage labor that would reestablish a staple crop economy and funnel cotton directly into northern textile mills. The freed slaves, however, preferred to grow crops for their families to eat rather than cotton to sell, relying on a system of barter and trade among networks of extended families. Their goal was to break free of white landlords, suppliers, and cotton merchants.

Meanwhile, in southern Louisiana, the Union capture of New Orleans in the spring of 1862 enabled northern military officials to implement their own free (that is, nonslave) labor system. General Nathaniel Banks proclaimed that U.S. troops should forcibly relocate blacks to plantations "where they belong"; there they would continue to work for their former owners in the sugar and cotton fields, but now for wages supposedly negotiated annually. The Union army would compel blacks to work if they resisted doing so. In defiance of these orders, however, some blacks went on strike for higher wages, and others refused to work at all. Moreover, not all Union military men relished the prospect of forcing blacks to work on the plantations where they had been enslaved. Thus, federal policies returning blacks to plantations remained contested even within the ranks of the army itself.

Not all Union military men relished the prospect of forcing blacks to work on the plantations where they had been enslaved.

The Lincoln administration had no hard-and-fast **Reconstruction** policy to guide congressional lawmakers looking toward the postwar period. In December 1863, the president outlined his Ten Percent Plan. This plan would allow former Confederate states to form new state governments once 10 percent of the men who had voted in the 1860 presidential election had pledged allegiance to the Union and renounced slavery. Congress instead passed the Wade-Davis Bill, which would have required a majority of southern voters in any state to take a loyalty oath affirming their allegiance to the United States. By refusing to sign the bill before Congress adjourned, Lincoln vetoed the measure (through a **pocket veto**). However, the president approved the creation of the Freedmen's Bureau in March 1865. The bureau was responsible for coordinating relief efforts on behalf of blacks and poor whites loyal to the Union, for sponsoring schools, and for implementing a labor contract system on southern plantations. At the time of his assassination, Lincoln seemed to be leaning toward giving the right to vote to southern black men.

Presidential Reconstruction, 1865–1867

When Andrew Johnson, the seventeenth president of the United States, assumed office in April 1865 after Lincoln's death, he brought his own agenda for the defeated South. Throughout his political career, Johnson had seen himself as a champion of poor white farmers in oppo-

CORBIS

■ Freedmen's Bureau agents distributed rations to former slaves and southern whites who had remained loyal to the Union. Agents also sponsored schools, legalized marriages formed under slavery, arbitrated domestic disputes, and oversaw labor contracts between workers and landowners. This photo shows the bureau office in Petersburg, Virginia.

sition to the wealthy planter class. A man of modest background, he had been elected U.S. senator from Tennessee in 1857. He alone among southern senators remained in Congress and loyal to the Union after 1861. Lincoln first appointed Johnson military governor of Tennessee when that state was captured by the Union in 1862 and then tapped him as his running mate for the election of 1864.

Soon after he assumed the presidency, Johnson disappointed congressional Republicans who hoped that he would serve as a champion of the freedpeople. He welcomed back into the Union those states reorganized under Lincoln's Ten Percent Plan. He advocated denying the vote to wealthy Confederates, though he would allow individuals to come to the White House to beg the president for special pardons. Johnson also outlined a fairly lenient plan for readmitting the other rebel states into the Union. Poor whites would have the right to vote, but they must convene special state conventions that would renounce secession and accept the Thirteenth Amendment abolishing slavery. Further, they must repudiate all Confederate debts. The president opposed granting the vote to the former slaves; he believed that they should continue to toil as field workers for white landowners. In fact, many former rebels gradually came to see Johnson as their postwar political ally.

Johnson failed to anticipate the speed and vigor with which former Confederate leaders would move to reassert their political authority. In addition, he did not gauge accurately the resentment of congressional Republicans, who thought his policies toward the defeated South were too forgiving. The southern states that took advantage of Johnson's reunification policies passed so-called **Black Codes**. These state laws were an ill-disguised attempt to institute a system of near-slavery. They aimed to penalize "vagrant" blacks, defined as those who did not work in the fields for whites, and to deny blacks the right to vote, serve on juries, or in some cases even own land. The Black Code of Mississippi restricted the rights of a freed-person to "keep or carry fire-arms," ammunition, and knives and to "quit the service of his or her employer before the expiration of his or her term of service without good cause." The vagueness of this last provision threatened any blacks who happened not to be working under the supervision of whites at any given moment. People arrested under the Black Codes faced imprisonment or forced labor.

DOCUMENT

The Mississippi Black Code

At the end of the war, congressional Republicans were divided into two camps. Radicals wanted to use strong federal measures to advance black people's civil rights and economic independence. In contrast, moderates were more concerned with the free market and private property rights; they took a hands-off approach regarding former slaves. But members of both groups reacted with outrage to the Black Codes. Moreover, when the legislators returned to the Capitol in December 1865, they were in for a shock: among their new colleagues were four former Confederate generals, five colonels, and other high-ranking members of the Confederate elite, including former Vice President Alexander Stephens, now under indictment for treason. All of these rebels were duly elected senators and representatives from southern states. In a special session called for December 4, a joint committee of fifteen lawmakers (six senators and nine members of the House) voted to bar these men from Congress.

By January 1865, both houses of Congress had approved the Thirteenth Amendment to the Constitution, abolishing slavery. The necessary three-fourths of the states ratified the measure by the end of the year. However, President Johnson was becoming more openly defiant of his congressional foes who favored aggressive federal protection of black civil rights. He vetoed two crucial pieces of legislation: an extension and expansion of the Freedmen's Bureau and the Civil Rights Bill of 1866. This latter measure was an unprecedented piece of legislation. It called on the federal government—for the first time in history—to protect individual rights against the willful indifference of the states (as manifested, for example, in the Black Codes). Congress managed to override both vetoes by the summer of 1866.

In June of that year, Congress passed the Fourteenth Amendment. This amendment guaranteed the former slaves citizenship rights, punished states that denied citizens the right to vote, declared the former rebels ineligible for federal and state office, and voided Confederate debts. This amendment was the first to use gender-specific language, guarding against denying the vote "to any of the male inhabitants" of any state.

Even before the war ended, Northerners had moved south, and the flow increased in 1865. Black and white teachers volunteered to teach the former slaves to read and write. Some white Northerners journeyed south to invest in land and become planters in the staple crop economy. White southern critics called all these migrants **carpetbaggers**. This derisive term suggested that the Northerners hastily packed their belongings in rough bags made of carpet scraps

and then rushed south to take advantage of the region's devastation and confusion. To many freedpeople, whether they worked for a carpetbagger or a Southerner, laboring in the cotton fields was but a continuation of slavery.

Some former southern (white) Whigs, who had been reluctant secessionists, now found common ground with northern Republicans who supported government subsidies for railroads, banking institutions, and public improvements. This group consisted of some members of the humbled planter class as well as men of more modest means. Southern Democrats, who sneered at any alliances with the North, scornfully labeled these whites **scalawags** (the term referred to a scrawny, useless type of horse on the Scottish island of Scalloway).

INTERPRETING HISTORY

A Southern Labor Contract

After the Civil War, many southern agricultural workers signed labor contracts. These contracts sought to control not only the output of laborers but also their lives outside the workplace.

On January 1, 1868, the planter John D. Williams assembled his workers for the coming year and presented them with a contract to sign. Williams owned a plantation in the lower Piedmont county of Laurens, South Carolina. He agreed to furnish "the said negroes" (that is, the three black men and two black women whose names were listed on the document) with mules and horses to be used for cultivating the land. The workers could receive their food, clothing, and medical care on credit. They were allowed to keep one-third of all the corn, sweet potatoes, wheat, cotton, oats, and molasses they produced. Presumably, they would pay their debts to Williams using proceeds from their share of the crop.

According to the contract, Williams's workers promised to

bind them Selves to be steady & attentive to there work at all times and to work at keeping in repair all the fences on Said plantation and assist in cuting & taking care of—all the grain crops on Said plantation and work by the direction of me [Williams] or my Agent.…

And should any of them depart from the farm or from any services at any time with out our approval they shall forfeit one dollar per day, for the first time and for the second time without good cause they shall forfeit all of their interest in the crop their to me the enjured person—they shall not be allowed to keep firearms or deadly wapons or ardent Spirits and they shall obey all lawful orders from me or my Agent and shall be honest—truthful—sober—civel—diligent in their business & for all wilful Disobedience of any lawful

After the Civil War, many rural southern blacks, such as those shown here, continued to toil in cotton fields owned by whites.

orders from me or my Agent drunkenness moral or legal misconduct want of respects or civility to me or my Agent or to my Family or any elce, I am permitted to discharge them forfeiting any claims upon me for any part of the crop.…

Moses Nathan	1 full hand
Jake Chappal	" "
Milly Williams	½ " "
Easter Williams	" "
Mack Williams	" "

At the end of the contract is this addition:

We the white labores now employed by John D. Williams on his white plains plantation have lisened and heard read the foregoing Contract on this sheet of paper assign equal for the black laborers employed by him on said place and we are perfectly Satisfied with it and heare by bind our selves to abide & be Governed & Controwed by it

Wm Wyatte	1 full hand
John Wyatte	1 full hand
Packingham Wyatte	½ " "
Franklin Wyatte	½ " "
R M Hughes	1 full hand
B G Pollard	1 full hand
George Washington Pollard	1 full hand

To sign the contract, all of the blacks and two of the whites "made their marks"; that is, they signed with an "X" because they were illiterate.

Questions

1. In what ways did sharecropping differ from wage labor?
2. Do you see evidence that family or kin members worked together on Williams's plantation?
3. What is the significance of the contract addendum signed by white laborers? ∎

Source: Rosser H. Taylor, "Postbellum Southern Rental Contracts" [from Furman University library, Greenville, South Carolina], *Agricultural History* 17 (1943): 122–123.

Library of Congress

■ Residents of Edisto Island, off the coast of South Carolina, pose with a U.S. government mule cart immediately after the Civil War. U.S. troops captured the island in November 1861. The following March, the government began to distribute to blacks the lands abandoned by their former masters. In October 1865, President Andrew Johnson halted the program. A group of angry and disappointed blacks appealed to the president, claiming, "This is our home, we have made these lands what they are." After meeting with the group, General Oliver O. Howard noted, "I am convinced that something must be done to give these people and others the prospect of homesteads."

Soon after the war's end, southern white vigilantes launched a campaign of violence and intimidation against freedpeople who dared to resist the demands of white planters and other employers. Calling itself the Ku Klux Klan, a group of Tennessee war veterans soon became a white supremacist terrorist organization and spread to other states. In May 1866, violence initiated by white terrorists against blacks in Memphis, Tennessee, left forty-six freedpeople and two whites dead, and in July, a riot in New Orleans claimed the lives of thirty-four blacks and three of their white allies. These bloody encounters demonstrated the lengths to which ex-Confederates would go to reassert their authority and defy the federal government.

Back in Washington, Johnson vetoed the Fourteenth Amendment, traveling around the country and urging the states not to ratify it. He argued that policies related to black suffrage should be decided by the states. The time had come for reconciliation between the North and South, maintained the president. (The amendment would not be adopted until 1868.)

H. P. Moore/Collection of the New-York Historical Society, Neg. #37497

Congressional Republicans fought back. In the election of November 1866, they won a two-thirds majority in both houses of Congress. These numbers allowed them to claim a mandate from their constituents and to override any future vetoes by the president. Moderates and radicals together prepared to bypass Johnson to shape their own Reconstruction policies.

The Postbellum South's Labor Problem

While policymakers maneuvered in Washington, black people throughout the South aspired to labor for themselves and gain independence from white overseers and landowners. Yet white landowners persisted in regarding blacks as field hands who must be coerced into working. With the creation of the Freedmen's Bureau in 1865, Congress intended to form an agency that would mediate between these two groups. Bureau agents encouraged workers and employers to sign annual labor contracts designed to eliminate the last vestiges of the slave system. All over the South, freed men, women, and children would contract with an employer on January 1 of each year. They would agree to work for either a monthly wage, an annual share of the crop, or some combination of the two.

> *While policymakers maneuvered in Washington, black people throughout the South aspired to labor for themselves and gain independence from white overseers and landowners.*

Most freedpeople understood they must find a way to provide for themselves first and foremost. They thought of freedom in terms of welfare for their family rather than just for themselves as individuals. Men and women embraced the opportunity to live and work together as a unit. For many couples, their first act as free people was to legalize their marriage vows. Black women shunned the advice of Freedmen's Bureau agents and planters that they continue to pick cotton. These women withdrew from field labor whenever they could afford to do so. Enslaved women had been deprived of the opportunity to attend to family life. Now freedwomen sought to devote themselves to caring for their families.

Blacks along the Georgia and South Carolina coast were determined to cultivate the land on which their forebears had lived and died. They urged General Sherman to confiscate the land owned by rebels in the area. In response, in early 1865, Sherman issued Field Order Number 15, mandating that the Sea Islands and the coastal region south of Charleston be divided into parcels of 40 acres for individual freed families. He also decreed that the army might lend mules to these families to help them begin planting. Given the provisions of this order, many freed families came to expect that the federal government would grant them "40 acres and a mule."

As a result of Sherman's order, 20,000 former slaves proceeded to cultivate the property once owned by Confederates. Within a few months of the war's end, however, the War Department bowed to pressure from the white landowners and revoked the order. The War Department also provided military protection for whites to return and occupy their former lands. In response, a group of black men calling themselves Commissioners from Edisto Island (one of the Sea Islands) met in committee to protest to the Freedmen's Bureau what they considered a betrayal. Writing from the area in January 1866, one Freedmen's Bureau official noted that the new policy must be upheld but regretted that it had brought the freedpeople in "collision" with "U.S. forces."

Southern Skepticism of the Freedmen's Bureau (1866)

During its brief life (1865 to 1868), the Freedmen's Bureau compiled a mixed record. The individual agents represented a broad range of backgrounds, temperaments, and political ideas. Some were former abolitionists who considered northern-style free labor to be "the noblest principle on earth." These men tried to ensure safe and fair working arrangements for black men, women, and children. In contrast, some agents had little patience with the freedpeople's drive for self-sufficiency. Some bureau offices became havens for blacks seeking redress against abusive or fraudulent labor practices, but other offices had little impact on the postwar political and economic landscape. For agents without means of transportation (a reliable horse), plantations scattered throughout the vast rural South remained outside their control. Because white landowners crafted the wording and specific provisions of labor contracts, the bureau agents who enforced such agreements often served the interests of employers rather than laborers.

A Sharecrop Contract

The outlines of **sharecropping**, a system that defined southern cotton production until well into the twentieth century, were visible just a few years after the Civil War. Poor families, black and white, contracted annually with landlords, who advanced them supplies, such as crop seed, mules, plows, food, and clothing. Fathers directed the labor of their children in the fields. At the end of the year, many families remained indebted to their employer and, thus, entitled to nothing and obliged to work another year in the hope of repaying the debt. If a sharecropper's demeanor or work habits displeased the landlord, the family faced eviction.

Single women with small children were especially vulnerable to the whims of landlords in the postbellum period. Near Greensboro, North Carolina, for example, planter Presley George Sr. settled accounts with his field worker Polly at the end of 1865. For her year's expenses, Polly was charged a total $69 for corn, cloth, thread, and board for a child who did not work. By George's calculations, Polly had earned exactly $69 for the labor she and her three children (two sons and a daughter) performed in the course of the year, leaving her no cash of her own. Under these harsh conditions, freedpeople looked to each other for support and strength.

Building Free Communities

Soon after the war's end, southern blacks set about organizing themselves as an effective political force and as free communities devoted to the social and educational welfare of their own people. Differences among blacks based on income, jobs, culture, and skin color at times inhibited institution-building. Some black communities found themselves divided by class, with blacks who had been free before the war (including many literate and skilled light-skinned men) assuming leadership over illiterate field hands. In New Orleans, a combination of factors contributed to class divisions among people of African heritage. During the antebellum period, light-skinned free people of color, many of whom spoke French, were much more likely to possess property and a formal education than were enslaved people, who were dark-skinned English speakers. After the Civil War, the more privileged group pressed for public accommodations laws, which would open the city's theaters, opera, and expensive restaurants to all blacks for the first time. However, black churches and social organizations remained segregated according to class.

AUDIO

"Free At Last"

For the most part, postbellum black communities united around the principle that freedom from slavery should also mean full citizenship rights: the ability to vote, own land, and educate their children. These rights must be enforced by federal firepower: "a military occupation will be absolutely necessary," declared the blacks of Norfolk, "to protect the white Union men of the South, as well as ourselves." Freedpeople in some states allied themselves with white yeomen who had long resented the political power of the great planters and now saw an opportunity to use state governments as agents of democratization and economic reform.

Networks of freedpeople formed self-help organizations. Like the sponsors of the Savannah Education Association, blacks throughout the South formed committees to raise funds and

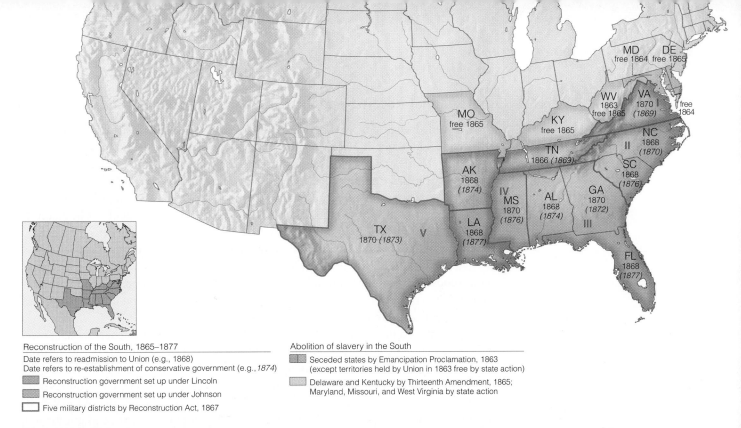

Reconstruction of the South, 1865–1877

Date refers to readmission to Union (e.g., 1868)
Date refers to re-establishment of conservative government (e.g., *1874*)

Reconstruction government set up under Lincoln

Reconstruction government set up under Johnson

Five military districts by Reconstruction Act, 1867

Abolition of slavery in the South

Seceded states by Emancipation Proclamation, 1863
(except territories held by Union in 1863 free by state action)

Delaware and Kentucky by Thirteenth Amendment, 1865;
Maryland, Missouri, and West Virginia by state action

■ **MAP 15.1**

RADICAL RECONSTRUCTION Four of the former Confederate states, Louisiana, Arkansas, Tennessee, and Virginia, were reorganized under President Lincoln's Ten Percent Plan in 1864. Neither this plan nor the proposals of Lincoln's successor, Andrew Johnson, provided for the enfranchisement of the former slaves. In 1867 Congress established five military districts in the South and demanded that newly reconstituted state governments implement universal manhood suffrage. By 1870 all of the former Confederate states had rejoined the Union, and by 1877 all of those states had installed conservative (i.e., Democratic) governments.

hire teachers for neighborhood schools. Small Georgia towns, such as Cuthbert, Albany, Cave Spring, and Thomasville, with populations no greater than a few hundred, raised up to $70 per month and contributed as much as $350 each for the construction of school buildings. Funds came from the proceeds of fairs, bazaars, and bake sales; subscriptions raised by local school boards; and tuition fees. In the cash-starved postbellum South, these amounts represented a great personal and group sacrifice for the cause of education.

All over the South, black families charted their own course. They elected to take in orphans and elderly kin, pool resources with neighbors, and arrange for mothers to stay home with their children. These choices challenged the power of former slaveholders and the influence of Freedmen's Bureau agents and northern missionaries and teachers. At the same time, in seeking to attend to their families and to provide for themselves, southern blacks resembled members of other mid-nineteenth-century laboring classes who valued family ties over the demands of employers and landlords.

Tangible signs of the new emerging black communities infuriated most southern whites. A schoolhouse run by blacks proved threatening in a society where most white children had little opportunity to receive an education. Black communities were also quick to form their own churches, rather than continue to occupy an inferior place in white churches. Other sights proved equally unsettling: on a main street in Charleston, an armed black soldier marching proudly or a black woman wearing a fashionable hat and veil, the kind favored by white women of the planter class. These developments help to account for the speed with which whites organized themselves in the Klan and various other vigilante groups, aiming to preserve "the supremacy of the white race in this Republic."

Reconstruction

Congressional Reconstruction: The Radicals' Plan

The rise of armed white supremacist groups in the South helped spur congressional Republicans to action. On March 2, 1867, Congress seized the initiative. A coalition led by two radicals, Senator Charles Sumner of Massachusetts and Congressman Thaddeus Stevens of Pennsylvania, prodded Congress to pass the Reconstruction Act of 1867. The purpose of this measure was to purge the South of disloyalty once and for all. The act stripped thousands of former Confederates of voting rights. The former Confederate states would not be readmitted to the Union until they had ratified the Fourteenth Amendment and written new constitutions that guaranteed black men the right to vote. The South (with the exception of Tennessee, which had ratified the Fourteenth Amendment in 1866) was divided into five military districts. Federal troops were stationed throughout the region. These troops were charged with protecting Union personnel and supporters in the South and with restoring order in the midst of regional political and economic upheaval.

Congress passed two additional acts specifically intended to secure congressional power over the president. The intent of the Tenure of Office Act was to prevent the president from dismissing Secretary of War Edwin Stanton, a supporter of the radicals. The other measure, the Command of the Army Act, required the president to seek approval for all military orders from General Ulysses S. Grant, the army's senior officer. Grant also was a supporter of the Republicans. Both of these acts probably violated the separation of powers doctrine as put forth in the Constitution. Together, they would soon precipitate a national crisis.

During the Reconstruction period, approximately 2,000 black men of the emerging southern Republican party served as local elected officials, sheriffs, justices of the peace, tax collectors, and city councilors. Many of these leaders were of mixed ancestry, and many had been free before the war. They came in disproportionate numbers from the ranks of literate men, such as clergy, teachers, and skilled artisans. In Alabama, Florida, Louisiana,

■ This drawing by famous political cartoonist Thomas Nast depicts the first black members of Congress. Left to right, front row: Senator Hiram Revels of Mississippi (the first African American to serve in the U.S. Senate), Representatives Benjamin S. Turner of Alabama, Josiah T. Walls of Florida, Joseph H. Rainey of South Carolina, Robert B. Elliott of South Carolina. Back row: Representatives Robert G. DeLarge of South Carolina, Jefferson Long of Georgia.

THE FIRST COLORED SENATOR AND REPRESENTATIVES.
In the 41ˢᵗ and 42ⁿᵈ Congress of the United States.

Mississippi, and South Carolina, black men constituted a majority of the voting public. Throughout the South, 600 black men won election to state legislatures. However, nowhere did blacks control a state government, although they did predominate in South Carolina's lower House. Sixteen black Southerners were elected to the U.S. Congress during Reconstruction. Most of those elected to Congress in the years immediately after the war were freeborn. However, among the nine men elected for the first time after 1872, six were former slaves. All of these politicians exemplified the desire among southern blacks to become active, engaged citizens.

Newly reconstructed southern state legislatures provided for public school systems, fairer taxation methods, bargaining rights of plantation laborers, racially integrated public transportation and accommodations, and public works projects, especially railroads. Nevertheless, the legislative coalitions forged between Northerners and Southerners, blacks and whites, were uneasy and, in many cases, less than productive. Southern Democrats (and later, historians sympathetic to them) claimed that Reconstruction governments were uniquely corrupt, with some carpetbaggers, scalawags, and freedpeople vying for **kickbacks** from railroad and construction magnates. In fact, whenever state legislatures sought to promote business interests, they opened the door to the bribery of public officials. In this respect, northern as well as southern politicians were vulnerable to charges of corruption. In the long run, southern Democrats cared less about charges of legislative corruption and more about the growing political power of local black Republican party organizations.

In Washington in early 1868, President Johnson forced a final showdown with Congress. He replaced several high military officials with more conservative men. He also fired Secretary of War Stanton, in apparent violation of the Tenure of Office Act. Shortly thereafter, in February, a newly composed House Reconstruction Committee impeached Johnson for ignoring the act, and the Senate began his trial on March 30. The president and Congress were locked in an extraordinary battle for political power.

The final vote was thirty-five senators against Johnson, one vote short of the necessary two-thirds of all senators' votes needed for conviction. Nineteen senators voted to acquit Johnson of the charges. Nevertheless, to win acquittal, he had had to promise moderates that he would not stand in the way of congressional plans for Reconstruction. Johnson essentially withdrew from policymaking in the spring of 1868. That November, Republicans urged Northerners to "vote as you shot" (that is, to cast ballots against the former Confederates) and elected Ulysses S. Grant to the presidency.

Political reunion was an uneven process, but one that gradually eroded the newly won rights of former slaves in many southern states.

TABLE 15-1			
The Election of 1868			
Candidate	**Political Party**	**Popular Vote (%)**	**Electoral Vote**
Ulysses S. Grant	Republican	52.7	214
Horatio Seymour	Democratic	47.3	80

By the end of 1868, Arkansas, North Carolina, South Carolina, Louisiana, Tennessee, Alabama, and Florida had met congressional conditions for readmission to the Union, and two years later, Mississippi, Virginia, Georgia, and Texas followed. The Fifteenth Amendment, passed by Congress in 1869 and ratified by the necessary number of states a year later, granted all black men the right to vote. However, in some states, such as Louisiana, reunification gave Democrats license to engage in wholesale election fraud and violence toward freed men and women. In 1870–1871, a congressional inquiry into the Klan exposed pervasive and grisly assaults on Republican schoolteachers, preachers, and prospective voters, black and white. The Klan also targeted men and women who refused to work like slaves in the fields. In April 1871, Congress passed the Ku Klux Klan Act, which punished conspiracies intended to deny rights to citizens. But Klan violence and intimidation had already taken their toll on Republican voting strength.

VIDEO

Legacies of
Reconstruction

Claiming Territory for the Union

While blacks and whites, northerners and southerners struggled for power in the south, poet Walt Whitman celebrated the "manly and courageous instincts" that propelled a brave, adventurous people west. Whitman hailed the march across the prairies and over the mountains as a cavalcade of progress. He and other Americans believed that the postbellum migration fulfilled a mission of national regeneration begun by the Civil War. Kansas's population grew by 240 percent in the 1860s, Nebraska's by 355 percent.

To unite the entire country together as a single economic and political unit was the Republican ideal. The railroads in particular served as vehicles of national integration. When the Central Pacific and Union Pacific Railroads met at Promontory Point, Utah, in 1869, the hammering of the spike that joined the two roads produced a telegraphic signal received simultaneously on both coasts, setting off a national celebration.

Meanwhile, regular units of United States cavalry, including two regiments of blacks, were launching attacks on Indians on the Plains, in the Northwest, and in the Southwest. Between 1865 and 1890, U.S. military forces conducted a dozen separate campaigns against western Indian peoples and met Indian warriors in battle or attacked Indian settlements in more than 1,000 engagements. In contrast to African Americans, who adamantly demanded their rights as American citizens, defiant western Indians battled a government to which they owed no allegiance.

Federal Military Campaigns Against Western Indians

In 1871 the U.S. government renounced the practice of seeking treaties with various Indian groups. This change in policy opened the way for a more aggressive effort to subdue native populations. It also hastened the expansion of the reservation system, an effort begun in the antebellum period to confine specific Indian groups to specific territories.

In the Southwest, clashes between Indians and U.S. soldiers persisted after the Civil War. In 1867 at Medicine Lodge Creek in southern Kansas, the United States signed a treaty with an alliance of Comanche, Kiowa, Cheyenne, Arapaho, and Plains Apache. This treaty could not long withstand the provocation posed by the railroad, as Indians continued to attack the surveyors, supply caravans, and military escorts that preceded the railroad work crews. The year before, the Seventh U.S. Cavalry, under the command of Lieutenant Colonel George Custer, had been formed to ward off native attacks on the Union Pacific, snaking its way across the central Plains westward from Kansas. In November 1868, Custer destroyed a Cheyenne settlement on the Washita River, in present-day Oklahoma. Custer's men murdered women and children, burned tipis, and destroyed 800 horses.

Geronimo and Natiche Surrender (1886)

The Apache Indians managed to elude General George Crook until 1875. Crook employed some of these Apache to track down the war chief Geronimo of the Chiricahua. Like many other Indian leaders, Geronimo offered both religious and military guidance to his people. He believed that a spirit would protect him from the white man's bullets and from the arrows of Indians in league with government troops. Yet Geronimo was tricked into a momentary surrender in 1877, and was held in irons for several months before gaining his release and challenging authorities for another nine years.

In 1874 Custer took the Seventh Cavalry into the Black Hills of the Dakotas. Supposedly, the 1868 Treaty of Fort Laramie had rendered this land off-limits to whites. Custer's mission was to offer protection for the surveyors of the Northern Pacific Railroad and to force Indians onto reservations as stipulated in the 1868 treaty. However, the officer lost no time trumpeting the fact that Indian lands were filled with gold. This report prompted a rush to the Black Hills, lands sacred to the Sioux. Within two years, 15,000 gold miners had illegally descended on Indian lands to seek their fortunes. The federal government proposed to buy the land, but leaders of the Sioux, including Red Cloud, Spotted Tail, and Sitting Bull, spurned the offer.

During the morning of June 25, 1876, Custer and his force of 264 soldiers attacked a Sun Dance gathering of 2,500 Sioux and Cheyenne on the banks of the Little Big Horn River in Montana. Custer foolishly launched his attack without adequate backup, and he and his men were easily overwhelmed and killed by Indian warriors, led by the Oglala Sioux Crazy Horse and others. Reacting to this defeat, U.S. military officials reduced the Lakota and Cheyenne to wardship status, ending their autonomy.

Indians throughout the West maintained their distinctive ways of life during these turbulent times. Horse holdings, so crucial for hunting, trading, and fighting, varied from group to group, with the Crow wealthy in relation to their Central Plains neighbors the Oglala and the Arikara. Plains peoples engaged in a lively trading system. They exchanged horses and their trappings (bridles and blankets) for eastern goods such as kettles, guns, and ammunition. Despite their differences in economy, these groups held similar religious beliefs about an all-powerful life force that governed the natural world. People, plants, and animals were all part of the same order.

The Postwar Western Labor Problem

In 1865 the owners of the Central Pacific Railroad seemed poised for one of the great engineering feats of the nineteenth century. In the race eastward from California, they would construct trestles spanning vast chasms and roadbeds traversing mountains and deserts. Government officials in Washington were eager to subsidize the railroad. What the owners lacked was a dependable labor force. The Irish workers who began the line in California struck for higher wages in compensation for brutal, dangerous work. These immigrants dropped their shovels and hammers at the first word of a gold strike nearby—or far away. As a result, in 1866 the Central Pacific had decided to tap into a vast labor source by importing thousands of Chinese men from their native Guangdong province.

Robert Benecke, photographer. DeGolyer Library, Southern Methodist University, Dallas, Texas, Ag1982.86.80

■ With this 1870 photograph, the Kansas Pacific Railroad advertised the opportunity for western travelers to shoot buffalo from the comfort and safety of their railroad car. The company's official taxidermist shows off his handiwork. Railroad expansion facilitated the exploitation of natural resources while promoting tourism.

■ Chinese construction workers labor on the Central Pacific Railroad, c. 1868. Many Chinese immigrants toiled as indentured laborers, indebted to Chinese merchant creditors who paid for their passage to California. Isolated in all-male work camps, crews of railroad workers retained their traditional dress, language, and diet. After the completion of the transcontinental railroad in 1869, some immigrants returned to China, and others dispersed to small towns and cities throughout the West.

Union Pacific Historical Collection

The Chinese toiled to extend the railroad tracks eastward from Sacramento, California, up to 10 miles a day in the desert, only a few feet a day in the rugged Sierra Nevada Mountains. In nerve-wracking feats of skill, they lowered themselves in woven baskets to implant nitro-glycerine explosives in canyon walls. Chinese laborers toiled through snowstorms and blistering heat to blast tunnels and cut passes through granite mountains. With the final linking of the railroad in Utah in 1869, many Chinese returned to California.

Signed in 1868, the Burlingame Treaty, named for Anson Burlingame, an American envoy to China, had supposedly guaranteed government protection for Chinese immigrants as visitors, traders, or permanent residents. Most immigrants were men. (Six out of ten California Chinese women were listed in the 1870 census as prostitutes, most the victims of their compatriots.) Yet the treaty did not inhibit U.S. employers, landlords, and government officials from discriminating against the Chinese.

By 1870, 40,000 Chinese lived in California and represented fully one-quarter of the state's wage earners. They found work in the cigar, woolen-goods, and boot and shoe factories of San Francisco; in the gold mining towns, now as laundry operators rather than as miners as they had before the Civil War; and in the fields as agricultural laborers. White workers began to cry unfair competition against this Asian group that was becoming increasingly integrated into the region's economy.

As a group, Chinese men differed from California Indians, who remained trapped in the traditional agricultural economy of unskilled labor. Whites appropriated Indian land and forced many men, women, and children to work as wage earners for large landowners. Deprived of their familiar hunting and gathering lands, and wracked by disease and starvation, California Indians had suffered a drastic decline in their numbers by 1870, from 100,000 to 30,000 in twenty years.

Land Use in an Expanding Nation

As with the labor force, the end of the Civil War prompted new conflicts and deepened long-standing ones over the use of the land in a rich, sprawling country. In the South, staple crop planters began to share political power with an emerging elite, men who owned railroads and textile mills. Despairing of ever achieving antebellum levels of labor efficiency, some landowners turned to mining the earth and the forests for saleable commodities. These products, obtained through extraction, included phosphate (used in producing fertilizer), timber, coal, and turpentine.

As European Americans settled in the West and Southwest, they displaced natives who had been living there for generations. For example, the U.S. court system determined who could legally claim property. Western courts also decided whether natural resources such as water, land, timber, and fish and game constituted property that could be owned by private interests. In the Southwest, European American settlers, including army soldiers who had come to fight Indians and then stayed, continued to place Hispanic land titles at risk. Citing pre-war precedents, American courts favored the claims of recent squatters over those of long-standing residents. In 1869, with the death of her husband (who had served as a general in the Union army), Maria Amparo Ruiz de Burton saw the large ranch they had worked together near San Diego slip out of her control. The first Spanish-speaking woman to be published in English in the United States, de Burton was a member of the Hispanic elite. Nevertheless, she had little political power. California judges backed the squatters who occupied the ranch.

In the 1870s, the so-called Santa Fe Ring wrested more than 80 percent of the original Spanish grants of land from Hispanic landholders in New Mexico. An alliance of European American lawyers, businesspeople, and politicians, the Santa Fe Ring defrauded families and kin groups of their land titles and speculated in property to make a profit. Whereas many ordinary Hispanic settlers saw land—with its crops, pasture, fuel, building materials, and game—as a source of livelihood, groups such as the Santa Fe Ring saw land primarily as a commodity to be bought and sold.

Seemingly overnight, boom towns sprang up wherever minerals or timber beckoned: southern Arizona and the Rocky Mountains west of Denver, Virginia City in western Nevada, the Idaho-Montana region, and the Black Hills of South Dakota. In all these places, increasing numbers of workers operated sophisticated kinds of machinery, such as rock crushers. When the vein was exhausted or the forests depleted, the towns went bust.

Railroads facilitated not only the mining of minerals but also the growth of the cattle-ranching industry. Rail connections between the Midwest and East made it profitable for Texas ranchers to pay cowboys to drive their herds of long-horned steers to Abilene, Ellsworth, Wichita, or Dodge City, Kansas, for shipment to stockyards in Chicago or St. Louis. Cattle drives were huge; an estimated 10 million animals were herded north from Texas alone between 1865 and 1890. They offered employment to all kinds of men with sufficient skills and endurance. Among the cowhands were African American horsebreakers and gunmen and Mexicans skilled in the use of the *reata* (lasso). Blacks made up about 25 percent and Hispanics about 15 percent of all cowboy outfits.

In knitting regional economies together, federal land policies were crucial to the Republican vision of a developing nation. The Mineral Act of 1866 granted title to millions of acres of mineral-rich land to mining companies, a gift from the federal government to private interests. The Timber Culture Act of 1873 allotted 160 acres to individuals in selected western states if they agreed to plant one-fourth of the acreage with trees. Four years later, the Desert Land Act provided cheap land if buyers irrigated at least part of their parcels.

The Apex Mining Act of 1872 legalized traditional mining practices in the West by validating titles approved by local courts. According to the law, a person who could locate the apex of a vein (its point closest to the surface) could lay claim to the entire vein beneath the surface.

TABLE 15-2

Estimates of Railroad Crossties Used and Acres of Forest Cleared, 1870–1910

Year	Miles of Track	Ties Renewed Annually (millions)	Ties Used on New Construction (millions)	Total Ties Annually (millions)	Acres of Forest Cleared (thousands)
1870	60,000	21	18	39	195
1880	107,000	37	21	58	290
1890	200,000	70	19	89	445
1900	259,000			91	455
1910	357,000			124	620

Source: Michael Williams, *Americans and Their Forests* (1989), 352.

The measure contributed to the wholesale destruction of certain parts of the western landscape as mining companies blasted their way through mountains and left piles of rocks in their wake. It also spurred thousands of lawsuits as claimants argued over what constituted an apex or a vein.

It was during this period that a young Scottish-born naturalist named John Muir began to explore the magnificent canyons and mountains of California. He contrasted nature's majesty with the artificial landscape created by and for humans. In the wilderness, there is nothing "truly dead or dull, or any trace of what in manufactories is called rubbish or waste," he wrote; "everything is perfectly clean and pure and full of divine lessons."

Muir was gratified by the creation of the National Park system during the postwar period. Painters and geologists were among the first Easterners to appreciate the spectacular vistas of the western landscape. In 1864 Congress set aside a small area within California's Yosemite Valley for public recreation and enjoyment. Soon after the war, railroad promoters forged an alliance with government officials in an effort to block commercial development of particularly beautiful pockets of land. Northern Pacific railroad financier Jay Cooke lobbied hard for the government to create a 2-million-acre park in what is today the northwest corner of Wyoming. As a result, in March 1872, Congress established Yellowstone National Park. Tourism would continue to serve as a key component of the western economy.

Muir and others portrayed the Yosemite and Yellowstone valleys as wildernesses, empty of human activity. In fact, both areas had long provided hunting and foraging grounds for native peoples. Yellowstone had been occupied by the people now called the Shoshone since the fifteenth century. This group, together with the Bannock, Crow, and Blackfoot, tried to retain access to Yellowstone's meadows, rivers, and forests after it became a national park. However, U.S. policymakers and military officials persisted in their efforts to mark off territory for specific commercial purposes, while Indians were confined to reservations.

Buying Territory for the Union

Before the war, Republicans had opposed any federal expansionist schemes that they feared might benefit slaveholders. However, after 1865 and the outlawing of slavery, some Republican lawmakers and administration officials advocated the acquisition of additional territory. Secretary of State William Seward led the way in 1867 by purchasing Alaska from Russia. For $7.2 million (about 2 cents an acre), the United States gained 591,004 square miles of land. Within the territory were diverse indigenous groups—Eskimo, Aleut, Tlingit, Tsimshian, Athabaskan, and Haida—and a small number of native Russians. Though derided at the time as "Seward's icebox," Alaska yielded enough fish, timber, minerals, oil, and water power in the years to come to prove that the original purchase price was a tremendous bargain.

The impulse that prompted administration support for the Alaska purchase also spawned other plans for territorial acquisitions. In 1870 some Republicans joined with Democrats in calling for the annexation of the Dominican Republic. These congressmen argued that the tiny Caribbean country would make a fine naval base, provide investment opportunities for American businesspeople, and offer a refuge for southern freedpeople.

However, influential Senator Charles Sumner warned against a takeover without considering the will of the Dominican people, who were currently involved in their own civil war. Some congressmen, in a prelude to foreign policy debates of the 1890s, suggested that the dark-skinned Dominican people were incapable of appreciating the blessings of American citizenship. In 1871 an annexation treaty failed to win Senate approval.

The Republican Vision and Its Limits

After the Civil War, victorious Republicans envisioned a nation united in the pursuit of prosperity. All citizens would be free to follow their individual economic self-interest and to enjoy the fruits of honest toil. In contrast, some increasingly vocal and well-organized groups saw the expansion of legal rights, and giving black men the right to vote in particular, as only initial, tentative steps on the path to an all-inclusive citizenship. Women, industrial workers, farmers, and African Americans made up overlapping constituencies pressing for equal political rights and economic opportunity. Together they challenged the mainstream Republican view that defeat of the rebels and destruction of slavery were sufficient to guarantee all people prosperity.

Government-business partnerships also produced unanticipated consequences for Republicans committed to what they believed was the collective good. Some politicians and business leaders saw these partnerships as opportunities for private gain. Consequently, private greed and public corruption accompanied postwar economic growth. Thus, Republican leaders faced challenges from two very different sources: people agitating for civil rights and people hoping to reap personal gain from political activities.

Postbellum Origins of the Woman Suffrage Movement

After the Civil War, the nation's middle class, which had its origins in the antebellum period, continued to grow. Dedicated to self-improvement and filled with a sense of moral authority, many middle-class Americans (especially Protestants) felt a deep cultural connection to their counterparts in England. Indeed, the United States produced its own "Victorians," so called for the self-conscious middle class that emerged in the England of Queen Victoria during her reign from 1837 to 1901.

At the heart of the Victorian sensibility was the ideal of domesticity: a harmonious family living in a well-appointed home, guided by a pious mother and supported by a father successful in business. Famous Protestant clergyman Henry Ward Beecher and his wife were outspoken proponents of this domestic ideal. According to Eunice Beecher, women had no "higher, nobler, more divine mission than in the conscientious endeavor to create a *true home*."

Yet the traumatic events of the Civil War only intensified the desire among a growing group of American women to participate fully in the nation's political life. They wanted to extend their moral influence outside the narrow and exclusive sphere of the home. Many women believed that they deserved the vote and that the time was right to demand it.

In 1866 veteran reformers Elizabeth Cady Stanton, Susan B. Anthony, and Lucy Stone founded the Equal Rights Association to link the rights of white women and African Americans. Nevertheless, in 1867, Kansas voters defeated a referendum proposing **suffrage** for both blacks and white women. This disappointment convinced some former abolitionists that the two causes should be separated—that women should wait patiently until the rights of African American men were firmly secured. Frederick Douglass declined an invitation to a women's suffrage convention in Washington, D.C., in 1868. He explained, "I am now devoting myself to a cause [if] not more sacred, certainly more urgent, because it is one of life and death to the long enslaved people of this country, and that is: negro suffrage." But African American activist and former slave Sojourner Truth warned, "There is a great stir about colored men getting their rights, but not a word about the colored women; and if colored men get their rights, and not colored women get theirs, there will be a bad time about it."

In 1869 two factions of women parted ways and formed separate organizations devoted to women's rights. The more radical wing, including Cady Stanton and Anthony, bitterly denounced the Fifteenth Amendment because it gave the vote to black men only. They helped to found the National Woman Suffrage Association (NWSA), which argued for a renewed commitment to the original Declaration of Sentiments passed in Seneca Falls, New York, two decades earlier. They favored married women's property rights, liberalization of divorce laws, opening colleges and trade schools to women, and a new federal amendment to allow women to vote. Lucy Stone and her husband, Henry Blackwell, founded the rival American Woman Suffrage Association (AWSA). This group downplayed the larger struggle for women's rights and focused on the suffrage question exclusively. Its members supported the Fifteenth Amendment and retained ties to the Republican party. The AWSA focused on state-by-state campaigns for women's suffrage.

In 1871 the NWSA welcomed the daring, flamboyant Victoria Woodhull as a vocal supporter, only to renounce her a few years later. Woodhull's political agenda ranged from free love and dietary reform to legalized prostitution, working men's rights, and women's suffrage. (In the nineteenth century, free love advocates denounced what they called a sexual double standard, one that glorified female chastity while tolerating male promiscuity.)

In 1872 one of Woodhull's critics successfully challenged her. Woodhull spent a month in jail as a result of the zealous prosecution by vice reformer Anthony Comstock, a clergyman who objected to her public discussions and writings on sexuality. Comstock assumed the role of an outspoken crusader against vice. A federal law passed in 1873, and named after him, equated information related to birth control with pornography, banning this and other "obscene material" from the mails.

Susan B. Anthony used the 1872 presidential election as a test case for women's suffrage. She attempted to vote and was arrested, tried, and convicted as a result. By this time, most women suffragists, and most members of the NWSA for that matter, had become convinced that they should focus on the vote exclusively; they therefore accepted the AWSA's policy on this issue. In the coming years, they would avoid other causes with which they might have allied themselves, including black civil rights and labor reform.

Workers' Organizations

Many Americans benefited from economic changes of the postwar era. Railroading, mining, and heavy industry helped fuel the national economy and in the process boosted the growth of the urban managerial class. In the Midwest, many landowning farmers prospered when they responded to an expanding demand for grain and other staple crops. In Wisconsin, wheat farmers cleared forests, drained swamps, diverted rivers, and profited from the booming world market in grain. Yet the economic developments that allowed factory managers and owners of large wheat farms to make a comfortable living for themselves did not necessarily benefit agricultural and manufacturing workers.

The economic developments that allowed factory managers and owners of large wheat farms to make a comfortable living for themselves did not necessarily benefit agricultural and manufacturing workers.

State Historical Society of Wisconsin, WHi (D32) 821

■ A Norwegian immigrant extended family in the town of Norway Grove, Wisconsin, poses in front of their imposing home and up-to-date carriage in this photograph taken in the mid-1870s. Linking their fortunes to the world wheat market, these newcomers to the United States prospered. Wrote one woman to her brother back home in Norway, "We all have cattle, driving oxen, and wagons. We also have children in abundance."

Indeed, during this period growing numbers of working people, in the countryside and in the cities, became caught up in a cycle of indebtedness. In the upcountry South (above the fall line, or Piedmont), formerly self-sufficient family farmers sought loans from banks to repair their war-damaged homesteads. To qualify for these loans, the farmer had to plant cotton as a staple crop, to the neglect of corn and other foodstuffs. Many sharecroppers, black and white, received payment in the form of credit only; for these families, the end-of-the-year reckoning yielded little more than rapidly accumulating debts. Midwestern farmers increasingly relied on expensive threshing and harvesting machinery and on bank loans to purchase the machinery.

Several organizations founded within five years of the war's end offered laborers an alternative vision to the Republicans' brand of individualism and nationalism. In 1867 Oliver H. Kelly, a former Minnesota farmer now working in a Washington office, organized the National Grange of the Patrons of Husbandry, popularly known as the Grange. This movement sought to address a new, complex marketplace increasingly dominated by railroads, banks, and grain elevator operators. The Grange encouraged farmers to form **cooperatives** that would market their crops and to challenge discriminatory railroad rates that favored big business.

Founded in Baltimore in 1866, the National Labor Union (NLU) consisted of a collection of craft unions and claimed as many as 600,000 members at its peak in the early 1870s. The group welcomed farmers as well as factory workers and promoted legislation for an eight-hour workday and the arbitration of industrial disputes.

In 1873 a nationwide depression threw thousands out of work and worsened the plight of debtors. Businesspeople in agriculture, mining, the railroad industry, and manufacturing had overexpanded their operations. The free-wheeling loan practices of major banks had contributed to this situation. The inability of these businesspeople to repay their loans led to the failure of major banks. With the contraction of credit, thousands of small businesses went bankrupt. The NLU did not survive the crisis.

However, by this time, a new organization had appeared to champion the cause of the laboring classes in opposition to lords of finance. Founded in 1869 by Uriah Stephens and other Philadelphia tailors, the Knights of Labor eventually aimed to unite industrial and rural workers, the self-employed and the wage earner, blacks and whites, and men and women. The Knights were committed to private property and to the independence of the farmer, the entrepreneur, and the industrial worker. The group banned from its ranks "nonproducers," such as liquor sellers, bankers, professional gamblers, stockbrokers, and lawyers.

This period of depression also laid the foundation for the Greenback Labor party, organized in 1878. Within three years after the end of the Civil War, the Treasury had withdrawn from circulation $100 million in wartime paper currency ("greenbacks"). With less money in circulation, debtors found it more difficult to repay their loans. The government also ceased coining silver dollars in 1873, despite the discovery of rich silver lodes in the West. To add insult to injury, the Resumption Act (1875) called for the government to continue to withdraw paper greenbacks. Thus, hard money became dearer, and debtors became more desperate. In 1878 the new Greenback Labor party managed to win 1 million votes and elect fourteen candidates to Congress. The party laid the foundation for the Populist party that emerged in the 1890s.

Several factors made coalition building among these American workers difficult. One was the nation's increasingly multicultural workforce. Unions, such as the typographers, were notorious for excluding women and African Americans, a fact publicized by both Frederick Douglass and Susan B. Anthony, to no avail. In 1869 shoe factory workers (members of the Knights of St. Crispin) went on strike in North Adams, Massachusetts. They were soon shocked to see seventy-five Chinese strikebreakers arrive by train from California. Their employer praised the new arrivals for their "rare industry." The shoemakers' strike collapsed quickly after the appearance of what the workers called this "Mongolian battery." Employers would continue to manipulate and divide the laboring classes through the use of ethnic, religious, and racial prejudices.

Political Corruption and the Decline of Republican Idealism

Out of the new partnership between politics and business emerged an extensive system of bribes and kickbacks. Greedy politicians of both parties challenged the Republicans' high-minded idealism.

In the early 1870s, the *New York Times* exposed the schemes of William M. "Boss" Tweed. Tweed headed Tammany Hall, a New York City political organization that courted labor unions and contributed liberally to Catholic schools and charities. Tammany Hall politicians routinely used bribery and extortion to fix elections and bilk taxpayers of millions of dollars. One plasterer employed on a city project received $138,000 in "payment" for two days' work. After the *Times* **exposé**, Tweed was prosecuted and convicted. His downfall attested to the growing influence of newspaper reporters.

Another piece of investigative journalism rocked the political world in 1872. In 1867 major stockholders of the Union Pacific Railroad had formed a new corporation, called the Crédit Mobilier, to build railroads. Heads of powerful congressional committees received shares of stock in the new company. These gifts of stock were bribes to secure the legislators' support for public land grants favorable to the new corporation. The *New York Sun* exposed a number of the chief beneficiaries in the fall of 1872, findings confirmed by congressional investigation. Among the disgraced politicians was Grant's vice president, Schuyler Colfax.

The 1872 presidential election pitted incumbent Grant against the Democratic challenger, *New York Tribune* editor Horace Greeley. Many Republicans, disillusioned with congressional corruption and eager to press forward with civil service reform, endorsed the Democratic candidate. Greeley and his Republican allies decried the patronage (or "spoils") system by which politicians rewarded their supporters with government jobs. Nevertheless, Grant won the election.

By 1872, after four bloody years of war and seven squandered years of postwar opportunity, the federal government seemed prepared to hand the South back to unrepentant rebels. The North showed what one House Republican called "a general apathy among the people concerning the war and the negro." The Civil Rights Act of 1875 guaranteed blacks equal access to public accommodations and transportation. Yet this act represented the final, half-hearted gesture of radical Republicanism. The Supreme Court declared the measure unconstitutional in 1883 on the grounds that the government could protect only political and not social rights. White Southerners reasserted their control over the region's political economy.

The presidential election of 1876 intensified public cynicism about deal making in high places. A dispute over election returns led to what came to be known as the Compromise of 1877. In the popular vote, Democrat Samuel J. Tilden outpolled Republican Rutherford B. Hayes, a former Ohio governor. However, when the electoral votes were counted, the Democrat had only 184, one short of the necessary number. Nineteen of the twenty votes in dispute came from Louisiana, South Carolina, and Florida, and these three states submitted two new sets of returns, one from each of the two main parties. A specially appointed congressional electoral commission, the Committee of Fifteen, was charged with resolving the dispute. It divided along

PLATE 17

Harper's Weekly, September 16, 1871

■ In 1871 Thomas Nast drew a series of cartoons exposing the corruption of New York City Democratic boss William M. Tweed and his political organization, Tammany Hall. In this drawing, published in *Harper's Weekly* in 1871, Nast depicts Tweed and his cronies engaging in a "wholesale" looting of the New York City treasury with the assistance of compliant police officers. Those same officers stand ready to crack down on the impoverished father who robs a bakery to feed his family. By portraying Tweed as an enemy of the poor, Nast ignored the fact that the political boss gained a large following among immigrant voters.

TABLE 15-3			
The Election of 1872			
Candidate	**Political Party**	**Popular Vote (%)**	**Electoral Vote**
Ulysses S. Grant	Republican	55.6	286
Horace Greeley	Democratic, Liberal Republican	43.9	66

TABLE 15-4			
The Election of 1876			
Candidate	Political Party	Popular Vote (%)	Electoral Vote
Rutherford B. Hayes	Republican	48.0	185
Samuel J. Tilden	Democratic	51.0	184

DOCUMENT

Samuel Tilden's
Speech to the
Manhattan Club
Conceding the
Election of 1876

partisan lines. The eight Republicans outvoted the seven Democrats to accept the Republican set of returns from Florida.

To break the logjam, the Democrats agreed that Hayes could assume office in return for the withdrawal of all remaining federal troops from the South. The Republicans tacitly agreed that their work there was finished and that blacks in the region should fend for themselves. Hayes declined to enforce the Civil Rights Act of 1875. White Southerners were free to uphold the principle of states' rights that had been traditionally invoked to deny blacks their rights in the region.

Conclusion

During the dozen or so years after the Civil War, both northern Republicans and southern Democrats registered a series of spectacular wins and crushing losses. Though humiliated by the Union victory, southern white supremacists eventually won for themselves the freedom to control their own local and state governments. As landlords, sheriffs, and merchants, these men defied the postwar federal amendments to the Constitution and deprived African Americans of basic citizenship rights. By the end of Reconstruction, northern Republicans had conceded local power to their former enemies. Even an aggressive nationalism, it turned out, could accept traditional southern hierarchies: white over nonwhite, rich over poor.

On the other hand, at the end of Reconstruction, Republicans remained in firm control of national economic policy. The white South had secured its right to conduct its own political affairs, but the Republican vision of economic growth and development had become the law of the land. This vision was a guiding principle of historic national and, increasingly, international significance. Economic innovation in particular proved to be a force of great unifying power, stronger than all the federal military forces deployed during and after the Civil War.

Sites to Visit

Impeachment of Andrew Johnson
www.impeach-andrewjohnson.com
   This HarpWeek site about the impeachment includes images and text from the Reconstruction period.

Diary and Letters of Rutherford B. Hayes
www.ohiohistory.org/onlinedoc/hayes/index.cfm
   The Rutherford B. Hayes Presidential Center in Fremont, Ohio, maintains this searchable database of his writings.

Freedmen and Southern Society Project (University of Maryland, College Park)
www.history.umd.edu/Freedmen/index.html
   This site contains a chronology and sample documents from several collections of primary sources about emancipation and freedom in the 1860s.

History of the Suffrage Movement
www.rochester.edu/SBA/
   This site includes a chronology, important texts relating to women's suffrage, and bibliographical information about Susan B. Anthony and Elizabeth Cady Stanton.

Indian Memorial at Little Big Horn Battlefield National Monument
www.nps.gov/libi/indmem.htm
   The Smithsonian Institution maintains this site, providing information about the museum.

National Museum of the American Indian
www..nmai.si.edu
   The Smithsonian Institution maintains this site, providing information about the museum.

Northern Great Plains, 1880–1920: Photographs from the Fred Hulstrand and F. A. Pazandak Photograph Collections
www.memory.loc.gov/ammem/award97/ndfahtml/ngphome.html
   This American Memory site from the Library of Congress contains two collections from the Institute for Regional Studies at North Dakota State University with 900 photographs of rural and small-town life at the turn of the century. Included are images of sod homes and the people who built them, farms and the machinery that made them prosper, and one-room schools and the children who were educated in them.

For Further Reading

General Works

Eric Foner, *Reconstruction: America's Unfinished Revolution, 1863–1877* (1988).

David Montgomery, *Beyond Equality: Labor and the Radical Republicans, 1862–1872* (1967).

Amy Dru Stanley, *From Bondage to Contract: Wage Labor, Marriage, and the Market in the Age of Slave Emancipation* (1998).

Ronald Takaki, *A Different Mirror: A History of Multicultural America* (1993).

Richard White, *"It's Your Misfortune and None of My Own": A History of the American West* (1991).

The Struggle over the South

Peter Bardaglio, *Reconstructing the Household: Families, Sex and the Law in the Nineteenth-Century South* (1995).

Ira Berlin and Leslie S. Rowland, eds., *Families and Freedom: A Documentary History of African-American Kinship in the Civil War Era* (1997).

Dwight B. Billings, *Planters and the Making of a "New South": Class, Politics, and Development in North Carolina, 1865–1900* (1979).

Frederick Cooper, Thomas C. Holt, and Rebecca J. Scott, eds., *Beyond Slavery: Explorations of Race, Labor, and Citizenship in Post-Emancipation Societies* (2000).

Michael Golay, *A Ruined Land: The End of the Civil War* (1999).

Thomas C. Holt, *Black over White: Negro Political Leadership in South Carolina During Reconstruction* (1977).

Jacqueline Jones, *Soldiers of Light and Love: Northern Teachers and Georgia Blacks, 1865–1873* (1980).

Claiming Territory for the Union

Stephen E. Ambrose, *Nothing Like It in the World: The Men Who Built the Transcontinental Railroad, 1863–1869* (2000).

Orin G. Libby, ed., *The Arikara Narrative of the Campaign Against the Hostile Dakotas, June, 1876* (1998).

Ruth B. Moynihan, Susan Armitage, and Christiane Fischer Dichamp, eds., *So Much to Be Done: Women Settlers on the Mining and Ranching Frontier* (1990).

Larry Sklenar, *To Hell with Honor: Custer and the Little Bighorn* (2000).

Robert Wooster, *The Military and United States Indian Policy, 1865–1903* (1988).

Judy Yung, *Unbound Feet: A Social History of Chinese Women in San Francisco* (1995).

The Republican Vision and Its Limits

Leon Fink, *Workingmen's Democracy: The Knights of Labor and American Politics* (1983).

Barbara Goldsmith, *Other Powers: The Age of Suffrage, Spiritualism, and the Scandalous Victoria Woodhull* (1998).

Heather Cox Richardson, *The Death of Reconstruction: Race, Labor and Politics in the Post-Civil War North* (2001).

Lyde Cullen Sizer, *The Political Work of Northern Women Writers and the Civil War* (2000).

Irwin Unger, *The Greenback Era: A Social and Political History of American Finance, 1865–1879* (1964).

For quizzes and other resources on these topics, go to www.longmanamericanhistory.com.

PART SIX

The Emergence of Modern America, 1877–1900

THE UNITED STATES BECAME A MODERN NATION DURING THE LAST quarter of the nineteenth century. Vast reserves of coal, timber, and water helped fuel a growing industrial economy. Railroad lines criss-crossed the nation and knit together regional economies. Large numbers of immigrants, many from eastern Europe, arrived in the United States, drawn by America's rising standard of living, high demand for labor, and religious and political freedom.

To raise the money needed to purchase expensive equipment and machinery, coal and oil producers and railroad owners formed modern corporations, businesses that were owned by stockholders rather than individuals. The largest businesses sought to dominate the marketplace by eliminating their competitors. Managers could cut production and operating costs by slashing the wages of workers or by installing labor-saving machinery. Either way, workers paid the price.

The generation that came of age after the Civil War witnessed a series of violent confrontations between workers and employers. Standards of industrial work discipline required workers to labor for long hours at dangerous, disagreeable jobs. Some workers formed new kinds of labor unions to combat the power of big business. Some organizations, such as the Knights of Labor, were national in scope and inclusive in their membership; others represented the interests of specific groups of workers. Employers, local and state law enforcement officials, and judges used a variety of means to suppress strikes and other forms of collective action among workers. Nevertheless, local communities often supported the strikers, who were their friends and neighbors.

During the late nineteenth century, the national economy began to shift to the production of consumer goods. New products gave Americans new ways to spend their money. Manufacturers of everything from toothpaste to bathtubs advertised their goods to a mass market. In cities, department stores offered a dazzling array of goods.

Even as the country was becoming more ethnically diverse, advertisers promoted a single standard of physical beauty and material well-being. At the same time, some scholars and politicians seized on a revolutionary new theory of natural history to argue for the superiority of white, middle-class Americans. Social Darwinism served as the intellectual justification for unfettered economic growth and for the subjugation of darker-skinned peoples, at home and abroad.

Many Americans rejected the trends toward economic standardization and cultural homogeneity. Native Americans in the West continued to resist the railroad and its profound threat to their way of life. By 1890 the U.S. military had forcibly subdued most of these Indians, relegating many to reservations. Together with industrial workers throughout the nation, Hispanic villagers in the Southwest and African American sharecroppers in the South disputed the notion that progress could be defined exclusively in terms of economic growth and development.

Middle-class reformers sought to mediate between what they perceived to be two dangerous groups: arrogant industrialists and discontented workers. These reformers feared that rapid urban and industrial growth would cause rifts in the social fabric. Middle-class women pioneered in the founding of social settlements and other urban institutions to ease the transition of immigrants into modern American society.

The lines between national standards and local cultural interests often blurred. For example, for a short time Sioux chief Sitting Bull (Tatanka Iyotake) appeared with William ("Buffalo Bill") Cody's "Wild West" show, which played to enthusiastic audiences in the United States and Europe. Yet this Indian leader also led the Plains Indians as they attempted to resist U.S. military authorities. Some groups of Americans who sought to preserve their own cultural traditions nonetheless aspired to a middle-class way of life and its material comforts. Elite Hispanic families in the Southwest remained devoted to their Roman Catholic faith and at the same time followed up-to-date clothing fashions marketed by East Coast department stores.

The promise and the conflicts inherent in the emerging modern social order met head on in the 1890s. A new political party called the Populists mounted a brief but potent challenge to entrenched economic and political power. The Populists failed in their attempt to capture the presidency in 1896, but they offered a vision of a new kind of political party, one that would bring black and white farmers and industrial workers together in opposition to landlords, employers, and bankers.

In 1898, in an effort to protect its interests in the Western Hemisphere and to extend those interests into the Pacific, the United States went to war with Spain. This imperialist venture suggested the links among several impulses, including missionary outreach, commercial expansion, and white supremacist racial ideologies. By 1900 the United States was fast becoming a world leader in terms of manufacturing, technological innovation, and the rapid growth of its prosperous middle class.

1891 Populist party formed
Eleven Italian immigrants are lynched in New Orleans

1892 Ellis Island opens as screening site for immigrants
Miners strike in Coeur d'Alene, Idaho
Steelworkers strike at Carnegie's Homestead plant near Pittsburgh

1893 Columbian Exposition opens in Chicago
Pro-American interests stage a successful coup against Queen Liliuokalani of Hawaii
Worst nationwide depression to date

1894 Coxey's Army marches on Washington, D.C.
Pullman workers strike

1896 Supreme Court decides *Plessy v. Ferguson*, upholds segregation
W. E. B. Du Bois is first black person to receive a Ph.D. from Harvard

1898 United States annexes Hawaii
Maine blows up in Havana Harbor

United States defeats Spain in Spanish-American-Cuban-Filipino War
Spain cedes Guam and Puerto Rico to United States, turns over Philippines in return for $20 million

1899 Gen. Emilio Aguinaldo leads Filipino revolt against 70,000 U.S. occupying forces

1900 U.S. troops sent to China to crush Boxer Rebellion

16

Standardizing the Nation: Innovations in Technology, Business, and Culture, 1877–1890

ANDREW CARNEGIE EVENTUALLY BECAME THE RICHEST MAN IN THE WORLD, but he began life in modest circumstances. In 1835 Will and Margaret Carnegie were living in the village of Dunfermline, Scotland, where Will was a skilled weaver. The couple had two sons—Andrew, born in 1835, and Tom, born eight years later. When steam-powered textile looms threw Will Carnegie and other handweavers out of work, the family emigrated to the United States and settled in Pittsburgh, Pennsylvania. Eager to work hard, Andrew took a series of jobs to help support the family: bobbin boy in a textile mill, tender of a steam boiler in a factory, clerk and then messenger in a telegraph office. By the time he was 18 years old, he was personal assistant to Thomas Scott, superintendent of the Western Division of the Pennsylvania Railroad. Three years later, after the death of his father, Andrew assumed the role of family breadwinner; he also took over the job of Thomas Scott, who became president of the railroad.

Working for the railroad, Andrew Carnegie learned a great deal about running a gigantic business efficiently and profitably. He also invested in oil and railroads. In 1872 he visited England and gained first-hand information about the production of steel, a lighter, stronger material than iron. Three years later he opened his own steel plant in Pittsburgh, then proceeded to buy rival steel mills.

In his business life, Andrew Carnegie was a man of strong principles. In 1868 he had promised himself that he would not hoard the money he made; instead he would promote the "education and improvement of the poorer classes." Earning $25 million a year by the early 1890s, he nonetheless believed that "The amassing of wealth is one of the worst species of idolatry." During the course of his career, Carnegie gave away 90 percent of his fortune, founding the Carnegie Endowment for International Peace, as well as many public libraries around the country.

It was significant that Carnegie spent his formative years in business learning about railroads. These lessons paved the way for his own success in the steel industry. By 1877 the emergence of a national rail system signaled the rise of big business. The railroad industry produced Amer-

HultonIArchive/Getty Images

■ When Andrew Carnegie retired in 1901, he sold the Carnegie Steel Company to American banker and financier J. P. Morgan for $480 million. Carnegie's personal fortune was about $500 million.

Carnegie Library of Pittsburgh (#P-1987)

■ **The "Great Labor Uprising" of July 1877 was the first national strike in U.S. history. As railroad lines proliferated, owners slashed wages in a bid to remain competitive. Railroad workers in some cities destroyed trains, tracks, and other equipment. Spreading eventually to fourteen states, the conflict claimed the lives of more than 100 people and resulted in the loss of millions of dollars worth of private property.**

ica's first business bureaucracies, employing gigantic workforces to maintain, schedule, operate, and staff trains that traversed 93,000 miles of track. By 1890 the Pennsylvania Railroad had become the nation's largest employer, with 110,000 workers on its payroll. About one out of seven people worked in the rail industry. The personnel in charge of coordinating these vast operations were among the country's first professional, salaried managers.

The railroad industry was both a great centralizer and a great standardizer. Trains ran on schedules that were set by a central office, and those schedules relied on definitions of actual time that were standard throughout the nation. Moreover, trains broke down regional boundaries by transporting goods to all areas of the country. For the first time, trains carried brand-name goods and commodities to a national market. A California wheat farmer could purchase replacement parts for his McCormick reaper manufactured in Chicago. An Iowa farm family ordered a new cookstove through a mail-order catalogue. Levi-Strauss, a small clothier in San Francisco, shipped its famous denim pants to cowboys in Texas. Pillsbury Flour of Minnesota distributed its products to bakeries throughout the Midwest. Armour Meatpacking of Chicago sent its sausages to the East Coast. With the introduction of the new refrigerated railroad car, trains also began carrying larger loads of fruits and vegetables over longer distances. The new traffic in produce stimulated commercial agriculture in the South and on the West Coast.

Few Americans amassed the fabulous fortunes of rich industrialists like Carnegie, yet most people aspired to a better life, even in modest terms. Proprietors, managers, and office workers filled the ranks of the comfortable middle class, men and women freed of the danger and drudgery of manual labor. Between 1880 and 1900, clerical workers tripled in number, and business managers increased from 68,000 to more than 318,000. Enjoying steady work and cash salaries, middle-class employees began to move their families out of the city. Urban areas were becoming increasingly befouled by smokestacks and congested with new factories and workshops.

Providers of goods and services celebrated a "standard" American viewed as white, native born, middle class, heterosexual, and Protestant. This image assumed special significance in the marketing of consumer products and in the appeal of new forms of leisure activities. With technical innovations came novel ways for people to spend their money. Athletic contests, traveling road shows, and amusement parks provided exciting sensory experiences for young and old alike. At the same time, the mass marketing of goods gave rise to a consumer culture that valued newness, fashion, and luxury.

Mass advertising techniques heightened distinctions that European Americans drew between themselves and people they considered inferior, exotic, or foreign. Yet the energy and vitality associated with American popular culture served as a magnet for people all over the world. Beginning in the 1880s, eastern European immigrants streamed to the United States. They were also eager to partake of the country's plentiful jobs, material prosperity, and democratic openness. Well into the twentieth century, the nation still showed the ethnic and cultural diversity that was shaped by patterns of immigration during the late nineteenth century.

The New Shape of Business

In 1882 prospectors discovered gold in the creeks of Idaho's Coeur d'Alene region (in Indian territory, about 90 miles east of Spokane, Washington). Multiethnic boomtowns mushroomed in the region. The Northern Pacific Railway promoted settlement, and the primitive techniques that had been used in surface mining soon yielded to far more efficient hydraulic methods of extraction (a process in which powerful water hoses wash the soil away to expose gold deposits).

The mining industry in the region soon emerged as a big business. In 1885 an unemployed carpenter named Noah S. Kellogg set in motion a dramatic chain of events. Kellogg discovered a lode containing not only gold but also zinc and lead. In short order, he sold his mines to a Portland businessman, who paid a whopping $650,000 for them. A group of eastern and California investors, and finally several large corporations, soon controlled major interests in the mines. By the mid-twentieth century, mining companies had dug more than a billion dollars' worth of metal out of Noah Kellogg's original stake.

Population growth spurred the growth of industries that exploited nature.

Population growth spurred the growth of industries that exploited nature. Immigrants streamed to American shores, particularly from eastern and southern Europe. Between 1880 and 1890, the U.S. population grew from 50 million people to almost 63 million, and six new states entered the Union: North Dakota, South Dakota, Montana, and Washington (all in 1889) and Idaho and Wyoming (both in 1890). Increased demand in turn hastened large-scale commercial mining, logging, and fishing.

Crucial to the process of innovation were engineers, who mastered the technical aspects of construction and design. Many American engineers were trained in Germany, but others attended such schools as the Massachusetts Institute of Technology (MIT) or Cornell University, in New York State, both of which introduced electrical engineering into their curricula in 1882. American engineers, such as those who worked in Mexico under the auspices of mining companies and the railroads, served as the vanguard of American capitalism throughout the world.

Advocates of standardized industrial processes and mass marketing hoped to break down regional barriers and create an integrated national economy. Whether they specialized in railroads or shoes, wheat or steel, business owners and managers who possessed the necessary resources and resourcefulness pursued similar goals: to mine, grow, manufacture, or process large quantities of goods and then market them as widely, cheaply, and quickly as possible. Business put a premium on technological innovation, on the efficient use of workers, and on the reduction of uncertainties that accompanied a competitive marketplace. These guiding principles, formulated during the late 1870s and 1880s, laid the foundations of economic progress in late nineteenth-century America.

New Systems and Machines—and Their Price

The free enterprise system thrived on innovation. Indeed, during the 1880s, new machines, new technical processes, new engineering feats, and new forms of factory organization fueled the growth and efficiency of U.S. businesses. Many devices that became staples of American life appeared during this period. Alexander Graham Bell invented the telephone in 1876. Thomas A. Edison developed the phonograph in 1877 and the electric light in 1879. Cash registers, stock tickers, and typewriters soon became indispensable tools for American businesses. Beginning in the 1880s, railroad cars installed steam heat and electric lights, boosting the comfort of passengers.

DOCUMENT

Edison, "The Success of the Electric Light"

During this period, more and more businesses perfected the so-called American system of manufacturing, which dated back half a century and relied on the mass production of interchangeable parts. Factory workers made large numbers of a particular part, each part exactly the same size and shape. This system enabled manufacturers to assemble products more cheaply and efficiently, to repair products easily with new parts, and to redesign products quickly. The engineers who designed the modern bicycle (which has wheels of equal size) used the American system to make their product affordable to almost anyone who wanted one. The bicycle craze of the late nineteenth century resulted from the novelty and cheapness of this new form of transportation and recreation, one enjoyed by males and females of all ages. Production techniques used to make bicycles were later adapted to the manufacture of automobiles.

New technical processes also facilitated the manufacture and marketing of foods and other consumer goods. Distributors developed pressure-sealed cans, which enabled them to market agricultural products in far-flung parts of the country. Innovative techniques for sheet metal stamping and electric resistance welding transformed a variety of industries. By 1880, 90 percent of American steel was made by the Bessemer process, which injected air into molten iron to yield steel.

The agriculture business benefited from engineering innovations as well, which often reached across national boundaries. As just one example, the first modern irrigation systems in the Southwest were constructed by Native Americans and *mestizos* (people of both indigenous and Spanish ancestry). And in the 1870s, Japan began importing American farm implements and inviting U.S. engineers to construct dams and canals for new steam- and water-powered gristmills and sawmills. Technology was a universal language, one that many peoples around the globe sought to master.

Long active in territorial exploration and land surveying, the federal government continued to assume a leading role in applied science. In 1879 the U.S. Geological Survey (USGS) was formed, charged with compiling and centralizing data describing the natural landscape, an effort that had originated in 1804 with the Lewis and Clark expedition. In the 1880s, the federal government also began to systematize and disseminate information useful to farmers through the U.S.

■ **MAP 16.1**

AGRICULTURAL REGIONS OF THE MIDWEST AND NORTHEAST By 1890 several Midwestern cities served as shipping centers, getting wheat and corn to the growing metropolitan areas of the Northeast and Mid-Atlantic. Farmers complained that the railroads gave discounts to large shippers, such as Standard Oil, and discriminated against small producers.

Resources and Conflict in the West

Department of Agriculture. In 1881, for example, the department's Entomology Bureau began to combine current research on insects with practical techniques for pest control.

Like factory machines, new agricultural machinery benefited consumers, but the need for hired hands evaporated. Early in the nineteenth century, producing an acre of wheat took fifty-six hours of labor; in 1880 that number dropped to twenty hours. One agricultural worker in Ohio observed, "Of one thing we are convinced, that while improved machinery is gathering our large crops, making our boots and shoes, doing the work of our carpenters, stone sawyers, and builders, thousands of able, willing men are going from place to place seeking employment, and finding none. The question naturally arises, is improved machinery a blessing or a curse?"

Alterations in the Natural Environment

Innovation altered the natural landscape and hastened the depletion of certain natural resources. By the mid-1870s, Texas had new steam-powered lumber mills equipped with saw rigs that could produce up to 30,000 board feet a day. This capacity made Texas lumbering a big business, especially when it was combined with infusions of capital and the expansion of railroad lines into the piney woods region, along the eastern edge of the state. Texas lumber mills were poised to benefit from the exhaustion of the great forests of the eastern and Great Lakes states.

In the Chesapeake Bay, dredge boats were becoming more efficient in harvesting oysters, and shellfish reserves began to decline. In the mid-1880s, oyster harvesters took a record 15 million bushels from the bay; the shellfish simply could not replenish themselves. New means of commercial fishing also reduced supplies of salmon in the Northwest.

Courtesy, the Burton Historical Collection, Detroit Public Library

■ Following the wholesale slaughter of buffalo on the Great Plains, settlers earned money by gathering the skeletons. "The bones are shipped East by the carloads," reported the Dodge City *Times*, "where they are ground and used for fertilizing and manufactured into numerous useful articles." This mound of buffalo bones at the Michigan Carlson Works in Detroit, c. 1880, suggests the extent of the devastation.

In 1884 in California, a federal court issued a permanent injunction against hydraulic mining, because it contributed to soil erosion and water pollution. Hydraulic mining had washed an estimated 12 billion tons of earth into San Francisco Bay, raising the floor of the bay several feet. At the same time, mercury flowing into nearby streams from gold mines in the San Jose hills was poisoning fish in the bay, creating pollution that would be felt well into the twentieth century. Similar cases of industrial pollution despoiled other parts of the country. In the absence of any laws to restrain them, Chicago meatpackers befouled the Chicago River with the byproducts of sausage, glue, and fertilizer.

By stimulating manufacturing and **extractive enterprises** alike, the railroads powered these great environmental transformations, for better or worse. Since buffalo herds impeded rail travel, railroads promoted the shooting of buffalo from trains, a "sport" that almost eradicated the species. By the mid-1880s, the great herds had disappeared, victims of ecological change (the incursion of horses into grazing areas), disease (brucellosis spread by domestic livestock), and commercial enterprise. Sioux leader Black Elk decried the slaughter and the "heaps of bones" left to rot in the sun.

Innovations in Financing and Organizing Business

As agents of economic development and cultural change, the railroads knew no peer. As private enterprises, however, they faced the same challenges that all big businesses ultimately must address. The proliferation of independent lines and the high fixed costs associated with the industry made profits slim and competition intense. As a result, railroad companies began to come together in informal pools to share equipment and set prices industrywide. In the 1880s, these pools gave way to consolidation, a process by which several companies merged into one large company.

In these years, U.S. businesses grew larger and more quickly than their western European counterparts. This difference stemmed in large part from America's astonishing population growth and its rich natural resources. Equally significant, the United States possessed a social and legal culture favorable to big business. The absence of an entrenched, conservative elite, along with the spread of state and national laws that protected private property, stimulated the entrepreneurial spirit. The U.S. government refrained from owning industries, although it heavily subsidized the railroad industry. It taxed business lightly and did not tax individual incomes at all until 1913. Finally, American bankers such as J. P. Morgan aggressively promoted growth through their lending practices and bond sales.

Several large enterprises began to conquer not just local but also national markets. Examples include Bell Telephone (founded in Boston), the Kroger grocery business (Cincinnati), Marshall Field department store (Chicago), and Boston Fruit Company. In the South, Midwest, and West, investors rushed to finance gigantic mining operations and agribusinesses, such as the 1.5 million acres devoted to rice cultivation in southeastern Louisiana and bonanza wheat farms (as large as 38,000 acres) in the Red River valley of North Dakota.

Owners of these enterprises devised new forms of business organization that helped their companies grow and survive in a dynamic economy. By combining, or integrating, their operations, manufacturers cut costs and monopolized an entire industry in the process. Unable to withstand the ruthless competition that favored larger enterprises, smaller companies folded. The two icons of American big business in the 1880s—Andrew Carnegie in steel and John D. Rockefeller in petroleum—proved master innovators in both the managerial and technical aspects of business.

In 1875 Carnegie opened the Edgar Thomson Steelworks in Pittsburgh. Within a year, he was producing steel at half the prevailing market price. Carnegie excelled at vertical integration, in which a single firm controls all aspects of production and distribution. Carnegie employed laborers in the Lake Superior region to mine the raw material, and he owned the ships and railroads that brought the ore to the mills in Pittsburgh.

■ Bonanza farms were huge agricultural enterprises, ranging in size from 15,000 to 50,000 acres. This photo shows a bonanza wheat farm in Oregon, c. 1890. Many of these farms relied not only on sophisticated machinery but also on transient labor forces (up to 1,000 workers at a time) to help plow, plant, harvest, and thresh the crop. Some of the largest landowners abandoned farming when they had an opportunity to sell their vast holdings for a profit.

Oregon Historical Society, OrHi 92918

Another form of business consolidation was horizontal integration, in which a number of companies producing the same product merge to reduce competition and control prices. In 1882 John D. Rockefeller, a former bookkeeper, horizontally integrated the petroleum industry by forming Standard Oil Trust. Stockholders in small companies turned over their shares to Standard Oil, which then coordinated operations and eliminated competition from other smaller firms. Standard Oil also practiced vertical integration. Soon Rockefeller had positioned himself to buy out his rivals—or ruin them. **Trusts** placed a premium on efficient production, but they also worked to the disadvantage of consumers, who were hostage to high prices within industries that lacked competition.

New Labor Supplies for a New Economy

To operate efficiently, expanding industries needed expanding supplies of workers to grow crops, extract raw materials, and produce manufactured goods. Many of these workers came from abroad. The year 1880 marked the leading edge of a new wave of immigration to the United States. Over the next ten years, 5.2 million newcomers entered the country, almost twice the previous decade's level of 2.8 million.

In the mid-nineteenth century, most immigrants hailed from western Europe and the British Isles—from Germany, Scandinavia, England, and Ireland. Between 1880 and 1890, Germans, Scandinavians, and the English kept coming, but they were joined by numerous Italians, Russians, and Poles. In fact, these last three groups predominated among newcomers for the next thirty-five years, their arrival rates peaking between 1890 and 1910. At the same time, immigrants from Asia, especially from China, were making their way to the Kingdom of Hawaii, which was annexed by the United States in 1898. Between 1852 and 1887, 26,000 Chinese arrived on the islands. Almost 40 percent of all immigrants to the United States during this period were known as "birds of passage," men who were recruited by American employers and who, after earning some money, migrated back to their native land.

The year 1880 marked the leading edge of a new wave of immigration to the United States. Over the next ten years, 5.2 million newcomers entered the country, almost twice the previous decade's level of 2.8 million.

Many of the new European immigrants sought to escape oppressive economic and political conditions in Europe, even as they hoped to make a new life for themselves and their families in the United States. Russian Jews fled discrimination and violent **antisemitism** in the form of pogroms, organized massacres conducted by their Christian neighbors and Russian authorities. Southern Italians, mostly landless farmers, suffered from a combination of declining agricultural prices and high birth rates. Impoverished Poles chafed under cultural restrictions imposed by Germany and Russia. Hungarians, Greeks, Portuguese, and Armenians, among other groups, also participated in this great migration; members of these groups too were seeking political freedom and economic opportunity.

Immigrants replenished America's sense of itself as a haven for the downtrodden, a place where opportunity beckoned to hard-working and ambitious people. "The New Colossus," written by American poet Emma Lazarus in 1883, pays tribute to the "huddled masses yearning to breathe free"—people from all over the world who sought refuge in the United States. The words of her poem are inscribed on the Statue of Liberty at the entrance to New York harbor.

The story of Rosa Cassettari, a young woman who emigrated from northern Italy to the United States in 1884, suggests the challenges that faced many newcomers during this period. Rosa's husband, Santino, had preceded her to America. He had settled in an iron mining camp in Missouri. Leaving her son with relatives, Rosa received the assurances of friends and relatives: "You will get smart in America. And in America you will not be so poor."

Life in the iron camp proved harsh—nothing like what Rosa had expected. Her husband, who was much older than she, neglected her; he preferred the company of prostitutes in the

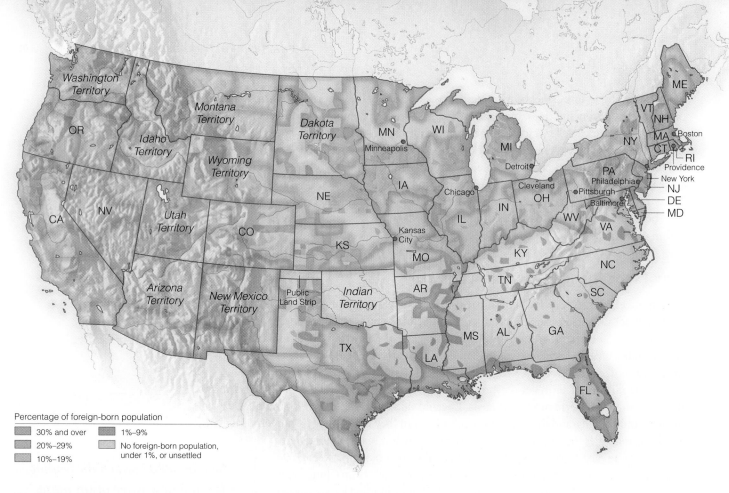

Percentage of foreign-born population

- 30% and over
- 20%–29%
- 10%–19%
- 1%–9%
- No foreign-born population, under 1%, or unsettled

■ **MAP 16.2**

POPULATION OF FOREIGN BORN, BY REGION, 1880 After the Civil War, large numbers of immigrants settled in northeastern cities. In addition, the upper Midwest and parts of the western mining frontier drew many newcomers from western Europe. The area along the country's southwestern border was home to immigrants from Mexico. Cuban cigar makers established thriving communities in southern Florida.

town. The iron was almost depleted, and some workers and their wives had moved on to a new mine in Michigan. Rosa's days centered on caring for her new baby and cooking for thirteen of the miners.

Despite these realities, within a couple of years, Rosa grew used to America and considered herself an American. She returned briefly to her hometown in Italy but expressed impatience with the rigid social etiquette that separated the rich from the poor. She also yearned for the hearty meals that had become her staple in the iron camp. Back in Missouri, she mustered enough courage to leave Santino, traveling to Chicago and making a new life for herself in the Italian *colonia* (community) there. She eventually married another Italian man (the two had fallen in love in Missouri) and found work as a cleaning woman at Chicago Commons, a social settlement house.

Specific groups of immigrants often gravitated toward particular kinds of jobs. For example, many Poles found work in the vast steel plants of Pittsburgh, and Russian Jews went into the garment industry and street-peddling trade in New York City. California fruit orchards and vegetable farms employed numerous Japanese immigrants. Cuban immigrants rolled cigars in Florida. In Hawaii, the Chinese and Japanese labored in the sugar fields; after they had accumulated a little money, they became rice farmers and shopkeepers. In Boston and New York City, second-generation Irish took advantage of their prominent place in the Democratic party to become public school teachers, firefighters, and police officers.

The experience of Kinji Ushijima (later known as George Shima) graphically illustrates the power of immigrant niches. Shima arrived in California in 1887 and, like many other Japanese immigrants, found work as a potato picker in the San Joaquin Valley. Soon, Shima moved up to become a labor contractor, securing Japanese laborers for the valley's white farmers. With the money he made, he bought 15 acres of land and began his own potato farm. Eventually he built a large potato business by expanding his holdings, reclaiming swampland, and investing in a fleet of boats to ship his crops up the coast to San Francisco. Taking advantage of a Japanese niche, Shima prospered through a combination of good luck and hard work.

Efficient Machines, Efficient People

VIDEO
The Industrial Revolution

By the late nineteenth century, the typical industrial employee labored within an immense, multistory brick structure and operated a machine powered by water or steam. Smoky, smelly kerosene lamps gave way to early forms of electric lighting, first arc and then incandescent light bulbs. Long-standing industries, such as textiles and shoes, were now fully mechanized. The new products flooding the economy—locomotives and bicycles, cash registers and typewriters—streamed from factories designed to ensure maximum efficiency from both machines *and* the people who tended them.

In the 1880s, a few factory managers hired efficiency experts. The experts' goal was to cut labor costs in the same way that industry barons had shaved the costs of extracting raw materials or distributing final products. With huge quantities of goods flowing from factories, even modest savings in wages could mean significant profits in the long run. Frederick Winslow Taylor, chief engineer for the Midvale Steel Plant outside Philadelphia, pioneered in the techniques of efficient "scientific management."

> *By the late nineteenth century, the typical industrial employee labored within an immense, multistory brick structure and operated a machine powered by water or steam.*

Southern textile mill owners in the Piedmont region of South Carolina and Georgia devised their own strategies for shaping a compliant workforce. They employed only white men, women, and children as machine operators, but threatened to hire blacks if the whites protested low wages and poor working conditions. Poor whites lived in company housing, their children attended company schools, and they received cash wages. In contrast, blacks remained in the countryside, impoverished and without the right to vote. In the cities of the North as well as the textile villages of the South, factory workers remained exclusively white until well into the twentieth century.

The Birth of a National Urban Culture

In the 1880s, visitors to the territory of Utah marveled at the capital, Salt Lake City, where Mormon pioneers had made the desert bloom. Situated at the foot of the magnificent snow-covered Wasatch Range, this oasis in the Great Salt Basin boasted a built landscape almost as impressive as the natural beauty that surrounded it. In the heart of Salt Lake City lay Temple Square. This broad plaza contained the Mormon Tabernacle, a huge domed structure. Next to it stood the Mormon Temple, a soaring six-spired granite cathedral still under construction. The city had the advantage of rail service (Promontory Point, where the transcontinental railroad was joined, was not far away). Mines in nearby Bingham Canyon yielded rich lodes of silver and large local smelters refined copper ores. Irrigation systems made the city self-sufficient in the production of foodstuffs. A settlement inspired by religious faith, Salt Lake City was at the same time thoroughly modern.

Not just Salt Lake City, but other cities around the country began to assume monumental proportions. In New York, the 1880s marked the completion of Central Park and the Brooklyn Bridge and the arrival of the Statue of Liberty from France. Chicago, rebuilding after a disastrous fire in 1871, became a sprawling rail hub dotted with yards for western cattle, northern timber, and the

■ Admirers hailed New York City's Brooklyn Bridge as the eighth wonder of the world when it was completed in 1883. With a central span of 1,595 feet, it became the largest suspension bridge in the world. Built over fourteen years, the bridge linked Brooklyn to Manhattan across the East River, using steel suspension cables that are nearly 16 inches thick. Its total cost was about $18 million.

trains that hauled them. In 1885 Chicago also became the location for a major architectural breakthrough by engineer William LeBaron Jenney. He designed the ten-story Home Insurance Building, the world's first metal frame skyscraper. The steel skeleton weighed only one third as much as the thick stone walls needed to support a similar masonry building, and the design left room for numerous windows. Urban architecture would never be the same again.

Cities in general represented American notions of progress and prosperity; they were places where innovation, consumer culture, and new forms of entertainment grew and flourished. From 1875 to 1900, American cities developed increasingly sophisticated systems of communications and transportation. Streetlights, transportation networks, and sewer lines provided basic services to swelling populations of immigrants and rural in-migrants. Cities also represented a new cultural diversity in American life. And they required larger local governments to manage the services necessary for daily life.

Economic Sources of Urban Growth

Northeastern and mid-Atlantic cities emerged as centers of concentrated manufacturing activity. Yet, with the aid of eastern capital, western cities also flourished. New York's Wall Street and Boston's State Street, home to the nation's largest investment bankers, financed the Main Streets of the Midwest and West. Some urban areas prospered through milling, mining, or other enterprises, such as lumber and flour milling in Minneapolis and ore smelting in Denver. Others focused on manufacturing to serve a growing western population. Chicago was rivaled only by New York in terms of its industrial economy and the vast territory that it supplied with raw materials, processed food, and manufactured goods. Salt Lake City produced goods for the so-called Mormon Corridor of settlements that stretched west from the city to southern California. By the 1880s, San Francisco had a commercial reach that encompassed much of the West as well as Hawaii and Alaska.

No trend supported urban growth more than the arrival of newcomers from abroad. To stoke its furnaces, mill its lumber, and slaughter its cattle, Chicago relied on immigrants from Ireland, Slovakia, Germany, Poland, and Bohemia. The three cities with the highest percentage of foreign-born residents in 1880 were San Francisco (45 percent), Chicago (42 percent), and New York (40 percent). Yet all large cities also attracted migrants from America's own countryside, as native-born men and women fled the hardships of life on the farm. Moreover, the use of increasingly efficient agricultural machines meant that rural workers had fewer job opportunities. Most of the immigrants from rural areas to the cities were young women; they included Yankee girls from the hardscrabble homesteads of New England, daughters of Swedish immigrants in Minnesota, and native-born farm tenants in Indiana.

Rural folk sought the steady work and wages afforded by jobs in the city, but they were also drawn to the excitement that had become the hallmark of the urban scene. In the early nineteenth century, Thomas Jefferson had located the heart of America in its sturdy yeoman farmers. By the late nineteenth century, that heart had shifted to the city.

Building the Cities

The American city was emerging as a technological marvel. Through a combination of money and engineering skill, cities managed to provide an adequate water supply for private and commercial purposes, move large numbers of people and goods efficiently, get rid of waste materials, and illuminate thoroughfares at night. Professionals, such as landscape contractors, construction architects, and civil engineers, designed the parks, bridges, public libraries, and museums that made cities so attractive to many.

Cities grew upward and outward as a result of developments in mass production and technology. Elevators extended living and office spaces upward. The invention of the electric streetcar in 1888 permitted cities to spread out. Soon, residential suburbs cropped up many miles from urban commercial cores. Wealthy and middle-class urban residents followed the streetcar lines out of the city, hoping to find a green refuge from the grime and noise of downtown while maintaining a manageable commute to work.

As cities expanded, the challenges associated with providing services also grew more complex and expensive. A polluted water supply, for example, meant epidemics of diphtheria and cholera, so city taxpayers demanded waterworks that delivered drinkable water through intricate systems of dams, pumps, reservoirs, and pipes. Chicago had long pumped its sewage into Lake Michigan, the source of its drinking water. In the 1880s, the city financed the building of a canal and the reversal of the flow of the Chicago River. These changes sent the city's sewage away from Lake Michigan and westward into the Mississippi River instead. Begun in 1889, the 28-mile Chicago Sanitary and Ship Canal was completed seven years later. One awed observer marveled at the "powerful machinery for digging and hoisting, steam shovels, excavators, inclines, conveyors, derricks, cantilevers, cableways, channelers, steam drills, pumps, etc." The cost: $54 million.

Local Government Gets Bigger

These new systems of services, combined with the mushrooming immigrant neighborhoods, changed both the quality and the quantity of urban problems. Zoning issues—who could build what, where, and when—became flashpoints for conflict as the interests of homeowners, developers, and municipal engineers collided. Urban political leaders struggled to improve the city's public works while meeting the needs of multiple ethnic groups. Governing a city was an expensive, full-time enterprise and one that had the potential to be very lucrative to businesspeople and politicians alike.

Although New York's "Boss" Tweed had been convicted on charges of corruption in the early 1870s, the infamous Tammany Hall gang carried on his legacy. The Democratic officials associated with this social and political organization perfected a system of kickbacks linked to municipal construction projects. Under this system, contractors paid politicians for city construction contracts. For example, a New York City courthouse that was supposed to cost a quarter of a million dollars ended up costing taxpayers fifty-two times that amount, or twice as much as the United States paid Russia for Alaska! In the 1880s, secretive networks of corruption linking law enforcement personnel, city officials, and construction contractors flourished in many cities. These webs, or "machines," characterized urban life for decades to come.

> *In the 1880s, secretive networks of corruption linking law enforcement personnel, city officials, and construction contractors flourished in many cities.*

Urban machines existed to secure jobs for their loyal supporters and line the pockets of those at the highest levels of power. Deal-making blurred the lines between private enterprise and public service as everyone from mayors to local ward organizers benefited from the modernization of the American city. In the process, urban bosses ensured that the streets were paved, tenement buildings erected, sewer lines laid, and trolley tracks extended. But taxpayers footed the bill, which included outrageous amounts of money used for bribes and kickbacks.

Money-grubbing politicians, judges, and police extorted "hush money" from brothels, gambling parlors, and unlicensed taverns. Urban bosses also had a vested interest in sponsoring new money-making venues for professional sports and supporting other forms of commercialized leisure activity. Baseball parks, boxing rings, and race tracks yielded huge sums in the form of kickbacks from contractors. Once built, stadiums and boxing rings generated profits indefinitely as fans filled the stands.

Thrills, Chills, and Bathtubs: The Emergence of Consumer Culture

On a hot summer day in 1890, a young mother named Emily Scanlon, with her three-year-old daughter in tow, paid the 5-cent admission fee to a popular ride called the Toboggan Slide at the Brandywine Springs Amusement Park near Wilmington, Delaware. The two of them ascended a stairwell to the top of the three-story-high structure and then stepped into a car that ran on a wooden trough. When the attendant released the brakes, the car descended, pulled by gravity. It moved slowly at first, then picked up speed around a curve. Suddenly, Emily Scanlon stood up in the car (perhaps to retrieve her hat, which had blown off), and she and her daughter were thrown from the car. Mrs. Scanlon died instantly of a broken neck, but the youngster survived. Significantly, the tragedy did not provoke a shutdown of the ride or the installation of safety measures. Instead, park managers simply posted a sign that read, "Passengers must keep their seats." Patrons continued to enjoy the thrills of the toboggan.

Brandywine Springs boasted an ornate gateway that proclaimed "Let All Who Enter Here Leave Care Behind." In cities around the country, amusement parks brought men and women, girls and boys together to enjoy merry-go-rounds, prizefights, and circus sideshows. By 1880 railroads and steamships were transporting crowds out of Manhattan to Coney Island, where working-class people mingled with the self-proclaimed "respectable" middle classes.

Americans of all kinds began to sample a new realm of sensual experience—one of physical daring, material luxury, and visual fantasy—either as participants or as observers. Central to this emerging consumer culture was mass advertising, a form of appeal that sought to instill in consumers the desire for things that were new and visually attractive. Colorful spectacles of all kinds—whether in the form of a department store window or a well-publicized athletic event—became an integral part of American life.

Shows as Spectacles

Public officials, college administrators, and ambitious entrepreneurs alike discovered that Americans craved new and stimulating forms of entertainment and were willing to pay for them. The traveling circus provides a case in point. By the 1870s, such shows were erecting their tents in small towns and big cities alike. The largest shows employed hundreds of people as performers, cooks, carpenters, and wagon drivers. Circus owners provided their customers with exciting sights and sounds—death-defying lion-tamers, gravity-defying gymnasts and tightrope walkers, exhibits of wild animals such as elephants and tigers, rollicking brass bands, and the hilarious antics of clowns.

In the quarter-century after Reconstruction, three major sports began to attract large national audiences. Organized baseball had existed since 1846, when the Knickerbocker Base Ball Club of New York met the New York Nine in Hoboken, New Jersey. (The score was 23 to 1, in favor of the Nine.) The National Baseball League, consisting of eight professional teams, was founded in 1876, the American League in 1900. In the 1880s, several new regulations—those governing the overhand pitch, foul balls, and swingless strikes—helped to standardize the game.

Also in the 1880s, Walter Camp, a former Yale University football player, introduced rules—for instance, the system of downs and the center snap to the quarterback—that made that sport quicker and more competitive. Camp was also behind the selection of the first "All America" team (1889) to stimulate fan interest. By this time towns, high schools, and colleges were fielding football teams.

Likewise, boxing emerged as a national, regulated sport. John L. Sullivan, an American, won renown as the world's bare-knuckled champion in 1882, even as more and more fighters had started wearing gloves. Sullivan then joined a traveling theatrical group and demonstrated gloved boxing to enthusiastic crowds all over the country. In 1889, Sullivan defeated an opponent in a seventy-five-round match, the last heavyweight, bare-knuckled championship.

Performances based on skills of all kinds gained national audiences, as the career of William "Buffalo Bill" Cody reveals. Born in Iowa in 1846, Cody parlayed his early years as a Pony Express postal rider, cavalry scout, Indian fighter, and buffalo hunter into a form of mass entertainment. In his "Buffalo Bill Combination" show, cowboy and Indian actors performed skits depicting dramatic events in western history (from a European American point of view, at least).

In 1882 Cody produced "Buffalo Bill's Wild West," a traveling road show that featured sharpshooter Annie Oakley, cowboy musicians, and Sioux warriors performing authentic Native American dances. Sioux leader Sitting Bull (Tatanka Iyotake), long an admirer of Annie Oakley (he called her "Little Sure Shot"), joined the show in 1885. Like other Indians who worked for Cody, Sitting Bull took advantage of the opportunity to escape the confines of the reservation (in his case, Standing Rock in North Dakota). As a member of the "Wild West" troupe, he also enjoyed decent food and accommodations. At a time when whites were denigrating Indian culture, Sitting Bull affirmed that culture by demonstrating his shooting and riding skills. However, white audiences jeered him—they saw him as less an entertainer and more an enemy warrior—and he left after just a year. By the 1890s, Cody was playing to audiences in Europe as well as the United States, dramatizing a West that was fast disappearing.

Denver Public Library/Western History/Genealogy Department (Neg. #B-133)

■ "Buffalo Bill" Cody and Sitting Bull pose for a promotional photo for the 1885 season of the "Wild West." Cody refrained from calling the production a "show," maintaining that it demonstrated frontier skills and recreated historical encounters (such as Custer's Last Stand and stagecoach robberies). The "Wild West" toured Canada and Europe and inspired many imitators.

Mass Merchandising as Spectacle

During the late nineteenth century, the act of shopping in cities for goods, especially luxury goods, became an adventure in itself. A new piece of the cityscape, the department store, welcomed customers into a world of luxury and abundance, a place of color, light, and glamour. These "palaces of consumption" showcased a variety of technological innovations. In Marshall Field's "Grand Emporium" (Chicago), Wanamaker's (Philadelphia), and Lord & Taylor (New York), shoppers glided from story to story on escalators and in elevators. Warmed by central heating, they browsed display cases, racks, and tables laden with enticing goods and illuminated by arc lighting. Their money streamed into cash registers or to a central clerk through cash conveyors.

Thus, department stores not only offered a dazzling array of goods but also made shopping an exciting experience. This appealed particularly to middle-class women, who had the leisure time and the cash to indulge in day-long shopping excursions. In 1880 a New Yorker could arrive at Macy's by taking the Sixth Avenue elevated train and spend the morning exploring any number of specialized departments: ribbons, women's and children's muslin underwear, toys, candy, books, men's furnishings, china and glassware, and so on. Fatigued at noon, she might visit the lunchroom to partake of a modest meal and then devote the rest of her day to examining the colored dress silks, a new department established the year before.

The department store was an exclusively urban phenomenon, but mass merchandising reached far beyond cities. The material riches of American society became accessible to rural people through the mail-order catalogue. This marketing device was pioneered in 1872 by the Chicago company Montgomery Ward, the official supply house for the Farmers' Grange. On homesteads throughout the Midwest, family members gathered to pore over the thousands of items displayed in "The Great Wish Book." The company's motto? "Satisfaction guaranteed or your money back." Farm wives delighted in the latest Parisian fashions, their husbands pondered the intricacies of McCormick threshing machinery, and the children studied the newest line of toys and fishing rods. Late in the decade, a competitor appeared on the scene in the form of the Sears, Roebuck Catalogue.

The mass production needed to satisfy eager customers depended on mass advertising, an enterprise still in its infancy in the 1880s. Yet some of the principles that would shape the future of this business were in place even at this early date. For instance, soon after the Civil War, the makers of Sozodont dentifrice (toothpaste) plastered the name of their product all over weekly religious magazines and more mainstream publications, such as *Harper's* and *Scribner's*. They labeled the natural landscape as well. Indeed, the word *Sozodont* on Maiden's Rock in Red Wing, Minnesota, was so large that steamboat passengers on the Mississippi River three miles away could plainly read it.

■ Refugio Amador and her five daughters, Emilia, Maria, Clotilde, Julieta, and Corina, were members of an elite Hispanic family in Las Cruces, New Mexico. Her husband, Martin Amador, was a prominent politician, merchant, hotel owner, and freighter. A subcontractor for the U.S. government, he supplied military troops in the area. The family shopped by mail-order catalogue from Bloomingdale's Department Store in New York City.

VIDEO

"Rural Free Delivery Mail"

Defending the New Industrial Order

By the late 1870s, as consumer culture expanded, intense conflict over fundamental issues all but evaporated from national politics. Although ethnic and cultural loyalties continued to inflame local and state elections, Republicans and Democrats at the national level disagreed about little except the tariff. Adhering to tradition, Republicans favored a higher tariff that would benefit domestic businesses by making imported goods more expensive. In contrast, Democrats argued that a higher tariff, and resulting higher prices for goods produced in the United States, would harm consumers. Members of the Republican party called themselves the Grand Army of the Republic; they "waved the **bloody shirt**"—that is, reminded voters that many of their Democratic opponents, especially those in the South, had supported secession a generation before. Still, the two major parties openly shared a similar goal: to win as many jobs as possible for their respective supporters. Politics served as a vehicle for patronage and favors rather than as a conduit for ideas and alternative visions of the nation's future.

Many politicians also shared a belief in the idea of ***laissez-faire*** (a French phrase meaning to leave alone, referring to the absence of government interference in the economy). Laissez-faire was actually a flexible concept, invoked to justify government indifference in some areas but government intervention in others. Indeed, politicians tended to favor laissez-faire in social matters more than in the economy. Thus, support for manufacturers and railroads in the form of tariff protection and land grants, for example, was justified. At the same time, however, Congress, the president, and the Supreme Court were reluctant to enact bold measures to redress the growing gap between rich and poor. In fact, certain clergy, businesspeople, and university professors sought to explain and defend the inequality between the captains of industry and the masses of ill-paid laborers. Their theory of **Social Darwinism** viewed the system of industrial capitalism as desirable because it was "natural."

In his first novel, *The Gilded Age* (1873), writer Mark Twain (Samuel Clemens) satirized the trend toward corruption in public affairs and the wild financial speculation that produced both poverty and great wealth. The growth of large businesses that received economic and political support from government officials served to enrich employers, investors, and politicians at the expense of workers and farmers. The term *Gilded Age* became synonymous with the excess and extravagance on the part of politicians and businessmen alike during the last quarter of the nineteenth century.

The Contradictory Politics of Laissez-Faire

In 1880 the undistinguished President Rutherford B. Hayes chose not to run for office again. That summer the Republicans nominated James A. Garfield of Ohio, a former mule driver who had become a Civil War general. To counter the "bloody-shirt" effect, Democrats put forth their own former Union general: Winfield S. Hancock, who had been wounded at Gettysburg. Garfield won the popular vote by a narrow margin but overwhelmed Hancock in the electoral college.

Garfield's arrival in the White House set off a race for patronage jobs among loyal Republicans. Indeed, overwhelmed by office-seekers, the new president remarked, "My God! What is there in this place that a man should ever want to get into it?" Then on July 2, 1881, Charles J. Guiteau, who had unsuccessfully sought the position of U.S. consul in Paris, shot Garfield in a Washington, D.C., train station. Garfield languished for a few months, finally dying on September 19.

Vice President Chester A. Arthur, a former New York politician, assumed the reins of government. Arthur's administration supported certain forms of government intervention in society, or "social engineering." Arthur and others believed that laissez-faire policies had their limits; strong measures were needed to counter what they and other conservatives considered immoral personal behavior. In 1882 Congress passed the Edmunds Act. Targeting Mormons, the act outlawed polygamy (the practice of having more than one wife at a time), took the right to vote away from the law's offenders, and sent a five-member commission to Utah to oversee local elections.

TABLE 16-1

The Election of 1880

Candidate	Political Party	Popular Vote (%)	Electoral Vote
James A. Garfield	Republican	48.5	214
Winfield S. Hancock	Democratic	48.1	155
James B. Weaver	Greenback-Labor	3.4	—

That same year, Congress responded to pressure from West Coast European American politicians, the San Francisco Workingmen's Party in particular, and approved the Chinese Exclusion Act. The act became the first piece of legislation to bar a particular group from entering the United States. Most Chinese immigrants took jobs that native-born whites shunned. Moreover, unemployment among California white manufacturing workers in the 1870s was caused not by Chinese competitors, but by the flood of cheap eastern-made goods carried into the state by the transcontinental railroad. As eastern goods entered California, manufacturers in the West laid off workers and closed factories. The Chinese thus became scapegoats for groups hit hard by larger economic changes.

In 1883 the Supreme Court hurt the cause of blacks' civil rights by declaring the Civil Rights Act of 1875 unconstitutional. The five cases involved in the Court's decision focused on exclusions of blacks from hotels, railroad cars, and theaters. The Court held that state governments could not discriminate on the basis of race but that private individuals could do so. This decision put an official stamp of approval on racist practices of employers, hotels, restaurants, and other providers of jobs and services.

Arthur surprised his critics by embracing the cause of civil service reform. This movement sought to inject professional standards into public service and rid the country of the worst excesses of the corrupt "spoils system," where political victors put loyal supporters into public jobs regardless of their qualifications. In response to Garfield's assassination by Guiteau, the disappointed patronage-seeker, Congress passed the Pendleton Act (1883). This measure established a merit system for federal job applicants and created the Civil Service Commission, which administered competitive examinations to candidates in certain classifications.

In 1884 Arthur fell ill (he would die shortly), and the Republicans nominated James G. Blaine of Maine as their candidate for the presidency. Blaine, who had benefited from corrupt deals in the past, offended the sensibilities of a group of reform-minded Republicans, who called themselves Mugwumps. (The term reportedly had its roots in an Indian word that meant "holier than thou.") As a result, Blaine was bested in the national election by the former mayor of Buffalo, Grover Cleveland, who became the first Democratic president in twenty-eight years.

TABLE 16-2			
The Election of 1884			
Candidate	Political Party	Popular Vote (%)	Electoral Vote
Grover Cleveland	Democratic	48.5	219
James G. Blaine	Republican	48.2	182

Resources and Conflict in the West

The Dawes Act

Throughout the 1880s, Congress and the chief executive applied the laissez-faire principle selectively—for example, to the status of Indians. Like other critics of federal Indian policy, writer Helen Hunt Jackson in her 1881 book *A Century of Dishonor* called for applying the "protection of the law to the Indian's rights of property." Moved to act, Congress passed the Dawes General Allotment (Severalty) Act in 1887. The new act was intended to improve the economic condition of Indians by eliminating common ownership of tribal lands in favor of a system of private property. The law distributed plots of land to individual Indians who renounced traditional customs. The law also encouraged these landowners to become sedentary farmers and to adopt "other habits of civilized life." In the end, however, the act amounted to little more than a land-grab on the part of whites; between 1887 and 1900, Indian-held lands decreased from 138 million acres to 78 million acres.

By the 1880s, local citizens, through the Grange and their elected public officials, were calling for the states to restrict the monopolistic practices of the railroads. Nevertheless, in *Wabash v. Illinois* (1886), the Supreme Court invalidated a state law regulating railroads, ruling that only Congress, and not the states, could control interstate transportation. The next year Congress passed the Interstate Commerce Act of 1887. This legislation mandated that the railroads charge all shippers the same rates and refrain from giving rebates to their largest customers. The act also established the Interstate Commerce Commission to oversee and stabilize the railroad industry. Congress thus acknowledged that the public interest demanded some form of business regulation, although enforcement of the act was less than vigorous.

DOCUMENT

Interstate Commerce Act

Cleveland invoked laissez-faire principles in 1887 when he vetoed legislation that would have provided seeds for hard-pressed farmers in Texas. As the president put it, "Though the people support the government, the government should not support the people." Cleveland also favored lower tariff rates, but most Americans favored government protection of domestic manufacturing in the form of higher tariffs. The Republicans exploited Cleveland's unpopular views on this issue in the 1888 campaign, nominating Benjamin Harrison, grandson of President William Henry ("Tippecanoe") Harrison. The younger Harrison defeated his rival in the electoral college but not in the popular vote.

TABLE 16-3			
The Election of 1888			
Candidate	Political Party	Popular Vote (%)	Electoral Vote
Benjamin Harrison	Republican	42.9	233
Grover Cleveland	Democratic	48.6	168
Clinton B. Fisk	Prohibition	2.2	—
Anson J. Streeter	Union Labor	1.3	—

The principle of government laissez-faire was of little use in addressing a central paradox of the late nineteenth century: the free enterprise system was being undermined by the very forms of business organization it had spawned and nourished. **Trusts** and combinations were inherently hostile to competition. In 1890 Congress passed a piece of landmark legislation, the Sherman Anti-Trust Act, designed to outlaw trusts and large business combinations of all kinds.

Social Darwinism and the "Natural" State of Society

In the late nineteenth century, human-made devices and engineering feats helped create a new social order, one marked by a few very wealthy industrialists, a growing middle class, and an increasingly diverse workforce of ill-paid field and factory hands. Brazenly borrowing from the theories of Charles Darwin, a British naturalist who had pioneered the study of evolution, some prominent clergy, businesspeople, journalists, and university professors sought to defend this new order as God-ordained or "natural." These observers drew parallels between Darwin's theory of "survival of the fittest" and the workings of modern society. (In his book *The Origin of Species*, Darwin had discussed the study of animals, not people or societies.) In the United States, Social Darwinists warned that "unnatural" forms of intervention—specifically, labor unions or social welfare legislation—were misguided, dangerous, and ultimately doomed to failure. In essence, Social Darwinists distorted a compelling scientific theory, misusing it to justify exploitation of the poor and laboring classes.

DOCUMENT

Herbert Spencer, Social Darwinism (1857)

The ideology of Social Darwinism evolved in response to class conflict and other forms of social turbulence in the 1870s and 1880s. Famed Brooklyn minister Henry Ward Beecher cited what he called "the great laws of political economy" to preach the virtues of poverty ("it was fit that man should eat the bread of affliction") and the evils of labor unions. Beecher and like-minded thinkers agreed that the government had the right and the obligation to come to the rescue of private companies threatened by angry workers or consumers. These observers also made a distinction between public subsidies to railroads and tariff protection for domestic manufacturers on one hand and public intervention on behalf of workers on the other.

Yale sociologist William Graham Sumner declared that society was like a living organism. For the species to remain healthy, individuals must prosper or decline according to their inherent characteristics. "Society, therefore, does not need any care or supervision," Sumner wrote in his 1883 treatise *What the Social Classes Owe to Each Other*. These views

INTERPRETING HISTORY

Andrew Carnegie and the "Gospel of Wealth"

In an article titled "Wealth," published in the North American Review *in 1889, steel manufacturer Andrew Carnegie defended the amassing of large fortunes on the part of a few. He hailed this trend as a sign of progress.*

The conditions of human life have not only been changed, but revolutionized, within the past few hundred years. In the former days there was little difference between the dwelling, dress, food, and environment of the chief and those of his retainers. The Indians are to-day where civilized man then was. When visiting the Sioux, I was led to the wigwam of the chief. It was just like the others in external appearance, and even within the difference was trifling between it and those of the poorest of his braves. The contrast between the palace of the millionaire and the cottage of the laborer with us to-day measures the change which has come with civilization.

This change, however, is not to be deplored, but welcomed as highly beneficial. It is well, nay, essential for the progress of the race, that the houses of some should be homes for all that is highest and best in literature and the arts, and for all the refinements of civilization, rather than that none should be so. Much better this great irregularity than universal squalor. . . . Whether the change be for good or ill, it is upon us, beyond our

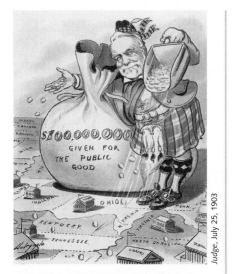

This *Judge* cartoon depicts Andrew Carnegie dispersing his fortune. Many of his donations were used for the establishment of public libraries, a worthy cause according to Carnegie's "gospel of wealth."

Judge, July 25, 1903

power to alter, and therefore to be accepted and made the best of. It is a waste of time to criticise the inevitable.

Carnegie believed that wealthy people had the responsibility to give away their money before they died, although he had distinct ideas about to whom—or to what—such money should be given. He elaborated on what came to be called the "gospel of wealth":

There remains, then, only one mode of using great fortunes; but in this we have the true antidote for the temporary unequal distribution of wealth, the reconciliation of the rich and the poor—a reign of harmony—another ideal, differing indeed, from that of the Communist in

requiring only the further evolution of existing conditions, not the total overthrow of our civilization. . . . Under its sway we shall have an ideal state, in which the surplus wealth of the few will become, in the best sense, the property of the many, because it is administered for the common good, and this wealth, passing through the hands of the few, can be made a much more potent force for the elevation of our race than if it had been distributed in small sums to the people themselves. Even the poorest can be made to see this, and to agree that the great sums gathered by some of their fellow-citizens and spent for public purposes, from which the masses reap the principal benefit, are more valuable to them than if scattered through the course of many years in trifling amounts.

In 1901 Carnegie sold his steel company to banker J. P. Morgan for $480 million. By the time of his death, Carnegie had given away an estimated $350 million to a variety of causes and institutions.

Questions

1. How does Carnegie link extremes of wealth and poverty with progress?
2. Why did Carnegie focus his philanthropic energies on building public libraries?
3. Why would Carnegie have rejected as impractical and unreasonable the argument that he should have paid his workers higher wages rather than distributing his profits to charity? ■

Source: Andrew Carnegie, "Wealth," *North American Review* (1889).

rationalized not only the hierarchies of the workplace but also the triumph of "Anglo Saxons" on the North American continent and beyond. Editors of the *New York Times* interpreted Darwin's ideas as suggesting that "the red man will be driven out, and the white man will take possession. This is not justice, but it is destiny." In his book *Our Country* (1885), the Reverend Josiah Strong also drew on the ideas of Social Darwinism to claim that just as the fittest plants and animals endure in the natural kingdom, so "civilized" whites would eventually displace "barbarous," dark-skinned peoples, whether on the High Plains of South Dakota or on the savannas of Africa.

Conclusion

Some historians suggest that the great captains of industry were the chief representatives of widely held values in late-nineteenth-century America. Men such as Carnegie and Rockefeller had the vision and personal ambition necessary to build large corporate enterprises. They became fabulously wealthy by providing the United States with the ingredients necessary to an economic revolution: steel, oil, and other materials. Their ideology of unbridled individualism encouraged many people to aspire to entrepreneurial independence: the tailor's hope that he would someday own his own store, the waiter's dream of opening his own restaurant. The explosion of economic activity during this period—a second American industrial revolution—widened the middle class and lent credence to the notion of widespread upward mobility, modest though it was in most cases.

Nevertheless, a case can be made that engineers were the true representatives of the age. As designers of railroad routes, gravity-defying skyscrapers, and new systems of shop-floor management, they oversaw the technical aspects of economic growth and development. Engineers melded science with mass production to yield a form of capitalism that thrived on consumers' deepest desires and anxieties, despite resistance from some who rejected standardization in favor of local tradition or new forms of collective action.

Sites to Visit

Alexander Graham Bell Family Papers

www.memory.loc.gov/ammem/bellhtml/bellhome.html

> This Library of Congress site contains papers from 1862 to 1939 as well as a chronology, images, selected documents, and interpretive essays about Bell.

John D. Rockefeller and Standard Oil

www.micheloud.com/FXM/SO/

> This study with accompanying images by François Micheloud tells of the rise of Rockefeller and his mammoth company.

Transcontinental Railroad

www.sfmuseum.org/hist1/rail.html

> This virtual Museum of the City of San Francisco site has excellent information on the railroad.

Touring Turn-of-the-Century America: Photographs from the Detroit Publishing Company, 1880–1920

www.memory.loc.gov/ammem/detroit/dethome.html

> This Library of Congress collection has thousands of photographs from turn-of-the-century America.

African American Perspectives: Pamphlets from the Daniel A. P. Murray Collection, 1818–1907

www.memory.loc.gov/ammem/aap/aaphome.html

> This collection includes writings of famous African Americans, including Frederick Douglass, Booker T. Washington, Ida B. Wells-Barnett, Benjamin W. Arnett, Alexander Crummel, and Emanuel Love.

Evolution of the Conservation Movement, 1850–1920

www.memory.loc.gov/ammem/amrvhtml/conshome.html

> This American Memory site brings together scores of primary sources and photographs about the historical formations and cultural foundations of the movement to conserve and protect America's natural heritage.

Inside an American Factory: The Westinghouse Works, 1904

www.memory.loc.gov/ammem/papr/west/westhome.html

> Part of the American Memory project at the Library of Congress, this site provides a glimpse inside a turn-of-the-century factory.

For Further Reading

General Works

Alfred D. Chandler, *The Visible Hand: The Managerial Revolution in American Business* (1977).

Jon Gjerde, *The Minds of the West: Ethnocultural Evolution in the Rural Middle West, 1830–1917* (1997).

Andrew C. Isenberg, *The Destruction of the Bison: An Environmental History, 1750–1920* (2000).

T. Jackson Lears, *Fables of Abundance: A Cultural History of Advertising in America* (1994).

Walter Licht, *Industrializing America: The Nineteenth Century* (1995).

The New Shape of Business

James R. Barrett, *Work and Community in the Jungle: Chicago's Packinghouse Workers, 1894–1922* (1987).

Ron Chernow, *Titan: The Life of John D. Rockefeller, Sr.* (1998).

Wendy Gamber, *The Female Economy: The Millinery and Dressmaking Trades, 1860–1930* (1997).

Thomas Parke Hughes, *American Genesis: A Century of Invention and Technological Enthusiasm, 1870–1970* (1989).

David E. Nye, *Electrifying America: Social Meanings of a New Technology, 1880–1940* (1990).

Donald J. Pisani, *Water, Land, and Law in the West: The Limits of Public Policy, 1850–1920* (1996).

C. J. Schmitz, *The Growth of Big Business in the United States and Western Europe, 1850–1939* (1993).

The Birth of a National Urban Culture

Edwin G. Burrows and Mike Wallace, *Gotham: A History of New York City to 1898* (1999).

Howard P. Chudacoff and Judith E. Smith, *The Evolution of American Urban Society*, 5th ed. (2000).

William Cronon, *Nature's Metropolis: Chicago and the Great West* (1991).

Robert V. Hine and John Mack Faragher, *The American West: A New Interpretive History* (2000).

Eric Monkkonen, *America Becomes Urban: The Development of U.S. Cities and Towns, 1780–1980* (1988).

David Nasaw, *Going Out: The Rise and Fall of Public Amusements* (1993).

Thrills, Chills, and Bathtubs

Bessie Louise Pierce, *As Others See Chicago: Impressions of Visitors 1673–1933* (2004).

Allen Guttmann, *A Whole New Ball Game: An Interpretation of American Sports* (1988).

John F. Kasson, *Amusing the Millions: Coney Island at the Turn of the Century* (1978).

Joy S. Kasson, *Buffalo Bill's Wild West: Celebrity, Memory and Popular History* (2000).

William Leach, *Land of Desire: Merchants, Power, and the Rise of a New American Culture* (1993).

Defending the New Industrial Order

Thomas L. Haskell, *The Emergence of Professional Social Science: The American Social Science Association and the Nineteenth-Century Crisis of Authority* (1977).

Richard Hofstadter, *Social Darwinism in American Thought, 1860–1914*, rev. ed. (1955).

Valerie S. Mathes, *Helen Hunt Jackson and Her Indian Reform Legacy* (1990).

Louis Menand, *The Metaphysical Club: A Story of Ideas in America* (2001).

For quizzes and other resources on these topics, go to www.longmanamericanhistory.com.

Challenges to Government and Corporate Power, 1877–1890

I N THE SPRING OF 1889, MEN IN SAN MIGUEL COUNTY, NORTHERN NEW MEXICO TERRITORY, armed themselves and donned masks. Mounting their horses, they rode out to attack their enemies. As members of a secret organization called *las Gorras Blancas* (the Whitecaps), they banded together in the dead of the night and destroyed the fences of local cattle ranchers, chopping the wooden posts to pieces and scattering the barbed wire. In some of their raids, the rebels shot and wounded ranchers. Over the next year and a half, *las Gorras Blancas* broadened their targets. They burned bridges, haystacks, and piles of lumber; cut telegraph wires; and took axes to electric light poles and to railroad ties belonging to the Atchison, Topeka, and Santa Fe Railroad. The membership of the group overlapped with that of the Knights of Labor, a national labor union that boasted twenty local assemblies in San Miguel County, east of Santa Fe. On the night of March 11, 1890, *las Gorras Blancas* nailed pieces of paper to the buildings of East Las Vegas, the largest town in the county. These pages, copies of the insurgents' "platform," declared, "Our purpose is to protect the rights and interests of the people in general; especially those of the helpless classes."

■ By 1889 Santa Fe had seen several centuries of cultural conflict.

Who were these determined nightriders? They consisted of Hispanos—Spanish-speaking natives of the area. Their movement began when Juan Jose Herrera, together with his two brothers, Pablo and Nicanor, organized their neighbors in an effort to block European American ranchers from fencing their land. Labeled *las masas de los hombres pobres* (the masses, the poor people) by a local newspaper, *las Gorras Blancas* were desperately struggling to preserve a traditional way of life that was rapidly disappearing. Fenced lands prevented the area's Hispanic settlers from grazing their stock herds in the customary, open-range manner.

Many Hispanos lived in adobe (baked-clay) dwellings in small river-valley villages surrounded by breathtaking mesas, ponderosa pine forests, and high dry plains. In addition to raising chickens and grazing sheep, families grew chiles, pinto beans, squash, and wheat. Together, villagers relied on the common lands that had come down to them from their ancestors—land originally bestowed through grants from Spain and then Mexico. After the Civil War, European American interlopers—

sheep and cattle ranchers, lawyers, speculators, commercial lumberers, and the railroads—began to encroach on these common lands. Through local courts, the newcomers installed a system of private property that granted exclusive ownership to single individuals. It was these groups, with their fences and their laws governing land title registration, that *las Gorras Blancas* targeted.

Las Gorras Blancas had only mixed success. They managed to discourage new European Americans from settling in the area, and they prevented the railroads from buying more rail ties in northern New Mexico. Yet the nightriders could not stem the tide of land loss throughout the Southwest. The Court of Private Land Claims, established in 1891 by the U.S. government, resolved land disputes between Hispanic and European American claimants. Of the more than 35 million acres of land in dispute in the early 1890s, Hispanic claimants received title to little more than 2 million acres—barely one-twentieth of the land they had held in common.

Las Gorras Blancas represented a unique response to local conditions. But it was also part of a growing, nationwide movement against the standards imposed by industrialization and capitalism. Around the country, a wide variety of individuals and organizations emerged in the late 1870s and the 1880s to challenge employers, landlords, and military and government officials. Members of these latter groups responded with a challenge of their own: business, they proclaimed, must be allowed to develop fully and freely without "unnatural" intervention in the form of regulatory legislation or grassroots rebellions such as that of *las Gorras Blancas*.

> *Around the country, a wide variety of individuals and organizations emerged in the late 1870s and the 1880s to challenge employers, landlords, and military and government officials.*

It is difficult to generalize about those who contested the emerging order. Even their own names could be misleading. In the early 1890s, another group called "white caps," this one in Mississippi, consisted of whites who terrorized black landowners and mill workers. And although the Knights of Labor was a national union, it shaped its program in accordance with local issues. In San Miguel County, for instance, the issue was land—who controlled it and under what conditions. In Washington, D.C., the Knights' concern was the welfare of workers in the building trades. The Richmond, Virginia, Knights pioneered interracial organizing, living up to the group's motto, "An injury to one is an injury to all." In contrast, the San Francisco Knights spearheaded the move to bar Chinese laborers from the United States and to limit job opportunities for those who remained. Indeed, groups that challenged the authority of government and large business interests often disagreed among themselves about goals and strategies for change.

Resistance to Legal and Military Authority

America's march toward national economic centralization and integration was not steady. On the battlefield and in the courts, European Americans pressed their advantage, but these efforts met with stiff resistance from a variety of aggrieved groups. Members of these groups rightly believed they had much to lose from so-called progress. European Americans repeatedly used the notion of "racial" difference as a justification for depriving darker-skinned peoples of their claims to land, jobs, and even life itself. For example, California lawmakers approved legislation that discriminated against the Chinese as workers and as parents of school-aged children. In an effort to seek redress, some Chinese took their claims to court.

In a similar vein, prejudice against African Americans assumed the form of discriminatory legislation and random violence. Blacks chafed under restrictions intended to bar them from good jobs and from associating with white people on an equal basis. Varieties of black resistance to white authority included migration out of the South to the West, creation of community institutions, and violent retaliation.

For their part, during the late 1880s, the Plains Indians responded to encroaching railroads, settlers, and military regiments by embracing a movement of spiritual regeneration. On the Plains, whites, and especially U.S. military officers, perceived this movement as more dangerous than an armed uprising, and they reacted accordingly.

Chinese Lawsuits in California

Throughout California, job-hungry whites agitated for the violent expulsion of Chinese from jobs. (Most of these immigrants received two-thirds the wages of their white counterparts for the same work.) Opposition to the Chinese hardened in the 1880s. In San Francisco, the Knights of Labor and the Workingmen's Party of California helped to engineer the passage of the Chinese Exclusion Act, approved by Congress in 1882. This measure denied any additional Chinese laborers entry into the country while allowing some Chinese merchants and students to immigrate. In railroad towns and mining camps, vigilantes looted and burned Chinese communities, in some cases murdering or expelling their inhabitants. In 1885 in Rock Springs, Wyoming, white workers massacred twenty-eight Chinese and drove hundreds out of town in the wake of an announcement by Union Pacific officials that the railroad would begin hiring the lower-paid immigrants. Cheered on by others, a mob burned the Chinese section of town to the ground.

Whites held that the Chinese, with their distinctive customs, would never fit into American life. Nevertheless, early on the Chinese demonstrated an understanding and appreciation of American political and legal processes. Beginning in Gold Rush days, Chinese immigrants had taken their grievances to court. In 1862 in San Francisco, Ling Sing protested

DOCUMENT

Farwell, The Chinese at Home and Abroad

Courtesy, California History Room, California State Library, Sacramento, California (Neg. #23,239)

■ In the West, Chinese mining companies used water-management techniques based on traditional Chinese machinery such as the waterwheel. This photo shows a Chinese river-mining operation in Siskiyou, California, c. 1890. Chinese workers also constructed flumes, dams, canals, tunnels, and pumps to drain areas efficiently.

the $2.50 personal tax levied on Chinese exclusively. The California Supreme Court agreed (in *Ling Sing v. Washburn*) that the group could not be singled out for special taxes. In the 1870s, Chinese merchants used the provisions of the Civil Rights Act to challenge state and local laws that forbade them from holding certain jobs, living in white neighborhoods, and testifying in court.

DOCUMENT

Yick Wo v. Hopkins

In San Francisco in 1885, laundry operator Yick Wo was convicted under an 1880 municipal law prohibiting the construction of wooden laundries without a license. A native of China, Yick Wo had arrived in the United States in 1861. By the time of his arrest, he had operated a legal laundry for twenty-two years. When he applied for a license, the board of supervisors turned him down, just as the board had denied licenses to all Chinese laundry operators who applied. In 1885 his lawyers petitioned the California Supreme Court, which upheld Yick Wo's arrest. The lawyers continued their appeal to the U.S. Supreme Court, maintaining that the board of supervisors intended to bar Chinese from independent laundry work altogether. In *Yick Wo v. Hopkins* (1886), the Supreme Court reversed the state court's decision. The higher court held that the San Francisco laundry-licensing board had engaged in the discriminatory *application* of a law that on the surface was nondiscriminatory.

Still, many cases challenging discriminatory laws never made it to the nation's highest court. And state and local courts in general often refused to acknowledge that Chinese immigrants had any civil rights at all. (Chinese immigrants were not granted citizenship until World War II, although their children born in this country qualified as citizens.) In 1885 the California Supreme Court heard the case *Tape v. Hurley*, brought by Joseph and Mary Tape on behalf of their daughter Mamie. Joseph Tape was a Chinese immigrant with some standing in the San Francisco Chinese community. Mary Tape had been raised in a Shanghai orphanage and had come to the United States with missionaries when she was eleven years old. She grew up to speak English fluently and dressed as a European American. Their daughter Mamie was quite westernized as well.

Even so, Mamie Tape was barred from the city's public school system. The school board claimed that Mamie's presence in the classroom would be "very mentally and morally detrimental" to her classmates. The Tapes sued the city and won, but the school board retaliated by creating a separate school for children of Asian descent within Chinatown. Mary Tape wrote an angry letter to the board: "Dear Sirs, Will you please to tell me! Is it a disgrace to be Born a Chinese? Didn't God make us all!!! What right! have you to bar my children out of the school?" In the end, the Tapes decided to enroll their two children in the segregated school. Yet their legal protest kept alive the ideal of equality under the law.

Blacks in the "New South"

In 1886 Henry Grady, the young editor of the Atlanta *Constitution*, traveled north to deliver a speech to the New England Society of New York. Grady hailed what he called the "New South." The former Confederate states, he claimed, were now forward looking, prepared to embrace industrialization and promote the reconciliation of blacks and whites. According to the journalist, it was time for the South to march forward and join with a larger, modernizing America.

Grady's speech about the "New South" provided a label that stuck. Yet he doubtless spoke too soon and in terms too grandiose. True, he could point with pride to some dramatic industrial developments in the South. Soon after James Bonsack invented a cigarette-rolling machine in 1880, James Buchanan Duke's Durham, North Carolina, company was selling 400,000 machine-made cigarettes each day. The southern textile labor force more than doubled between 1880 and 1890. And by the mid-1880s, with the backing of the Tennessee Coal, Iron, and Railway Company, the city of Birmingham, Alabama, specialized in pig iron production.

Factory and professional work in towns and cities offered new opportunities in the South as industry developed. However, these jobs were dominated by white men. Low-paid heavy

■ Some Chinese made a prosperous life for themselves in the United States. This photo shows Ah Sue, her husband, Ah Quin, and their twelve children. Ah Sue found refuge in the San Francisco Chinese Mission Home in 1879. Two years later she and Ah Quin celebrated their Christian wedding in the Mission Home. Ah Quin rose from the position of cook to become a successful railroad contractor and merchant in San Diego.

labor, primarily in rural areas, continued to be the primary source of work for black men. The hardest and lowest-paid jobs, such as digging ore out of a hill in northern Alabama or constructing a railroad through the swamps of Florida, often went to convicts whom private employers had leased from the state. Most of these "convict lease" workers were black men who had been arrested on minor charges and then bound out when they could not pay their fines or court costs. In Mississippi a black man could be picked up for "some trifling misdemeanor," in the words of one observer, fined $500, and compelled to work off the fine (at a rate of 5 cents a day) for a local planter. With an almost unlimited supply of such workers, employers had little incentive to ease the brutal living and working conditions endured by these convicts.

Some blacks fled the countryside and settled in southern cities, where good jobs were still limited but personal freedom was greater. Gradually, a new black elite arose. These physicians, lawyers, insurance agents, and undertakers reached out to an exclusively black clientele. They also nourished a sense of community. Black men and women continued to sustain their own institutions, such as schools, lodges, benevolent societies, burial organizations, and churches.

In the late 1880s, white Democrats feared the assertiveness of the new black elite. According to whites, this generation of men and women born as free persons and not as slaves must be "put in their place," quite literally. As a result, new state and local laws mandated separate water fountains for blacks and whites, restricted blacks to separate railroad cars and other forms of public transportation, and excluded them altogether from city parks and other public spaces. Long-standing customs barring black people from white-owned theaters, restaurants, and hotels now carried the weight of law. There were two separate school systems, one white and well funded, one black and starved of cash. Legal discrimination against blacks came to be called the **Jim Crow** system.

By the 1890s, a rising tide of lynching engulfed the South, but white officials did little or nothing to halt it. Black men, women, and children were all vulnerable to the fury of the white lynch mob—on the most flimsy pretext. Blacks throughout the segregated South rightly feared that they would be targeted if they spoke out against lynching. Yet northern blacks did not hesitate to highlight the hypocrisy of the federal government, which turned a blind eye toward this practice. Frances Ellen Watkins Harper, an educator and writer living in Philadelphia, issued the following challenge to an audience of white club women: "A government which has the power to tax a man in peace, draft him in war, should have the power to defend his life in the hour of peril." Harper condemned "the government which can protect and defend its citizens from wrong and outrage and does not."

"Jim Crow" in the West

Racial segregation was not limited to the South. The U.S. military enforced its own set of Jim Crow regulations. In 1869 Congress created the 24th and 25th Infantries (Colored), composed of African American soldiers. White officers were appointed to lead these segregated units. Consequently, black men who aspired to positions of military leadership found their way blocked. Some white officers, such as George Custer, refused to command black troops.

Military officials assigned black soldiers to the West, where they became known as buffalo soldiers. (The origins of the term are unclear. It may refer to the buffalo robes worn by many of the soldiers or to Plains Indians' respect for the black men's skills on horseback.) Many of these men were proud to wear a U.S. soldier's uniform, an emblem of their newly won citizenship rights. They helped to construct new roads and forts, protect wagon trains of settlers, and patrol the border between the United States and Mexico. They were an integral part of campaigns to subdue the Cheyenne, Comanche, Sioux, Ute, Kiowa, and Apache. They were among the soldiers deployed to quash strikes among workers (silver miners in Idaho, for example) and to fight forest fires in the Northwest.

■ Among the "buffalo soldiers" who served with the U.S. military were these Seminole scouts. The Seminole traced their history to the eighteenth century, when Creek Indians and runaway slaves of African descent established communities together in Florida. After the Seminole Wars (1818–1858), many Seminole were relocated to Indian Territory (present-day Oklahoma). Some fled to Mexico before the Civil War. In 1870 they were recruited by U.S. Army officers to serve as scouts. Their unit was disbanded eleven years later. Discriminatory policies of the military caused some to return to Mexico.

William Katz Collection

Often the buffalo soldiers encountered hostility from local townspeople, who resented their patronage of local establishments. In 1881 black Tenth Cavalry troops stationed at Fort Concho near San Angelo, Texas, reacted angrily when a local white man killed a black soldier in a saloon. Another soldier had died at the hands of a local white within the previous two weeks. In the absence of justice for the murderers, the soldiers blanketed San Angelo with handbills. Signed "U.S. soldiers," the message read, "If we do not receive justice and fair play . . . someone will suffer, if not the guilty, the innocent. It has gone far enough." When some of the soldiers attacked one of the men they believed guilty, the Texas Rangers entered the town to restore order. The army transferred the black companies out of the area and disciplined the leaders of the protest.

Once they were mustered out of the army, some black soldiers decided to settle permanently in the West. There they joined thousands of black migrants who were fleeing the Jim Crow South. In the late 1870s, 20,000 blacks from Tennessee, Mississippi, and Louisiana, called "Exodusters," migrated into western Kansas. The migrants cited the South's convict lease system, poor schools, and pervasive violence and intimidation as reasons for their flight. Some of these migrants established all-black towns in Kansas, Colorado, Nebraska, and New Mexico. Though generally small and poor, such towns provided places for blacks to live life on their own terms.

The Ghost Dance on the High Plains

Their lands and way of life threatened by whites, western Indians sought desperately to revitalize their culture and protect themselves. In 1889 an Indian named Wovoka offered the Plains Indians a mystical vision of the future, a vision that promised a return to the beloved past. A leader of the Paiute in Nevada, Wovoka preached what came to be called the Ghost Dance, part religion and part resistance movement. In 1889 a solar eclipse occurred while Wovoka was wracked by fever, and he claimed that the conjunction of the two events enabled him to glimpse the afterworld. The Indians could usher in a new day of peace, Wovoka proclaimed, and this new day would be a time free of disease and armed conflict. The buffalo would return, he promised, and the Indian men and women who had died would come back to replenish depleted villages.

VIDEO

Sioux Ghost Dance

Many of the Indians who performed the Ghost Dance fell into a trance-like state, bringing inspiration to impoverished and disheartened reservation communities. However, as the ritual spread across the Plains, U.S. military officials grew anxious. In November 1890, E. B. Reynolds, a Special U.S. Indian Agent, described to his superiors in Washington the strange, seemingly dangerous behavior that had gripped the Indians on Pine Ridge Reservation in South Dakota: "The religious excitement aggravated by almost starvation is bearing fruits in this state of insubordination; Indians say they had better die fighting than to die a slow death of starvation, and as the new religion promises their return to earth, at the coming of the millennium, they have no fear of death."

VIDEO

Westward Expansion and the Native Americans

As tensions between whites and Indians mounted, Sitting Bull emerged as a spiritual and political leader. After leading his followers into Canada, Sitting Bull returned to the United States in 1881 and later performed briefly with Buffalo Bill Cody in the Wild West show (see page 395). He surrendered at Fort Buford, Dakota Territory, where he was held prisoner for two years. Sitting Bull offered a pointed critique of the sedentary, materialistic way of life promoted by whites:

> The life of white men is slavery. They are prisoners in towns or farms. The life my people want is a life of freedom. I have seen nothing that a white man has, houses or railways or clothing or food, that is as good as the right to move in open country, and live in our own fashion.

Sitting Bull rejected white notions of "progress" in favor of his people's traditions.

In mid-December 1890, military officials ordered Indian police to arrest Sitting Bull at his cabin on the Standing Rock Reservation in South Dakota. Alarmed by what they perceived as rising Indian militancy, white settlers in Nebraska and South Dakota pressured the

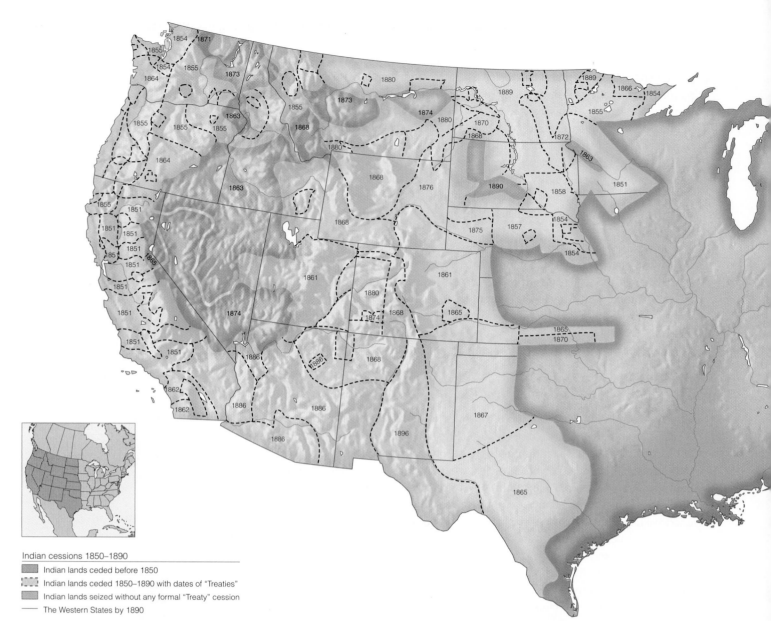

Indian cessions 1850–1890

▨ Indian lands ceded before 1850

▨ Indian lands ceded 1850–1890 with dates of "Treaties"

▨ Indian lands seized without any formal "Treaty" cession

—— The Western States by 1890

■ **MAP 17.1**

INDIAN LANDS LOST, 1850–1890   Between 1850 and 1890, many "treaties" signed by Indian groups and the U.S. government provided that Indians turn over land in exchange for cash payments. Yet U.S. military forces seized a large portion of western Indian lands by force, without signing any treaty agreements at all. By 1890 many Indians lived on reservations, apart from European American society.

DOCUMENT

Accounts of the Wounded Knee Massacre

government to rid the area of the "savages . . . armed to the teeth," men who were "traitors, anarchists, and assassins." While arresting Sitting Bull, his Indian captors killed him.

A week later, on December 28 and 29, soldiers of the Seventh Cavalry under Colonel James Forsyth attacked Indians at Wounded Knee Creek, South Dakota. Estimates of the number of Indians killed range from 150 to 250. More than sixty women and children were among those slain as they fled the oncoming troops. The massacre at Wounded Knee proved the last major violent encounter between Plains Indians and U.S. cavalry forces. By this time, many Indians throughout the Midwest lived on reservations and engaged in farming. Government agents, eager to create independent farmers, instructed Indian men in the use of the plow. But plowing became a collective effort, as bands would work together until their task was done. Thus some Indian groups attempted to maintain customs of collective endeavor in opposition to the European Americans' glorification of ambition and individualism.

Revolt in the Workplace

Workers launched different kinds of challenges against the system of industrial capitalism, which, many charged, enriched a few industrialists and bankers at the expense of the vast majority of laboring people. Workers joined together in unions, and in many cases they fought the violence of private company security forces with violence of their own. Some men and women destroyed the machinery that threatened to replace them in the workplace. By the early 1890s, critics of the new industrial and agribusiness order—a system driven by technological innovation—had come together in the form of a new political group, the People's party, or Populists. This organization aimed to bring together urban and rural, male and female, agricultural and industrial workers to protest the hardships suffered by laborers of all kinds and to demand that the federal government take strong action in rectifying social ills.

Nevertheless, in workplace conflicts, the lines were not always strictly drawn between employees and employers. For example, the late-nineteenth-century laboring classes never achieved the level of unity called for by the Populists. White workers often expressed intense hostility toward their African American and Chinese counterparts. Within small towns, shopkeepers and landlords at times showed solidarity with striking workers; in these cases, community ties were stronger than class differences. Also, despite their critique of big business, workers often embraced the emerging consumer culture. In fact, many of them fought for shorter work days and higher wages so that they could enjoy their share of the material blessings of American life—in department stores, movie theaters, and amusement parks. In the end, Populism was primarily a rural movement composed of small farmers, sharecroppers, and wage hands.

Trouble on the Farm

In the late summer of 1878, the combined effects of the recent national economic depression and the loss of jobs to labor-saving technology catalyzed a rash of machine breaking throughout rural Ohio. In the Midwest, displaced farmhands burned the reapers, mowers, and threshers of their former employers. Some wealthy farmers responded by abandoning their machinery and rehiring their farmhands. Technology, one noted, "ought to be dispensed with in times like these." By contrast, critics charged the machine-breakers with "short-sighted madness." The protests revealed that even family farming had become a business. Now farmers needed to secure bank loans, invest in new machinery, and worry about the price of crops in the world market.

In the mid-1880s, the plight of Plains farmers worsened when a series of natural disasters highlighted their vulnerability to the elements. Drought and declining wheat prices drove half the population of western Kansas and Nebraska back east to Iowa and Illinois between 1888 and 1892. Meanwhile, the bitterly cold winter of 1886–1887 decimated cattle herds throughout the region.

Things took a radical turn in the 1880s, when a national movement of farmers emerged and tapped into a wellspring of anger and discontent in farming regions throughout the nation. The Southern Alliance in Louisiana, Texas, and Arkansas pressed for an expanded currency, taxation reform, and government ownership of transportation and communication lines. Its members tended to ally with the Democratic party. The Northern Alliance from the Plains states also focused on the expansion of the currency supply—specifically, the coinage of silver—but advocated the formation of a third political party to advance its interests. Both of these large regional groups found adherents in the mountain West. There, miners and farmers joined together to protest the monopolistic powers of the railroads, privately owned water companies, and silver mining interests. These monopolies drove up consumer prices and depressed workers' wages.

■ A Nebraska farm family poses proudly with their new windmill, c. 1890. Such devices powered water pumps that reached deep into the earth. Though expensive, windmills were necessities for drought-stricken farmers on the Plains, especially during the harsh years of the mid-1880s to the mid-1890s.

Nebraska State Historical Society, Solomon D. Butcher Collection

Most Alliance men and women farmed modest parcels of land. As small producers, they felt powerless to influence the businesspeople and politicians who affected their livelihoods and their life possibilities. Members of the Alliance also presented themselves as the last line of defense for the noble yeoman in the face of the corrupting influences of modern corporate capitalism. In rural Alabama, where the Farmers' Alliance had links with local schools and churches, the group's newspapers railed against the "filthy city," a "wicked place" of vice, crime, and dissipation. Farm folk thus distanced themselves from the "New South Creed," which promoted materialism and industrialization.

Suffering from a recession in the late 1880s, farmers in the Dakotas, Nebraska, Kansas, and Texas began to mobilize into a new political party. Organizing work among Alliance members at the local level laid the foundation for the creation of the People's, or Populist, party. By representing the financial interests of all farmers and highlighting the vulnerabilities of debtors, the organization foreshadowed the wider national appeal of the Populist party in the 1890s.

Militancy in the Factories and Mines

The new economy wrought profound hardship on members of the urban laboring classes as well as on small farmers. Many industrial workers faced layoffs and wage cuts during the depressions of the 1870s and 1880s. The great railroad strikes of 1877 (see Chapter 16) foreshadowed an era of bitter industrial conflict. Because no laws regulated private industry, employers could impose ten- to fifteen-hour workdays, six days a week. Industrial accidents were all too common, and some industries lacked safety precautions. Steelworkers labored in excessive heat, and miners and textile mill employees alike contracted respiratory diseases. With windows closed and machines speeded up, new forms of technology created new risks for workers.

The Chicago meatpackers, who wielded gigantic cleavers in subfreezing lockers, and the California wheat harvesters, who operated complex mechanical binders and threshers, were among those confronting danger on the job.

Women wage-earners also faced dangerous working conditions. In 1884 the Massachusetts Bureau of Statistics of Labor issued a report outlining the occupational hazards for working women in the city of Boston. In button-making establishments, female workers often got their fingers caught under punch and die machines. Employers provided a surgeon to dress an employee's wounds the first three times she was injured; thereafter, she had to pay for her own medical care. Women operated heavy power machinery in the garment industry and exposed themselves to dangerous chemicals and processing materials in paper-box making, fish packing, and confectionery manufacturing.

Some women workers, especially those who monopolized certain kinds of jobs, organized and struck for higher wages. Three thousand Atlanta washerwomen launched such an effort in 1881 but failed to get their demands met. Most women found it difficult to win the respect not only of employers but also of male unionists. Leonora Barry, an organizer for the Knights of Labor, sought to change that. Barry visited mills and factories around the country. At each stop, she highlighted women's unique difficulties and condemned the "selfishness of their brothers in toil" who resented women's intrusion into the workplace. Barry was reacting to men such as Edward O'Donnell, a prominent labor official who claimed that wage-earning women threatened the role of men as family breadwinners.

For both men and women workers, the influx of 5.25 million new immigrants in the 1880s stiffened job competition at worksites throughout the country. To make matters worse, vast outlays of capital needed to mechanize and organize manufacturing plants placed pressure on employers to economize. Many of them did so by cutting wages. Like the family farmer who could no longer claim the status of the independent yeoman, industrial workers depended on employers and consumers for their physical well-being and very survival.

Yale Collection of Western Americana, Beinecke Rare Book and Manuscript Library

■ Mining was one of the most hazardous occupations in the United States. Below-surface miners worked with explosives and sophisticated kinds of machinery. As a result, the chances of explosions, cave-ins, rockslides, and fires increased. These conditions help to account for the labor militancy of miners throughout the country. This photo shows a mining operation at Marysville, near Helena, Montana, c. 1885.

Organizing American Labor in the Late 19th Century

Not until 1935 would American workers have the right to organize and bargain collectively with their employers. Until then, laborers who saw strength in numbers and expressed an interest in a union could be summarily fired, **blacklisted** (their names circulated to other employers), and harassed by private security forces. The Pinkerton National Detective Agency, founded in 1850 by a Scottish immigrant named Allan Pinkerton, initially found eager clients among the railroads. The Pinkertons, as they were called, served as industrial spies and policemen during some of the most bitter and violent strikes of the late nineteenth century.

The Knights of Labor under the leadership of Terence V. Powderly made impressive gains in the 1880s. In appealing to many different kinds of workers around the country, the Knights blended a critique of the late-nineteenth-century wage system with a belief in the dignity of labor and a call for collective action. According to the Knights, business monopolies and corrupt politicians everywhere shared a common interest in exploiting the labor of ordinary men and women. The Knights advocated a return to the time when workers controlled their own labor and received a just price for the products they made. "We declare an inevitable and irresistible conflict between the wage system of labor and republican system of government," the Knights proclaimed.

Bellamy, from *Looking Backward*

In condemning the concentration of wealth in the hands of a few, the Knights drew on the ideas of popular social critics of the day. In New York City, Henry George, an economist and land reformer, achieved national prominence with his book *Progress and Poverty* (1879), in which he advocated a single tax on property as a means of distributing wealth more equally. In his popular novel titled *Looking Backward* (1888), journalist-turned-novelist Edward Bellamy envisioned a "cooperative commonwealth" in the year 2000, a socialist paradise in which poverty and greed had disappeared and men and women of all classes enjoyed material comfort and harmonious relations with their neighbors.

Between 1885 and 1886, the Knights undertook the difficult task of organizing black workers. Many blacks remained suspicious of white-led unions, and for good reason. Historically, the white labor movement had conceived itself as a way to exclude black men and women from stable, well-paying jobs. Throughout the South, segregation was the norm within biracial unionism. Whites, whether New Orleans dockworkers, Birmingham District coal miners, or lumber workers in East Texas and Louisiana, insisted on separate locals from blacks. Yet African Americans did not necessarily acquiesce to this arrangement.

In 1886 workers around the country began to mobilize on behalf of the eight-hour day. "Eight hours to constitute a day's work" was their slogan. The issue had broad appeal, but the growing diversity of the labor force made unity difficult. In 1880, between 78 and 87 percent of all workers in San Francisco, St. Louis, Cleveland, New York, Detroit, Milwaukee, and Chicago were either immigrants or the children of immigrants. In many places, the laboring classes remained vulnerable to divisive social and cultural animosities. The diversity of ethnic groups, coupled with the fact that many newcomers from Europe adopted racist ideas to become "Americans," drove wedges between workers.

The Haymarket Bombing

The year 1886 marked the end of an era dominated by the Knights of Labor as the organization experienced the difficulties of overcoming its members' diverse crafts, racial loyalties, and political allegiances. Industrialists dug in their heels and, with the aid of hired detectives, took union leaders to court on charges of sabotage, assault, conspiracy, and murder.

On May 1, 1886, 350,000 workers in 11,562 business establishments went out on a one-day strike as part of the eight-hour workday movement. In Chicago, home to militant labor anarchists (men and women who opposed government authority of any kind), 40,000 workers participated in the strike. Among the Chicago leaders was Albert Parsons. A descendant of New England Puritans and a printer by trade, Parsons had lived in Waco, Texas, where he

"Albert Parsons's Plea for Anarchy"

On August 10, 1886, the New York Herald published an essay by convicted Haymarket defendant Albert R. Parsons. In it, Parsons defends his views on anarchism. His theories on the inevitable clash between workers and capitalists echo the arguments of Karl Marx, the German political theorist. Marx predicted that the capitalist system would inevitably self-destruct and that the working classes would rise to rule the world.

So much is written and said nowadays about socialism or anarchism, that a few words on the subject from one who holds to these doctrines may be of interest to the readers of your great newspaper.

Anarchy is the perfection of personal liberty or self-government. It is the free play of nature's law. . . . It is the negation of force or the domination of man by man. In the place of the law maker it puts the law discoverer and for the driver, or dictator, or ruler, it gives free play to the natural leader. It leaves man free to be happy or miserable, to be rich or poor, to be mean or good. The natural law is self-operating, self-enacting, and cannot be repealed, amended or evaded without incurring a self-imposed penalty. . . .

The capitalist system originated in the forcible seizure of natural opportuni-

Albert Parsons

Library of Congress

ties and rights by a few, and converting these things into special privileges, which have since become vested rights formally entrenched behind the bulwarks of statute law and government. . . .

And what of the laborer who for twelve or more hours weaves, spins, bores, turns, builds, shovels, breaks stones, carries loads, and so on? Does his twelve hours weaving, spinning, boring, turning, building, shoveling, etc. represent the active expression or energy of his life? On the contrary, life begins for him exactly where this activity, this labor of his ceases—viz: at his meals, in his tenement house, in his bed. His twelve hours work represents for him as a weaver, builder, spinner, etc., only so much earnings as will furnish him his meals, clothes, and rent. . . . The wage slaves are "free" to compete with each other for the opportunity to serve capital and capitalists to compete with each other in monopolizing the laborer's products.

Parsons argues that it is only a matter of time before the capitalist system "will collapse, will fall of its own weight, and fall because of its own weakness." He asserts that the fall of capitalism will usher in a new era of socialism, a system in which all property is held in common and workers can govern themselves. He concludes:

To quarrel with socialism is silly and vain. To do so is to quarrel with history; to denounce the logic of events; to smother the aspirations of liberty. Mental freedom, political freedom, industrial freedom—do not these follow in the line of progress? Are they not the association of the inevitable?

Ten days after this essay was published, Albert Parsons and the other Haymarket defendants were found guilty and sentenced to be hanged. Four of them, including Parsons, were executed on November 11, 1887. The true identity of the bomb-thrower remains a mystery to this day.

Questions

1. What is the significance of Parsons's claim that the triumph of socialism is "inevitable" and "natural"?
2. Why did many Americans identify anarchists with violence? ■

---

met his future wife, Lucia Gonzalez, an Afro-Latina (probably born a slave). In 1873 the Parsonses moved to Chicago to avoid Texas laws against "race mixing," which prohibited interracial marriage. There Albert joined the International Typographical Union, and Lucia took up dressmaking. They were counted among the most famous and feared radicals in the city.

On May 4, things took a bloody turn. Strikers called a rally in Chicago's Haymarket Square to protest the murder of two McCormick Reaper strikers the day before. During the rally, a bomb went off, killing a police officer and wounding seven others, who later died. Although the identity of the culprit was never discovered, eight **anarchists**, including Albert Parsons, were arrested, tried, and sentenced to death for conspiring to provoke violence.

The Haymarket hangings demoralized the labor movement nationwide. Now associated in the minds of the middle class with wild-eyed bomb throwers, the Knights saw their ranks plummet from 700,000 in 1886 to 100,000 by 1890. With the demise of the Knights of Labor,

DOCUMENT

Engel, Address by a Haymarket Anarchist

the American Federation of Labor (AFL) emerged to become the most powerful national labor movement. Samuel Gompers, an English immigrant cigarmaker, had founded the new group in 1886 partly in response to the Knights' attempts to usurp the Cigar Makers' International Union with a socialist-dominated local. The AFL garnered the allegiance of skilled trade workers (most of them white men) and promoted basic goals such as better wages and working conditions.

Yet the radical labor tradition persisted. Meeting in Paris in 1889, a congress of world socialist parties voted to set aside May 1, 1890, as a day of worldwide celebrations in support of labor and demonstrations in favor of the eight-hour workday. (May 1 became an international labor day, celebrated annually.) In the United States, the United Mine Workers (founded in 1890) and the American Railway Union (1893) followed the radical labor-organizing principles of the Knights of Labor long after the AFL attained its ascendancy.

Crosscurrents of Reform

In the 1880s, a young Danish-born journalist named Jacob Riis prowled New York's East Side slum district in search of stories for the New York *Tribune* and the Associated Press bureau. In this part of the city, more than 37,000 tenement buildings housed more than 1 million people in inhuman living conditions. In 1890 Riis published a collection of his own photographs, along with explanatory notes, under the title *How the Other Half Lives*. His book galvanized the public in support of slum clearance and housing codes. *How the Other Half Lives* is a powerful indictment of greedy landlords, indifferent city officials, and unscrupulous sweatshop owners.

■ Jacob Riis titled this photograph *Street Arabs in Sleeping Quarters [Areaway, Mulberry St.]*. Riis's photos, collected in his book *How the Other Half Lives*, exposed the poverty and wretched living conditions endured by many immigrants in New York's Lower East Side. In certain cases, Riis carefully positioned his subjects before photographing them. It is doubtful that these little boys were sleeping while the photographer noisily set up his equipment a few feet away.

During the last decades of the nineteenth century, reformers adopted a range of causes. Some, like Riis, focused on the plight of the urban poor. Others challenged the Indian reservation system, which, they charged, left Indians poor and dependent on the federal government. Settlement house workers aimed to improve the lives of immigrant families. Middle-class women sought to protect and empower women by aiding abused or vulnerable wives and mothers, promoting temperance in alcohol use, and supporting women's suffrage. Many reformers participated in a transatlantic community of ideas, learning about reform strategies and institutions from their European counterparts.

One factor leading to reform was middle-class Americans' fear that the poor would lash out in angry frustration in order to call attention to social injustice. The reformers reasoned that even modest improvements in the lives of the poor would stave off violent conflict between the classes. Dramatic labor disputes, from the railroad workers' "great uprising" of 1877 to the Haymarket bombing of 1886, frightened many well-to-do people, especially in the nation's largest cities. Although reformers professed to favor the full integration of various ethnic groups into American life, at times they could hardly help but look down on the people they aimed to help. Yet many reformers were also motivated by a genuine sense of concern for less privileged groups.

Transatlantic Networks of Reform

American reformers derived ideas and inspiration from their European counterparts. This transatlantic exchange of ideas was greatly facilitated by improvements in sea transportation. During the 1870s and 1880s, ocean travel became cheaper and safer as well as more efficient and comfortable. Writer Henry James (1843–1916) traveled extensively in Europe before making his home in London in the mid-1870s.

Contacts between European and American scholars, students, artists, clergy, writers, and reformers enriched the intellectual life of the United States and bolstered the reform impulse. American women's rights supporters conferred with their counterparts in London. American college students attended classes at German universities. Out of these contacts emerged the Social Gospel, a moral reform movement that stressed the responsibility of Christians to address the ills of modern urban life.

Contacts between European and American scholars enriched the intellectual life of the United States and bolstered the reform impulse.

An idealistic graduate of Rockford (Illinois) Female Seminary, Jane Addams journeyed to Europe for the first time in 1883. The sight of large numbers of poor people in London's East End made a lasting impression on her. In 1888 she went again to England and visited Toynbee Hall, a social settlement founded to alleviate the problems of the laboring classes. Back in Chicago, she and her friend and former classmate Ellen Gates Starr decided to open a settlement house of their own in 1889. Called Hull House, it was located in the Nineteenth Ward, home to 5,000 Greek, Russian, Italian, and German immigrants.

Social settlement houses—so-called because their goal was to help immigrants with the transition of settling in the United States—provided a variety of services for immigrants, including English language classes, neighborhood health clinics, after-school programs for children, and instruction in personal hygiene and infant care. In 1891 six settlements were in operation. By 1900 the number stood at 200.

The Goal of Indian Assimilation

In the mid-nineteenth century, many European Americans, including government officials, believed that the reservation system was a much-needed reform to protect western Indians. Whites reasoned that reservation Indians would remain separate from the rest of American society, to the benefit of everyone. Indians could preserve their own culture, and they would remain safe from the attacks of both homesteaders and U.S. Army troops. By segregating this

Courtesy, Hampton University Archives

■ Susan LaFlesche was the first Indian woman to become a physician in the United States. Together with her sisters Marguerite and Lucy, Susan attended Hampton Institute in Virginia, a vocational school for African Americans and Indians. This photo, c. 1885, shows Hampton students performing in a pageant at the school. Susan, center, and the woman on the right represented "Indians of the Past." The other students represented "Indians of the Present." Hampton's mission was to prepare its students for farming and the skilled trades.

AUDIO

Omaha Funeral Song

group, European Americans were free to settle on rich farmlands, mine for gold and silver, and take advantage of timber resources in the West.

By the 1870s, the harsh reality of the reservation system had prompted a group composed of both Native Americans and European Americans to call for reform. The reformers pointed out that many western Indians had previously roamed the Plains in search of buffalo and other sources of food, clothing, and shelter. Confining whole tribes to reservations meant that they lost not only their traditional means of feeding and housing themselves but their entire way of life. Reservation lands were often unsuitable for farming, leaving the residents to depend on supplies of food, blankets, and clothing provided by the federal government. Kept apart from the rest of American society, denied the rights of citizenship such as education and the vote, many Indians fell victim to self-destructive behavior, including alcoholism and suicide.

Convinced that the reservation system was a failure, in 1879 reformers began to call for the assimilation of Native Americans into American life. This cause was promoted by some Indians as well as Protestant missionaries. In 1879 Ponca chief Standing Bear toured the East Coast, speaking before large, receptive audiences in Chicago, Boston, New York, Philadelphia, and Washington.

Standing Bear's appeal helped to galvanize eastern reformers. The campaign for Indian assimilation bore a marked resemblance to the antislavery crusade before the Civil War. Both movements focused on the wrongs perpetrated by the U.S. government (slavery and the Indian reservation system). Both argued that the group in question deserved full citizenship rights. And both promoted the ideal of group self-sufficiency: blacks and Indians tilling the soil, embracing mainstream Christianity, and learning trades.

Beginning in 1883, advocates of Indian assimilation sponsored annual conferences at Lake Mohonk, New York, to plot strategy for the coming year. These conferences brought together scholars, clergy, reformers, and politicians, all of whom considered their cause as part of the tradition of Protestant missionary outreach work. The reformers believed that the values of white middle-class Protestants provided the best guide for Indians seeking to rid themselves of the hated reservation system. Advocates of assimilation also received support from people who simply wanted the Plains Indians removed from their land to make way for European American settlers.

Out of these conflicting impulses—one on behalf of the Indians' welfare, the other in support of the destruction of Indians' claims to large tracts of land—came two major initiatives that would shape federal Indian policy in the years to come. The first was the Indian boarding school movement, begun in 1879 with the founding of a school near Carlisle, Pennsylvania. The purpose of the movement was to convert Indian children to Christianity, and to force them to abandon their native culture and learn literacy skills. The second was the Dawes Severalty Act of 1887, allowing reservation land to be divided into separate farms for individual Native American families. Moreover, ambitious land speculators and corrupt government officials sought to enrich themselves from the provisions of the act which allowed the sell-off of Indian lands to white buyers.

Women Reformers: "Beginning to Burst the Bonds"

Like the Indian assimilation movement, women's reform work in general during this period had a strong missionary strain. In San Francisco, the Occidental Branch of the Women's Foreign Missionary Society enlisted the aid of well-to-do women in sponsoring a rescue home for Chinese prostitutes. Without the protection of traditional kin ties, these immigrants remained vulnerable to sexual and physical abuse. The rescue home enabled the young women to escape the men who exploited them and, in some cases, to reenter society, now as married women, factory wage-earners, or small merchants.

In Salt Lake City, a group of women challenged the Mormon practice of plural marriage. In 1886 their Industrial Christian Home Association received a subsidy from Congress to provide shelter for "women who renounce polygamy and their children of a tender age." That same year some Denver women founded the Colorado Cottage Home, a rescue home for pregnant girls and women.

The Women's Christian Temperance Union (WCTU) is an apt example of the missionary impulse behind late-nineteenth-century reform. Though best known for its antialcohol crusade, the WCTU also sponsored homes for unwed mothers and day and night nurseries for the children of working women. It also stressed the need for women's "purity," claiming that women and children were the chief victims of men's alcohol consumption. But the group went further to denounce women's victimization at the hands of men in general.

By the 1870s, the issue of women's suffrage had captured the attention of men and women throughout the country. The issue had special resonance in the West for several reasons. When European American women overcame the hardships associated with the challenge of settling the trans-Mississippi West, they considered themselves worthy of having an equal voice in the polling booth. Reflecting on her hard life as a settler in Circle Valley, Utah, Mrs. L. L. Dalton wrote in 1876 that she was "proud and thankful" to see women "beginning to burst the bonds of iron handed custom" and asserting their "co-heirship" with fathers, brothers, and husbands. Abigail Scott Duniway, who sympathized with the plight of overworked and often lonely farm wives, published a women's rights journal, *New Northwest*, in Portland, Oregon, from 1871 to 1887.

May Wright Sewall Collection/Library of Congress

■ Frances Willard (1839–1898) grew up on a farm in Wisconsin Territory. She served as the first dean of women at Northwestern University in Illinois. In the mid-1870s, she decided to devote her life to the cause of temperance. From 1879 until her death, she was president of the Woman's Christian Temperance Union. Willard developed what she called a "Do-Everything policy." Under her leadership, the WCTU addressed a range of issues, including women's suffrage and workers' rights.

Western politics pitted cattle ranchers against farmers, and religious and cultural groups against each other. These conflicts prompted the men of various groups to seek allies wherever they could find them—within their own households if necessary. The territorial legislature of Wyoming granted women the right to vote in 1869. Utah Territory followed suit in 1870, and Washington Territory in 1883. Then came the states of Wyoming (1890), Colorado (1893), and Utah and Idaho (1896).

Conclusion

In the 1870s and 1880s, the Americans who challenged the power of government and big business represented a wide spectrum of ideologies, tactics, and goals. Some resisted violently. Others formed new institutions such as settlement houses, reform associations, or political parties. Some people hoping to effect social change used the language of evangelical Protestantism, echoing the reform activities of persons who called for the abolition of slavery before the Civil War. Others collected data and interviewed specific groups of workers, women, or immigrants in an effort, first, to expose the conditions under which these groups lived and labored and, second, to propose specific legislation to remedy those conditions. Plains Indians embraced religious mysticism in a failed attempt to halt the incursion of European Americans into their ancient hunting grounds. Thus, powerful groups encountered much resistance from people opposed to their narrow idea of progress—the idea that bigger factories, more efficient farm machinery, and a nationwide network of railroad lines would bring prosperity to all Americans.

As Americans began to think more broadly about their place in the world, some men and women hoped to apply the principles of moral and civic reform to other countries west of the United States. The 1880s laid the foundations for a trans-Pacific empire of missionary work and trade. In the process, a new ideology of expansionism emerged, one that blended elements of economic gain, national security, and Christian missionary outreach to peoples in far-off lands.

Sites to Visit

Anarchy Archives at Pitzer University
dwardmac.pitzer.edu/Anarchist_Archives/
archivehome.html

This archive includes classic anarchist texts, especially information about and graphics of the Haymarket Riot.

Labor-Management Conflict in American History
http://www.publichistory.org/reviews/
view_review.asp?DBID=93

This Ohio State University site includes primary accounts of some of the major events in the history of the labor-management conflict in the late nineteenth and early twentieth centuries.

Samuel Gompers Papers at the University of Maryland

http://www.history.umd.edu/Gompers/index.html

This site includes information about the papers project. It also has a photo gallery, selected documents, and a brief history of the first president of the American Federation of Labor.

African American Perspectives: Pamphlets from the Daniel A. P. Murray Collection, 1818–1907

http://memory.loc.gov/ammem/aap/aaphome/html

This collection includes writings of famous African Americans, including Frederick Douglass, Booker T. Washington, Ida B. Wells-Barnett, Benjamin W. Arnett, Alexander Crummel, and Emanuel Love.

The Haymarket Affair Digital Collection

http://www.chicagohistory.org/hadc/index.html

The Chicago Historical Society maintains this site about a pivotal moment in American labor history.

African American Women Writers of the Nineteenth Century

digital.nypl.org/schomburg/writers_aa19/

The New York Public Library's Schomburg Center for Research in Black Culture maintains this site, which contains a large number of digital texts by African American women of the nineteenth century.

For Further Reading

General Works

Edward L. Ayers, *The Promise of the New South: Life After Reconstruction* (1992).

Sarah Deutsch, *No Separate Refuge: Culture, Class, and Gender on an Anglo-Hispanic Frontier, 1880–1940* (1987).

Lawrence Goodwyn, *Democratic Promise: The Populist Moment in America* (1976).

Patricia N. Limerick, *The Legacy of Conquest: The Unbroken Past of the American West* (1987).

David Montgomery, *The Fall of the House of Labor: The Workplace, the State, and American Labor Activism, 1865–1925* (1987).

Elizabeth Sanders, *Roots of Reform: Farmers, Workers, and the American State, 1877–1917* (1999).

Resistance to Legal and Military Authority

Tomás Almaguer, *Racial Fault Lines: The Historical Origins of White Supremacy in California* (1994).

Dee Brown, *Bury My Heart at Wounded Knee: An Indian History of the American West* (1970).

Steven Hahn, *A Nation Under Our Feet: Black Political Struggles in the Rural South from Slavery to the Great Migration* (2003).

Leon Litwack, *Trouble in Mind: Black Southerners in the Age of Jim Crow* (1998).

Robert J. Rosenbaum, *Mexicano Resistance in the Southwest: The Sacred Right of Self-Preservation* (1981).

Alexander Saxton, *The Indispensable Enemy: Labor and the Anti-Chinese Movement in California* (1971).

Robert M. Utley, *The Lance and the Shield: The Life and Times of Sitting Bull* (1993).

Revolt in the Workplace

Leon Fink, *Workingmen's Democracy: The Knights of Labor and American Politics* (1983).

Philip S. Foner, *The Great Labor Uprising of 1877* (1977).

Jacquelyn Dowd Hall, James Leloudis, Robert Korstad, Mary Murphy, LuAnn Jones, and Christopher B. Daly, *Like a Family: The Making of a Southern Cotton Mill World* (1987).

Stuart B. Kaufman, *Samuel Gompers and the Origins of the American Federation of Labor, 1848–1896* (1973).

Theodore R. Mitchell, *Political Education in the Southern Farmers' Alliance, 1887–1900* (1987).

Bruce Nelson, *Beyond the Martyrs: A Social History of Chicago's Anarchists, 1870–1900* (1988).

Richard Steven Street, *Beasts of the Field: A Narrative History of California Farmworkers, 1769–1913* (2004).

Crosscurrents of Reform

Jean Bethke Elshtain, *Jane Addams and the Dream of American Democracy* (2001).

Paula Giddings, *When and Where I Enter: The Impact of Black Women on Race and Sex and America* (1984).

Frederick E. Hoxie, *A Final Promise: The Campaign to Assimilate the Indians, 1880–1920* (1984).

Peggy Pascoe, *Relations of Rescue: The Search for Female Moral Authority in the American West, 1874–1939* (1990).

Jacob Riis, *How the Other Half Lives: Studies Among the Tenements of New York* (1971).

Daniel T. Rodgers, *Atlantic Crossings: Social Politics in a Progressive Age* (1998).

For quizzes and other resources on these topics, go to www.longmanamericanhistory.com.

Political and Cultural Conflict in a Decade of Depression and War: The 1890s

I N THE EARLY 1890s, LUTHER STANDING BEAR, A YOUNG MAN OF LAKOTA SIOUX ORIGIN, FOUND himself suspended between two worlds. Born in 1868 in South Dakota, he had learned to hunt buffalo in the traditional manner of the western Sioux. In 1879 he bowed to the wishes of his father, Standing Bear, who insisted that he learn the ways of "Long Knives," or whites. And so the youth was among the first pupils to attend the new federal Indian boarding school in Carlisle, Pennsylvania.

Called Ota Kte, or Plenty Kill, at home, now he was required to pick a new first name from among those listed on a classroom blackboard. He chose Luther. His teachers took away his blanket and moccasins and gave him a coat, pants, and vest to wear. They forbade him to speak his native language, and they cut his long hair. Like most other youths at Carlisle, Standing Bear learned to read and write English and to practice a craft (in his case, tin-smithing). His teachers encouraged him to embrace Christianity.

In 1884, as part of his government-sponsored training, Luther Standing Bear traveled to Philadelphia to work at the Wanamaker department store. After spending a year stocking shelves and performing other tasks at the famous store, Standing Bear returned to South Dakota. There he taught Sioux schoolchildren and married the daughter of an Indian mother and a white father.

After the massacre at Wounded Knee, South Dakota, in December 1890, the young man moved with his family to the nearby Pine Ridge Reservation, where he began work as a shopkeeper and postal clerk. In the late 1890s, Luther Standing Bear served

■ This group of Chiricahua Apache students arrived at the Carlisle Indian boarding school in 1890. Government-sponsored Indian education included dressing them in European American clothing and cutting their hair.

as an interpreter for Buffalo Bill's "Wild West" show during its tour in London. By 1912 he had become an American citizen and settled in southern California, where he began his acting career in the new motion picture industry. He appeared in some of the first movie westerns and became an Indian activist, speaking out against the "government prison" known as the reservation.

In the 1890s, Luther Standing Bear's journey took place amid economic depression, civil strife, and war. Throughout the decade, workers and owners showed that the United States was not immune to the bloody class conflict that had long plagued Europe. Some scholars lamented the closing of the western frontier, prompting fears that America's unique dynamic of growth and social improvement had come to an end. Native-born whites began to seize upon new categories of racial difference to draw distinctions between various groups in the United States and around the world. Faced with declining consumer demand at home, politicians and businesspeople joined forces to expand American markets and American influence abroad. America's imperialistic ventures would reveal a blend of economic interests and missionary outreach, particularly in Cuba and the Philippines.

> *Native-born whites began to seize upon new categories of racial difference.*

Whereas some Americans tried to define rigid racial and nationalistic boundaries, others sought avenues of connections. A new political party, the Populist, or People's, party, aimed to bring together men and women of all backgrounds and regions. By advocating **grassroots democracy** as well as government action to regulate the economy, the party paved the way for the Progressive reforms of the early twentieth century.

Frontiers at Home, Lost and Found

In 1893 historian Frederick Jackson Turner proposed a new way of thinking about American history. According to Turner, the process of settling the West had shaped all of American history. He argued that during the colonial period, the rigors of taming the land had transformed English colonists into more resourceful, more democratic people—in other words, into Americans. With each successive wave of western settlement, American society renewed itself. In his view, the West served as a safety valve, a place of opportunity that beckoned people out of crowded eastern cities. However, Turner noted, an 1890 Census Report had concluded that the frontier—the unsettled area of the western part of the country—had recently disappeared. "And now," Turner concluded, "four centuries from the discovery of America, at the end of a hundred years of life under the Constitution, the frontier has gone, and with its going has closed the first period in American history."

Turner's thesis promoted the idea of American "exceptionalism": the idea that its individualism and democratic values made the United States unique among the nations of the world. Yet, in his celebration of the sturdy frontiersman, Turner ignored the bloody legacy of western settlement and its devastating effects on native and Spanish-speaking peoples.

Nevertheless, at the end of the nineteenth century, Turner and others were asking questions. Did America need to conquer new lands and "tame" certain peoples to preserve its distinctive character? Now that the frontier had disappeared, what was to prevent the United States from becoming more like Europe? These urgent concerns led to efforts to assimilate and Americanize certain groups of people and to tighten systems of legal discrimination against others. In addition, some Americans turned their attention to "interior" frontiers of psychology, art, and spirituality.

National Archives

■ Frederick Jackson Turner's 1893 announcement that the western frontier had disappeared was premature. Here, homesteaders in Washington State cut down trees to carve a farm out of the forest, c. 1900. Felling gigantic hardwoods in the Northwest was a formidable challenge to family farmers.

Claiming and Managing the Land

As less and less land was available for cultivation, grazing, and mining, the politics of rural development entered a new phase. In the early 1890s, the last great parcel of Indian land was opened to European American farmers. Congress established the Territory of Oklahoma in 1890. Three years later, the Cherokee Outlet in the north-central part of the territory, combined with Tonkawa and Pawnee reservations, was thrown open to settlers and oil developers. On September 16, 1893, 100,000 people claimed 6.5 million newly opened acres in a single day. The "sooners," people who rushed to claim the land, gave the state of Oklahoma its nickname. The "Sooner State" was admitted to the Union in 1907.

Congress took other steps to manage western lands during the 1890s. The Court of Private Land Claims (1891) oversaw land disputes in New Mexico, Colorado, and Arizona. This court favored recent European American claimants over the Hispanic settlers who had received title to the lands from either Spain or Mexico generations earlier.

Land courts were only one example of an expanded federal role in the settlement of the West and management of the land. During the 1890s, the federal government continued to provide information and services for farmers through the U.S. Department of Agriculture. Policymakers argued over the proper balance between conserving natural resources for use by farmers, loggers, and oilmen and preserving the beauty of unspoiled panoramas for the enjoyment of all. In 1890 Congress established a national park in California's spectacular Yosemite Valley, where the Yosemite Indians had lived for hundreds of years. The 1891 Forest Reserve Act set aside forest reserves in the **public domain** (that is, vast tracts of land still owned by the federal government). Logging companies were allowed to exploit these areas for their timber.

With his appointment as chief of the Division of Forestry in 1898, Gifford Pinchot sought to bring the issue of natural resource conservation to national attention. He believed that a managed forest could provide lumber and then renew itself. By contrast, John Muir and others argued that uninhabited regions should be preserved in their natural state, unmarred by dams, mines, or logging operations. In 1892 Muir founded the Sierra Club, a group devoted

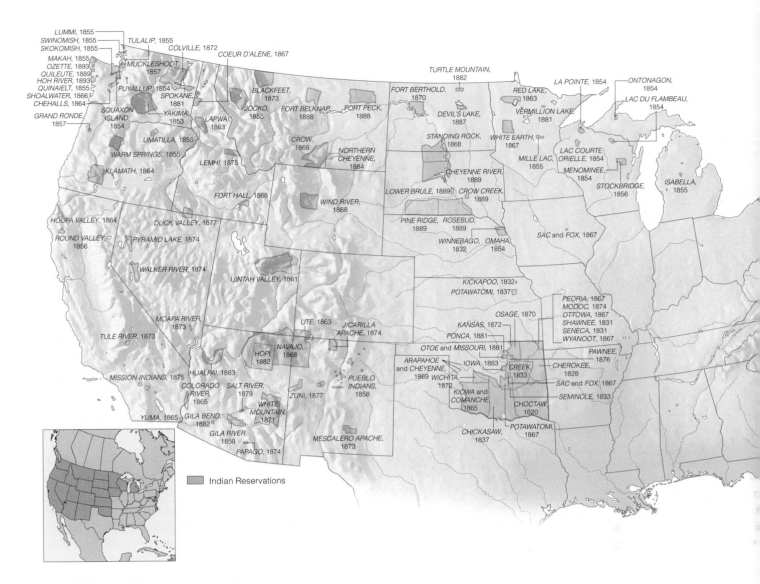

■ MAP 18.1

INDIAN RESERVATIONS, 1900   The Dawes Severalty Act, passed by Congress in 1887, intended to abandon the reservation system and integrate Indians into mainstream American society. Nevertheless, many reservations remained intact. As a group, Indians lived apart from European Americans. By the early twentieth century, the Indian as a "vanishing American" had become a stock character in novels and films. Yet Indian activists continued to press the cause of their people: to preserve native cultures and, at the same time, protest persistent poverty.

to preserving wilderness. In 1899 both Muir and the Northern Pacific Railroad lobbied successfully for two new national parks, Mount Rainier in Washington and Glacier in Montana, highlighting the ongoing significance of railroad tourism. "Rusticating," or hiking and enjoying the beauty of nature, became a popular pastime for many Americans in the 1890s.

The Tyranny of Racial Categories

The supposed closing of the western frontier, and with it the disappearance of the "safety valve" for restless Easterners, highlighted urban America's increasing class and cultural diversity. In an effort to categorize social groups, many national opinion-makers—scholars, journalists, and

National Anthropological Archives, Smithsonian Institution

■ A middle-class Powhatan Indian family in Virginia poses for the camera, c. 1900. Since the seventeenth century, the Powhatan had intermarried with the Nanticoke of Delaware as well as African Americans of the mid-Atlantic region. Communities such as these defied the efforts of scientists and others to rigidly categorize people according to race.

politicians—claimed that people should be distinguished from one another by their inborn, "natural" characteristics, ranging from skin color to facial bone structure and intelligence. Supposedly, these differences defined specific racial categories, such as Caucasoid, Mongoloid, and Negroid. In fact, so-called racial differences between groups were cultural differences. Late-nineteenth-century scientific racists ranked "superior" and "inferior" races on an elaborate hierarchy encompassing all groups, native and foreign born. Identification of racial categories pervaded the nation's popular, political, and legal cultures.

Several factors account for this renewed obsession with race in the 1890s. European and American efforts to colonize and explore the far reaches of the globe brought whites face to face with darker-skinned peoples, whom scholars in the new discipline of **anthropology** studied and classified. The "New Immigration" from eastern Europe raised concerns about conferring citizenship on non-Anglos, such as Russian Jews, Poles, and Italians. Persistent violence along the U.S.-Mexican border, combined with the resistance of Indians and African Americans to the authority of white people, alarmed local and federal officials. Theories of "racial difference" were used to justify attempts to subordinate these groups, by violence if necessary.

In the South, the doctrine of white supremacy had disastrous consequences for African Americans. Beginning with Mississippi in 1890, over the next twenty years, white Democrats in all the southern states met in state constitutional conventions and imposed restrictions on the voting rights of African American men, including literacy requirements and poll taxes (fees that people had to pay to vote).

In 1896 the Supreme Court put its stamp of approval on segregated schools, trains, and streetcars in its *Plessy v. Ferguson* opinion. By a seven-to-one majority, the Supreme Court ruled that such Jim Crow laws did "not necessarily imply the inferiority of either race." Justice John Marshall Harlan dissented from the majority view, pointing out the obvious: "The white race deems itself to be the dominant race," a view that conflicted with the "colorblind" U.S. Constitution.

Between 1882 and 1901, more than 100 people, most of them black men, were lynched every year in the United States; the year 1892 set a record of 230 deaths. In the South, lynch mobs targeted black men and women who refused to subordinate themselves to whites. Many black men victimized by lynch mobs were falsely accused of raping white women. Black Memphis newspaper editor Ida B. Wells charged that accusations of rape were merely a pretext for the murder of black men. The southern white man, wrote Wells, "had never gotten over his resentment that the Negro was no longer his plaything, his servant, and his source of income." Death threats forced the editor to move north.

Yet even in the South, racial definitions were never as clear-cut or self-evident as racists, scientific or otherwise, claimed. For example, Italians and Jews occupied a **middle ground** between black and white, as class issues intermingled with racial categories. In 1891 in New Orleans, the lynching of a group of eleven Italian prisoners accused of conspiring to murder the city's chief of police met with no public outcry. Instead, a local newspaper condemned the "lawless passions" and "the cutthroat practices" that it claimed were characteristic of all Italian immigrants. However, the Italian government protested loudly against the incident. Armed conflict between the two nations was averted only when the United States agreed to compensate the victims' families.

At the same time, Jewish shopkeepers and merchants in the South gained a conditional entry into the ranks of "whites." In Natchez, Mississippi, the small but prosperous Jewish community owned forty-five businesses, about a third of all in the town. However, living in an overwhelmingly Protestant region of the country, many southern Jews found themselves barred from local social organizations.

New Roles for Schools

Between 1890 and 1899, nearly 3.7 million immigrants entered the United States, fewer than 1.4 million of them English speakers from the United Kingdom and Ireland; nearly 2.3 million were non-English speakers from Germany, Italy, Austria-Hungary, and Russia. During this period, public displays of patriotism became increasingly characteristic of American life. The recitation of the Pledge of Allegiance was introduced into public classrooms and courtrooms in the 1890s.

Victorians (in England and the United States) saw formal education as a great equalizer of social groups. Moreover, many younger immigrants and the children of immigrants eagerly embraced American schooling as a means of upward mobility. However, schools did not always fulfill their promise as agents of equal opportunity for all. Increasingly, schools separated and grouped children according to their culture, religion, and class as well as race.

At the Carlisle Indian school, boys learned to make harnesses, tin pots and pans, wagons, and carriages, among other products, many of which were sold to local residents to raise money for the school. Girls took in laundry and ironed, also part of the school's money-making effort. The goal of such activities was to enable the pupils to become self-supporting upon graduation.

The school as a vehicle for vocational instruction also found support among northern philanthropists concerned about education for southern black children and young people. A generation after the Civil War, the persistent poverty of many rural southern blacks convinced northern reformers that this group of Americans should be educated for a distinct form of second-class citizenship. Philanthropists, such as Julius Rosenwald of Chicago, upheld the notion of segregated public education. They created new institutions, or modified existing ones, to stress the trades and "domestic arts" at the expense of such subjects as philosophy, mathematics, and foreign languages.

DOCUMENT

Booker T. Washington, Atlanta Exposition Address

This emphasis on vocational training evoked varied reactions from African American leaders. Born a slave in 1858, Booker T. Washington had labored in a West Virginia coal mine before attending Hampton Normal (teacher-training) and Agricultural Institute in Virginia. In 1881 he assumed the leadership of Tuskegee Institute, an Alabama school for blacks founded on the Hampton model. Speaking at the Cotton States Exposition, a fair held in Atlanta in 1895, Washington urged southern blacks to "Cast down your buckets where you are"—in other words, to remain in the South and to concentrate on acquiring manual skills that would bring a measure of self-sufficiency to black families and communities. In the same address, Washington proposed that blacks refrain from agitating for civil rights, such as the vote. In return, whites should refrain from attacking innocent men, women, and children. Ignoring this last part of the speech, whites hailed Washington's "Atlanta Compromise" proposal as one that endorsed racial segregation and second-class citizenship for blacks.

Challenging Washington's message, northern scholar-activist W. E. B. Du Bois ridiculed the notion that blacks should be content to become maids, carpenters, and sharecroppers. Similarly, in 1896 John Hope, a young professor at Roger Williams University in Nashville, Tennessee, and future president of Morehouse College and later Atlanta University, renounced Washington's apparent **accommodationist** stance: "If we are not striving for equality, in heaven's name for what are we living?" he demanded. "Rise, Brothers! Come let us possess this land. Never say, 'Leave well enough alone.'"

In many urban areas, Roman Catholic nuns founded and staffed **parochial** (parish) **schools** that appealed to certain immigrant communities. By 1900 Catholics constituted the largest single denomination in the country, with 9 million members from diverse backgrounds.

New forms of schooling reinforced class and cultural distinctions. No longer dependent on the income their children might earn in the workplace, late-nineteenth-century urban middle-class families could allow their sons and daughters to prolong their schooling. High school came to be considered a logical extension of public schooling. Between 1890 and 1900, the number of students graduating from high school doubled, from 43,731 to 94,883.

The spread of private institutions of higher education reflected the wealth of a new industrial owner class and new forms of socialization for young people of privilege. In 1891 Central Pacific Railroad builder Leland Stanford founded Stanford University in California in honor of his recently deceased son. The previous year, Standard Oil's John D. Rockefeller established the University of Chicago.

College life was becoming associated with a particular stage of personal development, a stage marked not only by academic endeavors, but also by uniquely American group activities, such as playing with or cheering for the school football team. The game of basketball was invented in 1891, and soon after, many colleges formed teams that played the new sport. In 1893 an editorial in the *Nation* magazine decried "the inordinate attention given to athletics in college" and suggested that "debt, drink, and debauchery" were the natural consequence. The writer singled out athletic scholarships and the recruitment of college baseball players by professional scouts as especially unfortunate developments.

Connections Between Consciousness and Behavior

In the 1890s, some scholars and writers proposed that, although America's geographic frontier was closed, the "interior" frontier (of the human will and imagination) still attracted the curious. In Vienna, professor-physician Sigmund Freud pioneered the study of the human unconscious, the mysterious realm of thought and feeling that lies hidden beneath the mundane activities of everyday life. Freud's *The Interpretation of Dreams* (1900) suggested that dreams reveal the dreamer's unconscious desires and that these desires shape routine behavior. In the United States, the new discipline of psychology owed much to the work of Harvard University professor William James. In his *Principles of Psychology* (1890), James described the human brain as an organism constantly adjusting itself to its environment; people's surroundings profoundly influence their behavior, he argued.

Novelist Stephen Crane combined an unflinching look at reality—a blood-soaked Civil War battlefield or the slums of New York City—with a sensitive probing of human psychology. In *The Red Badge of Courage* (1894), Crane explores the fears and self-delusions of a Union soldier, basing his account on firsthand descriptions of the fighting a generation before. By stripping the story of all ideology—northern soldiers are hardly distinguishable from southern soldiers, and political issues are never mentioned—Crane suggests that the real war was that of the combatants battling their own private demons.

> *The new discipline of psychology owed much to the work of Harvard University professor William James.*

Kate Chopin's novel *The Awakening* (1899) prompted outrage among critics. They objected to the sympathetic portrayal of the wealthy married heroine, Edna Pontellier, who anguishes over her inability to reconcile her artistic, free-spirited temperament with her roles of wife and mother. At the end of the story, set in New Orleans, she chooses to commit suicide rather than submit to a life of convention. The novel focuses on Edna's reaction to the expectations other people have of her and on her gradual awakening to the idea that she must live life—or die—on her own terms.

Religious leaders also explored the uncharted territory of the mind. In the late nineteenth century, the Church of Christ, Scientist, founded by Mary Baker Eddy in 1879, prospered and grew. Eddy held that physical illness was a sign of sin and that such illness could be healed by Christian faith and prayer. In 1892 she reorganized her Christian Science faith around a mother church in Boston. Through branch churches, the American-born sect spread to more than sixty countries throughout the world.

The Search for Alliances

In the 1890s, groups of Americans seemed to be estranged from each other as they rarely had been before. A few were enjoying the fruits of astonishing wealth, building for themselves magnificent, multimillion-dollar "summer cottages" reminiscent of glittering European palaces. In 1899 University of Chicago sociologist Thorstein Veblen coined the term **conspicuous consumption** to describe the expensive tastes of the ostentatious rich. Meanwhile, working men and women toiled long hours under dangerous conditions—when they had jobs. In 1895 the average worker was unemployed for three months of the year. Categories of race pitted various groups, native born and immigrant, against one another. Self-styled sophisticated city folk derided the **hayseeds** on the farm.

Still, the prosperous middle class hoped that certain unifying forces would connect different classes and ethnic groups. Businessmen, lawyers, and other professionals placed their faith in public schools, such cultural institutions as public museums and libraries, and the desire for a more comfortable life to instill "American" values in newcomers and the poor. The 1890s also witnessed some remarkable alliances between groups of people who had never before found common ground. The Populist party had a profound impact on the nation's political landscape in the 1890s. And women, through their local and national organizations, helped to blend domestic concerns with politics, offering a new model of civic involvement.

Class Conflict

Congress passed the Pension Act of 1890 to provide pensions for all disabled men who had served in the Union army during the Civil War. To pay for the pensions, Congress imposed a high tariff (named the McKinley Tariff after Representative William McKinley of Ohio) on a wide variety of imported goods. The northeastern states, dependent on domestic manufacturing, traditionally supported a high tariff. Western states supported the McKinley Tariff in return for the Sherman Silver Purchase Act of 1890, under which the federal government promised to buy a total of 4.5 million ounces of silver each month and to issue banknotes for that amount redeemable in gold or silver. As a result, Westerners benefited from the infusion of federal cash used to purchase silver mined in the West.

Political and Cultural Conflicts—1890s

However, the pairing of a high tariff with the purchase of silver produced explosive political and economic results. The tax on imported manufactured goods hurt consumers, and when wages did not keep pace with prices, workers revolted. In 1892 steel magnate Andrew Carnegie and his company chairman Henry Clay Frick initiated a drastic wage cut at the Carnegie Steel Company's Homestead plant, near Pittsburgh. Workers struck in June. They armed themselves with rifles and dynamite and engaged in a pitched battle with some 300 detectives from the Pinkerton agency, men hired by Frick to break the strike. (Homestead town officials had refused Frick's request to subdue the strikers.) Ten people died, and sixty were wounded. In response to the violence, the governor of Pennsylvania mobilized the state's

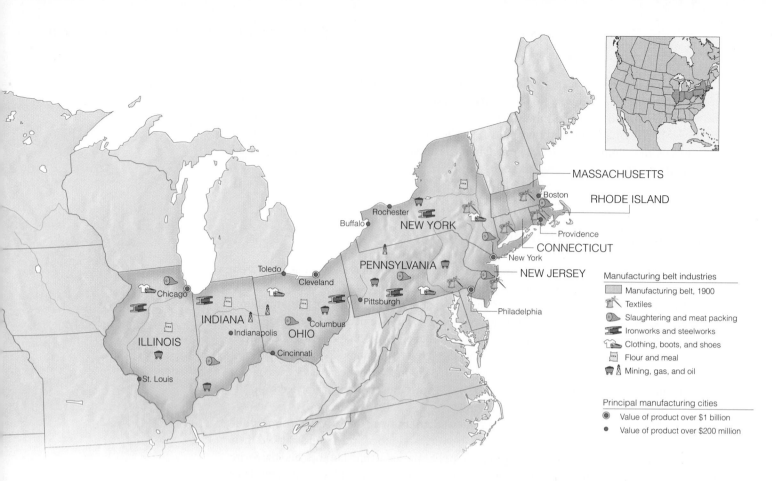

■ **MAP 18.2**

MANUFACTURING IN THE UNITED STATES, 1900   During the late nineteenth century, most manufacturing took place in the northeastern United States. Exceptions included flour milling in Minneapolis, the growing textile industry in the southern Piedmont, and the emergence of steel production in Birmingham, Alabama, thanks to rich local deposits of coal and iron ore.

National Guard. The troops escorted strikebreakers to work. The company cut its workforce by 25 percent and reduced the wages of the strikebreakers. The steelworkers' union lay in ruins. Gloated Frick, "Our victory is now complete and most gratifying."

In the West, gold, copper, and silver miners faced daunting barriers to labor organization from within and outside their ranks. Protestants harbored suspicions of Roman Catholics. Ancient hatreds prevented the Irish from cooperating with the English. European Americans disdained Mexicans and the Chinese. However, the workers in Idaho's Coeur d'Alene mines managed to overcome these animosities and strike for union recognition. In March 1892, mine owners in the region formed a "protective association" and slashed wages. When workers walked off the job, the owners imported strikebreakers from other areas of the West. The strikers retaliated by blowing up a mine with dynamite. Fifteen hundred state and federal troops arrived on the scene, and the resulting clash left seven miners dead. The troops confined 300 striking miners in bullpens, where they remained for several weeks before their trials. In this case, too, the strikers met with defeat. However, out of this conflict came a new organization, founded in Butte, Montana, in 1893: the Western Federation of Miners.

Widespread discontent over the tariff and simmering resentment on the part of debtors clamoring for unlimited coinage of silver helped unseat President Harrison in the election of 1892. The victorious Democratic candidate, Grover Cleveland, took office once more in 1893 (the only defeated president to be reelected). A new and noteworthy player in the election of 1892 was the People's (Populist) party, whose first national convention took place in Omaha, Nebraska, that summer. The party had emerged from the Farmers' Alliances that had so effectively organized black and white midwestern and southern farmers in the 1880s. In the 1890s, the plight of western farmers reflected the state of American agriculture in general. The price of wheat had been a dollar a bushel in 1870, but it was only 35 cents twenty years later. Dakota farmers lost 15 cents on every bushel of wheat they sent to market.

The Populist party platform endorsed at the Omaha convention supported "free and unlimited coinage of silver and gold at the present legal ratio of sixteen to one"; a graduated income tax; government ownership of railroad, telegraph, and telephone companies; and an end to land speculation. The delegates condemned government subsidies to private corporations and called for the direct election of U.S. senators. The Populists' 1892 platform also included resolutions sympathizing "with the efforts of organized workmen to shorten the hours of labor" to an eight-hour workday (many workers were forced to toil twelve to fourteen hours daily) and expressing solidarity with the Knights of Labor in their struggles against "tyrannical" employers.

TABLE 18-1

The Election of 1892

Candidate	Political Party	Popular Vote (%)	Electoral Vote
Grover Cleveland	Democratic	46.1	277
Benjamin Harrison	Republican	43.0	145
James B. Weaver	Populist	8.5	22
John Bidwell	Prohibition	2.2	—

The Populists gained strength when a national economic depression hit in 1893. This dramatic downturn stemmed from several causes. As debtors clamored for "free silver," foreign investors in the United States became nervous, and European bankers began to call in their loans. A bubble of overbuilding and land speculation burst.

The effects of the depression were widespread. Within six months, 8,000 businesses failed. As many as 20 percent of all workers lost their jobs. In 1894 Jacob S. Coxey, an Ohio quarry owner, dubbed himself a "general" and mobilized 5,000 men to march to Washington, D.C. There, "Coxey's Army" protested the failure of the federal government to provide relief, now that the country was in the midst of the worst depression ever.

Also in 1894, Eugene V. Debs, head of the American Railway Union (ARU), inspired the union's 150,000 members to protest conditions at the Pullman Palace Car Company. Employees in the company town of Pullman, near Chicago, felt squeezed when Pullman cut their wages by one-third but left intact the rents on their company-owned houses. The resulting strike crippled railroads from Chicago to California. President Cleveland declared that he could not stand by while the strikers interfered with the delivery of the U.S. mail. The president sent troops to quell the uprising, crushing the strike. For the first time, a federal court issued an **injunction** to force workers to go back to their jobs. Debs and other ARU leaders defied the order and went to jail.

To workers all over the country, the response to the Pullman strike signaled a troublesome alliance between government and big business, two powerful forces that the poor and the unemployed could not hope to counter. Judicial decisions confirmed the belief of many farmers and workers that all branches of the federal government were conspiring to favor the rich at the expense of the poor. In 1895 the Supreme Court rendered two opinions that favored big business and the wealthiest Americans. In *United States v. E. C. Knight*, the court ruled that the Sherman Anti-Trust Act of 1890 applied only to interstate commerce and not to manufacturers. The court had decided in favor of the subject of the suit, the sugar trust that controlled 98 percent of the industry. In *Pollock v. Farmers' Loan and Trust Company*, the court struck down a modest federal income tax (2 percent on incomes over $4,000 per year). These decisions helped set the stage for the showdown between the Populists and the two major parties in 1896.

Demise of the Populists

In 1896 the Republicans nominated Congressman William McKinley of Ohio, whose name had graced the widely unpopular tariff bill of 1890. The Democrats turned their back on Cleveland, regarded as a pariah by members of his own party for his ties to big business and his high-handed tactics against the Pullman strikers. Without an obvious presidential candidate at their convention in Chicago in July, the Democrats seemed at loose ends. Then, out of the audience, a young man rose to address the 15,000 delegates. William Jennings Bryan, a thirty-six-year-old Populist from Nebraska, electrified the assembly with his passionate denunciation of arrogant industrialists and indifferent politicians. The country must abandon the gold standard once and for all, he thundered: "You shall not press down upon the brow of labor this crown of thorns, you shall not crucify mankind upon a cross of gold." One awestruck listener, an alternate member of the Nebraska delegation, later said of Bryan's "Cross of Gold" speech, "There are no words in our language to picture the effect it produced upon the vast multitude which heard it." The next day, the Democrats chose Bryan as their candidate for president, too.

By nominating this eloquent upstart, the Democrats took on the Populist cause of free silver. Conservative Democrats bolted the party or sat out the election. Meeting in their own convention later in the summer, the Populists chose Bryan as their candidate for president.

TABLE 18-2			
The Election of 1896			
Candidate	Political Party	Popular Vote (%)	Electoral Vote
William McKinley	Republican	51.1	271
William J. Bryan	Democratic	45.5	176

In the general election, McKinley received much support from his friend and political supporter Marcus (Mark) Hanna. A wealthy iron magnate and chair of the Republican National Committee, Hanna coordinated an effort to raise large sums of money for the Republicans ($16 million in total, compared with the Democrats' $1 million). Hanna charged that Bryan as president would mean disaster for businessmen, bankers, and other creditors, who would now be at the mercy of working people, small farmers, and other debtors. McKinley triumphed in November and, as a national force, the People's party rapidly disintegrated after the election of 1896.

As a political movement encompassing disparate elements, the Populists left a mixed legacy. In some areas of the country, the party yielded some remarkable, if short-lived, interracial coalitions. In North Carolina, Republican-Populist **fusion** captured the state legislature in 1894 and the governorship in 1896. Throughout the South, however, the black population was growing—from 4.5 million on the eve of the Civil War to a total of 10 million people in 1890. Frightened by this development, white southern Democrats campaigned to disfranchise black men, beginning in the 1890s. Landless blacks and whites would find no common political ground again until the 1930s.

Barriers to a U.S. Workers' Political Movement

In the 1890s, workers in Europe were forging new political parties to represent their interests and, in some cases, to press a bold socialist agenda, in the forum of national politics. Although late-nineteenth-century America showed dramatic evidence of bitter class conflict, it produced no viable workers' party or socialist movement. Why? The answer is not simple. Together, farmers and members of the industrial laboring classes aspired to self-sufficiency, a life free of debt that released their wives and children from unremitting toil and provided some measure of material comfort. Nevertheless, both groups found it difficult to unify themselves.

The large influx of immigrants meant that competition for even low-paying jobs remained fierce among wage-earning men and women. Employers manipulated racial, ethnic, and religious prejudices among workers to keep them estranged. White Protestant workers seized on ethnic and religious distinctions to win for themselves advantages in the workplace. Their unions excluded certain racial and ethnic groups altogether. Even somewhat egalitarian unions fell prey to racial prejudice. In addition, skilled workers, taking pride in their craft and its traditions, distanced themselves from those who tended machines.

Many American workers, regardless of ethnicity, religion, or industry, continued to believe that they could eventually own their own businesses. They resisted casting their lot permanently with unions or other working-class organizations. High rates of **geographic mobility** also prevented workers from committing themselves to a particular union in a particular place. And the power of antistrike forces proved daunting. Private security agencies, such as the Pinkertons, as well as state-deployed National Guard troops, backed up the authority of employers, judges, mayors, and governors.

Challenges to Traditional Gender Roles

In the 1890s, the women's suffrage, club, missionary, and social settlement movements emerged as significant political forces. In 1890 the two major national women's suffrage associations, the National Woman Suffrage Association and the American Woman Suffrage Association, merged to form the National-American Woman Suffrage Association (NAWSA). Elizabeth Cady Stanton served as the new group's first president for two years. But the suffrage movement exhibited contradictory impulses. On one hand, it brought together supporters from around the country and yielded striking examples of international cooperation. On the other hand, white native-born Protestant American suffragists distanced themselves from the poor, immigrants, African Americans, and the laboring classes within their own country.

Identifying themselves primarily as wives and mothers, some women entered the political realm through local women's clubs. They believed that personal intellectual development and group political activity would benefit both their own families and society in general. In the 1880s, the typical club focused on self-improvement through reading history and literature. By the 1890s, many clubs had embraced political activism. They lobbied local politicians for improvements in education and social welfare and raised money for hospitals and playgrounds. The General Federation of Women's Clubs (GFWC), founded in 1892, united 100,000 women in 500 affiliate clubs throughout the nation.

Yet the GFWC specifically excluded African American clubs. Black women formed their own national federation, the National Association of Colored Women (NACW), in 1896. Through club work, they spoke out against lynch mobs and segregationists and worked to improve their local communities. In some areas of the country, black and white women did make common cause—to further the goals of temperance, for example—although white women embraced these alliances uneasily.

In the West, Protestant-sponsored "mission homes" ministered to women in need. The San Francisco Presbyterian Chinese Mission Home offered a safe haven for Chinese women fleeing abuse and exploitation. Eastern women supported not only the San Francisco mission but also shelters for unwed mothers and abused girls in other cities, in the name of virtuous womanhood.

Virginia Historical Society

■ In 1896 Charles H. Epps, the city sergeant of Richmond, Virginia, ran for reelection. He distributed these cards to prospective voters. The cards suggest the masculine nature of politics at this time. This one doubled as a scorecard for the city's professional baseball team and carried advertisements for a local whiskey manufacturer and liquor and tobacco store.

Women's Suffrage before the 19th Century

California Views Historical Photo Collection, Monterey, CA

■ The diversity of the American workforce and the American economy inhibited the development of a national workers' political party. By the 1890s, some industries were fully mechanized. Others relied on traditional forms of manual labor. In California, Asian workers faced persistent discrimination from labor unions. These immigrants are picking oranges near Santa Ana, c. 1895.

Social settlements were unique institutions, founded and staffed by well-educated women, many of whom had attended elite women's colleges. The daily operations of the settlement house reflected the priorities of its founders, who often brought activists, public health officials, journalists, and laboring men and women together around the dinner table to discuss problems of the poor. Settlement house workers hoped to instill in poor women the values of domesticity and pride in American citizenship. By 1900 more than 200 social settlement houses were helping to acculturate immigrants by offering classes in a variety of subjects, including English, health, and personal hygiene.

Although often associated with immigrants in the largest cities, settlement houses reached diverse populations. In the late 1890s, a coalition of the Kentucky Federation of Women's Clubs and other organizations sponsored several teachers who organized a summer settlement called Camp Cedar Grove in the eastern part of the state. This venture provided the foundation for the Hindman Settlement School. The school, still in existence, initially aimed to **acculturate** mountain people to middle-class ways in dress, eating habits, and manners and to preserve traditional mountain music and crafts.

Sensitive to the racial prejudices of their clients and their neighbors, most early settlements failed to reach out to African Americans. This policy stimulated the development of black-led settlements, such as the Phyllis Wheatley Settlement in Minneapolis and the Neighborhood Union in Atlanta. Founded by Lugenia Burns Hope in 1908, the Neighborhood Union aimed "to bring about a better understanding between the races."

Some women challenged traditional gender relations that relegated women to dependence on men. Emma Goldman, a Russian immigrant and self-proclaimed anarchist, paired the sexual liberation of women with the rights of workers to live a decent life. A radical by any measure, Goldman was, nevertheless, not alone in rejecting the idea that marriage should always be permanent. Between 1890 and 1900, the divorce rate increased from one out of every seventeen new marriages to one out of twelve. More and more couples, middle class and working class, native born and immigrant, were seeking means to dissolve marriages that had failed.

The daily operations of the settlement house reflected the priorities of its founders.

Charlotte Perkins Gilman was among the most prolific and well-known critics of the conventional division of labor in the home. She proclaimed that women, no longer content to remain dependent on men, must take their rightful place within the economy, working as equals with their brothers and husbands. Gilman proposed that housework be divided into its specialized tasks to be performed by professionals. This system would free women from the unpaid, mind-numbing task of combined "cook-nurse-laundress-chambermaid-housekeeper-waitress-governor." In her critique of gender conventions, Gilman anticipated the feminist movement of the 1960s.

Men also pondered the effects of industrializing society on their own roles. As assistant secretary of the U.S. Navy in the late 1890s, Theodore Roosevelt worried that, in this age of machines, young men lacked the opportunities for "the strenuous life" their grandfathers had enjoyed. He argued that unapologetic masculine bravado provided the key to American strength and **rejuvenation** on both a national and personal level. In his multivolume history *The Winning of the West* (1889–1896), Roosevelt extolled America's relentless march to the Pacific: "The rude, fierce settler who drives the savage from the land lays all civilized mankind under a debt to him." Imperialism at home and abroad, he declared, was a "race-important work," one that should claim the energies of men as politicians and soldiers.

American Imperialism

In the 1890s, the United States began to extend its political reach and economic dominance to other parts of the world. Americans looked beyond their borders and saw exotic peoples who represented a variety of opportunities—as consumers of American goods, producers of goods Americans wanted to buy, and objects of American benevolence. This view represented an extension of the reform impulse at home.

The country's mighty industrial manufacturing sector demanded new markets and a wider consumer base. The depression of 1893, in particular, raised fears that manufacturers would have to contend with surpluses of goods that Americans could not afford to buy. American businesspeople and State Department officials established a partnership that combined private economic self-interest with national military considerations. Some molders of public opinion used the new languages of race and masculine virility to justify an "Anglo-Saxon" mission of conquest of "childlike" peoples. Meanwhile, European countries were carving up Africa and making economic inroads into China. Many Americans believed their own country should join the "race" for riches and "march" to glory as part of the international competition to exploit the natural resources and trade potential of weaker countries.

> *American businesspeople and State Department officials established a partnership that combined private economic self-interest with national military considerations.*

Cultural Encounters with the Exotic

In early October 1897, 30,000 spectators paid their 25-cent fee to enter New York's Excursion Wharf and observe the strange cargo of the recently arrived steamship *Hope*. Arctic explorer Robert Peary had returned from Greenland, bringing with him six Greenland Eskimo and a 37.5-ton meteorite dislodged from the Cape York region. The American public hailed the intrepid explorer Peary as a hero. The American Museum of Natural History put the Eskimo on display, and New Yorkers regarded their odd clothing, language, and eating habits with intense curiosity.

During the late nineteenth century, Americans were fascinated by artifacts and images dealing with far-away places, especially Africa, the Middle East, and Asia. This impulse, revealed in high art as well as popular culture, stereotyped darker-skinned, non-Christian peoples as primitive, sensual, and inscrutable. Chicago's Columbian Exposition of 1893 featured exhibits depicting harems, spice merchants, and turbaned warriors and performances of "hootchy kootchy dancers," scantily clothed young women writhing to the music of exotic instruments.

Throughout the late nineteenth century, photographers took pictures of Middle Eastern nomads and African villagers. American artists traveled abroad to render romantic scenes of deserts, ancient ruins, and mysterious peoples in oils and in watercolors. These cultural tendencies could be used to sell products and entertainment. The glassmaker-jeweler Tiffany and Co. evoked Islamic art in its tea services and silver patterns. Tobacco companies marketed mass-produced cigarettes with "Oriental" brand names: "Fatima," "Omar," and "Camel."

American Museum of Natural History Library, Image No. 220545

■ The Greenland Eskimo Minik is shown here soon after his arrival in New York City in 1897 at age 7. Minik was devastated by the death of his widowed father, Qisuk; the two were among six Eskimo brought to New York by Arctic explorer Robert E. Peary. Later in his life, Minik spoke of his father to a newspaper reporter, saying, "He was dearer to me than anything else in the world, especially when we were brought to New York, strangers in a strange land."

Thus, a fascination with the exotic encompassed a wide range of impulses in American life and letters, bringing together explorers, scientists, artists, and advertising agents.

Initial Imperialist Ventures

The opening of Asia to American trade, combined with the military challenges posed by the major European imperial powers, stimulated the growth of the U.S. Navy in the 1880s. In his book *The Influence of Sea-Power in History, 1660–1763* (1890), Captain Alfred Thayer Mahan contended that if the United States aspired to be a world power, it must control the seas.

Seeking way stations for its ships, the United States negotiated control over both Pearl Harbor in Hawaii and the harbor at Pago Pago in Samoa in 1887. Three years later, Secretary of State James G. Blaine hosted the first Pan-American Conference in Washington, D.C., a gathering of representatives from nineteen independent Latin American republics.

In 1895 the United States signaled to Great Britain that it was prepared to go to war to bar Europeans from colonizing or intervening in the Americas, a policy outlined in the Monroe Doctrine more than seventy years before. Britain had persisted in its long-standing claims to the jungle boundary between its colony of British Guiana and the country of Venezuela on the north coast of South America. President Cleveland made clear his intention to enforce the Monroe Doctrine. Britain, sensitive to other threats posed by European imperial powers to the far-flung British empire, backed down. Thereafter, Britain began to concentrate on strengthening its diplomatic ties with the United States.

Meanwhile, in the Pacific, the Hawaiian Islands seemed to pose both a threat and an opportunity for American interests. Located 2,000 miles from the California coast, Hawaii had a population of 150,000 in 1890. In 1875 sugar planters and merchants, many of whom were related to missionaries, had negotiated a treaty with the United States that let them ship the crop to the United States duty free. Production of Hawaiian sugar increased from less than 10,000 tons in 1870 to 300,000 tons thirty years later.

By this time, Chinese, Koreans, Filipinos, Puerto Ricans, Japanese, and Portuguese had made their way to the Hawaiian Islands. These groups formed the bulk of the plantation labor force, for disease had decimated the native population. In the fields and in their barracks, immigrant contract workers followed a disciplined regimen under the supervision of mounted, whip-wielding overseers called *lunas*. Indeed, these laborers' workday bore a marked resemblance to that of sharecroppers on the largest cotton plantations of the U.S. South.

The McKinley Tariff of 1890 raised duties on imports of the islands' sugar. This served to overturn the 1875 pro-planter treaty, causing planters (mostly Americans) to panic about their livelihood. They received no support from the islands' native leader, Queen Liliuokalani, who believed foreigners should be barred from running the country. In 1893 the planters, backed by American marines, launched a successful revolt that deposed the queen. They then called for the United States to annex the islands as a territory. When President Cleveland discovered that native Hawaiians opposed annexation, he refused to agree to the move. His refusal incurred the wrath of American imperialists, who claimed that the "Hawaiian pear" had been "ripe for the plucking." Those seeking to expand American influence also looked just south of Florida.

The Spanish-American-Cuban-Filipino War of 1898

In the Caribbean, Cuban nationalists staged an uprising against the island's Spanish colonial authorities in 1895. Native *insurrectos* under the leadership of José Martí burned crops of sugar cane and attacked passenger trains. American companies with large investments in the Cuban sugar industry (a total of about $50 million) were outraged at the destruction of their property; they had no sympathy for the *insurrectos*. Yet the arrival of Spanish military officials, who herded the rebels into barbed-wire concentration camps, inflamed public opinion in the United States. By 1897, both businesspeople and humanitarians urged President McKinley to intervene in Cuba.

Activities of the United States in the Caribbean, 1898–1930s

Two major American newspaper publishers, William R. Hearst and Joseph Pulitzer, highlighted Spanish atrocities against Cubans. On February 9, 1898, Hearst published a letter written by the Spanish minister in Washington, D.C., Dupuy de Lôme, in which de Lôme denounced President McKinley as a spineless politician. Six days later, the American battleship *Maine*, which had been sent to Havana harbor to evacuate Americans should the need arise, exploded and sank. Two hundred sixty officers and men were killed. Subsequent investigations concluded that the heat from one of the coal bins had ignited an adjacent powder magazine. But the Hearst papers implied that the Spanish were responsible for the blast. Attempting to expand their readership, the Hearst and Pulitzer newspapers engaged in **yellow journalism**: sensational news reporting that blurred the line between fact and fiction, spontaneous reality and staged theater. War sold papers.

McKinley responded to American businesspeople who feared for their interests in Cuba and to other Americans who decried Spain's brutality toward the *insurrectos*. On April 11, 1898, McKinley called on Congress to declare war against Spain. To war supporters, much was at stake: the large American sugar investment, trade with the island, and American power and influence in the Western Hemisphere. Congress responded to McKinley's message by adopting

Granger Collection, New York

■ The battleship *Maine* exploded and sank in Havana harbor on February 15, 1898.

■ **MAP 18.3**
THE SPANISH-AMERICAN-CUBAN-FILIPINO WAR OF 1898
In Cuba, the United States combined a blockade of the island with an army invasion to defeat Spanish forces. In the Philippines, the U.S. triumph over the Spanish opened a wider war between American occupying forces and native Filipinos.

the Teller Amendment, which declared that the United States would guarantee Cuba its independence once the Spanish were driven from the island. America went to war on April 29.

McKinley hoped to hobble the Spanish navy by making a **preemptive attack** on the fleet in the Spanish colony of the Philippines. Commodore George Dewey, stationed with the American Asiatic Squadron in Hong Kong, was dispatched with his ships to Manila Bay, where on May 1, 1898, his force of four battleships sank all ten rickety Spanish vessels, killing 400, with only a few minor American casualties. Dewey waited in the harbor until American reinforcements arrived in August. Then, with the help of Filipino nationalists led by Emilio Aguinaldo, U.S. forces overran Manila on August 13.

Meanwhile, congressional Republicans had found the necessary votes to annex Hawaii. They claimed that the United States needed the Pacific islands to secure a refueling way station for Dewey's troops. McKinley signed the congressional resolution on July 7, 1898. Hawaiian residents were granted citizenship rights, and the islands became an official U.S. territory in 1900.

Earlier, in the summer of 1898, 17,000 American troops prepared for their incursion into Cuba. Among them were the Rough Riders, volunteers organized by Lieutenant Colonel Theodore Roosevelt, who had resigned his post as assistant secretary of the navy to serve as an officer. The troops landed near Santiago, Cuba, in late June. On July 1, Roosevelt and his men engaged an unprepared Spanish force of about 2,000 men at El Caney and San Juan Hill. The Rough Riders charged up nearby Kettle Hill (they were on foot, not on horses) and into American legend. They received crucial backup support from two African American regiments

VIDEO

Roosevelt's Rough Riders

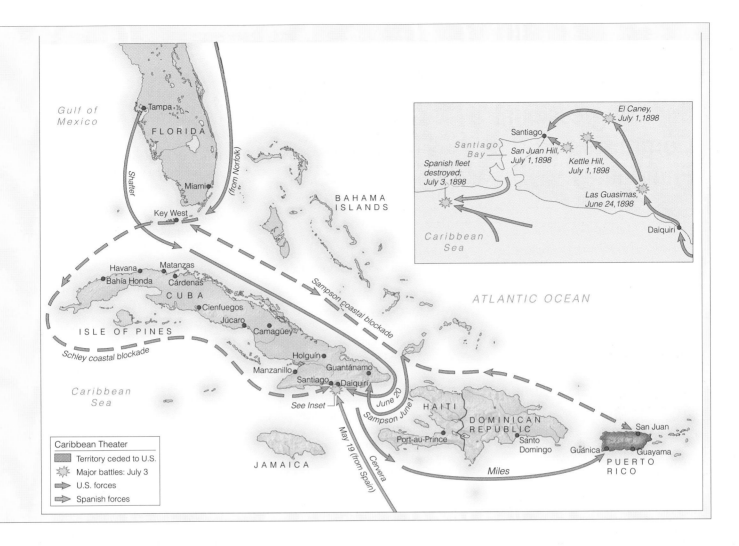

that day. By late July, American warships had destroyed the Spanish fleet in Santiago Bay. According to Secretary of State John Hay, it had been "a splendid little war," just 113 days long. Battles claimed 385 American lives.

On August 12, 1898, Spain signed an **armistice** and later in the year ceded its claim to remnants of its empire, including Cuba and Puerto Rico in the Caribbean and the island of Guam in the Pacific. The United States forced Cuba to incorporate into its constitution (written in 1901) the so-called Platt Amendment, which guaranteed continuing U.S. influence over the country, including the stationing of American troops at a naval station on Guantanamo Bay. Meeting with Spanish negotiators in Paris, the United States agreed to pay $20 million for the Philippines.

But Filipino rebels were not about to bow to a new colonial power. Over the next two years, the United States committed 100,000 troops to subdue the rebels, using tactics that foreshadowed the U.S. war in Vietnam seventy years later. Hunting down guerrillas hiding in the jungle, American soldiers torched villages and crops. They forced water down the throats of suspected rebel leaders—a form of torture known as the "water cure"—in an effort to extract information. Four thousand Americans and 20,000 Filipinos died in combat. As many as 600,000 Filipino civilians succumbed to disease and starvation.

Ownership of the Philippine Islands gave the United States a foothold in Asia. In 1894–1895, Japan had waged a successful war against China, and European traders rushed in to China to monopolize local markets and establish their own **spheres of influence**. Secre-

World Colonial Empires, 1900

Proceedings of the Congressional Committee on the Philippines

In January 1900, Congress established the Committee on the Philippines. Senator Henry Cabot Lodge of Massachusetts was appointed chair. The committee's task was to review the American conduct of the war. The testimony of two U.S. officers, which follows, foreshadows the difficulties faced by the United States in fighting a guerrilla war in Vietnam six decades later.

Brigadier General Robert P. Hughes testified in response to questions posed by committee members:

Q: In burning towns, what would you do? Would the entire town be destroyed by fire or would only offending portions of the town be burned?

GEN. HUGHES: I do not know that we ever had a case of burning what you would call a town in this country; but probably a *barrio* or a *sitio;* probably a half dozen houses, native shacks, where the *insurrectos* [rebels] would go in and be concealed, and if they caught a detachment passing they would kill some of them.

Q: What did I understand you to say would be the consequence of that?

GEN. HUGHES: They usually burned the village.

Q: All of the houses in the village?

GEN. HUGHES: Yes, every one of them.

Q: What would become of the inhabitants?

GEN. HUGHES: That was their lookout....The destruction was as a punishment.

Q: The punishment in that case would fall, not upon the men, who would go elsewhere, but mainly upon the women and little children.

GEN. HUGHES: The women and children are part of the family, and where you wish to inflict a punishment you can punish the man probably worse in that way than in any other.

Q: But is that within the ordinary rules of civilized warfare? Of course you could exterminate the family, which would be still worse punishment.

Gen. Hughes: These people are not civilized.

Sergeant Charles S. Riley also testified in response to the committee's questions:

Q: During your service there [in the Philippine Islands] did you witness what is generally known as the water cure?

A: I did.

Q: When and where?

A: On November 27, 1900, in the town of Igbaras, Iloilo Province, Panay Island.

Riley described to the committee a Filipino man, 40–45 years of age, stripped to the waist, with his hands tied behind him.

Q: Do you remember who had charge of him?

A: Captain Glenn stood there beside him and one or two men were tying him. . . . He was then taken and placed under the tank, and the faucet was opened and a stream of water was forced down or allowed to run down his throat; his throat was held so he could not prevent swallowing the water, so that he had to allow the water to run into his stomach. . . . When he was filled with water it was forced out of him by pressing a foot on his stomach or else with their hands. . . .

---

tary of State John Hay issued a communication called the Open Door note in the summer of 1899; in it, he urged the imperial powers to respect the trading interests of all nations. In 1900 the Boxer Uprising in China prompted cooperation among the western powers. The Boxers, radical Chinese nationalists, killed 200 foreign missionaries and other whites in an effort to purge China of outsiders. Together, the Germans, Japanese, British, French, and Americans sent 18,000 troops to quell the revolt. The United States and European nations continued to compete for the China market well into the twentieth century.

Critics of Imperialism

Theodore Roosevelt seemed to personify the late-nineteenth-century idea of American manifest destiny: the notion that the core of the nation's history was a militant mission to expand its territorial reach. However, not all Americans agreed with Roosevelt. New York financier Mark Hanna called him a "madman" and "that damned cowboy." Writer Mark Twain believed him "clearly insane" and "insanest upon war and its supreme glories." Twain and other prominent people founded the Anti-Imperialist League in 1898 in an attempt to stem the rising tide of militarism.

It is difficult to generalize about the politics of anti-imperialists during this period. Some critics of imperialism advocated a hands-off policy toward other nations in the belief that all peo-

This photograph of a United States soldier during the War of 1898 is titled *The Church Saint sat on by a Washington "Johnnie" [soldier]*. During the war, photographers produced vivid images that conveyed the dramatic effects of the U.S. invasion on the society and culture of the Philippines. Led by Emilio Aguinaldo, insurrectionists fought for Philippine independence, beginning in January 1899. Two years later, American forces captured Aguinaldo and established a colonial government in the country.

Q: What had been his crime?
A: Information had been obtained from a native source as to his being an insurgent officer. After the treatment he admitted that he held the rank of captain in the insurgent army—an active captain....

Q: His offense was treachery to the American cause?
A: Yes, sir.

Questions

1. In what ways did the Filipino insurrection challenge the conventions of what congressional committee members called "civilized warfare"?

2. How did General Hughes justify the destruction of whole villages as part of the U.S. effort to suppress the insurrectionists?

3. What are the arguments for and against the practice of torture as a means of extracting information from enemy combatants? ■

Source: Proceedings of the Congressional Committee on the Philippines, in Harvey Graff, ed., *American Imperialism and the Philippine Insurrection* (Boston, 1969),pp. 64–79.

---

ples were entitled to self-determination. In contrast, other anti-imperialists such as Social Darwinists used arguments about racial hierarchies to justify their opposition to expansion.

In the summer of 1900, the Democrats and Republicans prepared for the upcoming presidential election. Receiving the Democratic nomination once again, William Jennings Bryan was eager to press the outdated cause of free silver. He also condemned the American presence in the Philippines, although this issue, too, was rapidly losing the attention of the electorate. At the Republican convention, Roosevelt's supporters managed to win for him the slot as McKinley's running mate. That fall, the former Rough Rider waged an exuberant campaign. Accompanied by a retinue of gun-toting cowboys, he wrapped the Republicans in the American flag. When McKinley swept to reelection in the fall, few Americans could have anticipated how central Roosevelt's vision would become to the country over the next two decades.

Conclusion

As Americans greeted the twentieth century, they might have marveled at the dramatic changes that had occurred in their country over the last 100 years. In 1800 the United States was home to 5.3 million people who lived in sixteen states. One hundred years later, the country included forty-five states and boasted a population of 76 million people. Many workplaces, fields as well as factories, were dominated by machines and the people who tended them. The economy was shifting toward the mass production of consumer goods.

In 1900 the United States exerted control over the land and peoples of Alaska, the Hawaiian and Samoan Islands, the Philippines, Guam, Puerto Rico, and (through the Platt Amendment) Cuba as well. These holdings, notable for their strategic significance, illustrated the growing willingness of the United States to extend its influence and economic reach—by armed force if necessary—to the far corners of the earth. The new drive for worldwide economic and political power was fast eclipsing America's revolutionary heritage, with its values of democracy and self-determination.

Sites to Visit

Spanish-American War
www.loc.gov/rr/hispanic/1898

This site provides resources and documents about the Spanish-American War, the period before the war, and the people who participated in the fighting or commented on it.

The Age of Imperialism
www.smplanet.com/imperialism/toc.html

Focusing on the late nineteenth and early twentieth centuries, this site includes much information about American imperialism.

Hispanic Voices/Voces Hispanas
bancroft.berkeley.edu/collections/latinamericana.html

This interactive site on Latinos in California is maintained by the Bancroft Library in Berkeley. The autobiographical narratives include late-nineteenth-century oral histories with Latinos.

Late Nineteenth-Century Authors
xroads.virginia.edu/~hyper/hypertex.html

This University of Virginia site includes material on prominent nineteenth-century writers, including William Dean Howells, Mark Twain, and Joel Chandler Harris.

Mary Baker Eddy
www.tfccs.com/index.jhtml;jsessionid

Sponsored by the Christian Science Church, this site looks at the founding of Christian Science.

National Arts and Crafts Archives
www.arts-crafts.com/index.html

This site serves as a guide to materials related to the Arts and Crafts movement, which lasted from about 1890 to 1929.

Era of William McKinley
http://history.osu.edu/projects/McKinley/default.cfm

This Ohio State University site contains a bibliography and numerous images from various periods of McKinley's career. It also includes an excellent collection of McKinley-era cartoons.

"Votes for Women" Suffrage Pictures
http://lcweb2.loc.gov/ammem/vfwhtml/vfwhome.html

This site, part of the Library of Congress American Memory Series, includes images of parades and picket lines, as well as anti-suffragist activity.

Hawaii's Last Queen
http://www.pbs.org/wgbh/amex/hawaii/index.html

This site complements the PBS program on the overthrow of Hawaii's hereditary monarchy in 1893.

For Further Reading

General

Glenda Elizabeth Gilmore, *Gender and Jim Crow: Women and the Politics of White Supremacy in North Carolina, 1896–1920* (1996).

Matthew Frye Jacobson, *Barbarian Virtues: The United States Encounters Foreign Peoples at Home and Abroad, 1876–1917* (2000).

Emily S. Rosenberg, *Spreading the American Dream: American Economic and Cultural Expansion, 1890–1945* (1982).

Robert W. Rydell, *All the World's a Fair: Visions of Empire at American International Expositions, 1876–1916* (1984).

Frontiers at Home, Lost and Found

David Wallace Adams, *Education for Extinction: American Indians and the Boarding School Experience, 1875–1928* (1995).

Matthew Frye Jacobson, *Whiteness of a Different Color: European Immigrants and the Alchemy of Race* (1998).

Neil R. McMillen, *Dark Journey: Black Mississippians in the Age of Jim Crow* (1989).

Mark David Spence, *Dispossessing the Wilderness: Indian Removal and the Making of the National Parks* (1999).

David B. Tyack, *Managers of Virtue: Public School Leadership in America, 1820–1980* (1982).

Michael J. Pfeifer, *Rough Justice: Lynching and American Society, 1874–1947* (2004).

Jonathan Sarna, *American Judaism: A New History* (2004).

The Search for Alliances

Paul Buhle, *From the Knights of Labor to the New World Order: Essays on Labor and Culture* (1997).

Sarah Deutsch, *Women and the City: Gender, Space, and Power in Boston, 1870–1940* (2000).

Patricia R. Hill, *The World Their Household: The American Woman's Foreign Mission Movement and Cultural Transformation, 1870–1920* (1985).

Seymour Martin Lipset and Gary Marks, *It Didn't Happen Here: Why Socialism Failed in the United States* (2000).

Vicki L. Ruiz and Ellen Carol DuBois, eds., *Unequal Sisters: A Multicultural Reader in U.S. Women's History* (2000).

American Imperialism

Robert L. Beisner, *Twelve Against Empire: The Anti-Imperialists, 1898–1900* (1968).

H. W. Brands, *Bound to Empire: The United States and the Philippines* (1992).

Kenn Harper, *Give Me My Father's Body: The Life of Minik, the New York Eskimo* (2000).

Walter LaFeber, *The American Search for Opportunity, 1865–1913* (1993).

William Appleman Williams, *The Tragedy of American Diplomacy* (1972).

For quizzes and other resources on these topics, go to www.longmanamericanhistory.com.

PART SEVEN

Reform at Home, Revolution Abroad, 1900–1929

MANY AMERICANS GREETED THE FIRST YEARS OF THE TWENTIETH century with optimism. Developments at home and abroad seemed to promise a new era of prosperity and progress. The mass manufacturing of automobiles proved a boon to the economy and transformed patterns of travel, leisure, and consumption. The beginning of commercial air flights heralded a revolution in communication and transportation. Moving pictures and new musical forms such as jazz delighted millions.

Focused on the new challenges of urbanization and industrialization, Progressive reformers sought to use science to solve a wide range of problems related to public health and welfare. Some advocated overhauling the system of public education; others pressed for legislation banning the sale and distribution of alcohol. Some lobbied for worker health and safety legislation, and still others sought to exercise social control through eugenics and state-mandated sterilization.

A variety of groups challenged white men's exclusive claim to civil rights. African Americans took the national stage to argue for equality under the law and for freedom from state-sanctioned violence in the form of lynching and servitude for debt. Beginning with the Great Migration of World War I, southern blacks abandoned the cotton fields to seek jobs in northern cities.

The changing roles of women bolstered the women's suffrage movement. Growing numbers of women were becoming labor organizers, reformers, and college professors. Rising divorce rates and the emergence of birth control as a political as well as a medical issue signaled challenges to the traditional patriarchal family. At the same time, conflicts among reformers emerged. For example, white middle-class suffragists hoped to maintain their "respectability" in an effort to win the support of reluctant male leaders; in the process, these women distanced themselves from members of the working class and even the African American women active in the suffrage movement. Suffragists' efforts paid off in 1920, with the ratification of the Nineteenth Amendment to the Constitution.

With its lively consumer culture and rising standard of living, the United States continued to attract newcomers from abroad. Immigrants from Mexico and eastern Europe sought refuge from poverty, oppression, and civil strife at home. In 1914, 1.2 million immigrants came to America, the largest number in a single year before or since that date. Between 1900 and 1930, more than 1 million Mexicans migrated north, most settling in existing Mexican American communities in the Southwest or creating new communities there or in the Midwest.

World War I shattered the belief among many Progressives that conflicts could be solved in a rational, peaceful way. The end of the war had permanently entangled U.S. interests in European affairs. Moreover, revolutions in Mexico (1910) and Russia (1917) affected the United States directly, the former by spurring immigration across the country's southwest border, the latter by challenging the nation's system of industrial capitalism. Nevertheless, many Americans remained convinced that the country could and should isolate itself from world affairs.

Natural forces also remained beyond the control of reformers and government officials. The San Francisco earthquake of 1906, the great Mississippi flood of 1927, and the Florida hurricane of 1928 exacted devastating tolls in terms of human life and property damage. The local communities that were directly affected struggled for years to recover from these disasters.

But for many Americans, the 1920s were a period of peace and prosperity. New household appliances and conveniences lightened the burdens of housework. Radios and movies proved to be popular forms of entertainment. Traditional social mores gave way to expressions of sexual freedom. Progressive impulses waned as business values rose to take their place.

The decade after the end of World War I revealed both the persistence of old conflicts and the emergence of new conflicts within American society. Conservatives branded labor union organizers and socialists as unpatriotic and subversive. Asian immigrants on the West Coast and blacks in the rural South and urban North faced continued legal discrimination in the workplace and in the courts. Protestant fundamentalists challenged the move toward secularism and rationalism, claiming that religious faith, not science, set the standard for morality in modern life. Responding to those who feared that foreign immigration represented a threat to American society, Congress imposed immigration restrictions in 1924. Put into effect in 1920, the Eighteenth Amendment to the Constitution prohibited the sale and distribution of alcoholic beverages. The three Republican presidents who served during the 1920s—Harding, Coolidge, and Hoover—retreated from the activist stance favored by their predecessors, including Theodore Roosevelt and Woodrow Wilson.

The stock market crash of 1929 revealed fundamental weaknesses in the American economy. A tide of bank failures engulfed individual American families even as it threatened businesses abroad. As the depression deepened, Americans looked to the federal government to address the crisis.

1915	U.S. Marines occupy Haiti Germans sink *Lusitania* Film *Birth of a Nation* released
1916	Jeannette Rankin elected first female member of Congress U.S. Marines occupy Dominican Republic
1917	U.S. enters World War I U.S. Marines occupy Cuba Russian Revolution Residents of Puerto Rico granted U.S. citizenship
1918	Spanish influenza epidemic kills 20 million worldwide Sedition Act Wilson's "Fourteen Points" speech to Congress
1919	Versailles Treaty ends World War I U.S. Senate rejects League of Nations Eighteenth Amendment (prohibition) ratified
1920	Nineteenth Amendment (women's suffrage) ratified
1921	Tulsa whites attack black community Sheppard-Towner Act
1922	Five-Power Naval Treaty
1923	Equal Rights Amendment proposed
1924	Johnson-Reid Act Portable radio introduced
1925	Scopes trial, Dayton, Tennessee F. Scott Fitzgerald, *The Great Gatsby*
1926	Gertrude Ederle is first woman to swim across English Channel
1927	Charles Lindbergh flies nonstop from New York to Paris Al Jolson stars in *The Jazz Singer*, first talking movie Sacco and Vanzetti executed *Buck v. Bell* upholds compulsory sterilization laws
1928	Tamiami Trail across Florida Everglades completed
1929	Stock market crash

CHAPTER 19

The Promise and Perils of Progressive Reform, 1900–1912

"I AM A WORKING GIRL," DECLARED CLARA LEMLICH IN HER NATIVE YIDDISH, "ONE OF THOSE striking against intolerable conditions." Still in her teens, the petite young woman took the podium on the night of November 22, 1909, in front of thousands of striking workers in New York, and roused them with her passionate, direct call for action: "I am tired of listening to speakers who talk in generalities. What we are here for is to decide whether or not to strike. I offer a resolution that a general strike be declared—now." The next morning, 15,000 garment workers went on strike, demanding that the work week be reduced to fifty-two hours, with overtime pay and union recognition. Soon, the strikers swelled in number to more than 20,000. Observers at the time were astonished to see lively, fashionably dressed young women filling the picket lines. Ninety percent of the striking workers were women; they were over-whelmingly young Jewish immigrants, with Italian women constituting about 6 percent.

The strike was a demand for union recogni-tion, reasonable wages and hours, and safe and decent working conditions, including an end to sexual harassment on the job. But at the same time, the strikers insisted that they should be treated as "ladies" and have access to the con-sumer goods and leisure culture taking shape in American cities. Ultimately, the strike ended with a failed compromise when the striking workers over-whelmingly rejected an offer of better wages and working conditions that did not include recog-nition of their union. Calling the strikers "socialists," their more moderate allies broke

■ Victims of the Triangle Shirtwaist Company fire.

from the union and left the young female workers vulnerable to the power of the company owners. The coalition of support fell apart, and most of the strikers eventually went back to work.

Less than two years later, a fire broke out in the top floors of the Triangle Shirtwaist Company, one of the centers of the 1909 strike. Eight hundred workers, most of them young Jewish and Italian women, were trapped in the inferno because company officials had locked interior doors to prevent the women from taking unauthorized breaks or leaving work early. The flames tore through the building in less than half an hour, leaving 146 young women dead. Those who did not succumb to

CHAPTER OUTLINE

Immigration: The Changing Face of the Nation

Work, Science, and Leisure

Reformers and Radicals

Expanding National Power

Conclusion

Sites to Visit

For Further Reading

446

flames and smoke jumped to their deaths. One reporter wrote, "I looked upon the dead bodies and I remembered these girls were the shirtwaist makers. I remembered their great strike of last year in which the same girls had demanded more sanitary conditions and more safety precautions in the shops. Their dead bodies were the answer." In the investigation that followed, the owner of the factory was never charged with a crime or held responsible for the tragedy. He claimed that his building was in full compliance with safety laws, but compliance with the laws did not ensure safety for the workers. No laws required sprinklers, adequate fire escapes, or fire drills. Just a few months before the fire, the building had been inspected and declared "fireproof."

The "uprising of twenty thousand," as the 1909 strike came to be called, and the tragic factory fire that ignited in its aftermath, are two among many dramatic episodes in the early twentieth century that expose the fractures and tensions within the nation at the time. Immigrants and racial minorities demanded the full promise of American life; workers struggled against the exploitation, poor pay, and dangerous conditions that characterized industrial jobs; young women insisted on respect at work and access to the playful environment of urban fashion and popular culture; female voices called for full citizenship and the vote and claimed their right to be heard by male bosses and union leaders; and activists across the political spectrum tried to control and manage the changes taking place around them in accord with their widely differing values.

During the first years of the twentieth century, the nation began to emerge as something profoundly different than it had been in the past. Even the landscape changed as cities continued to grow not only outward but also upward, with the construction of towering skyscrapers, and downward, with the creation of subway systems. But human enterprise continued to be vulnerable to the forces of nature. On April 18, 1906, an earthquake virtually leveled San Francisco. The earthquake symbolized American life at the dawn of the twentieth century, as did

Library of Congress

■ An earthquake devastated San Francisco on April 18, 1906. Here a Chinese immigrant watches as the city goes up in flames. Chinatown was destroyed, along with much of the downtown.

one word: upheaval. The dramatic changes taking place in the nation at the dawn of the new century, from industry and technology down to the most intimate levels of life, sparked equally dramatic efforts to control, tame, and regulate them. Because of the flurry of reform activity during this period, historians call it the Progressive Era. Politicians from all parties participated in the wide range of reform efforts known as Progressivism, fueled by a faith in progress and a belief in the possibility for social improvement.

Immigration: The Changing Face of the Nation

Between 1900 and 1910, nearly 9 million immigrants entered the United States, the largest number for any single decade in the nation's history until the 1990s. They came particularly from southern and eastern Europe, as well as Mexico and Asia. The United States was one of several potential destinations for these courageous and hopeful sojourners. It was particularly appealing because of its often exaggerated, but nonetheless

VIDEO

Ellis Island
Immigrants, 1903

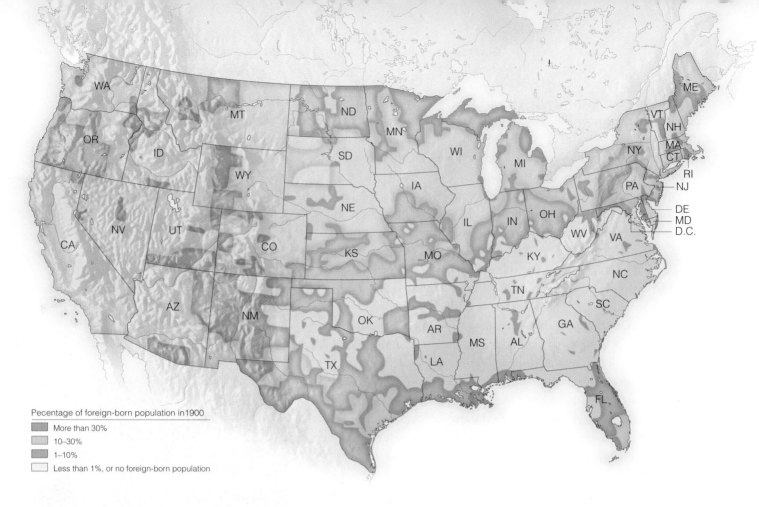

Pecentage of foreign-born population in1900

- ■ More than 30%
- ■ 10–30%
- ■ 1–10%
- □ Less than 1%, or no foreign-born population

■ **MAP 19.1**

FOREIGN-BORN POPULATION, 1900   Although the most famous points of entry for immigrants during the turn-of-the-century decades were New York's Ellis Island for people from Europe, and Angel Island in San Francisco Bay for people from Asia, most immigrants actually settled in the upper Midwest and the southwestern region bordering Mexico.

real, opportunities for jobs and economic advancement, its official commitment to freedom of religion and political thought, and its reputation as a nation that welcomed newcomers from abroad.

On arrival, many found that the "promised land" was not the paradise they expected. They faced crowded living conditions in urban tenements, jobs in sweatshops and factories with long hours, low wages, and miserable working conditions, and a hostile reception. Many Americans—including some whose own parents or grandparents had come to the United States as immigrants—looked down on the newcomers as "racially inferior" and morally suspect, feared competition for jobs, and worried that the masses of poor foreigners in their midst would become a burden on taxpayers and public institutions. The Statue of Liberty may have held up the torch of welcome, but many citizens, from union halls to legislative chambers, wanted the newcomers to leave.

Many did leave. One-third of immigrants to the United States returned to their home countries. Some came for only a few years and returned to their native lands, including nearly 90 percent of migrants from the Balkans. Other groups, especially those who faced severe hardships in the lands of their birth, were more likely to make the United States their permanent home, settling with their families and building communities. Only 11 percent of the Irish and 5 percent of the Jews returned between 1908 and 1923.

The Heartland: Land of Newcomers

At the dawn of the twentieth century, it was not the coastal cities, with their visible immigrant ghettos, but the settlements in the upper Midwest, along with the lower Southwest, where the greatest concentration of foreign-born residents lived. In the growing towns and cities of the Midwest, newcomers from central Europe and Italy joined the earlier settlers from Germany and Scandinavia to form farming and mining communities on the rich soil and abundant iron deposits of the region.

In the 1890s, the upper Midwest was sparsely settled. As a result of the Dawes Act of 1887, which divided tribal lands into individual parcels, much of the land originally held by Indians had been divided and sold. Most of the Indians who were native to that region were removed to reservations. The iron-rich areas near Lake Superior, previously the hunting, fishing, and gathering areas of the Native Americans, were now inhabited by lumberjacks who cut the forests. Mining companies discovered the iron deposits and began recruiting workers, first from northern Europe and then, after 1900, from southern and eastern Europe. By 1910 the iron range was home to thirty-five European immigrant groups. Gradually, these cohesive working-class communities, like others elsewhere, developed their own brand of ethnic Americanism, complete with elaborate Fourth of July celebrations and other festivities that expressed both their distinctive ethnic identities and their allegiance to their adopted country.

Jessie Tarbox Beals, *Women and Children in the Kitchen*, 1915. Community Service Society, New York, NY. © The Jewish Museum/Art Resource, NY

■ **An immigrant family manages the daily routines of life in a tenement flat in 1910. Crowded conditions, poor ventilation, and inadequate plumbing made it impossible for impoverished residents such as these to maintain a clean and healthy environment.**

The Southwest: Mexican Borderlands

In 1904 a train carrying Irish orphans from a Roman Catholic **foundling home** in New York chugged westward to deliver its small passengers to waiting Catholic families in Clifton and Morenci in the Arizona territory. Church officials at the New York orphanage had screened the families carefully to be certain that the couples hoping to adopt these children were devout churchgoing Catholics, industrious workers, and respectable members of the community. The local parish priest approved these couples, and on the appointed day, they waited eagerly as the orphans, dressed in their best clothes with their pink cheeks scrubbed clean, departed from the train. But when the Anglo-Protestant residents of the town discovered that Mexican Catholic foster parents claimed these fair-skinned children, they were outraged.

That night, the Anglo women gathered to mobilize their husbands into a vigilante posse. In the middle of the night, during a driving rainstorm, the men went to the homes of the Mexican couples and kidnapped the children at gunpoint. The next day, the children were distributed to the vigilantes' wives and other Anglo foster parents. Although the Catholic foundling home that had placed the children with the Mexican couples fought a lengthy legal battle to regain custody of the children, the Anglos managed to keep the orphans. The Arizona Supreme Court validated the kidnapping in the name of the "best interests of the children," and the U.S. Supreme Court let the ruling stand.

The struggle over the orphans reflected tensions and divisions in the region along lines of class as well as race. Longtime residents of this borderland region of Arizona included many

Mexicans, mainly farmers, ranchers, and miners. In the early twentieth century, Mexico's deteriorating economy and prolonged revolution after 1911 prompted large numbers of Mexicans to migrate to California and the Southwest, looking for work. The year before the arrival of the orphans, Mexican mine workers had struck for better wages and working conditions against the Anglo owners of the Arizona Copper Company. The owners put down the strike, and the conflict left bitter feelings on both sides. The vigilante kidnapping of the orphans was, in part, retaliation against the Mexican workers who had organized the strike the previous year.

Asian Immigration and the Impact of Exclusion

Asians continued to face the most severe restrictions on immigration. The Chinese Exclusion Act of 1882, which prohibited most Chinese from immigrating to the United States, was renewed and extended in 1902. As a result, the mostly bachelor Chinese community in the United States declined by nearly half between 1890 and 1920. Many died or returned to China, reducing the numbers from more than 107,000 to about 61,000. The sex ratio remained severely unbalanced, with about fourteen men for every woman.

During the exclusion era, certain categories of Chinese immigrants were allowed entry. Wives of Chinese men already in the United States could enter, as could teachers, students, and merchants. More than 20,000 Chinese arrived during the first decade of the new century. One such emigrant was Sieh King King, an eighteen-year-old student. In 1902, at a meeting of the Protect the Emperor Society, a reform party that advocated restoring the deposed emperor and establishing a constitutional monarchy in China, she addressed a packed hall in San Francisco's Chinatown. The *San Francisco Chronicle* reported that she "boldly condemned the slave girl system, raged at the horrors of foot-binding [a traditional Chinese practice in which girls' feet were tightly bound to keep them small] and, with all the vehemence of aroused youth, declared that men and women were equal and should enjoy the privileges of equals." Like Clara Lemlich, her eastern European Jewish peer in New York, Sieh King King expressed

■ **FIGURE 19.1**
NUMBER OF IMMIGRANTS ENTERING THE UNITED STATES, 1821–2000 The number of immigrants entering the United States spiked in the first decade of the twentieth century and then dropped drastically as a result of the immigration restriction laws passed by Congress in the 1920s. Immigration increased again as laws changed after World War II, allowing new immigrant groups to enter.

Asian immigration exclusion

▨ Immigration restricted by
Chinese Exclusion Acts (1882–1943)

▨ Asiatic barred zone (1917–1952)

▨ Japanese and Koreans restricted by
"Gentlemen's Agreement" (1907)
and barred in 1924

■ **MAP 19.2**

AREAS EXCLUDED FROM IMMIGRATION TO THE UNITED STATES, 1882–1952   In 1882 the United
States barred Chinese immigrants from entering the country; Japanese and Koreans were barred in 1924. In
1917 the exclusion was extended to people from India, Indonesia, and the Arabian Peninsula. Those laws
remained in effect until 1943 and 1952, respectively.

ideas that were emerging among urban radicals in the United States but also reflected political movements in their home countries.

Individual Chinese could also immigrate if they had family members in the United States. As a result, American-born Chinese frequently traveled back and forth, claiming on their return that they left a child in China and requesting permission for their offspring to emigrate. In this way they created spaceholders for imaginary kin, allowing other Chinese to enter the country. The American authorities knew of this system of "paper sons" and "paper fathers" and tried to stop the practice with elaborate and lengthy investigations that could last a year or more while hopeful Chinese immigrants waited as virtual prisoners in wretched conditions on Angel Island, the immigrant gateway in San Francisco Bay.

In the 1880s, there were only about 3,000 Japanese immigrants in mainland United States. Japanese immigrants could still enter the country, and nearly 300,000 did so between 1890 and 1920, when opportunities for higher-paying jobs in Hawaii and California offered an alternative to the economic crisis they faced in Japan. Marriages in Japan generally were arranged by families, and some men returned to Japan to meet and marry their brides. But cost and distance often prevented those meetings. Some women came to the United States as "picture brides" after an exchange of photographs. Although some women were disappointed with their often much older husbands, most accepted their fate as they would have accepted an arranged marriage in Japan. Others were delighted with the opportunity for adventure and life in the new land. As one picture bride explained, many of the people from her village had already gone

California Views Historical Photo Collection, Monterey, CA

■ **This young woman was a "picture bride" whose photograph secured her betrothal to her distant future husband. In this way, many men who emigrated from Asia arranged to marry women they had never met. The young fiancée then left her home to join a strange man in a strange land, hoping for the best.**

Foreign-Born Population, 1890

to the United States, and she wanted to go, too: "I didn't care what the man looked like."

Although the Japanese comprised less than 1 percent of California's population, they faced intense nativist hostility. The Japanese in California protested against the discrimination they faced, and in one case they successfully turned a local case of school segregation into an international incident. In response to the segregation of Japanese children in San Francisco, the Japanese government expressed its extreme displeasure. Hoping to avoid a confrontation with Japan—a significant military power that had just won a war with Russia—President Theodore Roosevelt interceded and convinced the San Francisco school board to rescind its segregation order. This incident led to the "Gentlemen's Agreement" of 1907, in which the Japanese government agreed to limit the number of immigrants to the United States. The numbers of immigrants from Japan dwindled, and Japanese immigrants instead began to settle in Brazil.

Newcomers from Southern and Eastern Europe

Eastern European Jews were among the most numerous of the "new" immigrants in the early twentieth century. In 1880 there were about 250,000 Jews in America; by 1920, there were 4 million, the vast majority from eastern Europe. During those forty years, a number of factors motivated Jews to leave their small towns, or *shtetls*. Economic turmoil and restrictions on Jewish land ownership, trade, and business left many Jews impoverished. Antisemitic policies in Russia and eastern Europe confined many Jews to live in restricted areas. Even more devastating was the increase in antisemitic violence in the form of riots, or *pogroms*, in which Jewish towns were attacked and many Jews were beaten and killed. Many young Jewish boys emigrated to avoid being conscripted into the czar's army.

One such immigrant was young Morris Bass. At age twelve, he left his family and ventured alone across the Atlantic. He did not wander long in the crowded Jewish ghetto of New York before a butcher offered him a job and a place to sleep on a straw mat behind the shop. Like many others, Morris prospered modestly. After a few years, he was able to strike out on his own as a pushcart peddler. Eventually, he sent home enough money to bring his parents and siblings to America. Some Jewish immigrants struggled to retain the faith and practices of Jewish orthodoxy that had defined their lives in the *shtetl*. But Morris was among those who wanted to assimilate into American life. He retained Jewish cultural practices but abandoned many religious rituals, such as refraining from work on Saturdays (the Jewish Sabbath) and wearing distinctive clothes.

Italian immigration also reached its peak between 1900 and 1914. While 90 percent of the Jews who migrated from Russia came to the United States, Italians ventured to many countries around the world. Turmoil in their home country, resulting from the political and economic consequences of unification of the Italian peninsula, prompted 27 million Italians—a third of Italy's population—to emigrate between 1870 and 1920. The majority of Italians who came to the United States arrived with their families and settled permanently, establishing strong communities and mutual aid societies. Most Italians were committed Roman Catholics, and they preserved their rituals, festivals, and faith in the new country.

International Museum of Photography at George Eastman House, Rochester, NY

■ At Ellis Island this immigrant family received identification tags, indicating that they had been examined and declared healthy. Those who were ill, or youngsters without relatives to meet them, were sent to quarantine houses. Some were refused entry and sent back to their home countries.

Work, Science, and Leisure

As the nineteenth century gave way to the twentieth, working women and men—both immigrants and native-born—could increasingly expect to be employed in industry rather than farms, in large organizations rather than small shops, and in enterprises that relied more on efficiency than craftsmanship. Towering skyscrapers began to dot the urban landscape, symbolic of the triumph of commerce and corporate power. Science and technology reigned, changing the nature of work as well as the fruits of production. Professional organizations of educators, social workers, physicians, and scientists emerged, while experts with academic credentials became leaders of many public institutions. It seemed as though science could solve virtually any problem. Advances in medical science contributed to improved public health. But in some cases, experts relied on scientific principles to address social problems rather than confronting the underlying structural causes, such as widespread poverty.

This more urban society developed new forms of leisure and entertainment. The film industry emerged in Hollywood, a suburb of Los Angeles. Amusement parks and nightclubs provided new venues for greater intimacy between unmarried men and women. And American art and literature began to emphasize the vitality and diversity of life in the nation's cities.

The Uses and Abuses of Science

Breakthroughs in science and medicine led to improvements in public health. Reformers exposed the dangers of potions and remedies sold by street vendors, as standards for medications improved. But crowding and lack of sanitation still fostered the spread of disease, especially among the poor. Lack of access to clean water was one of the major causes of disease, along with crowding, lack of medical care, and other chronic problems of poverty. Improved

Defining Whiteness

Naturalization laws pertaining to immigrants in the early twentieth century were based on racial categories. Asian immigrants, classified racially as "Mongolians," were not allowed to apply for U.S. citizenship. Naturalization was available only "to aliens being free white persons and to aliens of African nativity and to persons of African descent." Because racial theories were imprecise and fluid, and racial identities were not linked to nationality, immigrants occasionally challenged their racial classification to claim that they were "white." John Svan, who was Finnish, petitioned in federal court to contest the labeling of Finns as Mongolians, claiming that he was white

and, therefore, allowed to apply for U.S. citizenship. The petition demonstrates the acceptance of racial definitions based on phenotype—particularly skin color—as well as the imprecise nature of those definitions. In the case of "John Svan vs. the United States Government," the court granted Svan's petition, legally changing his racial identity from Mongolian to white and reclassifying Finns as white people. Here is the court's 1908 memorandum, which allowed Svan to become a citizen:

John Svan was born in Finland and calls himself a Finn. . . . According to ethnologists, the Finns in very remote times were of Mongol origin; but the various groupings of the human race into families is arbitrary and, as respects any particular people, is not permanent but is subject to change and modification through the influences of climate, employment, intermarriage and other causes. There are indications that central and western Europe was at one time overrun by the

Finns; some of their stock remained, but their racial characteristics were entirely lost in their remote descendants, who now are in no danger of being classed as Mongols. The Osmanlis, said to be of Mongol extraction, are now among the purest and best types of the Caucasian race. Changes are constantly going on and those occurring in the lapse of a few hundred years with any people may be very great.

The chief physical characteristics of the Mongolians are as follows: They are short of stature, with little hair on their body or face; they have yellow-brown skins, black eyes, black hair, short, flat noses, and oblique eyes. In actual experience we sometimes, though rarely, see natives of Finland whose eyes are slightly oblique. We sometimes see them with sparse beards and sometimes with flat noses; but Finns with a yellow or brown or yellow-brown skin or with black eyes or black hair would be an unusual sight. They are almost universally of light skin, blue or gray eyes, and light hair. No people of foreign births applying

public sanitation alleviated the problem considerably in the early years of the twentieth century, reducing the incidence of typhoid fever by 70 percent. Among those who contributed to better conditions were community nurses. In 1900 the New York Charity Organization Society hired Jessie Sleet Scales, the first African American public health nurse, to address problems related to tuberculosis. Scales and other public health professionals implemented sanitation standards and provided care for poor communities, helping to control the spread of disease. Public sanitation remained a problem, however, especially in crowded cities.

Reflecting an impulse to blame social problems on allegedly flawed individuals or groups was the eugenics movement, which advocated scientific breeding to improve the nation's racial stock. Drawing on theories of white racial superiority and unscientific notions of genetic inheritance, eugenicists believed that character traits were inherited, including tendencies toward criminality, sexual immorality, and lack of discipline leading to poverty. Eugenicists claimed that social problems resulted from the high birthrate of immigrants and others they considered to be racially inferior to educated middle-class Anglo-Saxon Americans with their low birthrate.

President Theodore Roosevelt was an outspoken advocate of eugenics reform. One of his major concerns was that Americans were shirking their duty to create a robust citizenry for the future. Alarmed by the dramatic decline in the birthrate of native-born Americans and the tendency of some college-educated women to remain single and childless, he feared that the immigrants, with their much higher birthrate, would overrun the nation. Roosevelt called upon Anglo-Saxon women to prevent what he called **race suicide**, much as male citizens had an obligation to defend the country if called to military duty.

These Finnish men living in Minnesota were among those whose racial classification was changed from "Mongolian" to "White" as the result of one Finnish immigrant's petition. Along with the Jews, Italians, Irish, and other immigrant groups now considered "white," Finns were classified as nonwhite until the laws and customs changed. Racial categories were fluid and imprecise, but whiteness conferred status and privileges.

Minnesota Historical Society, Negative #93125. Photo by Maki of Virginia, MN

in this section of the country for the full rights of citizenship are lighter-skinned than those born in Finland. In stature they are quite up to the average. Confessedly, Finland has often been overrun with Teutons and by other branches of the human family, who, with their descendants, have remained within her borders and are now called Finns. They are in the main indistinguishable in their physical characteristics from those of purer Finnish blood. Intermarriages have been frequent over a very long period of time. If the Finns were originally Mongols, modifying influences have continued until they are now among the whitest people in Europe. It would, therefore, require a most exhaustive tracing of family history to determine whether any particular individual born in Finland had or had not a remote Mongol ancestry. This, of course, cannot be done and was not intended. The question is not whether a person had or had not such ancestry, but whether he is now a "white person" within the meaning of that term as usually under-

stood. This is the practical construction which has uniformly been placed upon the law. . . . Under such law Finns have always been admitted to citizenship, and there is no occasion now to change the construction.

The applicant is without doubt a white person within the true intent and meaning of such law.

The objections, therefore, in my opinion should be overruled and it will be so ordered.

Questions

1. According to the court, what might cause changes in the "groupings of the human race into families" over time? How does the court's opinion reflect prevailing attitudes toward race during the Progressive Era?
2. How did the court explain the transformation of Finns from the classification as "Mongols" to becoming "among the whitest people in Europe"?

Some eugenics crusaders proposed compulsory sterilization of those they deemed unfit for parenthood. Indiana enacted a eugenic sterilization law in 1907, and other states soon followed. These laws gave legal sanction to the surgical sterilization of thousands of men and even greater numbers of women whom government and medical officials deemed "feeble-minded." The criteria for determining "feeblemindedness" were vague at best; often sexual impropriety or out-of-wedlock pregnancy landed young women—generally poor and often foreign-born—in institutions for the feebleminded, where the operations took place. The Supreme Court upheld compulsory sterilization laws in the 1920s. Increasingly, women of color were targeted, and the practice continued well into the 1980s.

Scientific Management and Mass Production

In 1911 Frederick Winslow Taylor wrote *The Principles of Scientific Management*, a guide to increased efficiency in the nation's industries. Taylor began his career as a laborer in the Midvale Steel Works near Philadelphia in 1878 and rose through the ranks to become the plant's chief engineer. There he developed a system to improve mass production in factories in order to make more goods more quickly. Taylor's principles included analysis of each job to determine the precise motions and tools needed to maximize each worker's productivity, detailed instructions for workers and guidelines for their supervisors, and wage scales with incentives to motivate workers to achieve high production goals. Over the next decades, industrial managers all over the country drew on Taylor's studies. Business leaders rushed to embrace Taylor's principles, and Taylor himself became a pioneering management consultant.

DOCUMENT

Taylor, Scientific Management

Henry Ford was among the most successful industrialists to employ Taylor's techniques. Born in 1863 on a farm near Dearborn, Michigan, the mechanically inclined Ford became an apprentice in a Detroit machine shop in 1879. Although he did not invent the automobile—the first motor cars were manufactured in Germany—he developed design and production methods that brought the cost of an automobile within the reach of the average worker. Experimenting with the new internal combustion engine in the 1890s, he built his first automobile in 1896. In 1903 Ford established the Ford Motor Company and began a profitable business. He introduced the popular and relatively inexpensive, mass-produced Model T automobile in 1908, which sold for $850. In 1913 Ford introduced the **assembly line**, a production system in which each worker performed one task repeatedly as each automobile in the process of construction moved along a conveyor. The assembly-line manufacturing increased production while cutting costs. In 1914 Ford increased his workers' wages to $5 per day at a time when industrial laborers averaged only $11 per week. By 1916 the price of the Model T dropped to $360. In this sense Ford was a pioneer not only in production but also in consumption.

New Amusements

As Americans increasingly moved from rural to urban areas, and from farms to factories, new institutions of leisure emerged in the growing cities. Consumer culture was the flip side of business culture in the early twentieth century. One of the great ironies of American history in the twentieth century is that its popular culture—which more than anything else identifies the United States to the rest of the world—was largely a creation of immigrants and people of color. During the very years when these groups faced intense discrimination, they developed the cultural products that came to define America itself.

The motion picture industry is a case in point. In 1888 Thomas Edison invented the kinetoscope, the early motion picture camera. The pragmatic Edison thought that his new device might be used in education and industry. But he did not see much commercial potential for the gadget. Not until the early twentieth century did the moving picture begin to reach a wide audience. Moviemakers left the East Coast and moved to the West, taking advantage of the even climate, cheap land, and nonunion labor. Within a few years, the moviemakers, mostly Jewish immigrants from Europe, established the film industry. Hollywood emerged as a major center of American popular culture, sending its products across the nation and abroad.

The first audiences for the motion pictures were in the working-class neighborhoods of the growing cities. In New York alone, by 1910, there were 1,000 small storefront theaters and fun houses known as penny arcades where there had been none twenty years earlier. The number of saloons also increased from 7,000 to 9,000, while the Coney Island amusement park drew thousands to its shimmering lights and thrilling rides. During these same years, the sounds of African American music began to attract audiences among immigrants as well as native-born whites, as youths from all ethnic groups flocked to dance halls. Glamorous nightclubs, known as cabarets, also began to appear, offering dining, dancing, music, and entertainment to the wealthy.

DOCUMENT

Coney Island, 1904

"Sex O'Clock in America"

The sexual mores and behavior of Americans seemed to be changing so dramatically that one observer announced that "sex o'clock" had struck. Indeed, the codes of the past were challenged at every turn. Among the middle class, unchaperoned dating began to replace the previous system of a man "coming to call" at the home of a woman he hoped to court.

Immigrants often brought traditional courtship patterns to the new world and extended them into the next generation. One Italian man described his thwarted efforts to woo his fiancée in private. When he visited her home, "She sat on one side of the table, and I at the other.

They afraid I touch." Finally, less than a month before their wedding, he got permission to take her to the theater. But the family was unwilling to let them go alone. "We came to the aisles of the theater. My mother-in-law go first, my fiancée next, my little sister, my father in law. I was the last one. I had two in between. . . . I was next to the old man." He tried to steal a kiss a few days before the wedding, but his fiancée rebuffed him: "No, not yet."

In spite of efforts by their elders, native-born as well as immigrant youth challenged the sexual codes of the past. Increasing sexual intimacy between unmarried men and women reflected heightened expectations for sexual satisfaction—for women as well as men. These years also witnessed a rise in the proportion of brides who were pregnant at marriage, from a low of 10 percent in the mid-nineteenth century to 23 percent by 1910.

Marriage increasingly held the promise not only of love, intimacy, and mutual obligation, as it had in the nineteenth century, but of sexual fulfillment and shared leisure pursuits. However, some women did not marry but instead formed lifelong attachments to other women. Rarely identified as lesbian but often described as **Boston marriages**, these unions signified long-term emotional bonds between women who lived together. The widely admired reformer Jane Addams shared her life with Mary Rozet Smith for more than thirty years. Meanwhile, lesbians, as well as gay men, gained greater visibility in the cities. They frequented bars and clubs in such places as Greenwich Village and Harlem, hoping to avoid the attention of police, who were likely to arrest them for indecent conduct.

> *Marriage increasingly held the promise not only of love, intimacy, and mutual obligation, but of sexual fulfillment and shared leisure pursuits.*

Artists Respond to the New Era

Artists of all kinds contributed to enriching, expressing, interpreting, and transforming the urban industrial landscape. Among the most controversial was a group of painters who focused their attention on portrayals of life in the cities—including urban amusements and diverse

George Luks, *The Café Francis*, c. 1909. Butler Institute of American Art, Youngstown, OH

■ *The Café Francis*, by George Luks, c. 1909. Luks was one of the "Ashcan School" artists who celebrated urban street life and popular culture. Their raw and sensual depictions of city entertainments stirred controversy among art critics at the time.

working-class subjects. This art exuded the vitality of urban life and conveyed a gritty reality without moral condemnation. Contemptuous critics referred to them as the "Ashcan School," a label they embraced.

Theodore Dreiser's 1900 novel *Sister Carrie* narrates the story of an independent young woman who comes to Chicago and uses her sexuality to advance her ambition. Contrary to the morality tales popular at the time, Carrie does not suffer for her sins. Rather, she prospers, while her male lovers are destroyed by their infatuation with her. Because of the novel's scandalous content, Dreiser's publisher did not promote the book, although it was revived and republished in later years.

Photography also began to exhibit a new realism. Documentary photographer Lewis Hine photographed immigrants, industrial work, and urban street life. Avant-garde artists Alfred Stieglitz and Edward Steichen drew inspiration from artistic innovations in Europe, such as Cubism. Popular music flourished in the first decade of the century, especially jazz. From its roots in African musical traditions, slave songs, spirituals, and ragtime, jazz brought together the various strains of African American music and developed new forms, centered in New Orleans.

Reformers and Radicals

ALL STAR FEATURE CORP. presents IN MOTION PICTURES
— UPTON SINCLAIR'S —
WONDERFUL STORY OF THE BEEF PACKING INDUSTRY
THE JUNGLE
FEATURING
GEORGE NASH · GAIL KANE
AND THE AUTHOR
5 DARING ACTS — 210 ASTOUNDING SCENES

DOCUMENT

Steffens, from
*The Shame of
the Cities*

DOCUMENT

Mother Jones,
"The March of the
Mill Children"

The broad movement for social reform known as **Progressivism** included two distinct impulses. On the one hand, many Anglo-Saxon Protestants tried to impose order on a rapidly changing nation. They hoped to stem the tide of immigration, bolster rapidly eroding sexual codes, and quell the movements for social change. On the other hand, women's rights activists, workers, and African Americans struggled to achieve the rights and privileges available to white men of property and standing. The tensions between these two very different approaches to reform shaped the politics of the era.

Muckraking, Moral Reform, and Vice Crusades

In the early twentieth century, a group of investigative journalists, the **muckrakers**, began to expose the ills of industrial life. Their best-known works illuminated corruption in business and politics. Ida Tarbell wrote a powerful exposé of the ruthless business practices of John D. Rockefeller, who transformed the Standard Oil Company into a monopoly. Lincoln Steffens unearthed scandals in city and state politics. Upton Sinclair's novel *The Jungle*, published in 1906, tells the story of Jurgis Rudkus, a Lithuanian immigrant, and his family and friends and provides a grim exposé of the squalid working conditions in the meatpacking plant where Rudkus worked. It led to the passage of the Pure Food and Drug Act (1906) and a Meat Inspection Act, which prohibited adulterated or fraudulently labeled food and drugs from interstate commerce.

Child labor was another concern of reformers. Children worked in fields and factories across the country, picking cotton in Texas, mining coal in West Virginia, working in the textile mills of North Carolina, and sewing buttons in urban sweatshops. Children of immigrants and rural migrants often assisted parents on farms or in shops, their labor an accepted part of the household economy. But the sorts of jobs available to children in the urban industrial world often were dangerous and unhealthy, characterized by long hours, low pay, and miserable working conditions. Reformers attempted to improve the conditions under which children worked and to establish age limits so that children could attend school and spend time in healthful recreation rather than in grim sweatshops and factories. Ultimately, child labor activists succeeded in passing legislation at the state level that restricted child labor, although these efforts were more successful in northern states than in the South.

Protective legislation for women was also controversial. Reformers campaigned for laws that would establish minimum wages, maximum hours, regulations against night work, and restrictions on heavy lifting. When they were unable to secure such safety measures for all workers, they argued that women needed special protections because of their physical frailty and their role as future mothers. Women's rights activists disagreed over these measures. Some argued that they were necessary to protect women from exploitation and dangerous working conditions. Others claimed that women should be treated the same as men, arguing that protective legislation implied that women needed special care and were not suited for particular kinds of work. The Supreme Court affirmed the ten-hour working day for women—and the principle of protective legislation—in its landmark 1908 decision *Muller v. Oregon*.

One noted reformer was Helen Keller, whose work on behalf of the blind called attention to the needs of the disabled. Keller lost her sight and hearing from an illness at the age of nineteen months and learned to communicate through Braille and sign language, which she mastered through touch, with the help of her extraordinary teacher, Anne Sullivan. Keller went on to study at schools for the deaf and graduated with honors from Radcliffe College in 1904. A passionate socialist and advocate of women's rights along with other radical causes, Keller wrote several books and lectured widely all over the world, with the assistance of interpreters.

Most Progressive reformers were prosperous American-born Anglo-Saxon Protestants. Along with their efforts to improve living and working conditions and alleviate the suffering of the poor, they also hoped to eradicate vice from their society. Vice crusaders in most of the nation's large cities tried to eliminate prostitution and to patrol dance halls, movie theaters, and saloons. Vice crusading culminated in the passage of the Mann Act in 1910, which made it illegal to transport women across state lines for "immoral purposes."

International Museum of Photography at George Eastman House, Rochester, NY

■ In the early twentieth century, many children such as this young boy worked long hours doing hard labor. Photographer Lewis Hine, who took this picture, worked for the National Child Labor Committee. His photographs documented the exploitation of child workers and helped to generate support for child labor laws.

Women's Suffrage

The movement for women's rights, including the effort to gain the vote, was already more than half a century old by 1900. But the movement gained momentum at the dawn of the twentieth century. A new generation of women's rights leaders came together in the suffrage movement. The militancy of the suffrage movement in England inspired American activists to develop new tactics and international alliances. These activists achieved legislative success when several western states granted women the right to vote: Washington in 1910, California in 1911, and three more states in 1912. Eventually the movement united around the goal of enacting a federal amendment.

The suffrage movement, for all its radicalism, was largely a movement of white middle-class women. White suffrage leaders feared that any alliance with women of color would alienate Southern voters whom they needed for ratification of the Nineteenth Amendment. They also hoped to win over to their cause racist and nativist critics in the North who feared that granting the vote to women would enfranchise "undesirable" voters, specifically immigrant and minority women. The suffrage movement also gained the support of conservatives who believed that women would vote for conservative causes such as prohibition and immigration restriction.

Many minority women, such as Hispana activist Adelina Otero Warren, supported the suffrage movement even though white leaders kept their distance and refused to embrace the antiracist campaigns of their nonwhite sisters. The African American antilynching activist Ida B. Wells (also known by her married name as Ida B. Wells-Barnett) supported women's suffrage but was unable to convince the white women's rights leaders to denounce lynching. Ultimately, the passage of the Nineteenth Amendment resulted from a combination of factors, including radical activism, strong support of a wide range of reformers, and an alliance with conservative, racist, and anti-immigrant forces.

Radical Politics and the Labor Movement

Progressive reformers believed that American capitalist democracy was a fundamentally sound system that simply needed to be fixed to achieve its full promise. Radicals of the era, by contrast, believed that the system itself was flawed and needed to be fundamentally transformed. Emma Goldman, a Russian Jewish immigrant, was one of many radical activists who gained both fame and notoriety for her outspoken support of radical causes. Like Sieh King King and Clara Lemlich, Goldman was among the growing numbers of women who were leaders in the labor struggles of the day, although women were excluded from most unions.

Socialism was never as strong in the United States as it was in Europe, but it did gain strength at the turn of the century. Socialists promoted labor unions and the rights of women and formed their own political party. Socialist leader Eugene V. Debs, who had gained national fame for his role in the 1894 railroad strike, became the spokesperson and leader of the Socialist party. Between 1900 and 1920, he was the party's candidate for president, gaining nearly a million votes, or 6 percent of the electorate, in the 1912 election. Although the socialists never gathered a large enough following to win national elections, they elected hundreds of candidates to local office.

Logo for the Industrial Workers of the World

The Industrial Workers of the World (IWW), also known as the **Wobblies**, offered another possibility for labor radicalism. It was organized in 1905 by socialists and labor militants. The IWW included women, blacks, immigrants, and unskilled and migratory laborers, workers generally shunned by the American Federation of Labor (AFL). The Wobblies organized workers in the mines of the Rocky Mountain states, in the lumber camps of the Pacific Northwest and the South, and in the eastern textile and steel mills. IWW membership reached about 3 million people, although no more than 150,000 were members at any one time.

Resistance to Racism

The Progressive Era was anything but progressive for nonwhite Americans. Although there were notable exceptions, such as Jane Addams, many white Protestant reformers were either indifferent to racial minorities or actively hostile to them. Moreover, most blacks lived in the rural South, not in northern cities where Progressives were most active. Lynching continued into the twentieth century, with nearly 100 lynchings per year between 1900 and 1910. African Americans were the primary targets of lynch mobs, although other minorities were also vulnerable. Between 1850 and 1930, 597 Mexicans died at the hands of vigilante mobs, half of them in Texas. Black leaders spoke out against lynching and other forms of racial injustice. Ida B. Wells-Barnett, who had launched an international crusade against lynching in the 1890s, worked to establish local and national networks of black women's clubs. Although she was unable to persuade white suffrage leaders to support the cause of racial justice, she worked closely with Jane Addams to prevent the establishment of segregated schools in Chicago.

A number of other black leaders came to prominence in the first decade of the twentieth century. In 1905 scholar and civil rights leader W. E. B. Du Bois joined with other black leaders to form the Niagara Movement, which called for an end to segregation and discrimination in unions, the courts, and public accommodations, as well as for equal economic and educational opportunity. In 1909 prominent African Americans joined with white progressive allies to establish the National Association for the Advancement of Colored People (NAACP). The new organization adopted the platform of the Niagara Movement, and Du Bois became the editor of its journal, *The Crisis.*

Expanding National Power

Along with flourishing radical and reform movements at the grassroots, the Progressive Era gave rise to a reformist impulse at the national level. The person who most fully embodied the national Progressive movement was Theodore Roosevelt, president from 1901 to 1908. Roosevelt used his power to regulate big business, intervene in labor disputes, control the uses of the natural environment, and extend the reach of the nation across the world. His hand-picked successor in the White House, William Howard Taft, followed mostly similar policies.

Theodore Roosevelt: The "Rough Rider" as President

Roosevelt rose to prominence in the Republican party in the 1880s and held a number of important political posts, including assistant secretary of the U.S. Navy (1897–1898) and governor of New York (1899–1900). In 1900 Roosevelt became vice president. But in September 1901, President McKinley was assassinated, and at age forty-two, Roosevelt became the youngest person ever to occupy the Oval Office. Roosevelt was a strong proponent of American military and commercial presence in the world. He expanded the power of the federal government both at home and abroad and used the "bully pulpit" of the presidency to exert moral leadership.

Using the Sherman Anti-Trust Act of 1890, which gave the federal government the power to break up monopolies, Roosevelt in 1902 ordered the Justice Department to prosecute the Northern Securities Company, a $400-million monopoly that controlled all railroad lines and traffic in the Northwest. Within a year, the company was dissolved. Although this bold act earned Roosevelt the title of "trust-buster," it was not his intention to weaken big business. In fact, he believed that a strong country needed large, powerful industries, and he hoped to regulate them to keep big business strong.

TABLE 19-1			
The Election of 1900			
Candidate	**Political Party**	**Popular Vote (%)**	**Electoral Vote**
William McKinley	Republican	51.7	292
William Jennings Bryan	Democratic-Populist	45.5	155

The same year that Roosevelt took on the Northern Securities Company, he also used the powers of the federal government to intervene in a labor dispute. Striking coal miners in eastern Pennsylvania wanted recognition of their union, a 10 to 20 percent increase in wages, and an eight-hour day. But the mine owners refused to negotiate. Roosevelt summoned the mine owners and John Mitchell, president of the United Mine Workers union, to the White House for a meeting. He threatened to send in troops if the mine owners did not agree to the union's request for arbitration. The mine owners backed down, and the arbitrators negotiated a compromise that awarded the miners a 10 percent wage increase and a nine-hour day.

Roosevelt's efforts to strengthen the state and foster American nationalism extended to his attitudes toward immigrants. He believed that discrimination against loyal newcomers harmed democracy: "It is a base outrage to oppose a man because of his religion or birthplace." He was proud of appointing a cabinet in which "Catholic and Protestant and Jew sat side by side." But

Yale Collection of Western Americana, Beinecke Rare Book and Manuscript Library

◼ Lumberjacks topple a giant spruce tree in a forest in Washington state around 1900. President Theodore Roosevelt believed that the federal government should manage timberlands and other natural resources to prevent depletion while allowing their use. Roosevelt preserved some Pacific Northwest forests in national parks and refuges but allowed others to be cultivated for timber.

to Roosevelt, becoming an American meant renouncing any loyalties to one's original homeland or culture. He did not believe in cultural pluralism, the idea that the United States could include citizens who retained their ethnic heritage. Rather, Roosevelt promoted the idea of a melting pot that would blend all diverse cultures into a unique American "race." Although Roosevelt was a firm believer in Anglo-Saxon superiority, he was also the first president to invite an African American leader, Booker T. Washington, to the White House.

Protecting and Preserving the Natural World

Industrial smoke had long been a problem in both European and American cities, and Progressive Era reformers established organizations in major cities to fight air pollution. At the same time, mining and other industries were depleting natural resources while destroying the natural beauty of the land. More than any previous president, Roosevelt used the federal government to manage the natural world. Although his actions did not please everyone on all sides of the debate, Roosevelt's environmental efforts were among his most enduring legacies.

Roosevelt advocated both preservation and conservation. His preservation policies doubled the number of national parks, created sixteen national monuments, and established fifty-one wildlife refuges. At the same time, he shared the view of **conservationists** that timberlands, areas for livestock grazing, water, and minerals needed federal government management. Roosevelt transferred 125 million acres of public land into the forest reserves to prevent the depletion of timber, and he set aside land for dam sites, oil and coal reserves, and grazing. John Muir and the Sierra Club campaigned to protect the beautiful Hetch Hetchy Valley in Yosemite National Park, but Congress passed the Raker Act in 1913, allowing the city of San Francisco to build a dam and a reservoir, flooding the valley. Residents of the Owens Valley in eastern California also protested the building of an aqueduct to divert water to the Los Angeles area. Dams, reservoirs, and aqueducts brought water and electricity to arid regions, allowing such cities as Las Vegas and Los Angeles to flourish in environments that would otherwise be unable to support large populations.

Expanding National Power Abroad

The decades surrounding the turn of the twentieth century marked the high point of European and American imperial expansion, bringing 75 percent of the world's land under the control of Europeans or their descendants. Roosevelt hoped to stengthen the federal government at home, develop the nation's military and commercial might, and extend American power abroad. To further these ends, he sent troops to China as part of the international expedition to crush the nationalist Boxer Uprising in 1900. He also proposed the construction of a canal across the Isthmus of Panama, which Congress approved in 1902. But Panama was still a province of Colombia, and Roosevelt was unhappy with the Colombia government's negotiating position regard-

TABLE 19-2			
The Election of 1904			
Candidate	Political Party	Popular Vote (%)	Electoral Vote
Theodore Roosevelt	Republican	57.9	336
Alton B. Parker	Democratic	37.6	155
Eugene V. Debs	Socialist	3.0	—

ing an American canal project. So he encouraged and aided Panamanian nationalists who seceded from Colombia in 1903. In return, the U.S. president got his canal deal with a newly independent Panama.

In 1904 Roosevelt further increased the authority of the United States to intervene in the affairs of nations in the Western Hemisphere through what came to be known as the Roosevelt Corollary to the Monroe Doctrine of 1823. Fearing political uprisings that might threaten American commercial interests, Roosevelt asserted that "chronic wrongdoing" might require the intervention by "some civilized nation" in the affairs of another. "In the Western Hemisphere," he concluded, this "may force the United States . . . to the exercise of an international police power." The Roosevelt Corollary justified later interventions in the Dominican Republic, Cuba, Nicaragua, Mexico, and Haiti. While the Monroe Doctrine had told Europeans to stay out of the hemisphere, the Roosevelt Corollary declared that the United States would intervene where it wanted to.

The bloody U.S. war against Filipino nationalists that began in 1899 lasted four years before the Americans crushed the revolt and established firm colonial rule in the Philippines. William Howard Taft became the colony's first governor-general in 1901. Taft developed a program of public works that included an infrastructure of roads, bridges, and schools. He also transferred government functions to those Filipinos who cooperated with American colonial powers. Although the United States promised to grant Philippine independence, that promise was deferred until 1946.

William Howard Taft: The One-Term Progressive

Roosevelt declined to run for reelection in 1908. The Republicans selected Roosevelt's hand-picked successor, William Howard Taft. Prior to his service in the Philippines, Taft had been a federal circuit judge. In 1904 Roosevelt appointed him secretary of war. Taft was a loyal ally who worked closely with Roosevelt on foreign and domestic policies. Roosevelt assumed that Taft, after his victory in the general election, would fulfill Roosevelt's reform agenda.

Taft's respect for the separation of powers spelled out in the U.S. Constitution made him dubious about some of Roosevelt's extensions of the powers of the presidency. Nevertheless, Taft initiated far more antitrust suits than Roosevelt had during his presidency. Despite similar political inclinations, Roosevelt's support for his protégé cooled. Although Roosevelt counted major business

TABLE 19-3

The Election of 1908

Candidate	Political Party	Popular Vote (%)	Electoral Vote
William H. Taft	Republican	51.6	321
William Jennings Bryan	Democrat-Populist	43.1	162
Eugene V. Debs	Socialist	2.8	—

leaders among his own advisors, he was displeased when Taft appointed corporate lawyers rather than activist reformers to his cabinet. Taft departed from Roosevelt's foreign policy as well. In contrast to Roosevelt, who emphasized military might, Taft claimed that "Dollar Diplomacy"—"substituting ballots for bullets"—was the best way for the United States to exert influence in the world. Taft took Roosevelt's military rule of the Philippines a step further by establishing U.S. business interests there.

When Taft signed the higher Payne-Aldrich Tariff in 1909, he disappointed progressive Republicans and aligned himself with the conservative old guard of the party, those who had been most critical of Roosevelt. The breach between Taft and the Progressives widened when Taft's secretary of the interior, Richard A. Ballinger, opened up for commercial development 1 million acres of land that Roosevelt had placed under federal protection. In a further affront to conservationists, Gifford Pinchot, still head of the National Forest Service, discovered that Ballinger had sold Alaskan coal deposits to corporate moguls J. P. Morgan and David Guggenheim. When Taft defended Ballinger, Pinchot leaked the news to the press and called for a

DOCUMENT

Dollar
Diplomacy—
William Howard Taft
(1912)

congressional investigation. Taft subsequently fired Pinchot, but Roosevelt publicly supported Pinchot and signaled his break from Taft.

Roosevelt returned from big-game hunting in Africa to enter the political spotlight once again. He toured the country in 1910, describing his plan for a "New Nationalism," a far-reaching expansion of the federal government to stabilize the economy and institute social reforms. The election of reformers of both parties to Congress in 1910 encouraged Roosevelt to challenge Taft for leadership of the Republican party. When the old guard managed to renominate Taft at the Republican National Convention, Roosevelt and his supporters withdrew from the Republican party and formed the Progressive party. Roosevelt boasted, "I am as strong as a bull moose," inspiring his followers to call themselves the **Bull Moosers**. Their reformist platform called for extensive controls on corporations, minimum wage laws, child labor laws, a graduated income tax, and women's suffrage.

TABLE 19-4			
The Election of 1912			
Candidate	Political Party	Popular Vote (%)	Electoral Vote
Woodrow Wilson	Democratic	41.9	435
Theodore Roosevelt	Progressive	27.4	88
William H. Taft	Republican	23.2	8
Eugene V. Debs	Socialist	6.0	—

Roosevelt argued for a "New Nationalism," in which a strong federal government would regulate the trusts and, if necessary, curb their power. Democratic candidate Woodrow Wilson, reluctant to vest so much power in the government, called his own approach the "New Freedom," believing that the government should dismantle the trusts and then revert to limited powers. The Republican vote split between Taft and Roosevelt, and the victory went to Wilson, former president of Princeton University and governor of New Jersey. Wilson took office amid an overwhelming popular mandate for reform.

Conclusion

When Woodrow Wilson entered the White House in 1913, the nation looked and behaved differently than it had at the turn of the century. Millions of immigrants from Europe, Asia, and Mexico had arrived in the United States and settled in towns and cities across the nation. Growing urban areas with new amusements and increasingly diverse populations emerged as centers of a national mass culture. New developments in science and technology brought the automobile and the motion picture to American consumers. At the same time, industrial production contributed to environmental damage, pollution, and dangerous working conditions.

Progressive reformers and labor activists mounted efforts to curb the ill effects of urban industrial society. Faith in science and expertise gave rise to pervasive optimism that social problems could be solved. Muckrakers exposed corruption, women's rights activists pushed for the vote, and African American leaders organized for civil rights and against lynching. In the West and Southwest, Mexicans and Asians challenged discriminatory laws and labor practices. At the same time, moralists and vice crusaders sought to tame what they considered dangerous challenges to the social order.

These years also witnessed a major expansion of national power. Presidents Roosevelt and Taft strengthened the role of the federal government through new efforts to regulate big business and by extending America's military and economic presence abroad. By 1912 most Americans supported a strong reform agenda. But within a few years, the nation became embroiled in a major world war that would challenge the inherent optimism of Progressivism, signaling the end of an era.

Sites to Visit

Touring Turn-of-the-Century America: Photographs from the Detroit Publishing Company, 1880–1920.

memory.loc.gov/ammem/detroit/dethome.html

This Library of Congress site includes thousands of photographs from turn-of-the-century America.

Coal Mining in the Gilded Age and Progressive Era

http://ehistory.osu.edu/osu/mmh/gildedage/default.cfm

This Ohio State University site examines the development of the coal industry, including experiences of miners and sometimes violent labor-management conflict.

W. E. B. Du Bois Resources

http://webdubois.org

Included here are writings by and about the great African American intellectual and civil rights leader W. E. B. Du Bois.

Triangle Shirtwaist Factory Fire, March 25, 1911

www.ilr.cornell.edu/trianglefire/

Oral histories, cartoons, images, and essays about the fire are included here.

Inside an American Factory: Films of the Westinghouse Works, 1904

lcweb2.loc.gov/ammem/papr/west/westhome.html

This site provides a glimpse inside a turn-of-the-twentieth-century factory.

Theodore Roosevelt

www.ipl.org/ref/POTUS/troosevelt.html

This Internet Public Library site contains biographical information about Theodore Roosevelt and his election to the presidency and links to Internet biographies and resources about him.

William Howard Taft

www.ipl.org/ref/POTUS/whtaft.html

This Internet Public Library site contains biographical information about William Howard Taft and his election to the presidency and links to Internet biographies and resources about him.

Emma Goldman Papers

sunsite3.berkeley.edu/Goldman/

This site includes information about the famous immigrant radical and selections of writings by and about her.

For Further Reading

General Works

Gail Bederman, *Manliness and Civilization: A Cultural History of Gender and Race in the United States, 1800–1917* (1995).

Steven J. Diner, *A Very Different Age: Americans of the Progressive Era* (1998).

Sara Evans, *Born for Liberty: A History of Women in America* (1989).

Gary Gerstle, *American Crucible: Race and Nation in the Twentieth Century* (2001).

Immigration: The Changing Face of the Nation

Matthew Frye Jacobson, *Barbarian Virtues: The United States Encounters Foreign Peoples at Home and Abroad* (2000).

Erika Lee, *At America's Gates: Chinese Immigration During the Exclusion Era, 1882–1943* (2003).

Riv-Ellen Prell, *Fighting to Become Americans: Jews, Gender, and the Anxiety of Assimilation* (1999).

Vicki L. Ruiz, *From Out of the Shadows: Mexican Women in Twentieth-Century America* (1998).

Ronald Takaki, *Strangers from a Different Shore: A History of Asian Americans* (1989).

Work, Science, and Leisure

John D'Emilio and Estelle Freedman, *Intimate Matters: A History of Sexuality in America* (1988).

Elaine Tyler May, *Great Expectations: Marriage and Divorce in Post-Victorian America* (1980).

Lary May, *Screening Out the Past: The Birth of Mass Culture and the Motion Picture Industry* (1980).

Stephen Meyer III, *The Five Dollar Day: Labor Management and Social Control in the Ford Motor Company, 1908–1921* (1981).

David Van Drehle, *Triangle: The Fire That Changed America* (2003).

Reformers and Radicals

Jane Addams, *Twenty Years at Hull House* (1910).

W. E. B. Du Bois, *The Souls of Black Folk* (1903).

Nan Enstad, *Ladies of Labor, Girls of Adventure: Working Women, Popular Culture, and Labor Politics at the Turn of the Twentieth Century* (1999).

Dorothy Herrmann, *Helen Keller: A Life* (1999).

Expanding National Power

Kathleen Dalton, *Theodore Roosevelt: A Strenuous Life* (2002).

Richard Drinnon, *Facing West: The Metaphysics of Indian-Hating and Empire-Building* (1980).

Richard Hofstadter, *The Age of Reform* (1960).

Walter LaFeber, *The American Search for Opportunity, 1865–1913* (1993).

Edmund Morris, *Theodore Rex* (2002).

Robert Weibe, *The Search for Order* (1967).

For quizzes and other resources on these topics, go to www.longmanamericanhistory.com.

War and Revolution, 1912–1920

20

ON THE MORNING OF APRIL 6, 1909, SIX PEOPLE ARRIVED AT THE TOP OF THE WORLD. THEY HAD fulfilled at last the dream of two generations of Arctic explorers to reach the North Pole. Exhausted from a month of walking across the treacherous ice of the Arctic Sea, they rested for thirty hours at their polar camp. Then they turned south—the only direction available—and raced for their lives against the brutal cold that threatened to kill them.

Who were these men? Four were Greenland Inuit ("Eskimo"), for whom the Arctic region was home, even if they rarely ventured out on the frozen sea that covered the last 400 miles to the Pole. Two were American. The leader of the party, Bowdoin College graduate and renowned Arctic adventurer Robert Peary, had already built a reputation as a leading figure in the explorations of the Earth's last remote places. The other American to reach the North Pole that day received no such fame. Yet by the accounts of his fellow travelers, Matthew Henson was the one person Peary said he could not get along without. Henson was also African American.

Twelve years after Henson and Peary stood together to plant the American flag in the Inuit world of the far North, the relations between white and black Americans appeared in a sharply different light in Oklahoma. The former Indian Territory had become a state in 1907 and had more than 50,000 Cherokee and other Native American residents, more than any other state. The discovery at the turn of the century of vast oil reserves along the Arkansas River made Tulsa a boom town, with all the social tensions that accompany rapid growth. The vibrant African American section of the segregated city along Greenwood Avenue offered a strong example of black economic independence.

That entire community was destroyed on the night of May 31, 1921, in the largest American race riot of the twentieth century. In previous years, similar riots had erupted in St.

■ American Robert Peary led the first expedition to reach the North Pole.

■ American Matthew Henson accompanied Peary on the epic 1909 expedition.

Louis, Chicago, and elsewhere, when white resentment over black mobility and declining deference exploded around a petty pretext. That night in Tulsa, white terrorists executed as many as 300 African Americans and burned the entire Greenwood district to the ground.

The decade that stretched from the discovery of the North Pole to the Tulsa race riot was marked by unusual turbulence in American life. From 1910 to 1914, optimism about solving the nation's social problems rose as reformers attempted to ameliorate some of the worst aspects of modern industrial life. International developments then turned American attentions abroad. Traumatic social revolutions swept through Mexico, China, and Russia, and the conflagration of the Great War—World War I—consumed all of Europe and eventually drew in the United States. What President Woodrow Wilson called the war "to make the world safe for democracy" encouraged people of color, both in the vast European-ruled colonies of Asia and Africa and in the segregated United States, to claim a place of greater equality. But at home the war also created pressures for conformity and intolerance for dissent. The United States emerged from the war with great prestige and power, although the Versailles Treaty ending World War I failed to create a lasting structure for world peace.

A World in Upheaval

American politics in the 1910s and the U.S. involvement in World War I must be understood within the context of change and uncertainty in the international system. While world affairs were still dominated by the wealthy nations of western Europe and North America, the first wave of the great revolutions of the twentieth century was beginning to wash away much of the old order. Tensions also sharpened within the United States over traditional hierarchies of color, gender, and class. The struggle between reform and reaction pervaded public life in the United States and much of the rest of the world.

The Apex of European Conquest

On the eve of World War I, all but a quarter of the world's population lived under the rule of Europeans or their descendants. Explorations of the most remote parts of the globe filled in the last blank spaces on world maps, including the North (1909) and South (1911) poles. The granting of statehood to Arizona and New Mexico in 1912 filled out the forty-eight mainland states.

Technological innovations in transportation and communication tied the world more closely together. Just as the Suez Canal (1870) and the trans-Siberian railroad (1904) linked Europe more directly to Asia, the Panama Canal (1914) cut in half the travel time by water between the East and West coasts of the United States. Cables laid on the floor of the Atlantic Ocean in 1914 inaugurated telephone service between Europe and the United States.

The competition that arose from the expansion of European power sowed the seeds of World War I. Germany, France, Britain, Italy, and Russia raced each other for new colonies and greater influence across Africa and Asia. The central rivalry emerged between a newly unified Germany (1871) and traditionally dominant Britain. Anticipating trouble, each of the major European powers sought allies to bolster its position. Britain, France, and Russia formed the Triple **Entente** against the Triple Alliance of Germany, Austria-Hungary, and Italy (when war came in 1914 Italy switched sides, and the Ottoman Empire—modern Turkey—joined Germany and Austria-Hungary as the Central Powers).

The United States emerged as a global power in this same period around the turn of the century. Fifteen years after the United States seized an overseas empire in 1898, U.S. economic growth was stunning. U.S. consumption of energy from modern fuels (coal and oil) in 1913 equaled that of Britain, Germany, France, Russia, and Austria-Hungary combined. The United States also brought a different history to the world stage. It had been born in 1776 in the first successful revolution by colonies against a European empire. Americans had long understood themselves as a people who opposed empires and supported self-government. The events of 1898 contradicted this legacy, and Americans remained ambivalent about their country's imperial venture. The U.S. Congress in 1916 promised eventual independence to the Philippines and granted U.S. citizenship to residents of Puerto Rico in 1917.

> *The United States had been born in the first successful revolution by colonies against a European empire.*

Confronting Revolutions Abroad

As nationalist movements in China, Russia, and Mexico overturned weak central governments controlled by foreign investors, American economic and security interests seemed to be at stake on three continents. In Asia, the Chinese deeply resented exclusive foreign enclaves that dominated their nation's coastal region and exempted foreigners from the constraints of Chinese laws. In 1911 nationalist revolutionaries inspired by Sun Yat-sen, a Hawaiian-educated democratic reformer, overthrew the Manchu dynasty that had proven unable to resist western incursions.

The American desire for an open door into China's trade—a door that no other powerful nation could close at will—conflicted with the rising imperial power of the region: Japan. The Tokyo government, which had annexed Korea in 1910, responded to the outbreak of World War I by seizing the valuable German-held Shantung Peninsula in northeastern China. In its Twenty-One Demands to China, issued in January 1915, Japan made clear its plans to dominate the development of the Chinese economy. The American relationship with both China and Japan was undercut at home by continued discrimination and violence against immigrants from Asia.

Revolutionary struggles with implications for America also threatened the monarchs who ruled eastern Europe. For Russians, defeat at the hands of Japan in 1905 helped precipitate a thwarted revolution that year, followed by two years of political turmoil. The **czar** survived to rule another decade, and thousands of political activists—unionists, anarchists, and socialists—joined a growing wave of immigration from Russia to the United States. The wave crested in 1914 at 1.2 million people, most of them from east or south of the Alps. That same year, the assassination of the heir to the Austro-Hungarian throne by a Serbian nationalist in Sarajevo provided the spark that ignited the Great War.

The most important region of the world for the United States before World War I was Latin America, especially Central America and the Caribbean islands. This area guarded the nation's strategic southern flank, and American citizens and corporations invested more money in Latin America than in any other region of the world. American anxieties about stability to the south centered on Mexico. "Land for the landless and Mexico for the Mexicans" became the slogan of revolutionaries there between 1910 and 1920. U.S. stakes in the Mexican revolution were high. American investors owned 43 percent of all Mexico's wealth (other foreigners owned another 25 percent), and more than half of the country's trade flowed north to the United States. Moreover, by 1921 Mexico was the world's second largest exporter of oil. Almost a million Mexicans crossed their northern border during the revolutionary decade, tripling the number of Americans with recent roots south of the Rio Grande.

■ MAP 20.1

U.S. INTERESTS AND INTERVENTIONS IN THE CARIBBEAN REGION, 1898–1939 By its size, wealth, and military power, the United States dominated the Caribbean region to its south. American capitalists invested heavily in Mexico, Central America, and the Caribbean islands, and U.S. troops often intervened to protect those investments. Puerto Rico (by acquisition from Spain) and the Panama Canal Zone (by lease from Panama) became particularly important territories ruled by the United States.

Many came through El Paso, the "Ellis Island" for immigrants from the south. Fleeing poverty and violence, they found both discrimination and employment. Whereas most immigrants sought unskilled positions, members of Mexico's professional classes came north for political asylum as well, including teachers, architects, and lawyers. New arrivals of all classes joined Mexican Americans who had lived in the region since it was part of Mexico. They had not crossed the border; in 1848 the border had crossed them.

Wilson sought unsuccessfully to reestablish in Mexico a political order respectful of the rights of foreign property owners. Wilson twice sent U.S. troops into Mexico, at Veracruz in April 1914 to block a German arms shipment and then in pursuit of Francisco ("Pancho") Villa and his army after their 1916 assault on Columbus, New Mexico. The American forces under General John J. Pershing withdrew in early 1917 as the president

> *Mexican Americans had lived in the region since it was part of Mexico. They had not crossed the border; in 1848 the border had crossed them.*

prepared to enter the much larger war in Europe. Land redistribution and national control of Mexico's abundant mineral wealth, particularly oil, were written into the new constitution passed a few days later, and the revolutionary upheaval ended by 1920.

Conflicts over Hierarchies at Home

Just as social upheaval threatened monarchies and international investors abroad, less privileged Americans contested traditional lines of hierarchy and control in the United States. The Wilson administration's "New Freedom" slogan did not apply to African Americans, who faced continuing discrimination in employment and housing. The president filled his cabinet with white Southerners who segregated the few federal agencies that had employed blacks. When Wilson took office, African Americans continued to be murdered publicly by vigilante mobs across the South at a rate of more than one person per week. But the president ignored requests from the recently formed NAACP for an antilynching law, and the United States remained one of the few societies in which human beings were burned at the stake.

Women of all colors lived under particular burdens of discrimination. Their uniquely intimate relationships—as daughters, wives, mothers—to those who did not treat them as equals complicated their efforts at reform. So did their dilemma about women's roles in society: some sought full legal equality with men, while others wanted special protections for women on the grounds that they were fundamentally different.

American women's long struggle to vote came to a head in this decade. By 1912 a growing number of European nations and nine American states, all in the West, granted the franchise to citizens of both sexes. The moderate National American Women Suffrage Association under the leadership of Carrie Chapman Catt worked within the political system, building an alliance

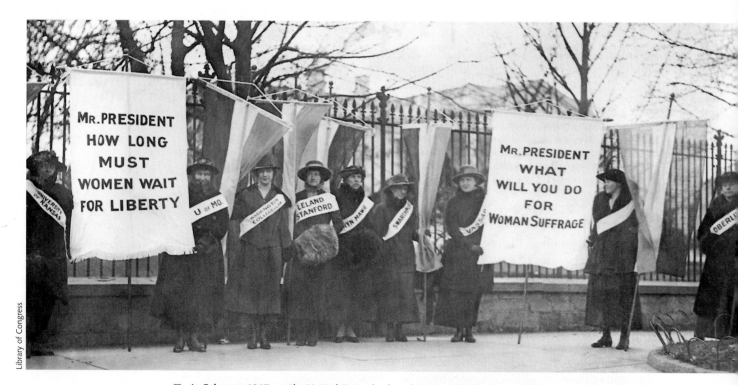

Library of Congress

■ In February 1917, as the United States broke relations with Germany and began to prepare to enter World War I, supporters of women's suffrage continued to picket on the sidewalk outside the White House. College women joined the effort to ensure that winning liberty at home would go hand in hand with fighting for democracy abroad.

with President Wilson after he endorsed women's suffrage in 1916 and supporting the U.S. entry into World War I the next year. Alice Paul and other militants formed the National Women's party and opposed the war effort as inherently undemocratic because half the adult population could not vote. In 1918 suffragist organizers helped elect a more sympathetic Congress that passed the Nineteenth Amendment, ending sex discrimination in voting two years later.

Most adult Americans—workers—continued to find themselves in frequent conflict with the owners who employed them. Industrial capitalism's efficiency produced great material wealth, but 60 percent of it belonged to 2 percent of the population, whereas two-thirds of Americans owned only 2 percent of the wealth. The anticapitalist aspirations of the Socialist party and the Industrial Workers of the World frightened both industrialists and the more conservative labor leaders of the American Federation of Labor, especially when the western-based IWW led two major strikes in the East, one a success in Lawrence, Massachusetts, in 1912 and the other a failure in Paterson, New Jersey, in 1913. The campaign against a wage cut at the vast Lawrence textile factory was especially impressive in uniting 20,000 workers of forty different national backgrounds.

■ The coal miners' tent colony outside Ludlow stood on the high plains of south-central Colorado, at the base of the mountains of the Front Range. Winter snows and cold temperatures made for a difficult life, as did the grueling and dangerous work of mining coal that was common across the state. Strikers along with their wives and children died in the Ludlow massacre on April 20, 1914.

Some business owners sought to undercut union campaigns by providing better working conditions and even company-run "unions." These carrots of concession were accompanied by the stick of force. Bolstered by sympathetic federal courts and state governors, companies usually refused to negotiate with workers who went on strike. This pattern reached a shocking climax on Easter night in 1914 outside Ludlow, Colorado, in a mining camp owned by John D. Rockefeller Jr.'s Colorado Fuel and Iron Company. State militia and company guards broke a strike there with torches and machine guns, burning the miners' tent colony and killing two women and eleven children.

Such brutality by owners against workers and their families appalled most Americans. The Wilson administration slowly began supporting the right of laborers to organize for collective bargaining with their employers. Wilson's strong backing from Samuel Gompers and the AFL in the 1912 election initiated the modern Democratic-labor alliance.

The Great War and American Neutrality

Most Americans had roots of some kind in Europe and had long defined themselves in relation to life on "the continent." But they also considered themselves part of the New World that was separate from the Old World of kings, castles, and rigid social classes. When Europe stepped off the precipice in August 1914 into a war larger than any previously fought or imagined, few Americans wanted any part of it. Make "no entangling alliances," George Washington had urged his fellow citizens. Europeans must stay out of our hemisphere, the Monroe Doctrine had declared. Americans focused instead on domestic political reforms and on an economy revived by European demands for war-related goods, which created new jobs that lured many black Southerners north. But international ties proved too important to the well-being of Americans for the country to remain indefinitely on the sidelines of World War I.

"The One Great Nation at Peace"

Following traditional U.S. policy, Wilson urged Americans to remain neutral "in fact as well as in name" to promote an eventual "peace without victory." Neutrality was profitable. Wilson stoutly defended the rights of neutrals to trade with belligerents, the same principle that had led the United States into the War of 1812 against England. After the recession of 1913–1914, war-related demands from abroad for American farm and factory products jump-started the economy. In the course of World War I, American bankers extended $10 billion in loans to the Entente (primarily Britain and France), and the United States changed from a debtor nation to the world's largest creditor.

The nature of the fighting in Europe bolstered the American determination to avoid being drawn into the conflict. Industrialized warfare brought fiendish new ways to kill human beings, including machine guns and poison gas. Gone were the days of bold maneuvers and dashing cavalry charges; now was the time of trench warfare, with its unrelenting misery, terror, and helplessness. Eight and a half million young men lost their lives and another 21 million were wounded, devastating an entire generation of European society. Eight million civilians also died as a result of the fighting, and an international outbreak of influenza in 1918 killed another 20 million around the world.

In the United States, neutrality also made political sense. Immigrants from every part of Europe lived and voted in the United States, so Americans had blood ties to all the belligerents. Commercial and political elites tended to identify with Britain and France, as did many other Americans. But among two of the largest groups of Americans, those with roots in Germany and Ireland, many took a different view. Few Irish Americans equated England with the cause of democracy after centuries of British rule in Ireland. Native-born white Americans were already concerned with preserving unity in their increasingly varied and urban society. Allowing in the hatreds from Europe's battlefields would only exacerbate the ethnic and class tensions that worried social reformers and many politicians, including President Wilson.

Reform Priorities at Home

Americans traditionally considered powerful government a primary threat to individual liberty, but the rise of mammoth corporations at the start of the twentieth century altered that calculation. Competition was disappearing, particularly in critical sectors of the economy such as oil production and railroads. Laissez-faire policies, by which federal agencies encouraged economic expansion, were no longer adequate; only government could balance the new might of the largest companies. This meant modest regulation of some aspects of the marketplace. Wilson's first term also encouraged such democratic reforms as the ratification of the Seventeenth Amendment for the direct popular election of U.S. senators (1913), previously chosen by state legislatures.

Three areas topped the Wilson administration's reform agenda: taxes, the money system, and monopolies. The Underwood-Simmons Tariff of 1913 cut duties—taxes—on imported goods by almost one-half, helping American consumers and promoting freer trade. The Sixteenth Amendment (1913) allowed a federal income tax, which the 1916 Revenue Act put into effect. This was a progressive tax, one that took a larger percentage of the income of the rich than it took from the poor. The legislation also levied higher taxes on corporate profits and created the first federal estate tax on inheritances.

Congress moved to regulate money in another new way as well. The absence of a centrally managed money system had long contributed to the exaggerated boom-and-bust cycles in the American economy. The Federal Reserve Act of 1913 created a system of twelve Federal Reserve Banks to control the amount of currency in circulation, increasing it in deflationary times and decreasing it when inflation threatened. The system aimed to abolish depressions and prevent bank closures. It did not fully succeed, as the years after 1929 showed, but the

Hulton I Archive/Getty Images

■ The body of a soldier lies caught in barbed wire in the "no-man's-land" between opposing trenches on the western front. Technological advances in weaponry helped make the fighting in World War I vastly more destructive than previous wars. The sheer scale of the slaughter stunned combatants and observers, both in Europe and America, and helped turn many in the postwar generation to deep skepticism regarding the use of military force.

Federal Reserve System stabilized the American banking industry and helped position the dollar to become the central global currency.

No issue so dominated American politics between 1913 and 1915 as the tension between huge new corporations and the nation's antimonopoly tradition. The size and market share of companies such as U.S. Steel, American Tobacco, and Du Pont (chemicals) inhibited competition. Congress created the Federal Trade Commission (1914) to investigate business practices that unfairly prevented competition. The Clayton Antitrust Act of 1914 supplemented the 1890 Sherman Antitrust Act by outlawing specific unfair business practices such as local price cutting and granting rebates to undermine competitors.

TABLE 20-1

The Election of 1916

Candidate	Political Party	Popular Vote (%)	Electoral Vote
Woodrow Wilson	Democratic	49.4	277
Charles E. Hughes	Republican	46.2	254
A. L. Benson	Socialist	3.2	—

Another kind of legislation focused on preserving natural landscapes. An increasingly urban, industrial society looked to its most beautiful rural places for solace. Local and state governments set aside parklands throughout the Progressive Era. Wilson followed in Roosevelt's conservationist footsteps by creating the National Park Service in 1916 to provide unified management of such new national treasures as Glacier National Park in Montana (1910), Rocky

Mountain National Park in Colorado (1915), Lassen Volcanic National Park in California (1916), and Acadia National Park in Maine (1919).

The Great Migration

Most African Americans lived in the South, where segregation and discrimination trapped the majority in poverty. Many therefore seized the unprecedented opportunity offered by the outbreak of the Great War. War-related orders created huge needs for workers in northern factories, and the war also closed the spigot of European immigration, drying up the standard source of new labor. Along with other cities, Chicago and Detroit became centers of the **Great Migration** of more than half a million African Americans out of Dixie during the war years.

African American Population, 1910 and 1950

Black Southerners still found plenty of discrimination in the urban North. But the large black communities of Philadelphia, Cleveland, and New York offered far greater independence than the rural South they left behind. African Americans could vote, earn higher wages, send their children to better schools, and even sit where they wanted on streetcars. One woman newly arrived in Chicago was stunned the first time she boarded a trolley and saw black people sitting next to whites. "I just held my breath, for I thought any minute they would start something. Then I saw nobody notices it, and I just thought this is a real place for Negroes."

When war in Europe shut off most Atlantic immigration after 1914, it opened the door to newcomers who did not have to cross the submarine-infested ocean. Blacks who boarded trains for the North were joined by a similar number of white Southerners leaving rural poverty to look for jobs. A small stream of French Canadians found work in New England factories. A much larger stream of Mexicans and Mexican Americans flowed to jobs across the American Southwest and Midwest. World War I and the Mexican Revolution increased their num-

Historical Pictures/Stock Montage, Inc.

■ A migrant family from the South arriving in Chicago, c. 1916. Southerners of all colors, like Europeans, were drawn by the lure of better jobs to the industrial cities of the American Northeast and Midwest. With immigration from Europe slowed to a trickle by the onset of World War I, industry's demand for southern immigrants increased sharply.

bers sharply, with the growing cities of Los Angeles, San Antonio, and El Paso remaining particular magnets for new immigrants. The number of Mexican Americans in Los Angeles soared from 6,000 in 1910 to nearly 100,000 in 1930.

Limits to American Neutrality

A steady undertow of interests and inclinations pulled against American neutrality after 1914. Most Americans who paid attention to events abroad favored the Entente over the Central Powers. The diversity of Americans' ethnic roots across Europe, Africa, Asia, and Latin America could not mask fundamental cultural and linguistic connections to England, the one-time "mother country." President Wilson deeply admired British political values and institutions, and most influential newspaper editors supported the British cause. Even Americans critical of the British Empire did not want to see the European continent under the autocratic rule of the German Kaiser.

Concrete economic interests also tied the United States to the Entente. During three years of neutrality, American bankers lent 85 times as much to the Entente nations as to the Central Powers ($2.3 billion versus $27 million), and agricultural and industrial workers earned decent wages in filling Entente war orders.

Certain powerful Americans, concentrated on the East Coast, tried from the start to prepare the country for entering the war. They emphasized that the U.S. military was much smaller than the forces of European states because of Americans' traditional aversion to large standing armies. Republicans such as Theodore Roosevelt and former Secretary of State Elihu Root led the war preparedness movement.

Progressives themselves split over the war. More radical reformers opposed joining it as a matter of principle. "Let the capitalists do their own fighting and furnish their own corpses," Socialist Eugene Debs wrote in 1914, "and there will never be another war on the face of the earth." They feared, presciently, that going to war would take the wind out of the sails of domestic reform.

DOCUMENT

Debs, Critique of
World War I

Most Progressives followed President Wilson's leadership, opposing U.S. involvement in Europe at first but gradually shifting to support it. The president squeaked by conservative Republican nominee Charles Evans Hughes in the 1916 election, winning a second term in the White House. "He kept us out of war," his supporters declared, but Wilson himself was less optimistic. He knew where German submarine warfare might lead: "Any little German lieutenant can put us into the war at any time by some calculated outrage."

The United States Goes to War

Like Lyndon Johnson in 1964 regarding Vietnam, Wilson won reelection as a liberal reformer and a man of peace, only to go to war within six months. On April 2, 1917, Wilson asked Congress for a declaration of war against Germany "to make the world safe for democracy." Congress agreed by a large majority, and four days later the United States entered the Great War. Mobilization went slowly. The government limited anti-war criticism, and it took almost a year before American soldiers in large numbers saw combat in the trenches of northern France. But American foodstuffs and munitions arrived more quickly, as did American naval ships protecting cargo vessels bound for England. The U.S. entry into the war ultimately provided the narrow margin of victory against the Central Powers.

The Logic of Belligerency

Wilson's insistence on the traditional rights of neutral nations to trade with belligerents clashed with German and British efforts to prevent trade destined for their enemy. The German use

DOCUMENT

Wilson's War Message to Congress

of the new submarines, or U-boats (from the German *Unterseeboote*), against superior British surface forces pulled Americans into the war. Submarines were extremely vulnerable when not submerged. Before firing on a merchant or passenger ship that might be armed or carrying contraband (war materials), they refused to surface and warn civilian passengers—as required under international law—to evacuate on lifeboats. With Britain arming merchant ships and stowing munitions in the holds of passenger ships, U-boats were the key element in the German campaign to weaken the enemy. The British navy, in turn, seized American goods bound for Germany. But Britain's blockade of the German coastline and neutral ports nearby did not endanger civilians in the same way. "One deals with life; the other with property," Secretary of State Robert Lansing explained.

The deaths of civilians without warning on the high seas shocked and angered the American public, especially the sinking of the magnificent British ocean liner *Lusitania* in May 1915, which killed 128 U.S. citizens and a thousand others. Hoping not to draw the United States into the war, the German government twice put its unrestricted submarine warfare on hold. But by January 1917 the British blockade had reduced German food rations per person to less than half the prewar level. Facing imminent starvation, Berlin decided to take one last chance with unrestricted submarine warfare. The German government calculated that it could force a British and French surrender before enough American assistance arrived.

Preparing for war with the Americans, German Ambassador Arthur Zimmermann secretly offered German aid to the revolutionary Mexican government "to reconquer the lost territory in Texas, New Mexico, and Arizona" if it joined the Central Powers. Mexico declined, but the Zimmermann telegram leaked to the press on March 1 and outraged Americans. One last hindrance to joining the Entente disappeared with the revolution that same month in Russia, which replaced the monarchy with a democratic government.

Still guarding American autonomy and wary of close identification with the French, British, and Russian empires, however, Wilson took the nation into war as an "Associated" power rather than a full-blown member of the Entente. The president believed that the United States, unique among the belligerents, sought only to defend principles rather than to acquire territory. "We have no quarrel with the German people" but only with the "Prussian autocracy" whose U-boats were engaged in "a warfare against mankind," Wilson declared in calling Americans to a great crusade in Europe.

Mobilizing the Home Front

America and the Great War

Going to war entailed a complete reorientation of the American economy. For the army and navy to succeed abroad, mass production of war materials had to be centrally planned, and only the federal government could fulfill this role. The Wilson administration created several new agencies to manage the war effort at home. The Selective Service Act established local boards to draft young men into the military. The U.S. Railroad Administration took control of the nation's primary transportation system to solve railroad tie-ups caused by heavy demands for war materials. The War Industries Board supervised all war-related production, allowing large manufacturers to coordinate their schedules without fear of antitrust action. The War Labor Board resolved disputes between workers and employers. The Committee on Public Information had the task of inspiring and maintaining public support for Wilson's war policies.

The close cooperation between industry and government, combined with strong demand for American goods from the Entente governments, caused corporate earnings to soar. "We are all making more money out of this war than the average human being ought to," one steel company official admitted privately. And some of the war gains were spread, for a collaborative effort entailed keeping workers productive and content. Taking a position unprecedented in the U.S. government, the War Labor Board promoted an eight-hour workday and the right of workers to form unions.

Courtesy, Hagley Museum and Library (Neg. #69.170.13.622)

■ European demand for war-related goods brought the U.S. economy out of the deep recession of 1913–1914 and created hundreds of thousands of new jobs. U.S. entry into the war in April 1917 took several million men into the armed forces, opening better-paying opportunities in manufacturing to many women. Four workers at the Westinghouse Electric Company pause from their labors in 1918.

Ensuring Unity

The deaths of U.S. soldiers and sailors made support for the war an emotional issue, and a pattern of repressing dissent took hold that outlasted the war. Several states banned teaching the German language. Sauerkraut became "liberty cabbage," frankfurters became hot dogs, and many German Americans anglicized their names. Temperance reformers cited German beer drinking in their successful campaign for a constitutional prohibition of alcohol production. Congress approved the controversial Eighteenth Amendment in December 1917 as a way to save grain for the war effort, and the states ratified it in 1919. Anti-German sentiment led to sometimes deadly violence against Americans of German descent by the summer of 1918. Congress passed sharply restrictive immigration legislation in 1917 as anti-German feelings fed broader prewar fears of new immigrants.

Most African Americans agreed with W. E. B. Du Bois's call to "close our ranks shoulder to shoulder" with white fellow citizens in support of the war effort, despite escalating antiblack violence. The arrival of half a million black Southerners in northern cities increased competition for jobs and housing, causing resentment among many whites. Employers contributed to tensions by recruiting African Americans as strikebreakers and pitting them against white workers. Whites rioted in East St. Louis on July 1, 1917, causing at least forty-seven fatalities, most of them black. Black soldiers from the North at times rebelled against the Jim Crow restrictions they found on southern military bases.

DOCUMENT

Buffington, "Friendly Words to the Foreign Born"

African American Women in the Great War

Just as black American men served in the American Expeditionary Forces in France in 1917–1918, black American women served in auxiliary organizations such as the Red Cross and the Young Men's and Women's Christian Associations (YMCA and YWCA), which worked to boost the soldiers' morale. They staffed canteens set up to provide social and educational support for American troops as an alternative to entertainments such as prostitution and gambling. Addie W. Hunton and Kathryn M. Johnson felt a particular calling to encourage African American soldiers, who suffered from discrimination and segregation even as they fought for democracy. As devout Christians, the two women believed they must model a life of service and compassion, even in the face of persecution. An account of their time in Europe published soon after they returned to the United States suggests some of the complications of a segregated society sending people abroad.

American women supported the war effort in many ways, including working in munitions factories, buying war bonds, single-parenting while husbands were away in the military, and volunteering as nurses for the armed forces in France. Here, African American women entertain black soldiers with music in a service club in Newark, New Jersey, 1918.

Two Colored Women with the American Expeditionary Forces

The relationship between the colored soldiers, the colored welfare workers, and the French people was most cordial and friendly and grew in sympathy and understanding, as their associations brought about a closer acquaintance. It was rather an unusual as well as a most welcome experience to be able to go into places of public accommodation without having any hesitations or misgivings; to be at liberty to take a seat in a common carrier, without fear of inviting some humiliating experience; to go into a home and receive a greeting that carried with it a hospitality and kindliness of spirit that could not be questioned.

These things were at once noticeable upon the arrival of a stranger within the gates of this sister democracy, and the first ten days in France, though filled with duties and harassed with visits from German bombing planes, were nevertheless a delight, in that they furnished to some of us the first full breath of freedom that had ever come into our limited experience.

The first post of duty assigned to us was Brest. Upon arriving there we received our first experience with American prejudices, which had not only been carried across the seas, but had become a part of such an intricate propaganda, that the relationship between the colored soldier and the French people is more or less a story colored by a continued and subtle effort to inject this same prejudice into the heart of the hitherto unprejudiced Frenchman.

[An order posted by a white officer of a black battalion read:] "Enlisted men of this organization will not talk to or be in company with any white women, regardless of whether the women solicit their company or not."

[Another order read:] "There are two Y.M.C.A.'s, one near the camp, for white troops, and one in town, for the colored troops. All men will be instructed to patronize their own Y."

The account also describes segregation imposed during the return voyage to the United States:

Quite a bit of unpleasantness was experienced on the boats coming home. . . . On [one] boat there were nineteen colored welfare workers; all the women were placed on a floor below the white women, and the entire colored party was placed in an obscure, poorly ventilated section of the dining-room, entirely separated from the other workers by a long table of Dutch civilians. The writer immediately protested; the reply was made that the southern white workers on board the ship would be insulted if the colored workers ate in the same section of the dining-room with them, and, at any rate, the colored people did not expect any such treatment as had been given them by the French.

Questions

1. *How did serving in France affect the ways African American men and women viewed their own country?*
2. *What might the impact of blacks' service in France have been on American society when they returned home after the war?* ■

Source: Addie W. Hunton and Kathryn M. Johnson, *Two Colored Women with American Expeditionary Forces* (New York: Brooklyn Eagle Press, 1920), pp. 28–30, 182–183, 186.

National Archives

■ MAP 20.2
WORLD WAR I IN EUROPE AND THE WESTERN FRONT, 1918 By the time U.S. troops arrived in force on the western front in northern France, the new Bolshevik (Communist) government of Russia had made peace with the Germans and withdrawn from the war. Germany now faced enemies only on one front—the western front—and moved all its troops there. In this dire situation for the French and British, American soldiers helped fill the gap in 1918.

The War in Europe

When the United States entered the war in Europe in 1917, crisis gripped the Entente. In the east, much of the war effort collapsed in the confusion of Russia's revolution against the czar. In the west, forty-nine divisions of the French army mutinied, refusing orders to make further suicidal advances. In the south, at Caporetto, Austro-Hungarian forces inflicted a disastrous defeat on the Italian army. It was not clear whether the Americans had joined soon enough to stave off defeat.

World War I

No battle-ready American army waited at ports for immediate shipment to the trenches of northern France. U.S. commanders instead had to conscript and train nearly 5 million young men for an American Expeditionary Force (AEF) under General Pershing, and 16,000 young women volunteered for service overseas as nurses and Red Cross workers. Although the veteran French and British lines had to stand largely on their own against the final German spring offensive, American soldiers later engaged in fierce combat at Belleau Wood, Château-Thierry, and St. Mihiel, ultimately losing 114,000 men. As the only army growing stronger in 1918, the AEF contributed crucially to the fall offensive that convinced Germany to surrender on November 11.

Events in Russia provoked the greatest long-term concerns. In October 1917, Vladimir Lenin and his fellow **Bolsheviks** seized control of the government, building a dictatorship of the Communist party in the name of the working class. The Bolsheviks opposed the Great War as a struggle among rival capitalists. In the czar's archives, they found and published the secret prewar treaties of the Entente for dividing up their prospective conquests after the war, both in Europe and in the colonies overseas. While Wilson spoke of a war for democracy, the Bolsheviks asked Russians, "Are you willing to fight for this, that the English capitalists should rob Mesopotamia and Palestine?"

The answer, as Wilson feared, was no. In January 1918, the president gave the famous "Fourteen Points" speech to the U.S. Congress, outlining his aims of a postwar world built not on expansion and revenge but on national self-determination, open diplomacy, and freedom of commerce and travel, to be guaranteed by a new League of Nations. He hoped to dissuade the Bolsheviks from making a separate peace with Germany that would allow Germany to move all its troops to the western front. But Lenin, facing civil war at home, conceded huge swaths of the old czarist empire in eastern Europe to the Germans to gain peace with the Brest-Litovsk Treaty of March 3, 1918.

The competing visions of Wilson and Lenin for world order contained the roots of the Cold War that would dominate American life after 1945. They agreed that the old diplomacy of imperialist states competing for pieces of property around the globe would no longer work and that only the creation of democratic states would prevent further wars. But they understood democracy very differently. For Wilson, it meant self-governing nations with capitalist economies and republican political practices (at least in Europe and North America, and eventually elsewhere). For Lenin, it meant workers in every land overthrowing the owners of capital and setting up Soviet governments. Whereas Wilson viewed the world as a collection of nations, Lenin saw it as a battleground between two classes.

ТОВ. ЛЕНИН ОЧИЩАЕТ ЗЕМЛЮ ОТ НЕЧИСТИ.

From Art of the October Revolution, Leningrad, Aurora Art Publishers, 1979

■ "Comrade Lenin Sweeps the Globe Clean." This Bolshevik (Communist) drawing shows Vladimir I. Lenin (1870–1924), the leader of the Russian revolution and founder of the world's first Communist government, ridding the world of capitalists and monarchs. But Lenin also sought western trade and investment, especially from the United States, as a stimulus to reconstructing the devastated postwar economy of the new Union of Soviet Socialist Republics (USSR).

The Struggle to Win the Peace

World War I killed more than 16 million people and wrought immeasurable physical, social, and psychological damage. Was it worth it? Citizens of the belligerent nations emerged from 1918 convinced that only a future free of war could legitimate such suffering. Some put their hopes in the radical solution unfolding in Russia. Some in the Entente states believed that severe measures against Germany would ensure peace. Most looked to Woodrow Wilson in the winter and spring of 1919, with his vision of a more peaceful, democratic postwar order. The president sailed for Europe in January to lead the

■ MAP 20.3
EUROPE AFTER WORLD WAR I   The outcome of World War I
led to significant changes in the boundaries of Europe, particularly
its eastern parts. Four great empires in the region—Russia, Germany,
Austria-Hungary, and the Ottomans—collapsed. Negotiations at Versailles
created a band of new nations, providing both self-determination and a bulwark
against Russian communism.

conference that would shape the peace. Vast crowds greeted him enthusiastically as he toured
England, Italy, and France.

Peacemaking and the Versailles Treaty

War and revolution destroyed the four great empires of Russia, Germany, Austria-Hungary, and the Ottomans (based in modern Turkey). Meeting in Paris from January to

June 1919, the "Big Three" of Wilson, French President Georges Clemenceau, and British Prime Minister David Lloyd George took on two major tasks to shape the postwar order. First, the three leaders redrew the map of eastern and central Europe to create nation-states out of the vanished empires. Second, they had to decide what to do about a defeated Germany. The possible spread of revolution gave the negotiations a particular urgency. Anticolonial revolts broke out in India and China, and pro-Soviet workers' councils seized power briefly in Hungary and southern Germany. "We are running a race with Bolshevism," Wilson warned, "and the world is on fire."

To put out the fire, the Big Three created a string of new nations running from Finland in the north to Yugoslavia in the south. Eastern Europeans were to be self-governing within the new political boundaries. How far would "self-determination" go? Secretary of State Lansing worried that the president's language of democracy was "loaded with dynamite." The world's nonwhite majority wondered whether it applied to them. The Big Three created the mandate system to provide for eventual self-determination for colonies after a period of tutelage under an established power, and they rejected Japan's proposal to include racial equality as a principle of the new League of Nations.

The German question predominated at the Paris conference. To create a long-term peaceful order in Europe, Wilson wanted lenient terms for Germany. But the French and British had lost much more in the war than the Americans, and they believed Germany must pay for that. To satisfy France and England, Germany had to admit guilt for causing the war and pay $33 billion in reparations, while losing much of its eastern territory to the new states of Poland and Czechoslovakia. For Wilson the League of Nations was the key: this new and unprecedented global organization would keep the peace by ensuring collective security for all nations.

DOCUMENT

Henry Cabot Lodge's Objections to Treaty of Versailles

Most Republicans objected on principle to one key aspect of the Versailles Treaty (named for the estate of King Louis XIV, where it was signed): Article 10 of the League of Nations charter, guaranteeing ahead of time a collective response to defend any member's territory from attack. Treaty opponents were determined to preserve complete American autonomy, including freedom of action in Latin America. Henry Cabot Lodge Jr. of Massachusetts, the powerful Republican chair of the Senate Foreign Relations Committee, organized the two Senate votes rejecting American membership in the league. Hoping to stave off defeat for his idealistic plan, Wilson undertook an ill-advised national speaking tour to promote the league. His strenuous effort failed to win American participation in the league, and it ultimately broke his fragile health. Wilson suffered a stroke on October 2, 1919, that left him incapacitated for the rest of his presidency.

Waging Counterrevolution Abroad

Soon after Russia withdrew from the war, Britain, France, and the United States intervened in the civil war there between the Bolsheviks (the "Reds") and the various counterrevolutionary forces (the "Whites"). The initial military rationale in the summer of 1918 was to reopen the eastern front against Germany. The United States landed 7,000 troops in Vladivostock, on Russia's far Pacific coast. In conjunction with the British, 5,000 U.S. soldiers went ashore at Archangel in northern Russia. They quickly became involved in fighting the Red Army. The Wilson administration meanwhile funneled money and military intelligence to leaders of the White forces.

The Bolsheviks rejected certain values cherished by most Americans: the sanctity of private property and contracts, political liberty, and religious freedom. They liberalized divorce laws and legalized abortion, challenging conservative American attitudes about the relationships between women and men. And they established the Comintern in 1919 to promote similar revolutions around the world. Intervention in the Russian civil war failed to overthrow Lenin's government, and American troops pulled out in 1920.

The Red and Black Scares at Home

Meanwhile, in the United States, the scale of industrial unrest provoked fears of a Soviet-style revolution. Four million American workers, one out of every five, went out on strike in 1919—the highest proportion of the workforce ever. They sought improved wages and working conditions as well as recognition of the right to collective bargaining. In Seattle a walkout by shipyard workers mushroomed into a general strike that shut down most of the city for a week. In Pittsburgh the AFL led a bitter strike against U.S. Steel in pursuit of union recognition. The United Mine Workers led walkouts by hundreds of thousands of coal miners, which evolved into open warfare between miners and coal companies in West Virginia over the next two years. In Boston three-quarters of the police force went on strike to protest wages lower than those of common laborers. Between April and June, anarchists mailed or delivered bombs to thirty-six prominent public figures, including Attorney General A. Mitchell Palmer. All were defused except two.

Museum of History and Industry, Seattle, WA/Pemco, Webster and Stevens Collection

■ **The Seattle General Strike Committee** took on the responsibility of keeping essential services running in the city. Here its members issue groceries to union families, January 1919. The cooperation necessary among organized workers to keep a strike going offered a different model of community interaction than did the individualism often touted by wealthier Americans.

Whereas many Americans sympathized with struggles for unionization, others viewed them as dangerous to private property and social order. They associated strikes with radical immigrants and anarchists and considered them "un-American." The **Red Scare** of 1919 associated reform and social justice of any kind with subversion. Attorney General Palmer directed the deportation to Russia of 249 foreign-born radicals aboard the *Buford* in December 1919, including anarchist and feminist Emma Goldman. "Palmer raids" led to the arrest of thousands more within a month.

Violence against workers extended to African Americans after World War I. An upsurge in lynching included at least ten black veterans still in uniform and was not limited to the South. White mobs burned entire black communities to the ground, including Tulsa's Greenwood neighborhood in 1921 and the all-black town of Rosewood, Florida, in 1923. The Red Scare merged with the "Black Scare" in Phillips County, Arkansas, where black sharecroppers, many of them veterans, formed a union in 1919 to pursue equitable crop settlements from landlords. Fearing insurrection, local white leaders used 2,500 federal troops and white vigilantes to massacre more than 200 sharecroppers. But any inclination toward deference in the face of brutality was gone, and African Americans fought back fiercely against white marauders in deadly riots in Washington and Chicago in the summer of 1919.

Where was the president during this turmoil? Incapacitated by his stroke, he lay resting in his bed in Washington, the administration managed largely by his wife, Edith, and his secretary, Joseph Tumulty. In any case, Wilson's segregationist policies suggested that he would have been unlikely to provide effective leadership in bridging the nation's racial divides.

Conclusion

How much success could a varied generation of Progressive reformers claim? Women had won the vote with the Nineteenth Amendment. Daily life for Americans of darker hue continued to entail picking one's way through a maze of discrimination. Most union campaigns stalled by 1920, beaten back by the physical force and cleverness of corporate employ-ers and their government sympathizers. When the Red Scare dissipated, Americans did not return to the reform spirit of Progressivism. Voter turnout in 1920 dipped below 50 percent for the first time in a century. Those who did vote that year gave the Republican party a sweeping victory and put Ohio Senator Warren G. Harding in the White House. His speeches may have been, as one rival said, "an army of pompous phrases moving over the landscape in search of an idea," but most of the nation sought calm after the upheavals of the previous decade.

American contributions to democracy abroad were similarly ambivalent. Whereas eastern Europeans named streets in their newly independent nations for President Wilson, few Latin Americans believed that U.S. invasions of Caribbean and Central American countries promoted self-government. Russians admired much about American society and the U.S. economy while resenting American troops in their land. Above all hung the problem of Germany, still the most potentially powerful single nation in Europe. The Versailles Treaty imposed harsh terms and embittered a generation of German people. "If I were a German, I think I should not sign it," Wilson admitted privately. The Weimar Republic that replaced the abdicated German Kaiser lasted through the 1920s. But the storms of the Great Depression after 1929 swamped Ger-many's republican experiment and gave rise to Adolph Hitler.

Sites to Visit

The Great War, 1914–1918
www.pitt.edu/~pugachev/greatwar/ww1.html
This site offers an array of narratives, photos, documents, statistics, maps, and bibliography, plus links to other useful World War I sites.

Women and Social Movements in the United States, 1600–2000
womhist.binghamton.edu
Maintained by two Binghamton University historians, this site has a rich trove of documents on the history of American women as well as excellent links to others.

Avalon Project at Yale Law School: Documents in Law, History and Diplomacy
www.yale.edu/lawweb/avalon/avalon.htm
Researchers can find here the texts of a large number of the most important primary documents illuminating U.S. relations with other countries, including materials on American responses to the Bol-shevik revolution in Russia.

Temperance and Prohibition
prohibition.osu.edu/
Cartoons, newspaper articles, and other primary documents avail-able here illuminate the struggle over whether to prohibit the sale of alcoholic beverages.

Emma Goldman Papers
sunsite3.berkeley.edu/Goldman/
This site has photos and excerpts from the writings and speeches of one of America's most influential radicals and feminists.

Religion Online
www.religion-online.org/
This site has essays by prominent scholars on diverse aspects of Christian theology and American church history.

Up South: African American Migration in the Era of the Great War
www.ashp.cuny.edu/video/south.html
Maintained by the American Social History Project at the Gradu-ate Center of the City University of New York, this site offers details of the mass migration of rural black Southerners to the urban north during World War I.

Influenza Pandemic of 1918
www.stanford.edu/group/virus/uda/
A variety of information, documents, and photos of the deadly global outbreak of the "Spanish flu" can be found here.

For Further Reading

General

Kendrick A. Clements, *Woodrow Wilson: World Statesman* (1987).
John M. Cooper, *Pivotal Decades: The United States, 1900–1920* (1990).
Alan Dawley, *Changing the World: American Progressives in War and Peace* (2003).
Nell Irvin Painter, *Standing at Armageddon: The United States, 1877–1919* (1987).

A World in Upheaval

John Mason Hart, *Empire and Revolution: The Americans in Mexico since the Civil War* (2002).
Arthur Link, ed., *Woodrow Wilson and a Revolutionary World* (1982).
Joseph A. McCartin, *Labor's Great War: The Struggle for Industrial Democracy and the Origins of Modern American Labor Relations, 1912–1921* (1997).

George J. Sánchez, *Becoming Mexican American: Ethnicity, Culture, and Identity in Chicano Los Angeles, 1900–1945* (1993).

The Great War and American Neutrality

John W. Coogan, *The End of Neutrality: The United States, Britain, and Maritime Rights, 1899–1915* (1981).

Steven J. Diner, *A Very Different Age: Americans of the Progressive Era* (1998).

James Grossman, *Land of Hope: Chicago, Black Southerners, and the Great Migration* (1989).

Vicki I. Ruiz, *From Out of the Shadows: Mexican Women in Twentieth-Century America* (1998).

The United States Goes to War

Edward M. Coffman, *The War to End All Wars: The American Military Experience in World War I* (1987).

Martin Gilbert, *The First World War: A Complete History* (1994).

David M. Kennedy, *Over Here: The First World War and American Society* (1980).

Kathleen Kennedy, *Disloyal Mothers and Scurrilous Citizens: Women and Subversion During World War I* (1999).

The Struggle to Win the Peace

Alfred W. Crosby, *America's Forgotten Pandemic: The Influenza of 1918*, 2nd ed. (2003).

David S. Foglesong, *America's Secret War Against Bolshevism: U.S. Intervention in the Russian Civil War, 1917–1920* (1995).

Thomas J. Knock, *To End All Wars: Woodrow Wilson and the Quest for a New World Order* (1992).

Gordon N. Levin Jr., *Woodrow Wilson and World Politics: America's Response to War and Revolution* (1968).

William M. Tuttle Jr., *Race Riot: Chicago in the Red Summer of 1919* (1970).

For quizzes and other resources on these topics, go to www.longmanamericanhistory.com.

The Promise of Consumer Culture: The 1920s

I N THE SUPERIOR COURT OF LOS ANGELES IN 1920, LORIMER LINGANFIELD, A RESPECTABLE BARBER, filed for divorce. Although his wife, Marsha, held him in "high regard and esteem as her husband," there were "evidences of indiscretion" in her conduct. She wore a new bathing suit, "designed especially for the purpose of exhibiting to the public the shape and form of her body." To his further humiliation, she was "beset with a desire to sing and dance at cafes and restaurants for the entertainment of the public." When Lorimer complained about her "appetite for beer and whisky" and extravagant tastes for luxury, she replied that he was "not the only pebble on the beach, she had a millionaire 'guy' who would buy her all the clothes, automobiles, diamonds and booze that she wanted." The ultimate insult was her refusal to have any sexual intercourse, claiming that she did not want any "dirty little brats around her." The judge was sympathetic, and Lorimer Linganfield won his suit.

The Linganfields' difficulties represent a larger struggle as Americans shifted from the **producer economy** of the nineteenth century, complete with clearly defined gender roles and sexual mores, to the **consumer economy** of the twentieth century and to new amusements, changing sexual behavior, and flamboyant "new women." Marsha Linganfield was a "**flapper**," one of the young women of the 1910s and 1920s who broke from time-honored conventions. With short, "bobbed" hair, knee-length dresses, and boyish styles unencumbered by layers of

■ Gertrude Ederle swims the English Channel.

CHAPTER OUTLINE

The Business of Politics

The Decline of Reform

Hollywood and Harlem: National Cultures in Black and White

Science on Trial

Consumer Dreams and Nightmares

Conclusion

Sites to Visit

For Further Reading

petticoats, flappers flirted, petted, and danced "wild" dances like the Charleston, an African American dance brought north from South Carolina **juke joints**. Flappers blurred the line between "good girls" and "bad girls" that had previously defined proper female behavior.

New forms of popular entertainment that developed in the 1920s, especially Hollywood movies and jazz music, became defining features of the nation itself. The popular arts offered Jews and blacks a space for innovation. At a time when white, Anglo-Saxon, Protestant (WASP) men had control of nearly all government and business institutions, Jewish moviemakers and African American musicians were creating the culture that would soon represent the nation.

The great heroes of the 1920s were celebrities admired for their individual achievements in sports and adventure. In 1927, the same year that Babe Ruth hit a record sixty home runs, Charles Lindbergh flew his small monoplane, *The Spirit of St. Louis*, nonstop from New York to Paris in thirty-three and one-half hours, a feat that electrified the world and made him an instant hero. Professional sports came of age in the 1920s. In 1926, nineteen-year-old Olympic gold medalist Gertrude Ederle became the first woman to swim the English Channel. She broke the world's record with her time of fourteen hours and thirty-one minutes, two hours shorter than those of the six men who had preceded her. On her return to the United States, 2 million cheering fans lined the streets of New York City to welcome her home. The nation idolized this new generation of heroes, who dominated headlines and drew cheering crowds wherever they went.

> *The great heroes of the 1920s were celebrities admired for their individual achievements in sports and adventure.*

The glamorous life, however, was out of reach for many. Often characterized as the "roaring twenties" of giddy prosperity and reckless good times, these were also years of widespread poverty, especially in rural areas and urban ghettos. But at the end of the decade, almost half of all households did own a car or a radio; almost a third owned a washing machine or a vacuum cleaner real wages rose steadily.

Conservative politics at the national level prevailed throughout the decade. An anti-radical immigrant Red Scare followed World War I, and Prohibition made alcohol consumption illegal until 1933. High-profile court cases revealed public ambivalence about the use of new scientific knowledge. Business values of material acquisition spread as the expansion of consumer credit weakened the traditions of saving and frugality. For those with money to invest, Wall Street beckoned. The stock market rose to perilous heights, only to collapse at the end of the decade.

The Business of Politics

In 1924 President Calvin Coolidge declared, "The business of America is business." Despite its many critics, with the support of national political leaders, business reigned. After an initial recession following World War I, the Republican U.S. economy grew steadily. The Gross National Product (GNP) increased 5.5 percent per year, from $149 billion in 1922 to $227 billion in 1929. Official unemployment remained below 5 percent throughout the decade, and real wages rose 15 percent. These trends fueled the popularity of the conservative, business-friendly presidents of the 1920s. Economic interests also drove foreign policy during the decade. After World War I, with much of Europe in shambles, the United States made loans to foreign countries, becoming the world's leading creditor nation. International markets opened up for American-made products, leading to a tremendous expansion in foreign trade.

Warren G. Harding: The Politics of Scandal

Warren G. Harding, a former newspaper editor and Republican U.S. senator from Ohio, won the 1920 presidential election by the biggest landslide since 1820. He established the conservative agenda that would last throughout the decade. Harding supported immigration restriction and opposed labor unions. In the wake of World War I, Harding distanced himself from Woodrow Wilson's peace settlement but promoted international treaties. In 1921 and 1922, Secretary of State Charles Evans Hughes achieved the first major disarmament accord, the Five-Power Treaty, signed by Japan, Britain, France, Italy, and the United States at the Washington Conference. The

VIDEO
Warren G. Harding

five nations agreed to scrap more than 2 million tons of warships in the first such pact of its kind. Hughes extended the power of the United States abroad through economic ties, encouraging banks to provide loans to war-ravaged Europe.

But Harding's presidency was marred by scandal. He had built his political base by handing out favors and deals to his friends, and he continued to do so as president. His buddies used their offices and influence for personal gain, while Harding caroused with them, drinking, despite Prohibition, and engaging in notorious extramarital affairs. At first, the press ignored these abuses, but by 1923, the many scandals finally broke. Harding's cronies were exposed for selling government appointments and providing judicial pardons and police protection for bootleggers.

The most serious scandal of Harding's presidency involved the large government oil reserves at Teapot Dome, Wyoming, and Elk Hills, California. At the urging of Secretary of the Interior Albert Fall, Harding transferred control over the reserves from the U.S. Navy to the Department of the Interior. After accepting a bribe of nearly $400,000 from two oil tycoons, Harry F. Sinclair and Edward L. Doheny, Fall secretly issued leases to them without opening up the competition to other oil companies. Fall went to jail for a year as a result. In another scandal, Charles R. Forbes, head of the Veteran's Bureau, went to prison for swindling the government out of $200 million worth of hospital supplies. When he learned of the scandals that occurred in his close circle, Harding grew deeply worried. The stress probably contributed to the illness that killed him in 1923.

TABLE 21-1

The Election of 1920

Candidate	Political Party	Popular Vote (%)	Electoral Vote
Warren G. Harding	Republican	60.4	404
James M. Cox	Democratic	34.2	127
Eugene V. Debs	Socialist	3.4	—

Calvin Coolidge: The Hands-Off President

DOCUMENT

Inaugural Address, Calvin Coolidge (March 1925)

Harding's vice president, Calvin Coolidge, took over the presidency. Sober and serious, this aloof New Englander was not vulnerable to scandal as his predecessor had been. Coolidge believed that the government should meddle as little as possible in the affairs of the nation. He took long naps every day and exerted little presidential leadership. Known mostly for his hostility to labor unions and his laissez-faire attitude toward business, he was a popular president during the complacent mid-1920s.

Not everyone was pleased with Coolidge's probusiness politics, and opposition mobilized for the 1924 election. Progressive Republicans formed a new Progressive party and nominated Robert M. La Follette of Wisconsin for president. The Progressive platform promoted conservation measures, higher taxes on the wealthy, doing away with the electoral college in favor of direct election of the president, and the abolition of child labor. The Democrats deadlocked between Catholic candidate Alfred E. Smith, an urban politician from New York, and Protestant William G. McAdoo, who had a base of support in the South and West. On the 103rd ballot, the delegates finally chose a compromise candidate, John W. Davis, a corporation lawyer. The Republicans nominated Coolidge, who claimed responsibility for the nation's prosperity and won easily, receiving more votes than the other two candidates combined.

TABLE 21-2

The Election of 1924

Candidate	Political Party	Popular Vote (%)	Electoral Vote
Calvin Coolidge	Republican	54.0	382
John W. Davis	Democratic	28.8	136
Robert M. LaFollette	Progressive	16.6	13

Coolidge took pride in measures that prevented the government from interfering in the economy, such as his vetoes of the 1926 and 1928 McNary-Haugen bills, which would have provided government subsidies to farmers if farm prices dropped. The passage of the Revenue

Act of 1926, a form of **trickle-down economics** intended to boost the economy, reduced the high income and estate taxes that Progressive reformers had put into place during World War I.

Herbert Hoover: The Self-Made President

The 1928 election was a major turning point for the presence of ethnic minorities in politics, for the Democrats broke tradition by selecting an Irish Roman Catholic, Alfred E. Smith, governor of New York, as their candidate. It was the first time a major party had nominated a Catholic for president. Coolidge decided not to run for reelection in 1928, and the Republican party selected Secretary of Commerce Herbert Hoover as its nominee. Prohibition—the Eighteenth Amendment banning the manufacture and sale of alcohol—figured prominently in the 1928 presidential campaign. Although the Democratic platform gave lukewarm support to the continuation of Prohibition, Smith made no secret of his support for the repeal of the Eighteenth Amendment. By contrast, Republican Herbert Hoover praised Prohibition as "a great social and economic experiment." The other major issue of the campaign was religion. Anti-Catholic sentiment was strong throughout the country, especially in the South, where Democrats either sat out the election or voted Republican. Smith's opponents attacked his Catholicism, charging that he was more loyal to the Vatican than to the United States.

TABLE 21-3			
The Election of 1928			
Candidate	**Political Party**	**Popular Vote (%)**	**Electoral Vote**
Herbert Hoover	Republican	58.2	444
Alfred E. Smith	Democratic	40.9	87
Norman Thomas	Socialist	0.7	—

Herbert Hoover epitomized the values of the self-made man. He was orphaned as a child and raised by relatives of modest means. After graduating from newly established Stanford University, Hoover went into mining and rose through the ranks to become a wealthy corporate leader. By age forty, he was already a millionaire. Hoover began his career in government during World War I, when he earned widespread admiration for handling the distribution of food relief to European war refugees. He then served ably as secretary of commerce in the Harding and Coolidge administrations. Shortly after the election, President Hoover predicted, "We in America today are nearer to the final triumph over poverty than ever before in the history of any land." But less than a year into his presidency, his optimism, along with the nation's economy, came crashing down.

The Decline of Reform

Reformers who had championed the causes of the marginalized and disadvantaged lost influence in the business-dominated 1920s. After achieving the vote, the women's rights movement splintered as younger women sought new freedoms not through politics but through a social and sexual revolution. Widespread hostility toward immigrants and various ethnic groups was at the root of the outlawing of liquor, new laws restricting immigration, and the rise of the Ku Klux Klan. But progressive political impulses did not entirely disappear, especially among African Americans, who continued to mobilize and organize for civil rights.

Women's Rights After the Struggle for Suffrage

One indication of the waning of progressive reform was the fragmentation of women's rights activism in the 1920s. The more radical wing of the suffrage movement, the National Woman's Party (NWP), in 1923 launched a campaign for the Equal Rights Amendment (ERA), which

Bettmann/CORBIS

■ Speakeasy hostess Mary Louise Guinan appears unrepentant as she is arrested for selling alcohol during the Prohibition era. Law enforcement was futile because speakeasies that were raided and closed simply reopened in new locations.

DOCUMENT

Eighteenth Amendment— Prohibition of Intoxicating Liquor (January 16, 1919)

declared simply: "Equality of rights under the law shall not be denied or abridged by the United States or by any state on account of sex."

The debate over the ERA in the 1920s reflected the fundamental divide that would permeate women's rights activism throughout the rest of the twentieth century. On one side were those who believed that women were fundamentally the same as men and deserved equal rights; on the other side were those who argued that women were different and deserved special privileges and protections. Many women's rights activists opposed the ERA because it would undercut efforts to gain special legislative protections for women based on their presumed physical weakness and their potential for childbearing, such as maximum hours, regulations against night work, and limitations on the weights they could lift. These women disapproved of the goals and tactics of the NWP and formed their own nonpartisan organization, the League of Women Voters, which promoted social and political reform.

Marital breakdown still carried a heavy negative stigma, especially for women. Nevertheless, the divorce rate doubled between 1900 and 1920 and continued to rise throughout the 1920s, in part the result of women's increasing independence. As job opportunities for women increased, more women felt able to abandon unhappy marriages.

Prohibition: The Experiment That Failed

The Eighteenth Amendment, prohibiting the manufacture and sale of alcohol, went into effect in January 1920. Several diverse interests came together to promote the ban on liquor. Temperance crusaders in the Anti-Saloon League and the Women's Christian Temperance Union had argued since the late nineteenth century that women and children suffered when men spent their paychecks at the saloon and returned home drunk and violent. World War I prompted others to support a ban on the manufacture of liquor to save grain for the war effort. Anti-immigrant "drys" had political motives for promoting prohibition. They hoped to undercut the power bases of immigrant and ethnic politicians who used local saloons to forge their constituencies and **political machines**. The "wets" included alienated intellectuals, Jazz Age rebels, and many city dwellers whose social lives revolved around neighborhood pubs, especially in Irish and German communities.

Enforcement was impossible. Federal agents had responsibility for enforcing the law, but their numbers were inadequate. In order to be effective, federal agents had to work closely with local law enforcement officials. In some urban areas, local officials refused to cooperate with federal agents. Americans who wanted to drink liquor found many ways to acquire it. Illegal "speakeasies" abounded where customers could buy drinks delivered by rumrunners who smuggled in liquor from Canada, Mexico, and the West Indies. Many people concocted their own "bathtub gin" or "moonshine whiskey," homemade brews using readily available ingredients and household equipment.

Prohibition was intended to cure society's ills. Instead, it provided vast opportunities for crime and profit. Organized crime received a major boost when violence erupted in the scramble to profit from illegal liquor. Chicago witnessed 550 gangland killings in the 1920s, with few arrests or convictions. By 1929 Chicago mob king Al Capone controlled a massive network of speakeasies that raked in $60 million annually.

Prohibition failed to live up to its promise. Although alcohol consumption declined by two-thirds within a year of the passage of the amendment, by 1929 the consumption of alcohol had climbed back up to 70 percent of its pre-Prohibition level.

AUDIO

"Prohibition is a Failure"

Reactionary Impulses

The Red Scare after World War I (see Chapter 20) inaugurated a decade of hostility to political radicals and foreigners. Shoemaker Nicola Sacco and fish peddler Bartolomeo Vanzetti were both: Italian **aliens** and self-proclaimed anarchists. In May 1920, the paymaster and guard of a South Braintree, Massachusetts, shoe company was robbed and murdered, and Sacco and Vanzetti were arrested and charged with the crime. Sacco testified that he was in Boston at the time, applying for a passport, and his alibi was corroborated. Both men proclaimed their innocence and insisted that they were on trial for their political beliefs rather than the crime itself. Their Italian accents and advocacy of anarchism in the courtroom did not help their case with many Americans suspicious of foreign radicals, including the judge presiding at their trial. Despite a weak case against them, Sacco and Vanzetti were convicted of first-degree murder and sentenced to death.

Lawyers for the two anarchists appealed the case several times to no avail. The convictions sparked outrage among Italian Americans, political radicals, labor activists, and liberal intellectuals who believed the two men were falsely convicted. The case soon generated mass demonstrations, appeals for clemency, and petitions from around the world. In response, the governor of Massachusetts appointed a commission to review the case, but the commission concluded that there were no grounds for a new trial. Finally, on August 23, 1927, Sacco and Vanzetti were executed by electric chair at Charlestown State Prison.

The case of Sacco and Vanzetti underscored the anti-immigrant sentiment that prevailed in the 1920s. In 1924 Congress passed the Johnson-Reid Act, imposing a limit of 165,000

Bettmann/CORBIS

■ Nicola Sacco and Bartolomeo Vanzetti, Italian aliens and self-proclaimed anarchists, were accused of murder in May 1920. The men and their supporters claimed they were on trial not for the crime but for their political beliefs and their immigrant status. After all appeals failed, the two were executed in 1927.

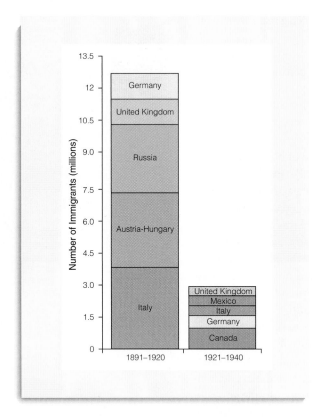

■ FIGURE 21.1
**NUMBER OF IMMIGRANTS AND COUNTRIES OF ORIGIN,
1891–1920 AND 1921–1940   Before the immigration restriction
laws passed in the 1920s, many immigrants came from Russia and
southern and eastern Europe. After immigration restriction, most
came from western Europe and Canada.**

immigrants from countries outside the Western Hemisphere and using a quota system for each country based on the year 1890, a time when British, German, and Scandinavian immigrants dominated the foreign-born population. The Johnson-Reid Act limited entry every year to 2 percent of the total number of immigrants from each country who were present in 1890. This measure effectively barred Jews, Slavs, Greeks, Italians, and Poles because their numbers were so small in 1890. In addition, the 1924 law reaffirmed the exclusion of Chinese immigrants and added Japanese and other Asians to the list, effectively closing the door to all migrants from Asia.

Agricultural interests in California and Texas lobbied hard to keep the door open to Mexicans because of the low-wage labor they provided. In the aftermath of the Mexican Revolution, many Mexicans hoped to find stability and jobs in the United States. Between 1910 and 1930, more than 1 million Mexicans, nearly one-tenth of Mexico's population, migrated to the United States, where they found work on farms, on railroads, and in mines.

One of the most reactionary developments of the 1920s was the revival of the Ku Klux Klan (KKK), which became the most powerful white supremacy group in the nation, remaining active throughout the twentieth century. Klan membership included laborers, businesspeople, physicians, judges, social workers, and women who felt that their homogenous small-town Protestant culture was threatened by the evils of modern life, brought on by the presence and influence of morally suspect outsiders. The Klan wielded considerable power in the 1920s in certain states, particularly Texas, Oklahoma, Oregon, and Indiana.

Marcus Garvey and the Persistence of Civil Rights Activism

In the midst of a decade of reactionary policies toward outsiders and political activists, African Americans continued their struggle for civil rights. Jamaican-born black nationalist Marcus Garvey moved to New York City's Harlem in 1916 and opened a branch of his Universal Negro Improvement Association (UNIA). Garvey urged black people to establish their own nation-state in Africa: "Africa was peopled with a race of cultured black men, who were masters in art, science, and literature. . . . Africa shall be for the black peoples of the world." By the 1920s, the UNIA had nearly 1 million followers and called for political justice and labor rights for black Americans.

In keeping with his belief in black-owned businesses, Garvey established the Black Star Line and encouraged his followers to invest in the shipping company. Nearly 40,000 African Americans invested three-quarters of a million dollars to purchase shares of Black Star stock. But the business ran into problems. Managers purchased ships that needed extensive and costly repairs, and the company ran up huge debts. Garvey claimed that he had paid for a ship that was never delivered. In 1922 Garvey was arrested and charged with mail fraud for advertising and selling stock for a ship that did not exist. Although the government lacked any concrete evidence to prove the case against him, Garvey was convicted and sentenced to five years in prison. Garvey kept up his political activities from prison, then was released after two years and deported to Jamaica as an undesirable alien. Nevertheless, the momentum he sparked continued.

Hollywood and Harlem: National Cultures in Black and White

In 1920, for the first time, the majority of Americans lived in towns and cities with populations greater than 2,500. Although this shift often is considered a watershed in the transformation from rural to urban America, it is worth noting that because the census defined any town with more than 2,500 inhabitants as urban, the majority of Americans still lived in small and ethnically homogeneous towns. Many small-town Americans still viewed big-city life with suspicion. They feared the decline of traditional Protestant American values of hard work, thrift, and discipline. Yet they were drawn to the new urban life.

Hollywood on the West Coast and Harlem on the East Coast became centers of cultural innovation that spanned the nation. Eventually, the artistic productions of both centers attracted audiences of all racial, class, and regional backgrounds. Increasingly, as Americans moved from place to place, they encountered similar entertainments, music, arts, and consumer products. Movies, automobiles, radios, and advertising all fostered this emerging national culture.

Hollywood Comes of Age

As movie theaters spread into towns and cities across the country, the messages of Hollywood began to reach a mass audience and forge a nationwide popular culture. Movie stars and their films provided models for how to adopt new styles of manhood and womanhood. Douglas Fairbanks showed middle-class men how to break free from the humdrum of white-collar work into the world of leisure. His attire of sports clothes changed the way men dressed in their off-work hours. Female stars, such as Clara Bow, epitomized the flapper and taught female viewers how to be "naughty but nice."

Ironically, as the nation closed its doors to immigrants, foreigners on screen captivated the imagination of a native-born population drawn to the allure of the outsider. Movie stars like Greta Garbo from Sweden, Dolores del Rio, Lupe Velez, and Ramon Navarro from Mexico, and Rudolph Valentino from Italy drew audiences with their foreignness. And yet, because movies were silent until the late 1920s, their accented voices were not heard. Sound arrived in the late twenties, bringing the voices and dialects of ethnic performers into the movies. For native-born Americans watching films in small towns and cities, sound movies brought the diverse voices of the cities into their communities. For immigrants, sound movies carried their own familiar accents and allowed for a greater sense of identification with the stars on the screen.

The Harlem Renaissance

While Hollywood in the 1920s developed on the West Coast, a flourishing center of African American culture emerged on the East Coast. The black arts movement known as the Harlem Renaissance drew on European as well as African and African American artistic traditions and gathered white as well as black intellectuals and artists. The young black poet Arna Bontemps was among the many artists drawn to Harlem. In 1924 he described Harlem as "a foretaste of paradise. A blue haze descended

■ **FIGURE 21.2**
URBAN AND RURAL POPULATION, 1890–1990   In the nineteenth century, the American population was primarily rural. During the twentieth century, the population became predominantly urban.

■ **Rudolph Valentino dances the tango in this famous scene from the 1920 film *The Four Horsemen of the Apocalypse*.** Films in the 1920s featured exotic locales with foreign stars such as the Italian-born Valentino. In keeping with the public's taste for grandeur, lavish movie palaces emerged in cities across the country.

VIDEO

Roaring 20's

at night and with it strings of fairy lights on the broad avenues. From the window of a small room in an apartment on Fifth and 129th Street, I looked over the rooftops of Negrodom and tried to believe my eyes. What a city! What a world!"

Harlem Renaissance writers laid claim to their identity as Americans while articulating the culture, aesthetics, and experiences of African Americans. The poet Langston Hughes challenged white America to accept African Americans in his 1925 poem "I, too, sing America:"

> I, too, sing America
> I am the darker brother
> They send me to eat in the kitchen
> When company comes,
> But I laugh
> And eat well
> And grow strong
> Tomorrow,
> I'll be at the table
> When company comes
> Nobody'll dare
> Say to me,
> "Eat in the kitchen,"

Then.
Besides,
They'll see how beautiful I am
And be ashamed—
I, too, am America.

The music of black America was such an important marker of the era that it provided the decade with its most lasting moniker, the Jazz Age. Emanating not from Harlem but from New Orleans, Chicago, and St. Louis, jazz was, nevertheless, central to the black arts movement and the emerging national culture. With the help of the recording industry and radio, jazz and the blues began to reach a wide audience, primarily among blacks but increasingly among whites as well. Blues lyrics expressed themes of working-class protest and resistance to racism. Women who sang the blues, including Bessie Smith, Ma Rainey, and Ethel Waters, asserted their sexuality, their passion for men or for women, their resistance to male domination, their sorrows, and their strength.

Radios and Autos: Transforming Leisure

Radio played a major role in linking people across regions through shared information, advertising, and entertainment. Annual radio production increased from 190,000 in 1923 to almost 5 million in 1929. Radios brought jazz and other forms of popular music to the airwaves, transforming the way music was enjoyed in American homes. Americans became more inclined to listen to music on their Victrolas and radios than to make music themselves. By the mid-1920s, sales of records surpassed those of sheet music; production and sales of pianos also dropped precipitously.

The number of radio stations soared from thirty in 1922 to 556 the following year, and national broadcasts began to supersede local ones. Airwaves became so cluttered that by the mid-1920s, the federal government, through the leadership of Secretary of Commerce Herbert Hoover, created the Federal Radio Commission to regulate and organize access. Meanwhile, American Telephone and Telegraph (AT&T) and the National Broadcasting Company (NBC) combined to form the first national network system, which gave programs and advertisers access to audiences across the country.

As radios entered millions of American homes, automobiles began to extend the mobility of Americans. The automobile offered the possibility of commuting to work without relying on public transportation, encouraging the expansion of suburban communities. The number of passenger cars in the nation more than tripled during the twenties. The Federal Highways Act of 1916 had produced a network of roads all over the country, providing construction jobs and a slew of new roadside businesses, from restaurants to garages. Automobiles also stimulated the tourist industry; Florida, California, and Arizona became vacation destinations in this period.

Automobile production also revolutionized the consumer industry. The pragmatic Henry Ford built inexpensive, functional automobiles that he expected his workers to be

Schomburg Center for Research in Black Culture, Portrait Collection

■ **Poet Langston Hughes as a student at Lincoln University, Pennsylvania, in 1927. One of the major literary figures of the Harlem Renaissance, Hughes expressed the hopes, dreams, and sorrows of black Americans.**

"Oh, I beg your pardon! I thought you were extinct."

■ This cartoon from *The New Yorker* reflects the intrusive aspects of tourism that developed in the Southwest, as well as the widespread erroneous assumption that Native American communities had died out by the twentieth century.

DOCUMENT

Wembridge, "Petting and the Campus"

able to purchase and keep. But Ford faced serious competition from General Motors' Alfred P. Sloan Jr., who developed the concept of **planned obsolescence** and put a new emphasis on auto styling to encourage customers to trade in their old cars for newer and more expensive models.

The automobile was part of a consumer society increasingly focused on leisure, pleasure, and intimacy. Courtship patterns changed, and sexual activity increased as young couples abandoned the front porch for the back seat. Women gained new freedom and autonomy when they, too, took the wheel. Moralists worried that the automobile would provide youth with too much independence and privacy. One juvenile court judge announced that "the automobile has become a house of prostitution on wheels."

Science on Trial

Although advances in technology and medicine improved the quality of life for many Americans in the early twentieth century, scientific efforts to alter the natural world did not always lead to expected social benefits. One case in point was the engineering project to build levees along the Mississippi River to prevent flooding. Scientific ideas were also tested in the nation's courtrooms. Two major cases, the Scopes trial and the Supreme Court's decision in *Buck v. Bell*, subjected scientific ideas to judicial and cultural scrutiny. Although decisions in both cases resolved the immediate legal issues, the questions they raised continued to generate controversy and debate throughout the rest of the century.

The Great Flood of 1927

For half a century the engineers of the Mississippi River Commission had adhered to a policy of building levees, assuming that strong barricades against the river's banks would prevent flooding. Presumably, the levees would allow the rich soil of the floodplains along the river to be settled and farmed rather than leaving the basins empty to provide places for the river to expand and contract with seasonal rains. But the levee policy proved to be a disastrous example of human efforts to master the natural contours of the land. In March 1927, the rains came, and the river rose. Public authorities and river experts assured those who watched and worried that the levees would hold. They were wrong. Torrential rains caused the river to rage across the levees and the land beyond, submerging 26,000 square miles of prime farmland in 170 counties across seven states. More than 900,000 people were forced from their homes. The flood caused more than $100 million in crop losses and $23 million in livestock deaths. Journalists at the time called it "America's greatest peacetime disaster."

With the help of the Department of Commerce and the National Guard, the Red Cross set up 154 relief camps for flood victims. The camps were racially segregated. Refugees in the white camps were free to come and go and had more comfortable and generous accommodations

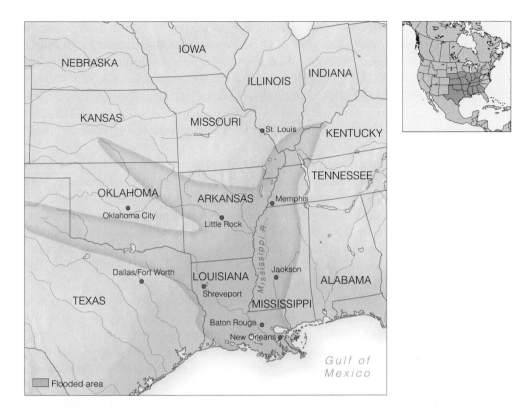

■ **MAP 21.1**
THE MISSISSIPPI RIVER FLOOD OF 1927   The Mississippi River flood in 1927 sent water across a huge area of the South, extending as far west as Texas, covering most of Louisiana, Arkansas, and Mississippi, and reaching north into Kansas, Illinois, and Indiana.

and rations than those in the black camps. Armed guards patrolled the camps for black refugees and restricted people attempting to enter or leave. Black laborers had to register and give the names of their employers to receive any shelter or assistance. Federal authorities, including Secretary of Commerce Herbert Hoover, refused to intervene in local camp management. As a result, southern whites were able to force black sharecroppers back to work on their plantations. Despite the prisonlike conditions, many African American refugees managed to escape and made their way north.

The Triumph of Eugenics: *Buck v. Bell*

Many Americans, including large numbers of policymakers, believed in white racial superiority. Supposedly scientific theories of race bolstered claims that distinct, biologically based characteristics divided humans into superior and inferior races. These theories had no scientific merit and were later thoroughly discredited. But in the 1920s, these dubious theories of racial superiority supported measures such as immigration restriction and eugenic sterilization laws. Eugenics was a pseudo-science based on notions of racial superiority. Eugenicists claimed that the Anglo-Saxon Protestant "race" was superior to all others, including Jews, Southern Europeans, and Catholics, as well as nonwhites. Racial superiority, according to eugenic reformers, might be compromised not only by mixing with inferior groups but also by the propagation of individuals whose mental or moral condition rendered them inferior, and whose offspring would diminish the quality of the Anglo-Saxon "stock."

Several states had enacted eugenic laws that allowed the state to sterilize "inferior" individuals without their knowledge or consent. These laws authorized government and medical officials to determine whether or not an individual was inferior, or "feebleminded," and to order that the person be sterilized. Opponents of eugenic sterilization, mostly Catholic activists, challenged these laws in several states. In an effort to put an end to such challenges, eugenic advocates decided to test the constitutionality of the Virginia compulsory sterilization law. Their plan was to bring the case all the way to the U.S. Supreme Court, which they expected to uphold the law.

The proponents of the law selected the case of Carrie Buck, in part because she was white. Eugenic advocates did not want race to be at the center of the case, especially because eugenic sterilization laws did not target particular races; they simply targeted the "feebleminded." Feeblemindedness was a loosely defined criterion often used to label poor, immigrant, or minority women who were sexually active. At the age of seventeen, Carrie Buck, the daughter of an unmarried woman, was raped and became pregnant; as a result, she was sent to a state institution for the feebleminded. Buck was labeled as feebleminded because she had borne a child out of wedlock and was therefore deemed morally unfit for parenthood.

Carrie Buck was sterilized in 1927. The following year, Buck's sister Doris was taken to the Virginia Colony for Epileptics and the Feebleminded and sterilized at age sixteen. She was told that she had had an appendectomy. Later, Doris Buck married and tried to get pregnant. None of the physicians she consulted told her why she could not conceive. She finally learned the truth in 1979. "I broke down and cried. My husband and I wanted children desperately. We were crazy about them. I never knew what they'd done to me."

No evidence established that Carrie Buck, her mother, or her daughter was below normal intelligence. Buck's daughter died as a child, but her teachers described the girl as bright. In writing the majority opinion for the Supreme Court that upheld the law, Justice Oliver Wendell Holmes wrote, "Three generations of imbeciles are enough." Within the next few years, thirty states had compulsory sterilization laws, and the number of operations rose dramatically. In the 1930s, the Nazis in Germany modeled their sterilization policies on the California law. Finally, in the 1980s, a rare alliance of traditional Catholics and feminist activists succeeded in repealing compulsory sterilization laws.

Science, Religion, and the Scopes Trial

Populist leader and longtime reformer William Jennings Bryan was among those troubled by eugenics. In his last public crusade, Bryan opposed another scientific theory in a courtroom in Dayton, Tennessee, in July 1925. Tennessee had recently enacted the Butler Act, which made it illegal to teach the theory of evolution in the schools. The American Civil Liberties Union (ACLU) announced that it would defend any teacher charged with violating the Butler Act. A twenty-four-year-old science teacher from the local high school, John Thomas Scopes, agreed to test the law. Using a state-approved textbook, Scopes taught a lesson on evolutionary theory on April 24 to his Rhea County High School science class. He was arrested on May 7 and quickly indicted by a grand jury. Bryan agreed to represent the prosecution; famed Chicago criminal lawyer Clarence Darrow headed the ACLU's team of defense lawyers.

Almost all advocates on both sides of the Scopes trial were Christians who disagreed over how to interpret the Bible.

Bryan did not oppose science, but he objected to its misapplication. Darrow did not oppose religion. But he argued that religious fundamentalists—"creationists" who believed in the literal interpretation of the Bible—should not determine the way science was taught in the schools. Reporters at the time, and since, cast the trial as a struggle between religion and science, with rural and small-town Americans on the side of creationism and secular urbanites supporting evolution. But the divide was not so clear-cut. Almost all advo-

The Rise and Fall of Man

Primate   **Neanderthal Man**   **Socrates**   **W.J.Bryan**

■ This satiric political cartoon, published during the Scopes trial, depicts the theory of evolution as the development of humans from their origins as apes to the "survival of the fittest," portrayed as William Jennings Bryan. Bryan argued the case against evolution in the famous courtroom drama.

cates on both sides of the Scopes trial were Christians who disagreed over how to interpret the Bible. They were also believers in science; those opposed to the teaching of evolution considered it to be an unscientific theory.

The Scopes trial also contained elements of popular entertainment. Dubbed "the Monkey trial" because Darwin's theory of evolution demonstrated that humans evolved from an earlier primate form from which monkeys and chimpanzees also descended, the trial was one of the first national media events. The judge invited reporters from around the country, including broadcast journalists. The Scopes trial was the first jury trial broadcast on live radio. More than 900 spectators packed the courtroom, and hundreds more gathered in the streets, where a carnival atmosphere prevailed, complete with souvenir stands, food vendors, itinerant preachers, and hucksters, including numerous chimpanzees accompanied by their trainers.

The jury reached a guilty verdict in just nine minutes. Bryan technically won the case, but most reporters deemed the spectacle a victory for Darrow and the teaching of evolution. That assessment was premature. The Tennessee Supreme Court overturned the verdict on a technicality, robbing Darrow of his chance to take the case to the U.S. Supreme Court. Before the trial, most science textbooks included discussion of evolution; after the trial, material on evolution began to disappear. Laws against the teaching of evolution remained on the books until the U.S. Supreme Court overturned an Arkansas law in 1968.

The Scopes trial did not resolve the debate between creationists and evolutionists, and the controversy continued throughout the century. As late as 2000, the Board of Education in Kansas ruled that creationism and evolution were both unproven theories and that both could be taught in the schools.

Consumer Dreams and Nightmares

Unlike faith and politics, the material prosperity of many in the Jazz Age seemed a unifying force. During the 1920s, spending on recreation nearly doubled. Faith in continuing prosperity promoted the extension of consumer credit to unprecedented heights. Previously, the only major item routinely purchased on credit was a house. But in the twenties, installment buying became the rage for a wide range of consumer goods, from autos and radios to household appliances. Consumer debt rose from $2.6 billion in 1919 to $7.1 billion in 1929. As one official in a midwestern loan company remarked, "People don't think anything nowadays of borrowing sums they'd never have thought of borrowing in the old days. They will assume an obligation for $2,000 today as calmly as they would have borrowed $300 or $400 in 1890." This habit of buying on credit boosted the standard of living for many but also left families in a precarious situation and vulnerable to the vagaries of the broader economy. The stock market crash and subsequent depresion made that vulnerability vividly clear.

Marketing the Good Life

DOCUMENT

Advertisements from 1925 and 1927

Advertising fueled much of the new spending. As one contemporary reporter noted, "Advertising is to business what fertilizer is to a farm." According to advertisers, consumer goods promised health, beauty, success, and the means to eliminate personal and embarrassing flaws, such as bad breath or dandruff. Cigarette companies used advertising to promote smoking as a symbol of independence for women and as a means to achieve beauty. Clever advertising campaigns promised women that if they would "reach for a Lucky Strike" instead of a sweet, they would remain slim, healthy, and sexually appealing.

Advertising also fostered a vision of big business as a benevolent force, promoting individual happiness. In his 1925 best-seller *The Man That Nobody Knows*, advertising executive Bruce Barton portrayed Jesus as a businessman who gathered a group of twelve followers who believed in his enterprise and, through effective public relations and advertising, sold his product to the world. The consumer culture had its temples: movie palaces, department stores, and the 1920s innovation, the shopping center. Kansas City's elegant Country Club Plaza was the first shopping center in the nation.

A much less successful venture was the Florida land boom, based on fantasies of a consumer paradise. When World War I closed off routes to the European playgrounds of American elites, shrewd developers in the sunshine state sparked a frenzy of investment in Florida real estate. To create "earthly paradises" and resorts, developers rushed to construct roads and find new land on which to build.

Human folly and nature's fury contributed to the Florida land boom and bust. The boom peaked in 1925 and quickly collapsed. In 1926 a hurricane hit Miami, killing 130 people and causing millions of dollars of property damage. Another hurricane in 1928 killed more than 1,000 people and destroyed several towns. The destruction wrought by the hurricanes, and the exposure of exaggerated promotional advertisements and inflated prices, quickly put an end to land speculation in Florida.

Writers and Critics

Some social critics claimed that consumerism fostered not only economic disasters such as the Florida land boom but also a stifling conformity. Sinclair Lewis was one of several

JUST GOING ALONG FOR THE RIDE

Many a General spare tire is never put to service during the single ownership of a car—they just go along for the ride. It is this year round freedom from tire worry that has spoiled General Tire users for any other tire. But more important is the factor of safety at today's high speeds. Generals are blowout proof and skid-safe and the exclusive low pressure feature makes comfort a luxurious reality. All of these advantages cost so little when you total up General's almost unheard of big mileage. The General Tire & Rubber Co., Akron, O.

The New GENERAL DUAL BALLOON —goes a long way to make friends

Advertising Archive Ltd.

■ In the 1920s, advertisers used sexualized images to sell all sorts of products. This advertisement for automobile tires provides very little information about the product but evokes images of fun and romance to capture consumers' attention.

novelists of the twenties whose books expressed biting criticism of the frantic pursuit of material gain and status. George Babbitt, the protagonist of Lewis's novel *Babbitt* (1922), struggles to become accepted and successful in his small town by conforming to the empty materialism and standardized opinions accepted and prized by his neighbors.

F. Scott Fitzgerald wrote not about small-town conformity, as Lewis did, but about the modern urban life that was its antithesis. Fitzgerald glamorized, criticized, and in many ways embodied the giddy nightlife and status seeking of the Jazz Age. Born in St. Paul, Minnesota, into a family of modest means, he grew up admiring and emulating the wealthy. He married glamorous flapper Zelda Sayre, daughter of a prominent Alabama judge, and together they embraced the dizzy, indulgent, free-spirited life of the decade. But Fitzgerald's novels, including *This Side of Paradise* (1920), *The Beautiful and the Damned* (1922), and *The Great Gatsby* (1925), criticized the era's obsessions with success, glamour, consumerism, advertising, and status. The Fitzgeralds, along with other writers who were critical of American superficiality and conformity, moved to Paris. Eventually, the life Fitzgerald both lived and criticized caught up with him. By the end of the decade, he—like the nation—was broken by his excesses. In 1931 he came home to Baltimore an alcoholic; Zelda was diagnosed with schizophrenia and spent the rest of her life in mental institutions.

Poverty amid Plenty

Most Americans in the 1920s were neither investing in Florida real estate nor frequenting expatriate American writer Gertrude Stein's Paris salon. Even so, they were not immune to the desires and dreams that the consumer society sparked. The middle class and the more prosperous members of the working class enjoyed many of the comforts, amusements, and appliances that the booming economy made available. The poor, by contrast, struggled just to make ends meet. Throughout the twenties, the nation's poorest people continued to be the most mobile, moving in search of jobs, security, and a place they could settle and call home. Henry Crews, son of a white Georgia sharecropper, longed for "that single house where you were born, where you lived out your childhood . . . your anchor in the world." But he never had such a

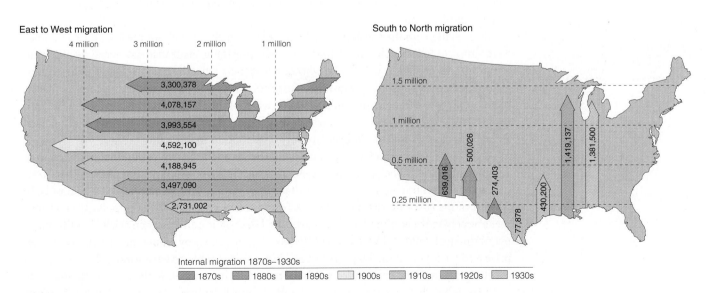

■ MAP 21.2
AMERICANS ON THE MOVE, 1870s–1930s   Between the 1870s and the 1930s, millions of Americans moved around the country, mostly from East to West, but also from South to North.

home. Like that of many other hardworking sharecroppers and factory workers, his family moved frequently in search of a better life, a dream that often proved elusive.

Sharecropping required hard work and careful planning to carve out a meager life, but many did so with pride. Ed Brown, a young black sharecropper, had no formal education but considered himself "pretty schemy." He worked on six different plantations, moving about in search of better circumstances or to escape from debt or threats of violence. Although he and his wife, Willie Mae, were never able to buy a place of their own, they did improve their circumstances over time. When they finally got out of debt and secured a bit of cash, they used it to adorn their meager cabin. In 1929 they bought an old Model T Ford. But finding it too costly to maintain, they swapped it for a cow and a butter churn and dasher, which provided more practical benefits. Meanwhile, Ed took odd jobs to earn extra money, while Willie Mae took care of the children, picked cotton, took in laundry, and, as Ed noted with appreciation, kept "things . . . lookin very pretty."

Industrial workers struggled throughout the decade, especially in a political climate hostile to unions. With the crushing of labor radicalism in the Red Scare after World War I, union organizing and strikes declined. But workers continued to protest low wages and poor working conditions. In March 1929, young women textile workers in Elizabethton, a small town nestled in the Blue Ridge Mountains of eastern Tennessee, closed down the American Glanzstoff plant in protest against low wages, petty rules, and arrogant employers. Soon, the protest spread to textile mills across the region. At Glanzstoff, the strikers returned to work when the company promised better pay and agreed not to discriminate against union members. But the employers broke their promises, so the women struck again. The governor sent in the National Guard, armed with machine guns. More than 1,000 people were arrested in confrontations with the troops.

The Stock Market Crash

The symbolic end of the 1920s arrived on "Black Tuesday," October 29, 1929, when the inflated and overextended stock market came crashing down. In one day, stocks fell in value $14 billion. By the end of the year, stock prices were down 50 percent; by 1932, they had dropped another 30 percent. In three years, $74 billion of the nation's wealth had vanished. The effect on the economy was catastrophic. Industrial production fell by half. More than 100,000 businesses went bankrupt. Banks failed at an alarming rate: more than 2,000 closed in 1931 alone. Unemployment rose to staggering levels, reaching 25 percent by 1932 and rarely dropping below 17 percent throughout the 1930s.

In keeping with the social policies that had prevailed throughout the 1920s, relief efforts were slim. No federal relief or welfare, no unemployment insurance, no Social Security, no job programs existed to help those who had lost their jobs, their savings, and their homes. Although many wealthy people lost their fortunes, which had been built on speculative investments, the poor suffered the most. People who lost their homes and farms moved into makeshift shelters in shantytowns, which they nicknamed "**Hoovervilles**" to mock the ineffectual efforts of President Herbert Hoover to respond to their plight.

The causes of the stock market crash and the decade-long depression that followed were complex and varied. Stock prices had risen dramatically, especially at the end of the 1920s. Speculators had been purchasing stocks on 10 percent margins, meaning they put down only 10 percent of the cost and borrowed the rest from brokers and banks. The popularity of installment buying in the consumer goods market had devastating effects when applied in this manner to the stock market. Investors expected to get rich quickly by selling their stocks at a higher price and paying back the loans from their huge profits. This system worked for a few years, encouraging investors with limited funds to make risky investments in the hope of gaining large fortunes. When the price of stocks spiraled out of control, far beyond their actual value, creditors demanded repayment of their loans, and investors were unable to pay their debts.

INTERPRETING HISTORY

Mario Puzo, *The Fortunate Pilgrim*

*I*talians, like most other European immigrants, established households where almost everyone worked to support the family. Fathers earned wages, mothers often took in boarders or did piecework at home to earn extra money, and sons and daughters found jobs in sweatshops and factories. Most immigrants married within their own ethnic groups. Often, immigrant families were torn by fierce generational conflicts, as old-world parents tried to maintain traditional ways while their American children struggled to break free. This generational struggle beset nearly every immigrant group.

Mario Puzo, the Italian American novelist best known for The Godfather, was among the many children of immigrants to express the cultures and experiences of newcomers through the arts. His autobiographical novel The Fortunate Pilgrim is a portrait of life in the Italian community of New York City in the early years of the century. The book depicts the struggles and triumphs of an Italian immigrant family. The men work long hours for meager wages while the women struggle to maintain the family. Mothers gather on tenement stoops to bemoan the behavior of their Americanized children, yet they dream the American dream of a better life. At the end of the book, the mother's dream comes true, and the family moves to a suburban home in Long Island. Yet it is a bittersweet ending, for she and her family realize the loss of the vibrant community that, for all its hardship and poverty, had sustained them in the city.

Each tenement was a village square; each had its group of women, all in black, sitting on stools and boxes and doing more

Mario Puzo, author of *The Fortunate Pilgrim* and *The Godfather.*

than gossip. They recalled ancient history, argued morals and social law, always taking their precedents from the mountain village in southern Italy they had escaped, fled from many years ago. And with what relish their favorite imaginings! Now: What if their stern fathers were transported by some miracle to face the problems *they* faced every day? Or their mothers of the quick and heavy hands? What shrieks if *they* as daughters had dared as these American children dared? If *they* had presumed.

The women talked of their children as they would of strangers. It was a favorite topic, the corruption of the innocent by the new land. Now: Felicia, who lived around the corner of 31st Street. What type of daughter was she who did not cut short her honeymoon on news of her godmother's illness, the summons issued by her own mother? A real whore. No no, they did not mince words. Felicia's mother herself told the story. And a son, poor man, who could not wait another

year to marry when his father so commanded? Ahhh, the disrespect. *Figlio disgraziato.* Never could this pass in Italy. The father would kill his arrogant son; yes, kill him. And the daughter? In Italy—Felicia's mother swore in a voice still trembling with passion, though this had all happened three years ago, the godmother recovered, the grandchildren the light of her life—ah, in Italy the mother would pull the whore out of her bridal chamber, drag her to the hospital bed by the hair of her head. Ah, Italia, Italia; how the world changed and for the worse. What madness was it that made them leave such a land? Where fathers commanded and mothers were treated with respect by their children.

Each in turn told a story of insolence and defiance, themselves heroic, long-suffering, the children spitting Lucifers saved by an application of Italian discipline—the razor strap or the *Tackeril.* And at the end of each story each woman recited her requiem. *Mannaggi a America!*—Damn America. But in the hot summer night their voices were filled with hope, with a vigor never sounded in their homeland. Here now was money in the bank, children who could read and write, grandchildren who would be professors if all went well. They spoke with guilty loyalty of customs they had themselves trampled into dust.

Questions

1. What seem to be the particular contrasts between cultural values in a southern Italian village and in New York City that these mothers worry most about?

2. Can you think of other, more recent immigrant groups in the United States who might be wrestling with similar dilemmas arising from inevitable cultural tensions in the immigrant experience? ∎

Source: Mario Puzo, *The Fortunate Pilgrim* (New York: Random House, 1997), pp. 10–11.

The collapse of the stock market alone would not necessarily have caused such a severe and prolonged depression. Poor decision making by financial and political leaders exacerbated underlying weaknesses in the economy. The Federal Reserve curtailed the amount of money in circulation and raised interest rates, making it more difficult for people to get loans and pay off their debts. These policies had profound worldwide implications and contributed to an international crisis. Banks in Germany and Austria, for example, depended on loans from the United States, and many went bankrupt, causing a ripple effect across Europe. The Hawley-Smoot Tariff of 1930 also contributed to the downward spiral. The new high tariff was intended to protect American commodities from competition from cheaper foreign goods. Foreign governments retaliated by raising their own tariffs to keep out American goods. These monetary and trade policies backfired, and the economic crisis spread throughout the western industrial world.

VIDEO
"Prosperity of the 1920s and the Great Depression"

Within the United States, the unequal distribution of wealth exacerbated the effects of the economic downturn. The nation may have looked prosperous, but most of the wealth was concentrated in the hands of a small number of people. If average Americans had been able to buy more cars, household appliances, and other products, those industries might have survived, and the economy might have recovered more quickly. Political leaders, and the business-oriented public policies they had promoted throughout the decade, left the country ill prepared to address the crisis and meet the needs of families deprived of their means of livelihood.

Conclusion

The stock market collapse, and the prolonged depression that followed, revealed the flaws in the economic system that spurred the apparent prosperity of the 1920s. Beneath the visible affluence was the hidden poverty that prevailed throughout the decade. National leaders promoted business interests and paid little attention to social welfare, the environment, or the need to regulate the economy. By the end of the 1920s, it was clear that Prohibition was a dismal failure and that the federal government was ill equipped to enforce it.

Although political reform withered, cultural vitality flowered. Hollywood emerged as a major industry, and the Jazz Age reflected the widespread appeal of African American music. A black arts movement flourished, centered in Harlem, and writers—disenchanted with the status quo—gathered in Greenwich Village or moved to France. Across the country, a youth culture challenged the gender and sexual mores of the past. Consumer culture expanded as increasing numbers of families purchased cars, radios, and new fashions. Few who were involved in the private preoccupations of the decade could have foreseen the disaster ahead, when the stock market crashed and the Depression set in.

Sites to Visit

Harlem: Mecca of the New Negro
etext.lib.virginia.edu/harlem/
This site is the online text of the March 1925 *Survey Graphic Harlem Number*, which includes writings of many Harlem Renaissance writers.

Calvin Coolidge
www.ipl.org/div/POTUS/ccoolidge.html
This site contains basic information about Coolidge's election and presidency and online biography.

Warren G. Harding
www.ipl.org/div/POTUS/wgharding.html
This site contains basic information about Harding's election and presidency and online biography.

Herbert Hoover
www.ipl.org/div/POTUS/hchoover.html
This site contains basic information about Hoover's election and presidency and online biography.

Harlem, 1900–1940: An African American Community
www.si.umich.edu/CHICO/Harlem/
> This site of the New York Public Library's Schomburg Center for Research in Black Culture includes information and articles about the history of Harlem as a center of African American cultural life.

Scopes Trial
xroads.virginia.edu/~UG97/inherit/1925home.html
> This site from the University of Virginia's American Studies program includes images, documents, and articles relating to the Scopes Trial.

Temperance and Prohibition
prohibition.osu.edu/
> This site from Ohio State University covers the history of temperance and prohibition in the United States.

Jazz Age: Flapper Culture and Style
www.geocities.com/flapper_culture/
> This site includes images, descriptions, and information on famous "flappers" of the 1920s.

For Further Reading

General

Ann Douglas, *Terrible Honesty: Mongrel Manhattan in the 1920s* (1995).

Lynn Dumenil, *The Modern Temper: American Culture and Society in the 1920s* (1995).

David J. Goldberg, *Discontented America: The United States in the 1920s* (1999).

Robert S. Lynd and Helen Merrell Lynd. *Middletown* (1929).

The Business of Politics

Kendrick A. Clements, *Hoover, Conservation, and Consumerism: Engineering the Good Life* (2000).

John Kenneth Galbraith, *The Great Crash, 1929* (1955).

William E. Leuchtenberg, *The Perils of Prosperity, 1914–1932* (1958, 1993).

David Farber, *Sloan Rules: Afred P. Sloan and the Triumph of General Motors* (2002).

The Decline of Reform

Nancy Cott, *The Grounding of Modern Feminism* (1987).

Matthew Frye Jacobson, *Whiteness of a Different Color: European Immigrants and the Alchemy of Race* (1998).

Desmond S. King, *Making Americans: Immigration, Race, and the Origins of the Diverse Democracy* (2000).

Nancy MacLean, *Behind the Mask of Chivalry: The Making of the Second Ku Klux Klan* (1994).

Hollywood and Harlem

Beth Bailey, *From Front Porch to Back Seat: Courtship in Twentieth-Century America* (1988).

Ray Batchelor, *Henry Ford, Mass Production, Modernism and Design* (1994).

Nathan Irvin Huggins, *The Harlem Renaissance* (1971).

Virginia Scharff, *Taking the Wheel: Women and the Coming of the Motor Age* (1991).

Science on Trial

John M. Barry, *Rising Tide: The Great Mississippi Flood of 1927 and How It Changed America* (1997).

Daniel Kevles, *In the Name of Eugenics: Genetics and the Uses of Human Heredity* (1985).

Garry Wills, *Under God: Religion and American Politics* (1990).

Consumer Dreams and Nightmares

William Frazer and John J. Guthrie Jr., *The Florida Land Boom: Speculation, Money, and the Banks* (1995).

Jacqueline Jones, *The Dispossessed: America's Underclass from the Civil War to the Present* (1992).

Jackson Lears, *Fables of Abundance: A Cultural History of Advertising in America* (1994).

For quizzes and other resources on these topics, go to www.longmanamericanhistory.com.

PART EIGHT

From Depression and War to World Power, 1929–1953

THE GREAT DEPRESSION AND WORLD WAR II TESTED AMERICANS' faith in their federal government to a degree unmatched in the nation's history. Economic collapse in the 1930s and the threat of Nazi and Japanese aggression from 1941 to 1945 presented challenges beyond the reach of ordinary citizens, local communities, and businesses acting alone. The federal government began to take more responsibility for economic and social well-being at home and for the spread of American values around the world.

The Great Depression resulted in a fundamental reordering of American politics. President Franklin Delano Roosevelt (FDR), who took office in 1933, believed that the federal government must assume an active role in banking, agriculture, and social welfare. He sponsored a large number of federal initiatives, known collectively as the New Deal. The New Deal aimed to put people back to work, restore faith in American businesses, boost purchasing power among consumers, and cushion the effects of economic downturns on industrial workers.

The effects of the New Deal were uneven. Many workers, including domestic servants, agricultural laborers, and part-time and seasonal employees, did not qualify for Social Security and other benefits. In the South, government policies that discouraged landowners from planting crops led to the displacement of many black and white sharecropping families. On the other hand, employees of many large companies won higher wages and improved job security as a result of militant labor protests. African American civil rights activists, local communist organizations such as urban Unemployed Councils, and southern sharecroppers' and tenants' unions gave voice to the groups hit hardest by the Depression.

The New Deal did not end the Depression. On the morning of December 7, 1941, the Japanese conducted a surprise air attack on the U.S. Pacific naval fleet stationed in Pearl Harbor, Hawaii. Americans reacted with shock and outrage to what the president called this "day of infamy." The U.S. entry into World War II put large numbers of Americans back to work, many of them in the expanding defense industries.

The conflict brought Americans together in shared hardship, sacrifice, and national purpose. At the same time, the war placed strains on the social fabric. All over the country, family members separated from one another to search for work. In the Midwest, blacks and whites competed for scarce wartime resources, such as housing. On the West Coast, more than 100,000 Japanese immigrants and U.S. citizens of Japanese descent were forced into internment camps.

Elected to an unprecedented fourth term in 1944, Roosevelt proved to be a commanding leader during wartime as well as economic depression. In the last stages of the war, the president met several times with his British and Soviet counterparts, Winston Churchill and Josef Stalin, to plan for the postwar reconstruction of Europe and Asia. Roosevelt's death in April 1945 catapulted Vice President Harry S. Truman into the presidency. Germany surrendered to the Allies the next month. In August 1945, the new president authorized the dropping of atomic bombs on the Japanese cities of Hiroshima and Nagasaki, effectively ending the war in the Pacific. Together, the two bombs killed 120,000 Japanese civilians and wounded at least 130,000 more. The Atomic Age ushered in a new chapter in the history of human warfare.

Together with its allies, the United States emerged victorious from the war, but unlike its allies, America escaped physical destruction. Yet in many respects the postwar world was radically different from the world of the 1930s. The Soviet Union, an ally in the war against Germany and Japan, emerged as America's greatest enemy. The development of weapons of mass destruction introduced a new and profound threat to the natural environment, as well as to humans. To secure its supremacy in world affairs, the United States helped to form the North Atlantic Treaty Organization (NATO). For the first time, Americans were part of a multinational peacetime alliance, one that required them to defend a member of the alliance even if they themselves were not attacked.

World War II also profoundly altered life in the United States. The perceived communist threat led some Americans to suspect domestic groups of internal subversion: African Americans agitating for their civil rights, labor leaders attempting to organize southern factories, and leftists who expressed support for communism in general and the Soviet Union in particular. Supported by government contracts, the defense industry became an integral part of the nation's economy.

Recovering quickly from the disruptions of war, returning soldiers and their wives hoped to settle down to a normal family life. These couples produced the baby boom, a generation that shaped American culture and society in significant ways. In the new and growing suburbs, many (predominantly white) Americans achieved their dream of home ownership, and businesses found plenty of room to expand in new industrial parks. Yet, not all Americans shared in this newfound prosperity and security, and not all were willing to forgo their rights to free speech and free assembly in the struggle against communism.

1943 Smith-Connally Act
Zoot-suit riots in Los Angeles. Attacks on blacks in Detroit

1944 Normandy invasion on D-Day (June 6)
Servicemen's Readjustment Act (GI Bill)

1945 Harry S. Truman becomes president upon death of Roosevelt
First test of atomic bomb, Alamogordo, New Mexico
Atomic bombs dropped on Hiroshima and Nagasaki
V-E Day (May 7); V-J Day (Sept. 2)
United Nations created

1946 *Morgan v. West Virginia* outlaws segregation in interstate transportation
Winston Churchill gives "Iron Curtain" speech, Fulton, Missouri

1947 Jackie Robinson joins Brooklyn Dodgers
Taft-Hartley Act
Truman Doctrine of containing communism announced

1948 New Mexico and Arizona grant Indians right to vote
Modern state of Israel founded
Armed Services desegregated
Organization of American States (OAS) founded

1949 Billy Graham launches his first evangelical crusade in Los Angeles
Establishment of People's Republic of China
USSR acquires nuclear weapons

1950 North Korean troops invade South Korea
Internal Security Act of 1950
Senator Joseph McCarthy accuses State Department of harboring communists

1951 Ethel and Julius Rosenberg convicted of treason

1952 McCarran-Walter Act
Puerto Rico becomes self-governing commonwealth

1953 Korean War ends
Soviet leader Josef Stalin dies

Hardship and Hope in the 1930s: The Great Depression

WILL ROGERS WAS A CHEROKEE, A COMEDIAN, A PLAINSPOKEN CRITIC OF THE NATION'S RICH and powerful, a movie star, a journalist, and an adviser to President Franklin Delano Roosevelt (FDR). Rogers articulated a new vision of American national identity that took shape in the 1930s. In contrast to an earlier notion of the United States as an Anglo-Saxon country into which newcomers might assimilate, this new Americanism included ethnic minorities, particularly those of European immigrant background. The Great Depression tarnished the status of the nation's business elite and opened up the political process to party realignments and new leaders. The popular culture expressed and reflected this new Americanism; Will Rogers was its most prominent voice.

In the 1930s, the Great Depression gave rise to a cultural and political upheaval that helped propel Rogers to stardom and political influence. President Franklin Roosevelt coveted his support, and Rogers obliged by promoting the New Deal, the president's program for economic recovery. However, Rogers also pushed the president to the left by advocating such measures as taxing the rich and redistributing wealth. In 1932 Oklahoma nominated Rogers for president as the state's favorite son; three years later, California Democratic leaders urged him to run for the Senate. But in 1935, before any of these possibilities could come to fruition, Rogers died in a plane crash.

The response to Rogers's death illustrates his stature as a national leader and spokesperson for a new multicultural Americanism. Congress adjourned in his memory, President Roosevelt sent a well-publicized letter to Rogers's family, the governor of California proclaimed a day of mourning, flags flew at

■ Presidential candidate Franklin Delano Roosevelt (left) delighted in the support of comic Will Rogers (right) in 1932.

half staff, bells rang in Rogers's honor in more than 100 cities, and nearly 100,000 people filed by his coffin at Forest Lawn Cemetery. Radio stations across the country broadcast his memorial service from the Hollywood Bowl, presided over by a Protestant minister and a Catholic priest, while a

Yiddish performer sang a Hebrew mourning chant. Across town, Mexican American citizen groups placed a wreath on Olvera Street that read "Nosotros Lamentamos la Muerte de Will Rogers" ("We Mourn the Death of Will Rogers"). In the predominantly black Los Angeles community of Watts, an African American fraternal group called the Friends of Ethiopia joined black performers from Rogers's films in a parade to honor the Cherokee movie star who had spoken out publicly against Italy's 1935 invasion of Ethiopia. Back in his hometown of Claremore, Oklahoma, Cherokee Indians performed a death dance in memory of their fallen kinsman.

This massive national grieving reveals not only Rogers's popularity, but also the culture of 1930s America. The economic crisis unleashed changes in society that opened the door for a politically radical Cherokee Indian to become one of the most popular figures of the Great Depression. Millions of Americans experienced poverty—many for the first time. The shared experience of loss and suffering permeated the country.

Roosevelt drew a new political coalition into the Democratic party that elected him to the presidency four times. The Great Depression gave him the opportunity to forge a strong national government and to promote a more representative democracy. His inclusiveness efforts brought citizens of recent immigrant background into the political mainstream but stopped short of the color line. Nevertheless, African American voters abandoned the Republican party to vote for FDR.

The New Deal, a package of remedies put together by Franklin Roosevelt to address the problems of the Depression, provided relief to many Americans in need but did not eradicate poverty or end the Depression. Yet, as American families from every region of the country drew around their radios to hear the president's **fireside chats**, as they made heroes of Will Rogers and other outsider celebrities, and as they held onto their faith in the nation's promise in spite of its worst economic crisis, they helped forge a more inclusive nation.

> *The economic crisis opened the door for a politically radical Cherokee Indian to become one of the most popular figures of the Great Depression.*

The Great Depression

The Great Depression defined the 1930s in the United States. Part of a global economic crisis, it shaped American culture, the political life of the nation, the public policies that resulted, and the cultural expressions that reflected the spirit of the people during a time of national crisis. Its effects permeated the lives of Americans from the mansions of the wealthy to the shanties of the poor and from the boardrooms to the bedrooms. The Depression drove thousands of farmers from the drought-striken southern Great Plains to California. But the story is not simply one of despair and hardship. It is also one of strong communities, resourcefulness, and hope.

> *The story of the Depression is not simply one of despair and hardship. It is also one of strong communities, resourcefulness, and hope.*

Causes of the Crisis

The Great Depression of the 1930s was the worst economic depression in the nation's history. But it was neither the first nor the last. **Capitalism**, the economic system that forms the basis of the American economy, has cycles of ups and downs. Under capitalism, the free market operates with minimal interference from the government. In the United States, prior to the 1930s, the government stepped in to regulate the

■ Margaret Bourke-White in this 1937 photograph, "At the time of the Louisville Flood," depicts the painful irony of poverty in the midst of affluence. Here, hungry Americans line up at a breadline in front of a billboard proclaiming American prosperity.

economy primarily to protect economic competition. Progressive Era reforms prevented corporations from establishing monopolies, so that competition could flourish. In the free market economy, consumers would determine which companies would succeed, based on the quality of their products and services. Because the government did not determine the levels of industrial or agricultural productivity, and did not set the prices, the economy was subject to changing circumstances that led to times of prosperity and times of recession or, in the case of severe economic downturns, depression.

Before the 1930s, the United States provided no **welfare-state** benefits, such as medical care, relief from poverty, income for the unemployed, or old-age insurance. Without any policies that would serve as a safety net for workers who lost their jobs, many wage earners and their families fell into poverty during times of economic downturn. In the Great Depression of the 1930s, the economic crisis was so severe that one-quarter of the nation's workers, nearly 14 million people, lost their jobs, leaving them and their families—40 million people in all—without any income or security. Many of these people had never known poverty before. Among the newly poor were thousands of middle-class Americans who now faced the loss of their homes and savings. For working-class and poor Americans, the impact of the Depression was devastating because they had little economic security to begin with.

The Depression was a global economic catastrophe. Of the major world powers, only the Soviet Union—as a communist society, with state-directed labor, agriculture, and industry—was immune to the collapse of the capitalist system after 1929. In fact, its economy grew throughout the 1930s. The relative health of the Soviet economy led many people in troubled capitalist systems to look to communism as an alternative. Socialism also gained many converts across Europe.

The Great Depression

For many Americans, the Depression really began in the 1920s. Food production and distribution stumbled along weakly throughout the 1920s, leaving widespread rural poverty in its wake. During the 1920s, 1,200 big corporations absorbed more than 6,000 independent businesses. By 1929, 200 corporations controlled nearly half of all industry, which limited competition and made it difficult for new, smaller businesses to flourish.

Although the economy looked healthy on the surface, prosperity rested on an unsound foundation. Many people obtained consumer goods on credit, so when people lost their jobs, they could not pay their debts. Throughout the 1920s, the gap between the rich and poor increased. Nearly 80 percent of the nation's families had no savings at all. Americans with high annual incomes of $10,000 or more—2.3 percent of the people—held two-thirds of all savings. The concentration of wealth among the richest Americans during the 1920s contributed to the persistence of the crisis in the 1930s.

International factors also played a role in the economic collapse. American overseas loans soared in the 1920s, reaching $900 million by 1924 and $1.25 billion by 1928. Germany was a large borrower, for example. Following its defeat in World War I, Germany had been required to make large reparation payments to France and other countries. The United States provided loans to Germany to help the country make its payments. When the stock market crashed, foreign economies like that of Germany also weakened and could not repay their debts. To make matters worse, the United States had established high tariffs to keep foreign goods out of the country so that Americans would buy only American-made goods. This, in turn, encouraged other countries to establish their own tariff barriers. American exports fell sharply.

Surviving Hard Times

In human terms, the Depression of the 1930s dealt a devastating blow to large numbers of Americans: crushing poverty, hunger, humiliation, and loss of dignity and self-worth. Many felt a profound shame that they could no longer earn a living and support their families. The few jobs available often went to the young, strong, well-fed, and well-groomed. Thousands of citizens poured out their hearts in letters to the president, hoping that the government could provide some assistance. In 1934 an Oklahoma woman lamented, "The unemployed have been so long without food-clothes-shoes-medical care-dental care etc—we look pretty bad—so when we ask for a job we dont' get it. And we look and feel a little worse each day—when we ask for food they call us bums—it isent our fault . . . no we are not bums."

Families provided the first line of defense against disaster, especially in the early days of the crisis. Many families adapted to hard times by abandoning time-honored gender roles. As men lost jobs, women went to work. Working women did not take jobs from men; rather, they held jobs defined as "traditional women's work" as secretaries, nurses, and waitresses. These jobs offered lower wages than most jobs held by men. A white woman working for wages earned, on average, 61 percent of a white man's wages; a black woman earned a mere 23 percent. Still, they provided at least a modicum of much-needed income.

Many parents struggled to provide for their families under difficult conditions, sometimes risking their health and safety to do so. Erminia Pablita Ruiz Mercer remembered when her father was injured while working in the beet fields in 1933. "He didn't want to live if he couldn't support his family," so he risked experimental back surgery and died on the operating table. Young Erminia then dropped out of school to work as "a doughnut girl" to support her mother and sisters.

Enduring Discrimination

For many poor families, hard times were nothing new. As one African American noted, "The Negro was born in depression. It only became official when it hit the white man." Throughout the 1930s, black Americans suffered the impact of economic hard times disproportionately. By 1932 black unemployment reached 50 percent. With local white authorities in charge of relief, impoverished southern blacks had few places to turn for assistance. African Americans also faced increasing violence; the number of lynchings increased from eight in 1932 to twenty in 1935.

Many poor people joined the growing ranks of **hobos**, riding the rails from town to town, looking for work. But poverty did not erase racial hierarchies or sexual codes, especially for nine young African Americans who came to be known as the "Scottsboro Boys." On March 25, 1931, the youths, ranging in age from thirteen to twenty-one, were taken from a train in Paint Rock, Alabama, after a fight with a group of white men. Two white women, also on the train, accused the nine of rape. Narrowly avoiding a lynching, the youths were taken to jail in Scottsboro, where they began a long ordeal. Within two weeks, an all-white jury convicted them of rape, and they were sentenced to death. But in November 1932, the U.S. Supreme Court ordered a new trial on the grounds that the defendants did not get a fair trial.

The first defendant to be retried was quickly convicted again and sentenced to death. At this point, the case became a major rallying point for civil rights activists, liberals, and radicals throughout the 1930s. Support for the young men came from all over the world, including the British Parliament and the Communist party. In 1935 the U.S. Supreme Court reversed the second set of convictions on the grounds that excluding blacks from the jury denied the defendants due process. Yet, in the next two years, five of the defendants were again tried and found guilty. Although none of the Scottsboro Boys was executed, they all spent long years in prison.

Mexican American families could barely survive on the low wages paid to Mexican laborers. According to a 1933 study, working children's earnings constituted more than one-third of their families' total income. The work was often grueling. Julia Luna Mount recalled her first day at a Los Angeles cannery: "I didn't have money for gloves so I peeled chilies all day long by hand. After work, my hands were red, swollen, and I was on fire! On the streetcar going home, I could hardly hold on my hands hurt so much." Young Julia was lucky—her father saw her suffering and did not make her return to the cannery. But Carmen Bernal Escobar's father could not afford to be soft-hearted about work: "My father was a busboy and to keep the family going . . . in order to bring in a little more money . . . my mother, my grandmother, my mother's brother, my sister and I all worked together" at the cannery.

Those with cannery work, hard as it was, were among the fortunate. Many more Mexicans were deported. Between 1931 and 1934, more than 500,000 Mexicans and Mexican Americans—approximately one-third of the Mexican population in the United States—were sent to Mexico. Most were children born in the United States. Throughout the century, the United States opened or closed its doors to Mexican immigrants depending on the need for their labor. They were deported during the Depression when unemployment was high, then recruited again during the labor shortage of World War II.

AUDIO

Interview about Life in a Government Camp

The Dust Bowl

Severe drought exacerbated the difficulties of farmers across Oklahoma, Texas, Kansas, Colorado, and New Mexico, an area that came to be known as the **Dust Bowl**. Farmers had used the land mainly for grazing until high grain prices during World War I enticed them to plow

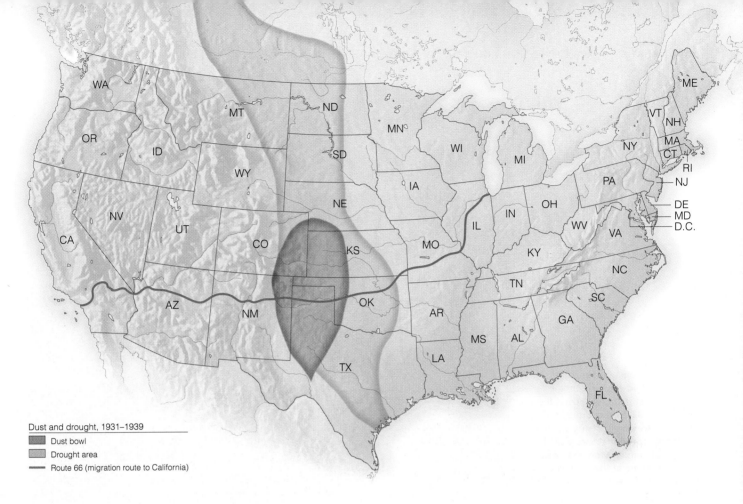

■ **MAP 22.1**
DUST AND DROUGHT, 1931–1939   Drought cut a giant swath across the middle of America during the years of the Great Depression. The hardest hit region was the Dust Bowl area of Oklahoma, Texas, New Mexico, Colorado, and Kansas. Many people fled the afflicted areas, abandoning farms, piling their belongings on their cars, and driving along Route 66 to California.

under millions of acres of natural grasslands to plant wheat. Plowing removed root systems from the soil, and years of little rainfall caused the land to dry up. By the middle of the decade, high winds picked up the loose topsoil, creating dust storms across the open plains. The ecological disaster drove 60 percent of the population out of the region.

Migrant farm families fleeing the Dust Bowl came to symbolize the suffering wrought by the Depression. The photographs of Dorothea Lange, the songs of Woody Guthrie, and the writings of John Steinbeck all immortalized their plight. Steinbeck's Pulitzer prize–winning novel *The Grapes of Wrath* (1939) and its film version have remained classics of American popular art. Writing in *The Nation* in 1936, Steinbeck described the Dust Bowl migrants streaming into California:

> Poverty-stricken after the destruction of their farms, their last reserves used up in making the trip, they have arrived so beaten and destitute that they have been willing at first to work under any conditions and for any wages offered. . . . They are not drawn from a peon class, but have either owned small farms or been farm hands in the early American sense, in which the "hand" is a member of the employing family. They have one fixed idea, and that is to acquire land and settle on it. . . . They are not easily intimidated. They are courageous, intelligent, and resourceful. Having gone through the horrors of the drought and with immense effort having escaped from it, they cannot be herded, attacked, starved, or frightened.

Thousands of **Okies** piled belongings on their cars and made their way to California in hopes of starting over. There they joined Mexican migrant farm workers, African American laborers, and others down on their luck, hoping for work.

Arthur Rothstein, 1936. Library of Congress

■ An Oklahoma farmer and his sons try to find shelter from the storm of dust that blew across the plains in 1935. Severe drought after years of excessive plowing created dry loose topsoil that was picked up by high winds. More than half of the residents of the Dust Bowl moved out of the area as a result of the devastation.

Presidential Responses to the Depression

Until the collapse of the economy, President Herbert Hoover's political achievements had earned wide admiration. He seemed the perfect embodiment of the spirit of the prosperous 1920s. But his ideas about politics and economics were ill suited to the crisis of the 1930s. Dissatisfaction with Hoover's response to the Depression gave Franklin Delano Roosevelt a landslide victory in the 1932 presidential election. Promising to take action to ease the nation's suffering, the optimistic Roosevelt seemed to embody hope for an end to the crisis.

Herbert Hoover: Tackling the Crisis

Had prosperity continued, Hoover might have left a legacy of presidential leadership to match his earlier achievements as a Progressive administrator of food relief in Europe. Declaring that "excessive fortunes are a menace to true liberty," he favored steeply graduated inheritance and income taxes on the wealthy, with no tax burden on the poor. He believed that society had a responsibility to care for those in need and that the prosperous should bear much of the burden. After the stock market crash, Hoover increased spending for public works—programs in which the government created jobs for people who needed employment—to the unprecedented sum of $700 million. He established the Reconstruction Finance Corporation to make government credit available to banks and other financial institutions. Seeking to restore confidence in the economy, he strove for a balanced budget by raising taxes and cutting spending—a strategy that underestimated the depth of the Depression and made the situation worse.

As the Depression set in and brought widespread misery, Hoover fully expected that charitable organizations would step in and provide aid to the poor. He believed that government relief to the needy had demoralizing effects on people. Even when it was clear that the crisis was beyond the help of charitable groups, Hoover remained strongly opposed to direct relief for the poor. Private giving did increase to record levels; unfortunately, it was not sufficient.

Hoover's popularity reached its lowest ebb in 1932. A group of World War I veterans in Portland, Oregon, organized a march on Washington, D.C., called the Bonus March. The veterans were due to receive a bonus of $1,000 each in 1945. The group had asked to have their bonuses early, in 1932, to help ease their suffering during the Depression. Hoover refused. More than 20,000 veterans traveled to Washington to petition Congress. The House passed a bill to pay the bonus immediately, but the Senate refused to follow suit. The determined veterans set up a tent city and settled in with their families. On the last day of the congressional session, when Hoover again refused to meet with the protesters, the veterans began to leave. But some did not depart quickly enough, and a police officer began shooting at the unarmed demonstrators, killing one person.

Army Chief of Staff Douglas MacArthur stepped in and escalated the violence. His troops used tear gas and bayonets to prod the veterans and their families to vacate the area, then set fire to the tent city. The attack injured more than 100 people and killed one baby. The image of federal troops assaulting a group of peaceful veterans stunned the public. Although MacArthur had ordered the brutality, the public directed its outrage against Hoover. As most people saw it, Hoover had heartlessly spurned the veterans' legitimate request. By the time of the 1932 election, Hoover had lost most of his public support.

IMAGE

Bonus Expeditionary Force March on Washington

Franklin Delano Roosevelt: The Pragmatist

In contrast to Hoover, Franklin Delano Roosevelt was born into a family of wealth and privilege whose ancestors included European aristocrats and passengers on the *Mayflower*. Pampered as a child, at age fourteen he went to Groton, then the nation's most exclusive boarding school; from there he attended Harvard College and Columbia Law School. In 1905, during his first year at Columbia, he married a distant cousin, Eleanor Roosevelt, the niece of President Theodore Roosevelt. Like Franklin, Eleanor came from a sheltered, upper-class background. But her early life, unlike his, was filled with sadness. Both her parents died when she was a young child, and at age ten she went to live with her grandmother, who left her in the care of a harsh governess. The young

Franklin D. Roosevelt Library

■ Franklin Delano Roosevelt during a radio broadcast, October 14, 1938. Roosevelt mastered the medium of radio and used it effectively to communicate directly to the people. In what came to be known as "fireside chats," Roosevelt addressed his millions of listeners as "my friends."

Songs of the Great Depression

Popular songs expressed the spirit, sorrows, and longings of Depression Era Americans. According to folk-music historian Alan Lomax, the 12-year-old daughter of a striking Harlan County, Kentucky, mineworker wrote "Which Side Are You On?" in 1937. The song became a popular anthem for labor militancy.

Woody Guthrie (1912–1967) wrote more than a thousand songs about the struggles of common people and the dispossessed. As a teenager, Guthrie left home to hitchhike, ride the rails, live in hobo camps, and follow migrant workers around the country. His song "Union Maid" expresses the hopes and spirit of union workers, and "So Long, It's Been Good to Know Yuh" captures the sorrows of Dust Bowl migrants.

Bettmann/CORBIS

Woody Guthrie, singer and songwriter, immortalized the spirit of ordinary Americans during the struggles of the Great Depression. His songs became anthems of the era and remain classics of American folk music.

Which Side Are You On? By Florence Reece (sung to the tune of an old English song, "Jack Munro")

Come all of you good workers
Good news to you I'll tell
Of how the good old union
Has come in here to dwell.

Chorus
Which side are you on,
Tell me, which side are you on?

My daddy was a miner,
He's now in the air an' sun,
Stick with him, brother miners,
Until this battle's won.

They say in Harlan County
There are no neutrals there
You'll either be a union man,
Or a thug for J. H. Blair.

O gentlemen, can you
stand it,
O tell me if you can,

---

woman began to flourish when she went abroad to study. The rigorous education developed her strengths and confidence, which would serve her well during her marriage to FDR.

Franklin Roosevelt was elected to the New York State Senate in 1911, and in 1913 he became Assistant Secretary of the Navy. He ran unsuccessfully as the Democratic vice presidential nominee in 1920. His political plans derailed suddenly in 1921 when he was stricken with polio. The painful and incapacitating illness threw the normally ebullient young man into despair. He had always assumed that he would control his own destiny. Now he could no longer use his legs. The formerly athletic Roosevelt depended on braces, crutches, and a wheelchair to move around. But his upbringing had given him extraordinary reserves of self-confidence and optimism, and these qualities helped to sustain him in the face of his paralysis.

FDR's bout with polio did nothing to dampen his political ambitions. He became governor of New York in 1928, following in the footsteps of Theodore Roosevelt. But, unlike

TABLE 22-1

The Election of 1932

Candidate	Political Party	Popular Vote (%)	Electoral Vote
Franklin D. Roosevelt	Democratic	57.4	472
Herbert Hoover	Republican	39.7	59
Norman Thomas	Socialist	2.2	—

Will you be a lousy scab,
Or will you be a man?

Don't scab for the bosses,
Don't listen to their lies,
Us poor folks haven't got a chance,
Unless we organize.

Union Maid By Woody Guthrie (first verse and chorus)

There once was a union maid
Who never was afraid
Of goons and ginks and company
    finks
And the deputy sheriffs who made
    the raids;
She went to the union hall
When a meeting it was called
And when the company boys
    came 'round
She always stood her ground.

Chorus
Oh, you can't scare me.
I'm sticking to the union, (3 times)
Oh, you can't scare me.
I'm sticking to the union, (2 times)
Till the day I die.

"So Long, It's Been Good to Know Yuh (Dusty Old Dust)" By Woody Guthrie (selected verses and chorus)

I've sung this song, but I'll sing it
    again,
Of the place that I lived on the
    wild, windy plains,
In the month called April, the
    county called Gray
And here's what all of the people
    there say:

Chorus
So long, it's been good to know ye;
    (3 times)
This dusty old dust is a-getting my
    home,
And I've got to be driftin' along.

A dust storm hit, and it hit like
    thunder;
It dustedus over, and it covered us
    under;
Blocked out the traffic and blocked
    out the sun.
Straight for home all the people did
    run.

The sweethearts sat in the dark and
    they sparked,
They hugged and kissed in that
    dusty old dark,
They sighed and cried, hugged and
    kissed

Instead of marriage, they talked like
    this:
Honey, so long, it's been good to
    know ye...

Now, the telephone rang, and it
    jumped off the wall;
That was the preacher a-making his
    call.
He said, "Kind friend, this may be
    the end;
You've got your last chance of sal-
    vation of sin."

The churches was jammed, and the
    churches was packed,
And that dusty old dust storm
    blowed so black;
The preacher could not read a word
    of his text,
And he folded his specs and he
    took up collection, said:
So long, it's been good to know
    ye. . . .

Questions

1. *What makes the songs emblematic of the era in which they were written?*

2. *How are issues of class addressed in these folk tunes?* ■

---

his Republican cousin, Franklin was a Democrat. In the 1932 presidential campaign, FDR made few specific proposals, but promised the American people a "New Deal."

"Nothing to Fear but Fear Itself"

In his inaugural address, Roosevelt endeavored to ease the nation's anxieties with reassuring words: "Let me assert my firm belief that the only thing we have to fear is fear itself—nameless, unreasoning, unjustified terror which paralyzes needed efforts to convert retreat into advance." Roosevelt launched his advance immediately. Panic had prompted many Americans to pull out their bank savings, causing many banks to fail. To stop the run on banks, FDR called Congress into a special session and announced a "bank holiday," temporarily closing all the nation's banks. He could have nationalized the banking system, a move toward socialism that would likely have received widespread support. But Roosevelt favored government regulation, not government ownership. He proposed the Emergency Banking Bill, providing government support for private banks. Congress passed the bill instantly, to the applause of the bankers who helped draft it.

In the first of his "fireside chats" to millions of radio listeners, whom he addressed as "my friends," Roosevelt assured citizens that the banks that reopened were sound. He

DOCUMENT

Franklin D. Roosevelt, First Inaugural Address (1933)

DOCUMENT

Franklin
Roosevelt,
fireside chat
(September
6, 1936)

used the medium of radio skillfully to explain his policies and to communicate comforting and reassuring messages that reached people in the intimate setting of their homes. The next day, bank deposits exceeded withdrawals as a result of the confidence he inspired.

The New Deal

The New Deal drew on Progressive Era reform impulses to extend the reach of the federal government to solve social problems. It provided assistance to many Americans suffering the effects of the Depression and established the welfare state that would last half a century. Based on pragmatism, experimentation, and shrewd political calculation, FDR's plan began with a flurry of activity in the first 100 days of his administration and developed into a more progressive agenda by 1935, often called the **second New Deal**. New Deal programs countered the cyclical nature of capitalism and offered a safety net for industrial workers. They legitimized labor unions and established a system of regulation and cooperation between industry and labor. They won Roosevelt a resounding reelection in 1936. Many New Deal programs failed, but those that succeeded created the foundation of the modern American state. The broad-based reform effort, however, did not end the Depression nor eradicate poverty.

The First Hundred Days

Roosevelt acted quickly and pragmatically. As one of his first acts, he encouraged Congress to repeal Prohibition. In 1933 the states quickly ratified the Twenty-First Amendment, repealing the Eighteenth. Repeal of Prohibition helped the economy by providing additional tax revenues from liquor sales, since they were once again legal, and a market for farmers' corn and wheat, which were used in the production of liquor. Congress created the Securities and Exchange Commission (SEC) to oversee the stock market and the Federal Deposit Insurance Corporation (FDIC) to reform the banking system and provide insurance for deposits.

One of FDR's most pressing challenges was to prop up prices for producers while keeping them low enough for consumers. Poverty in the midst of plenty was one of the Depression's cruelest ironies. Because farmers could no longer afford to transport their goods to market, food rotted while millions of people went hungry. Through the Agricultural Adjustment Act, the government sought to prop up farm prices by limiting supply. That is, it paid farmers to destroy livestock and take acreage out of production.

Library of Congress

■ **Dorothea Lange took photographs for the Farm Security Administration (FSA), documenting the lives of Depression-era migrants. This 1939 photo, "Mother and Children on the Road, Tulelake, Siskiyou County, California," is one of Lange's many portraits of impoverished families.**

Most Americans in need desperately wanted to work. They considered government relief a sign of failure and a source of deep shame and humiliation. Many citizens searched for ways to preserve their pride. One woman wrote to Eleanor Roosevelt asking to borrow money in order to avoid charity:

■ **MAP 22.2**
AREAS SERVED BY THE TENNESSEE VALLEY AUTHORITY The Tennessee Valley Authority (TVA) brought electricity to a large area in western Appalachia, one of the poorest regions in the country. The government-owned project strengthened the economy and improved living conditions in the area.

Please Mrs. Roosevelt, I do not want charity, only a chance from someone who will trust me. . . . I am sending you two of my dearest possessions to keep as security, a ring my husband gave me before we were married, and a ring my mother used to wear. . . . If you will consider buying the baby clothes, please keep them (rings) until I send you the money you spent. It is very hard to face bearing a baby we cannot afford to have, and the fact that it is due to arrive soon, and still there is no money for the hospital or clothing, does not make it any easier. I have decided to stay home, keeping my 7 year old daughter from school to help with the smaller children when my husband has work. . . . The 7 year old one is a good willing little worker and somehow we must manage—but without charity.

In March 1933, Congress passed the Federal Emergency Relief Administration (FERA), which provided $500 million in grants to the states for aid to the needy. Roosevelt placed Harry Hopkins in charge. Hopkins, an energetic and brash young reformer, disbursed $2 million during his first two hours on the job. He then persuaded Roosevelt to launch a temporary job program, the Civil Works Administration (CWA). The CWA provided government-sponsored jobs for more than 4 million workers. But the program came under fire from conservatives, and FDR ended it a few months later.

The New Deal included two major programs that addressed conservation and environmental issues. In 1933 Roosevelt combined his interest in conservation with his goal of providing work for unemployed young men. The Civilian Conservation Corps (CCC) operated under the control of the Army. CCC workers lived in camps, wore uniforms, and conformed to military discipline. They planted millions of trees, dug canals and ditches, built

New Deal

519

The Tennessee Valley Authority

Tennessee Valley Authority Act

more than 30,000 wilderness shelters, stocked rivers and lakes with nearly 1 billion fish, and preserved historic sites. Their work revived depleted forests and provided flood control. By 1935 the CCC had employed more than 500,000 young men and kept them, in FDR's words, "off the city street corners."

Another measure that linked natural resources to the recovery effort was the Tennessee Valley Authority (TVA), an experiment in government-owned utilities that brought power to rural areas along the Tennessee River in seven states in western Appalachia—among the poorest areas in the nation. This far-reaching government-owned project offered a radical alternative to American capitalism, based on private enterprise. Under the TVA, the government built five dams, improved twenty others, and constructed power plants; it produced and sold electricity to the valley's farmers and facilitated the development of industry in the region. The TVA also provided flood control. The TVA became one of the largest and cheapest suppliers of power in the nation.

The National Industrial Recovery Act (NIRA), passed by Congress in 1933, became the centerpiece of the first New Deal. The NIRA established the National Recovery Administration (NRA) to oversee regulation of the economy. In his second "fireside chat," Roosevelt called the NRA "a partnership in planning" between business and government. The NRA enabled businesses in each sector of the economy to form trade associations and set their own standards for production, prices, and wages. Section 7(a) of the NIRA also guaranteed collective bargaining rights to workers, sparking new hope for union organizers.

FDR's first 100 days also included the creation of the Home Owners' Loan Corporation, providing refinancing of home mortgages at low rates. Because the plan helped stem the tide of foreclosures and also guaranteed the repayment of loans, it pleased homeowners, banks, and real-estate interests. It helped gain for FDR the support of a large segment of the middle class.

One of the boldest New Dealers was John Collier, whom Roosevelt appointed as Commissioner of Indian Affairs. Collier opposed the policy of land allotment that the Dawes Act of 1887 had enacted. Under allotment, Native American land holdings had dwindled from 130 million acres to 49 million acres—much of it desert. Collier rejected the assumption that Indians' survival depended on their assimilation into white culture. He altered the government

■ On October 28, 1935, John Collier, Commissioner of Indian Affairs, stands with a group of Flathead Indian chiefs as Secretary of the Interior Harold L. Ickes signs the first constitution providing for Indian self-rule. Franklin Roosevelt appointed Collier to bring the New Deal to Native Americans.

AP/Wide World Photos

boarding schools' curriculum to include bicultural and bilingual education and eliminated military dress and discipline.

Collier's ideas came to fruition in the 1934 Indian Reorganization Act, which recognized the autonomy of Indian tribes, did away with the allotment program, and appropriated funds to help Indians add to their land holdings. It also provided for job and professional training programs as well as a system of agricultural and industrial credit. In keeping with Collier's goal of Indian self-government, each tribe decided whether to accept the terms of the Indian Reorganization Act. In the end, 181 tribes voted to accept the law, while seventy-seven opted out of it.

Monumental Projects Transforming the Landscape

The New Deal years gave rise to monumental construction projects that altered the landscape and affected the natural environment. In addition to the dams built as part of the TVA, gigantic new dams provided electricity and irrigation in the arid West. Construction on Hoover Dam on the Colorado River 30 miles from Las Vegas began in 1931. The huge Grand Coulee Dam across the Columbia River in Washington State provided electricity to much of the Northwest and irrigation for over half a million acres of land in the Columbia basin.

The Golden Gate Bridge, another Depression-era project, spanned the entrance to San Francisco Bay. When the bridge opened in 1937, 32,000 vehicles and 19,000 pedestrians passed over the picturesque engineering marvel on the first day. Monumental architecture also soared skyward in other cities. In 1930, construction began on the Empire State Building in New York City, the tallest building in the world up to that time.

Protest and Pressure from the Left and the Right

Despite these accomplishments, challenges to Roosevelt's New Deal took many forms. In spite of FDR's efforts to help businesses survive and remain profitable during the Depression, many business leaders continued to oppose the New Deal, charging that FDR was a dictator and that his program amounted to socialism. At the same time, FDR faced criticism from the left. Many people believed that Roosevelt's policies did not go far enough to ease the suffering caused by the economic crisis. Some thought that New Deal policies aimed at bolstering capitalism were ill-advised, and that capitalism itself was the problem. Disenchantment with capitalism drew many Americans to the cause of socialism and swelled the ranks of the small Communist party.

Many people believed that Roosevelt's policies did not go far enough to ease the suffering caused by the economic crisis.

By 1934 and 1935, much of the pressure on Roosevelt came from workers, whose hopes that the NIRA would guarantee collective bargaining rights were dashed by the intransigence of employers. In 1934 nearly 1.5 million workers participated in 1,800 strikes. Although most African Americans supported FDR and the Democratic party during the Depression, between 3,000 and 4,000 members of the black community of Birmingham, Alabama, joined the Communist party and related organizations during the 1930s. One successful effort at biracial organizing occurred in the Arkansas delta in 1934. The Southern Tenant Farmers' Union (STFU) brought together black and white tenants and sharecroppers to fight for better working conditions.

In addition to the communists, socialists, labor unions, and grassroots organizations that sprang up all over the country, a number of individuals proposed alternatives to Roosevelt's program and gained large followings. The most influential of these were Dr. Francis Townsend, Father Charles E. Coughlin, and Senator Huey P. Long. In 1934 Townsend, a retired physician and health commissioner from Long Beach, California, introduced an idea for a pension plan that sparked a nationwide grassroots movement. Townsend proposed a 2 percent national sales tax that would fund a pension of $200 a month for Americans over age sixty. The **Townsend Plan** became hugely popular, especially among elderly Americans. In 1936 a national survey indicated that half of all Americans favored the plan. Though the plan was never implemented, the groundswell of support that it generated probably hastened the development and passage of the old-age insurance system contained in the 1935 Social Security Act.

Coughlin also inspired a huge following. A Catholic priest from Canada, he served as pastor of a small church outside Detroit, Michigan. He began to broadcast his sermons on the radio, using his magnetic personality to address political as well as religious issues. Soon he became a media phenomenon, broadcasting through twenty-six radio stations to an audience estimated at 40 million. The "Radio Priest" called for a redistribution of wealth and attacked Wall Street, international bankers, and the evils of capitalism. But his message turned from social justice populism to right-wing bigotry. His virulent anti-Semitism and admiration for the fascist regimes of Adolf Hitler in Germany and Benito Mussolini in Italy drove away many of his followers. By 1940 Coughlin had ceased broadcasting and abandoned all political activities, under orders of the Catholic Church.

Huey P. Long was among the most powerful, and colorful, politicians of the era. He rose from modest origins to become a lawyer and a public service commissioner. In 1928 Long won the governorship of Louisiana. His progressive leadership inspired tremendous loyalty, especially among poor workers and farmers. He did more for the underprivileged people of

Huey P. Long was among the most powerful, and colorful, politicians of the era.

Louisiana than any other governor. He expanded the state's infrastructure; developed social services; built roads, hospitals, and schools; and changed the tax code to place a greater burden on corporations and the wealthy. He proved unique among southern politicians in that his public statements were free of racial slurs. But he also trampled the democratic process. His ambition had no bounds, and he used any means to accumulate power.

In 1932 Long resigned the governorship and won election to the U.S. Senate. Soon, he gained a huge national following. Initially he supported FDR, but by 1933 he had broken with the president and forged his own political movement based on his Share-Our-Wealth Plan. Giving voice to the resentments many Americans felt toward "wealthy plutocrats," Long advocated a radical redistribution of the nation's wealth. He called for new taxes on the wealthy and proposed to use the funds to guarantee a minimum annual income of $2,500 for all those in need. As he put it, "How many men ever went to a barbecue and would let one man take off the table what was intended for nine-tenths of the people to eat? The only way you'll ever be able to feed the balance of the people is to make that man come back and bring back some of the grub he ain't got no business with." By 1935 he was planning to challenge FDR in the next presidential election. But he never had the chance. In September 1935, the son-in-law of one of his vanquished political opponents assassinated him.

Eleanor Roosevelt also pushed FDR to the left, particularly on the issue of civil rights. Although FDR was reluctant to support an antilynching bill in Congress for fear of alienating southern white voters, the First Lady campaigned vigorously against lynching. When the Daughters of the American Revolution (DAR) denied the African American opera star Marian Anderson the right to perform at Constitution Hall in Washington, D.C., Eleanor promptly resigned from the DAR in protest and arranged for Anderson to perform at the Lincoln Memorial on Easter Sunday 1939, where a huge audience stood in the cold to hear her sing.

The Second New Deal

FDR was careful not to alienate southern Democrats by cultivating African American voters. However, he did reach out to industrial workers. In the spring of 1935, Congress passed the National Labor Relations Act, also known as the Wagner Act, which strengthened and guaranteed collective bargaining and gave a huge boost to labor unions.

Also in 1935, Congress passed the Social Security Act, perhaps the most important and far-reaching of all New Deal programs. The act established a system of old-age pensions,

TABLE 22-2

Key New Deal Legislation, 1933–1938

Year	Act or Agency	Key Provisions
1933	Emergency Banking Act	Reopened banks under government supervision
	Civilian Conservation Corps (CCC)	Employed young men in reforestation, flood control, road construction, and soil erosion control projects
	Federal Emergency Relief Act (FERA)	Provided federal funds for state and local relief efforts
	Agricultural Adjustment Act (AAA)	Granted farmers direct payments for reducing crop production; funds for payment provided by a processing tax, later declared unconstitutional
	Farm Mortgage Act	Provided funds to refinance farm mortgages
	Tennessee Valley Authority (TVA)	Constructed dams and power projects and developed the economy of a seven-state area in the Tennessee River Valley
	Home Owners' Loan Corporation	Provided funds for refinancing home mortgages of nonfarm homeowners
	National Industrial Recovery Act (NIRA)	Established a series of fair competition codes; created National Recovery Administration (NRA) to write, coordinate, and implement these codes; NIRA's Section 7(a) guaranteed labor's right to organize (act later declared unconstitutional)
	Public Works Administration (PWA)	Sought to increase employment and business activity by funding road construction, building construction, and other projects
	Federal Deposit Insurance Corporation (FDIC)	Insured individual bank deposits
	Civil Works Administration (CWA)	Provided federal jobs for the unemployed
1934	Securities and Exchange Act	Created Securities and Exchange Commission (SEC) to regulate trading practices in stocks and bonds according to federal laws
	Indian Reorganization Act	Restored ownership of tribal lands to Native Americans; provided funds for job training and a system of agricultural and industrial credit
	Federal Housing Administration (FHA)	Insured loans provided by banks for the building and repair of houses
1935	Works Progress Administration (WPA)	Employed more than 8 million people to repair roads, build bridges, and work on other projects
	National Youth Administration (NYA)	WPA program that provided job training for unemployed youths and part-time jobs for students in need
	Federal One	WPA program that provided financial assistance for writers, artists, musicians, and actors
	National Labor Relations Act (Wagner Act)	Recognized the right of employees to join labor unions and to bargain collectively, reinstating the provisions of NIRA's Section 7(a); created the National Labor Relations Board (NLRB) to enforce laws against unfair labor practices
	Social Security Act	Created a system of social insurance that included unemployment compensation and old-age survivors' insurance; paid for by a joint tax on employers and employees
1938	Fair Labor Standards Act	Established a minimum wage of 25 cents an hour and a standard work week of 44 hours for businesses engaged in interstate commerce

unemployment insurance, and welfare benefits for dependent children and the disabled. The framework of the Social Security Administration shaped the welfare system for the remainder of the century. But the welfare state established by the Social Security Act left out many of the most needy. It also established a two-track system of welfare. One track provided workers with unemployment insurance and support in their old age (the Social Security program). But Social Security did not cover domestics, seasonal or part-time workers, agricultural laborers, or housewives. The other track made matching funds available to states to provide relief for the needy, mostly dependent women and children with no means of support. Unlike Social Security, which was provided to all retired workers regardless of their circumstances, relief programs, which came to be known as "welfare," were administered according to need.

The architects of this welfare system included top New Deal advisers, many of them women who had been active reformers, such as Eleanor Roosevelt. These advocates hoped to protect women and children from the destitution that almost certainly resulted if a male breadwinner lost his job, deserted his family, or died. The system presumed that a man ordinarily earned a **family wage** that let him support his wife and children and that women were necessarily economically dependent on men. Thus, a deeply entrenched gender system prevailed through the 1930s. As a result, some—though not all—male breadwinners received benefits like Social Security. Impoverished women and children, on the other hand, received public charity. These payments were usually meager, not enough to lift a woman and her children out of poverty.

Because there were no nationally established guidelines on how to distribute welfare funds, states could determine who received assistance. As a result, the Social Security Act did little to assist African Americans, especially in the South, where black women were deliberately excluded by local authorities who preferred to maintain a pool of cheap African American labor rather than to provide relief for black families.

WPA Project at Tonawanda Reservation

In 1935 Congress allocated the huge sum of nearly $5 billion for the Emergency Relief Appropriation. Roosevelt used a significant portion of the money to expand his public works program. By executive order, he established the Works Progress Administration (WPA), which provided millions of jobs for the unemployed. The project mandated that WPA jobs would make a contribution to public life and would not compete with private business. The jobs included building streets, highways, bridges, and public buildings; restoring forests; clearing slums; and extending electricity to rural areas. The WPA National Youth Administration gave work to nearly 1 million students.

The most effective WPA program was Federal One, which provided financial support for writers, musicians, artists, and actors. The Federal Theater Project, under the direction of Hallie Flanagan, former head of Vassar College's Experimental Theater, shaped the project into an arena for experimental community-based theater. The Federal Theater Project included sixteen black theater units. Federal One supported thousands of artists and brought the arts to a wide public audience through government-funded murals on public buildings, community-theater productions, local orchestras, and the like.

The New Deal did not reach everyone. Programs were geared toward full-time industrial workers, most of whom were white men. Domestic workers, Mexican migrant laborers, black and white sharecroppers, Chinese and Japanese truck farmers—all were among those ineligible for Social Security, minimum wages and maximum hours, unemployment insurance, and other New Deal benefits. But the New Deal established the national welfare state and provided assistance and security to millions of working people along with disabled, dependent, and elderly Americans. Such sweeping programs also solidified Roosevelt's popularity among the poor, workers, and much of the middle class.

FDR's Second Term

In the 1936 campaign, FDR claimed that the election was a battle between "the millions who never had a chance" and "organized money." He boasted that the "forces of selfishness and of lust for power" had united against him: "They are unanimous in their *hate* for *me—and I welcome their hatred*." His strategy paid off. Roosevelt won the election by a landslide of more than 60 percent of the popular vote. Six million more voters cast ballots than had done so in

Ralph Stackpole, *Industries of California,* 1934. © 1981 Don Beatty Photo

■ In this mural on San Francisco's Coit Tower, "Industries of California," Works Projects Administration (WPA) artist Ralph Stackpole depicts the city's diverse workforce. Across the country, government-funded artists created works of public art that portrayed life in local communities.

1932, and 5 million of those new votes went to Roosevelt. His strongest support came from the lower ends of the socioeconomic scale. The election also swept Democrats into Congress, giving them a decisive majority in both the House and the Senate.

With such a powerful mandate, Roosevelt was well positioned to promote a new legislative program. As his first major effort, he took on the Supreme Court. Dominated by conservative justices, the Court had invalidated some major legislation of Roosevelt's first term, including the AAA and the NIRA. Roosevelt feared that the justices would unravel the New Deal by striking down its progressive elements. To shift the balance of power on the Court, he proposed a measure that would let the president appoint one new justice for every one on the Court who had at least ten years of service and who did not retire within six months after turning seventy.

Emboldened by his landslide victory, FDR believed that he could persuade Congress and the nation to go along with any plan he put forward, but he was mistaken. Many viewed his "court packing" plan as a threat to the funda-

TABLE 22-3			
The Election of 1936			
Candidate	**Political Party**	**Popular Vote (%)**	**Electoral Vote**
Franklin D. Roosevelt	Democratic	60.8	523
Alfred M. Landon	Republican	36.5	8
William Levine	Union	1.9	—

mental separation of powers and feared that it would set a dangerous precedent. Powerful Republicans in Congress forged an alliance with conservative Democrats, mostly from the South, to defeat the plan. This informal alliance dominated Congress for the following two decades. The Court blunder cost Roosevelt considerable political capital and empowered his opponents. In the end, his plan proved unnecessary anyway. The Court did not undercut the New Deal. Within the next few years, retirements allowed Roosevelt to appoint several new justices who tipped the balance in his favor.

A New Political Culture

FDR continued to face strong opposition from conservatives on the right and from radicals, communists, and socialists on the left. But his political fortunes benefited from the emergence of a new and more inclusive national culture. This new Americanism emanated from the working class and found expression in the labor movement, the popular culture, and the political coalition that came together in the Democratic party. These nationalizing forces cut across lines of class and region and occasionally challenged hierarchies of gender and race.

The Labor Movement

The labor insurgency that erupted during the early years of the New Deal demonstrated the need for a new national labor movement. The American Federation of Labor (AFL), restricted to skilled workers, left out most of the nation's less skilled industrial laborers. John L. Lewis of the United Mine Workers (UMW) and Sidney Hillman of the Amalgamated Clothing Workers of America were among several union leaders from a number of industries—including mining, steel, rubber, and automobile—who left the AFL to form a new and more broad-based labor organization, the Congress of Industrial Organizations (CIO). Hillman and others argued that higher wages were good for the economy because workers would then be able to purchase consumer products, benefiting industry as well as workers. Lewis and Hillman played key roles in the CIO's growth into a national force, but the impetus came from the workers themselves.

The CIO's first major action came in 1936 in Akron, Ohio, where workers in the rubber industry organized a **sit-down strike**, a new strategy whereby laborers stopped work and simply sat down, shutting down production and occupying plants so that strikebreakers could not enter and take their jobs. Sit-down strikes became a prominent labor tactic during 1936 when forty-eight strikes broke out across the nation. The numbers shot up the following year to about 500 strikes that lasted more than one day.

■ These sit-down strikers at the Dodge Main plant in Hamtramck, Michigan, slept on their sewing tables while occupying the factory, shutting down production. The sit-down strike became an effective form of labor protest during the 1930s.

Courtesy, Wayne State University Archives

The most powerful demonstration of workers' discontent came in the automobile industry, where speed-ups of the assembly line drove workers to rebellion. In 1936 a spontaneous strike erupted against General Motors in Atlanta; it soon spread to Kansas City, Missouri; Cleveland, Ohio; and the main plants at Flint, Michigan. Two weeks into the strike, workers clashed with police. Frank Murphy, Michigan's pro-labor governor, refused to use National Guard troops against the strikers, and Roosevelt declined to send in federal troops. John L. Lewis negotiated on behalf of the workers, who demanded recognition of their union.

Women as well as men participated actively in the Flint strike. Twenty-three-year-old Genora Johnson Dollinger, wife of a striker and mother of two young sons, organized 500 women into the Women's Emergency Brigade, made up primarily of strikers' wives, sisters, and girlfriends. Wearing red berets and armbands, they ran soup kitchens and first-aid stations. They also entered the fray when necessary, as when they broke plant windows so that the company could not use tear gas effectively against the strikers inside.

Dollinger arranged a children's picket line as well, in which her two-year-old carried a sign that read, "My daddy strikes for us little tykes."

The sit-down strike at Flint lasted forty-four days and forced General Motors to recognize the United Auto Workers (UAW), which was a CIO union. The strike scored a clear victory for the workers and boosted the CIO's stature as a national union of industrial workers. Membership in the UAW quadrupled in the next year. Bowing to the formidable power of the national union in the wake of the UAW success, U.S. Steel conceded to the CIO even without a strike, ending its policy of hiring nonunion workers and signing an agreement with the Steel Workers' Organizing Committee. The CIO brought together workers from all over the country. Most of its member unions were open to racial and ethnic minorities and women.

The New Deal Coalition

FDR's support of labor unions brought workers solidly into the Democratic fold. They joined a coalition that included voters who had never before belonged to the same party, particularly northern blacks and southern whites. Although African Americans in the South were disenfranchised, blacks in the North had voted Republican for sixty years, loyal to the party of Lincoln. In a dramatic shift, black voters in northern cities overwhelmingly backed FDR in 1936 and remained in the Democratic party for the rest of the century.

Other racial and ethnic minorities also joined the New Deal coalition. In 1939 Latinos organized their first national civil rights assembly, El Congreso de Pueblos de Habla Española (the Spanish-Speaking People's Congress), which opened with a congratulatory telegram from Eleanor Roosevelt. Immigrants from Europe and their children also became loyal Democratic voters.

In spite of this diverse coalition, many Americans remained bitterly opposed to FDR. On the left, socialists and communists criticized the New Deal for patching up capitalism rather than transforming the economic system. On the right, conservative business leaders despised Roosevelt for the constraints he placed on business and the intrusion of the government into the economy. Critics from the political right considered the New Deal akin to communism. In 1938 Congress created the House Un-American Activities Committee (HUAC), chaired by Martin Dies of Texas. Formed ostensibly to investigate American fascists and Nazis in the United States, the committee instead pursued liberal and leftist groups throughout World War II and the Cold War.

A New Americanism

The New Deal coalition reflected not only Roosevelt's popularity but also a new and more inclusive American identity. An expanding mass culture fostered this sensibility, spread largely through the national media. It is no accident that Franklin Roosevelt found his way into the homes and hearts of Americans through his "fireside chats" over the radio; his mastery of that technology made him the first media-savvy president. During the 1930s, 70 percent of all households owned a radio—more than owned a telephone. The motion-picture industry also expanded into small towns across the country. Talking films brought vernacular speech and a variety of accents to diverse audiences who gathered in neighborhood theaters.

Movie plots portrayed the triumph of common people over the rich and powerful and celebrated love across class and ethnic lines. Although racial stereotypes persisted in motion pictures throughout the decade, notable exceptions, such as Will Rogers's films, featured strong minority characters. Popular movies also challenged traditional gender and class hierarchies. Female stars, such as Katharine Hepburn, Rosalind Russell, Bette Davis, and Mae West, portrayed feisty, independent women.

New sports celebrities also embodied the nation's diversity. Baseball star Joe DiMaggio, son of an Italian immigrant fisherman, became a national hero. African American boxer Joe Louis, the "Brown Bomber" who was born into a sharecropper family in Alabama, became

Air & Space Museum, Smithsonian Institution

■ Amelia Earhart was the first woman to fly solo across the Atlantic. The legendary aviator gave preliminary flying lessons to her friend Eleanor Roosevelt. FDR convinced his wife not to take up flying, but the First Lady always regretted her decision.

heavyweight champion of the world at age twenty-three. In 1938, when Louis fought German boxer Max Schmeling at Yankee Stadium, the fight attracted 70,000 fans and grossed more than $1 million. When the black fighter knocked out Schmeling in the first round, he seemed to strike a blow for America against Hitler's Nazi Germany.

A number of women also became heroes in the 1930s for their daring exploits, personal courage, and physical prowess. Athletes like tennis champion Helen Wills and Olympic track star and brilliant golfer "Babe" (Mildred) Didrikson (later Zaharias) greatly expanded the popularity of women's sports. Renowned aviator Amelia Earhart, the first woman to fly solo across the Atlantic, devoted her life to advancing both feminism and commercial aviation. When her plane disappeared during an attempted round-the-world flight in 1937, many of her admirers were so convinced of her invincibility that they refused to believe she had died. Even today, people still speculate about her fate.

Conclusion

The New Deal set in place a welfare state that established the principle of government responsibility for the well-being of vulnerable citizens. Before the New Deal, people suffered the fluctuations of the market economy with no recourse beyond the assistance of kin, communities, and charities. Older Americans who could no longer work had no government-guaranteed pensions and often faced poverty in old age. Bank failures could wipe away life savings. Unemployment could mean starvation for a worker's family. The New Deal provided Social Security for the elderly, unemployment compensation for workers who had lost their jobs, minimum standards for hours and wages, and economic aid to women and children who had no means of support. It established national economic regulations and regulatory agencies as well as the right of workers to unionize and engage in collective bargaining. These government protections offered many Americans an unprecedented level of economic security.

Most New Deal policies protected factory workers in large companies. The safety net did not extend to many of the neediest Americans, including Mexican American migrant workers, African American and white sharecroppers, seasonal agricultural laborers, and domestic workers. FDR was reluctant to press for antilynching legislation for fear of alienating southern congressmen who still retained enormous power. Although FDR's conservative opponents accused him of socialist leanings, the New Deal actually rescued and shored up capitalism.

The New Deal was the Roosevelt administration's response to a global economic crisis. With the exception of the communist Soviet Union, which had already abandoned capitalism, all industrialized nations responded to the Depression by increasing the role of the state in the economy. Italy, Germany, and Japan moved to fascism and the nearly total state direction of the economy, while Britain and France established welfare states that would become more fully developed after World War II. The U.S. system of social welfare was not as extensive and inclusive as those that emerged in some western European democracies. But it was part of a larger trend toward government intervention in the economy and greater protections for citizens.

Sites to Visit

African American Odyssey: The Depression, New Deal, and World War II

memory.loc.gov/ammem/aaohtml/exhibit/aopart8.html

This Library of Congress site covers the history of African Americans during the years of the Depression and World War II.

Southern Mosaic: The John and Ruby Lomax 1939 Southern States Recording Trip

memory.loc.gov/ammem/lohtml/lohome.html

This site from the American Folklife Center, Library of Congress, provides audio, text, and photos of the Lomax collection of American folk songs collected and recorded across the South.

Voices from the Dust Bowl: The Charles L. Todd and Robert Sonkin Migrant Worker Collection, 1940–1941

memory.loc.gov/ammem/afctshtml/tshome.html

This Library of Congress site includes Farm Security Administration studies of migrant work camps in California in 1940 and 1941, with audio, images, manuscripts, and publications.

New Deal Network

newdeal.feri.org

This site includes images, documents, texts, artifacts, and other materials from the New Deal era.

Crash of 1929

www.btinternet.com/~dreklind/thecrash.htm

This site includes a discussion of the causes of the 1929 stock market crash, along with audio clips of songs related to the crash.

Franklin D. Roosevelt Presidential Library and Museum

www.fdrlibrary.marist.edu/

This site includes documents, images, audio, and other primary source material from the Franklin D. Roosevelt Library.

New Deal for the Arts

www.archives.gov/exhibits/new_deal_for_the_arts/index.html

This site of the National Archives includes artwork, documents, photographs, and information from the New Deal programs that funded artists in the 1930s.

For Further Reading

General

Steve Fraser and Gary Gerstle, eds., *The Rise and Fall of the New Deal Order, 1930–1980* (1989).

Robert S. McElvaine, *The Great Depression: America, 1929–1941* (1984, 1993).

James R. McGovern, *And a Time for Hope: Americans in the Great Depression* (2000).

Studs Terkel, *Hard Times: An Oral History of the Great Depression* (1986).

The Great Depression

Glen Elder Jr., *Children of the Great Depression: Social Change in Life Experience* (1974).

Robert S. McElvaine, ed., *Down and Out in the Great Depression: Letters from the Forgotten Man* (1983).

Vicki L. Ruiz, *From Out of the Shadows: Mexican Women in Twentieth-Century America* (1998).

Judith Smith, *Family Connections: A History of Italian and Jewish Immigrant Lives in Providence, Rhode Island, 1900–1940* (1985).

Presidential Responses to the Depression

Edward D. Berkowitz, *America's Welfare State: From Roosevelt to Reagan* (1991).

Blanche Wiesen Cook, *Eleanor Roosevelt* (1999).

Frank Friedel, *Franklin D. Roosevelt: A Rendezvous with Destiny* (1990).

Lawrence W. Levine and Cornelia R. Levine, *The People and the President: America's Conversation with FDR* (2002).

The New Deal

Anthony Badger, *The New Deal* (1988).

Alan Brinkley, *Voices of Protest: Huey Long, Father Coughlin and the Great Depression* (1982).

Steven Fraser, *Labor Will Rule: Sidney Hillman and the Rise of American Labor* (1991).

Linda Gordon, *Pitied but Not Entitled: Single Mothers and the History of Welfare* (1994).

A New Political Culture

Lizabeth Cohen, *Making a New Deal: Industrial Workers in Chicago, 1919–1939* (1992).

Michael Denning, *Cultural Front: The Laboring of American Culture in the Twentieth Century* (1998).

Lary May, *The Big Tomorrow: Hollywood and the Politics of the American Way* (2000).

For quizzes and other resources on these topics, go to www.longmanamericanhistory.com.

CHAPTER

23

Global Conflict: World War II, 1937–1945

O N DECEMBER 7, 1941, KEITH LITTLE WAS OUT HUNTING RABBITS WITH FRIENDS AT THEIR boarding school on the Navajo reservation of Ganado, Arizona. When they heard the news that the Japanese had attacked the U.S. naval base in Hawaii at Pearl Harbor, the teenage boys pledged to fight for their country. The next morning, Little and his friends showed up with their hunting rifles at the office of the reservation superintendent, ready to enlist. The previous year, the Tribal Council had voted unanimously to defend the United States against invasion. "There exists no purer concentration of Americanism than among the First Americans," the council declared.

Little and about 400 other Navajo became part of a special unit that developed an intricate code, based on the Navajo language, to transmit top-secret information without risk of detection. The Navajo language was particularly well suited to code because very few people besides Navajo knew it. In a process code named "Magic," the all-Navajo 382nd Platoon of the U.S. Marine Corps encoded and decoded sensitive military information almost instantly and flawlessly. In two days on the Pacific island of Iwo Jima, six "Code Talkers" transmitted more than 800 messages, working around the clock, without a single error. Signal Officer Major Howard Conner recalled, "Without the Navajos the Marines would never have taken Iwo Jima."

The experiences of the Navajo "Code Talkers" echo many larger themes of America's involvement in World War II. Along with other ethnic and racial minorities, the Navajo willingly fought—and many died—

■ Navajo "Code Talkers" operate a portable radio in the Pacific combat zone in 1943.

for a country that had treated them as second-class citizens. African Americans also joined the war effort, though in segregated units, to fight for the **Double V**—victory against fascism abroad and racial discrimination at home. Young Japanese Americans left internment camps where their families had been forcibly detained to join a war against the land from which their parents came.

World War II was a global war, affecting countries and peoples all over the world. The huge scale of destruction was unlike that of any previous war. At least 55 million people died, including 25 million in the Soviet Union, 10 million in China, and 6 million in Poland. In the Holocaust, Nazi

Germany's campaign of genocide, 6 million European Jews perished along with thousands of Romani (Gypsies), Poles, mentally and physically disabled people, homosexuals, and others deemed "racially inferior." The war also had a tremendous impact on countries under colonial rule. Germany's bombardment of England and occupation of France, Holland, and Belgium weakened these countries' hold over their vast colonies. Japan's defeat of the American, British, Dutch, and French forces in Southeast Asia from 1940 to 1942 shocked the Western powers and ended white rule in the region, setting in motion a wave of decolonization in Asia and Africa after the war.

The United States was the only major combatant that did not suffer massive destruction on its home territory. It had two powerful advantages: an ocean barrier on its east and west coasts, plus tremendous natural resources that could provide the materials needed for modern warfare, such as steel and oil. In order to minimize American casualties, President Franklin Delano Roosevelt (FDR) pursued a strategy to make the United States the "arsenal of democracy," providing armaments and supplies to the other Allied powers so that their armies would do most of the fighting. Although the Soviet Union carried the largest burden of fighting the war and suffered the highest losses, millions of Americans also fought, and many died in the conflict. Military service had a leveling effect on social relations, as soldiers came together from all classes and ethnic groups. The vast majority of the troops—more than 85 percent—were white men from a wide variety of backgrounds. Soldiers of color generally fought in segregated units, but their battlefield successes and sacrifices gave them a sense of belonging to the nation and fueled postwar movements for equality and civil rights.

The United States was the only major combatant that did not suffer massive destruction on its home territory.

No bombs dropped on the American mainland, yet the war reached into every aspect of national and personal life. Although wartime brought prosperity, the rationing of essential goods and the scarcity of consumer products brought nearly all Americans into the war effort. As soldiers and war industry workers moved around the country, local and regional sensibilities gave way to a stronger national identity. The U.S. military and defense establishment expanded to the formidable scale it would maintain during and after the war, making the United States the most powerful nation in the world.

Mobilizing for War

During the 1930s, the rise of **fascism** and militarism in Italy, Germany, and Japan created a terrible dilemma for Americans. Disillusioned by World War I and preoccupied with the hardships of the Great Depression, they disagreed strongly with each other about how to respond to overt aggression in Africa, Europe, and Asia. The ensuing "Great Debate" became a turning point in the nation's relationship with the outside world. Mobilizing for the enormous crusade of World War II gave rise to a unity of purpose that lasted throughout the war and into the postwar era.

The Rise of Fascism

In the 1930s, Depression-era Americans grappled with their problems at home and avoided entanglements abroad. But they found it difficult to ignore events in Europe and Asia. In Italy, Spain, and Germany, where a weak economy and high unemployment created political unrest, fascist leaders rose to power with strong popular support. These new leaders promised economic recovery through strengthening military and national expansion. They also encouraged intense nationalist sentiments, urging people to identify strongly with the state. Fascist governments were antidemocratic, antiparliamentary, and frequently antisemitic. These governments generally ruled by police surveillance, coercion, and terror.

Germany emerged as the most powerful fascist state in Europe. After Germany's defeat in World War I and the severe economic depression that Germany experienced in the 1920s, Adolf Hitler's National Socialist (Nazi) party won broad support in the weakened country. On January 30, 1933, Hitler became chancellor of Germany. Extolling fanatical nationalism and the racial superiority of "Aryan" Germans, Hitler blamed Jews for Germany's problems. He began a campaign of terror against Jews, homosexuals, suspected communists, and anyone else he saw as promoting "un-German" ideas. Hitler vowed to unite all German-speaking peoples into a new empire, the "Third Reich."

The fascist governments forged alliances to increase their power and launched campaigns of aggression and expansion. In 1935 Italy invaded Ethiopia, the sole independent African nation. The following year, Nazi troops occupied the Rhineland, in the western region of Germany, in violation of the Versailles agreement. Hitler and Mussolini signed the **Axis Pact**, and Japan forged an alliance with Germany. Soon after that, civil war erupted in Spain. Hitler and Mussolini extended aid to the fascist General Francisco Franco, who was trying to overthrow Spain's republican government.

Although Spanish republicans appealed to antifascist governments for help in the fight against Franco, only the Soviet Union came to their assistance. The United States maintained an official policy of neutrality. American Catholics and State Department conservatives believed that the anticommunist Franco would promote social stability. Many on the left, including large numbers of writers and intellectuals, championed the beleaguered Spanish government and denounced the fascists. Some joined Soviet-organized international forces to fight against Franco.

Aggression in Europe and Asia

In the spring and summer of 1938, Hitler annexed Austria to the Third Reich and then demanded that the Sudetenland be turned over to Germany. In the breakup of the Austro-Hungarian Empire after World War I, this German-speaking area had become part of the newly formed Czechoslovakia. Soviet leader Josef Stalin offered to join France and Britain to keep Hitler out of the Sudetenland and halt his aggression. But the leaders of France and Britain rebuffed Stalin's suggestion. In September they met with Hitler in Munich and agreed to let him have the Sudetenland in return for his promise that he would seek no more territory. Stalin feared that the anticommunist leaders of France and Britain were trying to turn Hitler's aggression toward the Soviet Union. To prevent that possibility, Stalin signed a nonaggression pact with Hitler. Eventually, Hitler broke all his promises. Throughout the war and after, the Munich meeting became the symbol of "appeasement," a warning that compromise with the enemy leads only to disaster.

Hitler and Mussolini in Munich, 1940

In 1939, with the help of the Soviet Union and in violation of the Munich agreement, Germany invaded Poland, which fell quickly. At that point Britain and France declared war on Germany. That same year, Madrid finally fell to Franco's forces.

By 1940 Hitler was sweeping through Europe, invading Denmark, Norway, Holland, Belgium, Luxembourg, and then France. In just six weeks, the Nazis had seized most of western Europe. Hitler then turned his forces on Great Britain. In the summer and fall of 1940, German raids on British air bases nearly destroyed the British Royal Air Force (RAF). Hitler ordered the bombing of London and other English cities, attacking civilians day and night in what came to be called the Battle of Britain.

In the Far East, events had taken an equally alarming turn. Nationalistic militarists gained control of the Japanese government in Tokyo and began a course of expansion. In 1931–1932,

Japanese troops occupied the large Chinese province of Manchuria. Five years later, the Japanese launched a full-scale war against China. The United States extended aid to China and discontinued trade with Japan. In 1940 Japan joined Germany and Italy in the Axis alliance and invaded the French colony of Indochina.

The Great Debate: Americans Contemplate War

In the mid-1930s, the overwhelming majority of Americans opposed intervention in foreign conflicts. Congress passed the Neutrality Acts of 1935, 1936, and 1937, outlawing arms sales or loans to nations at war and forbidding Americans from traveling on the ships of belligerent powers. In 1937 a Gallup poll indicated that 70 percent of Americans believed that the United States should have stayed out of World War I.

When Japan invaded China in 1937, FDR refused to comply with the provisions of the latest Neutrality Act, on the technicality that neither combatant had officially declared war. By creatively interpreting the law, he was able to offer loans to the embattled Chinese. Roosevelt felt strongly that the United States should actively help to resist the Axis powers.

The largest organization to oppose Roosevelt's effort was the America First Committee. With 450 chapters, the group claimed several hundred thousand members, including famed aviator Charles Lindbergh. Centered largely in the Midwest, the America Firsters included some active Nazi supporters. But conservative businesspeople also took part. Some members believed that war would impede American prosperity. Others, long opposed to Roosevelt and the New Deal, feared that war would give additional power to the already strong federal government. In 1940, the popular FDR nonetheless became the first president elected to a third term.

Despite intense nonintervention sentiments, public opinion began to shift. Many Americans were shocked when Hitler swiftly conquered much of Europe. News reports of the German occupation of France and the intense bombardment of England in the Battle of Britain bolstered FDR's efforts to take action. In his "Four Freedoms" speech to Congress in January 1941, FDR cited the four freedoms he considered necessary for the postwar world: freedom of speech and expression, freedom of worship, freedom from want, and freedom from fear. At that time, the United States was not yet officially at war. But the president pledged his support for England against the Nazis. A few months later, Congress approved the Lend-Lease agreement to lend rather than sell munitions to the Allied countries.

When Hitler broke his promise to Stalin and attacked the Soviet Union in June 1941, FDR extended Lend-Lease to the Soviets. During the summer, FDR and British Prime Minister Winston Churchill met on a ship off the coast of Newfoundland

TABLE 23-1

The Election of 1940

Candidate	Political Party	Popular Vote (%)	Electoral Vote
Franklin D. Roosevelt	Democratic	54.8	449
Wendell L. Willkie	Republican	44.8	82

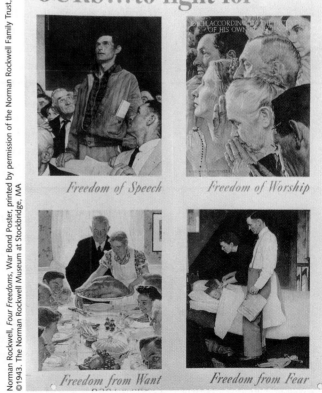

Norman Rockwell, *Four Freedoms*, War Bond Poster, printed by permission of the Norman Rockwell Family Trust, ©1943. The Norman Rockwell Museum at Stockbridge, MA

■ Norman Rockwell's depiction of the "Four Freedoms," which adorned the cover of the *Saturday Evening Post*, inspired the purchase of war bonds and came to symbolize the democratic values for which the nation was fighting. These four scenes by the popular artist evoked an American ideal of close families and harmonious communities.

to develop a joint declaration known as the Atlantic Charter. The two leaders announced that the United States and Britain sought no new territories, they recognized the right of all peoples to choose their own form of government, and they called for international **free trade** and navigation. Realizing the possible cost of losing colonies, Churchill retreated from the global implications of the charter, while Roosevelt walked a fine line between contradicting Churchill and supporting the idea of empire. However, the charter emboldened anticolonial activists around the world.

Pearl Harbor: The United States Enters the War

The Japanese attack on Pearl Harbor shocked the nation and catapulted the United States immediately into World War II. President Roosevelt somberly told millions of Americans gathered around their radios that the day of the attack would "live in infamy." Most former doubters now joined the war effort. The entire nation shifted into high gear to defeat brutal, aggressive regimes intent on conquering much of the world. For some, wartime mobilization offered new opportunities; for others, it brought sacrifice.

December 7, 1941

For nearly a decade, tensions had been mounting between the United States and Japan as American leaders tried to contain Japan's expansion in Asia. Roosevelt assumed that a strong U.S. military presence in the Pacific would persuade Japan's premier, General Hideki Tojo, to avoid a confrontation with the United States. When Japan continued its aggression in Asia, FDR froze Japanese assets in the United States, putting trade with Japan under presidential control. This move, he hoped, would bring Japan to the bargaining table. Instead, on November 25, the Japanese dispatched aircraft carriers toward Hawaii and sent troops to the border of Malaya in the South Pacific.

Although U.S. intelligence sources had broken the codes with which the Japanese encrypted messages about their war plans, they did not realize that the Japanese intended to strike Hawaii. At 7:55 a.m. on December 7, Japanese planes swooped over Pearl Harbor and bombed the naval base. The assault caught the American forces completely off guard and destroyed most of the U.S. Pacific fleet. Only a few aircraft carriers that were out at sea survived. Two hours after the attack on Pearl Harbor, the Japanese also struck the main U.S. base at Clark Field in the Philippines, destroying half of the U.S. Air Force in the Far East.

At roughly the same time that Keith Little heard the news about Pearl Harbor at his Navajo reservation boarding school, another sixteen-year-old, John Garcia, watched flames rising at Pearl Harbor from his house four miles away. The young Hawaiian reached the scene in time to witness the second round of bombings. "I spent the rest of the day swimming inside the harbor, along with some other Hawaiians. I brought out I don't know how many bodies, and how many were alive and how many dead. . . . We worked around the clock for three days."

When the smoke cleared, 2,323 American service personnel were dead. Congress immediately declared war against Japan. Three days later, Germany and Italy declared war against the United States.

VIDEO
Pearl Harbor

Japanese American Relocation

The assault on Pearl Harbor sparked widespread rumors along the U.S. West Coast that Japanese and Japanese Americans living there planned to sabotage the war effort. Although no charges of criminal activity or treason were ever brought against any Japanese Americans, powerful white farming interests eager to eradicate Japanese American competition pushed for an evacuation.

Not everyone supported the internment idea. U.S. Attorney General Francis Biddle protested that there was "no reason" for a mass relocation. J. Edgar Hoover, director of the FBI, also opposed the plan, arguing that it reflected "hysteria and lack of judgment." Nevertheless, the Roosevelt administration gave in to the pressure, with the support of California Attorney General Earl Warren. In February 1942, Roosevelt signed Executive Order 9066, which suspended the civil rights of American citizens of Japanese descent. The order authorized the removal of 110,000 Japanese and Japanese Americans from the West Coast. Of those, 70,000 were *Nisei*, native-born American citizens. Families received at most a week's notice to evacuate their homes and move to prisonlike camps surrounded by barbed wire and guarded by armed soldiers. There were ten such camps in seven states, most of them located in arid, desolate spots in the West. At the camps, internees lived in makeshift wooden barracks, where entire families crowded into one room.

While the internment experience alienated some Japanese Americans, fully 33,000 joined the armed services—including 1,200 who enlisted from the internment camps—and proved their patriotism on the battlefield. In the Pacific, their knowledge of the Japanese language proved critical in translating intercepted Japanese military documents. General Charles Willoughby, chief of intelligence in the Pacific, estimated that Japanese American military contributions shortened the war by two years. The Japanese also served ably in Europe, suffering huge casualties. The Japanese Americans of the 442nd Regiment lost one-fourth of their soldiers in battles in North Africa and Italy. They suffered another 800 casualties rescuing the Texan "Lost Battalion," 211 men surrounded by German troops in the Vosges Mountains of France. As one Texan recalled, "We were never so glad to see anyone as those fighting Japanese Americans."

DOCUMENT

Executive Order 9066: Resulting in the Relocation of Japanese

AP/Wide World Photos

■ On December 7, 1941, the Japanese launched a surprise attack on the U.S. naval base at Pearl Harbor, Hawaii. The attack brought the United States immediately into World War II and was the only time that the war came to American soil.

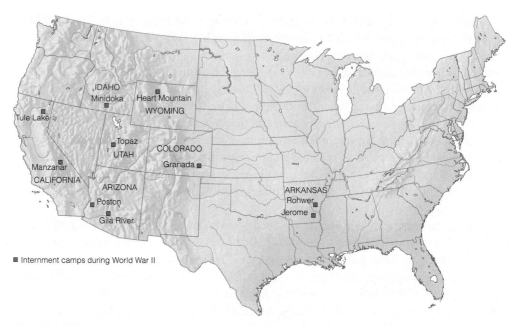

Internment camps during World War II

■ MAP 23.1

INTERNMENT OF JAPANESE AMERICANS DURING WORLD WAR II   After the Japanese attack on Pearl Harbor, President Franklin Delano Roosevelt signed an order authorizing the removal of people of Japanese descent from the West Coast. These Japanese Americans were relocated to internment camps built in arid and isolated areas in the West, as well as in two locations in Arkansas.

Nevertheless, the U.S. government would take its time acknowledging that the internment had been a grave injustice. The Supreme Court upheld the constitutionality of the policy, and Roosevelt would not rescind the evacuation order until after his reelection in 1944. The camps finally closed in 1945. All told, Japanese Americans lost property valued at $500 million. In 1988 Congress enacted legislation awarding restitution payments of $20,000 each to 60,000 surviving internees—a small gesture for Americans whose only "crime" was their Japanese ancestry.

Foreign Nationals in the United States

Although Japanese Americans were the only U.S. citizens interned solely on the basis of their ancestry, German and Italian nationals living in the United States were also subject to new regulations, and in some cases relocation and incarceration. The Smith Act of 1940 required all foreign-born residents to be registered and fingerprinted, and broadened the grounds for deportation.

Six hundred thousand Italians and 314,000 Germans living in the United States were subject to these requirements. Several hundred were deemed potentially dangerous and interned for the duration of the war. Approximately 10,000 Italian nationals were forced to relocate from their homes on the West Coast. A few hundred German and Italian immigrants who were naturalized U.S. citizens were also relocated from designated coastal areas.

Wartime Migrations

Even before the United States officially entered World War II, the conflict had begun to change the face of the nation. The sleepy town of Richmond, California, perched near the north end of San Francisco Bay, underwent a profound transformation when the nation stepped up war production. The town's mostly white population of 23,000 ballooned to 120,000 after industrialist Henry Kaiser constructed four shipyards there. The yards employed over 150,000 workers, more than one-fourth of them African American. Most were young, married migrants from the South, and there were slightly more women than men. They came to Richmond attracted by the better pay and benefits, along with the opportunity for greater freedom than they had known in the Jim Crow South.

National Archives

■ The family pictured here was among thousands of loyal citizens of Japanese ancestry removed from their homes on the West Coast and relocated to internment camps. Here, the Hirano family, George, Hisa, and Yasbei (left to right), pose at the Colorado River Relocation Center in Poston, Arizona. Hisa holds a photo of her son, an American soldier, who is off fighting the war.

Many cities, however, were ill equipped to handle the influx of migrants. An estimated 60,000 African Americans moved into Chicago, for example, causing an enormous housing crisis. Many newcomers lacked even a modicum of privacy as they crowded into basements and rooms rented from total strangers. Huge numbers of whites also came north, many leaving hardscrabble farms and hoping to prosper in booming war industries.

Wartime also saw new migration from abroad and a reversal of earlier immigration policies. Because of the alliance with China in the war against Japan, in 1943 Congress repealed the Chinese Exclusion Act, and migrants from China became eligible for citizenship for the first time. An executive agreement between the United States and Mexico created the ***bracero*** program, under which 300,000 Mexican laborers, mostly agricultural workers, came to rural areas like California's San Joaquin Valley. By the mid-1960s, nearly 5 million Mexicans had migrated north under the program.

The Home Front

Wartime mobilization brought Americans from all regions and backgrounds together in shared service and sacrifice. Automobile manufacturers stopped making cars and instead turned out tanks, jeeps, and other military vehicles. Citizens made do with government-rationed basic staples, from food to gasoline. As able-bodied men left their jobs to fight the war, new work opportunities opened up for women as well as for disabled Americans. Cities and centers of war production brought together young women and men who found new opportunities for sexual experimentation, while gay men and lesbians discovered newly visible communities in both military and civilian life. The war raised expectations of women and minorities that they would achieve full inclusion in the American promise.

Many Americans hoped that the liberal spirit of the New Deal would endure during the war; others were eager for an end to what they perceived as Depression-era class conflict and hostility to business interests. To some extent, both sides got their wish. Full employment, the increasing strength of unions, and high taxes on the wealthy pleased New Deal liberals. Profit guarantees, freedom from antitrust actions, no-strike pledges, and low-cost imported labor gratified probusiness conservatives. And Roosevelt was elected to an unprecedented fourth term in 1944.

TABLE 23-2			
The Election of 1944			
Candidate	Political Party	Popular Vote (%)	Electoral Vote
Franklin D. Roosevelt	Democratic	53.5	432
Thomas E. Dewey	Republican	46.0	99

Building Morale

The United States, like all other major powers involved in the conflict, mounted a propaganda drive to promote support for the war effort. Roosevelt created the Office of War Information (OWI) in 1942 to coordinate morale-boosting and censorship initiatives. Working in partnership with the motion picture industry and other media outlets, the OWI sponsored movies, radio programs, publications, and posters. These productions portrayed the war as a crusade to preserve the "American way of life" and encouraged American women and men to work in war industries, enlist in the armed forces, and purchase war bonds. Eric Johnston, head of the Motion Picture Producers' Association and FDR's business adviser, insisted that Hollywood remove class conflict from its films: "We'll have no more *Grapes of Wrath*, we'll have no more *Tobacco Roads*, we'll have no more films that deal with the seamy side of American life. We'll have no more films that treat the banker as a villain."

Within the United States, government censors made sure that no photographs showing badly wounded soldiers or mutilated bodies reached the public. The censors also removed any images that might elicit sympathy for the enemy, such as pictures of injured or frightened enemy soldiers suffering at the hands of American soldiers. Photographs that appeared in the American media generally sanitized the horror of war, depicting noble American soldiers and a shadowy, faceless enemy. Rarely, if ever, did those on the home front see the true extent of the war's destructiveness and brutality. When men returned home severely traumatized by what they had seen, even their trauma was censored. As just one example, for more than three decades, the army suppressed John Huston's *Let There Be Light*, a film documentary of World War II veterans in a psychiatric hospital suffering from post-traumatic stress disorder.

Home Front Workers, "Rosie the Riveter," and "Victory Girls"

Wartime opened up new possibilities for jobs, income, and labor organizing, for women as well as for men, and for new groups of workers. Disabled workers entered jobs previously considered beyond their abilities, fulfilling their tasks with skill and competence. Norma Krajczar, a visually impaired teenager from North Carolina, served as a volunteer aircraft warden where her sensitive hearing gave her an advantage over sighted wardens in listening for approaching enemy planes. Deaf people streamed into Akron, Ohio, to work in the tire factories that became defense plants, making more money than they ever made before.

Along with new employment opportunities, workers' earnings rose nearly 70 percent. Income doubled for farmers and then doubled again. Labor union membership grew 50 per-

■ Eight American presidents elected consecutively following World War II were veterans of that war. Pictured in wartime service, from top left, are: Dwight D. Eisenhower, John F. Kennedy, Lyndon Johnson, Richard Nixon, Gerald Ford, Jimmy Carter, Ronald Reagan, and George H. W. Bush.

cent, reaching an all-time high by the end of the war. Women and minorities joined unions in unprecedented numbers. Energetic labor organizers like Luisa Moreno and Dorothy Ray Healy organized Mexican and Russian Jewish workers at the California Sanitary Canning Company into a powerful CIO cannery union that achieved wage increases and union recognition.

World War II ushered in dramatic changes for American women. Wartime scarcities led to increased domestic labor as homemakers made do with rationed goods, mended clothing, collected and saved scraps and metals, and planted "victory gardens" to help feed their families. Employment opportunities for women also increased. As a result of the combined incentives of patriotism and good wages, many women took "men's jobs" while the men went off to fight.

Rosie the Riveter became the heroic symbol of the woman war worker. Pictures of attractive "Rosies" building planes or constructing ships graced magazine covers and posters. Future Hollywood star Marilyn Monroe first gained attention when her photograph appeared in *Yank*, a magazine for soldiers. The magazine pictured her not as the sex goddess she later became, but as a typical Rosie the Riveter clad in overalls, working at her job in a defense plant.

For the first time, married women joined the paid labor force in droves and public opinion supported them. During the Depression, 80 percent of Americans had objected to the idea of wives working outside the home; by 1942 only 13 percent still objected. However, mothers of young children found very little help. In 1943 the federal government finally responded to the needs of working mothers by funding some day-care centers. But meager to begin with and conceived as an emergency measure, government funding for child care would end after the war.

New opportunities for women also opened up in the armed services. All sectors of the armed forces had dwindled in the years between the two wars and needed to gain size and strength. Along with the 10 million men aged twenty-one to thirty-five drafted into the armed services and the 6 million who enlisted, 140,000 women volunteered for the Women's Army Corps (WACs; originally the Women's Army Auxiliary Corps, WAAC) and 100,000 for the Navy WAVES (Women Accepted for Voluntary Emergency Service).

Most female enlistees and war workers enjoyed their work and wanted to continue after the war. The extra pay, independence, camaraderie, and satisfaction that their jobs provided had opened their eyes to new possibilities. Edith Speert, like many others, was never again content as a full-time housewife and mother. Edith's husband, Victor, was sent overseas in 1944. During the eighteen months of their separation, they penned 1,300 letters to each other, sometimes two or three times a day. The letters revealed the love and affection they felt for one another, but Edith did not hesitate to tell Victor how she had changed. In a letter from Cleveland, dated November 9, 1945, she wrote:

> Sweetie, I want to make sure I make myself clear about how I've changed. I want you to know *now* that you are not married to a girl that's interested solely in a home—I shall definitely have to work all my life—I get emotional satisfaction out of working; and I don't doubt that many a night you will cook the supper while I'm at a meeting. Also, dearest—I shall never wash and iron—there are laundries for that! Do you think you'll be able to bear living with me? . . .
> I love you, Edith

Wartime upheaval sent the sexual order topsy-turvy. For many young women, moving to a new city or taking a wartime job opened up new possibilities for independence, excitement, and sexual adventure. Some young women, known as "victory girls," believed that it was an act of patriotism to have a fling with a man in uniform before he went overseas. The independence of these women raised fears of female sexuality as a dangerous, ungoverned force.

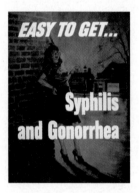

The worry extended beyond the traditional concern about prostitutes and "loose women" to include "good girls" whose sexual standards might relax during wartime. Public health campaigns warned enlisted men that "victory girls" would have their fun with a soldier and then leave him with a venereal disease, incapable of fighting for his country.

Wartime also intensified concerns about homosexuality. Urban centers and the military provided new opportunities for gay men and lesbians to form relationships and build communities. Although the military officially banned homosexuals from the forces, many served by keeping their orientation secret. If discovered, gay men faced severe punishment, including confinement in cages called "queer stockades" or in psychiatric wards. Lesbians faced similar sanctions, although the women's corps, in an effort to assure the civilian world of their recruits' femininity, often looked the other way.

Race and War

The Holocaust, Nazi Germany's campaign to exterminate European Jews, demonstrated the horrors of racial hatred taken to its ultimate extreme. The U.S. government did little to help Jewish refugees or to stem the slaughter of Jews in Europe. Official indifference and widespread antisemitism prevailed throughout the war. Nevertheless, Nazi policies against the Jews discredited racial and ethnic prejudice, forcing Americans to confront the reality of racism in their own country. Anthropologist Ruth Benedict, in her 1943 book *The Races of Mankind*, urged the United States to "clean its own house" and "stand unashamed before Nazis and condemn, without confusion, their doctrines of a Master Race." As black leader W. E. B. Du

Bois noted, World War II was a "War for Racial Equality" and a struggle for "democracy not only for white folks but for yellow, brown, and black."

The Holocaust

Nazi Murder Mills

Hitler's war aims included conquering all of Europe and destroying European Jewry. Throughout the war, Nazi anti-Jewish policies escalated from persecution and officially sanctioned violence to imprisonment in concentration camps, slave labor, and ultimately Hitler's "Final Solution," genocide. Nazis developed increasingly efficient means of killing Jews. In the infamous Nazi death camps, guards herded prisoners into "shower rooms" that were actually gas chambers.

American officials knew of the Nazi persecution of the Jews but did little about it. Throughout the 1930s, American Jewish groups pressured the Roosevelt administration to ease immigration laws to allow Jewish refugees to enter the country. But the United States raised the legal quota of Jewish immigrants only slightly.

When the Nazis began their policy of extermination in 1941, they tried to keep it a secret. U.S. State Department officials heard reports of the Holocaust but decided to keep the information quiet. Despite official silence, Rabbi Stephen S. Wise, a prominent American Jewish leader, heard the news and held a press conference in November 1942. But the American press, preoccupied with military events and reluctant to publish stories of atrocities without official verification, gave the Holocaust little coverage. Meanwhile, despite reports of Nazi genocide, the U.S. government turned away boatloads of Jewish refugees, sending them back to Germany to their deaths.

Nazi persecution of the Jews raised American sensitivity to the issue of racism but did little to diminish antisemitism within the United States. In fact, American hostility toward Jews reached new heights during World War II and exceeded the level of prejudice against any other group. In 1944, when asked to identify the greatest "menace" to the nation, 24 percent of Americans polled listed Jews—more than those who listed Germans, Japanese, radicals, Negroes, and foreigners. In Europe, American military strategists knew of the existence and location of Nazi death camps, but they chose not to try to bomb them or the railroad lines leading to the camps.

> *The U.S. government turned away boatloads of Jewish refugees, sending them back to Germany to their deaths.*

Racial Tensions at Home

Randolph, "Why Should We March"

Throughout the war years, racial tensions within the United States persisted. Black workers, who were excluded from the best-paying jobs in the defense industry, mobilized against discrimination on the job. Their most powerful advocate was African American civil rights leader A. Philip Randolph, who had organized the overwhelmingly black Brotherhood of Sleeping Car Porters and won the union a contract with the railroads in 1937. At the beginning of American involvement in the war in 1941, Randolph pressured FDR to ban discrimination in defense industries. He threatened to organize a massive march on Washington if Roosevelt did not respond. Roosevelt issued Executive Order 8802, which created the Fair Employment Practices Commission (FEPC) to ensure that blacks and women received the same pay as white men for doing the same job. The FEPC narrowed pay gaps somewhat, but it did not solve the problem. The American Federation of Labor, which included the highest-paid workers, still refused to accept blacks as members and fought with the FEPC over the equal-pay policy.

Sometimes the presence of racial minorities in previously all-white work settings led to hostilities. In 1943 in Detroit, white workers at the Packard auto plant walked off the job when three black employees were promoted. With increasing numbers of white and black Southerners arriving to work in the city's war industries, overcrowding strained the boundaries of traditionally segregated neighborhoods. Clashes at a new housing complex escalated into several days of rioting, resulting in thirty-four deaths and 1,800 arrests.

Zelda Webb Anderson, "You Just Met One Who Does Not Know How to Cook"

*Z*elda Webb Anderson became one of the first black women to enter military service during World War II. She served as an officer in the Women's Army Auxiliary Corps (WAACS), renamed the Women's Army Corps (WAC) in 1943. After the war she earned a doctorate in education at the University of California, Berkeley. Her 42-year career in education included a stint teaching at the University of East Africa in Dar-es-Salaam, Tanzania. She related her wartime experiences to the University of Nevada Oral History Program in 1995.

I reported for duty in January 1942. . . . This was so exciting to me. We had black officers, and our basic training was the same as for men. They would simply tell us, "You wanted to be in a man's army, so now you got to do what the men do." We learned military courtesy, history, how to shoot an M-1, go on bivouac, bathe in a teacup of water, eat hardtack rations. . . .

Every evening troops of male soldiers would march by our barracks en route to the mess hall. I told the commanding officer that we would like to have some shades at the windows. "Oh, no. You wanted to be in the man's army. Fine—you have to do what the men do." I told all the girls, "Listen, they won't give us any shades. So I want you to get right in front of the windows buck naked." The next day we had shades at all the windows. . . .

They pulled me out of basic training the third week and sent me to officer training in Des Moines. All of the instruc-

Courtesy, Zelda Webb Anderson and University of Nevada Oral History Project

Zelda Webb Anderson

tors were white, but white and black officers were being trained in the same facility, in the same classes, and we slept in the same barracks. After OCS I was assigned to a laundry unit.

A black enlisted WAAC could either be in the laundry unit or she could be in the hospital unit. In the laundry unit, if she had a college degree, she could work at the front counter. . . . If she had less than that, then she did the laundry—very demeaning. And in the hospital unit they let her wash walls, empty basins, wash windows—all that menial work. . . .

I was assigned to duty at Fort Breckenridge, Kentucky. The post commander's name was Colonel Throckmorton. In a pronounced southern accent he told me, "You're going over to that colored WAC company, and you're going to be the mess officer."

I said, "Sir, I have not had any mess training."

"All you nigras know how to cook."

I said, "You just met one who does not know how to cook; but if you send me to Fort Eustis, Virginia, for training I

will come back and be the best mess officer you have on this post."

"I ain't sending you to no school, and you're going over there to be a mess officer." When I about-faced, I kept on going. I didn't even salute him. . . .

[Much later, after developing a more cordial relationship with Colonel Throckmorton,] I told him that segregation has not allowed white people to know black people: "We know you very intimately, but you don't know how we think, how we react, and so you just try to push your stuff on us, not giving a damn about how we feel about this. And then when we rebel, or you meet somebody like me, who decides that you can't do this to me, then you think I'm cantankerous; you think I'm an agitator. I'm just trying to give you an education. . . ."

I lived out the rest of my days very happy in the Army. If I had succumbed to the treatment that they had given other blacks before, and not spoken up for myself, my morale would have been down. . . . In this life, you've got to speak up for yourself. You can't go around shuffling your feet with your head hung down acting apologetic. If you see something you want, you must go after it. One day somebody will recognize it, and it's a victory for you, especially when it's somebody who has denigrated you because of your race. . . .

Our country has not solved all of its problems. You have to live democracy before you can preach democracy. I've got four granddaughters, and I don't want them put in a position where they don't have equal opportunities, equal chances, and then they have to fight the same old battles that I fought again.

Questions

1. *Why do you think Anderson, as a woman and an African American, would choose to enlist in the U.S. Army during World War II?*

2. *According to Anderson, in what ways did the segregation of the armed forces distort white officers' views of blacks?* ■

In Los Angeles, the death of a Mexican American youth, José Diaz, at a gravel pit called Sleepy Lagoon sparked sensational news coverage and whipped up anti-Mexican fervor. Although police never determined the cause of Diaz's injuries, they filed first-degree murder charges against twenty-two Mexican American boys from the neighborhood. The jury found the young men guilty, but an appeals court overturned the convictions. Nevertheless, hostility continued to mount against Mexican American youths, particularly *pachucos* who sported **zoot suits**, distinctive attire with flared pants, long coats, and wide-brimmed hats. Pachucos wore the zoot suit as an expression of ethnic pride and rebelliousness, as well as incipient political consciousness.

For eight days in June 1943, scores of soldiers hunted zoot-suiters in Los Angeles bars, theaters, dance halls, and even in their homes, pulling off their clothes and beating them. Soon the attacks expanded to all Mexican Americans, and then to African Americans as well, some of whom also wore the zoot-suit style. The Los Angeles police sided with the rioters. They stood by during the beatings and then arrested the naked and bleeding youths and charged them with disturbing the peace. The rioting raged until the War Department made the entire city of Los Angeles off limits to military personnel.

Fighting for the "Double V"

In spite of discrimination at home, members of minority groups responded enthusiastically to the war effort. The numbers of blacks in the U.S. army soared from 5,000 in 1940 to 700,000 by 1944, with an additional 187,000 in the U.S. Navy, Coast Guard, and Marine Corps. Four thousand black women joined the WACs. Almost all soldiers fought in segregated units, despite protests by the NAACP that "a Jim Crow army cannot fight for a free world." African Americans fought for the "Double V"—victory over fascism abroad and racial discrimination at home.

Like Keith Little and his boarding-school buddies who became Navajo "Code Talkers" (described at the beginning of this chapter), American Indians all over the country declared their willingness to fight for the cause. Fully 25,000 Native Americans, including 800 women, served in the military during the war. By 1945 nearly one-third of all able-bodied Native American men between eighteen and fifty had served. Five percent of them were killed or wounded in action. Native Americans enlisted at a higher rate than the general population, prompting the *Saturday Evening Post* to editorialize, "We would not need the Selective Service if all volunteered like the Indians."

In addition to those who enlisted, half of all able-bodied Native American men not in the service and one-fifth of women left reservations for war-industry jobs. At the beginning of the war, men on reservations earned a median annual income of $500, less than one-fourth the national average. One-third of all Native American men living off reservations were unemployed. Worse, the average life expectancy for Native Americans in 1940 was just thirty-five years, compared with sixty-four years for the population at large. Like others who found new opportunities during the conflict, Native Americans hoped that the economic progress they had made would be permanent. But the boom would end for them when the war ended. Fewer than 10 percent of Native Americans who relocated to cities found long-term employment after the war.

Total War

World War II consisted of two wars, one centered in Europe and the other in the Pacific. Combatants in both conflicts engaged in **total war**—the targeting of civilian as well as military targets. Of all the combatants, only the United States escaped physical destruction on its own national soil (with the exception of Pearl Harbor). Coming out of the war physically unscathed, economically sound, and politically strong, the United States became the most prosperous and powerful nation in the world.

World War II in Europe

The War in Europe

The attack on Pearl Harbor brought the United States immediately into the war in both Europe and the Pacific. The leaders of the Allied powers, including the United States, Britain, and the Soviet Union, had to develop a strategy to defeat the Axis powers. But the **Allies** did not always agree on how to conduct the war, and relations between the United States and the Soviet Union remained strained. Unable to fully overcome the hostility and suspicion that had marked their earlier encounters, leaders of both countries fought the war with postwar power considerations in mind.

Like the United States at Pearl Harbor, the Soviet Union suffered a shocking blow when Germany launched a surprise invasion in June 1941 in violation of the nonaggression pact Hitler had signed with Stalin in 1938. With the full might of the Nazi forces now concentrated on the front lines against the Russians in eastern Europe, Soviet premier Joseph Stalin wanted the United States to open a second front in western Europe to divert the Nazis toward the west and relieve pressure on the Soviet

■ **MAP 23.2**
WORLD WAR II IN EUROPE   Along the eastern front of the war in Europe, Soviet troops did the bulk of the Allied fighting in Europe and sustained the highest casualties. The Battle of Stalingrad, in which Soviet troops finally drove back the Nazis after months of brutal fighting, was a major turning point in the war.

Union. In May 1942, Roosevelt assured Stalin that the United States would support an Allied invasion across the English Channel into France. But the British prime minister, Winston Churchill, persuaded FDR to delay that dangerous maneuver and instead to launch an invasion of French north Africa, which was controlled by the Nazi occupation forces in Vichy, France.

While the Allies turned their attention to north Africa, the Soviets managed single-handedly to force the German army into retreat at Stalingrad, where fierce fighting lasted from August 1942 to January 1943. The Battle of Stalingrad was a major turning point in the war. Axis soldiers in north Africa also surrendered in May 1943. The following summer, the Allied forces overran the island of Sicily and moved into southern Italy. Italians overthrew Mussolini and opened communication with General Dwight D. Eisenhower, commander of the Allied forces in Europe. By 1944 the Allied forces reached Rome.

National Archives

■ A photograph taken on D-Day, June 6, 1944, as U.S. troops waded to shore from their landing craft and faced German artillery fire on Omaha Beach. This is a rare surviving photograph from the initial Normandy invasion because so many of the photographers, along with thousands of soldiers, died at the scene.

The long-awaited Allied invasion across the English Channel finally began on June 6, 1944, code named D-Day. At dawn, in the largest amphibious landing in history, more than 4,000 Allied ships descended on the French beaches at Normandy. As the troops splashed onto shore, they met a barrage of German fire. Many thousands died on the beach that day. Over the next ten days, more than 1 million soldiers landed at Normandy, along with 50,000 vehicles and more than 100,000 tons of supplies, opening the way for an advance into Nazi-occupied France.

In the months after D-Day, the western Allies liberated Paris and went on to defeat the Germans in Belgium at the Battle of the Bulge, sending the Nazis into full retreat. The Allied armies then crossed the Rhine River and headed for Berlin. Eisenhower stopped his troops at the Elbe River to let Soviet troops take Berlin. Eisenhower hoped that giving the Soviets the final triumph would ease postwar relations with the Soviet Union—but he also wanted to save American lives. Huge numbers of Soviet troops died in the siege of Berlin, but the war in Europe was nearly over. With the Soviets approaching his bunker in April 1945, Hitler committed suicide. Germany surrendered on May 7, 1945—V-E (Victory in Europe) Day. FDR himself had died suddenly of a cerebral hemorrhage on April 12, 1945.

The War in the Pacific

As the conflict in Europe came to an end, the war in the Pacific continued to rage. Following the attack on Pearl Harbor, Japan continued its conquests in the Pacific. In April 1942, General Douglas MacArthur, driven from the Philippines to Australia, left 12,000 American and 64,000 Filipino soldiers to surrender on the Bataan peninsula and the island of Corregidor. On the infamous "Bataan Death March" to the prison at Camp O'Donnell, the Japanese beat, tortured, and shot the sick and starving troops. As many as 10,000 men died on the march.

World War II in the Pacific

Now in control of Indochina, Thailand, the Philippines, and the chain of islands from Sumatra to Guadalcanal, Japan's military leaders planned to destroy what remained of the U.S. fleet. But MacArthur marshaled his forces and achieved a major victory in the Battle of the Coral Sea in May 1942. U.S. intelligence sources discovered that the Japanese were planning a massive assault on Midway Island, a naval base key to Hawaii's defense. Under the command of Admiral Chester Nimitz, the United States launched a surprise air strike on June 4,

World War II in the Pacific

- Allies
- Areas under Japanese control
- Neutral
- Japanese perimeter 1944
- Allied forces
- Major battles
- Atomic bomb

SOVIET UNION
(U S S R)

MONGOLIA

MANCHUKUO

Vladivostok

CHINA

Beijing

Seoul

Hiroshima

Tokyo

JAPAN

Nanjing

Nagasaki

Yellow
Sea

Shanghai

TIBET

Okinawa
April–June, 1945

Iwo Jima
Feb., 1945

Midway
June, 1942

MARSHALL
ISLANDS

PACIFIC
OCEAN

Tarawa
Nov., 1943

BURMA
(Britain)

Hong Kong

Bay of
Bengal

Manila

PHILIPPINES
(U.S.A.)

Saipan
June, 1944

THAILAND

South
China
Sea

SOLOMON
ISLANDS

Bangkok

INDOCHINA
(France)

Saigon

NORTH
BORNEO

Guadalcanal
Aug., 1942–
Feb., 1943

MALAYA
(Britain)

BRUNEI

NORTHEAST
NEW GUINEA

Coral Sea
May, 1942

Singapore

BORNEO

PAPUA
NEW GUINEA

DUTCH EAST INDIES

AUSTRALIA

■ **MAP 23.3**

WORLD WAR II IN THE PACIFIC   During World War II, the Japanese occupied vast territories in Asia and the Pacific. The Battle of Midway in 1942 was the first major victory for the United States in the Pacific and helped turn the tide of the war in favor of the Allies.

1942, sinking four Japanese carriers, destroying 322 planes, and virtually eliminating Japanese offensive capabilities. Two months later, Nimitz's forces landed at Guadalcanal in the Solomon Islands, subduing the Japanese in five months of brutal fighting. Having seized the offensive, U.S. troops continued toward Japan. MacArthur's forces took New Guinea, and, by February 1944, Nimitz secured the Marshall Islands and the Marianas. Next came Saipan, Iwo Jima, and Okinawa in the spring of 1945.

The war in the Pacific was particularly vicious. Racism on both sides fueled acts of extreme brutality. Japan's leaders believed that their racial superiority gave them a divine mission to conquer Asia. The Japanese tortured prisoners of war and civilians in their conquered lands. They tested biological weapons and conducted medical experiments on live subjects. Japanese troops forced Chinese and Korean women into sexual slavery, euphemistically calling them "**comfort women.**"

Racial hostility also promoted American battlefield savagery. U.S. troops in the Pacific often killed the enemy instead of taking prisoners and desecrated the enemy dead with disrespect equal to that meted out by the Japanese on the bodies of their foes. War correspondent Ernie Pyle explained that "in Europe we felt that our enemies, horrible and deadly as they were, were still people. But . . . the Japanese were looked upon as something subhuman and repulsive, the way some people feel about cockroaches or mice."

The End of the War

Allied leaders met several times to plan for the postwar era. Roosevelt hoped to ensure American dominance and to limit Soviet power. At a conference in Teheran, Iran, in 1943, Roosevelt insisted that the eastern European states of Poland, Latvia, Lithuania, and Estonia should be independent after the war. As the war wound down, Churchill, Stalin, and Roosevelt met again at Yalta, in Ukraine, in February 1945. They agreed to demand Germany's unconditional surrender and to divide the conquered nation into four zones to be occupied by Britain, the Soviet Union, the United States, and France. It became obvious at Yalta that separate spheres of influence would prevail after the war. Poland was a source of contention. Although Stalin nominally agreed to allow free elections in eastern Europe, he intended to make sure that the countries bordering the Soviet Union would be under his control. He also pledged to enter the war against Japan and received assurances that the Soviet Union would regain the lands lost to Japan in the 1904–1905 Russo-Japanese War.

In July 1945, the newly sworn-in American president, Harry Truman, joined Stalin and Churchill (replaced by Clement Attlee after Churchill's election loss) at Potsdam, near Berlin. The three leaders issued a statement demanding "unconditional surrender" from Japan while privately agreeing to let Japan retain its emperor. The rest of the conference focused on postwar Europe.

As the war ended in Europe, Allied troops liberated the Nazi concentration camps. At that moment, the world finally learned the extent of Hitler's "Final Solution." Among the soldiers who first entered the camps were a number of Japanese Americans. Ichiro Imamura described the sight at Dachau: "When the gates swung open, we got our first good look at the prisoners. . . . They were like skeletons—all skin and bones. . . . They were sick, starving and dying." Some of the survivors saw the Japanese American soldiers and feared that they were Japanese allies of the Germans. A *Nisei* soldier reassured them, "I am an American soldier, and you are free."

The atomic bomb offered Truman a new means to end the war. In 1942 Roosevelt had authorized the Manhattan Project, the research program to develop nuclear weapons, at a top-secret laboratory in Los Alamos, New Mexico. The building of the bomb was the work of 125,000 people and cost nearly $2 billion.

When Truman learned of the successful test on July 16, 1945, while at the Potsdam conference, he hoped to avoid an invasion of Japan that would have cost the lives of many American soldiers, and he wanted to send a message to the Soviet Union that the United States would be the dominant power in the postwar world. But some of the scientists who had developed the bomb urged a "demonstration" in a remote, unpopulated area that would impress the Japanese but would not cause loss of life. General George C. Marshall and other military leaders argued in favor of dropping the bomb on military or industrial targets, with ample warning ahead

DOCUMENT

Manhattan Project Notebook

National Archives

■ On V-J Day, August 14, 1945, New Yorkers of Italian descent celebrate Japan's surrender. Although the United States fought against the country of their ancestors, these Americans showed their spirited support for the Allied cause.

of time to enable civilians to leave target areas. But others agreed with Truman that dropping the bomb on a major city, without warning, would be the only way to persuade the Japanese to surrender unconditionally.

When the first bomb exploded over Hiroshima on August 6, 1945, and the second on Nagasaki two days later, the horrifying destructiveness of nuclear weapons became apparent. Even though the American public saw few images of the carnage on the ground, the huge mushroom cloud and the descriptions of cities leveled and people instantly incinerated shocked the nation and the world. In addition to the immediate devastation wreaked by the bomb, deadly radioactive fallout remained in the atmosphere, causing illness and death for months and even years after the attack. On August 14, 1945—V-J (Victory in Japan) Day—the Japanese agreed to surrender, and the official ceremony of surrender took place on September 2.

Conclusion

World War II left massive devastation in its wake all across the globe. Although 400,000 Americans died in the conflict, American casualties were far below those suffered by other countries. The wartime economy provided full employment and brought the nation out of the Great Depression.

The war changed life for Americans in profound ways. Although wartime forged a sense of unity as the nation came together to fight against fascism, it also highlighted fissures within American society. Members of minority groups fought in segregated units. Racial tensions and conflicts erupted at home, even as the country fought against a racist foe. Women joined the paid labor force and the armed services in unprecedented numbers, while at the same time being bombarded by official and cultural messages reminding them that their ultimate service to the nation was as wives and mothers.

While life at home changed dramatically, so did the place of the United States in the world. The war's conclusion did not usher in the era of peace Americans expected. European empires staggered on the brink of collapse. Only the United States and the Soviet Union remained as major military powers, shifting the international balance of power from a multipolar to a bipolar system. For the next half-century, the fallout from World War II, as well as the power struggle between the United States and the Soviet Union, would shape political relationships across the globe.

Sites to Visit

Powers of Persuasion—Poster Art of World War II
www.archives.gov/exhibits/powers_of_persuasion/powers_
of_persuasion_home.html
This Library of Congress site includes posters created during World War II to encourage support for the war and to build morale.

A-Bomb WWW Museum
www.csi.ad.jp/ABOMB/
This site includes information about the impact of the atomic bombs dropped on Japan during World War II as well as materials and images about the development of nuclear weapons.

A People at War
www.archives.gov/exhibits/a_people_at_war/a_people_at_
war.html
This National Archives site includes materials and images about the contributions millions of Americans made to the war effort.

U.S. Holocaust Memorial Museum
www.ushmm.org/
This official Web site of the U.S. Holocaust Memorial Museum in Washington, D.C., covers the history and documents of the Holocaust.

Tuskegee Airmen

www.wpafb.af.mil/museum/history/prewwii/ta.htm

> This site of the Air Force Museum at Wright-Patterson Air Force Base includes information and photographs of the African American pilots of World War II.

Abraham Lincoln Brigade Archives

www.alba-valb.org/aboutalb.htm

> This site has information and articles about the Spanish Civil War and the unit of American volunteers who fought in it.

Zoot Suit Riots

www.pbs.org/wgbh/amex/zoot/

> This Web site from the Public Broadcasting Service (PBS) documentary series *The American Experience* covers the World War II Zoot Suit riots in Los Angeles.

William P. Gottlieb Photographs of the Golden Age of Jazz

memory.loc.gov/ammem/wghtml/wghome.html

> This Library of Congress site includes images, audio, and articles from *Down Beat* magazine in the 1940s.

For Further Reading

General

Paul Fussell, *Wartime: Understanding and Behavior in the Second World War* (1989).

John Keegan, *The Second World War* (1990).

Studs Terkel, *"The Good War": An Oral History of World War II* (1984).

Mobilizing for War

Justus D. Doenecke, *Storm on the Horizon: The Challenge to American Intervention, 1939–1941* (2000).

Thomas J. Fleming, *The New Dealers' War: Franklin D. Roosevelt and the War Within World War II* (2001).

Cecelia Lynch, *Beyond Appeasement: Interpreting Interwar Peace Movements in World Politics* (1999).

Pearl Harbor: The United States Enters the War

Allan Berube, *Coming Out Under Fire: The History of Gay Men and Women in World War Two* (1990).

Akira Iriye, *Pearl Harbor and the Coming of the Pacific War: A Brief History with Documents and Essays* (1999).

Michael S. Sherry, *The Rise of American Air Power: The Creation of Armageddon* (1987).

The Home Front

John Morton Blum, *V Was for Victory: Politics and American Culture During World War II* (1976).

Lewis A. Erenberg and Susan E. Hirsch, *The War in American Culture* (1996).

Elaine Tyler May, *Pushing the Limits: American Women, 1940–1961* (1994).

Race and War

Beth Bailey and David Farber, *The First Strange Place: The Alchemy of Race and Sex in World War II Hawaii* (1992).

Aaron Berman, *Nazism, the Jews and American Zionism, 1933–1948* (1990).

John W. Dower, *War Without Mercy: Race and Power in the Pacific War* (1987).

Barbara Dianne Savage, *Broadcasting Freedom: Radio, War, and the Politics of Race, 1938–1948* (1999).

Total War

Ronald Powaski, *March to Armageddon: The United States and the Nuclear Arms Race, 1939 to the Present* (1987).

George H. Roeder Jr., *The Censored War: American Visual Experience During World War Two* (1993).

Michael S. Sherry, *In the Shadow of War: The United States Since the 1930s* (1995).

Gerhard L. Weinberg, *A World at Arms: A Global History of World War II*, 2nd ed. (2005).

For quizzes and other resources on these topics, go to www.longmanamericanhistory.com.

CHAPTER

24

Cold War and Hot War, 1945–1953

A T 11:30 A.M. ON APRIL 25, 1945, U.S. ARMY PRIVATE JOSEPH POLOWSKY GLIMPSED WHAT looked like the future. The young Chicago native was riding in the lead jeep of an American force along the Elbe River in central Germany when he spotted Russian soldiers on the far side, their medals glistening in the morning sun. Elated, he and five of his comrades found a small boat and paddled across to the eastern bank. Using Polowsky's knowledge of German to communicate, the American soldiers embraced their Soviet allies with laughs and tears. The Russians produced bottles of vodka, and toasts, pledges, singing, and dancing followed. After years of pressing Germany from east and west, the Allies had finally linked up in the heart of Hitler's empire. A reporter wrote of the scene, "You get the feeling of exuberance, a great new world opening up."

Despite his conservative Republican background, Polowsky spent much of the rest of his life advocating American-Russian friendship. He could not forget the transforming experience of that April day along the Elbe and the hopes it engendered for a peaceful future. However, what followed the Allied victory turned out to be not a "great new world" of international peace and brotherhood but the **Cold War** of U.S.-Soviet hostility that lasted for more than four decades. The opposing ideologies—**communism** and capitalist democracy—joined with conflicting national interests to produce this armed stand-off. The American effort to contain the expansion of communist influence entailed a radical reorientation of American involvement abroad in peacetime, including the nation's first peacetime military alliance, the North Atlantic Treaty Organization (NATO). At times the Cold War turned into a hot war of actual shooting, most importantly in the Korean War of 1950–1953 and the Vietnam War in the following decade.

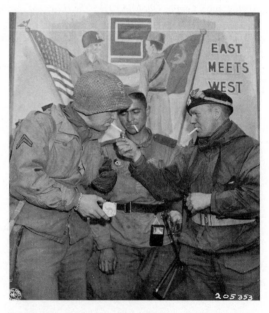

■ Soviet and American troops meet in central Germany in May 1945.

In some ways, the Cold War encouraged efforts at social reform. America's new leading role in world affairs brought its domestic life into the spotlight of world attention. Racial discrimination and violence at home embarrassed American leaders as they spoke of leading the anticommunist "free world" abroad.

But in other ways, the Cold War constrained efforts to bring American life more fully into line with its democratic and egalitarian promise. Rising tensions with communist movements and governments overseas stimulated great anxieties about possible subversion within the nation's own borders. Anticommunist fervor put unions on the defensive and encouraged women to shun the workplace in favor of family life and parenting, particularly in the nation's growing suburbs. This second Red Scare—the first had followed World War I in 1919—reached flood tide by 1950 with the rise to prominence of Senator Joseph McCarthy, a Republican from Wisconsin. McCarthy made a career of blaming supposedly disloyal Americans at home for setbacks to U.S. goals abroad in places such as China and Korea. He left a bitter legacy that long outlasted his political demise in 1954.

The Uncertainties of Victory

Franklin Roosevelt's death in April 1945 stunned the nation and the world. Elected four times to the presidency, he had dominated American politics like no figure before or since. Just as the unprecedented destruction of World War II was finally ending, the leadership of the nation passed into the new and less tested hands of Harry Truman. Peace brought an array of uncertainties and immediate needs. The victors had to reconstruct a world that had been damaged, physically and psychologically, almost beyond recognition. Spared the destruction visited elsewhere, the United States faced the different challenge of demobilizing its military forces and reconverting to a peacetime economy. Intense conflicts along the color line and in the workplace revealed real differences among Americans about the shape of the democracy they had fought to defend.

Ed Clark/TimePix

■ Franklin D. Roosevelt's death at his vacation home in Warm Springs, Georgia, stunned a nation and a world that had not known another U.S. president for 13 years. Navy bandsman Graham Jackson was one of Roosevelt's favorite musicians. As the procession began to transport the president's body north for burial in Hyde Park, New York, Jackson captured the grief of millions of Americans as he played the sweet, slow strains of "Going Home."

Global Destruction

World War II wrought death on a scale that defies comprehension. From England in the west to the islands of New Guinea in the east, from the Baltic Sea in the north to the Sahara Desert in the south, much of Europe and Asia was left in ruins. Soviet and American power had finally crushed the Axis, with Berlin now a "city of the dead" and Japan's urban landscape devastated by firebombing and nuclear attacks. Most of the victors were only marginally better off.

Only one of the major combatants emerged from the war in better shape than at the beginning. The American people, one official remarked in 1945, "are in the pleasant predicament of having to learn to live 50 percent better than they have ever lived before." Many Americans suffered terribly in the war, of course; 400,000 died, leaving behind desolate families, and millions of veterans returned with traumas that colored the remainder of their lives. But such casualties paled in comparison to those of other belligerent nations. With just 6 percent of the world's population and 50 percent of its wealth, the United States enjoyed a position of staggering economic advantage in comparison with the rest of the world.

Americans' overriding fear was that the end of the fighting might return the country to the state it had faced when the war began: economic depression. The nation's awesome industrial productivity depended on government spending, which was now to be cut back sharply. International trade might pick up much of the slack, but the war had destroyed most of the purchasing power of U.S. trading partners in Europe and Asia. Rising tensions between the two primary victors—the United States and the Soviet Union—hampered the process of postwar reconstruction. President Truman showed his frustration with the Soviet military occupation of eastern Europe by lecturing Soviet diplomats and abruptly cutting off Lend-Lease aid to the USSR. Soviet dictator Joseph Stalin feared America's new global military power, manifest in its monopoly of the atomic bomb, and was determined to secure his European border against future invasion from the West.

Vacuums of Power

World War II altered the world's ideological and physical landscape. Japan and Germany, the centers of prewar power in Asia and continental Europe, were vacuums waiting to be filled and reshaped by their conquerors. In addition to defeating two nations, the Allies had also discredited the right-wing ideas on which those governments had been built: fascism and militarism. Fascism's murderous character tarred those who had collaborated with the Axis during the war, primarily conservatives in countries such as France who preferred fascism to socialism.

Into many of the postwar vacuums of power flowed a newly prominent worldwide left. Socialists, communists, and other radicals espoused communal rather than individualistic values. The occupying Soviet forces installed communist governments in eastern Europe by force (sometimes called "Red Army socialism"), and Socialist and Communist parties rose sharply in popularity in France, Italy, Belgium, and Scandinavia. The nominally socialist Labor party took power in Great Britain, defeating war leader Winston Churchill and his Conservative party at the polls. Europeans across the continent established welfare states to provide a minimum standard of living for all their citizens.

This turn to the left encompassed most of the globe. Africans began organizing for eventual independence from European rule, and Asians launched the final phase of their anticolonial struggle for liberation. Indonesia fought its way free from the Dutch, and India gained its freedom from Britain. In French Indochina, Ho Chi Minh quoted from Thomas Jefferson's Declaration of Independence as he announced the creation of an independent Vietnam. The Allies established the new United Nations (UN) in San Francisco in April 1945. Eventually housed in New York, its General Assembly gave all nations an equal voice and vote in deliberations, and its small Security Council—responsible for guiding any UN military actions—gave a permanent seat and veto power to five nations: the United States, the USSR, Britain, France, and China. The 1948 UN Human Rights Charter helped put practitioners of colonialism and racial discrimination on the defensive by declaring worldwide support for the principles of national self-determination and equal treatment for all peoples.

Postwar Reconversion

The fundamental task for Americans at home was to convert from a wartime society back to a peacetime one. They were especially eager to bring home the 12 million men in uniform serving abroad. Eager to resume civilian life, the veterans walked off ships' gangplanks into a country in transition. Wartime rationing was lifted on goods such as sugar and gasoline, and the 35-mph speed limit was withdrawn. But as orders for war materials dried up, taking jobs with them, wartime inflation persisted. Housing remained especially scarce. In the richest country in the world, one-third of the citizens still lived in poverty, with neither running water nor flush toilets.

To ease the transition home, Congress had passed the Servicemen's Readjustment Act of 1944 (the GI Bill) to provide crucial financial aid to veterans. It gave low-cost mortgages that helped create an explosion in home ownership. It created Veterans Administration hospitals to provide lifetime medical care. And it paid tuition and stipends for college and vocational training, making higher education broadly available for the first time. The 2 percent of veterans who were women also made use of these benefits. In the postwar era, when American politics generally became more conservative—shifting away from the New Deal reform spirit and toward an anticommunist emphasis—the GI Bill was the one area in which the United States expanded its own welfare state.

The postwar transition presented particular challenges to American women. Millions of them had gone to work outside the home during the war and found economic independence in doing so. Now they faced powerful pressures to leave the workforce and return to a domestic life of old and new families. Many women accepted this return to the domestic sphere, content to focus on marriage and family life. Others felt differently. "War jobs have uncovered unsuspected abilities in American women," one argued. "Why lose all these abilities?"

Contesting Racial Hierarchies

African Americans faced a similar problem. After finding new opportunities in industrial employment during the war, they were laid off afterward in favor of returning white veterans. Like women, blacks were expected by others to retreat into deference. Black veterans spearheaded the resistance to this notion.

African American efforts to overcome discrimination met fierce white resistance in 1946 and 1947. In the South, where most black Americans still lived, a wave of beatings and lynchings greeted black veterans in uniform and their attempts to register to vote. White Northerners also used violence to preserve the segregated character of neighborhoods in Chicago, Detroit, and other cities. They destroyed the property and threatened the lives of blacks who dared to move to previously all-white blocks, effectively confining African Americans to impoverished areas.

VIDEO

Post-World War II Society

John Vachon

■ **Japanese American women pack lima beans into boxes for freezing at Seabrook Farms, near Bridgeton, New Jersey, in 1947. Unlike the northern part of the state, which was closely tied to New York City, rural southern New Jersey was a rich fruit-and-vegetable-growing region. After their release from the internment camps of World War II, Americans of Japanese descent joined their fellow citizens in finding work where they could in a peacetime economy no longer shrouded by the Great Depression.**

The retreat of European colonialism and American competition with the Soviet Union nonetheless encouraged many white Americans to acknowledge the contradiction between leading the "free world" and limiting the freedoms of Americans of color. A series of Supreme Court decisions validated the long-term strategy of the National Association for the Advancement of Colored People (NAACP) for contesting segregation in the courts. Court rulings outlawed segregation in voting primaries (*Smith v. Allwright*, 1944), interstate transportation (*Morgan v. Virginia*, 1946), contracts for house sales (*Shelley v. Kraemer*, 1948), and graduate schools (*Sweatt v. Painter* and *McLaurin v. Oklahoma*, 1950).

Popular culture moved in the same direction of breaking down racial barriers. *Billboard* magazine in 1949 changed the category of "race music" to "rhythm and blues" as white record producers and radio disc jockeys such as Alan Freed began to bring the early rock 'n' roll of African American musicians to mainstream white audiences. By 1955 young white musicians such as Bill Haley and Elvis Presley joined black stars such as Chuck Berry and Little Richard in creating a wildly popular sound that transcended racial categories. Professional baseball erased its color line when Jackie Robinson, a former four-sport star at the University of California–Los Angeles and lieutenant in the U.S. Army, joined the Brooklyn Dodgers in 1947.

Native Americans and Mexican Americans faced similar discrimination in the Southwest and elsewhere. With war veterans in the fore, they also organized to contest unfair education and election practices. "If we are good enough to fight, why aren't we good enough to vote?" asked returning Navajo soldiers in New Mexico and Arizona, where the state constitutions prohibited Indian residents from voting, until successfully challenged in 1948. The League of United Latin American Citizens (LULAC) followed a strategy similar to that of the NAACP regarding educational discrimination, leading to a federal Court's decision in *Mendez v. Westminster* (1946) outlawing segregated schools for Mexican Americans in California. In parallel fashion, indigenous Alaskans organized in the Alaska Native Brotherhood successfully lobbied the territorial legislature in Juneau to pass an antidiscrimination law in 1945.

Class Conflict

In many ways, 1946 seemed like 1919. A world war had just ended, in which corporations had made handsome profits. American workers had enjoyed nearly full employment and improving wages and had joined unions in large numbers. In 1946 one-third of the workforce held a union card, the largest portion ever. But the end of war-related orders led to job cuts and the loss of overtime wages, and by the spring of 1946, 1.8 million workers were out on strike.

Mirroring World War I, the conclusion of hostilities in 1945 revealed rising tensions between the United States and the Soviet Union. The spread of leftist revolutions abroad amplified fears of communist influence in American unions, especially because a few of the most effective Congress of Industrial Organizations (CIO) organizers were Communist party members or at least sympathetic to an emphasis on class conflict between owners and workers. As in 1919, a Red Scare began to develop, egged on by a business community that used the supposed threat of the tiny U.S. Communist party to weaken the much larger and less radical union movement. In contrast to the end of World War I, however, federal law guaranteed the right of workers to bargain collectively, and the strikes of 1946 resulted in some negotiated wage increases.

The tide turned against unions as anticommunism intensified. The Republican party claimed a sweeping victory in the 1946 congressional elections, taking control of both the House and the Senate in a stark rejection of Truman's leadership. Republicans and conservative Democrats then passed the Taft-Hartley Act in 1947 over the president's veto, weakening unions by prohibiting secondary boycotts (against the products of a company whose workers were on strike) and requiring union officials to swear anticommunist oaths. Two years later, the increasingly conservative CIO expelled eleven unions that still had leftist and communist leadership. At the same time, the expanding U.S. economy after 1947 pulled many skilled workers up into the middle class and gave them a larger stake in the status quo.

The Quest for Security

On February 21, 1947, a British official in Washington informed the U.S. government that Britain could no longer provide financial assistance to the anticommunist governments of Greece and Turkey. This marked a watershed in modern world history. Long the greatest imperial power and the dominant outside force in the Middle East, Britain was beginning a protracted, slow retreat. Left in its wake were vacuums of power, particularly in the Middle East, South Asia, and Africa. President Truman and his advisers believed that either Soviet or American influence would flow into these regions. The Truman administration formulated a policy to contain communism in the eastern Mediterranean that it quickly expanded to encompass the entire noncommunist world. Powerful new nuclear weapons increased anxieties about the nation's security.

Redefining National Security

U.S. policymakers had ended World War II with one primary goal. They were determined to revive the global capitalist economy that had nearly dissolved in the Great Depression of the 1930s and had then been battered by the war. American prosperity and freedom, they believed, depended on a world system of free trade because Americans simply could not consume all the products of their efficient farms and factories. If they could not sell the surplus abroad, the United States would slide back into an economic depression.

"National security" was expanding to mean something very different from simply defending the nation's territory against invasion. For the disproportionately powerful United States, national security after 1945 came to be identified with the creation and preservation of a free-trading capitalist world order. American national security was seen to be at stake almost everywhere around the globe.

The primary threat to that security came from the Soviet Union. The danger lay in Soviet encouragement, by example and assistance, of revolutions that rejected market economies and individualist ethics. Demoralized by the war's destruction and by grim postwar economic conditions, western Europeans and others seemed to be considering the paths of socialism and communism. "Hopeless and hungry people," Secretary of State Dean Acheson warned, "often resort to desperate measures."

> *"Hopeless and hungry people," Acheson warned, "often resort to desperate measures."*

Conflict with the Soviet Union

The antifascist alliance of the Soviet Union and the United States dissolved rapidly as their conflicting interests reemerged after the war. Long skeptical of the capitalist world it wanted to replace, the Soviet government viewed expansive U.S. interests as evidence of "striving for world supremacy." Yet Moscow was just as clearly expanding its own sphere of national security, with Soviet troops remaining in areas they had occupied during the war: Manchuria, northern Korea, Iran, and especially eastern and central Europe. Each side spoke of the other's goal as "world domination."

Contrasting experiences in World War II amplified historical and ideological differences. Whereas the war brought the United States out of the global capitalist depression (which the

Soviets had avoided), it brought the USSR into a depression caused by the invading Germans' destruction of the western portion of the country. With a decimated population, a battered economy, and minimal air and naval forces, the postwar Soviet Union remained a regional power based on its army. The United States was the only truly global power, with a vast naval armada and air force projecting military might onto every continent, undergirded by the most productive economy in world history.

The two nations' visions of the postwar world order reflected these relative positions. Americans sought an open world for the free flow of goods and most ideas and proved willing to tolerate and even embrace dictatorial governments as long as they were anticommunist and open to foreign trade and investment. Meanwhile, the Soviets called for a more traditional division into separate spheres of influence for the great powers.

Conflicts over specific areas liberated from the Nazis hastened the onset of the Cold War in the first eighteen months after the end of World War II. Whereas the Soviets wanted reparations and a deindustrialized Germany that could never threaten it again, the United States considered a rebuilt industrial German state crucial for a healthy, integrated western European economy. Britain and France had gone to war in defense of an independent Poland, but for Stalin control of Poland was not negotiable because it had been "the corridor for attack on Russia." Moscow and Washington also clashed over Iran, where the Soviets briefly encouraged a leftist uprising in the northern part of the oil-rich country to counteract British and American influence in the capital city of Teheran. U.S. policymakers worried about Soviet requests to Turkey for greater control of the straits leading out of the Black Sea into the Mediterranean.

The Policy of Containment

DOCUMENT

Churchill's "Iron Curtain" Speech

Diplomat George Kennan best articulated the policy of **containment** in an influential telegram sent from his post at the U.S. embassy in Moscow in February 1946. Kennan explained Soviet hostility as a function of traditional Russian insecurity overlaid with newer Marxist justifications. He called for "the adroit and vigilant application of counterforce" against all Soviet efforts at expanding their influence. One month later, on March 5, 1946, former British prime minister Winston Churchill warned that a Russian "iron curtain" had descended across Europe, imprisoning all those to the east of it. "The reins of world leadership are fast slipping from Britain's competent but now very weak hands," the State Department argued. "These reins will be picked up either by the United States or by Russia."

"The reins of world leadership are fast slipping from Britain's . . . hands. These reins will be picked up either by the United States or by Russia."

Picking up those reins meant a fundamental reorientation for the United States. No longer just the dominant force in the Western Hemisphere, it would have to maintain its wartime projection of military forces around the globe—permanently. In an address to Congress on March 12, 1947, asking for $400 million in aid for Greece and Turkey, Truman simplified the world system into two "ways of life," those of "free peoples" and those of "terror and oppression" under communist rule. All nations must choose between them, he declared, and the United States must support "free peoples who are resisting attempted subjugation by armed minorities or outside pressures."

The **Truman Doctrine**, as it became known, exaggerated a real problem in order to win public support for a new international role for the United States. It funded the governments of Turkey and Greece, but it framed the new policy broadly, opening the path to supporting anticommunist regimes and opposing revolutions around the world for decades to come. The most important immediate step was the reconstruction of a vibrant, reintegrated western European economy. The United States provided $13 billion

Members of NATO (1949)
Members of Warsaw Pact (1955)
Nonaligned counties
($) Participants in the Marshall Plan, 1947–1952
Year first atomic device was tested by that country

ICELAND ($)

NORWAY
Oslo

SWEDEN
Stockholm

FINLAND
Helsinki

U.S.S.R.
1949

IRELAND
Dublin ($)

U.S loan of $3.5 billion, 1946

GREAT BRITAIN
1952
London ($)

DENMARK
($) Copenhagen

Baltic Sea

Berlin blockade, 1948–1949

NETHERLANDS
Amsterdam

Berlin

POLAND
Warsaw

ATLANTIC OCEAN

Brussels
BELGIUM ($)
Bonn

EAST GERMANY

Prague
CZECHOSLOVAKIA

Communist coup, 1948
U.S.S.R. invasion, 1968

Paris
LUX.
WEST GERMANY
Joined NATO, 1955

Anti-communist revolution failed, 1956

Withdrew forces from NATO, 1966

SWITZ.
AUSTRIA
Vienna
HUNGARY
Budapest

FRANCE
1960 ($)

Zones of occupation ended, 1955

ROMANIA
Bucharest

Belgrade
YUGOSLAVIA

Black Sea

PORTUGAL
Lisbon ($)
Madrid

SPAIN
Joined NATO, 1982

Tito–Stalin Schism, 1948

BULGARIA
Sofia

ITALY
Rome

GREECE
Athens
ALBANIA

Ankara
TURKEY

Withdrew from Warsaw Pact, 1968

Truman Doctrine, 1947 joined NATO, 1952

■ **MAP 24.1**

EUROPE DIVIDED BY THE COLD WAR   For centuries Europe had controlled much of the rest of the world. After 1945, Russians occupied the eastern half of the continent and Americans wielded dominant influence in the western half. This division of Europe into communist and noncommunist blocs lasted until the end of the Cold War in 1989.

between 1948 and 1952 to fund the European Recovery Program, commonly known as the Marshall Plan for its chief architect, Secretary of State George Marshall (1947–1949).

Ensuring western European security against the Red Army also entailed the first U.S. military alliance in peacetime. The victors of World War II divided a defeated Germany into separate zones of occupation. The British, French, and American decision in March 1948 to create

DOCUMENT

The Marshall Plan

a unified state out of the western sectors of Germany led a few months later to a year-long Soviet blockade of western access to Berlin and fears of a general war. The creation of the North Atlantic Treaty Organization (NATO) in 1949 made the American military commitment to Europe permanent. The point of NATO for western Europe, its British first secretary general said, was to "keep the Americans in, the Russians out, and the Germans down."

VIDEO
The Onset of Cold War

The onset of the Cold War determined the fate of the defeated powers of World War II. The Truman administration was committed to "push ahead with the reconstruction of those two great workshops of Europe and Asia—Germany and Japan." This agenda replaced initial concerns about rooting out Nazism and punishing war criminals, as at the Nuremberg trials of surviving Nazi leaders in 1945–1946. The American occupation of Japan under General Douglas MacArthur initially (1945–1947) emphasized democratization of Japanese society, including building labor unions, weakening corporate monopolies, ensuring women's political rights, and punishing war criminals. But rising U.S. tensions with the Soviets and the imminent victory of the Communist forces in China's civil war prompted American officials to shift course by 1948. Henceforth, they focused on rebuilding as quickly as possible Japan's industrial economy as the hub of capitalist Asia.

Colonialism and the Cold War

The world's nonwhite majority still lived under European colonial control, and for them the struggle for national independence and racial equality was the great issue of the late 1940s and 1950s. In this North-South conflict, as opposed to the East-West conflict of the Cold War, the United States held an awkward position. Its primary NATO partners included the greatest colonial powers: Britain, France, Belgium, the Netherlands, and Portugal. Racial segregation in the United States further undercut American leadership of the "free world."

For the world's nonwhite majority, the struggle for national independence and racial equality was the great issue of the late 1940s and 1950s.

With European rule in Asia and Africa on the way out, the Truman administration sought a gradual transfer of colonial rule into the hands of local pro-West elites. The U.S. grant of official independence to the Philippines in 1946 was offered as a model, as was the British departure from India a year later. However, the importance of Europe for America meant supporting even those imperialists who did not leave peacefully, such as the French who dug in against communist-led revolutionaries in Vietnam (part of French Indochina).

DOCUMENT
Press Release Announcing U.S. Recognition of Israel

The British withdrawal from Palestine in 1948 created a peculiar dilemma for the United States. Jewish settlers—primarily from Europe and often survivors of the Holocaust—proclaimed the new state of Israel against the wishes of the Arab majority. Secretary of State Marshall and others urged Truman not to recognize Israel in order to avoid imperiling U.S. relations with the Arab oil-producing states. The president sympathized with the Jewish desire for a homeland, however, and understood the importance of American Jews as constituents of the Democratic party in the 1940s. His decision to recognize Israel, which most Middle Easterners viewed as a new colonial state, set the United States on a course of enduring friendship with that nation and enduring conflict with Israel's Arab neighbors and the Palestinians.

The Impact of Nuclear Weapons

Scientists in the 1940s dramatically increased Americans' sense of personal safety by introducing the use of antibiotics. "Miracle drugs" such as penicillin cured common bacterial infections that had previously been debilitating or fatal. What science gave with one hand

■ Soldiers watch as "Dog," a 21-kiloton nuclear device, is dropped from a bomber at the Nevada Test Site at Yucca Flat, northwest of Las Vegas, in November 1951. U.S. atomic specialists tested nuclear weapons first in the Marshall Islands of the western Pacific Ocean, especially the Bikini atoll, beginning in 1946, and then in Nevada beginning in January 1951. Residents downwind from the test sites suffered various adverse health effects from radiation exposure, including high cancer rates.

it threatened to take away with the other, however. The use of atomic weapons on Japan foreshadowed a future of utter insecurity in which instantaneous destruction of entire nations could occur without warning.

Even without being fired again in war after 1945, nuclear weapons altered the American environment. Weapon tests released vast quantities of radiation into the atmosphere. Local cancer rates spiked upward for Bikini Islanders in the Pacific, where the first tests occurred, and then for farmers and ranchers in Utah and Nevada, when tests began 65 miles northwest of Las Vegas in 1953. Navajo Indians mining uranium in the Southwest paid dearly for their intensive exposure to the poisonous material, as did thousands of workers involved in nuclear weapon production. Weapon assembly plants in Hanford, Washington, and Rocky Flats, Colorado, leaked radioactivity into the groundwater. In combination with the nuclear power industry, atomic weapon development resulted in an enormous supply of radioactive waste—deadly for 10,000 more years—that the U.S. government still does not know how to dispose of safely.

The government offered reassurances about the safety of the atom, and the Atomic Energy Commission covered up evidence of radioactivity's ill effects. But many Americans were deeply anxious about this destructive new power that loomed over their lives, especially as the Soviet-American arms race intensified. Science fiction movies painted

VIDEO
Duck and Cover

frightening pictures of a future devastated by nuclear war and haunted by exposure to radiation. Concerns about a nuclear world escalated with the successful 1952 test of an American hydrogen bomb, a thousand times more powerful than the device that destroyed Hiroshima.

A Cold War Society

Expanding economic opportunities and narrowing political freedoms characterized American society in the first decade of the Cold War. A withering fire of anticommunist repression pushed dissident views to the margins of the nation's political life. Americans largely accepted this new conformity for two reasons: their desire to support their government during international crises, especially the Korean War (1950–1953), and a consumer cornucopia that surrounded them with attractive material goods. Americans moved to the suburbs, and to the South and West.

By 1947 the United States was launching into an era of extraordinary economic expansion that continued for twenty-five years. Since Ben Franklin's time, Americans had been known for thrift in their pursuit of wealth, but after 1945 the long-cherished principle of delaying gratification declined steeply. "Buy now, pay later," General Motors urged as it offered an installment plan to customers. Diner's Club introduced the first credit card in 1950. In a formulation breathtaking for its distance from Puritan and immigrant traditions of saving for the future, writer William Whyte observed that "thrift is now un-American."

> *Expanding economic opportunities and narrowing political freedoms characterized American society in the first decade of the Cold War.*

Family Lives

IMAGE
Levittown

Many white Americans embraced the opportunity to move to the suburbs after World War II. Seeking larger homes and yards and quieter neighborhoods, they flocked to new developments such as Levittown outside New York City on Long Island. Suburbs were not for everyone, however. Even as federal courts struck down segregation laws in some spheres of American life, agencies such as the Veterans Administration and the Federal Housing Administration were encouraging residential separation by race. Private banks did the same. Other government policies, including highway construction and tax benefits for homeowners, promoted the growth of suburbs at the cost of cities. A third epoch in American residential history began by 1970 when more Americans resided in suburbs than cities, parallel to the 1920 shift from a rural majority to an urban one.

Suburban life encouraged a sharpening of gender roles among the growing middle class. Men commuted to work while women were expected to find fulfillment in marriage and motherhood, including a nearly full-time job of unpaid housework. "We married what we wanted to be," one female college graduate recalled. "If we wanted to be a lawyer or a doctor we married one." Despite this partial retreat from wartime employment, however, fully one-third of American women continued to work for pay outside the home. The economic circumstances of most black women offered them little choice, and most wound up doing double housework: their own and that of families employing them as domestics.

From 1946 to 1964, women giving birth at a younger age to more children created the demographic bulge known as the baby boom. Large families reinforced the domestic focus of most women, putting the work of child-rearing at the center of their lives. Fatherhood became increasingly a badge of masculinity. Family physician Benjamin Spock published *Baby and Child Care* (1946), a runaway best-seller that helped shift the emphasis in American parenting from strictness to greater nurturance.

Married mothers were celebrated, but unmarried ones were rebuked. Despite the greater freedom of the war years, the sexual double standard remained in place, with women's virtue linked directly to virginity in a way that men's was not. Birth control devices such as the diaphragm were legal only for married women and only in certain states. Women seeking to terminate unwanted pregnancies had to consider illegal abortions, the only kind available before 1970; millions did so, including one-fifth of all married women and a majority of single women who became pregnant. Two studies of American sexual behavior by Dr. Alfred Kinsey of Indiana University in 1948 and 1953 shocked the public with their revelation of widespread premarital and extramarital sexual intercourse as well as homosexual liaisons.

The Growth of the South and the West

Before World War II, American cultural, industrial, and financial power had always been centered in the urban North, but federal expenditures during the war began to change this. The U.S. Army built most of its training bases in the South, where land close to the coasts was thinly populated and inexpensive. Military bases and defense industries sprang up along the West Coast to project power into the Pacific against Japan. U.S. troops built the Alcan (Alaska–Canada) Highway, and millions of GIs passed through Hawaii en route to the Pacific battlefront. Fighting against the Japanese to defend Pearl Harbor and the Aleutian Islands brought the once-distant territories of Hawaii and Alaska more into Americans' consciousness, setting them on the path to statehood in 1959.

Bettmann/CORBIS

■ A new cloverleaf intersection on a freeway arches across the northern New Jersey suburbs in 1949. Multilane, limited-access highways became common after World War II. A new word, "smog" (neither smoke nor fog), appeared to describe the urban pollution caused by trucks and commuter vehicles.

**Population Shifts,
1940—1950**

The **Sunbelt** of the South, the Southwest, and California grew rapidly after the war, whereas older Rustbelt cities of the Northeast and Midwest such as Buffalo and Detroit began to lose manufacturing jobs and population. Like the 440,000 people who moved to Los Angeles during the war, postwar migrants to California and Arizona appreciated the weather and the economic opportunities. Military spending underwrote half the jobs in California during the first decade of the Cold War. Migrants from south of the border, meanwhile, found work primarily in California's booming agricultural sector.

Two industries particularly stimulated the growth of the Sunbelt: cars and air conditioning. Automobiles helped shape the economies of western states, where new cities were built out of sprawling suburbs. New car sales shot up from 70,000 in 1945 to 7.9 million in 1955. Inexpensive gasoline, refined from the abundant crude oil of Texas and Oklahoma, powered this fleet. Automobile exhaust pipes replaced industrial smokestacks as the primary source of air pollution. Air conditioning also became widely available after World War II and contributed to the breakdown of the South's regional distinctiveness. From Miami and Atlanta to Houston and Washington, D.C., the new Sunbelt depended on the indoor comfort brought by controlling summertime heat and humidity.

Harry Truman and the Limits of Liberal Reform

On the political front, the onset of the Cold War narrowed the range of American political discourse. In seeking to consolidate the New Deal legacy, President Truman found himself boxed in by conservative Republican opponents. Allied governments in western Europe had embraced the idea that access to health care was a right of every citizen in a modern democratic state. But when Truman proposed a system of national health care, conservatives quashed the legislation in Congress.

Perhaps the most blatant omission of the New Deal had been protection against racial discrimination. As the Cold War intensified, the fact that millions of Americans still lacked basic guarantees for their civil rights was an embarrassing contradiction to rhetoric about ensuring rights and liberties throughout the "free world." Truman campaigned for reelection in 1948 on a platform of support for civil rights that was unprecedented in the White House. That summer he ordered the desegregation of the armed forces and the federal civil service.

African American voters in Chicago, Cleveland, and other northern cities played a key role in swing states; their solid support lifted Truman to a narrow and surprising victory over the heavily favored Republican candidate, New York governor Thomas Dewey. Truman's reelection was all the more impressive because of the fracturing of the Democratic party. Alienated by the civil rights plank, white Southerners walked out of the Democratic convention and ran South Carolina governor Strom Thurmond as an independent candidate. The "Dixiecrats" won four states in the Deep South, foreshadowing the abandonment by white Southerners of the party of their parents in the 1960s. Truman won as a man of the moderately liberal center, fierce against communism, usually supportive of the rights of organized labor, and opposed to discrimination.

The Cold War at Home

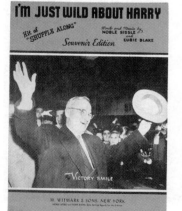

In a pattern that became known as **McCarthyism**, mostly Republican conservatives attributed communist successes abroad—especially in China and Korea—to liberal Democrats in the Truman administration, accusing them of sympathizing with and even spying for the Soviet Union. The hunt for domestic subversives to explain international setbacks was grounded in the reality of a handful of actual Soviet spies, most notably Julius Rosenberg (who was executed for treason in 1953 along with his apparently innocent wife, Ethel) and nuclear scientist Klaus Fuchs. But this second Red Scare expressed primarily the frustration of being unable to translate vast U.S. power into greater control of world events. And it served, above all, to cast suspicion on the patriotism of liberals at home.

Despite his general support for civil liberties, Truman helped set the tone for pursuing suspected traitors. In an unsuccessful effort to fortify his right flank against Republican attacks, he established a federal employee loyalty program in March 1947 as the domestic equivalent of the Truman Doctrine. Attorney General Tom Clark drew up a list of supposedly subversive organizations that the FBI and state committees on "un-American activities" then hounded. In a case with sobering implications for free speech, federal courts in 1949 convicted the leaders of the U.S. Communist party of promoting the overthrow of the U.S. government. Words alone, the courts ruled, could be treasonable—the same logic as the wartime Sedition Act of 1918 (see Chapter 20).

Republicans reaped the benefits of the Red Scare. Most Americans who had sympathized in any way with the Soviet Union in the Depression years were by the late 1940s merely liberal Democrats, but the House Un-American Activities Committee (HUAC) zeroed in on their earlier records. Investigating Hollywood, the television industry, and universities as well as the executive branch of the U.S. government, HUAC destroyed the careers of prominent figures as well as average Americans.

The era found its name in the previously obscure junior senator from Wisconsin, Republican Joseph McCarthy. With a single speech in Wheeling, West Virginia, on February 9, 1950, this ambitious politician soared to prominence. "I have here in my hand a list of 205" Communist party members working in the State Department, he declared. Over the next four years, the numbers and names changed as McCarthy stayed one step ahead of the evidence while intimidating witnesses before his Senate Permanent Subcommittee on Investigations. He talked about communists, but his show was about Democrats. As the war in Korea raged, he mercilessly red-baited (attacked as "soft" on communism) the Truman administration. But after the Republican electoral victory in 1952, his excesses lost their partisan utility. With the end of the war in Korea and his ill-advised attacks on the U.S. Army as supposedly infiltrated by communists (the Army-McCarthy hearings), he was at last censured by his Senate colleagues in 1954 and died an early, alcohol-related death in 1957.

TABLE 24-1			
The Election of 1948			
Candidate	Political Party	Popular Vote (%)	Electoral Vote
Harry S. Truman	Democratic	49.5	304
Thomas E. Dewey	Republican	45.1	189
J. Strom Thurmond	State-Rights Democratic	2.4	38
Henry A. Wallace	Progressive	2.4	—

DOCUMENT

McCarthy, Wheeling, West Virginia Speech

McCarthy talked about communists, but his show was about Democrats. As the war in Korea raged, he mercilessly red-baited the Truman administration.

Who Is a Loyal American?

The Cold War politics of inclusion and exclusion established a new profile for loyal Americans. Private familial and material concerns were expected to replace public interest in social reform. Anticommunists launched a withering assault on homosexuals as "perverts" and threats to the nation's security. Church membership climbed in tandem with condemnations of "godless communism," and Congress added the words "under God" to the Pledge of Allegiance. Discrimination against Roman Catholics and Jews, though still evident, declined as Catholics such as McCarthy proved intensely anticommunist and as pictures and stories emerged to reveal the horrors of the Nazi Holocaust against the Jews. More inclusive references to the "Judeo-Christian tradition" became common.

■ From 1951 to 1953, Mexican American miners went on strike against the Empire Zinc Mining Company in Silver City, New Mexico. Women took on major roles in this labor action, which inspired a famous movie, *Salt of the Earth*. Defiant in the face of police and company shotguns and billy clubs, Elvira Molano (center) served as cochair of the union negotiating committee and became known as "the most arrested woman" during the strike.

American leadership of the global anticommunist cause strengthened the struggle for racial equality at home, within certain limits. The **NAACP** and most African Americans took an anticommunist position in accord with Truman, in return for his support of civil rights. They downplayed their concern for colonial independence in Africa and Asia to support NATO. The American GI Forum (Latino veterans) and the Japanese American Citizen League also worked within the confines of Cold War politics to end discrimination.

For impoverished Native Americans, the government seemed to give with one hand and take away with the other. In 1946 Truman established the Indian Claims Commission to consider payment for lands taken and treaties broken. But Dillon S. Myer, director of the Bureau of Indian Affairs, closed reservation schools, withdrew support for traditional cultural activities, and launched an urban relocation program, all intended to move Native Americans into the mainstream and get the government "out of the Indian business."

Immigrants, too, received mixed messages. The McCarran-Walter Act (1952) ended the long-standing ban on allowing people of Asian descent not born in the United States to become U.S. citizens. But it preserved the discriminatory 1924 system of "national origins" for allocating numbers of immigrants from different countries. The bill also strengthened the attorney general's authority to deport aliens who were suspected of subversive intentions. The powerful 1953 film *Salt of the Earth*—with its pro-union, prosocialist, pro-feminist, and pro-Latino sympathies—was condemned as subversive and rarely screened until the 1970s.

The United States and Asia

Japan did not conquer independent nations in its sweep southward at the start of World War II. Instead it defeated the forces of imperial powers: the French in Indochina, the Dutch in Indonesia, the British in Singapore and Malaya, and the Americans in the Philippines. In a single swoop, Japanese soldiers demonstrated the absurdity of white supremacy and cleared the way for the end of colonialism in Asia. Then Japan's retreat in 1945 left vacuums of power throughout the region. Into them flowed two contenders: the returning but gravely weakened European imperialists, and Asian nationalists such as Ho Chi Minh in Vietnam. Americans were not passive observers of this struggle, as they sought to establish a new free-trading order in the region. As communist forces won a civil war in China, the U.S. government bulked up its military and intelligence capacities and went to war in Korea.

The Chinese Civil War

Americans had long felt a special connection to China. Half of the thousands of Christian missionaries sent out by American churches in the early twentieth century had been posted there. Entrepreneurs eyed the Chinese market, home to one-fifth of the world's potential consumers. During World War II, Chinese resistance to Japan's invasion occupied millions of Tokyo's soldiers who would otherwise have been shooting at American GIs. The close U.S. alliance with the government of Jiang Jieshi seemed to confirm American hopes that Asia's largest nation would follow a pro-American path.

But the partisans of the Chinese Communist Party (CCP) under Mao Zedong's leadership fought more effectively against the Japanese than Jiang's soldiers did. Japan's withdrawal from China in 1945 initiated four years of warfare between the Communists and Jiang's anticommunist Nationalists. The Truman administration provided $3 billion in aid to Jiang. Americans watched in frustration as the CCP defeated the Nationalists, who retreated to the island of Taiwan. On October 1, 1949, Mao announced the establishment of the People's Republic of China (PRC).

This was the first communist government created without the presence of Soviet troops. Profound suspicions on both sides prevented any Sino-American accommodation, and the U.S. government refused to recognize the People's Republic. Faced with U.S. hostility and sharing a common ideology with the Soviet Union, Mao papered over historic Chinese-Russian tensions and signed a mutual defense pact with Moscow in February 1950. The so-called loss of China increased the importance for American policymakers of building capitalist societies in the rest of Asia, particularly Japan and—fatefully—South Korea and Vietnam. China's revolution also became a major issue in American politics. "Who lost China?" Republicans demanded rhetorically and effectively, presuming that it had once been America's to lose.

The Creation of the National Security State

A week before Mao's announcement that China had become a communist country, President Truman shared some equally grim news with the American public: the Soviet Union had

■ Were all communists conspiring together against the United States and its interests? New Chinese leader Mao Zedong (left) helps Soviet ruler Josef Stalin celebrate his birthday on December 21, 1949. Two months later, the two men signed a mutual defense treaty. But, as their expressions suggest, they shared little personal warmth. Conflicting Chinese and Russian national interests soon strained—and eventually broke—their alliance.

ChinaStock

detonated its first nuclear device. The United States had lost the atomic monopoly that for four years assured Americans of their unique position of military strength. Truman asked his advisers for a full reevaluation of the nation's foreign policy.

The result was the top-secret National Security Council document 68 (**NSC-68**), which articulated the logic of what became the **national security state**: a government focused on the imperatives of military power, global involvement, and radically increased defense spending. NSC-68 argued that the United States had entered an era of permanent crisis because of the expansion of communism and the hostile intentions of the Soviet Union. America's worldwide interests meant that it must oppose revolutions or radical change anywhere on the globe. NSC-68 went beyond the containment policy of the Truman Doctrine to call instead for fostering "a fundamental change in the nature of the Soviet system." This armed struggle necessitated secrecy and centralization of power in the hands of the federal government.

The National Security Act of 1947 and its 1949 amendments created the institutions of the new national security state. The Central Intelligence Agency (CIA) organized spying and covert operations, the Department of Defense unified the separate branches of the military, and the National Security Council (NSC) coordinated foreign policy information for the president. NSC-68's call for secrecy encouraged government deception of the public in the interest of "national security," with a consequent decline in democratic input into the nation's foreign relations.

At War in Korea

Two months after NSC-68 arrived on the president's desk, troops from communist North Korea poured across the thirty-eighth parallel into South Korea on June 25, 1950. The alarmist recommendations of NSC-68 now seemed fully justified to U.S. policymakers. But the origins of the conflict on the Korean peninsula were complicated.

NSC-68

Concerned about the trend of international events in the wake of the Communist revolution in China and the Soviet Union's acquisition of nuclear weapons, President Truman ordered his National Security Council on January 31, 1950, to conduct "a reexamination of our objectives in peace and war and of the effect of these objectives on our strategic plans." The resulting study, known as NSC-68, called for a military buildup to counter Soviet expansionism. Some specialists on the USSR, such as George Kennan, questioned NSC-68's accuracy regarding Soviet intentions and successes. But the subsequent North Korean invasion of South Korea seemed to confirm the idea of "international communism" on the march.

Workers at the Douglas Aircraft Company's Santa Monica factory assemble Nike guided missiles for the U.S. Army in 1955. Large military contracts proliferated during the Cold War and stimulated the growth of Sunbelt states like California.

Bettmann/CORBIS

From NSC-68: U.S. Objectives and Programs for National Security (April 14, 1950)

The Soviet Union, unlike previous aspirants to hegemony, is animated by a new fanatic faith, antithetical to our own, and seeks to impose its absolute authority over the rest of the world. . . .

Any substantial further extension of the area under the domination of the Kremlin would raise the possibility that no coalition adequate to confront the Kremlin with greater strength could be assembled. It is in this context that this Republic and its citizens in the ascendancy of their strength stand in their deepest peril.

The issues that face us are momentous, involving the fulfillment or destruction not only of this Republic but of civilization itself. . . . The assault on free institutions is world-wide now, and in the context of the present polarization of power a defeat of free institutions anywhere is a defeat everywhere. . . .

Our policy and actions must be such as to foster a fundamental change in the nature of the Soviet system. . . . In a

shrinking world, which now faces the threat of atomic warfare, it is not an adequate objective merely to seek to check the Kremlin design, for the absence of order among nations is becoming less and less tolerable. . . .

The integrity of our system will not be jeopardized by any measures, covert or overt, violent or non-violent, which serve the purposes of frustrating the Kremlin design, nor does the necessity for conducting ourselves so as to affirm our values in actions as well as words forbid such measures. . . .

The total economic strength of the U.S.S.R. compares with that of the U.S. as roughly one to four. . . . The military budget of the United States represents 6 to 7 percent of its gross national product (as against 13.8 percent for the Soviet Union). . . . This difference in emphasis between the two economies means that the readiness of the free world to support a war effort is tending to decline relative to that of the Soviet Union.

It is true that the United States armed forces are now stronger than ever before in other times of apparent peace; it is also true that there exists a sharp disparity between our actual military strength and our commitments. . . . It is clear that our military strength is becoming dangerously inadequate. . . .

In summary, we must. . . [engage in] a rapid and sustained build-up of the political, economic, and military strength of the free world.

Questions

1. *What is the precise problem that the United States faces, according to NSC-68?*

2. *How does NSC-68's analysis of the Soviet threat in 1950 compare with American understandings today of the threat from Islamic terrorist organizations such as Al Qaeda?* ■

Sfc. Al Chang/Defense Visual Information Center (Department of Defense), HD-SN-99-03118

■ Near Haktong-ni, Korea, on August 28, 1950, an Army corpsman fills out casualty tags while one American soldier comforts another who has just seen a friend killed in action. Men who fought together on the front lines in Korea, as in other wars, experienced physical and psychological traumas unparalleled in civilian life. They often developed strong friendships with each other but sometimes had difficulty making the transition back to peacetime routines at home.

Korea had been colonized by Japan since 1910. After Japan's defeat in 1945, Soviet and U.S. forces each occupied half of the peninsula. In the north, the Soviets installed a dictatorial Communist regime under Kim Il Sung, who had fought with the Chinese Communists in their common struggle against Japan. In the south, the Americans established an authoritarian capitalist regime led by Syngman Rhee, who had lived in the United States most of the previous four decades. The thirty-eighth parallel was an arbitrary dividing line for a nation that had been unified for 1,300 years, and both governments sought to reunite Korea under their control. Border skirmishes intensified after the Soviets and Americans withdrew in 1948, and leftist rebellions continued across much of the south. Some 100,000 Koreans lost their lives in the fighting between 1945 and 1950.

U.S. forces arrived in late June 1950, just in time to prevent the South Korean army from being driven off the peninsula, and then slowly pushed the North Koreans back toward the thirty-eighth parallel in hard fighting. Truman received UN approval for this "police action," along with a small number of troops from several other nations.

Americans assumed the North Korean invasion had been orchestrated by Moscow as part of a plan of worldwide communist aggression. The Truman administration considered defense of South Korea crucial to demonstrate the credibility of U.S. power. The U.S. government took preemptive actions against possible aggression elsewhere. It sent the Seventh Fleet to defend Taiwan, which it had previously assumed China would eventually conquer and reabsorb; it increased assistance to anticommunist forces in the Philippines and Vietnam; and it rearmed West Germany as part of NATO. The U.S. annual military budget increased from $13 billion in 1950 before the war to $50 billion in 1953, setting a pattern for vast military expenditures ever since.

General Douglas MacArthur's brilliantly executed landing of fresh U.S. and UN troops at the port of Inchon behind North Korean lines on September 15, 1950, created a turning point in the war. South Korea was retaken; containment had succeeded. Should American commanders now shift to rolling back communism by proceeding north of the thirty-eighth parallel? The opportunity was irresistible, despite Truman's determination to keep this a limited war. MacArthur ignored signals that the Chinese would not allow U.S. soldiers to come all the way to their border at the Yalu River—the equivalent for Americans of having the Soviet Army arrive at the Rio Grande. On November 27, 200,000 Chinese soldiers struck hard, driving American soldiers south of the thirty-eighth parallel again in the longest retreat in U.S. military history.

MacArthur wanted to take this "entirely new war" directly to the Chinese, using conventional or nuclear bombing campaigns against the People's Republic of China. His growing insubordination forced Truman to fire the popular general in April 1951 because the president had no desire to start a larger war that would draw in the USSR. The bloody fighting in Korea stalemated that spring close to the original dividing line, where the front remained as the two sides negotiated for two years before signing a ceasefire in July 1953. American deaths totaled 37,000, and China lost nearly a million soldiers. Three million Koreans on both

TABLE 24-2			
The Election of 1952			
Candidate	Political Party	Popular Vote (%)	Electoral Vote
Dwight D. Eisenhower	Republican	55.1	442
Adlai E. Stevenson	Democratic	44.4	89

■ **MAP 24.2**

THE KOREAN WAR, 1950–1953   The strategic location of the Korean peninsula enhanced the importance of what had originally been a civil conflict among Koreans. Korea's close proximity to China, the Soviet Union, and U.S.-occupied Japan made the outcome of that conflict very important to all of the great powers. The Americans and Chinese wound up doing the bulk of the fighting against each other in the full-scale war that unfolded in 1950.

sides died—10 percent of the population of the peninsula—and another 5 million were made refugees. Containment succeeded at enormous cost, and the Korean peninsula is still divided and heavily armed today.

The Korean War shaped subsequent American politics and society in critical ways. The stalemate frustrated Americans, who agreed with MacArthur that there was "no substitute for victory." But the ominous threat of nuclear weapons meant that wars had to be limited. The fighting in Korea enabled McCarthy and the Red Scare to dominate political life in the United States. Republican presidential nominee General Dwight Eisenhower was perhaps the most popular American alive because of his leadership of the Allied victory in Europe in World War II, and he swept into the White House in 1952 over Democrat Adlai Stevenson, the governor of Illinois.

MAP

The Korean War, 1950–1953

Conclusion

The war in Korea ensured a generation of hostility between the United States and China. It tied the People's Republic more closely to the USSR, strengthening the common belief that international communism was a unified movement. The United States committed itself to defending Taiwan from recapture by the Beijing government. The Korean War also jump-started the moribund Japanese economy as American dollars poured into Japan, where the U.S. war effort was based.

Frustrations with the course of war in Korea affirmed the inward focus of American society in the 1950s. Despite the organizing efforts of political activists such as civil rights workers, most citizens seemed to look increasingly to their personal and familial lives for satisfaction and meaning. From the powerful U.S. economy flowed an unprecedented river of consumer goods, including the new artificial materials—plastic, vinyl, nylon, polyester, Styrofoam—that have pervaded and polluted American life ever since. As the ceasefire in Korea ended the fighting, and U.S. soldiers returned from across the Pacific, Americans sought the good life at home.

Sites to Visit

National Security Archive at George Washington University
www.gwu.edu/~nsarchiv/

This superb site includes the most recent declassified documents on the making of U.S. foreign policy.

Cold War International History Project
http://wilsoncenter.org/index.cfm?fuseaction=topics.home&topic_id=1409

The Woodrow Wilson International Center for Scholars maintains this excellent site, which offers newly released documents and up-to-date interpretive essays on the American-Soviet struggle.

The Ad*Access Project of Duke University Library
scriptorium.lib.duke.edu/adaccess/

This site presents images from over 7,000 advertisements in U.S. and Canadian newspapers and magazine between 1911 and 1955, offering insights into popular culture and consumer life.

Truman Presidential Museum and Library
www.trumanlibrary.org/index.php

The Harry Truman Presidential Library maintains this site, which contains an especially useful collection of documents regarding foreign policy decisions in the early Cold War.

Avalon Project at the Yale Law School: Documents in Law, History, and Diplomacy
www.yale.edu/lawweb/avalon/avalon.htm

Researchers can find here the texts of a large number of the most important primary documents illuminating U.S. relations with other countries.

Korea + 50: No Longer Forgotten
www.trumanlibrary.org/korea/

The Truman Library's site on the Korean War has documents, photos, and interpretative essays by prominent historians.

Bancroft Library Collections
bancroft.berkeley.edu/collections/

The Bancroft Library of the University of California at Berkeley has extensive collections, exhibits, and links revealing the history of California, the nation's most populous state.

For Further Reading

General

William H. Chafe, *The Unfinished Journey: America Since World War II*, 5th ed. (2006).
Alonzo Hamby, *Man of the People: A Life of Harry S. Truman* (1995).
Godfrey Hodgson, *America in Our Time* (1976).
Walter LaFeber, *America, Russia, and the Cold War, 1945–2002*, 9th ed. (2002).
James T. Patterson, *Grand Expectations: The United States, 1945–1974* (1996).

The Uncertainties of Victory

Thomas Borstelmann, *The Cold War and the Color Line: American Race Relations in the Global Arena* (2001).
Robert R. Korstad, *Civil Rights Unionism: Tobacco Workers and the Struggle for Democracy in the Mid-Twentieth-Century South* (2003).
Melvyn P. Leffler, *The Specter of Communism: The United States and the Origins of the Cold War, 1917–1953* (1994).

Suzanne Mettler, *Soldiers to Citizens: The G.I. Bill and the Making of the Greatest Generation* (2005).
Thomas Sugrue, *The Origins of the Urban Crisis: Race and Inequality in Postwar Detroit* (1996).

The Quest for Security

Carolyn Woods Eisenberg, *Drawing the Line: The American Decision to Divide Germany, 1944–1949* (1996).
Walter Isaacson and Evan Thomas, *The Wise Men: Six Friends and the World They Made: Acheson, Bohlen, Harriman, Kennan, Lovett, McCloy* (1986).
Melvyn P. Leffler, *A Preponderance of Power: National Security, the Truman Administration, and the Cold War* (1992).
Thomas G. Paterson, *On Every Front: The Making and Unmaking of the Cold War* (1992).

A Cold War Society

Paul S. Boyer, *By the Bomb's Early Light: American Thought and Culture at the Dawn of the Atomic Age* (1985).

Kenneth T. Jackson, *Crabgrass Frontier: The Suburbanization of the United States* (1985).

Elaine Tyler May, *Homeward Bound: American Families in the Cold War Era* (1988).

Ellen Schrecker, *Many Are the Crimes: McCarthyism in America* (1998).

Stephen J. Whitfield, *The Culture of the Cold War* (1991).

The United States and Asia

Warren I. Cohen, *America's Response to China: A History of Sino-American Relations*, 4th ed. (2000).

Jon Halliday and Bruce Cumings, *Korea: The Unknown War* (1988).

Michael J. Hogan, *A Cross of Iron: Harry S. Truman and the Origins of the National Security State, 1945–1954* (1998).

Christine Klein, *Cold War Orientalism: Asia in the Middlebrow Imgaination, 1945–1961* (2003).

Walter LaFeber, *The Clash: A History of U.S.-Japan Relations* (1997).

For quizzes and other resources on these topics, go to www.longmanamericanhistory.com.

P A R T   N I N E

The Cold War at High Tide, 1953–1979

URING THE THIRD QUARTER OF THE TWENTIETH CENTURY, THE Cold War cast a long shadow over the United States and the rest of the world. Tensions mounted at home and abroad as the United States and the Soviet Union vied for power among the world's nations. In poor Third World countries, insurgents attempted to throw off the yoke of colonialism and play the two superpowers against each other. The United States used a variety of strategies to counter Soviet influence in Latin America, Africa, the Middle East, and Southeast Asia, including military force in Korea and Vietnam, white-knuckle diplomacy in Cuba, extensive aid to nonaligned countries, and covert operations worldwide.

Soviet advances in science and technology spurred the U.S. government to sponsor bold new domestic initiatives in the areas of public education and space exploration. The Cold War even helped to shape a post–World War II domestic ideal: a nuclear family living in a house in the suburbs, with a breadwinner father and a full-time homemaker mother. Many Americans believed that their prosperous, consumer-oriented economy, with its emphasis on individualism and personal choice, was a key weapon in the fight against communism.

In a feverish arms race, both the United States and the USSR rushed to stockpile weapons of mass destruction. Constant innovations in the technology of nuclear weaponry (such as intercontinental ballistic missiles) made the bombers used in World War II obsolete. The hydrogen bomb, tested successfully for the first time in 1953, dwarfed the power of the atomic bomb that had leveled Hiroshima. Nevertheless, citizens who criticized the arms buildup risked being branded unpatriotic. More than ever before, domestic policy was intertwined with foreign policy.

The rise of multinational corporations meant that large, impersonal institutions, whether government or private, were shaping American life. Middle-level managers—men in "grey flannel suits"—represented the corporate ethos of loyalty to the company above all else. At the same time, many Americans sought to work within their local communities for social and political change. In the South, African American men and women launched a dramatic assault on the system of legal segregation known as "Jim Crow." Working at the grassroots level, these activists boycotted buses, marched, engaged in sit-ins at lunch counters, and went to jail. Their efforts provoked the courts and Congress to act, culminating in the Civil Rights Acts of 1964 and 1965. For the first time in American history, the federal government assumed responsibility for eliminating discrimination in the workplace and guaranteeing all its citizens the right to vote.

Other groups also organized and entered the political arena. Indians, disabled Americans, California farm workers, and gay men and lesbians all formed organizations to counter discrimination and advance their civil rights. The women's movement affected all aspects of American society, enabling women to play a fuller role in the political and economic life of the country. A new environmental movement secured legislation protecting wilderness areas and endangered species and ensuring that Americans had clean air to breathe and clean water to drink.

Lyndon B. Johnson assumed the presidency after the assassination of John F. Kennedy in 1963. Johnson hoped to revitalize the New Deal legacy by expanding social welfare programs. His program, called the Great Society, sought to address seemingly intractable problems such as poverty, lack of health care for the elderly, and the deterioration of inner-city neighborhoods. But Johnson also expanded the U.S. military presence in Vietnam, an effort that cost an increasing number of American lives. Even constant bombing proved futile to stem the civil war that pitted Americans and anticommunist Vietnamese against the National Liberation Front of South Vietnam and their comrades in the north. Johnson's successor, Richard M. Nixon, also found himself mired in a war that was becoming increasingly unpopular among Americans.

Protests against the war in the late 1960s and early 1970s highlighted an emerging youth culture. The baby boom generation, born in the two decades after World War II, embraced sexual freedom and new forms of music (such as rock 'n' roll) in an apparent attempt to defy their parents and "the Establishment" in general. Many Americans felt betrayed by both Johnson and Nixon, believing that tens of thousands of American soldiers had died in vain in Vietnam. The Watergate break-in at Democratic headquarters, leading eventually to Nixon's resignation, contributed to a growing, widespread disenchantment with government authority.

By the late 1970s, developments abroad had greatly complicated Cold War politics. Middle Eastern oil-producing nations imposed an oil embargo on the United States, highlighting U.S. dependence on fossil fuels. Islamic fundamentalists were beginning to retaliate violently against the spread of American influence and culture in Muslim countries. And at home, a conservative backlash emerged to counter the expansion of the welfare state, the heightened visibility of the feminist movement, and widening civil rights protests.

1968 Martin Luther King Jr. assassinated
Robert Kennedy assassinated
My Lai massacre
Wild and Scenic Rivers Act
Tet offensive

1969 Huge antiwar protests in Washington, D.C.
Indians occupy Alcatraz, San Francisco Bay
Stonewall raid, New York City
Astronauts Neil Armstrong and Buzz Aldrin walk on the moon

1970 United States invades Cambodia
National Guardsmen kill four students, Kent State University

1971 Pentagon Papers published
Nixon administration creates "plumbers" for illegal activities

1972 Watergate break-in
Nixon visits China
Founding of *Ms.* magazine

1973 *Roe v. Wade* legalizes abortion

American Indian Movement members occupy Wounded Knee
Endangered Species Act
OPEC oil embargo
American troops withdrawn from Vietnam

1974 Nixon resigns presidency; Gerald R. Ford becomes president

1975 *Mayaguez* incident
Vietnam reunified under communist rule
Congressional investigations of CIA covert operations

1976 Hyde Amendment prohibits use of Medicaid funds for abortions
Nation celebrates bicentennial

1977 President Jimmy Carter issues general amnesty for draft evaders
Trans-Alaska pipeline system completed
ABC airs miniseries *Roots,* based on book by Alex Haley

1978 *Bakke* Supreme Court decision
California Proposition 13

1979 Camp David peace accords
Partial meltdown of nuclear core at Three Mile Island nuclear plant
Iranian Revolution

CHAPTER
25
Domestic Dreams and Atomic Nightmares, 1953–1963

Dr. Tom Dooley was known as the "jungle doctor." A native of St. Louis and a devout Roman Catholic, Dooley joined the Navy medical corps during World War II and remained in the Navy reserves until 1950. After earning his medical degree, he moved to Southeast Asia, where he set up clinics to provide medical care for impoverished villagers. He quickly became a major celebrity. In a 1960 Gallup poll, Dooley was among the ten most admired Americans. President Dwight D. Eisenhower said of Dooley, "Few, if any, men have equaled [Dooley's] exhibition of courage, self-sacrifice, faith in his God and his readiness to serve his fellow man." When Dooley died of cancer in 1961 at the age of 34, he was honored by Congress and posthumously awarded the U.S. Navy's Legion of Merit. His legacy helped inspire John F. Kennedy's creation of the Peace Corps.

Although he was a practicing Catholic, Dooley rejected the role of the religious missionary—a role largely discredited in the anticolonial post–World War II years as tied to racist and imperialist designs. Rather, Dooley promoted modernization and development, embracing an internationalist vision that was grounded in respect and appreciation for the local culture and customs of the people with whom he lived.

Dooley's zeal to help the people of Southeast Asia went far beyond medical care. A passionate anticommunist, in 1956 he assisted the Central Intelligence Agency (CIA) and the U.S. Navy in leading the exodus of 900,000 Catholic refugees from newly created communist North Vietnam to South Vietnam, where the United States backed a

AP/Wide World

Dr. Tom Dooley is pictured here providing medical care to Laotian children. Known as the "jungle doctor," he represented American expertise and benevolence, as well as fervent anticommunism, during the early years of the Cold War.

noncommunist dictatorship under Ngo Dinh Diem. He recounted that experience in a best-selling book, *Deliver Us from Evil,* and wrote two other books that chronicled his activities at the clinics he founded in the villages and jungles of Laos. His books praised Diem's regime in South Vietnam and promoted the cause of anticommunism in Southeast Asia.

Dooley's work in Southeast Asia provided essential medical care to people in need and also served American interests in the early years of the Cold War. But his decision to live and work in the remote villages of Laos was not based simply on self-sacrifice. As a homosexual, Dooley would have had a difficult life within the United States in the 1950s. Anticommunist crusaders purged homosexuals from government employment, and gay men and lesbians faced harassment, ostracism, and often the loss of their jobs. Dooley escaped the intense homophobia of his home country by creating communal living situations with other men in remote areas of Laos, far from public view. There he could keep his sexual orientation private. If he had remained in the United States, the anticommunists whose political passions he shared would have purged him from their ranks.

It is fitting that a doctor spreading the benefits of American medicine to Asia would become a Cold War hero. Science and expertise reigned supreme during the Cold War years. Parents turned to another famous physician, Dr. Benjamin Spock, whose 1946 guide to raising children, *Baby and Child Care,* became an instant best-seller. Unlike prewar child-rearing experts who encouraged discipline and discouraged coddling, Dr. Spock emphasized nurture and affection. Dr. Jonas Salk became a hero for developing a vaccine against polio in 1955. The oral contraceptive pill, which came on the market in 1960, provided relatively safe and effective birth control. Hailed initially as a boon to family planning, the pill also helped to usher in the sexual revolution of the 1960s. The National Aeronautics and Space Administration (NASA), established in 1958, sent the first American into space in 1961. But science also brought pesticides, smog, and other pollutants. Americans, at the time, rarely considered the environmental effects of consumer goods, cars, petrochemicals, or nuclear power.

The decade from 1953 to 1963, under the presidencies of Dwight Eisenhower and John Kennedy, was a time of expansive optimism about the future. Hawaii and Alaska became states in 1959. The **baby boom** demonstrated widespread faith in the future for American children. It was also a decade of growth for U.S. influence abroad, the domestic economy, consumer culture, and television. Suburbs, highways, and shopping malls expanded to meet the needs of increasing numbers of families with young children. Some teenagers and others rebelled against what they saw as conformity in American life. But African Americans organized in the civil rights movement to gain full access to the freedoms and comforts of this increasingly middle-class society.

It was also a decade of anxiety. Americans worried about the perils of the atomic age as the nuclear arsenals of both superpowers continued to grow. Science fiction films about alien invaders reflected concerns about foreign dangers. The Soviet Union's 1957 launching of *Sputnik,* the first artificial satellite to orbit the Earth, alarmed Americans and forced the nation to confront the possibility of Soviet technological superiority. The United States appeared to be at the height of its strength and power, yet at the same time, more vulnerable than ever before.

Cold War, Warm Hearth

The postwar era was a time of deep divisions in American society, yet in certain ways Americans behaved with remarkable conformity. This is nowhere more evident than in the overwhelming embrace of the nuclear family. The GI Bill, with its provisions for home mortgage loans, enabled veterans of modest means to purchase homes. Although residential segregation prevailed throughout the postwar era, limiting most suburban developments

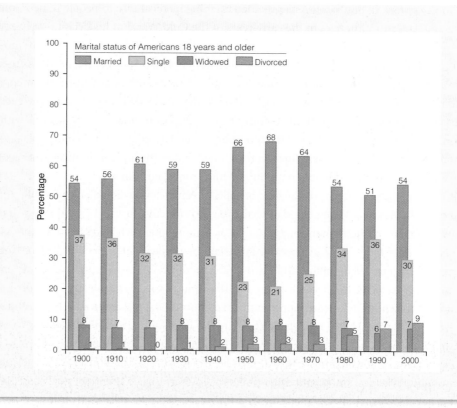

■ FIGURE 25.1
MARITAL STATUS OF THE U.S. ADULT POPULATION, 1900–2000
Following World War II, Americans married in record numbers. The high rate of marriage corresponded with a relatively low divorce rate. Beginning in the 1970s, the marriage rate plummeted and the divorce rate rose dramatically.

to prosperous white middle- and working-class families, many veterans of color were able to buy their first homes. Americans of all racial, ethnic, and religious groups, of all socioeconomic classes and educational levels, brought the marriage rate up and the divorce rate down. The "American way of life" embodied in the suburban nuclear family, as a cultural ideal if not a universal reality, motivated countless postwar Americans to strive for it, to live by its codes, and—for Americans of color—to demand it.

Consumer Spending and the Suburban Ideal

Between 1947 and 1961, national income increased more than 60 percent. Rather than putting this money aside for a rainy day, Americans were inclined to spend it. Investing in one's home, along with the trappings that would enhance family life, seemed the best way to plan for a secure future.

Between 1950 and 1970, the suburban population more than doubled, from 36 million to 74 million. Fully 20 percent of the population remained poor during this prosperous time. But most families of ample as well as modest means exhibited a great deal of conformity in their consumer behavior, reflecting widely shared beliefs about the good life. They poured their money into homes, domestic appliances, televisions, automobiles, and family vacations.

Nuclear families who settled in the suburbs provided the foundation for new types of community life and leisure pursuits, sometimes at the expense of older ones grounded in ethnic neighborhoods and kinship networks. Family-oriented amusement parks such as Disneyland in Anaheim, California, which opened in 1955, catered to middle-class tastes, in contrast to older venues such as Coney Island, known for their thrill rides, class and ethnic mixing, and romantic environments. Religious affiliation rose to an all-time high as Americans built and joined suburban churches and synagogues, complete with youth programs and summer camps. In 1949 fewer than 1 million American homes had a television. Within the next four years, the number soared to 20 million.

The Cold War made a profound contribution to suburban sprawl. Congress passed the Federal-Aid Highway Act of 1956, which provided $100 billion to cover 90 percent of the cost for 41,000 miles of national highways. When President Dwight D. Eisenhower signed the bill into law, he stated one of the major reasons for the new highway system: "[In] case of atomic attack on our key cities, the road net must permit quick evacuation of target areas."

The worst-case scenario was communist takeover and the defeat of the United States in the Cold War. Pentagon strategists and foreign policy experts feared that the Soviet Union might gain the military might to allow its territorial expansion and, eventually, world domination. But observers also worried that the real dangers to America were internal: racial strife, emancipated women, class conflict, and familial disruption. To alleviate these fears, Americans turned to the family as a bastion of safety in an insecure world. Most postwar Americans longed for security after years of economic depression and war, and they saw family stability as the best bulwark against the new dangers of the Cold War.

Race, Class, and Domesticity

After World War II, the nation faced a severe housing shortage. The federal government gave developers financial subsidies to build affordable single-family homes and offered Federal Housing Authority (FHA) loans and income tax deductions to homebuyers. These benefits enabled white working-class and middle-class families to purchase houses. Postwar prosperity, government subsidies, and the promise of assimilation made it possible for white-skinned Americans of immigrant background to blend into the suburbs.

Park Forest, Illinois, 1953. Courtesy, Sandra Weiner. Photo by Dan Weiner.

■ Commuters, mostly men, left their suburban homes each morning to go to jobs in the cities, returning home at night. Suburbs served as "bedroom communities," inhabited mostly by women and children during the day.

Despite the expansion of the black and Latino middle class and the increase in home ownership among racial minorities, most suburban developments excluded nonwhites. The FHA and lending banks maintained policies known as **red lining**, which designated certain neighborhoods off limits to racial minorities. Although Americans of color remained concentrated in urban and rural areas, some did move to the suburbs, usually into segregated communities.

For Americans of color, suburban home ownership offered inclusion in the postwar American dream. In her powerful 1959 play *A Raisin In the Sun*, African American playwright Lorraine Hansberry articulated with great eloquence the importance of a home in the suburbs, not to assimilate into white America but to live as a black family with dignity and pride. Asian Americans also had good reason to celebrate home and family life. With the end of the exclusion of Chinese immigrants during World War II, wives and war brides began to enter the country, helping to build thriving family-oriented communities. After the disruptions and anguish of internment, Japanese Americans were eager to put their families and lives back together. Mexican Americans and Mexican immigrants, including *braceros*, established flourishing communities in the Southwest. Puerto Ricans migrated to New York and other eastern cities, where they could earn four times the average wage on the island.

Racial segregation did not prevail everywhere. For example, in Shaker Heights, Ohio, a suburb of Cleveland, white residents made a conscious decision, as a community, to integrate their neighborhood. Drawing on postwar liberal ideals of civil rights and racial integration, they welcomed black homeowners. They succeeded in this effort by emphasizing class similarity over racial difference. White residents encouraged other white families to move into Shaker Heights, pointing out that their prosperous black neighbors were "just like us."

As residents and businesses migrated to the suburbs, slum housing and vacant factories remained in the central cities. The Housing Acts of 1949 and 1954 granted funds to municipalities for urban renewal. However, few of those federal dollars provided low-income housing. Mayors, bankers, and real estate interests used the money to bulldoze slums and build gleaming office towers, civic centers, and apartment complexes for affluent citizens, leaving the poor to fend for themselves in the remaining dilapidated corners of the cities.

Although intended to revitalize cities, urban renewal actually accelerated the decay of inner cities and worsened conditions for the urban poor. Federally funded projects often disrupted and destroyed ethnic communities. In St. Paul, Minnesota, the construction of U.S. Highway 94, while enabling suburbanites to commute to the city, obliterated the thriving urban African American neighborhood of Rondo. In Los Angeles, the Dodgers' stadium built in Chávez Ravine offered baseball fans and their families access to the national pastime, but it destroyed the historically rooted Mexican American neighborhood in its path. The $5 million project displaced 7,500 people and demolished 900 homes.

Along with the urban poor, rural Americans reaped few benefits of postwar affluence. The 1950s marked the greatest out-migration from the South as the mechanization of farms—particularly the mechanical cotton picker—reduced the number of workers on the land. More than one-fourth of the population left Kentucky and West Virginia, where unemployment in some areas reached 80 percent.

Women: Back to the Future

The nuclear family ideal of the 1950s included a full-time wife and mother and a breadwinner husband. This vision of domesticity marked a giant step backward for many women, whose opportunities and experiences had expanded dramatically during World War II. The elevation of the housewife as a major cultural icon contrasted sharply with the reality. The proportion of women who fit the mold of full-time homemaker was rapidly shrinking. Although most American women married, had children, and carried the lion's share of responsibility for housework and child-rearing, increasing numbers of married women also held jobs outside the home. The employment of married women began to rise during World War II and kept rising after the war, even though most of the well-paying and highly skilled jobs returned to men at the war's end.

Many women worked part-time while their children were at school, as they considered themselves homemakers not wage earners. With few other opportunities for creative work, women embraced their domestic roles and turned homemaking into a profession. Many fulfilled their role with pride and satisfaction and extended their energies and talents into their communities, where they made important contributions as volunteers in local parent-teacher associations (PTAs) and other civic organizations. Most postwar mothers finished childbearing by the time they were thirty and had many years ahead of them when their child-rearing responsibilities ended. Some expanded part-time employment into full-time occupations when their children left the nest. Others felt bored and frustrated and drowned their sorrow with

Betty Engle/Minnesota Historical Society, Neg. #64025

■ **The Women's Council of St. Paul, Minnesota, was one of many service organizations in which black and white women joined in common projects. Volunteer activities enabled women to serve their communities as well as develop important political and leadership skills.**

alcohol or tranquilizers. In 1963 author Betty Friedan described the constraints facing women as the "problem that has no name" in her feminist manifesto *The Feminine Mystique.*

Education was one avenue available to women, as students as well as teachers. But higher education did not open its doors fully to women. Because few women gained access to graduate and professional schools and most well-paying jobs were reserved for men, college degrees for white women did not necessarily open up career opportunities or greatly improve their job and earning prospects. By 1956 one-fourth of white female students married while still in college. Many of these women dropped out of school to take jobs in order to support their husbands through college. But the situation was quite different for black women. Like their mothers and grandmothers, most black women had to work to help support their families. Even in the prosperous postwar years, few black families could survive on the meager earnings of a single breadwinner. Job prospects for black women generally were limited to menial, low-paying occupations. Young black women knew that a college degree could mean the difference between working as a maid for a white family and working as a secretary, teacher, or nurse. Although few in number, more than 90 percent of black women who entered college completed their degrees.

Black women also aspired to the role of homemaker, but for very different reasons than white women. Although poverty still plagued large numbers of black citizens, the black middle class expanded during the 1950s. Postwar prosperity enabled some African Americans, for the first time, to strive for family life in which the earnings of men were adequate to allow women to stay home with their own children rather than tending to the houses and children of white families. For black women, domesticity meant "freedom and independence in her own home." It is no wonder that in the early 1960s, women of color bristled when white feminists such as Betty Friedan called upon women to break free from the "chains" of domesticity.

The Civil Rights Movement

As the civil rights movement gained momentum in the South, African American activists faced fierce opposition from local white authorities and contempt from national leaders. Persistent racial discrimination proved to be the nation's worst embarrassment throughout the Cold War. The Soviet Union and other communist countries pointed to American race relations as an indication of the hypocrisy and failure of the American promise of freedom for all. Yet national leaders paid only lip service to racial justice and failed to provide the strong support necessary to defeat the system of racial segregation in the South known as the "Jim Crow" system. Jim Crow was a legal, or *de jure*, set of institutions that prevailed throughout the South. Although the nation's leaders acknowledged the need to address Southern segregation, they did nothing to address the unofficial, or *de facto*, segregation that prevailed throughout the rest of the country.

Nevertheless, at the grassroots level, racial minorities continued to work for equal rights. For example, Mexican Americans in the Southwest continued to press for desegregation of schools, residential neighborhoods, and public facilities through organizations such as the middle-class League of United Latin American Citizens (LULAC) and the Asociación Nacional México-Americana (ANMA), a civil rights organization that emerged out of the labor movement. It was not until 1963 that the power of the civil rights movement—and the violence of southern white opposition—finally compelled the federal government to take action.

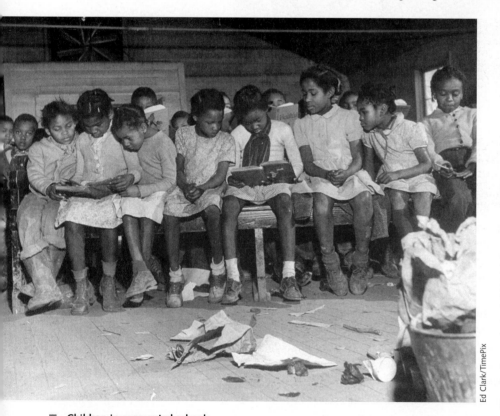

Ed Clark/TimePix

■ **Children in segregated schools studied in wretched physical conditions but benefited from dedicated African American teachers. The Supreme Court struck down school segregation in the landmark 1954 case *Brown v. Board of Education*, arguing in its unanimous decision that separate facilities were inherently unequal.**

Brown v. Board of Education

The first major success in the struggle to dismantle the Jim Crow system in the South came in the 1954 Supreme Court decision *Brown v. Board of Education*. Civil rights strategists decided to pursue their cause in the courts rather than through Congress. They knew that southern Democrats in Congress, who held disproportionate power through their seniority and control of major committees, would block any civil rights legislation that came before the House or Senate. They believed that they had a better chance of success through the courts.

NAACP lawyers filed suit against the Topeka, Kansas, Board of Education on behalf of Linda Brown, a black child in a segregated school. They were targeting the 1896 *Plessy v. Ferguson* decision, which had justified Jim Crow laws on the grounds that they provided "separate but equal" facilities. The case reached the U.S. Supreme Court, where NAACP general counsel Thurgood Marshall argued that separate facilities, by definition, denied African Americans their equal rights as citizens.

In 1953, during the three-year period that the Supreme Court had the *Brown* case before it, President Eisenhower appointed Earl Warren as chief justice. Warren had been state attorney general and then governor of California during World War II and had approved the internment of Japanese Americans—a decision he later deeply regretted. He now used his political and legal skills to strike a blow for justice. He knew that such a critical case needed a unanimous decision to win broad political support. One by one, he persuaded his Supreme Court colleagues of the importance of striking down segregation. On May 17, 1954, Warren delivered the historic unanimous ruling: "To separate [black children] from others of similar age and qualifications solely because of their race generates a feeling of inferiority as to their status in the community that may affect their hearts and minds in a way unlikely ever to be undone. . . . Separate educational facilities are inherently unequal."

Brown v. Board of Education of Topeka, Kansas

White Resistance, Black Persistence

Winning the *Brown* case was a great triumph, but it was only the first step. Desegregation would be meaningful only when it was enforced, and that was another matter entirely. At first, there seemed to be some cause for optimism. Although a few white officials in the South protested vehemently, many others seemed resigned to accept the decision. However, few were willing to initiate action to implement desegregation. Even the Supreme Court delayed its decision on implementation for a full year and then simply called for the process to begin "with all deliberate speed" but specified no timetable. Political leaders did not come forward to work on the task, leaving sympathetic educators and eager black Americans with no support.

The leader who could have done the most but in fact did the least was President Eisenhower. Expressing neither "approbation nor disapproval," Eisenhower said, "I don't think you can change the hearts of men with laws or decisions." Just before the Court's ruling, he told Chief Justice Warren that southern white segregationists simply wanted to make sure "that their sweet little girls are not required to sit in schools alongside some big overgrown Negroes." After the decision went against his wishes, Eisenhower remarked that his decision to appoint Warren to the court was the "biggest damn fool mistake" he ever made.

In 1955, the year after the *Brown* decision, white Mississippians murdered fourteen-year-old Emmett Till for allegedly whistling at a white woman. The boy had come from Chicago to Mississippi, where he was visiting relatives. His mutilated body was found in the Tallahatchie River. Although Till's killers later confessed to the murder, an all-white jury found them not guilty. Eisenhower remained silent about Till's murder and the travesty of justice, even when E. Frederick Morrow, his one black adviser, beseeched him to condemn the lynching.

Eisenhower's hands-off policy emboldened southern segregationists to resist the Supreme Court's desegregation decision. When it became clear that the federal government would do nothing to enforce the ruling, white resistance spread across the South. State legislatures passed resolutions vowing to protect segregation, and most southern congressmen signed the 1956 "Southern Manifesto," promising to oppose federal desegregation efforts.

A crisis at Central High School in Little Rock, Arkansas, finally forced Eisenhower to act. Under a federal district court's order to desegregate, school officials were prepared to comply and had carefully mobilized community support. But Arkansas Governor Orville Faubus, facing reelection, instructed National Guard troops to maintain "order" by blocking the entry of black students into the school. Eisenhower initially refused to intervene in the crisis. Hoping for a compromise, he met with Faubus, who agreed to allow the school to integrate peacefully. But Faubus broke his word, withdrew the National Guard troops, and left Little Rock, leaving the black students unprotected.

Executive Order 10730: Desegregation of Central High School

On September 23, 1957, as nine black students attempted to enter Central High, a huge angry crowd of whites surrounded them. With international news cameras broadcasting pictures of the shrieking and menacing mob, Eisenhower was forced to federalize the Arkansas National Guard and send 1,000 paratroopers to Little Rock. Eisenhower acted to maintain federal authority rather than to support integration.

> *Eisenhower acted to maintain federal authority rather than to support integration.*

Boycotts and Sit-Ins

Under Jim Crow laws in the South, black passengers were required to sit in the back section of buses, leaving the front of the bus for whites. If the "white" section at the front of the bus

MAP 25.1

MAJOR EVENTS OF THE AFRICAN AMERICAN CIVIL RIGHTS MOVEMENT, 1953–1963 Most of the major events of the early stages of the black freedom struggle took place in the South. Black southerners formed the backbone of the movement, but the grassroots protest movement drew participants from all regions of the country, all racial and ethnic groups, cities and rural areas, churches and universities, old and young, lawyers and sharecroppers.

filled up, black passengers were required to give up their seats for white passengers. On December 1, 1955, Rosa Parks and the black community of Montgomery, Alabama, were ready to take on the system. Parks, who worked as a seamstress, was a widely respected leader in Montgomery's black community, active in her church, and secretary of the local NAACP. On her way home from work that day, sitting in the first row of the "colored" section of the bus when the front of the bus filled with passengers, she refused to move when a white man demanded her seat. Parks was arrested, and black Montgomery sprang into action.

Literally overnight, the Montgomery bus boycott was born. For 381 days, more than 90 percent of Montgomery's black citizens sacrificed their comfort and convenience for the sake of their rights and dignity. As one elderly black woman replied when a white reporter offered her a ride as she walked to work, "No, my feets is tired but my soul is rested."

Martin Luther King Jr., pastor of the Dexter Avenue Baptist Church, was a newcomer to Montgomery when the bus boycott began. He embraced the opportunity to become the leader of the boycott and, eventually, the most powerful spokesperson for the civil rights movement. His stirring and impassioned words inspired thousands of black citizens to join the cause. As he told the 5,000 listeners who gathered in his church on the first night of the boycott, "If you will protest courageously and yet with dignity and Christian love, in the history books that are written in future generations, historians will have to pause and say, 'there lived a great people—a black people—who injected a new meaning and dignity into the veins of civilization.' This is our challenge and our overwhelming responsibility."

The bus boycott ended a year later when the Supreme Court ruled that Montgomery's buses must integrate, but the momentum generated by the boycott galvanized the civil rights movement. King and other leaders formed the Southern Christian Leadership Conference (SCLC), which united black ministers across the South in the cause of civil rights. The boycott tactic spread to other southern cities. As boycotts continued, a new strategy emerged: the **sit-in**.

On February 1, 1960, four African American students at North Carolina Agricultural and Technical College in Greensboro, inspired by the example of the bus boycott, entered the local Woolworth store and sat down at the lunch counter. When they were told "We do not serve Negroes," they refused to leave, forcing the staff at Woolworth's to physically remove the nonviolent protesters. Undaunted, they returned to the lunch counter the next day with twenty-three classmates. By the end of the week, more than a thousand students joined the protest. By this time, white gangs had gathered, waving Confederate flags and menacing the black undergraduates. But the students responded by waving American flags.

In May 1961, members of the Congress of Racial Equality (CORE) organized the Freedom Rides, in which black and white civil rights workers attempted to ride two interstate buses from Washington, D.C., to New Orleans in an effort to challenge segregation at facilities used in interstate travel. Their journey began peacefully, but when they reached Rock Hill, South Carolina, a group of whites beat John Lewis, one of the young black riders, for entering a whites-only rest room. In Anniston, Alabama, a mob slashed the tires of one of the buses, threw a fire bomb through a window, and pummeled the riders with fists and pipes. After the brutal beatings, reinforcements from the Student Nonviolent Coordinating Committee (SNCC) arrived to continue the Freedom Rides. They persevered, facing beatings along the way until they reached Jackson, Mississippi, where they were immediately arrested and jailed. The spirit and strength of the civil rights workers inspired many others to join them in the movement.

The Eisenhower Years

The presidency of Dwight D. Eisenhower was notable largely for moderation and maintaining the status quo, with very few major new initiatives and a style of leadership that rested more on his personal stature than his actions. Ike, as he was known, presided over the nation during a time of great prosperity, and his policies encouraged business expansion. However, the former general did try to stem the defense buildup. In his farewell address at the end of his second term as president, Eisenhower warned the nation against the growing power of the "military-industrial complex," the term he coined to describe the armed forces and the politically powerful defense industries that supplied arms and equipment to them. Eisenhower tried to fight the Cold War in a fiscally responsible manner.

TABLE 25-1			
The Election of 1956			
Candidate	Political Party	Popular Vote (%)	Electoral Vote
Dwight D. Eisenhower	Republican	57.6	457
Adlai E. Stevenson	Democratic	42.1	73

The Middle of the Road

As president, the Kansas-bred Eisenhower pursued a path down the middle of the road. His probusiness legislative agenda and appointments pleased conservatives, and he placated liberals by extending many of the policies of the welfare state enacted during the New Deal. He agreed to the expansion of Social Security and unemployment compensation and an increase in the minimum wage. He also made concerted efforts to reduce defense spending, believing that continued massive military expenditures would hinder the nation's economic growth. In December 1953, Eisenhower announced the New Look, a streamlined military that relied less on expensive conventional ground forces and more on air power and advanced nuclear capabilities.

Eisenhower's plans to reduce defense spending derailed on October 4, 1957, when the Soviet Union launched *Sputnik*, the first artificial Earth satellite. Although *Sputnik* could not be seen with the naked eye—it was only 22 inches in diameter and weighed only 184 pounds—

SEE THAT YOUR CANDIDATE WINS! *Only* WEAR A PAIR AND SHOW YOUR FRIENDS it emitted a beeping noise that was broadcast by commercial radio stations in the United States, making its presence very real and causing near hysteria among the public. The Soviet's launching of *Sputnik II* a month later seemed to confirm widespread fears that the United States was behind in the space race and, more significantly, in the arms race. Eisenhower's popularity in the polls suddenly dropped 22 points.

Acquiescing to his critics, the president allotted increased funds for military, scientific, and educational spending. NASA, which developed the program of space exploration, was one result of this increase. But Eisenhower believed that "the most critical problem of all" was the lack of American scientists and engineers. He led the federal government to subsidize additional science and math training for both teachers and students.

MISSION CONTROL CENTER

"What's Good for General Motors . . . "

Eisenhower's secretary of defense, former head of General Motors Charles Wilson, made the memorable comment that "what's good for General Motors business is good for America." But not everyone agreed. Eisenhower's probusiness policies had a deleterious impact on the nation's environment. He promoted the passage of the Submerged Land Act, which removed from federal jurisdiction more than $40 billion worth of oil-rich offshore lands. Under the control of state governments, oil companies could—and did—gain access to them. The *New York Times* called the act "one of the greatest and surely the most unjustified give-away programs" in the nation's history. The administration's willingness to allow businesses to expand with little regulation, and with virtually no concern for the environment, contributed to increasing pollution of the air, water, and land during the 1950s and helped spark the environmental movement of the 1960s and 1970s.

DOCUMENT

National Defense Education Act

Eisenhower also supported the Federal-Aid Highway Act of 1956. As the largest public works project the nation had ever mounted, this centrally planned transportation system was a boon to the auto, trucking, oil, concrete, and tire industries. In addition, it contributed to the national pastime of family road vacations and tourism. Cheap gas also fueled America's car culture. Cars gave Americans increased mobility and enabled suburban dwellers to drive to work in the cities. But reliance on the automobile doomed the nation's passenger train system and led to the decline of public transportation. Cars also contributed to suburban sprawl, air pollution, and traffic jams.

Eisenhower's Foreign Policy

The New Look, while containing military spending, also shifted American military priorities from reliance on conventional weapons to nuclear deterrence and covert operations. During Eisenhower's presidency, the United States and the Soviet Union both solidified their separate alliances. The twelve original NATO nations agreed that an attack on any one of them would be considered an attack on all, and they maintained a force to defend the West against a possible Soviet invasion. NATO expanded in 1952 to include Greece and Turkey, and West Germany joined in 1955. The Soviet Union formed a similar alliance, the Warsaw Pact, with the countries of eastern Europe. Confrontations between the United States and the Soviet Union over the fate of Europe gave way to more subtle maneuvers regarding the Third World—a term originally referring to nonaligned nations in the Middle East, Africa, Asia, and Latin America.

After Joseph Stalin died in 1953, Nikita Khrushchev became the new leader of the Soviet Union and called for peaceful coexistence with the United States. To limit military expenditures and improve relations, the superpowers arranged high-level summit meetings. In 1955 delegates from the United States, the Soviet Union, Britain, and France met in Geneva. Although the meeting achieved little of substance, it set a tone of cooperation. In 1959 Khrushchev came to the United States, met with Eisenhower, and toured the country. Despite the Soviet downing of an American U-2 spy plane in 1960 and the capture of American pilot Gary Powers, the superpowers began to discuss arms limitation. Both countries agreed to limit aboveground testing of nuclear weapons in light of the health and environmental risks such tests posed. Soviet negotiations with the United States did not, however, mean greater liberty in eastern Europe, where Soviet forces crushed a 1956 uprising in Hungary.

The Eisenhower administration continued to distrust countries that maintained neutrality in the Cold War, fearing that those not aligned with the United States might turn to communism and become allies of the Soviet Union. Through covert operations in 1953, the Central Intelligence Agency (CIA) helped to overthrow the elected government in Iran—which had seized control of Western-owned oil fields in the country—and to restore the dictatorship of Shah Reza Pahlavi, whose unpopular Western-leaning regime would be overthrown by Muslim fundamentalists in 1979. In 1954 the CIA helped overthrow the elected government of Jacobo Arbenz in Guatemala. U.S. officials considered Arbenz a communist because he sought to nationalize and redistribute large tracts of land, much of it owned by the Boston-based United Fruit Company.

> *Anticommunism became the guiding principle behind nearly all U.S. foreign policy, taking precedence over other American ideals.*

In 1959 revolutionary leader Fidel Castro overthrew Cuba's U.S.-friendly dictator Fulgencio Batista. Castro established a regime in Cuba based on socialist principles. His government took control of foreign-owned companies, including many owned by Americans. Castro's socialist policies alarmed U.S. officials and investors in Cuba. Eisenhower's hostility encouraged Castro to forge an alliance with the Soviet Union. The CIA then launched a plot to overthrow Castro. In 1960–1961, the CIA also helped orchestrate the overthrow and assassination of the charismatic left-leaning Patrice Lumumba, the first minister of the Republic of the Congo in Africa, soon after its independence from Belgium.

U.S. policymakers, with their anticommunist preoccupations, and people in Third World countries, with their campaigns against colonialism and racism, had little interest in each other's priorities. A case in point was Egypt, where in 1952 Gamal Abdul Nasser overthrew the corrupt monarchy of King Farouk and established a government neutral in the Cold War. In 1954 Nasser declared himself prime minister of the new government and accepted aid from both the United States and the Soviet Union. When Nasser engaged in trade with Soviet-bloc countries and extended diplomatic recognition to communist China, the United States canceled loans that were to support the building of the huge Aswan Dam, a major development project for the Egyptian economy. In response, Nasser nationalized the British-controlled Suez Canal in 1956, arguing that canal tolls would provide alternative funding for the dam. The British government, with the help of France and Israel, launched an attack against Egypt to regain control of the canal.

Although he distrusted Nasser, Eisenhower strongly criticized Britain for its effort to retain its imperial position in the Middle East. To avoid further antagonizing Nasser and other Third World leaders, Eisenhower denounced Britain's Suez attack and threatened economic sanctions, forcing the British to back down. Although leaders in Africa and Asia applauded Eisenhower's actions, the episode weakened U.S. relations with Nasser, who forged ties with the Soviet Union. Eisenhower now feared that "Nasserism" might spread throughout the Middle East.

In the spring of 1957, Congress approved the Eisenhower Doctrine, a pledge to defend Middle Eastern countries "against overt armed aggression from any nation controlled by international communism." However, U.S. policymakers rarely distinguished between nationalist movements and designs by "international communism," which they defined as Soviet aggression. Because American leaders believed that struggles for national self-determination in Third World countries were inspired and supported by the Soviet Union, they used the Eisenhower Doctrine to provide justification for U.S. military intervention to support pro-Western governments.

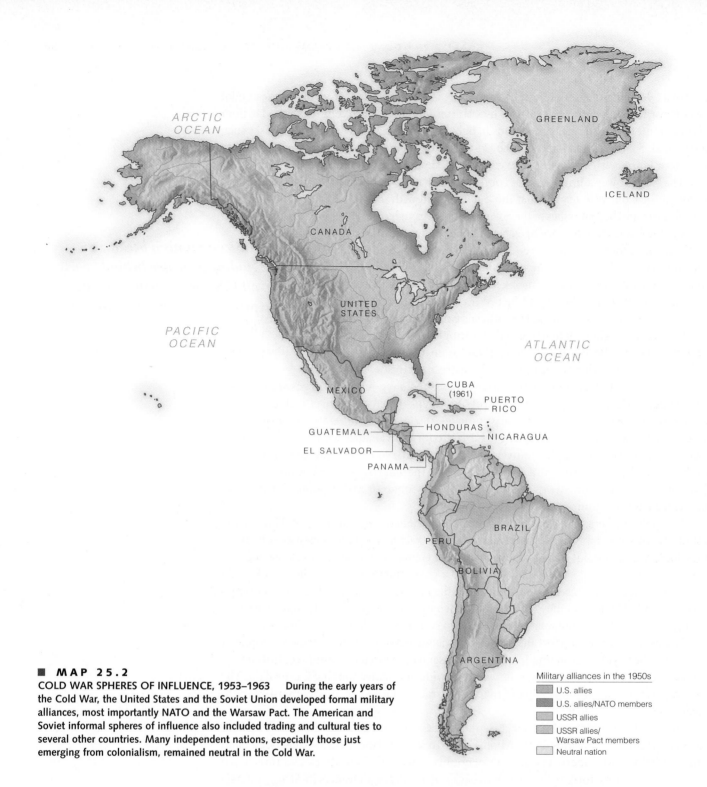

ARCTIC
OCEAN

GREENLAND

ICELAND

CANADA

PACIFIC
OCEAN

UNITED
STATES

ATLANTIC
OCEAN

MEXICO

CUBA
(1961)

PUERTO
RICO

GUATEMALA

HONDURAS

NICARAGUA

EL SALVADOR

PANAMA

BRAZIL

PERU

BOLIVIA

ARGENTINA

Military alliances in the 1950s
- U.S. allies
- U.S. allies/NATO members
- USSR allies
- USSR allies/ Warsaw Pact members
- Neutral nation

■ **MAP 25.2**
COLD WAR SPHERES OF INFLUENCE, 1953–1963 During the early years of
the Cold War, the United States and the Soviet Union developed formal military
alliances, most importantly NATO and the Warsaw Pact. The American and
Soviet informal spheres of influence also included trading and cultural ties to
several other countries. Many independent nations, especially those just
emerging from colonialism, remained neutral in the Cold War.

Outsiders and Opposition

The 1950s often are remembered as a time of political and cultural complacency among
white Americans, with most of the opposition to the nation's institutions emanating
from people of color. But some young whites, in the South as well as North, joined in
the struggle for civil rights; their numbers increased in the 1960s. Others were drawn to the
music and dance of black America, especially the fusion of rhythm-and-blues with country-
and-western, which took the form of early rock 'n' roll. Distinct forms of protest also emerged
from within the white middle class: the rebellion of the Beats who rejected staid conformity,

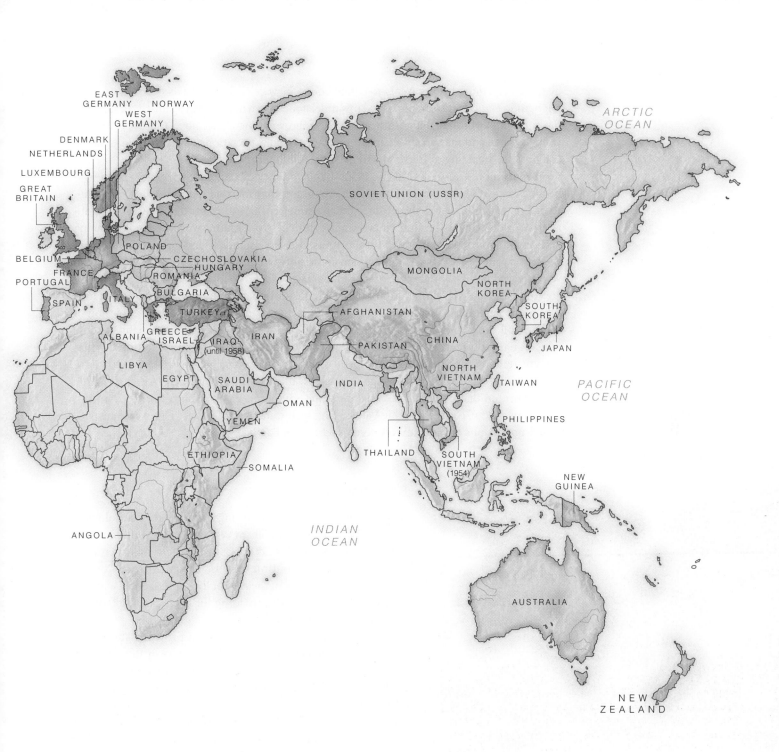

the stirrings of discontent among women, and the antinuclear and environmental movements. The arts also reflected a rejection of mainstream values, as Jackson Pollock and other abstract expressionist painters challenged the artistic conventions of the time and shifted the center of the art world from Paris to New York. Even the sexual revolution of the 1960s had its roots in widespread defiance of the rigid sexual codes of the 1950s.

Youth, Sex, and Rock 'n' Roll

One clue that all was not tranquil was the widespread panic that the nation's young were out of control. Adult authorities worried about an epidemic of juvenile delinquency, blaming everything from parents to comic books. New celebrities such as movie stars Marlon Brando and James Dean portrayed misunderstood youth in rebellion against a corrupt and uncaring adult world. In their films, and in J. D. Salinger's now-classic novel *Catcher in the Rye*, young women and men strain against the authority and expectations of their parents and the adult world, dreaming of freedom and personal fulfillment.

Sexual mores were rigid in the 1950s—and widely violated. Single young women who became pregnant faced disgrace and ostracism unless they married quickly, which many did. Abortion, which had been illegal since the late nineteenth century but tacitly accepted until after World War II, became increasingly difficult to obtain, with hospitals placing new restrictions on legal therapeutic abortions. A double standard encouraged men to pursue sexual conquest as a mark of manhood and virility but tarnished the reputation of women who engaged in sexual intercourse prior to marriage.

In many ways, the youth of the 1950s were already undermining the constraints that toppled in the next decade. Nowhere is this development more obvious than in the explosion of rock 'n' roll, with its roots in African American rhythm-and-blues, its raw sexuality, and its jubilant rebelliousness. Rock 'n' roll emerged out of the fusion of musical traditions. Artists from many ethnic backgrounds experimented with a variety of forms. Jewish songwriters Jerry Leiber and Mike Stoller wrote songs such as "Hound Dog" for black artists such as Willie Mae Thornton that were later recorded by white Southerner Elvis Presley. The first Mexican American rock 'n' roll star, Ritchie Valens, sang such romantic ballads as "Donna" along with jazzed-up versions of Mexican folk songs such as "La Bamba."

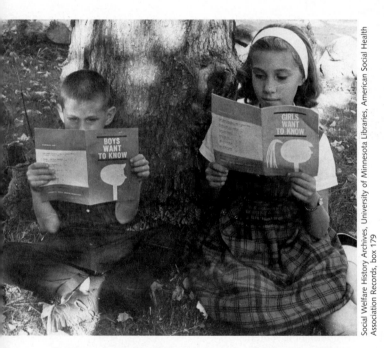

Since sex was rarely discussed in most middle-class families, many parents relied on schools to provide elementary sex education, and a generation of suburban children learned the facts of life from nervous teachers and a variety of simplified texts.

Social Welfare History Archives, University of Minnesota Libraries, American Social Health Association Records, box 179

Rebellious Men

Men, too, were in revolt. According to widely read sociological tracts of the time, such as William Whyte's *The Organization Man* and David Reisman's *The Lonely Crowd*, middle-class men were forced into boring, routinized jobs, groomed to be "outer-directed" at the expense of their inner lives, and saddled with the overwhelming burden of providing for ever-growing families with insatiable consumer desires.

A few highly visible American men provided alternative visions. Hugh Hefner built his Playboy empire by offering men the trappings of the "good life" without its burdensome responsibilities. The Playboy ethic encouraged men to enjoy the sexual pleasures of attractive women without the chains of marriage and to pursue the rewards of consumerism in well-appointed "bachelor flats" rather than appliance-laden homes. *Playboy* magazine celebrated this lifestyle.

Beat poets, writers, and artists offered a very different type of escape. In their literary works, such as Allen Ginsberg's poem *Howl* and Jack Kerouac's novel *On the Road*, and in their highly publicized lives, the Beats celebrated freedom from conformity, eccentric artistic expression, playful obscenity, experimentation with drugs, open homosexuality, and male bonding. While eschewing the sort of luxurious consumerism Hefner extolled, the Beats shared with the Playboy ethic a vision of male rebellion against conformity and responsibility. The mainstream men who indulged in these fantasies were more likely to enjoy them vicariously than to bolt from the breadwinner role. The dads who were honored on the new consumer holiday of Father's Day far outnumbered the freewheeling Beats and bachelors.

Mobilizing for Peace and the Environment

Some women did not wait for the new feminist movement to make their voices heard. Rachel Carson was one such woman. A marine biologist and a popular author, Carson became increasingly concerned about the impact of manufactured chemicals on the environment, especially the insecticide DDT, which had been poisoning the earth since World War II. Her last book, *Silent Spring*, published in 1962, brought attention to the worldwide problem of pesticide poisoning and helped launch the environmental movement that has flourished ever since.

Women also led the movement to stop the testing and proliferation of nuclear weapons. On November 1, 1961, 50,000 suburban women in more than sixty communities staged a protest, Women Strike for Peace (WSP). Participants lobbied government officials to "End the Arms Race—Not the Human Race." Within a year their numbers grew to several hundred thousand. Despite FBI surveillance, these women carried the banner of motherhood into political activism, much as their nineteenth-century predecessors had done.

Washington Post. Reprinted by permission of the D.C. Public Library

■ On November 1, 1961, 50,000 women in communities across the country took to the streets to protest nuclear testing. Under the sponsorship of Women Strike for Peace, these demonstrators used their authority as mothers, and brought along their children, to highlight their stake in the future.

The Kennedy Era

John Fitzgerald Kennedy was the first American president born in the twentieth century and the first Roman Catholic president. In his inaugural address, he claimed that "the torch has been passed to a new generation." It was a fitting metaphor for a young man who had been reared to compete and to win, whether the contest was athletic, intellectual, or political. But at the time of his election, it was not clear that a new generation had grabbed the torch. The young candidate was largely the creation of his father, Joseph, whose forebears had emigrated from Ireland during the 1840s. Joseph Kennedy rose to power and wealth as a financier, Hollywood executive, and ambassador to England. Ambitious and demanding, the elder Kennedy was known for his ruthlessness in business and politics and for his blatant philandering. He groomed his oldest son, Joseph P. Kennedy Jr., for greatness, specifically for the presidency. But when young Joe was killed in World War II, the father's ambitions settled on the next in line, John.

John (Jack) Kennedy became a hero during World War II, winning military honors for rescuing his crewmates on his patrol boat, PT-109, when it was rammed by a Japanese destroyer. The rescue left him with a painful back impairment and exacerbated the symptoms of Addison's disease, which plagued him all his life and necessitated daily cortisone injections. His father coached him to bear up under the pain, hide his infirmity, and project

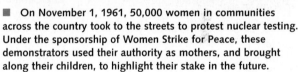

TABLE 25-2			
The Election of 1960			
Candidate	Political Party	Popular Vote (%)	Electoral Vote
John F. Kennedy	Democratic	49.9	303
Richard M. Nixon	Republican	49.6	219

Rachel Carson, *Silent Spring*

In 1962, Silent Spring, *Rachel Carson's eloquent exposé of the chemical industry's deadly impact on the health of the planet, landed on the best-seller list, where it stayed for months. The book, which eventually sold 1.5 million copies and remains in print today, galvanized the environmental movement of the 1960s and 1970s. Carson called the chemical industry "a child of the Second World War" and creator of "elixirs of death." She reported that annual pesticide production increased from 124 million pounds in 1947 to 637 million pounds by 1960. Twenty years later it had reached 2.4 billion pounds. "In the course of developing agents of chemical warfare," she noted, "some of the chemicals created in the laboratory were found to be lethal to insects. The discovery did not come by chance: insects were widely used to test chemicals as agents of death for man."*

It took hundreds of millions of years to produce the life that now inhabits the earth—eons of time in which that developing and evolving and diversifying life reached a state of adjustment and balance with its surroundings. The environment, rigorously shaping and directing the life it supported, contained elements that were hostile as well as supporting. Certain rocks gave out dangerous radiation; even within the light of the sun, from which all life draws its energy, there were short-wave radiations with power to injure. Given time—time not in years but in millennia—life adjusts, and a balance has been reached. For time is the essen-

Environmentalist Rachel Carson, author of *Silent Spring*.

Alfred Eisenstaedt/TimePix

tial ingredient; but in the modern world there is no time.

The rapidity of change and the speed with which new situations are created follow the impetuous and heedless pace of man rather than the deliberate pace of nature. Radiation is no longer merely the background radiation of rocks, the bombardment of cosmic rays, the ultraviolet of the sun that have existed before there was any life on earth; radiation is now the unnatural creation of man's tampering with the atom. The chemicals to which life is asked to make its adjustment are no longer merely the calcium and silica and copper and all the rest of the minerals washed out of the rocks and carried in rivers to the sea; they are the synthetic creations of man's inventive mind, brewed in his laboratories, and having no counterparts in nature.

To adjust to these chemicals would require time on the scale that is nature's; it

would require not merely the years of a man's life but the life of generations. And even this, were it by some miracle possible, would be futile, for the new chemicals come from our laboratories in an endless stream; almost five hundred annually find their way into actual use in the United States alone. The figure is staggering and its implications are not easily grasped—500 new chemicals to which the bodies of men and animals are required some-how to adapt each year, chemicals totally outside the limits of biologic experience.

Among them are many that are used in man's war against nature. Since the mid-1940s over 200 basic chemicals have been created for use in killing insects, weeds, rodents, and other organisms described in the modern vernacular as "pests"; and they are sold under several thousand different brand names.

These sprays, dusts, and aerosols are now applied almost universally to farms, gardens, forests, and homes—nonselective chemicals that have the power to kill every insect, the "good" and the "bad," to still the song of the birds and the leaping of fish in the streams, to coat the leaves with a deadly film, and to linger on in the soil—all this though the intended target may be only a few weeds or insects. Can anyone believe it is possible to lay down such a barrage of poisons on the surface of the earth without making it unfit for all life? They should not be called "insecticides" but "biocides."

Questions

1. *What connection does Carson make between time and the environment?*
2. *Why does Carson believe insecticides should be called biocides?* ■

an image of health and vitality. "Vigor" was a word Kennedy used often and an aura he projected, inspiring a national craze for physical fitness that survives to this day. Young JFK also emulated his father's brash sexual promiscuity, even after his marriage to Jacqueline Bouvier in 1953.

In 1946 Kennedy won election to the House of Representatives, and in 1952 he defeated incumbent Republican Henry Cabot Lodge to become the Democratic senator from Massachusetts. JFK's father financed all of his political campaigns, and in 1960 the elderly Kennedy bankrolled and masterminded JFK's narrowly successful run for the White House. Kennedy selected as his running mate the powerful Senate majority leader, Lyndon B. Johnson of Texas, whom he had battled for the nomination.

VIDEO

Kennedy-Nixon Debate

Domestic Policy

With such a thin margin of victory, Kennedy lacked a popular mandate for change. But he quickly established himself as an eloquent leader. In his inaugural address, the new president inspired the nation with his memorable words "And so, my fellow Americans, ask not what your country can do for you; ask what you can do for your country." Focusing his address on foreign policy, he declared, "Let every nation know . . . that we shall pay any price, bear any burden, meet any hardship, support any friend, oppose any foe to assure the survival and the success of liberty." In his first two years, he sought mainly to avoid division at home and to wage the Cold War forcefully abroad. He believed that prosperity was the best way to spread the fruits of affluence, rather than government programs that would promote a redistribution of wealth. Accordingly, he supported corporate tax cuts to stimulate the economy, which grew at a rate of 5 percent each year from 1961 to 1966.

Although Democrats held strong majorities in both houses, powerful southern conservatives often teamed up with Republicans to form a functional majority in Congress to defeat reform legislation. Kennedy knew that it would be futile to champion the cause of civil rights in the face of that alliance. But he did support issues important to his working-class constituents and proposed a number of legislative initiatives, including increasing the minimum wage, health care for the aged, larger Social Security benefits, and the creation of the Department of Housing and Urban Development (HUD).

Foreign Policy

Kennedy was the first U.S. president to understand and recognize the legitimacy of movements for national self-determination in the Third World. He endeavored to support movements to end colonial rule while at the same time containing the spread of communism. His efforts earned him a great deal of good will among Africans and other non-Europeans. But if nationalist movements appeared friendly to the Soviet Union, Kennedy worked against them. He sharply increased military spending and nuclear arms buildup as a show of strength and preparedness against possible Soviet aggression.

One of Kennedy's most popular initiatives was the creation of the Peace Corps, a program that sent Americans, especially young people, to nations around the world to work on development projects. In 1961 Kennedy signed the Charter of Punta del Este with several Latin American countries, establishing the Alliance for Progress, a program designed to prevent the spread of anti-Americanism and communist insurgencies in Latin America. The alliance offered $20 billion in loans to Latin American countries for democratic development initiatives.

Kennedy continued the strategies of Truman and Eisenhower to fight communism in South Vietnam by supporting the corrupt regime of Ngo Dinh Diem. But the National Liberation Front (NLF), founded in 1960 and supported by Ho Chi Minh's communist regime in North Vietnam, gained the upper hand in its struggle against Diem. In response, Kennedy increased the number of military advisers there from 800 to 17,000. By 1963 it was obvious that Diem's brutal regime was about to fall to the NLF, and Kennedy allowed U.S. military advisers and diplomats to encourage Diem's dissenting generals to depose Diem.

Kennedy also faced a crisis brewing in Cuba. Fidel Castro's revolution initially represented the sort of democratic insurgency that Kennedy wanted to support. But Castro's socialism turned the United States against him, and he established close ties with the Soviet Union. During the Eisenhower administration, the CIA began planning an invasion of Cuba with the help of Cuban exiles in Florida. Kennedy's national security advisers persuaded Kennedy to allow the invasion to proceed.

On April 17, 1961, U.S.-backed and -trained anticommunist forces, most of them Cuban exiles, landed at the Bahia de Cochinas (Bay of Pigs) on the southern coast of Cuba. Castro expected the invasion—his agents in Florida had infiltrated the Cuban exiles—so his well-prepared troops quickly surrounded and captured the invaders. No domestic uprising against Castro occurred to support the invasion. Kennedy pulled back in humiliating defeat. Nevertheless, the president continued to support covert efforts that tried but failed to destabilize Cuba and assassinate Castro.

Another crisis soon erupted in Berlin. Located 200 miles deep in East Germany, with only two highways connecting it to West Germany, West Berlin was a showcase of western material superiority and an espionage center for the western powers. In June 1961, Khrushchev threatened to end the western presence in Berlin and unite the city with the rest of East Germany. His plan was motivated in part to stop the steady stream of East Germans into West Berlin. Kennedy refused to relinquish West Berlin. On August 13, 1961, the East German government constructed a wall to separate East and West Berlin. Two years later, Kennedy stood in front of the wall and pledged to defend the West Berliners.

The most serious foreign policy crisis of Kennedy's presidency came in 1962, when the Soviet Union, at Castro's invitation, began to install intermediate-range nuclear missiles in Cuba. Kennedy's close advisers presented a series of options for actions that could be taken in response. The most dramatic and dangerous would be a full-scale military invasion of the island, which would topple Castro but would surely have prompted military retaliation by the Soviet Union. Another option was a more limited military intervention, an air strike to destroy the missiles before they became operational. Others proposed a blockade of Cuban ports to prevent the missiles from entering. Another possibility was to negotiate secretly with Castro, Soviet leaders, or both. Kennedy decided against behind-the-scenes negotiations as well as the drastic move of military intervention and instead established a "quarantine" around the island to block Soviet ships from reaching Cuba, hoping that the Soviet Union would back down and withdraw the missiles. A quarantine, unlike a blockade, was not considered an act of war; nevertheless, Kennedy put the Strategic Air Command on full alert for possible nuclear war.

> *Kennedy put the Strategic Air Command on full alert for possible nuclear war.*

VIDEO

The Cuban Missile Crisis

DOCUMENT

Test Ban Treaty

It was a risky move. On national television, Kennedy warned the Soviet Union to remove the missiles or face the military might of the United States. For the next five days tensions mounted, as Russian ships hovered in the water beyond the quarantine zone. Finally Khrushchev proposed an agreement, offering to remove the missiles if the United States would agree not to invade Cuba. Kennedy also privately promised to remove Jupiter missiles in Turkey as soon as the crisis was over. The two leaders managed to diffuse the crisis, but they were both sobered by the experience of having come to the brink of nuclear war. In 1963 they signed a nuclear test ban treaty.

A Year of Turning Points

In 1963 the President's Commission on the Status of Women, which Kennedy had appointed under the leadership of Eleanor Roosevelt, published a report that documented widespread discrimination against women in jobs, pay, education, and the professions. In response, Kennedy issued a presidential order requiring the civil service to hire people "without regard to sex," and he supported passage of the Equal Pay Act of 1963.

Also in 1963, in Birmingham, Alabama, Martin Luther King Jr. led a silent and peaceful march through the city. Chief of Police Bull Connor unleashed the police, who blasted the demonstrators with fire hoses and attacked them with vicious police dogs. Four black children were later killed when segregationists bombed an African American church. The Kennedy administration responded by bringing the full force of its authority to bear on the officials in Birmingham. But the crisis intensified. Alabama's segregationist governor, George Wallace, refused to admit two black students to the University of Alabama, threatening to stand in the doorway to block their entrance.

Civil Rights March
on Washington

Finally, on June 10, 1963, Kennedy federalized the Alabama National Guard and for the first time went before the American people to declare himself forcefully on the side of the civil rights protesters and to propose a civil rights bill. A few months later, on August 28, more than 250,000 people gathered at the nation's capital in front of the Lincoln Memorial for the culmination of the March on Washington, a huge demonstration for jobs as well as freedom, where Martin Luther King Jr. delivered his inspiring "I Have a Dream" speech.

In the fall of 1963, a confident Kennedy began planning his reelection campaign for the next year. To mobilize support, he visited Texas. "Here we are in Dallas," he said on November 22, 1963, "and it looks like everything in Texas is going to be fine for us." Within an hour of uttering those optimistic words, the president lay dying of an assassin's bullet.

As shock and grief spread across the nation, a bizarre series of events confounded efforts to bring the assassin to justice. Police arrested Lee Harvey Oswald, who had previously lived in the Soviet Union and who had loose ties to organized crime and to political groups interested in Cuba. Oswald claimed that he was innocent. But before he could be brought to trial, Oswald was murdered. Jack Ruby, a nightclub owner who also had links to organized crime, shot Oswald while he was in the custody of the Dallas police—an event witnessed by millions on live television. Ruby later died in prison. The newly sworn-in president, Lyndon B. Johnson, appointed a commission to investigate the assassination under the leadership of Supreme Court Chief Justice Earl Warren. The Warren Commission eventually issued a report concluding that Oswald and Ruby had both acted alone, although the report failed to end speculation about a possible conspiracy.

Conclusion

During the decade between the election of Dwight D. Eisenhower and the assassination of John F. Kennedy, the nation experienced unprecedented prosperity as increasing numbers of Americans moved into middle-class suburbs and enjoyed the fruits of a rapidly expanding consumer economy. Men and women rushed into marriage and childbearing, creating the baby boom and a powerful domestic ideology resting on distinct gender roles for women and men. At the same time, fears of nuclear war, intense anticommunism, and pressures to conform to mainstream political and cultural values contributed to anxieties and discontent.

Beneath the apparently tranquil surface, some Americans began to resist the limitations and exclusions of the widely touted "American way of life." African Americans in the South demanded their rightful place as full citizens, challenging the Jim Crow system and accelerating the civil rights movement through nonviolent protests, boycotts, and sit-ins. Young people created a vibrant youth culture to the pulsating rhythms of rock 'n' roll. Beatniks, peace activists, and environmentalists expressed incipient political and cultural dissent. The rumblings of vast social change had already begun and would explode in the years ahead, pushed along by a divisive war in Vietnam.

Sites to Visit

We Shall Overcome: Historic Places of the Civil Rights Movement
www.cr.nps.gov/nR/travel/civilrights/

> This site of the National Register of Historic Places provides maps and information about the historic locations of the civil rights movement.

Dwight David Eisenhower
www.ipl.org/div/POTUS/ddeisenhower.html

> This site contains basic information about Eisenhower's election and presidency, and online biography.

Literature and Culture of the American 1950s
www.writing.upenn.edu/~afilreis/50s/home.html

> This site by University of Pennsylvania Professor Al Filreis contains a large array of 1950s documents, literature, and images.

Levittown: Documents of an Ideal American Suburb
tigger.uic.edu/~pbhales/Levittown/

> Peter Bacon Hales of the Art History Department at the University of Illinois at Chicago developed this site, which includes images, articles, and information about the post–World War II Levittown suburb.

Hollywood and the Movies During the 1950s
lib.berkeley.edu/MRC/50sbib.html

> This site from the University of California at Berkeley libraries includes information about Hollywood during the 1950s, and links to related sites, such as the Hollywood blacklist and film noir.

Rock and Roll
www.rockhall.com/home/default.asp

> This Web site of the Rock and Roll Hall of Fame and Museum includes information about the history and major artists of rock and roll.

Little Rock 1957: Pages from History—The Central High Crisis
www.ardemgaz.com/prev/central/

> This site documents the events surrounding the effort to desegregate Central High in Little Rock, Arkansas, in 1957.

From *Plessy v. Ferguson* to *Brown v. Board of Education*: The Supreme Court Rules on School Desegregation
www.yale.edu/ynhti/curriculum/units/1982/3/82.03.06.x.html

> This site includes information about the landmark Supreme Court decisions compiled by the Yale-New Haven Teachers Institute.

Civil Rights Era
lcweb2.loc.gov/ammem/aaohtml/exhibit/aopart9.html

> This Library of Congress site includes information about the people, events, and developments of the civil rights movement.

John F. Kennedy
www.ipl.org/div/potus/jfkennedy.html

> This site contains basic information about Kennedy's election and presidency, and online biography.

For Further Reading

General

Taylor Branch, *Parting the Waters: America in the King Years, 1954–1963* (1988).

William H. Chafe, *The Unfinished Journey: America Since World War II*, 5th ed. (2006).

Pete Daniel, *Lost Revolutions: The South in the 1950s* (2000).

Eric Foner, *The Story of American Freedom* (1998).

Cold War, Warm Hearth

Barbara Ehrenreich, *The Hearts of Men: American Dreams and the Flight from Commitment* (1984).

Ruth Feldstein, *Motherhood in Black and White: Race and Sex in American Liberalism, 1930–1965* (2000).

Kenneth T. Jackson, *Crabgrass Frontier: The Suburbanization of the United States* (1985).

Elaine Tyler May, *Homeward Bound: American Families in the Cold War Era* (1999).

The Civil Rights Movement

Clayborne Carson, *In Struggle: SNCC and the Black Awakening of the 1960s* (1981).

Mary Dudziak, *Cold War Civil Rights: Equality as Cold War Policy, 1946–1968* (2000).

Steven F. Lawson, *Running for Freedom: Civil Rights and Black Politics in America Since 1941* (1990).

Harvard Sitkoff, *The Struggle for Black Equality, 1954–1992* (1993).

The Eisenhower Years

Stephen E. Ambrose, *Eisenhower* (1983–1984).

Thomas Borstelmann, *The Cold War and the Color Line: American Race Relations in the Global Arena* (2001).

Peter B. Dow, *Schoolhouse Politics: Lessons from the Sputnik Era* (1991).

Fred I. Greenstein, *The Hidden-Hand Presidency: Eisenhower as Leader* (1994).

Outsiders and Opposition

Rachel Carson, *Silent Spring* (1962).

Betty Friedan, *The Feminine Mystique* (1963).

James Gilbert, *A Cycle of Outrage: America's Reaction to the Juvenile Delinquent in the 1950s* (1986).

Joanne Meyerowitz, ed., *Not June Cleaver: Women and Gender in Postwar America, 1945–1960* (1994).

Rickie Solinger, *Wake Up Little Susie: Single Pregnancy and Race Before Roe v. Wade* (1992).

The Kennedy Era

Elizabeth Cobbs Hoffman, *All You Need Is Love: The Peace Corps and the Spirit of the 1960s* (1998).

James N. Giglio, *The Presidency of John F. Kennedy*, 2nd ed. (2006).

Herbert S. Parmet, *J.F.K.: The Presidency of John F. Kennedy* (1983).

Arthur M. Schlesinger Jr., *A Thousand Days: John F. Kennedy in the White House* (1965).

For quizzes and other resources on these topics, go to www.longmanamericanhistory.com.

The Nation Divides: The Vietnam War and Social Conflict, 1964–1971

CHAPTER

26

THE SOFT-SPOKEN BLACK MAN WITH THE STRANGE NORTHERN ACCENT FIRST SHOWED UP IN small-town McComb, Mississippi, in the summer of 1961. Robert Parris Moses had come on a mission of democracy. An organizer for the new Student Nonviolent Coordinating Committee (SNCC), he was there to encourage impoverished African Americans to register to vote. Over the next four years in the Deep South, Bob Moses paid a price for his commitments. Local police imprisoned him, and white supremacists beat him severely and murdered dozens of his fellow activists in the black freedom movement. But Moses remained committed to nonviolence and racial integration. His quiet courage became legendary in the movement. One summer night in 1962, he returned to a deserted SNCC office in Greenwood, Mississippi, that had just been ransacked by a white mob. Three other SNCC workers had barely escaped with their lives. Moses looked around, made up a bed in the corner of the devastated main room, and went to sleep. He refused to be intimidated.

■ A native of New York City, Bob Moses graduated from Hamilton College in upstate New York and did graduate work at Harvard University. He was inspired by the sit-in movement that began in 1960 in the American South and soon moved south to join SNCC.

During the 1960s, an extraordinary number of idealistic young people became involved in public life in an effort to make real their nation's promises of freedom, justice, and equality. The civil rights movement inspired the social movements that followed: for ending the war, for preserving the environment, and for liberating women, Latinos, Indians, and gay men and lesbians. But organizing for change inevitably brought activists up against fierce resistance from what they called "the establishment." Disillusionment and radicalization often followed. Public life became deeply contentious by 1968 as young radicals challenged more conservative citizens on issues of race, war, and gender.

The escalating American war in Southeast Asia loomed over all. Lyndon Johnson brought the nation to its apex of liberal reform with his extensive Great Society legislation. However, the high-flying hopes of Democratic liberals crashed to earth with the destructive war that the Johnson administration waged against seasoned communist revolutionaries in far-off Vietnam. Out of the wreckage of 1968 emerged a Republican president, Richard Nixon, and a growing conservative backlash against the social changes advocated by people of color, the counterculture, the antiwar movement, and the rising tide of women's liberation.

Lyndon Johnson and the Apex of Liberalism

Wealth provided the foundation on which the Great Society was built. American economic expansion after World War II had created history's richest nation by 1960. From 1961 to 1966, the economy accelerated at an annual growth rate of more than 5 percent with very low inflation, stimulated by large tax cuts and extensive military spending. The 41 percent increase in per capita income during the 1960s was not evenly distributed, however. Economist Paul Samuelson explained in 1970, "If we made an income pyramid out of a child's blocks, with each layer portraying $1000 of income, the peak would be far higher than the Eiffel Tower, but almost all of us would be within a yard of the ground." And the distribution of wealth (stocks and real estate) was far more skewed than that of income. The president and the Congress believed that economic expansion would continue indefinitely and the nation could therefore afford government policies to improve the welfare of less affluent Americans. The Supreme Court expanded individual liberties.

The New President

Lyndon Baines Johnson was one of the most remarkable American characters of the twentieth century, both a giant among political leaders and a bully with those who worked for him. Johnson grew up in a family struggling to stay out of poverty in the Texas hill country west of Austin. He entered Democratic politics early as an avid supporter of Franklin Roosevelt and the New Deal, aided by the business savvy and loyalty of his wife, Lady Bird Johnson, who grew wealthy through ownership of TV and radio stations. As First Lady, she became

■ Lyndon Johnson took the presidential oath of office on board *Air Force One*, returning to Washington from Dallas, where John Kennedy had just been assassinated on November 22, 1963. Johnson's wife, Lady Bird, is on his right, and Jacqueline Kennedy, still in blood-stained clothes, stands on his left. Johnson adroitly channeled the public outpouring of grief for the murdered young president into support for their shared legislative goals.

Lyndon Baines Johnson Library & Museum. Photo by Cecil Stoughton widely known for her leadership in highway beautification. Lyndon Johnson rose like a rocket through Congress to become perhaps the most powerful Senate majority leader ever (1954–1960) and then vice president (1961–1963). Kennedy's assassination catapulted him into the Oval Office as the nation's first Texan president.

Johnson retained Kennedy's cabinet and advisers and used the memory of the fallen young president to rally support for his administration. Johnson turned out to be the more liberal of the two men, in part because his early years in Texas had given him a visceral understanding of poverty and discrimination that his predecessor lacked. Johnson's focus was different, too. He retained Kennedy's anticommunist commitments abroad, but his heart remained at home, where he wanted to perfect American society.

First he had to win reelection. Less than a year remained until voters went to the polls in 1964. The Republicans nominated right-wing Senator Barry Goldwater of Arizona, a sign of the party's sharp swing away from its moderate eastern elements toward its fiercely conservative western and southern constituencies. Goldwater believed in unrestricted markets and a minimal role for the federal government in every aspect of American life except the military. He spoke casually about using nuclear weapons against communists abroad. Goldwater declared that "extremism in the defense of liberty is no vice," but Johnson zeroed in on that extremism and swept to the largest electoral majority of any president (61 percent).

TABLE 26-1

The Election of 1964

Candidate	Political Party	Popular Vote (%)	Electoral Vote
Lyndon B. Johnson	Democratic	61.1	486
Barry M. Goldwater	Republican	38.5	52

The Great Society: Fighting Poverty and Discrimination

In pursuit of what he called the Great Society, Johnson first declared a "War on Poverty." No citizen in the richest nation on earth should live in squalor, he believed. More than one out of five Americans still lived below the conservatively estimated official poverty line ($3,022 for a nonfarm family of four in 1960), and 70 percent of these citizens were white.

The president and a large congressional majority passed several measures to alleviate poverty. They sharply increased the availability of money and food stamps through the Aid to Families with Dependent Children ("welfare") program, and they raised Social Security payments to older Americans. Several programs focused on improving educational opportunities as an avenue out of poverty: Head Start offered preschool education and meals for youngsters, the Elementary and Secondary Education Act sent federal funds to the least affluent school districts, and an expanded system of student loans facilitated access to college. The Job Corps provided employment training, and Volunteers in Service to America (VISTA) served as a domestic Peace Corps, funneling people with education and skills into poor communities to serve as teachers and providers of other social services.

DOCUMENT

Johnson, "The War on Poverty"

No barrier to opportunity in the early 1960s was higher than the color bar. Both opportunist and idealist, Johnson as president shed his segregationist voting record (necessary for election in Texas before 1960) and became the most vocal proponent of racial equality ever to occupy the Oval Office. Two factors facilitated his change in position. One, blatant inequalities for American citizens weakened the United States in its competition with the Soviets and Chinese for the loyalty of the nonwhite Third World majority. Two, the African American freedom struggle in the South had reached a boiling point. Black frustration was mounting over white brutality and the seeming indifference or even hostility of the national government.

The Civil Rights Act of 1964 fulfilled the implicit promise of the *Brown v. Board of Education* decision a decade earlier. The 1964 act made desegregation the law of the land as it outlawed discrimination in employment and in public facilities such as

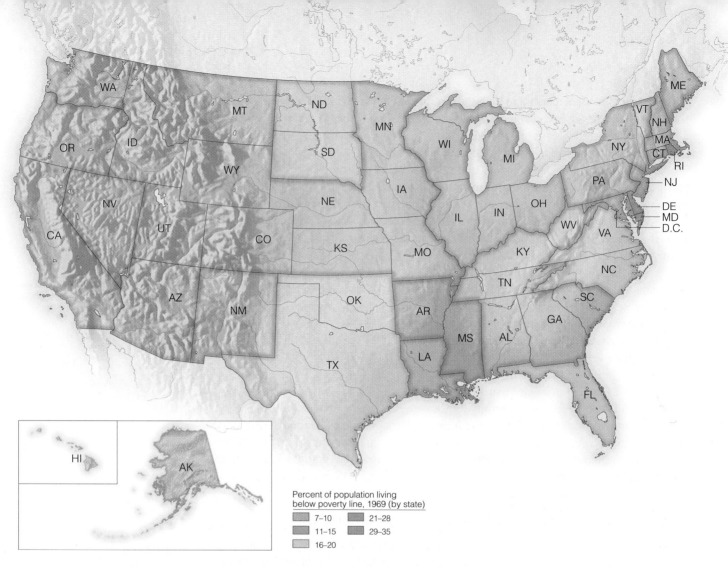

Percent of population living
below poverty line, 1969 (by state)

- 7–10
- 11–15
- 16–20
- 21–28
- 29–35

■ **MAP 26.1**

PERCENTAGE OF POPULATION LIVING BELOW THE POVERTY LINE, 1969 (BY STATE)   The United States in the 1960s was a nation of unprecedented wealth and comfort. Yet millions of Americans still lived in poverty. Prodded by other reformers, President Johnson sought to reduce the number of impoverished citizens through the Great Society programs. The southeastern and south-central states had the highest poverty rates, a legacy of slavery and limited industrialization.

Impact of the Voting Rights Act of 1965

restaurants, theaters, and hotels. The Voting Rights Act of 1965 outlawed poll taxes and provided federal voting registrars in states that refused the ballot to African Americans. The single most important legislation of the twentieth century for bringing political democracy to the South, the Voting Rights Act increased the percentage of blacks voting in Mississippi from 7 percent to 60 percent in two years.

The Great Society: Improving the Quality of Life

Johnson's vision of the Great Society extended to the broader quality of life in the United States. Health care was perhaps the most fundamental issue for citizens' sense of personal security. After 1965, the new Medicare system paid for the medical needs of Americans age sixty-five and older, and Medicaid underwrote health care services for the poor. In 1964, when more than half of adults smoked tobacco, the surgeon-general issued the first government report linking smoking to cancer. Higher federal standards for automotive safety followed a year later. Public pressures also led to the establishment of new requirements for publishing the nutritional values of packaged food. The federally funded Public Broadcasting System (PBS) was established to provide television programs that were more educational than the fare tied to advertising on the three corporate networks (NBC, CBS, and ABC). In fact, most Great Society measures targeted all Americans rather than just the disadvantaged.

Nothing more directly threatened the quality of American life than the degradation of the natural environment. The costs of the unrestrained and much-heralded economic growth since World War II showed up in the nation's air, water, and land. The leaded gasoline that fueled products of the booming auto industry created smog; industrial effluents polluted lakes and rivers; and petrochemical wastes poisoned the ground. The products of science that had contributed so much to the creation of wealth were turning out to have hidden costs, and a new wave of citizen action to protect the environment began to build.

Growing public awareness prompted the Clean Air Act (1963) and the Clean Waters Act (1966), which set federal guidelines for reducing smog and preserving public drinking sources from bacterial pollution. Even the long dam-building tradition in the American West faced new questions, with the Wild and Scenic Rivers Act enacted in 1968. Meanwhile, Congress passed the Wilderness Act in 1964, setting aside 9 million acres of undeveloped public lands as a place "where man is a visitor who does not remain."

The Liberal Warren Court

The Supreme Court under the leadership of Earl Warren steadily expanded the constitutional definition of individual rights. This shift reached even those deemed to have lost many of their rights: prisoners. *Gideon v. Wainwright* (1963) established the right of indigent prisoners to legal counsel, and *Escobedo v. Illinois* (1964) confirmed the right to counsel during interrogation, a critical hindrance to the use of torture. After *Miranda v. Arizona* (1966), police were required to inform people they arrested of their rights to remain silent and to speak to a lawyer.

The Warren Court bolstered other rights of individuals against potentially coercive community pressures. Decisions in 1962 and 1963 strictly limited the practice of requiring prayers in public schools. In 1963 the Court narrowed standards for the definition of "obscenity," allowing freer expression in the arts but also in pornography. *Griswold v. Connecticut* (1965) established the use of contraceptive devices by married people as a matter of private choice protected by the Constitution. In 1967 the Court heard the case of Mildred Jeter, a black woman, and Richard Loving, a white man, Virginians who had evaded their state's ban on interracial marriage by traveling to Washington, D.C., for their wedding and then returned to Caroline County to live. In the aptly titled *Loving v. Virginia*, the Court declared marriage one of the "basic civil rights of men" and overturned the laws of the last sixteen states restricting interracial unions.

The Supreme Court's interpreting of the Constitution to expand individual rights disturbed many conservative Americans. They saw the Court as another arm of an intrusive national government that was extending its control over matters previously left to local communities. For them, the goal of integration did not justify the busing of school children. Rising crime rates troubled them more than police brutality. Many Roman Catholics were unhappy with the legalization of contraceptives. Incensed by the ban on requiring school prayer, Protestant fundamentalists sought redress through political involvement, which they had previously shunned, initiating a grassroots religious conservative movement that helped bring Ronald Reagan to power in 1980.

Into War in Vietnam

The 1960s also marked the culmination of the U.S. government's efforts to control revolutionary political and social change abroad. The Truman Doctrine's logic of containing communism spanned the entire globe, but few imagined that the United States would overreach itself, tragically, in Vietnam. Johnson's accomplishments at home were forever overshadowed by the war he sent Americans to fight in the quiet rice paddies and beautiful highland forests of Southeast Asia. An aggressive U.S. anticommunist policy abroad collided with leftist revolutionaries throughout the Third World, and it was ill fortune for the Vietnamese that this collision struck them hardest of all.

The Vietnamese Revolution and the United States

The conflict in Vietnam began as one of many efforts to end European colonialism. Vietnamese nationalists, varying in ideologies but led by Ho Chi Minh and the Indochinese Communist party, had sought since the 1930s to liberate their country from French colonial rule. Japanese advances during World War II put the Vietminh (Vietnamese nationalists) on the same side as the Americans, and Ho worked closely with the U.S. Office of Strategic Services (OSS), precursor to the Central Intelligence Agency (CIA).

After the defeat of Germany and Japan, however, the French wanted to regain control of their colonies in Africa and Asia, including Vietnam. The British provided troop transport ships for French soldiers, and the United States provided most of the funds to support France in its war against the Vietminh (1946–1954). Cold War priorities won out: a weakened France had to be bolstered as the linchpin of a reintegrated, anticommunist western Europe, while the Vietminh were led by Communist party members. But the Vietnamese defeated the much more heavily armed French at the battle of Dien Bien Phu in May 1954. Two months later, the Geneva Accords divided the country temporarily at the seventeenth parallel until national elections could be held within two years to reunify Vietnam. Ho's forces solidified their control of the north, the French pulled out entirely, and the Eisenhower administration made a fateful decision to intervene directly to preserve the southern part of Vietnam from communism. The United States created a new government led by the Roman Catholic, anticommunist Ngo Dinh Diem in a new country called "South Vietnam."

The Vietnamese Revolution was only half over, however. The French colonialists withdrew, but the Saigon regime did not hold elections. In the North, the sometimes brutal internal revolution for the creation of a socialist society proceeded with an extensive program of land redistribution. In the South, Diem ruled for eight years with increasing repression of communists and other dissenters. U.S. funding kept him in power. Southern members of the old Vietminh began a sabotage campaign against the Saigon government and formed the National Liberation Front (NLF) in 1960, with the support of North Vietnam. Diem and his American supporters called them Viet Cong or VC, roughly equivalent to the derogatory American term *Commies*. As the struggle to overthrow Diem intensified, several of his own generals assassinated him in November 1963 with the tacit support of U.S. officials in South Vietnam and Washington.

Johnson's War

Lyndon Johnson inherited his predecessors' commitment to preserving a noncommunist South Vietnam. Bolstered by Kennedy's hawkish advisers, he believed that American credibility was at stake. But Johnson faced a swiftly deteriorating military situation. The NLF, which the administration portrayed as merely a tool of North Vietnam, was winning the political war for the South, taking control of the countryside from the demoralized Army of the Republic of Vietnam (ARVN). Faced with the choice of escalating U.S. involvement to prevent an NLF victory or withdrawing entirely from the country, Johnson escalated.

How he did so was crucially important. There was neither a national debate nor a congressional vote to declare war. Johnson did not want to distract Congress from his Great Society agenda, nor did he want to provoke the Soviet Union or China. But he believed he had to preserve a noncommunist South Vietnam or else face a debilitating backlash from Republicans, who would skewer him as McCarthy had done to Truman over the "loss" of China fifteen years earlier. So the president used deception, describing offensive American actions as defensive and opening up a credibility gap between a committed government and a skeptical public.

In August 1964, North Vietnamese ships in the Gulf of Tonkin fired on the U.S. destroyer *Maddox*, which was aiding South Vietnamese sabotage operations against the North. The president portrayed the incident as one of unprovoked communist aggression, and Congress expressed almost unanimous support through its Gulf of Tonkin Resolution. With this substitute for a declaration of war, Johnson ordered American planes to begin bombing North Vietnam, and the first American combat troops splashed ashore at Da Nang in South Vietnam on March 8, 1965. In July the administration made the key decision to add 100,000 more soldiers, with more to follow as necessary.

DOCUMENT

Johnson, The Tonkin Gulf Resolution Message

American strategy had two goals: to limit the war so as not to draw in neighboring China (to avoid a repeat of the Korean War) and to force the NLF and North Vietnam to give up their struggle to reunify the country under Hanoi's control. The problem was the political nature of the guerrilla war in the South: a contest for the loyalty of the population, in which NLF operatives mingled easily with the citizenry. This kind of war made the enemy difficult to find, as had often been true for the British in fighting the American revolutionaries in the 1770s. The "strategic hamlet" program uprooted rural peasants and concentrated them in fortified towns, creating "free fire zones" in their wake where anything that moved was a target. The U.S. Air Force pounded the South as well as the North, dropping more bombs on this ancient land (smaller than either Germany or Japan) than had been used in all theaters on all sides in World War II. These tactics destabilized and traumatized society in South Vietnam as one-fourth of the population became refugees.

> *American strategy had two goals: to limit the war so as not to draw in neighboring China (to avoid a repeat of the Korean War) and to force the NLF and North Vietnam to give up their struggle to reunify the country under Hanoi's control.*

Americans in Southeast Asia

Given America's wealth, size, and superior weaponry, most U.S. soldiers who went to Vietnam in 1965–1966 had no doubt they would win the war. They typically looked down on Asians. Very few knew anything about Vietnamese history or culture, and almost none spoke the Vietnamese language. Although a small number of Americans worked closely with their South Vietnamese allies, most GIs encountered Vietnamese in subservient roles as laundry workers, prostitutes, waitresses, and bartenders. Blinkered by anticommunism and far removed from their own revolutionary roots, Americans from the top brass to the lowest "grunts" marched into a country they did not understand but assumed they could control.

MAP

The Vietnam War

President Johnson spoke of the conflict in Vietnam as a case of one sovereign nation—the North—invading another one—the South. However, few Vietnamese saw the war in those terms. The United States, dismissing the failure of the French before them, had intervened not so much in an international war as in an ongoing revolution that aimed to reunify the country. Few Vietnamese, whatever their opinions of communism, viewed the corrupt Saigon regime as legitimate or democratic. After all, it was kept in place by foreigners, whereas the North was ruled by people who had expelled the French foreigners.

Initial U.S. optimism reflected a grave underestimation of the NLF and the North Vietnamese. Ho Chi Minh was an extremely popular leader, and intervention from the other side of the world only strengthened his position. As the war expanded, NLF recruiting in the South snowballed, and the people of North Vietnam remained loyal to their authoritarian government. Communist forces proved willing to endure fantastic hardship and sacrifices to prevail. Their morale was much higher than that of the ARVN.

Who were the 3 million Americans who went to Vietnam? The initial forces contained experienced soldiers, but as the war escalated, this professional army was diluted with hundreds of thousands of young draftees. Student deferments protected more comfortable Americans, so GIs were predominantly those who lacked money and education. Although 70 percent were

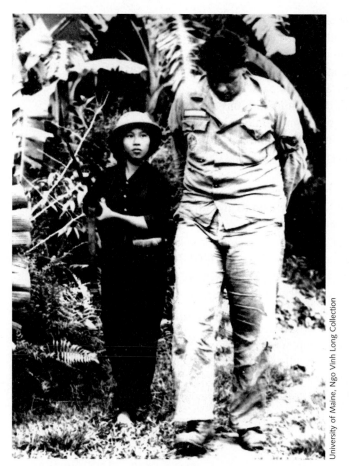

University of Maine, Ngo Vinh Long Collection

■ A North Vietnamese militia fighter named Kim Lai escorts an American pilot whom she captured after his plane crashed over the North. American GIs often were struck by the diminutive size of the average Vietnamese in comparison to the average American. Bigger, better equipped, and much more well-armed than their opponents, most U.S. soldiers and officers before 1968 went into the field in Vietnam certain that they would be victorious.

white men, black, Hispanic, and Native American enlistees shipped out in disproportionate numbers. In sharp contrast to the motives of the NLF and the North Vietnamese army, few of these young men (along with 10,000 women who volunteered as nurses) were in Vietnam to win the war regardless of the cost or duration. They had only to survive twelve months before returning home to the safety of a peacetime society.

North Vietnamese regular army units came South to match the growing number of U.S. forces, and they occasionally engaged the Americans in large set battles, as at Ia Drang Valley in the fall of 1965. U.S. troops fought well in such firefights, making devastating use of their superior weapons and air power. However, the bulk of the fighting consisted of smaller engagements with deceptive enemies on their home turf who faded in and out of the civilian population with ease. Ambushes and unexpected death haunted Americans on patrol, and relentless heat and humidity wore them down.

American soldiers felt mounting frustration and rage over the nature of the war that they were ordered to fight. Lacking a clear battlefront and an understandable strategy for winning the war, they were commanded simply to kill the often mysterious enemy. Yet distinguishing civilians from combatants in a popular guerrilla war was not always easy, especially when so many civilians evidently supported the NLF and so few Americans spoke Vietnamese. Realizing that few of the people they were supposed to be defending actually wanted them there but under orders to produce enemy bodies, U.S. troops on the ground began to slide toward a racial war against all Vietnamese.

Many GIs resisted this logic, sometimes showing real kindness to Vietnamese civilians. But atrocities on both sides inevitably followed from this kind of war. The worst came in the village of My Lai on March 16, 1968, where 105 soldiers from Charlie Company—enraged by the recent deaths of several comrades in ambushes—slaughtered, often after torturing or raping, more than 400 Vietnamese women, children, and old men. The army covered up the massacre for a year and a half, and eventually found only Lieutenant William Calley, the leader of Charlie Company's First Platoon, guilty of murdering Vietnamese civilians.

1968: The Turning Point

In late 1967, the public face of the war effort remained upbeat, as General William Westmoreland declared that he could now see "some light at the end of the tunnel." But hopes of an imminent victory were crushed by the startling Tet Offensive (named for the Vietnamese New Year) that began on January 30, 1968. NLF insurgents and North Vietnamese troops attacked U.S. strongholds throughout South Vietnam. The blow to American public confidence in Johnson and his military commanders proved irreversible. Far from being on the verge of defeat, as the administration had been claiming, the communists had shown that they could mount simultaneous attacks around the country.

The Tet Offensive coincided with two other crises in early 1968 to convince American political and business elites that U.S. international commitments had become larger than the nation could afford. First, a week before Tet began, the North Korean navy seized the U.S. intelligence ship *Pueblo* in the Sea of Japan and temporarily imprisoned its crew. U.S. commanders

■ **MAP 26.2**

THE AMERICAN WAR IN VIETNAM   Before U.S. combat troops entered Vietnam in 1965, few Americans knew where this Southeast Asian country was. Vietnam's geography and place names quickly became familiar in the United States as hundreds of thousands of young Americans served there and some 58,000 died there. Vietnam's elongated shape, its borders with Cambodia and Laos, and its proximity to China all affected the course of the fighting between 1965 and 1973.

were left scrambling to find enough forces to respond effectively without weakening American commitments in Europe and elsewhere. Second, a British financial collapse devalued the pound and caused the London government to announce its imminent withdrawal from its historic positions east of the Suez Canal, placing new military burdens on the United States in the Middle East. These events reduced international confidence in the U.S. economy, causing a currency crisis in March 1968 as holders of dollars traded them in for gold.

The political career of Lyndon Johnson was a final casualty of these events. His support on the left withered as the antiwar and **black power** movements expanded. Meanwhile, his more centrist supporters were joining the backlash against civil rights, urban violence, and antiwar protesters, peeling off to the Republican party. On March 12, antiwar challenger Senator Eugene McCarthy of Minnesota nearly defeated the incumbent president in the New

Hampshire Democratic primary. Johnson's vulnerability was clear. Senator Robert Kennedy of New York joined the race two weeks later. In a televised speech on March 31 that caught the divided nation by surprise, Johnson announced an end to U.S. escalations in the war, the start of negotiations in Paris with North Vietnam, and an end to his own political career. He would not seek reelection.

The Movement

While national leaders were defending what they called the "frontiers of freedom" abroad, young Americans in the mid- and late 1960s organized to expand what they considered the frontiers of freedom at home. Television for the first time tied the country together in a common culture whose shared images were transmitted simultaneously around the nation. The expanding war in Vietnam radicalized people who had initially been optimistic about reforming American society. Black power, the New Left, the counterculture, women's liberation, and other liberation movements often had quite divergent goals. But participants overlapped extensively and activists spoke of "the Movement" as if it were a unified phenomenon. At the heart of the youth movements of the decade lay a common quest for authenticity—a rejection of hypocrisy and a distrust of traditional authorities—that fused cultural and political protest.

From Civil Rights to Black Power

By 1966 the civil rights movement fractured as it confronted the limits of its success. It had achieved the goals of ending legal discrimination and putting southern African Americans in the voting booth, but it had not brought about a colorblind society. Racial prejudice among white conservatives remained virulent, and white liberals, such as those in the Kennedy and Johnson administrations, revealed themselves as not always trustworthy allies. Expecting only hostility from conservatives, civil rights workers were more disillusioned with what they saw as liberal betrayals.

■ A leading spokesman for the Black Muslims, Malcolm X converted to orthodox Islam and softened his antiwhite rhetoric in the two years before his murder in 1965. Like SNCC's Bob Moses, Malcolm increasingly identified with the Third World. Here he is shown in Egypt on a 1964 pilgrimage to Mecca, Saudi Arabia.

The Justice Department and the Federal Bureau of Investigation (FBI) did little to restrain the violence of the Ku Klux Klan until the murders of white organizers Michael Schwerner and Andrew Goodman in the summer of 1964—along with black co-worker James Chaney. Two months later, at the national Democratic party convention in Atlantic City, New Jersey, Johnson crushed the effort of the biracial Mississippi Freedom Democratic party to replace the state's regular, all-white Democratic delegates. The president was determined to avoid further alienating white southern voters as he pursued a huge victory margin in the November elections.

The black freedom struggle for centuries had woven together elements of racial separatism with elements of integration into the larger American culture. For many younger African Americans, the pendulum now swung toward a need for greater independence from the white majority. They took inspiration from Malcolm X, the fiery and eloquent minister of the Nation of Islam (Black Muslims), who until his murder in 1965 captivated listeners with denunciations of white perfidy and demands for black self-respect. In 1966 SNCC members began to speak of the need for "black power" rather than for the integrated "beloved community" they had initially sought in 1960.

The Black Panther party formed in Oakland, California, in response to police brutality. The heavily armed Panthers engaged in several shootouts with police and were eventually decimated by an FBI campaign against them. White Americans were shocked by the uprisings and riots that swept through black urban communities during the summers of 1964–1968. Triggered by the actions of white police, the riots expressed the fierce frustrations of impoverished people whose lives remained largely untouched by the achievements of the civil rights struggle. The most destructive outbreaks occurred in the Watts district of Los Angeles in 1965 and in Detroit and Newark in 1967.

Black power thrived primarily as a cultural movement that promoted pride in African American and African history and life. The slogan "black is beautiful" captured this spirit: long degraded by their white compatriots as inferior, black Americans in the late 1960s and 1970s reversed this equation to celebrate their cultural heritage. This could be as basic as a hairstyle, the natural Afro replacing hair straightened to look like Caucasian hair. At universities, new departments of African American studies fostered the exploration of black history. Unlearning habits of public deference to whites, most African Americans began referring to themselves as "black" rather than "Negro."

Cultural black power mixed with a different kind of political black power by the late 1960s: the election of black officials. Although militant black power advocates garnered the most media attention, most African Americans supported Lyndon Johnson and used the Voting Rights Act to pursue their goals in the realm of electoral politics. In 1966 Carl Stokes of Cleveland was elected the first black mayor of a major American city, and African Americans won local offices across the South.

The New Left and the Struggle Against the War

In 1962 a group of liberal college activists founded the Students for a Democratic Society (SDS). They called for a rejuvenation of American politics and society to replace the complacency that they saw pervading the country. Racial bigotry and poverty particularly troubled these optimistic young reformers, along with the overarching threat of nuclear destruction (highlighted anew by the missile crisis in Cuba). They hoped to become a kind of "white SNCC," promoting participatory democracy to redeem the promise of Cold War America.

VIDEO

"Protests Against the Vietnam War"

SDS served as the central organization of the New Left. Communism was simply not important to these activists. Nor was conservatism, which was then at its lowest point. They focused instead on the behavior of the liberals who ran the U.S. government from 1961 to 1968. They developed a critique of "corporate liberalism" as promoting the interests of the wealthy and the business community far more than providing for the needs of the disadvantaged.

After 1965, SDS's initially broad reform agenda narrowed to stopping the Vietnam War. SDS members organized the first major antiwar protest outside the White House on April 17, 1965, bringing their organization into alliance with the small group of religious and secular pacifists already working against the war. Mainstream Democrats also began abandoning Johnson over the war as it grew. The president had alienated the powerful chair of the Senate Foreign Relations Committee, J. William Fulbright of Arkansas, with his misleading reports during the brief U.S. military intervention in the Dominican Republic in April 1965 to defeat a left-leaning but not communist coup attempt. Fulbright then held televised hearings on the American war in Southeast Asia in January 1966, raising grave doubts about its wisdom. Draft resistance increased: young men moved to Canada, as did SNCC's Bob Moses, or went to jail, as did champion boxer Muhammad Ali.

Antiwar protesters followed the same trajectory of radicalization as black power advocates. Their dismay turned to rage as the Johnson administration continued to expand a war that was destroying much of Vietnam while killing tens of thousands of American soldiers for no reason its opponents considered legitimate. In combination

INTERPRETING HISTORY

Martin Luther King Jr. and the Vietnam War

Most Americans approved of the war in Vietnam until at least 1968. Appreciative of Lyndon Johnson's commitment to reduce poverty and end racial discrimination at home, African Americans generally supported the president's policies in Southeast Asia. However, younger, more radical civil rights workers were among those who opposed the first insertion of U.S. combat troops in 1965. Within two years, the nation's most prominent black leader, Martin Luther King Jr., decided that he could no longer keep quiet about his growing unease with the American war effort. A storm of criticism greeted his public denunciation of the war, most of it suggesting that he should limit himself to domestic civil rights work. But King no longer believed that events at home and abroad could be separated. The following excerpt is from his speech at Riverside Church, New York City, April 4, 1967.

A few years ago there was a shining moment in that struggle [against poverty and discrimination]. It seemed as if there was a real promise of hope for the poor—both black and white—through the Poverty Program. There were experiments, hopes, new beginnings. Then came the build-up in Vietnam and I watched the program broken and eviscerated as if it were some idle political plaything of a society gone mad on war. . . . I was increasingly compelled to see the war as an enemy of the poor and to attack it as such. . . .

We were taking the black young men who had been crippled by our society and sending them 8,000 miles away to guarantee liberties in Southeast Asia which they had not found in Southwest Georgia and East Harlem. So we have been repeatedly faced with the cruel irony of watching Negro and white boys on TV screens as they kill and die together for a nation that has been unable to seat them together in the same schools. . . .

As I have walked among the desperate, rejected and angry young men [in the ghettos of the North the last three summers] I have told them that Molotov cocktails and rifles would not solve their problems. I have tried to offer them my deepest compassion while maintaining my convictions that social change comes most meaningfully through non-violent action. But they asked—and rightly so—what about Vietnam? They asked if our own nation wasn't using massive doses of violence to solve its problems, to bring about the changes it wanted. Their questions hit home, and I knew that I would never again raise my voice against the violence of the oppressed in the ghettos without having first spoken clearly to the greatest purveyor of violence in the world today—my own government. . . .

[Our troops in Vietnam] must know after a short period there that none of the things we claim to be fighting for [such as freedom, justice, and peace] are really involved. Before long they must know that their government has sent them into a struggle among Vietnamese, and the more sophisticated surely realize that we are on the side of the wealthy and the secure while we create a hell for the poor.

His birthday now a national holiday, Martin Luther King Jr. has become widely accepted as a heroic figure in the American past. But in the last few years of his life, King's increasingly sharp criticisms of injustice in American society disturbed many fellow citizens.

Questions

1. How does King believe that the U.S. war in Vietnam is related to problems at home in American society?
2. What might have been the more negative and positive racial aspects of the Vietnam War?
3. What precisely does King believe to be wrong with the U.S. war in Vietnam? ■

Source: Bruce J. Schulman, Lyndon B. Johnson and American Liberalism (Boston: Bedford, 1995), pp. 208–212.

with or in support of black militants, white radicals took over buildings on university campuses in 1968–1969: Columbia, Cornell, Harvard, San Francisco State, and many others. SDS ultimately broke apart in the confusion and exhilaration of its growing demand for revolution against the larger systemic enemies, imperialism and capitalism, not just corporate liberalism. But radical rage could not be understood apart from the ongoing destruction of Vietnam by a government acting in the name of all Americans.

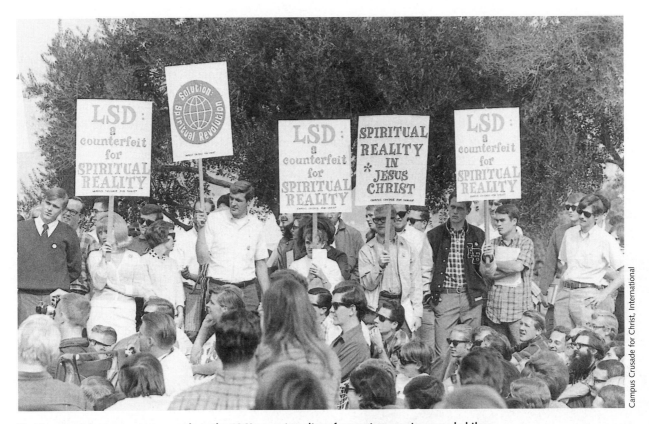

Campus Crusade for Christ, International

■ The search by many young people in the 1960s counterculture for greater consciousness led them to a spiritual path. These young evangelists held a Campus Crusade for Christ rally at the University of Texas at Austin in 1969. The emphasis of evangelical Christians on the person of Jesus rather than on a particular denominational tradition attracted many converts. The sandals, long hair, and gentleness associated with Jesus made a particularly good fit with the style and values of the "hippies," although most evangelicals appeared traditionally clean-cut and held conservative political views.

Cultural Rebellion and the Counterculture

While the New Left moved from wanting to reform American society to wanting to overthrow it, the counterculture sought to create an alternative society. Called "hippies" by those who disliked them, these young people were alienated by the materialism, competition, and conformity of American life in the Cold War. They tried to live out alternative values of gentleness, tolerance, and inclusivity. Sporting headbands, long hair, and beads, many identified with traditional Native Americans. In place of junk foods, they promoted health foods; in place of profit-seeking businesses, they established co-ops. "Do your own thing" was a common slogan.

In reaction against the conformity of mainstream society, members of the counterculture explored the limitations of consciousness to expand their self-knowledge. They went beyond the nicotine and alcohol that were the common stimulants of their parents' culture to experiment with such mind-altering drugs as marijuana, peyote, hashish, LSD, and cocaine. Spirituality was an important path into consciousness for many in the counterculture. Religious traditions associated with Asia, particularly Buddhism, gained numerous adherents, as did the spiritual customs and traditional practices of Native Americans. Others rediscovered the "authentic" Jesus obscured by the institutional structures of the formal Christian church (earning themselves the nickname "Jesus freaks"); Campus Crusade for Christ, InterVarsity, and other evangelical college groups spread across the country. Music served as the most common coin of the countercultural realm, from the political folk sound of Joan Baez and Bob Dylan to the broadly popular Beatles and the more distinctly countercultural rock 'n' roll of the Grateful Dead and Jefferson Airplane.

Older Americans experienced the counterculture largely as spectacle. The mainstream media emphasized the alternative aspects of the hippie lifestyle in its coverage. Viewers were varyingly disgusted by, attracted to, and titillated by the hair, clothing, nudity, and blurred gender distinctions. Meanwhile, entrepreneurs realized that they could market the antimaterialist counterculture profitably. Young Americans eagerly bought up records, clothing, jewelry, and natural foods—a revealing demonstration of how consumer values pervaded American life.

One of the most visible changes of the 1960s was often called the sexual revolution. Changes in Americans' sexual behavior in the 1960s reflected in part the counterculture's goal of living an authentic, honest life in which words matched actions. The sexual revolution removed some of the penalties for the premarital and extramarital sex that had previously been fairly common but unacknowledged. The appearance of the birth control pill in 1960 underpinned the shift to more open sexual relationships by freeing women from the fear of pregnancy. Attitudes toward abortion also became more tolerant. New York passed the first state law legalizing some abortions in 1970, and three years later the Supreme Court established a woman's constitutional right to abortion in the landmark case of *Roe v. Wade*.

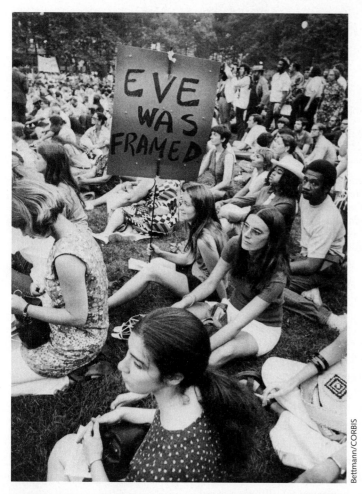

Bettmann/CORBIS

■ The new wave of organizing for women's rights that emerged in the late 1960s had many faces. Some protests against sex discrimination and disrespect for women were angry and others were gentle, as in this 1970 scene. "Raising consciousness" was a central strategy of the movement, as women and men became more aware of the gendered assumptions that had long governed—and channeled—their lives and their thoughts.

Women's Liberation

The movement for women's liberation built on developments earlier in the decade, including Betty Friedan's *The Feminine Mystique* (1963), a widely read book that captured the frustrations of many women who had accepted the role of suburban homemaker after World War II. Friedan and other liberal feminists founded the National Organization for Women (NOW) in 1966 to lobby against sexual discrimination in the public sphere in such areas as employment, wages, education, and jury duty. These challenges had radical implications for women's and men's earnings and thus for responsibilities within families, but NOW did not yet focus on issues inside the private sphere of the home.

The shift to the view that "the personal is political" came from younger, mostly white women who had been active in the civil rights and antiwar struggles. Inspired by the courage and successes of the protest movements in which they figured prominently, these female activists had also learned that traditional gender roles restricted them even in organizations dedicated to participatory democracy. Ironically, radical men could be as patronizing and disrespectful of women's abilities as mainstream men. Younger feminists in 1967 and 1968 agreed with NOW's challenge to discrimination in the public sphere, but they focused even more on the personal politics of women's daily lives, on critical issues such as parenting, child care, housework, and abortion.

The new wave of **feminism** that washed through American culture at the end of the 1960s triggered fierce debates about the nature of gender. Was there a uniquely feminine way of knowing, seeing, and acting, or were women in essence the same as men, distinguishable ultimately by their individuality? Was womanhood biologically or only culturally constructed? Feminists disagreed sharply in their answers.

However, diversity within the feminist movement did not hide a common commitment to expanding women's possibilities. The women's movement that emerged out of the 1960s permanently transformed women's lives and gender relations in American society, in areas ranging from job and educational opportunities, sexual harassment, and gender-neutral language to family roles, sexual relations, reproductive rights, and athletic facilities.

DOCUMENT

National Organization of Women, Statement of Purpose

The Many Fronts of Liberation

Like the women's movement, the Chicano, pan-Indian, and gay liberation movements of the late 1960s were grounded in older organizing efforts within those communities. The struggles for "brown power," "red power," and "gay power" also reflected the newer influence of black power and its determination to take pride in what the dominant American society had denigrated for so long. Activists on college campuses successfully pressured administrations to establish interdisciplinary ethnic studies programs, such as the first Chicano studies program at California State University at Los Angeles in 1968. Ethnic cultural identity went hand in hand with the pursuit of political and economic integration into mainstream American life.

The most prominent push to organize Latinos was the effort led by Cesar Chávez to build a farm workers' union in California and the Southwest. These primarily Mexican American migrant workers harvested most of the hand-picked produce that Americans ate, but their hard work under severe conditions failed to lift them out of poverty. National consumer support for boycotts of table grapes and iceberg lettuce helped win recognition for the United Farm Workers (UFW) union and better pay by 1970. Younger Mexican Americans across the Southwest looked with pride on their Mexican heritage, even appropriating the formerly pejorative term *Chicano*.

DOCUMENT

Cesar Chavez, From "He Showed Us the Way," April 1978

Puerto Ricans, the largest Spanish-speaking ethnic group located primarily on the East Coast, experienced a similar growth in militancy and nationalist sentiment during the late 1960s. By the 1960s, more than a million islanders had moved to the East Coast, most to the New York City area. Despite being the only Latino immigrants already holding American citizenship when they arrived, Puerto Ricans experienced similar patterns of both discrimination and opportunity as Mexican Americans.

The most destitute of Americans, Indians also sought to reinvigorate their communities. On the Northwest Coast, they staged "fish-ins" in the mid-1960s to assert treaty rights, and in 1968 urban activists in Minneapolis formed the American Indian Movement (AIM). On November 20, 1969, just days after the largest antiwar march in Washington, seventy-eight Native Americans seized the island of Alcatraz in San Francisco Bay "in the name of all American Indians by right of discovery." For a year and a half, they used their occupation of the former federal prison site to publicize grievances about anti-Indian prejudice and to promote a new pan-Indian identity that reached across traditional tribal divisions. In 1973 armed members of AIM occupied buildings for two months at Wounded Knee, South Dakota, site of the infamous 1890 U.S. Army massacre of unarmed Sioux. Tribal governments sought "red power" in their own quieter way. They asserted greater tribal control of reservation schools across the country.

Although they lacked a unifying ethnic identity, gay men and lesbians also found opportunities to construct coalitions in the more open atmosphere of the late 1960s. Building on the earlier community organizing of older homosexuals in New York, San Francisco, and Los Angeles, more militant youth began to express openly their anger at the homophobic prejudice and violence prevalent in American society. This demand for tolerance and respect reached the headlines when gay patrons of the Stonewall Bar in New York fought back fiercely against a typically forceful police raid on June 27, 1969. Activists of the new Gay Liberation Front emphasized the importance of "coming out of the closet": proudly acknowledging one's sexual orientation as legitimate and decent.

The Conservative Response

The majority of Americans had mixed feelings about the protests that roiled the nation. They were impressed by the courage of many who stood up against discrimination, and by 1968 they wanted to find a way out of the war in Southeast Asia. But they were alienated by the style and values of others who loudly demanded change in American society. Moderate and conservative citizens and generations of recent European immigrants resented what they saw as a lack of appreciation for the nation's virtues and successes. The political and social upheavals of 1968 opened the door to a Republican return to the White House, and Richard Nixon slipped through.

Backlashes

A backlash developed in response to the increasing assertiveness of people of color. European Americans in every part of the United States had long been accustomed to deference from nonwhites and racial segregation, either by law in the South or by custom elsewhere. Conservatives resented what they considered blacks' ingratitude at the civil rights measures enacted by the federal government, including black power's condemnation of whites as "crackers" and "honkies." Urban riots and escalating rates of violent crime, along with the Supreme Court's expansion of the rights of the accused, deepened their anger. They associated crime with urban African Americans, for although whites were still the majority of criminals, blacks (like any other population with less money) were disproportionately represented in prisons. The rise of often angry nonwhite nationalism dismayed most European Americans. They were troubled by the militancy of Chicanos in the Southwest, Puerto Ricans in the Northeast, Indians on reservations and in cities, and African Americans almost everywhere.

Another backlash developed as a defense of traditional hierarchies against the cultural rebellions of the 1960s. Proud of their lives and values, conservatives rejected a whole array of challenges to American society. Raised to believe in respecting one's elders, they resented the disrespect of many youth, who warned, "Don't trust anyone over 30." A generation that had fought and sacrificed in the "good war" against the Nazis found the absence of patriotism among many protesters unfathomable. The United States remained one of the most religious

Jules Fieffer

■ Cartoonist Jules Fieffer portrayed the generation gap that separated many younger Americans from many older ones by the early 1970s. Movements for black and Native American civil rights and against the U.S. war in Vietnam led to a profound shift in how many citizens, especially younger ones, understood their nation and its politics. A new generation of historians began to cast serious doubts on many long-accepted truisms about the American past.

of industrialized societies, and conservative churchgoers emphasized obedience to authorities. They feared the effects of illegal drugs on their children.

The backlash against the social changes of the 1960s contained elements of class antagonism as well. Working-class whites resented the often affluent campus rebels and the black and Latino poor targeted by some Great Society programs. They believed that their values of hard work, restraint, and respectability were increasingly unappreciated and even mocked. Republican leaders from Goldwater to Nixon to Reagan gave voice to these resentments and drew votes away from Democratic blue-collar strongholds. Democratic governor George Wallace of Alabama also became a spokesperson for the anger of many "forgotten" whites on both sides of the Mason-Dixon line.

The Turmoil of 1968 at Home

The traumas of 1968 brought the conservative backlash to the critical stage. First came the Tet Offensive in Vietnam, creating fears that the war might become an interminable quagmire. Then, on April 4, a gunman named James Earl Ray assassinated Martin Luther King Jr. in Memphis, where he had gone to support a strike by sanitation workers. King had become more openly radical in his final years, opposing the war and working on class-based organizing of poor people. But he remained the nation's leading apostle of nonviolence, and his murder evoked despair among millions of citizens, especially African Americans. Police battled rioters and arsonists in black neighborhoods of 130 cities across the nation, with forty-six people dying in the clashes.

Summer brought more shocking news. Charismatic senator Robert Kennedy's entry into the presidential campaign had inspired renewed hopes among Democratic liberals. But on the night of his victory in the June 5 California primary, Kennedy was killed by a deranged gunman. Vice President Hubert Humphrey seemed assured of the nomination at the Democratic convention in Chicago in August, despite his association with Johnson's war policies. Some 10,000 antiwar activists, including hundreds of FBI *agents provocateurs* (spies seeking to provoke violence), showed up to engage in protests outside the convention. Chicago's Democratic mayor Richard Daley unleashed thousands of police on protesters, bystanders, and photographers in an orgy of beatings that subsequent investigations called a police riot. Ninety million Americans watched on television as a deeply divided Democratic party appeared helpless before the violence.

Into the vacuum of public anger and alienation that accompanied the liberals' self-destruction in Chicago stepped two men. The spread of the conservative backlash from 1964 to 1968 gave George Wallace a wider constituency for his right-wing populist message of hostility to liberals, blacks, and federal officials. With the national Democratic party committed to racial integration, Wallace ran for president as an independent candidate and won 13.5 percent of the popular vote in November. Republican candidate Richard Nixon campaigned as the candidate of "law and order" and promised that he had a secret plan to end the war in Vietnam. Nixon won the popular vote by less than 1 percent.

The Nixon Administration

A lonely, aloof man of great tenacity and ambition, Richard Nixon had worked hard to remake his public image for 1968. Widely viewed as a somewhat unscrupulous partisan since his early career in Congress, he had refashioned himself as a statesman with a broad vision for reducing international tensions between the great powers. He sounded like a conservative in the campaign

TABLE 26-2

The Election of 1968

Candidate	Political Party	Popular Vote (%)	Electoral Vote
Richard M. Nixon	Republican	43.4	301
Hubert H. Humphrey	Democratic	42.7	191
George Wallace	American Independent	13.5	46

against Humphrey, but once in the White House he governed as the most liberal Republican since Theodore Roosevelt, pressed by a Congress still controlled by Democrats.

Nowhere was this clearer than on issues related to natural resources. Much had happened to the environment since Republican Theodore Roosevelt's conservation efforts, little of it for the better. A powerful movement was building to protect natural resources and human health from the effects of air and water pollution. Biologist Paul Ehrlich's best-selling *The Population Bomb* (1968) warned of the dire consequences of the globe's runaway growth in human population. In 1969 the government banned the carcinogenic pesticide DDT. That same year, a huge oil spill off Santa Barbara fouled 200 miles of pristine California beaches, and the Cuyahoga River in Cleveland, its surface coated with waste and oil, caught fire and burned for days. Environmentalists around the country proclaimed April 22, 1970, as "Earth Day."

Congress responded with legislation that mandated the careful management of the nation's natural resources. The Environmental Protection Agency was established in 1970. Amendments to the Clean Air (1970) and Clean Water (1972) Acts tightened restrictions on harmful emissions from cars and factories. The Endangered Species Act (1973) created for the first time the legal right of nonhuman animals to survive, a major step toward viewing the quality of human life as inextricable from the earth's broader ecology.

What Nixon did care deeply about at home was politics, not policy. Antiwar demonstrations reached their height during Nixon's first two years in the White House (1969–1970). He and Vice President Spiro Agnew loathed the protesters, whom they saw as weakening the nation. The two men pursued what Agnew called "positive polarization": campaigning to further divide the respectable "silent majority," as the president labeled his supporters, from voluble liberal Democrats in Congress and radical activists on the streets, whom they associated with permissiveness and lawlessness. In this broad cultural battle for political supremacy, the president appealed to conservative white southern and northern ethnic Democrats.

> *Antiwar demonstrations reached their height during Nixon's first two years in the White House (1969–1970).*

Early in his administration, Nixon began wielding the power of the federal government to harass his political opponents. Johnson had used the FBI, the CIA, and military intelligence agencies to infiltrate and thin the ranks of antiwar demonstrators and nonwhite nationalists. Nixon continued those illegal operations, agreeing with his predecessor that radical activists constituted a threat to national security. Nixon went beyond other presidents in assembling an "Enemies List" that included prominent elements of the political mainstream, especially liberals, the press, and his Democratic opponents. The president was particularly concerned about controlling secret information. The Pentagon Papers were a classified Defense Department history of U.S. actions in Vietnam, revealing that the government had been deceiving the American public about the course of the war. When disillusioned former Pentagon official Daniel Ellsberg leaked the study to the *New York Times* for publication in 1971, Nixon was enraged. The White House created a team of covert operatives nicknamed the Plumbers to "plug leaks" by whatever means necessary.

Escalating and De-escalating in Vietnam

Nixon and his national security adviser, Henry Kissinger, had ambitious plans for shifting the relationships of the great powers to America's advantage. To deal with China and the Soviet Union, they first had to reduce the vast U.S. engagement in the small country of Vietnam, which had grown wildly out of proportion to actual U.S. interests there. Under the Nixon Doctrine, the United States would provide military hardware rather than U.S. soldiers to allied governments, which would have to do their own fighting against leftist insurgencies. In South Vietnam, this doctrine required "Vietnamization," or withdrawing American troops so ARVN could shoulder the bulk of the war.

The key to a successful withdrawal from Vietnam for Nixon was to preserve U.S. "credibility." The perception of power could be as important as its actual exercise, and the president wanted other nations, both friend and foe, to continue to respect and fear American military might. There was no immediate pullout but a gradual process that lasted for four years (1969–1973), during which almost half of the total U.S. casualties in Vietnam occurred. Nixon did his utmost to weaken the communist forces during the slow withdrawal. The president ordered the secret bombing and invasion of neighboring Cambodia and Laos, an intensified aerial assault on North Vietnam, and the mining of Haiphong Harbor near Hanoi. Enormous protests rocked the country after the announcement of the Cambodian invasion on April 30, 1970. National Guard troops killed four students at a demonstration at Kent State University in Ohio and two at Jackson State College in Mississippi, deepening the sense of national division.

Kent State Demonstrations

A majority of Americans now opposed the nation's war effort, a level of dissent unprecedented in U.S. history. Most telling of all was the criticism of some veterans returning from Vietnam. The morale of American soldiers still in Vietnam plummeted as the steady withdrawal of their comrades made clear that they were no longer expected to win the war. Drug abuse and racial conflict increased sharply among GIs. Even "fragging" (killing one's own officers) escalated before the peace accords were signed in Paris and the United States evacuated its last combat troops in 1973.

Richard Nixon, "Peace With Honor" (1973)

Conclusion

Between 1964 and 1971, young, nonwhite, and female Americans laid claim to greater equality. The ratification of the Twenty-Sixth Amendment in 1971 reduced the voting age from twenty-one to eighteen, in acknowledgment of the sacrifices of young people sent to fight in Vietnam. In large numbers, women challenged and overcame traditional limits on their personal and work lives. Racial discrimination and segregation were outlawed.

These years also witnessed striking disjunctures. The nation accomplished humanity's age-old dream of walking on the surface of the moon when Neil Armstrong stepped out of the *Apollo 11* spacecraft on July 20, 1969, while at home the country sometimes appeared to be coming apart at the seams. Poverty rates dropped to their lowest point ever, yet violence seemed to pervade the land. The slaughter of forty-three people (mostly African Americans) by white state police retaking the Attica prison in upstate New York after an inmate insurrection in 1971 was one of the single most deadly confrontations between Americans since the Civil War.

The deceptive manner in which Johnson and Nixon waged the war in Vietnam eroded Americans' faith in their public officials, a process that the Watergate scandal accelerated between 1972 and 1974. American life also grew more informal as the egalitarian style of the various social movements of the 1960s spread into the broader culture. But the removal of some of the most blatant distinctions of race and gender did not extend to differences of class. In the watershed cases of *San Antonio Independent School District v. Rodriguez* (1973) and *Milliken v. Bradley* (1974), the Supreme Court ruled that wealthier districts did not have to share financing with poorer ones, nor did they have to share students by means of busing. The Court found that there was no constitutional right to an education of equal quality. The ladder of social mobility remained slippery in a nation whose neighborhoods were still stratified between the affluent and the poor.

Sites to Visit

The Sixties Project
lists.village.virginia.edu/sixties/
This University of Virginia site has extensive exhibits, primary documents, and personal narratives from the 1960s.

Lyndon B. Johnson Library and Museum
www.lbjlib.utexas.edu/
This presidential library site has images and online exhibits.

The Wars for Vietnam: 1945 to 1975
http://vietnam.vassar.edu/
Historian Robert Brigham's site offers an excellent overview of the U.S. war in Vietnam, along with critical documents and helpful links to other sites.

My Lai Courts-Martial (1970)
www.law.umkc.edu/faculty/projects/ftrials/mylai/mylai.htm
This site contains images, chronology, and court and official documents maintained by Dr. Doug Linder at the University of Missouri–Kansas City Law School.

Digger Archives
www.diggers.org
This site provides information about the San Francisco Diggers, a prominent countercultural group in the Haight-Asbury scene of 1966–1968.

U.S. Latino History and Culture
www.si.edu/resource/faq/nmah/latino.htm
This Smithsonian Institution site offers exhibits, photos, resources, and links to other useful sites on the lives of Latino Americans.

Gay Rights Movement
www.columbia.edu/cu/lweb/eresources/exhibitions/sw25/
This site includes articles from the New York City press as well as first-hand accounts of the 1969 Greenwich Village riots that are commemorated throughout the country during Gay Pride celebrations.

For Further Reading

General

William H. Chafe, *The Unfinished Journey: America Since World War II*, 5th ed. (2006).
David Farber, ed., *The Sixties: From Memory to History* (1994).
Maurice Isserman and Michael Kazin, *America Divided: The Civil War of the 1960s*, 2nd ed. (2004).
James T. Patterson, *Grand Expectations: The United States, 1945–1974* (1996).
Jeremi Suri, *Power and Protest: Global Revolution and the Rise of Détente* (2003).

Lyndon Johnson and the Apex of Liberalism

Robert Dallek, *Flawed Giant: Lyndon Johnson and His Times, 1961–1973* (1998).
Lucas A. Powe Jr., *The Warren Court and American Politics* (2000).
Bruce J. Schulman, *Lyndon B. Johnson and American Liberalism* (1995).

Into War in Vietnam

Michael Herr, *Dispatches* (1977).
George C. Herring, *America's Longest War: The United States and Vietnam, 1950–1975*, 4th ed. (2001).
Robert D. Schulzinger, *A Time for War: The United States and Vietnam, 1941–1975* (1997).
Marilyn B. Young, *The Vietnam Wars, 1945–1990* (1991).

The Movement

Terry H. Anderson, *The Movement and the Sixties: Protest in America from Greensboro to Wounded Knee* (1995).
Sara Evans, *Personal Politics: The Roots of Women's Liberation in the Civil Rights Movement and the New Left* (1979).
Malcolm X, *The Autobiography of Malcolm X* (1965).
Timothy Miller, *The '60s Communes: Hippies and Beyond* (1999).
William L. Van Deburg, *New Day in Babylon: The Black Power Movement and American Culture, 1965–1975* (1992).
Tom Wells, *The War Within: America's Battle over Vietnam* (1994).

The Conservative Response

Dan T. Carter, *The Politics of Rage: George Wallace, the Origins of the New Conservatism, and the Transformation of American Politics*, 2nd ed. (2000).
Lisa McGirr, *Suburban Warriors: The Origins of the New American Right* (2001).
Hal K. Rothman, *The Greening of a Nation? Environmentalism in the United States Since 1945* (1998).
Melvin Small, *The Presidency of Richard Nixon* (1999).

For quizzes and other resources on these topics, go to www.longmanamericanhistory.com.

Reconsidering National Priorities, 1972–1979

ABC TELEVISION NEWS ANCHOR HOWARD K. SMITH BEGAN HIS COVERAGE OF A WOMEN'S RIGHTS march in New York City in 1970 by quoting with approval the words of Vice President Spiro Agnew: "Three things have been difficult to tame. The ocean, fools, and women. We may soon be able to tame the ocean, but fools and women will take a little longer." Condescension toward women still pervaded American society, and few men even noticed it. The political upheavals of the 1960s had barely touched the relationships between most women and men by the start of the new decade. But all this changed as the 1970s unfolded. The spread of ideas about women's liberation in the 1970s transformed the personal lives of almost every American, female and male alike. Feminism challenged the most basic and intimate assumptions about relationships, family, work, and power. It also sharply expanded women's opportunities. At the end of the decade, Dr. Martha Hurley of Kansas City recalled, "In the middle of an operation today, I looked around the room—to the first assistant, my scrub nurse, and circulating nurse, the anesthesia doctor, nurse anesthetist, and the patient—and suddenly realized that we were performing major surgery and there was not a man in the room!"

Feminism joined with other developments of the decade to force Americans to reexamine much that they had taken for granted. Elected on the promise to end the war in Southeast Asia "with honor," President Nixon escalated the fighting before eventually withdrawing U.S. forces from Vietnam. At the same time, he repaired relations with both China and the Soviet Union as those two communist powers drew apart. Americans thus suffered their first clear defeat in war while also seeing the Cold War splinter. Scandal in the White House then forced the first resignation of a U.S. president and deepened public distrust of political authorities. American economic growth—the foundation of the country's power—stumbled

■ President Nixon met the premier of the People's Republic of China, Mao Zedong, in Beijing on February 29, 1972. The U.S. government had shunned China since its communist revolution in 1949. Richard Nixon's amiable visit there stunned observers and altered the dynamics of the Cold War.

because of spending on the Vietnam War and oil shortages. High-paying manufacturing jobs declined as factories began to move overseas in pursuit of cheaper labor, and skilled blue-collar workers saw their status as middle-class Americans start to slip. Unemployment grew sharply. A growing environmental movement raised disturbing questions about whether an expanding economy and exploitation of natural resources should continue to top the country's list of priorities.

The nation celebrated its 200th birthday in 1976 amid these uncertainties. That year, one-term Georgia governor Jimmy Carter won election to the White House by promising to restore honesty and trust to the federal government. In his first two years in office, Carter shifted the nation's foreign policy focus away from fighting communism toward building warmer relations with the Third World. He saw Americans' dependence on imported oil as a primary national security problem and implored citizens to scale back their lavish consumption of fossil fuels. But his presidency eventually foundered on persistent economic stagnation and inflation at home, upheavals abroad, and Carter's own limitations as chief executive.

Journalist Tom Wolfe dubbed the 1970s the "Me Decade," a phrase that proved even more appropriate for the 1980s. The label did have some merit: many Americans turned away from the public sphere after the exhilarating but divisive politics of the 1960s and pursued self-exploration and self-fulfillment instead. Crime, divorce, premarital and extramarital sex, and drug use all increased while the nation's economic health and international status declined. But the 1970s also witnessed a rethinking of long-standing assumptions: about how democracy should work at home, what role the nation should play in international affairs, how people ought to treat the environment, and how men and women should relate to each other. The decade offered a window of opportunity for Americans to reimagine their values and priorities for the future.

Twin Shocks: Détente and Watergate

Richard Nixon had long been the nation's leading anticommunist. No one had more fiercely opposed leftists at home and communists in China and the Soviet Union. However, the president was more a savvy political opportunist than an ideologue. He and his national security adviser, Henry Kissinger, saw a chance to use mounting Chinese-Soviet tensions to the advantage of the United States as they withdrew American armed forces from Vietnam.

At the same time that Nixon manipulated the Cold War abroad, the Republican president initiated a campaign of illegal actions at home to destroy his political opponents in the Democratic party. This strategy backfired in a scandal that drove him from office in 1974. Having undercut the logic of anticommunism abroad by warming relations with communist leaders in Beijing and Moscow, Nixon eroded the bipartisan consensus at home that had long supported the Cold War.

Triangular Diplomacy

Nixon and Kissinger prided themselves on their "realpolitik" approach to foreign policy: their pragmatic assessment of other powers' security needs, regardless of ideology, and their collaboration with those powers on issues of common concern. In 1969 China and the USSR gave Nixon and Kissinger an ideal opportunity to exercise their realpolitik skills. That year, tensions that had been building between the two communist states erupted in brief skirmishing between Chinese and Soviet troops on their shared border. Nixon envisioned a "triangular diplomacy" that he hoped would divide the communist world.

The president and Kissinger, a former Harvard professor with an intriguing German accent, also shared a commitment to secrecy. Any fundamental revision of the nation's foreign policy, they believed, could happen only if they concentrated all decision-making in the White House. They set out to keep Congress, the press, and even their own State Department in the dark. Diplomatic innovation thus went hand in hand with an unprecedented extension of the secretive national security state.

Nixon's 1972 visit to China brought a host of benefits. Live television coverage showed Nixon toasting Mao Zedong, premier of the People's Republic of China, while a Chinese military band played "America the Beautiful" and "Home on the Range." Americans' impression of the People's Republic as a grim, forbidding land began to give way to a renewed interest in China as an exotic but intriguing place. Cultural exchanges soon proliferated: first ping-pong teams, eventually legions of students. U.S. businesses also cast a covetous eye at the immense China market. Trade between the two nations rose dramatically over the next three decades.

Nixon and Kissinger now constructed the other leg of their diplomatic triangle. As they anticipated, the Soviets had taken alarm at the warming of relations between their two greatest rivals. Nixon flew to Moscow for a summit meeting with Soviet leader Leonid Brezhnev in May 1972 that initiated a policy of **détente** (relaxation of tensions). A trade pact quickly followed. The two superpowers also agreed to limit offensive nuclear weapons (the Strategic Arms Limitations Treaty, or SALT I) and to ban antiballistic missile defense systems (the ABM treaty).

Like the Soviet leaders, Nixon and Kissinger sought to preserve the existing international balance of power. Deal-making with China and the USSR constituted one step in this process. In another, the two men sought to stifle socialist revolutions in Third World nations by bolstering pro-American allies there. For instance, the duo feared that the democratic election of socialist Salvador Allende in Chile in 1970 would lead to "another Cuba." A socialist leader might nationalize the investments of U.S. corporations in Chile and perhaps challenge Washington's capitalist hegemony in the Western Hemisphere. Determined to block these possibilities, the CIA secretly funded a right-wing military coup in Chile in September 1973. Allende died in the assault on the presidential palace, and the rebel forces murdered thousands of his supporters and established a brutal military dictatorship under General Augusto Pinochet. "I don't see why we need to stand by and watch a country go Communist because of the irresponsibility of its own people," Kissinger explained privately.

Scandal in the White House

Meanwhile, on the domestic front, Washington police caught agents of Nixon's reelection campaign breaking into the Democratic National Committee headquarters in the **Watergate** hotel and office complex on June 17, 1972. The burglars' goal was to put in place secret listening devices, or "bugs." Later, the White House tried to cover up its connections to the crime.

The Watergate break-in was only one step in Nixon's broader campaign of illegal warfare against his political opponents. An insecure and unhappy loner, Nixon harbored an almost paranoid suspicion when he took office in early 1969. The president and his aides regularly discussed "how we can use the available federal machinery to screw our political enemies," in the words of White House counsel John Dean. They persuaded the FBI and the CIA to monitor and harass antiwar activists and pushed the Internal Revenue Service to investigate prominent Democrats. They extorted large contributions to the Republican party from corporate executives by making it clear that federal agencies would otherwise impede the pursuit of their business interests. The *New York Times*'s publication of the classified Pentagon Papers in 1971 stiffened the resolve of the Committee to Reelect the President (CREEP) to stop any further leaks. The committee assembled a group of undercover operatives (the "plumbers") to stop leaks and to engineer "dirty tricks" against the Democrats.

TABLE 27-1			
The Election of 1972			
Candidate	Political Party	Popular Vote (%)	Electoral Vote
Richard M. Nixon	Republican	60.7	520
George S. McGovern	Democratic	31.5	17

After the "plumbers" bungled Watergate break-in, the president directed the cover-up from the beginning, then lied about it to the public. He also used the CIA to hinder the FBI's

VIDEO

Richard Nixon, "I am not a crook"

investigation into the matter. He approved payments of hush money to the burglars to keep them quiet about their ties to the White House. Nixon's abuse of power escalated as he pressured his subordinates to perjure themselves in court. For most of a year the cover-up held, and Nixon won reelection in 1972.

But the persistent investigations by *Washington Post* journalists Bob Woodward and Carl Bernstein kept the heat on. In early 1973, the administration began to crack due to a grand jury probe in the federal court of Judge John Sirica. The president's men lost confidence that the cover-up would hold and began looking for ways to save their own skins. Congress initiated its own televised investigations that mesmerized a national audience. The Senate Watergate committee, chaired by eloquent conservative North Carolina Democrat Sam Ervin, methodically exposed the criminal actions in the White House, with growing bipartisan support. The key issue, as framed by Republican committee member Howard Baker of Tennessee, became, "What did the president know, and when did he know it?"

> *After the bungled Watergate break-in, the president directed the cover-up from the beginning, then lied about it to the public.*

On July 16, 1973, White House aide Alexander Butterfield told the Senate committee that a built-in recorder taped all conversations in the Oval Office. Almost certainly, these tapes would provide answers to questions about the president's role. Both Congress and Justice Department special prosecutor Archibald Cox subpoenaed the White House tapes, but Nixon refused to hand them over. Instead, he fired Cox on October 20 in what became known as the Saturday Night Massacre. Outraged, Congress initiated impeachment proceedings against the president. In the spring of 1974, the House Judiciary Committee passed bills of impeachment for his specific abuses of power. Before the full House could vote to impeach him and the Senate decide on his guilt or innocence, the Supreme Court ruled that the White House had to turn over the subpoenaed tapes. The tapes revealed the extent of the president's involvement in the cover-up and his personal crudeness, vindictiveness, and ethnic and racial prejudices. Facing a certain guilty verdict, Nixon resigned on August 9, 1974, less than halfway through his second term.

DOCUMENT

Committee's Conclusion on Impeachment

The Nation After Watergate

Never before had a U.S. president resigned from office. Many citizens celebrated the outcome of the Watergate investigations as evidence of democracy's resilience and power to uncover criminal activity in the White House and bring down a corrupt president. But the affair also discredited political institutions Americans had long respected. Indeed, the Nixon administration proved quite corrupt. A whole raft of senior officials, including the president's closest aides, H. R. Haldeman and John Ehrlichman, went to prison. Even Vice President Spiro Agnew had been forced to resign amid the Watergate investigations when a Maryland jury found him guilty of tax evasion dating back to his years as governor there. Congress swung strongly to the Democrats in the 1974 elections, slowing the Republicans' rise to the status of majority party.

■ Many South Vietnamese fled the communist victory in their country in 1975, including this woman and her children crossing the Mekong River. Most of the refugees undertook extremely perilous journeys by boat to other Southeast Asian nations, and hundreds of thousands eventually made their way to the United States.

The man who replaced Nixon in the White House faced a daunting situation. Gerald Ford, longtime Republican congressman and House minority leader from Grand Rapids, Michigan, had been tapped by Nixon to replace Agnew as vice president. Well liked by members of both parties, Ford seemed to embody the antidote to the extreme styles of both Nixon and Agnew. To restore decency and trust in the government, Ford saw his role as healing what he called "the wounds of the past." Within a month, he granted a "full, free, and absolute pardon" to Nixon for any crimes he may have committed as president, precluding any trial and punishment within a court of law. However, most Americans believed that Nixon should have faced justice for his actions, just as the people did who carried out his orders. Ford's popularity plummeted overnight from 72 percent to 49 percent and never fully recovered.

If Ford inherited the fallout from Watergate at home, abroad he inherited the pending defeat in Vietnam. U.S. soldiers returned to a nation determined to ignore or demean their sacrifices, and they quickly learned to keep their combat-induced traumas to themselves. When Saigon finally fell to the combined invasion of National Liberation Front and North Vietnamese fighters on April 30, 1975, Americans watched the televised images with both bitterness and relief. Two weeks later, Cambodian communist forces briefly seized the U.S. container ship *Mayaguez*, provoking Ford to demonstrate that the United States was still ready and willing to flex its military muscle. But forty-one U.S. soldiers died in the rescue mission to save thirty-nine sailors whom, it turned out, Cambodia had already released. Ford and Kissinger, serving as the new president's secretary of state, continued to pursue détente with the Soviets at summit meetings in Vladivostock (1974) and Helsinki (1975). At the same time, they supported anticommunist forces in various Third World conflicts, such as the civil war that erupted in Angola after that country achieved its independence in 1975.

Discovering the Limits of the U.S. Economy

Defeat in Vietnam and corruption in the White House were soon joined by grim economic news. Generation after generation of Americans had watched their incomes rise, and most children expected to be wealthier than their parents had been. Since World War II had pulled the U.S. economy out of the Great Depression, median family income had doubled. But by 1973, the famous American standard of living began to decline. The three pillars of postwar prosperity—cheap energy, rising wages, and low inflation—simultaneously crumbled. The costs of the Vietnam War struck home at the same time that an oil embargo spawned by conflict in the Middle East gripped the country. Moreover, a widening environmental movement raised questions about the pursuit of endless economic growth on a planet that more and more people realized had limited natural resources.

The End of the Long Boom

During the 1970s, a new economic scourge dubbed "stagflation" hit the United States. For the first time, employment and wages stagnated while prices climbed. What explained this phenomenon? Spending on the Vietnam War and on Great Society programs had pulled prices upward. The government had never raised enough taxes to cover the expense of the war, so it paid the bills by simply printing more dollars. In 1971 annual inflation stood at 4.5 percent, more than twice the pre-Vietnam rate; two years later it reached 10 percent, and by 1980 it topped out at 18 percent.

These figures devastated Americans' sense of economic security. Average real wages (income adjusted for inflation) dropped by an average of 2 percent a year from 1973 to the 1990s. Unemployment rose to 9 percent in 1975. Only the continued flow of women into the workforce, seen by most families as an economic necessity, kept the majority of U.S. families afloat financially. The number of citizens living in poverty, which had dropped sharply through the 1960s to 11 percent in 1973, rose again, hitting 15 percent by 1982. The gap between rich and poor began widening, a process that has persisted into the new millennium.

> *Only the continued flow of women into the workforce, seen by most families as an economic necessity, kept the majority of U.S. families afloat financially.*

Perhaps the most telling evidence of the weakening economy came with the drop in the growth of productivity: output per worker-hour had risen at an annual average of more than 3 percent during the postwar boom. From 1974 to 1992, it rose at less than half that rate.

This decline stemmed in part from competition from abroad, particularly West Germany and Japan. With U.S. assistance (and without the military expenditures that so burdened the United States), those countries had finally rebuilt their economies after World War II and boasted new, more efficient industrial facilities. The trade surplus that had long symbolized global U.S. economic superiority evaporated in 1971. That year, U.S. imports overtook exports for the first time in the twentieth century. Worried international investors traded in dollars for gold, forcing Nixon to end the twenty-seven-year-old monetary system formulated at the UN Monetary and Financial Conference at Bretton Woods, New Hampshire, in July 1944, that had linked all other currencies to the dollar at fixed exchange rates. Freed from the fixed rate of $35 per ounce of gold, the value of the dollar dropped like a stone; by the end of the decade, it took $800 to buy an ounce of gold.

In this competitive environment, the *Wall Street Journal* reported, American companies "seek places where labor, land, electricity, and taxes are cheap." Corporations found those places in the American South and Southwest, regions characterized by scarce unions, low wage rates, minimal taxes, and negligible local government regulations. Many more such places were in neighboring Mexico, where U.S. companies established *maquiladoras*. These assembly plants, often just a few hundred yards across the Mexican-U.S. border, allowed corporations to hire primarily female workers at low wages and avoid strict U.S. environmental, labor, and safety laws. The long-term decline of the Rustbelt—the series of urban industrial centers strung across the American Northeast and Midwest—accelerated in the 1970s.

High unemployment and shrinking real wages contributed to rising anti-immigrant sentiment. Two white autoworkers in Detroit in 1982 got into an altercation in a bar with Vincent Chin, a Chinese American (and son of a World War II veteran) whom they called a "Jap." Angered that Japanese auto sales were undercutting jobs in Detroit, they made Chin a scapegoat for their rage, chasing him down the street and beating him to death with a baseball bat.

Black Americans also faced an increasing backlash against hard-won civil rights gains. While court-ordered busing to integrate schools in segregated neighborhoods proceeded slowly but peacefully in the South, northern urban whites dug in their heels. In Boston, violence erupted in the school hallways and the streets from 1975 to 1978 as economically vulnerable working-class whites harassed African Americans attending schools in white ethnic neighborhoods of South Boston, and blacks defended themselves.

Stanley J. Forman, The Soiling of Old Glory, Pulitzer Prize 1976

■ White resistance to school busing in Boston sometimes turned violent in the mid-1970s. On April 5, 1976, white high school students from South Boston and Charlestown met with a city councilwoman who supported their boycott of classes. Outside City Hall, they chanced upon lawyer Theodore Landsmark and assaulted him. Photographer Stanley J. Forman won the Pulitzer Prize for this photo.

The Oil Embargo

Nothing revealed Americans' newfound economic vulnerability more than the 1973–1974 boycott initiated by the Oil Producing and Exporting Countries (OPEC). The largest producers of oil were the Arab countries around the Persian Gulf, especially Saudi Arabia. These nations resented the creation of Israel in 1948 and the resulting displacement of the Palestinians.

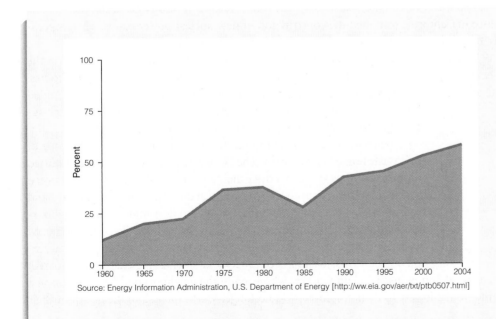

Source: Energy Information Administration, U.S. Department of Energy [http://ww.eia.gov/aer/txt/ptb0507.html]

■ **FIGURE 27.1**
IMPORTED PETROLEUM AS SHARE OF U.S. PETROLEUM CONSUMPTION   Abundant natural resources, especially coal and oil, encouraged Americans' long-standing feeling of national strength and autonomy. After World War II, however, the United States switched from exporting oil to importing oil. Conservation measures in the 1970s temporarily reversed America's growing dependence on oil from abroad.

Hostility intensified in 1967 when Israel seized control of the West Bank of the Jordan River and the Gaza Strip. Six years later, Egypt and Syria struck back, attacking and threatening to overrun Israel, but the United States gave the Israeli army a critical resupply of weapons that helped turn the tide of battle.

Henry Kissinger then shuttled between Tel Aviv and Cairo to negotiate a ceasefire. His diplomatic skills won him the Nobel peace prize and laid the groundwork for a warming of U.S. relations with Egypt (the most populous Arab nation though not an oil producer). However, the other Arab states expressed outrage at this demonstration of America's close links with the Israelis, and Arabs of all political persuasions were determined to voice their displeasure.

In October 1973, the OPEC nations initiated an embargo on selling oil to the United States and to western European nations that had supported Israel in the war. Oil supplies dwindled, and prices at gas pumps skyrocketed to four times their previous levels. Even when OPEC lifted the embargo after five months, it kept prices high by limiting production.

Steeper energy costs powerfully accelerated inflation. Decades of easy access to cheap gasoline came to a sudden halt. As American drivers formed long lines at the pump, President Ford urged them to drive at lower speeds to conserve gas. Americans confronted new and sobering limits on their mobility.

The Environmental Movement

The oil embargo encouraged many U.S. citizens to rethink the nation's cavalier use of natural resources. Environmental consciousness spread rapidly in the 1970s as evidence revealed the impact of industrial growth on the quality of life in the United States. Environmental organizations such as the Sierra Club, the National Wildlife Federation, and the Audubon Society saw their memberships soar. For the first time, the media began to examine the daunting range

of environmental problems plaguing the United States and the rest of the world: acid rain, groundwater contamination, smog, rainforest destruction, oil spills, nuclear waste disposal, species extinction, ozone depletion, and global warming.

Environmentalists argued that the idea of unlimited consumption of natural resources was fundamentally irresponsible, both to future human generations and to other species. They urged Congress and the Environmental Protection Agency (EPA) to require fuel-efficient engines from carmakers and to promote renewable energy sources such as water, solar, and wind power. Citizen groups such as the Clamshell Alliance in New England and the Abalone Alliance in California protested the construction of new nuclear power plants. These operations, they pointed out, had no reliable method in place for disposing of nuclear waste.

A broad critique of the chemical industry's impact on public health also emerged in the 1970s. As it turned out, pesticides worked their way up the food chain into people's bodies. Some artificial sweeteners proved carcinogenic, and the lead that manufacturers had added to gasoline and house paint for generations caused brain damage. Long-standing industrial dumping of toxic chemicals made headlines.

Discovering the limits of the U.S. economy so soon after the Vietnam War and the Watergate scandal spawned a crisis of confidence.

The crisis at Love Canal in upstate New York helped bring the issue of toxic waste home to Americans. The Hooker Chemical Company had buried tons of poisonous waste in a dry canal in the town of Niagara Falls between 1947 and 1952 and then covered it over with dirt. The company gave the land to the town, which promptly built a school on it. A middle-class neighborhood soon grew up around the site. But the ground smelled odd and oozed mysterious substances. Sometimes it even caught on fire for no apparent reason. By the 1970s, local rates of cancer and other severe illnesses had soared. The chemical and industrial plant workers who lived in the neighborhood began to suspect that their quiet loyalty to their employers was no longer worth the risk to the health of their

■ Thousands of runners surge up the Hayes Street hill in San Francisco in the annual 7-mile Bay-to-Breakers race across the city. In the 1970s, regular exercise began to become a common part of daily life for many Americans. At the same time, fast food and higher-fat diets contributed to a growing pattern of Americans being overweight and even obese.

Peter Menzel/StockBoston

families. Persistent activism by community members finally overcame local, state, and company officials' efforts to keep the contents of the buried canal secret. In August 1978, New York Governor Hugh Carey at last agreed to buy out the entire neighborhood, seal it off, and move residents elsewhere.

Discovering the limits of the U.S. economy so soon after the Vietnam War and the Watergate scandal spawned a crisis of confidence. Many Americans resented the idea of limits. But others began to embrace the idea of creating a healthier lifestyle that focused less on material consumption. Exercise, especially running, began to become an increasingly common activity for middle-class adults. The wildly successful Nike athletic shoe company was founded in 1972, and entrants in the New York City Marathon ballooned from 126 in 1970 to 10,000 by 1978. Interest in outdoor recreation—hiking, camping, and bicycling—grew exponentially. Recycling also started its climb from a fringe activity to common practice in a few parts of the country.

Reshuffling Politics

The skepticism toward authority and tradition spawned by the counterculture, the Vietnam War, and the Watergate scandal spread through American culture in the 1970s. The use of illegal drugs, especially marijuana, was widespread. Casual sexual relationships proliferated in a decade when contraceptive pills had become widely available and the AIDS virus had not yet appeared. Popular and critically acclaimed films featured tales of malfeasance in high places. *All the President's Men* (1976) told the story of the Nixon administration's Watergate crimes. *Apocalypse Now* (1979) revealed the madness of the American war in Vietnam. *Three Days of the Condor* (1975) portrayed the CIA as a rogue agency beyond democratic

The Church Committee and CIA Covert Operations

In 1975–1976 the U.S. Senate Select Committee to Study Governmental Operations with Respect to Intelligence Activities engaged in the first comprehensive review by Congress of the actions of the Central Intelligence Agency. Under the leadership of Frank Church (D-Idaho), the committee investigated both intelligence gathering ("spying") and covert operations, the secret side of American foreign policy during the Cold War. One of the most controversial issues that the Church committee examined was evidence of the CIA's attempted use of assassination as a means of dealing with key figures in Cuba, the Congo, the Dominican Republic, South Vietnam, and Chile.

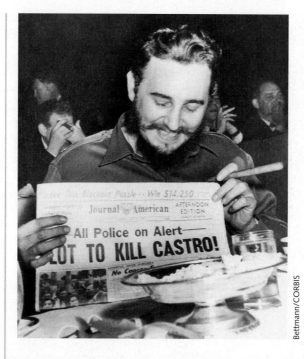

A star baseball pitcher who once turned down an offer to sign with the New York Giants, Fidel Castro led a leftist, anti-American revolution in Cuba in 1959. U.S. hostility and Castro's evolving politics moved him to declare Cuba a communist state in 1961. The CIA tried unsuccessfully to arrange for Castro's assassination.

Bettmann/CORBIS

Alleged Assassination Plots Involving Foreign Leaders (Interim Report, November 20, 1975)

The Committee has received evidence that ranking Government officials discussed, and may have authorized, the establishment with the CIA of a generalized assassination capability. . . .

The evidence establishes that the United States was implicated in several assassination plots. . . . Our inquiry also reveals serious problems with respect to United States involvement in coups directed against foreign governments. . . .

Once methods of coercion and violence are chosen, the probability of loss of life is always present. There is, however, a significant difference between a coldblooded, targeted, intentional killing of an individual foreign leader and other forms of intervening in the affairs of foreign nations. . . .

Non-attribution to the United States for covert operations was the original and principal purpose of the so-called doctrine of "plausible denial."

Evidence before the Committee clearly demonstrates that this concept, designed to protect the United States and its operatives from the consequences of disclosures, has been expanded to mask decisions of the President and his senior staff members. . . .

"Plausible denial" can also lead to the use of euphemism and circumlocution, which are designed to allow the President and other senior officials to deny knowledge of an operation should it be disclosed. . . .

It is possible that there was a failure of communication between policymakers and the agency personnel who were experienced in secret, and often violent, action. Although policymakers testified that assassination was not intended by such words as "get rid of Castro," some of their subordinates in the Agency testified that they perceived that assassination was desired and that they should proceed without troubling their superiors. . . .

Running throughout the cases considered in this report was the expectation of American officials that they could control the actions of dissident groups which they were supporting in foreign countries. Events demonstrated that the United States had no such power. This point is graphically demonstrated by cables exchanged shortly before the coup in Vietnam. Ambassador Lodge cabled Washington on October 30, 1963, that he was unable to halt a coup; a cable from William Bundy in response stated that "we cannot accept conclusion that we have no power to delay or discourage a coup." The coup took place three days later. . . .

Officials of the CIA made use of persons associated with the criminal underworld in attempting to achieve the assassination of Fidel Castro. These underworld figures were relied upon because it was believed that they had expertise and contacts that were not available to law-abiding citizens. . . .

It may well be ourselves that we injure most if we adopt tactics "more ruthless than the enemy."

Questions

1. What are the dangers to the United States of using assassination as a tool of U.S. foreign policy? Is the use of assassination compatible with the practice of democracy? How might it affect American society at home, as well as the way other nations perceive the United States?

2. Did the attacks of September 11, 2001, change the way Americans view the possible use by their government of assassination and other covert operations abroad? Should the attacks have altered Americans' attitudes about these issues? ■

control. *Chinatown* (1974) suggested the vast corruption marring the early-twentieth-century growth of Los Angeles. *Blazing Saddles* (1974) hilariously spoofed the heroic Westerns that had long served as the staple of American moviegoers' diet. *One Flew over the Cuckoo's Nest* (1975) used novelist Ken Kesey's story of an insane asylum to imply that those in charge were more dangerous than the inmates. In this atmosphere Congress began to reassert its authority against the "imperial presidency," and in 1976 voters put an obscure, devout, Georgia peanut farmer and former one-term governor in the White House.

Congressional Power Reasserted

The double shock of defeat in Vietnam and the Watergate scandal reawakened a Congress that had grown accustomed to deferring to the White House in foreign affairs. Tellingly, Congress had never formally declared war on North Korea or North Vietnam, although such declaration is its constitutional duty. Angered by the illegalities and deception in both the Johnson and Nixon administrations, Congress passed the War Powers Act in 1973 to limit the president's capacity to wage undeclared wars. The bill required the chief executive to obtain explicit congressional approval for keeping U.S. troops in an overseas conflict longer than ninety days.

> *Defeat in Vietnam and the Watergate scandal reawakened a Congress that had grown accustomed to deferring to the White House in foreign affairs.*

With encouragement from voters and journalists, Congress also uncovered its eyes and began to investigate the covert side of American foreign policy that had gathered momentum since 1945. After Watergate popped the cork on the bottled-up secret abuses of the executive branch, other troubling news spilled out about the nation's intelligence agencies, including CIA "dirty tricks" and the agency's Operation Chaos. The latter program of illegal domestic espionage against antiwar dissidents paralleled FBI abuses such as the COINTELPRO campaigns to defame Martin Luther King Jr. and destroy the Black Panthers and the American Indian Movement. Congressional investigators documented CIA involvement in assassination attempts against foreign leaders such as Fidel Castro of Cuba and Patrice Lumumba of the Congo.

These revelations stirred fierce controversy among those who took an interest in national and international politics. Many citizens decried what their government had done in their names and without their knowledge. However, officials claimed that the extreme conditions of the Cold War and the duplicity of the Soviets necessitated secrecy. At the core of this controversy were two burning questions. How transparent could a democratic society and its government afford to be when they also had global interests to protect? And when democratic openness and imperial self-interest conflicted, which should win out?

"I Will Never Lie to You"

In the backwash of Watergate, two presidential candidates—both outsiders to national politics—became advocates for opposing sides in the debate about power and openness in 1976. Former California governor Ronald Reagan made a strong run at the Republican nomination, falling just short at the Kansas City convention as incumbent Gerald Ford held on to head the GOP ticket. Reagan articulated conservative Americans' anger at seeing U.S. autonomy and power abroad hemmed in. He opposed détente with the Soviets, supported anticommunists everywhere, and warned

TABLE 27-2

The Election of 1976

Candidate	Political Party	Popular Vote (%)	Electoral Vote
Jimmy Carter	Democratic	50.0	297
Gerald R. Ford	Republican	47.9	241

against a treaty that would return control of the Panama Canal to the Panamanians. Ford found himself burdened by the faltering economy, weakened by Reagan's criticisms from the right, and hampered by widespread resentment of his pardon for Nixon.

Jimmy Carter was the winner. The former Georgia governor based his candidacy on moral uplift. Contrasting himself to the Nixon administration, he told audiences, "I will never lie to you." Instead, Carter promised openness, accountability, and a government "as good and decent as the American people."

Carter was also a Naval Academy graduate, a former nuclear engineer, a successful peanut farmer and businessperson, and the first president from the Deep South in more than a century. A born-again Christian, he had supported civil rights during his governorship in Georgia. Carter kept his diminutive first name: Jimmy, not James nor even Jim. He wore denim, and he carried his own bags. At his inaugural parade, he and his wife Rosalynn chose to walk down Pennsylvania Avenue rather than ride in a limousine.

The new president entered the White House at a time of unusual resistance to executive authority. He encountered an assertive and suspicious Congress. He faced an economy still mired in stagflation as unemployment and prices kept rising and interest rates reached 21 percent.

Politics and ideology also hamstrung the new president, limiting his ability to lead his own party in governing the nation. The Georgian was the first Democratic president since the 1930s who did not fully subscribe to the New Deal principle of government regulation of the economy. As a social moderate but an economic conservative, Carter had a strong desire to balance the federal budget. This vision placed him closer to the Republicans than to many in his own party. A businessperson, he also considered fiscal responsibility a primary virtue. Powerful liberal Democrats in Congress, by contrast, remained committed to government spending on programs such as Social Security and welfare, which Carter supported with less enthusiasm.

Carter's tendency to take moralistic stands did not mesh well with the horse-trading style of compromise that characterized Congress. The president and his aides tried to govern as outsiders to the federal government. They viewed insiders as selfish and narrow-minded. They failed to cultivate relationships with Democratic leaders in Congress such as powerful House Speaker Thomas ("Tip") O'Neill of Massachusetts. Meanwhile, seasoned legislators of both parties looked down on the new administration as inexperienced and naive.

Rise of a Peacemaker

Carter's idealism proved more effective, at least during his first two years, in refashioning U.S. foreign policy. The president started the national healing process with his first official act in office: he granted a "full, complete, and unconditional pardon" to those who had evaded the draft during the Vietnam War. He also tried to replace indiscriminate anticommunism with the promotion of human rights as the main theme in international affairs. "We are now free of that inordinate fear of Communism which once led us to embrace any dictator who joined us in that fear," he told an audience at Notre Dame University.

All presidents since 1945 had loudly supported human rights in the Soviet bloc. Carter defended dissidents in authoritarian countries friendly to the United States as well. His commitment to ending racial discrimination at home and his promotion of human rights abroad led to his administration's strong support for an end to white minority rule in southern Africa, including the establishment of Zimbabwe out of the old white-ruled Rhodesia in 1980.

Carter encouraged Americans to shift their attention from the East-West Cold War to the burgeoning problems between industrialized nations of the North and mostly poor countries of the Southern Hemisphere. The president made control over the Panama Canal a test case for this reorientation. The huge canal symbolized U.S. dominance of the hemisphere and served as a focus of resentment among many Latin Americans. Since 1903, the United States had ruled the 10-mile-wide Canal Zone as its own colony. Acknowledging this colonialist past, Carter signed treaties on September 7, 1977, to return sovereignty of the canal to Panama.

The Carter administration's other great diplomatic achievement came with the Camp David accords, an agreement between Egypt's president Anwar Sadat and Israel's prime minister Menachem Begin. The Arab-Israeli conflict had remained one of the most intractable problems in modern diplomacy. Sadat created an opening for diplomacy in 1977 by becoming the first Arab leader to visit Israel. Carter then invited Sadat and Begin to Camp David, the presidential retreat in rural western Maryland. There his persistence, plus promises of American aid to all parties, kept the marathon negotiations on track. In March 1979, the Egyptian and Israeli leaders signed two accords: Egypt became the first Arab state to grant official recognition to Israel. In turn, Israel agreed to withdraw its troops from the Sinai peninsula and apparently to stop building additional settlements on the Palestinian West Bank of the Jordan River. The framework for peace implied eventual autonomy for the Palestinians in the West Bank and the Gaza Strip.

Though promising, the Camp David accords failed to bring peace to the Middle East. Israeli settlements in the West Bank continued to proliferate, and anti-Israeli terrorism by Palestinians persisted. But Carter had persuaded two major players in the region to take a big step back from open hostility. The world rightly proclaimed him a peacemaker.

■ After his inauguration as president, Jimmy Carter got down to work in the Oval Office. Serious, conscientious, and extremely hard-working, Carter immersed himself in many of the details of his administration's policies. The image of him sequestered and industrious at his desk came to symbolize, for many, both the strengths and weaknesses of his presidency.

The War on Waste

Within three months of taking office, Carter called for the "moral equivalent of war" to meet the deepening national energy crisis. He exhorted his fellow citizens to stop being "the most wasteful nation on Earth." Conserve energy, he implored them. Switch off lights and turn down thermostats.

The administration created the Department of Energy and granted tax incentives to promote development of alternative sources such as solar energy. The EPA required U.S. automakers to meet stricter fuel efficiency standards for their engines. High prices encouraged a renewed search for domestic sources of oil. In 1977 workers completed the 800-mile-long, 48-inch-wide Trans-Alaska Pipeline System. The system linked the state's northern oil fields at Prudhoe Bay on the Arctic Ocean with a tanker terminal in Valdez, on Alaska's southern coast on the Pacific Ocean. With new oil now flowing freely, Carter worked with Congress to pass the 1980 Alaska National Interest Lands Conservation Act. This legislation created the single largest addition ever to the nation's wilderness system, 47 million acres, and the new Wrangell–St. Elias National Park.

The most controversial power alternative came in the form of nuclear energy. Obtained by harnessing the force of splitting atoms, nuclear energy seemed to promise unlimited pollution-free power. But it entailed the use of a deadly radioactive fuel, uranium. In March 1979, a partial meltdown of the nuclear core of the Three Mile Island reactor near Harrisburg, Pennsylvania, leaked radiation and forced a major evacuation. Nevertheless, existing nuclear power plants continued to generate 11 percent of the nation's electricity in 1979, a figure that climbed to 22 percent by 1992 as other plants under construction came on line. However, because of negative public opinion and the high cost per unit of nuclear power, no new plants ordered by utility companies after 1974 were ever completed.

Jimmy Carter Library

Danny Lehman/CORBIS

■ Mt. McKinley in Alaska's Denali National Park rises to 20,320 feet above sea level, the tallest peak in North America. Its scale and beauty inspired many supporters of the Alaska National Interest Lands Conservation Act of 1980, which dramatically expanded the nation's parklands and wilderness areas. The Alaska Lands Act and the new Trans-Alaska oil pipeline, completed three years earlier, helped residents of the lower forty-eight learn more about the nation's largest and most remote state.

Diffusing the Women's Movement

"Good morning, boys and girls!" This standard classroom greeting suggests the central place of gender in how Americans identify people from a young age. Few people consider the phrase offensive, even though they probably would protest if a teacher addressed class members as "blacks and whites" or "tall people and short people." Should one's sex (a biological characteristic) or gender (the social assumptions associated with sex) constitute the fundamental dividing line among human beings? The spread of feminism through U.S. society from the 1970s onward raised this question.

The Meanings of Women's Liberation

In a decade marked by hard rethinking of major issues, feminists provided one of the most profound challenges of all. Few American households avoided at least some reconsideration of the roles of men and women. Just as the nation reimagined its foreign policy in less assertive terms and with greater concern for human rights, feminists called for equality between the sexes while honoring their differences. The new title "Ms."—like Mr.—symbolized a desire not to have one's marital status revealed through the title of "Miss" or "Mrs." Thousands of consciousness-raising meetings also made women aware that their own experiences with discrimination were part of a broader pattern of injustice toward women.

■ MAP 27.1

BUILDING NUCLEAR POWER PLANTS   Between 1969 and 1980, all of the nation's 103 commercial nuclear power reactors either came on line (fifty-six) or were in the process of being planned or built (forty-seven). The United States has roughly one-quarter of the 434 commercial nuclear power reactors in the world. Despite nuclear energy's important role in U.S. electricity production, there is still no system in place for the permanent disposal of radioactive waste.

The millions of American women who found their lives changing in the 1970s did not agree on all issues. African American and Latino American women balanced identities as women with identities as people of color, which aligned them closely with men of their communities. Working-class women of all colors often focused on issues common to all workers, including wages, workplace conditions, and union representation. Community organizers such as Lois Gibbs of Love Canal zeroed in on neighborhoods and families. The educated white women who formed the most visible part of the movement for equality differed among themselves on such issues as pornography: some found it inherently exploitive of women, while others considered it primarily a matter of free expression.

However, all women shared certain concerns. Even as many female Americans remained wary of the label *feminist*—fearing associations with anger, militancy, and dislike of men—they nonetheless tended to side with feminist positions on issues from equal pay for equal work, to abortion rights, to more egalitarian distribution of household chores within families. Even women who still chose to wear makeup and dress in traditionally feminine fashion shared a desire for men to take women more seriously for their ideas and beliefs than for their appearance. The women's movement also sought to unmask the violence constraining all women's lives: sexual harassment, domestic abuse, and rape.

New Opportunities in Education, the Workplace, and Family Life

In the 1970s, educated women gained access to a host of new opportunities in the workplace. Young women in college, unlike their mothers, expected to choose and develop a career after

■ Gloria Steinem, kneeling, speaks at a meeting of a women's consciousness-raising group in the early 1970s. Similar groups gathered informally in homes around the country and helped women articulate their common struggles against discrimination.

Sophia Smith Collection, Smith College. Gloria Steinem Papers

graduation even more than they anticipated getting married. The number of women entering graduate and professional schools soared. The percentage of female students in law school shot up from 5 percent to 40 percent between 1970 and 1980. Most single-sex private colleges went coeducational. Many dormitories housed both men and women, allowing young people from the middle and upper classes to live in close physical proximity for the first time.

A similar process unfolded in the workplace. Employment in the United States, formerly divided into "men's" and "women's" work, saw a blurring of those lines. Help-wanted advertisements stopped categorizing jobs as male or female, and women joined the ranks of police officers and truck drivers. In 1980 more than half of women with children under six years old had paying jobs outside the home.

Not surprisingly, family life also changed shape in these years. In the 1950s, more than 70 percent of American families with children had a father who worked outside the home and a mother who stayed at home. By 1980, only 15 percent of families were configured that way. Yet society's growing acceptance of mothers in the workforce did not necessarily mean that these women enjoyed a lighter domestic load. Most working mothers still bore the brunt of the "second shift": child-rearing and housework in addition to a full-time paid job.

Changing roles brought new marital stresses, and divorce rates climbed in this decade. In 1970, one-third as many divorces as marriages occurred annually; in 1980, the figure was one-half. No-fault divorce laws, beginning with California's in 1970, eased the process and the stigma attached to divorce, although its emotional impact on adults and children remained difficult to measure. Men benefited financially when marriages split up. Their average living standard rose sharply, whereas that of women and their children plummeted.

Equality Under the Law

Paralleling the logic of the black civil rights movement, the modern women's movement pressured lawmakers to eliminate the legal underpinnings of sex-based discrimination. Title IX of the Educational Amendments of 1972 required schools to spend comparable amounts on women's and men's sports programs. This critical step symbolized women's shift away from spectatorship and cheerleading to the female athleticism that helped define American popular culture by the end of the twentieth century.

After languishing for decades among failed proposals in Congress, the proposed Equal Rights Amendment to the Constitution finally rode to an overwhelming victory among senators and representatives in 1972. The legislature then sent it to the states for possible ratification by 1980. Simple in its language, the ERA declared: "Equality of rights under law shall not be denied or abridged by the United States or by any State on account of sex."

DOCUMENT

Roe v. Wade

On January 22, 1973, in the landmark case of *Roe v. Wade*, the Supreme Court ruled (by a 7–2 vote) that constitutional privacy rights were "broad enough to encompass a woman's decision whether or not to terminate her pregnancy" in its first six months. This decision established women's constitutional right to determine the course of their own pregnancies.

Backlash

Even as the majority of Americans accepted the fundamental tenets of feminism, some fiercely defended existing gender roles. The mainstream media often painted women's rights activists as angry man-haters. Indeed, the media seized the opportunity to associate feminism with "bra-burning," a titillating way to blend women's rights with the sexual revolution and thus avoid the serious issues that women were raising. One Chicana worker involved in a strike against the Farah slacks company in Texas responded, "I don't believe in burning your bra, but I do believe in having our rights."

The women's movement posed a daunting challenge to traditional ideas about masculinity. Men wondered what equality for women really meant and how it might change their intimate and professional relationships with women. Should men still open doors for women? Should they begin to do half (or more) of housework and parenting? Should they not comment on a female colleague's appearance? Women's growing economic independence and educational opportunities often altered the dynamics of power in male-female relationships. Many men from all classes and ethnicities, feeling defensive about assumptions and behaviors that were increasingly labeled sexist, resisted these changes. Some found the increasingly open acknowledgment of lesbianism threatening because it implied their potential irrelevance to women.

> *Should men still open doors for women? Should they begin to do half (or more) of housework and parenting?*

That men would have mixed feelings about women's liberation surprised no one. But some of the stiffest resistance came from certain women. Those who had built their identities on motherhood and homemaking fiercely defended that tradition. They sought to uphold an established family structure that they believed divorce, gay rights, abortion, and day-care would destroy. In their view, femininity meant service to one's family. "Feminists praise self-centeredness," antifeminist Phyllis Schlafly declared, "and call it liberation." In addition to defending their own choices, female antifeminists worried about the impact of dual-career families on children.

Opponents of women's liberation made two major legislative gains in the late 1970s. First, Congress passed the Hyde Amendment in 1976, which forbade the use of Medicaid funds for abortions. In practice, the amendment limited access to abortion to those women who could afford to pay for it themselves. Second, Schlafly's Stop-ERA campaign helped defeat the Equal

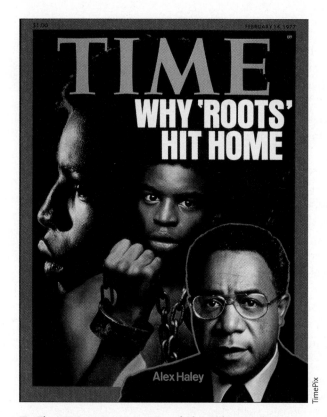

■ The 1977 miniseries version of Alex Haley's *Roots* captured the largest television audience ever to that time. The powerful drama about Haley's ancestors offered tens of millions of Americans an intimate and sympathetic understanding of the horrific story of black slavery and survival. *Roots* also represented the post-1960s emphasis on preserving and respecting group histories and identities rather than emphasizing only individual success and assimilation into the mainstream.

Rights Amendment by limiting its ratification to only thirty-five of the required thirty-eight states. Schlafly claimed that the amendment would "destroy the family, foster homosexuality, and hurt women." Opponents of the ERA argued that it would also draw out the worst in men, letting husbands opt out of supporting their wives and freeing divorced men from paying alimony. Antifeminists resented the disrespect for motherhood that they felt from some feminists. Still, they agreed with feminists that tens of millions of American women were just one man removed from welfare. The two sides differed on the best way to protect women's interests: should women be more economically independent, or should men be tied more tightly to their families?

Though discouraging for some, the narrow defeat of the ERA could not mask feminism's growing influence throughout American culture. The "first woman" stories that began showing up in the media during the 1970s marked the entrance of women into previously all-male roles. Like physicians, lawyers, and other figures of cultural authority, religious leaders now increasingly consisted of women, including the first Lutheran pastor (1970), the first Jewish rabbi (1972), and the first Episcopal priest (1974). In 1981 Sandra Day O'Connor became the first female Supreme Court justice. And mainstream organizations such as churches and municipalities ran feminist-created community institutions, including rape crisis centers, women's health clinics, and battered women's shelters.

Conclusion

In 1978 a divided U.S. Supreme Court handed down a ruling on the contentious policy of affirmative action. The justices decided by a 5–4 vote in the *Bakke* case that strict racial quotas were unconstitutional, but that universities could consider race as one of several factors in determining a candidate's qualifications for admission. The Court, like the American public, was wrestling with the broader 1970s problem of how to reform American society in ways that would preserve its historic strengths while removing the ills that the previous decade's political activism had laid bare. One specific problem was the tension between the ideal of colorblind integration and new expressions of pride in distinctive racial and ethnic identities. Many white ethnic Americans in these years leavened their long-standing cultural assimilation with renewed attention to their own roots in particular European countries, especially Ireland and Italy.

Americans' self-confidence and pride as a nation had been deeply shaken by the combination of the Vietnam War, the Watergate scandal, and the economic downturn after 1973. Disillusioned by the corruptions of public life, many citizens turned inward and heeded the advice of Robert J. Ringer in his 1977 bestseller, *Looking Out for Number One*. But others found motivation in the decade's events—especially the revelation that presidents, corporate executives, and other authorities had lied to them. They learned what earlier Americans had discovered in the 1760s and 1770s about imperious British officials and the corrupting effects of managing a global empire. Like the revolutionaries of George Washington's generation, they sought to strengthen democracy.

Sites to Visit

Divining America: Religion and the National Culture

www.nhc.rtp.nc.us/tserve/divam.htm

This site has essays by prominent historians on diverse aspects of the religious history of the United States.

Documents from the Women's Liberation Movement

scriptorium.lib.duke.edu/wlm/

Provocative and fascinating articles from feminists of the late 1960s and 1970s make this site worthy of a visit.

National Security Archive at George Washington University

www.gwu.edu/~nsarchiv/

This excellent site includes the most recent declassified documents on the making of U.S. foreign policy.

Natural Resources Defense Council

www.nrdc.org/

This site contains considerable information and links about environmental issues, particularly those that emerged into public consciousness in the 1970s.

Oyez Project of Northwestern University

http://www.oyez.org/oyez/frontpage

Arguments from important Supreme Court cases plus information about Supreme Court justices make this a most useful site for legal history.

Gerald R. Ford Library and Museum

www.ford.utexas.edu/

The Ford presidential library maintains this site, with documents and photographs from the mid-1970s.

The Watergate Story

www.washingtonpost.com/wp-srv/onpolitics/watergate/splash.html

The *Washington Post* created this informative site about the Watergate scandal twenty-five years after the event took place.

For Further Reading

General

Edward D. Berkowitz, *Something Happened: A Political and Cultural Overview of the Seventies* (2006).

Peter N. Carroll, *It Seemed Like Nothing Happened: America in the 1970s* (1990).

E. J. Dionne Jr., *Why Americans Hate Politics* (1991).

Bruce J. Schulman, *The Seventies: The Great Shift in American Culture, Society, and Politics* (2001).

Twin Shocks: Détente and Watergate

Walter Isaacson, *Kissinger* (1992).

Andreas Killen, *1973 Nervous Breakdown: Watergate, Warhol, and the Birth of Post-Sixties America* (2006).

Stanley I. Kutler, *The Wars of Watergate: The Last Crisis of Richard Nixon* (1992).

Melvin Small, *The Presidency of Richard M. Nixon* (1999).

Discovering the Limits of the U.S. Economy

Allen J. Matusow, *Nixon's Economy: Booms, Busts, Dollars, and Votes* (1998).

Thomas J. McCormick, *America's Half-Century: United States Foreign Policy in the Cold War and After*, 2nd ed. (1995).

Hal K. Rothman, *The Greening of a Nation? Environmentalism in the United States Since 1945* (1998).

Daniel Yergin, *The Prize: The Epic Quest for Oil, Money, and Power* (1991).

Reshuffling Politics

Samuel P. Hays, *Beauty, Health, and Permanence: Environmental Politics in the United States, 1955–1985* (1987).

Burton I. Kaufman, *The Presidency of James Earl Carter, Jr.* (1993).

John Ranelagh, *The Agency: The Rise and Decline of the CIA* (1986).

Gaddis Smith, *Morality, Reason, and Power: American Diplomacy in the Carter Years* (1986).

Diffusing the Women's Movement

Susan J. Douglas, *Where the Girls Are: Growing Up Female with the Mass Media* (1994).

Sara M. Evans, *Tidal Wave: How Women Changed America at Century's End* (2003).

Arlie Russell Hochschild, *The Second Shift: Working Parents and the Revolution at Home* (1997).

Ruth Rosen, *The World Split Open: How the Modern Women's Movement Changed America* (2000).

For quizzes and other resources on these topics, go to www.longmanamericanhistory.com.

1979	Iranian revolution; militants take American hostages
	Soviet Union invades Afghanistan
	Sandinista rebels seize control of Nicaragua
1980	Failed attempt to rescue American hostages in Iran
	Ronald Reagan elected president
1981	Iran releases American hostages
	U.S. funds "Contras" to try to overthrow Nicaraguan government
1982	Recession hits United States
	Nuclear freeze movement holds large protests in the United States and western Europe
1983	HIV identified as virus that causes AIDS
	First compact discs (CDs) marketed
	241 U.S. Marines killed in bombing of Beirut barracks
	Martin Luther King Jr.'s birthday designated a national holiday
1984	Russia boycotts summer Olympic Games in Los Angeles
1985	First Reagan-Gorbachev summit in Geneva
1986	Chernobyl nuclear power plant disaster (Ukraine)
	Iran-Contra scandal revealed
	Congress passes sanctions against South African apartheid government
1987	Intermediate Nuclear Force Treaty
	Stock market crash
1988	Indian Gaming Regulatory Act
	Libyan terrorist bomb downs Pan Am Flight 103 over Lockerbie, Scotland
	United States invades Panama to seize Manuel Noriega
1989	Grounding of oil tanker *Exxon Valdez* off Alaska coast
	Last Soviet troops withdraw from Afghanistan
	Berlin Wall falls
1990	Nelson Mandela freed from prison in South Africa
	Iraq invades and occupies Kuwait
1991	Clarence Thomas–Anita Hill congressional hearings
	Persian Gulf War against Iraq
	Los Angeles police beat, arrest Rodney King
	Soviet Union dissolves into Russia and other component states
1992	South Central Los Angeles riots follow acquittal of police in Rodney King case
	FBI shootout at Ruby Ridge, Idaho

P A R T   T E N

Global Connections at Home and Abroad 1979–2006

A FTER THE UNCERTAINTIES AND REFORMS OF THE 1970S, many Americans sought reassurance about their country's direction. In the 1980s, President Ronald Reagan left his imprint on both domestic and foreign affairs. Reagan gave voice to conservatives, including those who favored a federal retreat from social welfare programs. Bolstered by the Moral Majority and other fundamentalist Christian groups, conservatives engaged in the so-called culture wars with liberals. Conservatives disapproved of feminists, black power advocates, gay rights activists, and environmentalists. Reagan and Congress implemented policies that shrank the federal government's commitment to social welfare programs. Reagan also reinvigorated Cold War rhetoric—he denounced the Soviet Union as an "evil empire"—and pushed military spending to unprecedented levels. Yet Reagan welcomed the initiatives of Soviet leader Mikhail Gorbachev, who sought to ease tensions with the West.

Unable to meet the basic needs of its own people and bogged down in an unwinnable war in Afghanistan, the Soviet Union disintegrated in 1991. Simultaneously, the United States embarked on a remarkable period of economic growth and expansion. President Bill Clinton favored free trade policies, such as the North American Free Trade Agreement (NAFTA), which he and others hoped would knit the world's nations together in pursuit of political and economic progress.

Nevertheless, domestic and foreign conflicts thwarted much of this hopeful vision. At home, the AIDS epidemic and drug addiction claimed many lives. Clashes among African Americans, Latinos, and Koreans in Los Angeles in 1992; the bombing of an Oklahoma City federal building by domestic antigovernment terrorists in 1995; attacks on abortion clinics; and a series of shootings by high school students revealed persistent faultlines in American society. Backed by the Supreme Court, a number of state and local governments passed anti-immigrant and anti–affirmative action laws. The culture wars were hot and, in some cases, deadly.

The most violent assault on the United States came from forces outside as well as within it. The Middle East had become a tinderbox of fears and resentments. In Iran, Islamic militants overthrew the U.S.-backed Shah in 1979. Throughout the region, many Islamic fundamentalists expressed their resentment over the military and political presence of the United States in Israel and Saudi Arabia. During the 1991 Persian Gulf War, the United States successfully reversed Iraq's seizure of oil fields in Kuwait. Yet U.S. attempts to protect its economic and political interests in the Middle East continued to outrage Islamic militants.

By the end of the 1990s, some Americans were able to focus inward and enjoy prosperity. The stock market was booming. Cheap gas prices encouraged affluent Americans to purchase huge sport utility vehicles with little regard for their environmental impact. However, ten years of high employment masked the hidden effects of a transformed economy, one characterized by a decline in labor union membership and the rise of an ill-paid service sector. A substantial proportion of Americans lived from paycheck to paycheck.

On September 11, 2001, Americans were forced to confront their own vulnerabilities. Anti-U.S. terrorists hijacked commercial airliners and flew them into the Twin Towers of the World Trade Center in New York City and into the Pentagon outside Washington, D.C. Some 3,000 people were killed. Within a month, anthrax-laced letters caused death and havoc in the offices where they were delivered and the postal centers that processed them, heightening pervasive fear and insecurity among Americans.

The events of September 11 highlighted a grim reality: certain foreign groups despised such cherished American values as democracy, liberalism, and consumerism. Moreover, U.S. foreign policies in the Middle East fanned the fires of anti-western extremism. Terrorists were becoming more successful in enlisting people who were willing to die in attacks on the United States and more resourceful in using modern technology in those attacks. These terrorists were stateless, freed from the political tasks of protecting their own citizens, monitoring national borders, or dealing with internal dissidents. In contrast to the cold warriors, fighters against terrorism faced an elusive, dispersed, and, in some cases, suicidal enemy. In 2002 these realities prompted the United States to invade Afghanistan and displace the ruling Taliban, hosts to Al Qaeda's training network. The following year the United States attacked Iraq, a preemptive attack on what the Bush administration called a dangerous, destabilizing regime—the dictatorship of Saddam Hussein. At home, issues related to war, terrorism, and civil liberties became increasingly divisive and bitter among Americans.

1993 FBI storms compound of the Branch Davidian cult in Waco, Texas
Congress approves North American Free Trade Agreement (NAFTA)
Arab-Israeli peace talks
18 American soldiers die in Somalia; United States withdraws

1994 House Republican leadership announces "Contract with America"
Republicans win majority in House of Representatives
O. J. Simpson murder trial
Freedom of Access to Clinic Entrances Act

1995 Truck bomb destroys federal building in Oklahoma City
Congress revokes 55-mph speed limit

United States intervenes against Serbs in war in Bosnia
Dayton peace accords signed

1996 Welfare Reform Act

1997 Dow Jones average passes 8,000

1998 Lewinsky-Clinton affair revealed
Clinton impeached by House of Representatives

1999 Senate acquits Clinton
Dow Jones passes 10,000
U.S. bombing campaign frees province of Kosovo from Serbian rule
Elian Gonzales affair

2000 Supreme Court decides contested election; George W. Bush becomes president
Scientists map human genome

2001 Democrats regain control of Senate after Sen. James Jeffords leaves Republican party
Terrorists attack World Trade Center and Pentagon
U.S. forces attack Afghanstan and overthrow Taliban regime

2003 Space shuttle Columbia destroyed during re-entry into earth's atmphsere
U.S. and allied forces invade and occupy Iraq
Supreme Court legalizes gay sexual conduct

2004 George W. Bush reelected president

2005 Hurricane Katrina devastates New Orleans

2006 130,000–160,000 U.S. troops in Iraq

CHAPTER 28

The Cold War Returns— and Ends, 1979–1991

On July 16, 1979, just west of Albuquerque, New Mexico, a dam holding wastewater and residue from a uranium mine broke. Some 94 million gallons of radioactive water flooded into the Rio Puerco. Nearby, the Anaconda Copper Company operated the nation's largest uranium mine, producing the fuel for nuclear power. The mine closed in the early 1980s. At public hearings in 1986 concerning the future of the mine and its small mountain of poisonous tailings, Anaconda's scientists argued that the mine did not threaten human health in the area. Thus, they said, the tailing piles and the polluted ponds did not need to be cleaned up. Herman Garcia, a Laguna Indian who lived in the adjoining village of Paguate, listened carefully but remained unconvinced. "We lost five people from cancer" last year in tiny Paguate alone, he explained. "I'm no expert," he concluded, but "I'd like for some of these experts to go out there and swim in those ponds. Then when I see them swim, then maybe I feel more secure."

The Native American West and the nuclear West have overlapped to a remarkable extent ever since participants in the Manhattan Project began building the first atomic bomb in 1942. Repeatedly, the U.S. government constructed major nuclear sites in the West on lands surrounded by Indian settlements. These included the laboratories of Los Alamos, New Mexico; the bomb factories and nuclear waste dumps of Hanford, Washington; the Nevada Test Site for atomic weapons north of Las Vegas; and uranium mines in the Black Hills of South Dakota. Some of this overlap resulted from geological coincidence: almost 90 percent of the nation's

■ Ronald Reagan loved spending time outdoors at his ranch near Santa Barbara, California.

uranium lay on or adjacent to Indian lands. Some of it stemmed from politics. The sparse populations of Pueblo, Western Shoshone, and Yakima lacked the political clout to prevent their lands from becoming what the National Academy of Science called "national sacrifice areas."

In the 1980s, nuclear weapons and waste sparked controversy in the United States. President Ronald Reagan expanded the nation's nuclear arsenal, and his administration publicly discussed fighting and winning a nuclear war against the Soviet Union. An accident in 1986 at the Chernobyl nuclear power plant outside the Soviet city of Kiev only heightened public concerns. The disaster killed more than 100 people and irradiated hundreds of thousands more. Frightened by rising U.S.-Soviet tensions, citizens in western Europe and the United States organized an international movement to freeze further development of nuclear weapons.

In 1979 two international incidents raised questions about U.S. military effectiveness. A revolution in Iran led to the taking of American hostages and a dramatic rejection of American cultural values, and the Soviet Union sent troops into Afghanistan to prop up a Soviet-allied but weakening government. Angered, Americans put tough-talking Republicans in the White House for twelve years. These leaders' emphasis on military power challenged the Soviet leadership, while changes in eastern Europe and the USSR brought an end to the Cold War and the breakup of the Soviet Union.

The Reagan administration also avidly promoted free markets. Its policies produced enormous wealth at the top of the socioeconomic ladder, increasing the distance between the daily experiences of the rich and the poor. These policies also catalyzed bitter struggles over natural resources, particularly those on western public lands.

Finally, the newly organized religious right clashed with liberal opponents over such issues as abortion and homosexuality. In these years, Christian fundamentalists and their allies sought to reverse cultural liberties that had emerged since the late 1960s.

Anticommunism Revived

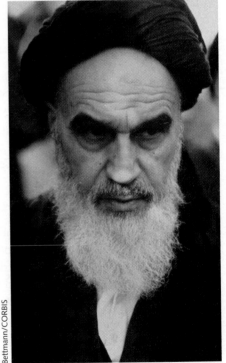

W e're going down!" cried U.S. political officer Elizabeth Swift on the phone to the State Department. These were her last words as a crowd of young Iranians poured into the U.S. embassy in Teheran on the morning of November 4, 1979, and cut telephone lines. In a move that shocked Americans, Islamic militants seized fifty-two embassy personnel and held them hostage for over a year.

In the late 1970s, revolutionaries of a different political bent—that of socialism and the left—took the offensive against authoritarian regimes in Central America. Indeed, the Third World seemed to be turning away from U.S. leadership in the wake of the American defeat in Vietnam. To make matters worse, the Soviet Union stepped up its support for leftists abroad. In December 1979, the Red Army invaded Afghanistan. Fed up with these humiliating events overseas and with relentless inflation at home, American voters elected Ronald Reagan as president—the most conservative chief executive since Calvin Coolidge. Reagan promised to resurrect the Cold War, and he delivered.

Iran and Afghanistan

In January 1979, the Iranian people overthrew the longtime authoritarian government of Shah Reza Pahlavi. Under the shah's rule, the nation's enormous oil wealth had flowed into the hands of a small elite. Meanwhile, the impoverished majority of devout Shi'ite Muslims grew increasingly resentful of the shah's closeness with his American allies. His secret police had detained 50,000 political prisoners. The revolution found its leader in the austere religious figure Ruhollah Khomeini, who shouldered aside more moderate opposition groups. Returning from exile in Iraq and then Paris, Ayatollah Khomeini created a popular **theocracy**, state grounded in a strict interpretation of Islamic law.

Bettmann/CORBIS

■ Ruhollah Khomeini led the 1979 revolution in Iran that established the modern world's first Islamic theocratic state. The events in Iran encouraged Islamic revolutionaries across the Middle East, Asia, and North Africa. For Americans, the closest analogy was the Bolshevik revolution of 1917 in Russia, which provided a model for other communist revolutions abroad.

Hunted by the rebels, the shah took his money and fled Iran. Several months later, the Carter administration let him fly to New York to seek treatment for cancer. Enraged that the United States harbored their nation's most wanted criminal, Iranians demanded the shah's extradition to Teheran to stand trial. Washington refused. Within a month, militants stormed the U.S. embassy—"that nest of spies," Khomeini called it, referring to the CIA's considerable presence in Iran.

The hostages' captors paraded them before television cameras to force Washington to return the shah. Carter refused to give in. In April 1980, he finally approved a military rescue effort. But mechanical failures forced the mission to abort, and the collision of two helicopters during the attempt killed several U.S. soldiers. Secretary of State Cyrus Vance resigned in protest against the attempted use of force. Americans' resentment of anti-American radicals in the Third World intensified. Not until after the shah's death in 1980 did the two governments finally negotiate the hostages' release in January 1981.

Khomeini and his followers despised the values they associated with modern U.S. culture: secularism, materialism, gender equality, alcohol consumption, and sexual titillation. They sought to export the cleansing power of a puritanical Islamic faith throughout the Middle East and beyond. Indeed, the revolutionaries condemned the atheistic Soviets just as fiercely as they did the materialistic Americans.

> *Khomeini and his followers despised the values they associated with modern U.S. culture.*

Just seven weeks after the seizure of hostages in Teheran, the first of 110,000 Soviet troops rolled south across the USSR's border into neighboring Afghanistan. Their goal: to stabilize the pro-Soviet government there against anticommunist Islamic guerrilla fighters. Moscow had resolved to prevent the spread of Islamic revolution into the heavily Muslim southern regions of the USSR.

But few Americans saw this invasion as a defensive operation. Rather, they feared a push toward vulnerable Iran as Red Army troops marched beyond eastern Europe for the first time in more than thirty years. The Carter administration halted most trade with the Soviets and withdrew the nuclear Strategic Arms Limitation Treaty (SALT II) from Senate consideration. In addition, the president organized a western boycott of the 1980 Olympics in Moscow and increased military spending. The "Carter Doctrine" proclaimed the U.S. commitment to preserve the status quo in the Persian Gulf region, even if it meant the use of military force. And the CIA began funding Afghan guerrillas.

The Conservative Victory of 1980

By mid-1980, Carter's public approval rating had dropped to the lowest level of any modern president. Inflation reached 17 percent. Even the president acknowledged a "crisis stage." With their dollars no longer buying what they used to, Americans wondered what the future would bring. For many voters, Carter's inability to free the hostages in Teheran or reverse the Soviet occupation of Afghanistan symbolized the limitations of his presidency.

Onto this stage strode Ronald Reagan. Long considered too conservative to win the presidency, the former California governor projected the confidence and strength that many Americans wanted, even if they did not share all of his views. The sixty-nine-year-old one-time actor sailed through the Republican primaries. For his main tactic, he appealed to nostalgia, particularly among whites, for a rosier past—a time of rising wages and U.S. military might. While Carter spoke of learning to live within limits, Reagan insisted that "we are too great a nation to limit ourselves to small dreams."

The media loved Reagan. Indeed, his presidency fit with the new emphasis on constant entertainment, as cable television, VCRs (1976), MTV (1981), and CDs (1983) swept the culture. Daily newspaper readership plummeted from 73 percent to 50 percent during the 1980s. Equally telling, the average length of an uninterrupted "sound bite" on the evening news dropped from forty-two seconds in 1968 to fewer than ten seconds in 1988. Anything longer,

■ MAP 28.1

TROUBLE SPOTS IN THE MIDDLE EAST, 1979–1993   Oil production around the Persian Gulf and the close American relationship with Israel made political instability in the Middle East a central concern of the U.S. government. American leaders particularly feared the spread of either Soviet influence or Islamic revolution, both of which opposed American cultural values and U.S. strategic interests.

the networks believed, would bore viewers. And no one projected simplicity with greater warmth or sincerity than Reagan.

Yet the 1980 election was about more than just Reagan's likable personality. It revealed the nation's renewed interest in conservative ideas. Republicans won control of the Senate for the first time since 1952. Several basic values united the Republican party: an unhindered private sector and entrepreneurial initiative to create affluence, plus free markets and individual responsibility to solve the nation's social problems. Republicans, like most Democrats, also believed that the United States had a moral obligation to preserve world order and halt further expansion of communist influence. Reagan proclaimed that "government was the problem, not the solution."

Renewing the Cold War

"Sometimes in our administration," Reagan once joked, "the right hand doesn't know what the far-right hand is doing." But all hands in the White House agreed on the importance of restoring confidence in the nation's engagements abroad, particularly in the Third World. In the 1970s, leftist insurgencies in Asia, Africa, and Latin America—especially Vietnam, Cambodia, Angola, Ethiopia, El Salvador, and Nicaragua—had suggested the retreat of U.S. power.

TABLE 28-1

The Election of 1980

Candidate	Political Party	Popular Vote (%)	Electoral Vote
Ronald Reagan	Republican	50.7	489
Jimmy Carter	Democratic	41.0	49
John B. Anderson	Independent	6.6	—

DOCUMENT

Reagan, "Evil Empire" Speech

Reagan blamed the Soviet Union for "all the unrest that is going on." He rejected the 1970s policy of détente that had emerged during the Nixon administration and had taken further shape under Ford and Carter. Often, Reagan spoke as though the Chinese-Soviet split had never happened. His was "a kind of 1952 world," one aide recalled. "He sees the world in black and white terms." Pointing to the Soviet occupation of Afghanistan and its 1983 shoot-down of a Korean Air Lines civilian jet that had strayed into Soviet airspace, the president denounced the USSR as "an evil empire."

Sacramento Bee

■ Critics of Reagan's policies toward Central America believed that he ignored the indigenous problems encouraging revolutions there, blaming instead the USSR and Cuba. The cartoon suggests that the Democratic party took a different view than the president. Many Democrats in Congress did, and they were responsible for limiting Reagan's promotion of the Nicaraguan Contras. But many others went along with the popular president in defending the Contras and supporting right-wing regimes in the region.

The Reagan administration backed up the president's words by launching the largest peacetime military buildup in American history. The Pentagon's budget ballooned 40 percent between 1980 and 1984. The new president also revived covert operations. He gave CIA director William Casey the green light to provide secret assistance to anti-communist governments and insurgencies throughout the Third World.

In Central America, extreme inequalities between landowning elites and vast peasant majorities had fueled insurgencies against the authoritarian governments of El Salvador, Guatemala, and Nicaragua. Moreover, some small assistance from Cuba and the Soviet Union had found its way to the rebels. Reagan passionately opposed these insurgents. He authorized the CIA to work hand in hand with the regimes, even though they used death squads to torture and murder dissidents and sometimes slaughtered whole villages and towns to wipe out possible resistance.

In Nicaragua, the Sandinista rebels managed to overthrow the pro-American dictatorship of Antonio Somoza in 1979. The Sandinistas set about building a more egalitarian and socialistic state while still preserving 60 percent of the nation's wealth in private hands. Carter had adopted a wait-and-see attitude. But after Reagan took office in 1981, the CIA created the counterrevolutionary "Contras," recruited primarily from Somoza's murderous former National Guard. The Contras waged an undeclared war on the new government in the Nicaraguan capital of Managua. By 1987, 40,000 Nicaraguans had died in the fighting, most of them civilians. Reagan called the Contras "freedom fighters" and declared them "the moral equal of our Founding Fathers."

Nevertheless, several European and Latin American allies considered the Contras an illegitimate force of terrorists. A large coalition of church and university groups in the United States agreed. They organized fact-finding visits to Nicaragua and lobbying trips to Washington. Christian activists formed the "Sanctuary" movement to aid refugees from the right-wing dictatorships in Central America that sympathized with the Contras. The Pentagon, for its part, had no interest in sending troops to fight a popular government abroad. The opposition finally prevailed; Congress passed the Boland Amendments of 1982 and 1984 to restrict U.S. assistance to the Contras.

Republican Rule at Home

While reasserting U.S. power abroad, Reagan also aimed to reorient domestic policies toward the free market. Lori was what the president called a "welfare cheat." Writer Barbara Ehrenreich told the story of a young neighbor in New York City representative of welfare recipients: a single white mother with one child. Lori had been married for two years to a man who beat her and once chased her around the house with a gun.

Welfare had made it possible for her to leave him, a move she described as like being born again, "as a human being this time." Lori sometimes earned close to $100 a week from cleaning houses and waiting tables—not enough to support herself and her daughter, but a useful supplement to the small government payments. She chose not to report this to the welfare office, spending it instead on little things deemed inessential by welfare regulations: deodorant, hand lotion, and an occasional commercial haircut.

Lori's story helps illuminate some of the major trends of the 1980s. Inflation finally eased and the stock market perked up. Congress and the White House slashed taxes. However, annual budget deficits and the national debt soon soared as tax revenues declined and military spending increased. The administration shrank government programs for the poor and portrayed welfare recipients like Lori as lazy and irresponsible. Washington turned a cold shoulder to concerns over the environment and opened public lands in the West to new commercial uses. By the 1990s, the gap between rich and poor widened noticeably and the vaunted American middle class worried about its declining economic security.

"Reaganomics" and the Assault on Welfare

Taxes played a crucial role in the Reagan administration's efforts to reduce government involvement in the economy. In 1981 the president proposed a new tax law to lower federal income tax rates by 25 percent over three years. Congress passed the legislation, and the top individual rate—paid only by the wealthiest Americans—dropped from 70 percent to 28 percent. Congress also slashed taxes on corporations, capital gains, and inheritances, further benefiting the most affluent Americans.

As taxes shrank, federal spending on the military soared. The Pentagon bolstered its conventional and nuclear arsenals and gave service personnel a morale-boosting salary increase. After 1983, billions of dollars poured from the U.S. Treasury into the president's proposed Strategic Defense Initiative (SDI) for a missile defense system.

> *Congress slashed taxes on corporations, capital gains, and inheritances, further benefiting the most affluent Americans.*

The funds for the weapons buildup could come from only one source: social programs at home. However, most domestic spending went to popular programs, such as Social Security and Medicare, which primarily benefited the middle class. Leaving those in place, Reagan instead reduced funding for welfare programs, including food stamps, school lunches, job training, and low-income housing.

The Republican desire to transfer the responsibility for citizens' well-being from the national government to the states resonated with opponents of the civil rights movement. The Reagan administration opposed any form of affirmative action, calling instead for the "colorblind" application of law. The president and his supporters argued that prejudice no longer had any significant effect on the decisions that employers and others made. Ironically, Reagan's own Justice Department demonstrated the opposite: it sought unsuccessfully to win tax-free status for Bob Jones University in Greenville, South Carolina, and other schools and colleges that discriminated against people of color.

Reducing welfare spending did not close the budgetary gaps that lower taxes and higher military outlays had opened. To close these gaps, the government resorted to borrowing money. Formerly the world's largest creditor nation, the United States became its largest debtor nation. Between 1981 and 1989, the national debt ballooned to almost $3 trillion. Moreover, during twelve years of Republican rule ending in 1993, annual budget deficits jumped from $59 billion to $300 billion.

Despite these problems, "Reaganomics" did help the national economy recover somewhat from the traumas of the 1970s. The tight

TABLE 28-2

The Election of 1984

Candidate	Political Party	Popular Vote (%)	Electoral Vote
Ronald Reagan	Republican	59.0	525
Walter Mondale	Democratic	41.0	13

■ James Watt, Reagan's first secretary of the Interior Department, became one of the most polarizing figures in a polarized decade. He made clear that he considered environmentalists to be his opponents as he worked to promote the interests of mining and timbering companies as well as ranchers. The Interior Department manages the national parks, monuments, and wildlife refuges, as well as the Bureau of Land Management's extensive lands (national forests fall under the Department of Agriculture's jurisdiction).

money policies of the Federal Reserve Board after 1979 eventually tamed inflation, which dropped from 14 percent in 1980 to less than 2 percent in 1983. The Fed's high interest rates also choked off the nation's cash flow and provoked a severe recession in 1981–1982, with unemployment reaching above 10 percent. However, the economy revived again in 1983 and was growing at a robust annual rate of 6.8 percent by 1984. Rising confidence in the economy helped Reagan soar to reelection over his opponent, Carter's former vice president Walter Mondale.

An Embattled Environment

The 1980 election marked the sharpest turn ever in American environmental policy. The new administration reversed two decades of growing bipartisan consensus on the need for greater protection of the environment. Reagan instead supported corporations' demands for fewer environmental regulations and easier access to natural resources on public lands. The president ridiculed the idea of preserving wilderness for its own sake. He even claimed in 1980 that "trees cause more pollution than automobiles do."

The officials Reagan appointed to oversee these lands and assume responsibility for protecting them had little respect for the agencies they ran. Critics described the situation as "foxes guarding the chicken house." The officials openly disdained environmentalists, including those in the moderate wing of the Republican party. Anne Gorsuch at the Environmental Protection Agency (EPA), Robert Burford at the Bureau of Land Management (BLM), and John Crowell in charge of the Forest Service explicitly rewrote regulations to favor private enterprise. They sold grazing, logging, and mining rights on public lands at prices far below market value, despite their stated commitment to market economics.

Gorsuch, Burford, and Crowell were moderates, however, in comparison to James Watt, the new Secretary of the Interior who controlled national parks and wildlife refuges. A native of Wheatland, Wyoming, Watt declared that only two kinds of people lived in the United States: "liberals and Americans." Watt was also a Christian fundamentalist. In his Senate confirmation hearings, he suggested that the nation had little need for long-term public land management because Christ would soon be returning and the known world would pass away—an interpretation of stewardship that not even all fundamentalists shared, much less the broader American public. Watt's abrasive personal style eventually alienated even the White House, and he resigned in 1983.

The administration's reversal of federal environmental policies alarmed a wide range of citizens and stimulated a powerful backlash. Membership in environmental organizations soared, in such traditional groups as the Sierra Club and the Audubon Society, as well as in more radical ones, such as Greenpeace. Most Americans wanted to breathe cleaner air, drink safe water, and make recreational use of national parks, national forests, and BLM lands. In much of the rural West, jobs in the recreation industry outnumbered those in the logging, mining, and ranching businesses. In 1989 concern intensified when the oil tanker *Exxon Valdez* ran aground in Prince William Sound in Alaska, coating 1,000 miles of pristine coastline with crude oil.

A Society Divided

As the Reagan administration eased corporate access to the nation's natural resources, the disparity between rich and poor expanded further. Whereas most Americans' real wages (wages after inflation is factored in) declined, the professional classes fared well, and the wealthiest citizens gained enormously. For example, the salary of an average corporate chief executive officer was forty times greater than that of a typical factory worker in 1980; by 1989, it was ninety-three times greater. The top 1 percent of American families now possessed more assets than the bottom 90 percent—a ratio typical of Third World nations.

A series of corporate mergers and consolidations further enriched well-off Americans, as did financial speculation and manipulation on Wall Street. *Business Week* wrote of a "Casino Economy" in which insider trading and leveraged buyouts (business takeovers financed by debt) created paper wealth rather than actual products. This explosion of wealth at the top fueled an emerging culture of extravagance, reminiscent of similar trends in the late nineteenth century and in the 1920s. Newly identified "yuppies" (young urban professionals) embodied the drive for material acquisition, in contrast to the anticonsumerist inclinations of the late 1960s and early 1970s. Jerry Rubin, a member of the anarchist "yippies" in the 1960s, once dropped dollar bills onto the floor of the New York Stock Exchange—which traders scurried madly to grab—to dramatize the stock market's pursuit of profit. By the 1980s, however, Rubin was working as an investment banker. Ronald and Nancy Reagan were older but shared similar values. They relished lavish amenities like those made popular on the television shows *Dynasty*, *Dallas*, and *Lifestyles of the Rich and Famous*.

As the affluence gap widened, the broad middle class watched its job security slip. Early in the decade, the recession had prompted factory shutdowns and mass layoffs. More than a million industrial jobs disappeared in 1982 alone. Manufacturers' decisions to keep moving plants abroad for cheaper labor only worsened the situation. Although the 1980s saw the creation of 20 million new jobs, most of these were in the nonunionized service sector and offered low pay and few benefits.

The poorest Americans fared badly in the 1980s. The bottom tenth saw their already meager incomes decline by another 10 percent. In 1986 a full-time worker at minimum wage earned $6,700 per year—almost $4,000 short of the poverty level for a family of four. Homelessness worsened in cities as the government cut funding for welfare and institutional care for the mentally ill while housing costs rose. More than 1 million people lived on the streets, one-fifth of them still employed. One out of eight children went hungry and 20 percent lived in poverty, including 50 percent of black children. These Americans received minimal

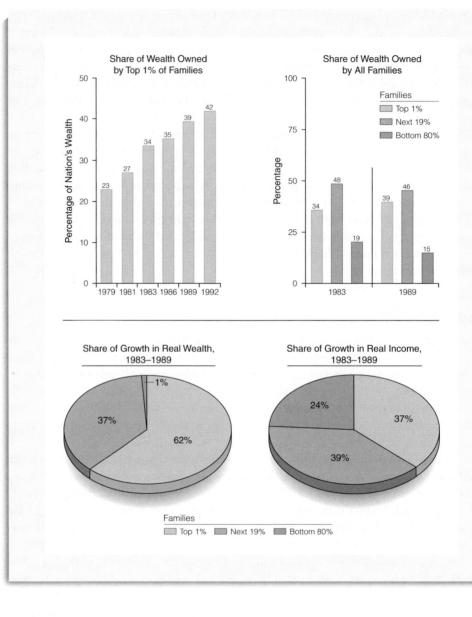

■ **FIGURE 28.1**
UNEQUAL DISTRIBUTION OF WEALTH AND INCOME   The 1980s were excellent years for wealthy Americans. The "trickle-down" effect touted by some Reagan administration officials—predicting that greater wealth accumulation among the rich would trickle down to the less affluent—had little impact.

sympathy from the nation's political leaders. By contrast, Congress and the White House provided large federal subsidies to "needy" businesses such as the Chrysler Corporation and the savings and loan industry.

Despite Reagan's record, 40 percent of union household members and 50 percent of all blue-collar workers cast their ballots for this staunch opponent of unions. Why? Part of the explanation lies in the decline of working-class voting during the 1970s. Disillusioned with a political process they saw as corrupt, numerous workers neglected to go to the polls on voting day. Many of those who did vote decided that the Democratic party had become increasingly co-opted by cultural **liberalism** and no longer spoke for the working class. Reagan's charisma and appeal to patriotism also attracted many citizens who might once have voted for their economic interests instead. Finally, white Americans increasingly defined their political loyalties on the basis of social and cultural issues—such as opposition to abortion, homosexuality, and affirmative action—rather than economic interests. Conservative Christians, in particular, strongly supported the Republican cause.

Cultural Conflict

One of the nation's foremost religious figures, Reverend Pat Robertson, controlled the Christian Broadcasting Network and ran unsuccessfully for the 1988 Republican presidential nomination. Like other social conservatives of this era, he promoted "family values" and traditional gender roles. Robertson went so far as to declare that feminism "encourages women to leave their husbands, kill their children [and] practice witchcraft." In contrast, author Susan Faludi wrote the 1991 best-seller *Backlash* about opposition to the women's movement. She became an important critic of gender roles in American society and how they limit people's life experiences and possibilities. In contrast to Robertson, Faludi concluded, "All women are feminists. It's just a matter of time and encouragement."

> *Americans argued primarily about issues that had come to the fore during the social movements of the 1960s and 1970s.*

Throughout the 1980s, Americans embroiled themselves in a contentious debate about values. Their society had changed in the previous generation in ways that some citizens disdained but others applauded. Americans argued primarily about issues that had come to the fore during the social movements of the 1960s and 1970s: sexuality, gender roles, the place of religion in public life, and multiculturalism. These often bitter "culture wars" dominated talk shows and newspaper editorial pages throughout much of the last two decades of the twentieth century.

The Rise of the Religious Right

Some of the Americans most troubled by the state of American society were conservative white Protestants, disproportionately from the South. Along with conservative Catholics, they bemoaned the post-1960s shift in mainstream values away from respect for traditional authorities—the church, political leaders, and the military—and toward freer sexual expression and general self-indulgence. What the nation needed, they believed, was a return to reverence for God. The growth of Christian fundamentalism paralleled rising religious fundamentalism around the globe, whether among Jews in Israel, Hindus in India, or Muslims in Iran and the Arab Middle East. For all their differences, religious people in these cultures shared a common quest: preserving spiritual purity and cultural traditions in an increasingly secular, integrated world.

Conservative Christians were not a fringe group. As many as 45 million Americans—20 percent of the population—identified themselves as fundamentalist Christians in 1980. In combination with a similar number of Catholics, they represented a vast potential force in American politics. And their ranks were growing, while membership in the more liberal mainline Protestant denominations, such as the Presbyterians and Episcopalians, declined steadily after the 1960s.

Conservative Christians mobilized in the 1980 campaign to support Reagan's candidacy. Critics noted that Reagan himself attended church only occasionally and seemed an indifferent father. They contrasted the divorced candidate with his born-again, Sunday-school–teaching opponent, Jimmy Carter. But Reagan's conservative views on abortion and gay rights and his support for school prayer resonated with fundamentalists. They flocked to the Republican party and to new right-wing religious organizations, such as the Moral Majority, founded in 1979 in Lynchburg, Virginia, by Reverend Jerry Falwell. More than 60 million people each week watched—and many sent money to—"televangelists," including Falwell, Robertson, and Jim Bakker.

Suffusing the GOP with a distinctly southern, grassroots flavor, the religious right also highlighted a major faultline in the modern Republican party: the tension between social conservatives, who emphasized community and tradition, and free marketeers, who promoted entrepreneurial capitalism. In its quest for profits, unrestrained capitalism had no inherent respect

Religion and Politics in the 1980s

In 1979, Baptist minister Jerry Falwell founded the Moral Majority in Lynchburg, Virginia. The organization represented the growing engagement of conservative evangelical Christians in American politics, and Falwell emerged as the most prominent figure of the new religious right. However, not all Christians were conservative. Robert McAfee Brown, a Presbyterian minister and theologian, represented more liberal elements of the church that understood both the Bible and the problems of American society differently than Falwell.

The Goals of the Moral Majority (1980) by Jerry Falwell

We must reverse the trend America finds herself in today. Young people. . . have learned to disrespect the family as God established it. They have been educated in a public-school system that is permeated with secular humanism. They have been taught that the Bible is just another book of literature. They have been taught that there are no absolutes in our

Before he became involved in politics, Jerry Falwell had already made a name for himself as a prominent preacher in his hometown of Lynchburg, Virginia, as the senior minister of the large Thomas Road Baptist Church and the founder of Liberty University. His organization, the Moral Majority, became the most well-known conservative evangelical Christian organization of the 1980s.

William E. Savro/*New York Times*, Nov. 11, 1980

for tradition. Indeed, it could bring unwelcome changes, as Rustbelt industrial workers had discovered when their employers moved south and overseas. Marrying Jesus to the market proved difficult: should the state play a minimal role in the economy and society, as free-market libertarians believed, or should it monitor personal behavior, as social conservatives implied?

Gender and sexuality issues particularly aroused the ire of religious conservatives. They blamed feminism for weakening male authority in the family and for increasing divorce rates. A growing antiabortion movement gained national visibility by 1980, and religious conservatives opposed Americans' slowly increasing acceptance of gays and lesbians. Dismayed by the prevalence of casual sexual relationships in the 1970s, church conservatives urged abstinence on young Americans.

The heyday of the sexual revolution ended in the early 1980s, when researchers identified the human immunodeficiency virus (HIV), which causes acquired immunodeficiency syndrome (AIDS). The deadly epidemic spread swiftly through the gay male communities of San Francisco and New York as a result of unprotected sex. AIDS continued to spread during the 1990s and beyond, among gays and heterosexuals, both in the United States and abroad—especially in such places as China, southern Africa, and Russia. New drugs slowed the onset of actual AIDS in many HIV-infected Americans while scientists continued the frustrating quest for a cure.

Yet another epidemic swept through the United States during the 1980s, striking impoverished urban neighborhoods especially hard. The culprit was crack cocaine. Powerfully addicworld today. . . . These same young people have been reared under the influence of a government that has taught them socialism and welfarism. . . .

I personally feel that the home and the family are still held in reverence by the vast majority of the American public. I believe there is still a vast number of Americans who love their country, are patriotic, and are willing to sacrifice for her. I remember that time when it was positive to be patriotic. . . . I remember as a boy. . . when the band struck up "The Stars and Stripes Forever," we stood and goose pimples would run all over me. . . .

It is now time to take a stand on certain moral issues. . . . We must stand against the Equal Rights Amendment, the feminist revolution, and the homosexual revolution. . . .

Americans have been silent much too long. We have stood by and watched as American power and influence have been systematically weakened in every sphere of the world. . . .

The hope of reversing the trends of decay in our republic now lies with the Christian public in America. We cannot expect help from the liberals. They certainly are not going to call our nation back to righteousness and neither are

the pornographers, the smut peddlers, and those who are corrupting our youth.

The Politics of the Bible (1982) by Robert McAfee Brown

In Christian terms, and I think in terms with which all Jews could also agree, my real complaint about the Moral Majority's intrusion of the Bible into American politics, is that they are not biblical enough. . . .

The Moral Majority's biblically inspired political agenda involves a very selective, very partial, and therefore very distorted use of the Bible. They have isolated a set of concerns that they say get to the heart of what is wrong with America—homosexuality, abortion, and pornography. . . .

Take the issue of homosexuality. If one turns to the scriptures as a whole, to try to come up with their central concerns, homosexuality is going to be very low on such a list even if indeed it makes the list at all. There are perhaps seven very ambiguous verses in the whole biblical canon that even allude to it. . . . [But there are] hundreds and hundreds of places where the scriptures are dealing over and over again with question of social justice,

the tendency of the rich to exploit the poor, the need for all of us to have a commitment to the hungry, . . . [and] the dangers of national idolatry, that is to say, making the nation into God, accepting uncritically whatever we have to do as a nation against other nations. . . .

When one looks over the agenda of the Moral Majority there is absolutely no mention of such things. . . . We seem to be living in two different worlds, reading two different books.

Questions

1. Which specific issues in American society most trouble Jerry Falwell? What specifically about "liberals" does he seem most unhappy about?

2. What does Robert McAfee Brown find most unpersuasive about Jerry Falwell's use of the Bible to understand American society and its problems?

3. Which of these two interpretations do you find most persuasive, and why? ■

Source: Irwin Unger and Robert R. Tomes, *American Issues*, 2nd ed. (Prentice-Hall, 1999), vol. 2, pp. 362–364, 375–377.

tive, it contributed to gang violence and record homicide rates in several cities. Drug-related convictions skyrocketed, stimulating a boom in prison building, a doubling of the nation's inmate population, and new police special weapons and tactics (SWAT) teams to deal with heavily armed drug operators.

Dissenters Push Back

The liberal and radical reform energies that had percolated in the late 1960s and early 1970s did not evaporate entirely in the conservative 1980s. Nuclear threats engaged activists from both the peace and environmental movements. The accidents at Three Mile Island (1979) and Chernobyl (1986) intensified public anxieties about the dangers of nuclear energy and nuclear weapons. The sharp increases in both Soviet and U.S. nuclear arsenals alarmed residents in those countries and across Europe, where many of the missiles were located. The broad-based nuclear freeze movement that emerged in the United States and western Europe in the early 1980s encouraged arms control negotiations that would bear fruit a few years later.

Racial justice remained a primary concern for Americans of color and liberal and leftist activists, particularly in light of the Republican administration's opposition to affirmative action. Determined to honor the foremost leader of the civil rights movement, antiracists convinced Congress in 1983 to designate Martin Luther King Jr.'s birthday a national holiday. By 1985 a robust antiapartheid movement successfully campaigned to reduce U.S. investments in racially segregated South Africa. Perhaps the most prominent face of left-leaning politics in the decade was that of Reverend Jesse Jackson, a former aide to Martin Luther King Jr. Jackson sought the Democratic nomination for president in 1984 and 1988, winning a handful of primaries in 1988 with his multiracial Rainbow Coalition. Jackson's candidacy encouraged several million African Americans to register to vote for the first time.

> *Gays and lesbians remained the only Americans against whom tens of millions of their fellow citizens openly believed it acceptable to discriminate.*

Gay rights advocates also raised their voices in the 1980s. Faced with the twin scourge of AIDS and homophobic violence, homosexuals and their heterosexual supporters lobbied for the inclusion of sexual orientation as a category of discrimination in civil rights laws. Others took to the streets, organized by the militant organization AIDS Coalition to Unleash Power (ACT-UP). In October 1987, nearly half a million Americans marched in Washington in support of gay rights. A few widely admired figures, such as tennis champion Martina Navratilova, publicly acknowledged their homosexuality, helping others to view this sexual orientation as acceptable rather than deviant. By the end of the 1980s, the record was mixed. Gays and lesbians remained the only Americans against whom tens of millions of their fellow citizens openly believed it acceptable to discriminate, but the rights of homosexuals, nonetheless, had much wider support than ever before.

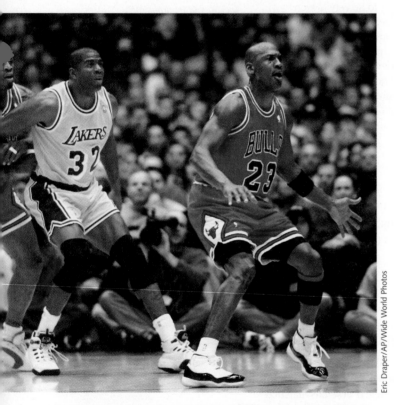

Eric Draper/AP/Wide World Photos

■ While immigrants brought their own distinctive cultures to the United States, American popular culture spread abroad. The broadcast of National Basketball Association (NBA) games in dozens of other countries helped basketball climb to being the world's second most popular game (after soccer). Personable stars like Earvin "Magic" Johnson of the Los Angeles Lakers and particularly Michael Jordan of the Chicago Bulls became popular icons around the world.

The New Immigration

For two decades after the restrictive immigration law of 1924, the flow of newcomers from abroad had slowed to a trickle. The trickle became a stream again after World War II, and then legislation in 1965 opened the gates even wider. As a result, a wave of new immigrants, 3.3 million in the 1960s and 4.5 million in the 1970s, hit the United States. In the 1980s 7.3 million people entered the country legally, along with a similar number without documentation.

These newcomers brought an unprecedented cultural and ethnic diversity. Only 10 percent of the most recent arrivals in the United States were Europeans. Forty percent came instead from Asia—particularly China, the Philippines, and South Korea—and 50 percent from Latin America and the Caribbean, particularly Mexico. From 1965 to 1995, 7 million Latinos and 5 million Asians moved to the United States.

The new immigrants came for the same reasons their predecessors had. Many were fleeing political and religious persecution in their home countries, but most sought new economic opportunity. A small number, primarily from South Korea and Hong Kong, arrived with some assets that helped them get started in business. However, most came with few resources and took what work they could find in garment sweatshops, on farms, as domestic servants and janitors, and as gardeners. These immigrants willingly endured profound hardship to build better lives for their families. They also rekindled the nation's long-standing cultural diversity, especially in Sunbelt cities from Miami, Florida, to San Diego, California. In 1981 citizens of San Antonio elected Henry Cisneros as the first Mexican American mayor of a major city. In Los Angeles, one-third of residents were foreign born by 1990.

Most Americans had foreign-born ancestors who had come to the United States with the same dreams that motivated the newest arrivals. Still, the non-European origins of the latest immigrants troubled some white citizens. Conservatives, in particular, worried about the growing diversity of American society and feared a decline of the Eurocentric culture they had grown up with. They were also anxious that poor immigrants might drain taxpayers' dollars by winding up on welfare. The Immigration and Naturalization Service (INS) stepped up patrols of the 2,000-mile U.S. border with Mexico to limit the rising number of undocumented Mexican workers heading north. By the early 1990s, the INS was apprehending and expelling 1.7 million undocumented workers every year.

America' Move to the Sunbelt, 1970–1981

The End of the Cold War

For Americans, the greatest surprise of the 1980s was the warming of U.S.-Soviet relations after 1985. Few imagined such a scenario during Reagan's first two years in office, when his administration became the first in four decades not to collaborate on nuclear arms control with the USSR. But in the Soviet Union, the rise to power of Communist party reformer Mikhail Gorbachev permanently changed the face of international politics. The American president finally agreed to work toward the common goal of reducing tensions between the two superpowers. Reagan eventually traveled to Moscow, embraced Gorbachev in front of Lenin's tomb, and announced that the Soviets had changed.

At the same time, the Reagan administration stumbled badly at home when a scandal involving Iran and the Nicaraguan counterrevolutionaries (Contras) came to light in 1986. The disaster revealed a secret foreign policy apparatus and a president out of touch with the daily governance process. Dramatic events in Europe then unfolded with little input from the administrations of either Reagan or George H. W. Bush, his successor in the White House. In 1989 eastern Europeans tore down the Berlin Wall and ended Soviet rule in their countries. Two years later, the Soviet Union unraveled into its separate components, Russia being the largest. The end of the Cold War enabled Bush to focus on the Middle East, where an international force drove Iraq out of occupied Kuwait and reestablished the status quo in that oil-rich region.

From Cold War to Détente

By the 1980s, the USSR's state-run economy was creaking to a halt. It simply could not provide the consumer products that Soviet citizens had learned about from the world outside their borders. Events further weakened the authority of the Soviet government. The USSR's occupation of Afghanistan became a quagmire resembling the United States' disastrous involvement in Vietnam, and the last Soviet troops finally withdrew in 1989. Initial government efforts to cover up the nuclear accident at Chernobyl only worsened matters, revealing the costs of corrupt communist rule. Nationalist movements for independence in the Baltic states, the Caucasus region, and central Asia gathered momentum. In his six years in power (1985–1991), Gorbachev tried to preserve the Soviet system by reforming it through *glasnost* (greater political liberty) and *perestroika* (economic restructuring allowing some private enterprise). However, his government proved unable to control the forces for change that it had helped unleash.

Reagan's primary role in ending the Cold War was to support Gorbachev's quest for change within the Soviet Union. To that end, Reagan moved from confrontational rhetoric to pursuing a policy of détente. Gorbachev became head of the Soviet Communist party in 1985, at the start of Reagan's second term. The American president had already built up the U.S. military and was now thinking about his place in history. He wanted to leave office having earned a reputation as a peacemaker.

Beneath Reagan's strident rhetoric about national military strength ran a streak of radical idealism, including a desire to eliminate the threat of nuclear warfare. The Soviet downing of a Korean Air Lines civilian jet in 1983 reminded him and others of the tragic costs of making mistakes with weapons. Once he felt convinced of Gorbachev's seriousness about internal reform and rapprochement with the United States, Reagan took action. In 1987 the two leaders signed the Intermediate Nuclear Force (INF) treaty. The agreement removed short-range and intermediate-range missiles from Europe and enabled each side to conduct on-site verification of the other side's compliance. The INF treaty marked the first actual reduction in the total number of nuclear weapons stored in the two nations' arsenals.

The Iran-Contra Scandal

Failures elsewhere offset Reagan's success with the Russians. His administration suffered its worst damage when it tried through illegal means to solve two foreign policy challenges with one stroke. Its main strategy consisted of linking a problem in the Middle East with one in Central America.

Revolutionary fervor intensified in the Middle East after the 1979 Iranian revolution, and hostage-taking and terrorism—the "poor man's nuclear bomb"—proliferated. In 1986 Americans bombed the Libyan capital of Tripoli in retaliation for apparent Libyan involvement in the killing of two U.S. soldiers in Germany. In 1988 things took an even nastier turn when an American warship in the Persian Gulf killed 290 civilians by shooting down an Iranian airliner, apparently by mistake. In revenge, pro-Iranian agents exploded a bomb on Pan Am Flight 109 over Lockerbie, Scotland, before the end of the year, killing eleven on the ground and 259 aboard the plane, including thirty-five students from Syracuse University.

Islamic revolutionaries also threatened moderate Arab leaders and assassinated Egyptian president Anwar Sadat in 1981. Lebanon became the center of a radical anti-Israeli campaign to seize Americans as hostages, especially after the United States' 1983 engagement against Muslim forces in the civil war there. Despite his 1980 campaign promise never to negotiate with terrorists, Reagan approved the illegal sale of U.S. arms to Iran in return for the freeing of a handful of hostages held by pro-Iranian radicals in Lebanon.

Events were heating up in Central America as well. The CIA-created Contras failed to overturn the new Sandinista government in Nicaragua. Even though the Contras lacked public support in Nicaragua and the United States, the president and his advisers were determined to keep them afloat. But they had a problem: how to fund the effort. Most Americans did not share Reagan's enthusiasm for the Contras and feared greater U.S. military involvement in Central America. Congress passed the Boland Amendments, restricting aid to the Nicaraguan counterrevolutionaries. Faced with their chief's expressed desire to shore up the Contra cause, the president's men found an alternative solution.

The National Security Council (NSC) established a secret operation run by staff member Lieutenant Colonel Oliver North. Free from public or congressional oversight, North worked closely with CIA director William Casey. North and his colleagues solicited funds for the Contras from wealthy, conservative Americans and from sympathetic foreign governments, including Saudi Arabia and Taiwan. Then North hit on what he called the "neat idea" of "using the Ayatollah Khomeini's money to support the Nicaraguan freedom fighters." Iran desperately needed weapons for its war against neighboring Iraq (1980–1988), so North and his colleagues started diverting profits to the Contras from new sales of U.S. Army property to Teheran.

The NSC's action was illegal: it sold U.S. government property without authorization from the Pentagon, and it broke U.S. laws banning aid to the Contras. When news of the operation finally leaked out in November 1986, it shocked the nation. What did the president know, and when did he know it? The old Watergate question about Richard Nixon came to the fore again. Reagan called North a "national hero" but claimed ignorance of any illegal activities, including the diversion of funds from Iranian arms sales to the Nicaraguan rebels.

But in early 1987, 90 percent of Americans did not believe Reagan was telling all he knew. His job approval ratings dropped from 67 percent to 46 percent. The first round of memoirs by former aides also appeared in the final years of his administration, revealing an isolated president out of touch with the government he nominally headed. For example, the former actor breezily admitted that he was happiest when "each morning I get a piece of paper that tells me what I do all day long."

A Global Policeman?

Despite running a bruising presidential campaign in 1988, Reagan's vice president, George H. W. Bush, proved cautious once in office. Hemmed in by a Democratic-controlled Congress, he had what his chief of staff called a "limited agenda" at home. His most enduring domestic action came with his 1991 appointment of archconservative Clarence Thomas, an African American lawyer from Georgia, to fill the seat of retiring Supreme Court justice Thurgood Marshall. Only forty-three years old and with little experience as a judge, Thomas was chosen because of his conservative views and his race.

TABLE 28-3			
The Election of 1988			
Candidate	Political Party	Popular Vote (%)	Electoral Vote
George H. W. Bush	Republican	53.4	426
Michael S. Dukakis	Democratic	45.6	111

The Senate narrowly confirmed him, 52–48, after contentious hearings in which a former aide, Anita Hill, accused Thomas of sexual harassment.

DOCUMENT

George H.W. Bush, Inaugural Address (January 1989)

"I much prefer foreign affairs," the president once confided in his diary. Some of the most dramatic events of the twentieth century unfolded during his presidency. Poles, Czechs, and Hungarians—encouraged by Gorbachev's promise not to intervene militarily in other Warsaw Pact nations—peacefully overthrew their communist rulers in 1989. East Germans did the same. The Berlin Wall—the twenty-eight-year-old symbol of Cold War tensions—finally toppled on November 8. Three months later, anti-apartheid leader Nelson Mandela walked out of the South African prison where he had been held for twenty-seven years. The white supremacist government there agreed to hold the first elections in which all South Africans could vote. The Baltic states of Lithuania, Latvia, and Estonia seceded from the USSR in 1990 and 1991. After a failed coup attempt by Communist hard-liners in August 1991, the Soviet Union broke into its sixteen constituent states. Russian president Boris Yeltsin replaced Gorbachev as the major figure in Moscow.

In Panama, under the brutal leadership of Manuel Noriega, tensions grew between the Panamanian Defense Forces (PDF) and U.S. soldiers based in the Canal Zone. Noriega deepened his lucrative role as an intermediary in smuggling Colombian cocaine into the United States. Meanwhile, the crack-cocaine epidemic tightened its grip in poor American neighborhoods. Rising popular concern about crack-related violence increased Americans' willingness to take action against Noriega. When the dictator overturned Panamanian election results that went against him and further confrontations erupted between American and Panamanian soldiers, Bush decided to step in.

In December 1989, 24,000 U.S. troops invaded the small Central American nation. They crushed the PDF, and thousands of civilians died in the crossfire. Noriega eventually surrendered and was brought to Miami, where he was convicted of drug trafficking and imprisoned.

Developments in the Middle East provoked the most important move of the George H. W. Bush administration: the initiation of the Persian Gulf War of 1991. In 1990 Iraq invaded tiny, neighboring, oil-rich Kuwait, annexing it as Iraq's "nineteenth province." With Americans and their Japanese and European allies dependent on Middle Eastern oil, Bush declared the invasion unacceptable. He rushed more than 200,000 troops to Saudi Arabia in "Operation Desert Shield" to discourage further aggression by Iraqi leader Saddam Hussein. At the same time, the United Nations slapped economic sanctions on Iraq.

Within three months, Bush shifted his attention to liberating Kuwait. He doubled the number of U.S. troops in the region to 430,000. He also gained the support of the UN, which demanded Iraqi withdrawal by January 15, 1991. The U.S. Congress backed him as well, voting to support any actions necessary to drive Iraq out of Kuwait. Bush went on the offensive because he faced a shrinking window of opportunity. He had wide international support, including troops from several Arab nations, but growing clashes in Jerusalem between Israelis and Palestinians threatened to break up this alliance by rekindling Arab anger at Israel.

Bush's Early Response in the Persian Gulf War

■ **MAP 28.2**
THE SOVIET BLOC DISSOLVES   No change in world politics since World War II was greater than the collapse of the Soviet Union and its satellite states in eastern Europe. Eastern European countries soon sought membership in NATO and post-Communist Russia built closer relations with the United States and western Europe. The transition from socialist to capitalist economies was difficult, however, and many poorer citizens found daily life little easier than it had been before.

The Soviet Union and the Communist bloc in Eastern Europe dissolve

Former Union of Soviet Socialist Republics (USSR), dissolved 1991

Eastern European countries that overturned Communist rule, 1989–1990

On January 16, 1991, U.S.-led coalition forces began five and a half weeks of bombing against Iraq. Then, on February 25, coalition forces poured across the border from Saudi Arabia in "Operation Desert Storm." The offensive freed Kuwait and sent Iraqi troops in headlong retreat toward Baghdad. The Iraqis burned oil wells as they fell back, blanketing the battlefield in smoke. Four days later, Bush halted the U.S.-led advance, having restored Kuwaiti sovereignty. Saddam Hussein remained in power and later crushed uprisings by Iraqi dissidents. The politics of coalition warfare helped prohibit further U.S. action, for no Arabs wanted Americans ruling Iraq.

The Gulf War's outcome seemed to validate two strategic lessons that U.S. commanders had learned during the Vietnam War. The first was the importance of preserving absolute control of the media. During the Persian Gulf conflict, the Pentagon kept journalists away from most of the action to control the images that Americans saw of the fighting. The public viewed endless videos of "smart" bombs hitting their targets in Baghdad but none of the tens of thousands of Iraqi soldiers being slaughtered during their retreat from Kuwait. Second, General Colin Powell, the African American chair of the Joint Chiefs of Staff who emerged from the war as a national hero, insisted on marshaling overwhelmingly superior forces before going into battle, thus ensuring the success of the operation.

The Gulf War seemed to demonstrate a U.S. willingness to act as a global police force in the post–Cold War era. Bush claimed at a 1992 international environmental conference that, when it came to oil, "the American lifestyle is not negotiable." But the war also stimulated the further growth of anti-Americanism among Islamic revolutionaries, including Saudi-born Osama bin Laden; they considered it sacrilege for non-Muslim American soldiers to operate bases in Saudi Arabia, home to Mecca, Islam's holiest site.

MAP

The Middle East in the 1980s and 1990s

Conclusion

The Republican era of Ronald Reagan and George H. W. Bush reshaped American relations with the rest of the world, as well as politics and economics in the United States. Both sets of changes hinged on the elevation of individualism and market forces above communal values and government planning. The collective dreams represented by the Soviet experiment evaporated into history in these years, leaving capitalism unchallenged as a system of economic organization across most of the globe. U.S. military power stepped into the vacuum left by the Soviet demise, most visibly in the 1991 Persian Gulf War. But that military revival came at the cost of vast deficit spending and a sharp recession in 1991–1992, which paved the way for Bill Clinton's victory over Bush in the 1992 presidential campaign.

Sites to Visit

Digital Atlas of the United States, 1990
http://geogdata.csun.edu/USpage1.html
This site offers an overview of the geography and demography of the U.S. population in 1990.

Immigrant Fact Sheet, 1996
www.uscis.gov/graphics/shared/aboutus/statistics/110.htm
The U.S. Immigration and Naturalization Service posted this site with historical statistics about immigration into the United States, especially from 1981 to 1996.

Divining America: Religion and the National Culture
www.nhc.rtp.nc.us:8080/tserve/divam.htm
This site has essays by prominent historians on diverse aspects of the religious history of the United States.

Ronald Wilson Reagan
www.ipl.org/div/potus/rwreagan.html
The Internet Public Library maintains this site, which has essential information about Reagan and his presidential administration as well as his most important speeches.

National Security Archive at George Washington University
www.gwu.edu/~nsarchiv/

> This excellent site includes the most recent declassified documents on the making of U.S. foreign policy.

Cold War International History Project
http://www.wilsoncenter.org/
index.cfm?topic_id=1409&fuseaction=topics.home

> The Woodrow Wilson International Center for Scholars maintains this site, which offers newly released documents and up-to-date interpretive essays on the American-Soviet struggle.

Persian Gulf War
www.pbs.org/wgbh/pages/frontline/gulf/

> The Public Broadcasting System's *Frontline* series created this site with information about the Persian Gulf War, including oral histories of U.S. commanders and of Americans taken as prisoners of war.

For Further Reading

General

Frances FitzGerald, *Way Out There in the Blue: Reagan, Star Wars, and the End of the Cold War* (2000).

James Patterson, *Restless Giant: The United States from Watergate to Bush v. Gore* (2005).

Neil Postman, *Amusing Ourselves to Death: Public Discourse in the Age of Show Business* (1985).

Ronald Reagan, *Reagan, In His Own Hand: The Writings of Ronald Reagan That Reveal His Revolutionary Vision for America* (2001).

Michael Schaller, *Reckoning with Reagan: America and Its President in the 1980s* (1992).

Anticommunism Revived

James A. Bill, *The Eagle and the Lion: The Tragedy of American-Iranian Relations* (1988).

David Farber, *Taken Hostage: The Iran Hostage Crisis and America's First Encounter with Radical Islam* (2004).

Thomas Ferguson and Joel Rogers, eds., *The Hidden Election: Politics and Economics in the 1980 Presidential Campaign* (1981).

Walter LaFeber, *Inevitable Revolutions: The United States in Central America*, 2nd ed. (1993).

William E. Pemberton, *Exit with Honor: The Life and Presidency of Ronald Reagan* (1998).

Republican Rule at Home

Thomas Byrne Edsall and Mary D. Edsall, *Chain Reaction: The Impact of Race, Rights and Taxes on American Politics* (1991).

Barbara Ehrenreich, *The Worst Years of Our Lives: Irreverent Notes from a Decade of Greed* (1990).

J. R. McNeill, *Something New Under the Sun: An Environmental History of the Twentieth-Century World* (2000).

Kevin Phillips, *The Politics of Rich and Poor: Wealth and the American Electorate in the Reagan Aftermath* (1990).

Cultural Conflict

Todd Gitlin, *The Twilight of Common Dreams: Why America Is Wracked by Culture Wars* (1995).

Martin E. Marty and R. Scott Appleby, *The Glory and the Power: The Fundamentalist Challenge to the Modern World* (1992).

David M. Reimers, *Still the Golden Door: The Third World Comes to America*, 2nd ed. (1992).

Randy Shilts, *And the Band Played On: Politics, People and the AIDS Epidemic* (1987).

The End of the Cold War

Theodore Draper, *A Very Thin Line: The Iran-Contra Affairs* (1991).

John Robert Greene, *The Presidency of George Bush* (2000).

Dilip Hiro, *Desert Shield to Desert Storm: The Second Gulf War* (1992).

Michael J. Hogan, ed., *The End of the Cold War: Its Meanings and Implications* (1992).

For quizzes and other resources on these topics, go to www.longmanamericanhistory.com.

Post–Cold War America, 1991–2000

O N A COLD DECEMBER NIGHT IN 1997, TWENTY-THREE-YEAR-OLD JULIA BUTTERFLY HILL climbed onto a small platform that had been constructed 180 feet above ground in a giant redwood tree in a forest in Humboldt County, California. She remained there for two years, trespassing in an act of civil disobedience on the property of the Pacific Lumber Company, which was threatening to cut down the 1,000-year-old tree as part of its logging operations. Julia Hill had not planned to become an internationally famous environmental activist. She grew up in Arkansas, the daughter of an itinerant preacher. When friends invited the restless young woman to join them on a drive to California, she eagerly went along. "I had been on a journey, searching for my purpose in life," she recalled. "I ended up finding it in the redwoods."

Hill's spiritual connection to the forest drew her to political activism, and she joined Earth First!, an environmental group that was working to save the redwoods from the logging industry. She discovered that 97 percent of the old-growth redwoods had already been destroyed and that the rest were threatened by clear-cutting, toxins, and diesel fuel. Tree sitting was a strategy the Earth First! activists developed to protest the destruction of the trees.

Those two years were rough. The young woman survived rain and hail storms, 90-mile-per-hour winds that tossed the tiny platform into the air, and bone-chilling cold that turned her feet black. Friends and supporters provided her with food and other supplies using a rope pulley. She ate mostly raw fruits and vegetables, slept in a hammock, took sponge baths, and used a bucket for a toilet. She faced harassment from

■ Julia Butterfly Hill in the giant redwood tree she named "Luna."

the logging company and derision from some skeptics. But she also had a powerful network of supporters and celebrities who raised money, brought her food, and publicized her protest.

Hill's effort to save an ancient tree as old as the last millennium was conducted using the global technology of the new millennium. Critical to the success of her protest was her ability to communicate with the entire world from her treetop perch. She set up an Internet Web site on the Internet visited by people from across the globe. She used a solar-powered cell phone to speak with radio stations, schools, rallies, religious groups, reporters, and talk-show hosts. The lumber company also used state-of-the-art technology in its efforts to stymie her protest, cutting down trees to make them fall in her direction, flying helicopters to hover noisily over her head, and using air horns to keep her awake at night.

The president of Pacific Lumber, John Campbell, eventually came to the tree to negotiate with Hill, and they made a deal. The company agreed never to cut down the tree or other trees in a 2.9-acre buffer zone. Hill agreed to come down. For her civil disobedience, she paid a $50,000 fine, contributed by supporters, which the court designated to Humboldt State University for forestry research.

Activists such as Julia Butterfly Hill addressed political concerns through personal beliefs and direct action. They were part of social movements that evolved out of a century of such protests. In the 1990s, the issues had reached a global scale. Internationally, Cold War power struggles gave way to other issues: regional and civil wars, ethnic strife, the environment and global warming, trade and labor relations, and terrorism.

In the United States, the economy expanded throughout the 1990s. Increasing numbers of Americans invested in the soaring stock market, many for the first time. The crime rate declined. Yet the strong economy also emboldened consumers to buy and use products and resources, such as huge gas-guzzling sport utility vehicles, with little concern for their environmental impact.

In national politics, the rifts between liberals and conservatives that had opened up in the 1960s persisted. Struggles over cultural issues such as abortion and gay rights polarized the political climate. In 1992 Democrats took back the White House, but in 1994 Republicans swept into control of Congress with a conservative agenda, hemming in President Bill Clinton, a Democrat of liberal social inclinations who, nonetheless, presided over the final destruction of the Aid to Families with Dependent Children (AFDC) program, the central feature of the national welfare system since the New Deal of the 1930s. In 2000 the Supreme Court decided one of the closest and most divisive elections in the nation's history, handing the White House to the Republican candidate, George W. Bush, son of the former president.

The post–Cold War era raised new questions about the role of the United States in the world. Americans no longer looked to Russia as a threat but to new international foes, especially terrorist networks operating outside the authority of particular countries. Within the nation, episodes of domestic terrorism, such as the bombing of a federal building in Oklahoma City and a series of school shootings by children, made Americans aware that dangers lurked within their previously safe havens.

The Economy: Global and Domestic

After the sharp recession of 1991–1992, by nearly all measures, the economy expanded in the 1990s. The stock market boomed, unemployment declined, and most Americans appeared to be better off financially at the end of the decade than at the beginning. But the overall growth of the economy did not benefit everyone, and many actually lost ground—especially those who lost jobs to mechanization, nonunionized workers who toiled for low wages under grim working conditions, and the nation's most vulnerable workers: poor single mothers, new immigrants, and unskilled people of color.

The Post–Cold War Economy

The end of the Cold War had a profound effect on the nation's economy. The demise of the Soviet Union put a final end to the arms race against a superpower foe and made cutting the defense budget politically acceptable. But the closing of defense-related plants in southern California, once the center of the nation's Cold War defense contracts that absorbed nearly a fifth of all federal defense dollars, devastated the regional economy. By the mid-1990s, half the workers in the southern California aerospace industry had been laid off.

While defense industries shrank, the technology sector of the economy expanded, opening up new opportunities for young computer experts and entrepreneurs and generating fortunes for corporate executives. At the same time, mergers of giant multinational companies concentrated wealth and power in an ever-smaller number of ever-larger corporations. In the last three years of the decade, mergers totaled $5 trillion. Media giants America Online and Time-Warner merged in 2000. In 2001 Nestlé bought Ralston-Purina for $10 billion. Many of the largest mergers crossed national boundaries, such as German automobile maker Daimler-Benz and U.S. Chrysler.

While corporations expanded, so did efforts to control their power. Microsoft initially lost an antitrust suit that ordered the computer software giant to be split into two companies. Microsoft appealed the ruling in 2001, and ultimately the Justice Department settled the suit with minor sanctions against the company. The controversial settlement generated opposition. Nine states that participated in the original suit refused to endorse the agreement, and calls for tougher penalties continued. In several states, civil suits against huge tobacco companies limited cigarette advertising and marketing and levied fines on tobacco companies totaling in the billions of dollars.

The nation's elite were not the only ones to capitalize on new entrepreneurial opportunities. The 1988 Indian Gaming Regulatory Act enabled Native Americans to build lucrative Las Vegas–style casinos on tribal lands, bringing new jobs and an estimated $4 billion a year to formerly impoverished communities. The Mashantucket Pequot east of Hartford, Connecticut, opened Foxwoods in 1992, and it quickly became the largest casino in the Western Hemisphere. The Oneida followed suit a few years later with the Turning Stone casino near Utica, New York. In Arizona casinos brought in $830 million a year. Some Indian casinos failed, however, and gambling always took a largely hidden toll in the losses of already poor local residents. Native Americans remained divided about the wisdom of trying to profit from America's growing inclination to take risks in hopes of winning big.

The Widening Gap Between Rich and Poor

In the last decade of the century, the bottom 60 percent of the population saw their real income decline, even as the economy boomed. Accumulated wealth—property and investments—was an even better measure of security and influence, and the top 1 percent of Americans owned more wealth than the bottom 90 percent combined. Microsoft chair Bill Gates alone was wealthier than the bottom 45 percent of all U.S. households together. Famed capitalist J. P. Morgan had maintained a century earlier that no corporate chieftain should earn more than twenty times what his workers were paid, but by 1980 a typical chief executive of a large U.S. company took home forty times the earnings of an average factory worker; by 1990 the ratio had grown to eighty-five times, and by 2004 it reached 431 times.

Miguel Gandert/CORBIS

■ Casino Sandia on the Sandia Pueblo in New Mexico. Many Native American communities across the country built gambling facilities on tribal lands. Although casinos brought needed income, they remained controversial.

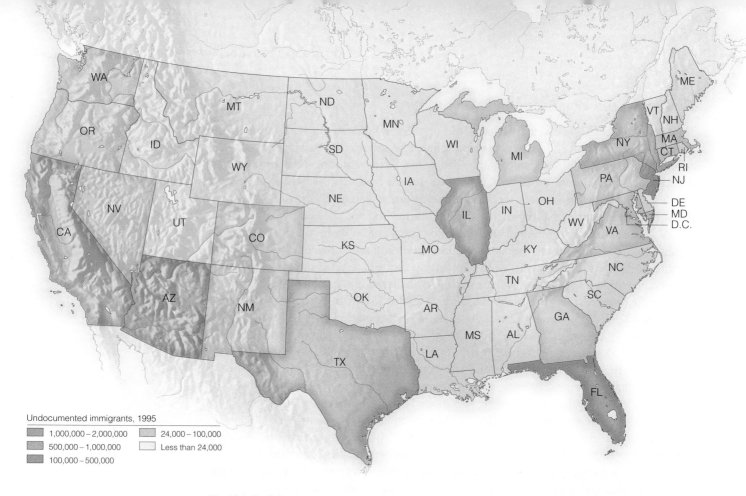

Undocumented immigrants, 1995

- 1,000,000 – 2,000,000
- 500,000 – 1,000,000
- 100,000 – 500,000
- 24,000 – 100,000
- Less than 24,000

■ **MAP 29.1**

STATES WITH LARGE NUMBERS OF UNDOCUMENTED IMMIGRANTS, 1995 Fully 77 percent of all undocumented immigrants entered the country legally, with visas in hand. During the 1990s, the total proportion of the foreign born in the United States, including those with and without legal status, increased from 9 to 11 percent, still less than the 15 percent in 1900. Immigrants paid $133 billion dollars annually in local, state, and federal taxes, and generated an annual contribution to the American economy in the range of $25 to $30 billion.

Although one-third of the nation's African Americans were part of the middle class, black families had fewer assets and resources, making their hold on middle-class status more precarious than that of their white peers. The poorest African Americans were concentrated in low-paying jobs, lacking the quality health care and education that would make social and economic mobility possible. Full-time employment did not necessarily mean an escape from poverty. Among fully employed black heads of households without a high school education, 40 percent of the women and 25 percent of the men did not earn enough to achieve economic self-sufficiency. Almost 50 percent of all black children lived in households below the poverty line, compared to 16 percent of white children. The rate of unemployment was more than twice as high for blacks as for whites.

Recent immigrants from Asia, Africa, and Latin America joined African Americans in jobs at the bottom of the economy. Despite the controversy over illegal immigration, a quarter of a million undocumented workers toiled in the fields of agribusiness. At the same time, 2 percent of able-bodied citizens were in jail, nearly half of them black, because of the arrest and incarceration policies of the "war on drugs" that hit minority communities particularly hard. Prisoners were often required to work while incarcerated. Convicts provided data entry, packed golf balls, and filled a wide array of jobs for less than minimum wage, and most of their earnings went back to the government. These and other workers at the bottom of the labor force gained little or nothing from the economic boom of the 1990s.

Labor Unions

Low-wage workers in the service industries had one advantage over laborers working for multinational corporations: their jobs could not be exported. Many service workers organized successfully for better wages and working conditions. In 2000, for example, striking janitors of Service Employees International Union Local 1877 in Los Angeles achieved a wage increase of 26 percent, raising their hourly pay from less than $8 to more than $10. This was a tremendous triumph for a union whose membership was 98 percent immigrant: 80 percent Central Americans, more than half women, and all of them poor.

Other service workers also won improved contracts. Unionized hotel workers in San Francisco negotiated a five-year contract that increased pay for the lowest-paid workers, room cleaners and dishwashers, by 25 percent, from $12 to $15 an hour. In Las Vegas, African American hotel worker Hattie Canty helped organize 40,000 employees of large casino hotels. Yatta Staples went out on the picket line in front of the Minneapolis hotel where she worked as a waitress, telling reporters, "I'll stay here as long as it takes." In the summer of 1997, 185,000 Teamsters went on strike against the United Parcel Service and won an improved contract with higher wages and benefits for part-time as well as full-time workers.

Strikes did little to benefit nonunionized workers, especially undocumented immigrants, and sweatshop laborers both inside and outside the United States. There were some attempts to improve working conditions for those most exploited by the global economy. In April 1997, representatives from clothing manufacturers, human rights groups, and labor organizations drafted an agreement that tried to

M. Sofronski/Sipa Press

■ Sweatshops like this one in the 1990s resemble those of a century earlier. Immigrant women labor in garment factories, working long hours in difficult conditions for meager wages.

improve conditions for garment workers around the world. Companies that agreed to the voluntary pact would limit work weeks to sixty hours, with a maximum of twelve hours of overtime. The companies had to pay "at least the minimum wage required by local law or the prevailing industry wage, whichever is higher." The pact forbade children under fifteen to work and contained policies protecting workers from harassment and unsafe working environments.

Tolerance and Its Limits

Racial discrimination had eased over the course of the twentieth century, but persistent inequalities of power and economic opportunity continued to disadvantage Americans of color, who remained disproportionately poor, in prison, and on welfare. The economic downturn of the early 1990s widened the chasm between affluent white and poor nonwhite Americans. Highly publicized incidents of police brutality directed against Americans of color generated protests and, occasionally, violence. Nevertheless, there were signs that Americans were becoming more tolerant of one another and more willing to accept and even appreciate their diversity.

"We Can All Get Along"

Shortly after midnight on March 3, 1991, police pulled over Rodney King, an African American motorist, after a high-speed chase on a Los Angeles freeway. The four officers dragged the unarmed black man from his car and kicked and beat him with their batons for fifteen minutes. A bystander recorded the beating on videotape, which was broadcast repeatedly on national television, sparking outrage among Americans of all races.

At the highly publicized trial in April 1992, defense lawyers for the police officers argued that King, who was clearly cowering on the videotape, was resisting arrest and that the police responded appropriately. The jury of ten whites, one Asian, and one Latino acquitted the officers. The acquittal ignited five days of rioting in the African American community of South Central Los Angeles, leaving fifty-eight people dead and $1 billion in property destroyed. Community leaders called for calm; even Rodney King implored the public: "We can all get along. We've just got to." Months later, a federal court in Los Angeles convicted two of the officers involved in the beating of violating King's civil rights—too late to avert the violence that erupted after the initial verdict.

Of the fifty-eight people who died in the violence, eighteen were Latino, twenty-six were black, ten were white, and two were Asian. Of the 4,000 businesses that were destroyed, most belonged to Latinos and Koreans. Perpetrators of the violence, as well as the victims, came from all racial groups. Antonia Hernandez, president of the Mexican American Legal Defense and Educational Fund, noted, "The hardest part is rebuilding the spirit of the city—what holds us together as Angelinos. It's the rebuilding of trust. . . . It's connecting communities that have never been connected." Several community groups came together in an effort to ease tensions, including the Japanese American Citizens League, Chinese for Affirmative Action, and the League of United Latin American Citizens.

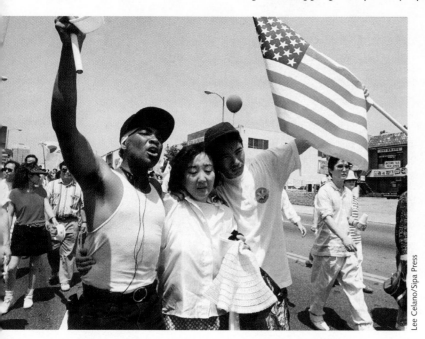

Lee Celano/Sipa Press

■ In the aftermath of the violent uprising that followed the acquittal of police officers in the beating of motorist Rodney King, Koreans and African Americans in Los Angeles express their solidarity, hoping to heal the wounds and divisions that had torn apart their city.

Values in Conflict

Many citizens worried that the bonds holding Americans together might be fraying. In 1991 former University of Colorado football coach Bill McCartney formed the Promise Keepers, a fundamentalist Christian group dedicated to restoring the traditional privileges and responsibilities of husbands and fathers in the home. The Promise Keepers held evangelical revivals that drew tens of thousands of mostly working-class white and some black men to rallies across the country. They believed that men should be good providers for their families, strong role models for their children, and committed spouses.

Although white men continued to control nearly all the major economic and political institutions in the nation, a 1993 poll found that a majority of white men believed that their advantage in terms of jobs and income, along with their influence over American culture, was declining. African American men also felt the need to bolster manhood and fatherhood. Efforts geared specifically toward African American men included the 1995 Million Man March, organized by Nation of Islam Reverend Louis Farrakhan, which drew hundreds of thousands of black men to demonstrate their solidarity at a rally in Washington, D.C.

At the same time, gay men and lesbians mobilized to gain acceptance and legitimacy for the families that they formed. Although a 1994 poll showed that 52 percent of respondents "claimed to consider gay lifestyle acceptable," 64 percent were opposed to legalizing gay marriage or allowing gay couples to adopt children. In 2000, Vermont became the first state to grant legal status to civil unions between same-sex couples, although a fierce backlash threatened to overturn the legislation.

Values also collided around the rights and traditions of Native Americans as tribal communities came into conflict with non-Native environmentalists, sports enthusiasts, and scientists. In the upper Midwest, treaties with the government in 1837 and 1842 granted the Chippewa hunting, fishing, and gathering rights in the territories ceded to the United States. Federal courts consistently upheld these treaties, which include rights to take up to half of the fish and game allowed by state conservation requirements and to use methods such as spear fishing that are illegal for non-Indians. In the 1980s and 1990s, non-Indians challenged these policies and accosted Native Americans in fishing boats with rocks and insults. Native American cultural practices also clashed with environmentalist sensibilities over religious practices involving the gathering and sacrificing of golden eaglets.

Courtroom Dramas

Two of the most controversial legal clashes of the decade centered on accusations against successful black men and exposed deep chasms along class and gender as well as racial lines. The first of these episodes was the Senate hearing of October 1991 to confirm the appointment of conservative Judge Clarence Thomas to the U.S. Supreme Court. Although President George H. W. Bush claimed that Thomas was the "best man for the job," the American Bar Association gave him the lowest rating of any justice confirmed in the previous three decades. When University of Oklahoma law professor Anita Hill accused Thomas of sexual harassment when she had worked for him at the Equal Opportunity Employment Commission in the early 1980s, the question of Thomas's professional qualifications faded to the background and the hearings focused exclusively on Hill's accusations.

In live televised hearings, the African American law professor testified that Thomas had made crude remarks to her as well as unwanted sexual overtures. Several of the all-white-male panel of senators questioned Hill's credibility, wondering why she continued to work for Thomas after the alleged harassment. Thomas drew on the long history of black men being falsely accused of sexual aggression to counter the charge of sexual harassment, accusing his Democratic opponents of conducting a "high-tech lynching." In the end, Thomas was confirmed. But Hill's testimony, and what appeared to her supporters as the insensitive behavior of the senators, brought the issue of sexual harassment to a high level of national consciousness. The hearings also highlighted the fact that Congress was overwhelmingly white and male, motivating female candidates and their supporters to alter that reality the following year. As a result of the 1992 elections, the number of female senators tripled from two to six, including the first black female senator, Carol Moseley Braun, Democrat from Illinois. The number of congresswomen rose from twenty-eight to forty-seven.

In 1994 television viewers were again riveted by a media spectacle, this time a sensational murder case in Los Angeles. The victims were the white ex-wife of black celebrity O. J. Simpson, former football star and film actor, and a male companion. Simpson's blood was found at the scene, hair and other forensic and DNA evidence linked him to the crime, he had no reliable alibi, and a motive was evident in his pattern of jealous rage and brutality against the murdered woman. No other suspects in the case were ever identified. But Simpson's

Vermont Civil Union Law

On April 26, 2000, Vermont became the first state to grant legal recognition to same-sex couples, affording them all the legal protections, privileges, and responsibilities of married couples. The law unleashed a storm of controversy and raised questions about the legal status in other states of civil unions contracted in Vermont. Nevertheless, in the first year after its enactment, 2,479 same-sex couples forged civil unions in Vermont, 478 of them among Vermonters, and the rest from other states. Two-thirds were lesbian unions. Several states began to consider similar bills, but others moved to prohibit such unions. Nebraska amended its state constitution to outlaw same-sex marriage and civil unions. On the national level, conservative lawmakers endeavored to introduce a constitutional amendment that would ban civil unions and restrict marriage to heterosexual couples. Among other provisions, the Vermont Civil Union Law stipulated that

(1) Civil marriage under Vermont's marriage statutes consists of a union between a man and a woman. . . .

(2) Vermont's history as an independent republic and as a state is one of equal treatment and respect for all Vermonters. . . .

(3) The state's interest in civil marriage is to encourage close and caring families, and to protect all family members from the economic and social consequences of abandonment and divorce, focusing on those who have been especially at risk.

(4) Legal recognition of civil marriage by the state is the primary and, in a number of instances, the exclusive source of numerous benefits, responsibilities and protections under the laws of the state for married persons and their children.

(5) Based on the state's tradition of equality under the law and strong families, for at least 25 years, Vermont Probate Courts have qualified gay and lesbian individuals as adoptive parents.

Kathleen Peterson and Carolyn Conrad exchange vows in front of Justice of the Peace T. Hunter Wilson. The ceremony in Brattleboro, Vermont, on July 1, 2000, marked the first legal union under Vermont's Civil Union Law. Vermont was the first state to provide recognition and legal status to gay and lesbian couples.

Getty Images

(6) Vermont was one of the first states to adopt comprehensive legislation prohibiting discrimination on the basis of sexual orientation. . . .

(7) The state has a strong interest in promoting stable and lasting families, including families based upon a same-sex couple.

(8) Without the legal protections, benefits and responsibilities associated with civil marriage, same-sex couples suffer numerous obstacles and hardships.

(9) Despite long-standing social and economic discrimination, many gay and lesbian Vermonters have formed lasting, committed, caring and faithful relationships with persons of their same sex. These couples live together, participate in their communities together, and some raise children and care for family members together, just as do couples who are married under Vermont law.

(10) While a system of civil unions does not bestow the status of civil marriage, it does satisfy the requirements of the Common Benefits Clause. Changes in the way significant legal relationships are established under the constitution should be approached carefully, combining respect for the community and cultural institutions most affected with a commitment to the constitutional rights involved.

Granting benefits and protections to same-sex couples through a system of civil unions will provide due respect for tradition and long-standing social institutions, and will permit adjustment as unanticipated consequences or unmet needs arise.

(11) The constitutional principle of equality embodied in the Common Benefits Clause is compatible with the freedom of religious belief and worship guaranteed in Chapter I, Article 3rd of the state constitution. Extending the benefits and protections of marriage to same-sex couples through a system of civil unions preserves the fundamental constitutional right of each of the multitude of religious faiths in Vermont to choose freely and without state interference to whom to grant the religious status, sacrament or blessing of marriage under the rules, practices or traditions of such faith.

Questions

1. What political principles and values provided the foundation for Vermont's civil union law?

2. In what ways does the Vermont civil union law distinguish between civil marriages and civil unions? ■

team of lawyers unearthed evidence that, before the Simpson case, white police detective Mark Fuhrman had boasted of planting evidence and had made racist comments. The mostly black and female jury was sympathetic to the possibility that Fuhrman had framed Simpson. In Los Angeles, in the wake of the Rodney King beatings, African Americans had good reason to distrust the police.

Finally, in early October 1996, after a trial that lasted nearly a year, it took the jury only two hours to acquit Simpson of all charges. Pundits focused on the racial divide: blacks were more inclined to believe Simpson was innocent, and whites more likely to consider him guilty. Simpson was later convicted in a wrongful death civil suit (with lower standards for conviction than a criminal case), which found him responsible for the deaths, and he was ordered to pay damages.

The Changing Face of Diversity

These highly charged events illuminated racial tensions, but there was also evidence that Americans were accepting the nation's diversity and adopting a more inclusive vision. The number of immigrants represented 10 percent of the population, the highest proportion of foreign-born residents since the 1930s. The numbers of Asians and Pacific Islanders increased by 45.9 percent, with those of Chinese ancestry comprising the largest group, followed by those with origins in the Philippines. The Latino population grew by 39.7 percent. Among the nation's Latinos, nearly two-thirds were of Mexican ancestry.

Not everyone celebrated these developments. In California, with one-third of the nation's Latino population, voters responded with Proposition 187 to deny public education and most other public social services to undocumented immigrants, and Proposition 227 to end bilingual education. Large numbers of Latino voters opposed these measures. In subsequent elections, many young Latinos and new citizens marshaled their political power and voted for the first time. By 2000 whites no longer constituted a majority of California's multiethnic population, dropping from 57 percent in 1990 to 47 percent in 2000.

At the same time, politics and ideas based on distinct and rigid racial lines gave way to a growing recognition of intermixing. In the world of sports, young golfer Tiger Woods, son of a black Vietnam-veteran father and a Thai mother, became the reigning superstar of the sport most closely identified with the world of the white elite. Pop star Prince was one of many artists who crafted a persona that highlighted both racial and gender ambiguity. On job and college application forms, a growing number of mixed-race Americans refused to be identified as belonging to one particular racial group. Reflecting this development, the U.S. Census of 2000 allowed people to check more than one box to indicate their racial identity.

Jack Smith/AP/Wide World Photos

■ Golf superstar Tiger Woods celebrates his triumph at the U.S. Amateur Championships in North Plains, Oregon, August 25, 1996. Woods, the son of an African American father and a Thai mother, was one of several mixed-race celebrities in the 1990s.

Violence and Danger

Violence was nothing new in American society, but new types of mayhem in the 1990s—including domestic terrorism and school shootings–sparked national soul-searching and wide-ranging debate over the causes of violence and what to do about them. Meanwhile, ordinary Americans inflicted various harms on themselves, often in class-distinct ways. Eating disorders and obesity reached epidemic proportions, and Americans continued to turn to drugs, most of them legal, to make them feel better.

Domestic Terrorism

On the morning of April 19, 1995, a 2-ton homemade bomb exploded at the Alfred P. Murrah Federal Building in Oklahoma City. The huge building crumbled, killing 168 people, including nineteen children. The attack was the worst act of terrorism in the nation's history to that date. Initial news reports speculated that the terrorists were Arabs, but it turned out that the attack was carried out by American citizens with a hatred for the government. Timothy McVeigh, a Persian Gulf War veteran turned antigovernment terrorist, and his accomplice, Terry Nichols, were found guilty of the bombing.

Antigovernment individuals and groups had long operated within the United States. During the 1990s, their activities—as well as FBI efforts to curtail them—intensified. Investigations throughout the decade uncovered networks of antigovernment militias, tax resisters, and white supremacist groups, many of them heavily armed and isolated in remote rural areas. The FBI tried to prevent these extremists from causing harm, but some of their efforts went awry. In 1992 an FBI agent shot and killed the wife and son of Randall Weaver, a former Green Beret and antigovernment militia supporter who had failed to appear for trial on weapons charges, in a shootout at their Idaho home.

The following year in Waco, Texas, the FBI stormed the heavily armed compound of an antigovernment religious sect known as the Branch Davidians. The leader of the group, David Koresh, had barricaded the compound. The FBI, acting on reports of abuse of members, particularly women and children, tried to force Koresh and his group out of the building. But a fire broke out, killing eighty men, women, and children inside. The FBI came under intense criticism for its aggressive tactics in these cases. For antigovernment extremists, these actions prompted revenge. The Oklahoma City bombing apparently was intended in part as retaliation for the FBI assault against the Branch Davidians precisely two years earlier.

The Oklahoma City bombing was the worst but not the only example of domestic terrorist attacks. After the Supreme Court's 1973 decision in *Roe* v. *Wade* legalized abortion, antiabortion activists worked to have the decision reversed. Most antiabortion protesters were peaceful and law abiding. But a small militant fringe of antiabortion crusaders switched their targets of protest from elected officials to abortion providers and turned to violence. In 1993 half of all abortion clinics reported hostile actions, including death threats, fires, bombs, invasions, blockades, and shootings. In 1993 and 1994, vigilantes shot and killed one abortion provider, tried to kill another, and shot employees at two clinics in Brookline, Massachusetts. The violence spurred Congress to pass the Freedom of Access to Clinic Entrances Act in 1994, making it a federal crime to block access to clinics. But ultimately, the intimidation and violence were effective. Although abortion remained legal, the procedure became increasingly difficult to obtain.

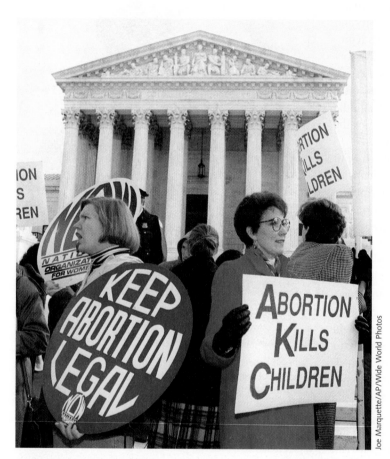

■ Abortion remained one of the most controversial political issues throughout the 1990s. Here abortion rights advocate Inga Coulter of Harrisburg, Pennsylvania, and antiabortion crusader Elizabeth McGee of Washington, D.C., take opposing sides in a demonstration outside the Supreme Court building on December 8, 1993.

Joe Marquette/AP/Wide World Photos

Kids Who Kill

Although violent crime declined throughout the decade, especially crimes committed by youths, a spate of school shootings in which children murdered other children sparked national soul-searching and finger-pointing as Americans wondered whom and what to blame. The murderers were mostly white middle-class boys who appeared to be "normal kids." The worst of these shootings occurred on April 20, 1999, at Columbine High School in a suburb of Denver, Colorado, where two boys opened fire and killed twelve of their schoolmates and a teacher before killing themselves.

The common factors in all of these killings were that the children used guns and that they got the weapons easily, often from their own homes. **Gun-control** advocates noted that the easy access to firearms in the United States was unique among western industrial nations. In 1992, 367 people were killed by handguns in Great Britain, Sweden, Switzerland, Japan, Australia, and Canada combined. The total population of those countries equaled that of the United States, where in that same year, handguns killed 13,220 people. Public opinion polls showed that most Americans favored gun control, but the powerful gun lobby and the National Rifle Association argued that the Second Amendment to the Constitution guaranteed individuals the unlimited right to bear arms. Congress enacted the Brady Bill, a gun control measure named for James Brady, the White House press secretary who was gravely wounded in the 1981 assassination attempt on President Ronald W. Reagan. The bill required a waiting period for handgun purchases and banned assault rifles. Nevertheless, access to firearms remained easy.

A Healthy Nation?

Despite the nation's near obsession with fitness, both the wealthy and the poor suffered from a number of afflictions. Eating disorders plagued millions of Americans. Among the affluent, anorexia nervosa (self-starvation) and bulimia (frequent bingeing and purging) affected an estimated 5 million Americans, especially young women, fed in part by a fashion fad that glamorized emaciated bodies. Men also strove for the fashionable body, sometimes with the aid of drugs to enhance athletic performance or muscle buildup. In 2000 the Mayo Clinic reported a 30 percent annual increase in eating disorders. The opposite problem plagued the lower end of the class ladder, where obesity increased dramatically, especially among children. With popular fast-food chains offering "supersized" high-fat meals, the proportion of overweight children jumped from 5 percent in 1964 to 20 percent in 2000.

Illegal drugs, including marijuana, cocaine, and heroin, remained popular in spite of official efforts to curb the trade. However, illegal drugs represented only one dimension of Americans' desire to solve their problems through the use of chemical substances. Some mind-altering drugs were legal and available by prescription, such as Prozac and other antidepressants. These psychopharmaceuticals saturated the prescription drug market. Some mental-health experts worried that these drugs were being overprescribed, especially for children, as life's normal ups and downs were increasingly diagnosed as maladies such as depression and attention deficit disorder. Aging **baby boomers** also boosted the profits of pharmaceutical companies. Women turned to hormone replacement therapies to offset the effects of menopause. Skyrocketing sales of Viagra, a drug for treating male impotence, reflected middle-aged men's concerns about waning sexual potency.

■ FIGURE 29.1
CHILDHOOD OVERWEIGHT RATES FOR BOYS AND GIRLS AGE 6–17, 1960s AND 1990s During the last half-century, obesity rates among children rose dramatically, especially in the 1990s. Childhood obesity is associated with a wide range of medical problems that can affect the health of overweight children throughout their lives. In the 1960s, boys and girls were equally likely to be more than 20% overweight. But by the 1990s, obesity had become more prevalent among boys.

Medical developments brought new worries and new cures. Antibiotics were so widely prescribed that forms of drug-resistant bacteria began to proliferate. In 1997 researchers in Scotland cloned a sheep, raising hopes that cloning could lead to new medical breakthroughs and fears that human cloning might be next. In 2000 scientists charted the entire human genome, or genetic code, offering the hope of finding causes and cures for genetically linked diseases.

The Clinton Presidency

VIDEO

Clinton
Presidential
Campaign Ad
(1992)

William Jefferson Clinton was the first American president born after World War II. Raised in Arkansas in a working-class family, Clinton attended Georgetown University and studied at Oxford University in England as a Rhodes Scholar. Like many college students of his generation, he opposed the Vietnam War and avoided the draft. He attended Yale Law School, where he met Hillary Rodham from Illinois, whom he married in 1975. In 1978, at the young age of thirty-three, he was elected governor of Arkansas. After one term, he was defeated in his bid for reelection. He made a comeback by defining himself as a New Democrat with centrist political inclinations and reclaimed his job as governor. When he ran for president in 1992, Clinton received the support of the Democratic Leadership Council, a group of **New Democrats** who shifted the national party to the right of its previous New Deal liberal position.

Clinton: The New Democrat

In 1992 the incumbent president, George H. W. Bush, faced an uphill battle. The recession of 1991–1992 hit white-collar as well as blue-collar workers as unemployment climbed above 8 percent. During twelve years of Republican presidents, the national debt had more than quadrupled to $4.4 trillion. The Republican party platform, reflecting pressures from the right wing of the party, attacked permissiveness in American society, opposed abortion and gay rights, and called for a smaller government. The Democrats nominated the forty-six-year-old Clinton. A wildcard in the election was the Reform party candidacy of H. Ross Perot, a Texas billionaire who financed his own campaign and used the national media to tap into voter discontent with the two major parties.

Much of the campaign reflected the culture wars, pitting what many saw as the socially permissive legacy of the 1960s against conservative efforts to restore traditional "family values" to American public life. Many Americans worried that the prevalence of single-parent families, the high rate of divorce, and the pervasiveness of sex and violence in the popular culture all reflected a decline in moral standards and an erosion of American society.

Clinton won the election by a comfortable margin, but Perot garnered 19 percent of the popular vote, the largest showing for a third-party candidate since Theodore Roosevelt ran on the Progressive party ticket in 1912. Clinton began his term with a solidly Democratic House and Senate, which included a new infusion of women, along with the nation's first senator of American Indian descent, Ben Nighthorse Campbell of Colorado. Saying that he wanted his advisers to "look like America," Clinton appointed two Latinos, three blacks, and three women to the fourteen-member cabinet.

TABLE 29-1			
The Election of 1992			
Candidate	Political Party	Popular Vote (%)	Electoral Vote
William J. Clinton	Democratic	43.1	370
George H. W. Bush	Republican	37.4	168
H. Ross Perot	Independent	18.8	—

Clinton's Domestic Agenda and the "Republican Revolution"

Clinton ran into trouble early in his administration when he tried to fulfill his campaign promise to allow gays and lesbians to serve openly in the military, reversing a policy that dated back half a century. Top military officials, already unhappy with having a new commander in chief who had avoided military service during the Vietnam War, vehemently opposed lifting the ban against gays. Ultimately, Clinton compromised and established a new policy of **"don't ask, don't tell,"** which allowed homosexuals to serve as long as they did not make their sexual orientation known.

Clinton's effort to reform the health care system was equally unsuccessful. With rising health care costs and millions of uninsured citizens, Clinton's campaign promises to provide national health insurance and reduce the cost of health care had wide public support but fierce opposition from the medical establishment and the pharmaceutical industry. Clinton appointed his wife, Hillary Rodham Clinton, an attorney and longtime advocate on behalf of children and families, to head a task force to develop a plan. But the task force, deliberating behind closed doors, failed to come up with a workable strategy acceptable to all sides. After a year of hearings and no action in Congress on the complicated task force proposal, the Clintons abandoned the effort.

DOCUMENT

Clinton Healthcare Reform Proposals

Clinton achieved a major success when he pushed through Congress a budget that raised taxes on the wealthiest Americans, cut spending to reduce the deficit, and expanded tax credits for low-income families. In the next three years, the economy markedly improved. Other legislative successes included the Family and Medical Leave Act, which required employers to grant unpaid medical leave for up to twelve weeks. Clinton appointed two relatively liberal new Supreme Court Justices, Ruth Bader Ginsburg in 1993 and Stephen Breyer in 1994.

The 1994 congressional elections dealt a devastating blow to Clinton's legislative agenda. In the midst of the campaign, about 300 Republican congressional candidates, under the leadership of Speaker of the House Newt Gingrich, stood on the Capitol steps and endorsed a "Contract with America," calling for welfare reform, a balanced budget, more prisons and longer sentences, increased defense spending, an end to legal abortion, and other conservative measures. Only 39 percent of the electorate voted, and a whisker-thin majority of those voted Republican. Nevertheless, the Republicans declared a "Republican Revolution" as they took control of both the House and Senate for the first time in forty years and pushed Congress to the right of center.

The new Congress passed a large tax cut and a tough anticrime bill, increased military spending, and reduced federal regulatory power over the environment. Clinton used his veto power to limit the Republican agenda, but he also undercut the conservative momentum by taking on some of their issues as his own, such as free trade and welfare reform. In his 1996 State of the Union address, Clinton announced that the "era of big government is over," and he signed the Welfare Reform Act, abolishing the sixty-year-old program Aid to Families with Dependent Children (AFDC). Clinton won reelection easily in 1996. Republicans lost some seats but stayed in control of both houses of Congress.

TABLE 29-2			
The Election of 1996			
Candidate	**Political Party**	**Popular Vote (%)**	**Electoral Vote**
William J. Clinton	Democratic	49.24	379
Robert Dole	Republican	40.71	159
H. Ross Perot	Reform	8.4	—

The Impeachment Crisis

Clinton's personal behavior left him vulnerable to political enemies, who took full advantage of every opportunity to discredit him. In 1993 the Clintons were investigated for possible complicity in a failed Arkansas investment scheme known as Whitewater. Although a few of the Clintons' close associates were found guilty of conspiracy, tax evasion, and mail fraud in the deal, four years of persistent investigation cleared the Clintons of any wrongdoing. Nevertheless, the Whitewater scandal activated the Office of the Independent Counsel, an independent investigative unit put into place during the Nixon administration to investigate the

Watergate break-in. The independent counsel, former judge Kenneth Starr, with the help of the congressional Republicans, pursued Clinton throughout his two terms and nearly brought down his presidency.

Clinton's sexual behavior became an issue well before he entered the White House. During the 1992 campaign, Gennifer Flowers, a former nightclub singer, told a tabloid that she and Clinton had an affair when he was governor. Early in his presidency, Paula Jones, a former Arkansas state employee, filed a sexual harassment suit against Clinton, claiming that he had propositioned her when he was governor of Arkansas. Eventually, the case was dismissed, but it came back to haunt him later.

In 1998 Kenneth Starr reported to the House Judiciary Committee that he had evidence that Clinton had an extramarital affair with a young White House intern, Monica Lewinsky. Starr claimed that Clinton had broken the law in an effort to cover up the affair. Lewinsky and Clinton had both been called to testify in the Paula Jones case, and both denied having had a sexual relationship. Starr claimed that Clinton had lied under oath and had instructed his close adviser and friend, Vernon Jordan, to find Lewinsky a job to keep her quiet. Starr charged Clinton with perjury, witness tampering, and obstruction of justice. As proof of the affair, Starr produced twenty hours of taped phone conversations recorded by Lewinsky's co-worker and confidante, Linda Tripp. Clinton vehemently denied the charges, but Lewinsky had saved a dress with a stain containing the president's DNA, providing the investigation with the "smoking gun" it needed.

As Starr and congressional Republicans pressed the investigation with relentless determination, the media saturated the nation and the world with sordid and graphic details of the president's sexual encounters with the young intern. Polls showed that Americans disapproved of Clinton's personal behavior, but they did not want him removed from office. With the economy booming and the country running smoothly, Clinton garnered high job performance ratings, rising to 79 percent at the height of the scandal. Negative sentiment against Kenneth Starr and congressional Republicans mounted as the investigation dragged on for four years at a cost to taxpayers of $40 million.

Public opinion notwithstanding, the House of Representatives impeached—that is, brought charges against—Clinton on December 19, 1998, accusing him of perjury and obstruction of justice, based on Clinton's false testimony in the Paula Jones case. But the majority of senators determined that Clinton's misdeeds did not meet the standard for "high crimes and misdemeanors" required to remove a president from office, and acquitted him.

DOCUMENT

Articles of
Impeachment
Against Clinton
(1999)

The Nation and the World

Stymied in Congress by Republican opposition, the president turned his attention increasingly to foreign policy. In foreign affairs, Clinton focused on peacekeeping and peacemaking while expanding trade and diplomatic relations, especially to countries that had been considered unfriendly during the Cold War. Clinton took on the role of peace broker by facilitating negotiations in long-standing conflicts in Northern Ireland and the Middle East. But hostilities in those areas proved too deep to be fully resolved. Military interventions in Somalia, Haiti, and Kosovo yielded mixed results, and trade agreements generated heated controversy. Episodes of international terrorism against U.S. embassies and military personnel killed hundreds of people and highlighted the strength of extremist groups whose members were deeply hostile to the United States and its interventions around the world.

Trade Agreements

In 1993, with the president's strong encouragement, Congress approved the North American Free Trade Agreement (NAFTA), eliminating tariffs and trade barriers among the United States,

Mexico, and Canada and thus creating the largest free trade zone in the world. In 1994 Congress approved the General Agreement on Tariffs and Trade (GATT), which reduced tariffs on thousands of goods and phased out import quotas imposed by the United States and other industrialized nations. Supporters argued that these measures would increase global competition and improve the U.S. economy. Businesses would benefit from the easing of trade barriers, and consumers would have access to lower-priced goods.

NAFTA and GATT barely passed Congress. Clinton faced strong opposition from liberal Democrats in industrial areas and from labor unions, who feared that these measures would result in jobs going abroad, declining American wages, and a relaxation of environmental controls over companies moving outside U.S. borders. In the first few years of NAFTA and GATT, these fears seemed justified. Some jobs went abroad, and threats of moving gave employers a negotiating edge over workers. In Mexico the impact of NAFTA was even worse. The peso collapsed as money and goods flowed across the border, and the average wages for workers fell from $1.45 to $.78 per hour.

Equally controversial were Clinton's efforts to grant China **most-favored-nation status,** which would designate China as a full trading partner with the United States. Human rights activists argued that China's dismal record of violent suppression and imprisonment of political dissenters should preclude favorable trading terms. But with an eye to China's huge potential market for American goods and favorable site for U.S.-owned factories, Congress approved Clinton's proposal.

Reuters NewMedia Inc./CORBIS

■ Activists protest at the opening of the meeting of the World Trade Organization (WTO) in Seattle, Washington, on November 1, 1999. During the four days of the meeting, hundreds of demonstrators took to the streets in opposition to the organization's environmental and labor policies.

Efforts at Peacemaking

Less controversial than relations with China were Clinton's peacemaking efforts. Northern Ireland had been fraught with violent conflict for thirty years. Irish Catholic nationalists wanted to break ties with England and join the Republic of Ireland; Protestants loyal to Great Britain wanted to remain part of the United Kingdom. The United States, with political and diplomatic connections to London as well as strong ties to the Irish, wanted to help resolve the crisis. Clinton made several trips to Ireland to promote peace. He appointed former Senator George Mitchell of Maine as negotiator, who spent months working on a settlement. Despite dissent and violence by extremists on both sides, by the time Clinton left office, an agreement had been reached that established a shared coalition government.

In the Middle East, Clinton brought Yasser Arafat, leader of the Palestinian Liberation Organization (PLO), and Yitzak Rabin, Israeli prime minister, to Washington for talks that led to an historic 1993 handshake and pledges to pursue a peace agreement. As in Northern Ireland, those efforts were hampered by violent extremists on both sides. Rabin was assassinated by a fanatical right-wing Israeli, leading to the election of a hawkish new prime minister, Benjamin Netanyahu. The peace process fell apart for several years until negotiations finally resumed in the late 1990s. But just when an agreement seemed to be within reach, large-scale violence between Palestinians and Israelis erupted again in the summer of 2000. Clinton left office with no agreement in sight.

In the final weeks of Clinton's presidency in 2000, he made a historic visit to Vietnam—the first by an American president since the war. Because Clinton had protested against the war decades earlier, his visit held great symbolic power and his administration was the first to reopen formal relations with the Vietnamese government. Although the United States lost the war, westernization had taken hold in Vietnam, with investment beginning to flow in from Europe, the United States, and Japan, as well as American popular culture and technology. Cheering crowds welcomed the president of the superpower that had been vanquished twenty-five years earlier.

Military Interventions and International Terrorism

The end of the Cold War raised new questions about how and when to use American military force. Most of the overseas crises stemmed from problems of national disintegration, ethnic conflict, and humanitarian disasters resulting from political chaos and civil wars.

On the Caribbean island of Haiti, a military coup in 1991 had ousted the democratically elected President Jean Bertrand Aristide. In a striking departure from former Cold War policies, Clinton backed the black populist Aristide against the coup leaders, who had strong ties to the CIA. In 1994 the United States received UN support for an invasion to restore Aristide to power. To avert a large-scale military conflict, Clinton sent former President Jimmy Carter to Haiti to negotiate a settlement. The resulting agreement allowed the coup members to leave the country, and Aristide returned. Six years later, however, the United States criticized Aristide for corruption and fraud in his 2000 reelection.

In 1992 President George H. W. Bush had sent U.S. marines to Somalia in east Africa as part of a UN effort to provide famine relief and to restore peace in the war-torn nation. After Clinton took office, Somali warlord Mohammed Farah Aidid killed fifty Pakistani UN peacekeepers. The U.S. forces then mobilized against Aidid, shifting the peacekeeping mission to military engagement. As part of the effort to hunt down Aidid, U.S. soldiers killed hundreds of Somali citizens, creating intense anti-American sentiment among the population. Amid that hostile atmosphere, in September 1993, Aidid's forces killed eighteen American soldiers under the UN command in a firefight and dragged one of their bodies through the streets. The outraged American public viewed the grim spectacle on TV, and the experience left Clinton with no clear guidelines on **humanitarian intervention** abroad. Largely as a result of the disaster in Somalia, when ethnic conflict led to genocide in Rwanda in central Africa in 1994, the United States and other western nations refused to intervene.

DOCUMENT

The Balkan Proximity Peace Talks Agreement

Ethnic conflict was also the cause of trouble in the Balkans. From 1945 to 1980, Marshal Josip Broz Tito ruled over a unified communist Yugoslavia, maintaining stability by suppressing ethnic rivalries. But after Tito's death in 1980 and the end of the Cold War in 1989, ethnic nationalism pulled Yugoslavia apart, with Slovenia and Croatia breaking away in 1991–1992. The region erupted in bloody conflicts. After sustained Serbian attacks on Muslims in Bosnia between 1992 and 1995, Clinton reluctantly agreed to air strikes against the Serbs, leading to the 1995 Dayton Accords, which brought an end to the war. When Serbian president Slobodan Milosevic embarked on a murderous campaign to drive the majority Muslim ethnic Albanians out of Serbia's southern province of Kosovo, Clinton finally ordered airstrikes in 1999 that forced the Serbs to retreat.

In some regions of the world, resentment against the United States found expression in violence and terrorism. In June 1996, a truck bomb killed nineteen U.S. airmen in Dhahran, Saudi Arabia. Two years later, bombs exploded at two U.S. embassies in east Africa, killing 224 people in Nairobi, Kenya, and Dar es Salaam, Tanzania. Four men were convicted of conspiracy in the terrorist attacks. They were identified as followers of Islamic militant Osama bin Laden, who was also indicted in connection with the embassy bombings. Bin Laden, originally from Saudi Arabia, was living in Afghanistan under the protection of the fundamentalist Taliban regime and remained a fugitive. He was known to be the leader of Al Qaeda, a terrorist network operating in several countries throughout the Middle East. On October 12, 2000, a small boat pulled up next to the destroyer USS *Cole* in Yemen's port of Aden.

■ **MAP 29.2**

THE BREAKUP OF THE FORMER YUGOSLAVIA   Created in 1919 as a multiethnic nation, Yugoslavia split apart in 1991–1992. After Slovenia and Croatia gained their independence swiftly, Bosnia deteriorated into fierce ethnic fighting dominated by Serb atrocities and encouraged by the Serbian government of Slobodan Milosevic. A brief U.S. bombing campaign in 1995 finally brought the Serbs to peace negotiations. Similar ethnic fighting in the province of Kosovo in 1999 led to another U.S. bombing campaign and Kosovo's current quasi-independence under NATO guidance. In 2006 Montenegro's citizens voted narowly to establish their full independence from Serbia.

A bomb exploded and ripped a hole in the destroyer, killing seventeen Americans and wounding thirty-nine others.

Terrorists also struck at home. On February 26, 1993, a bomb exploded in the parking garage underneath the World Trade Center, the skyscrapers dominating the New York skyline in Lower Manhattan. Five people were killed and more than a thousand were injured. Eight years later, the same twin towers were attacked again, with far more devastating consequences.

The Contested Election of 2000

The first presidential election of the new millennium was the most bitterly contested in more than a century. The Democratic candidate won the national popular vote, but with ballot counts disputed in the key state of Florida, a Supreme Court decision ultimately made the Republican candidate the victor. The election exposed defects in the election process, from faulty ballots and voting machines to the role of the media, and raised serious questions about the value of the electoral college. The election also revealed that flaws in the system disfranchised large numbers of poor and minority voters. But in the end, the transfer of power took place smoothly, and the nation accepted the outcome.

The Campaign, the Vote, and the Courts

The Democrats nominated Vice President Al Gore, who hoped to benefit from Clinton's high approval rating and the healthy economy. The Republicans nominated George W. Bush, governor of Texas and son of the former president. Only half of the nation's eligible voters turned out to vote. Even before all the polls had closed, the national media began to report the results.

Early in the evening, they declared that Florida, a key state with twenty-five electoral votes, had gone to Gore. But soon after that announcement, they changed their projection and put Florida back into the "undecided" group of states. It became clear that whoever took Florida, where Bush's brother Jeb Bush was governor, would win the election. By the next day, Gore had won the national popular vote by half a million votes, but Bush was ahead in Florida. Bush's lead was so narrow that it triggered an automatic recount.

TABLE 29-3			
The Election of 2000			
Candidate	Political Party	Popular Vote (%)	Electoral Vote
George W. Bush	Republican	47.88	271
Al Gore	Democratic	48.39	266*
Ralph Nader	Green	2.72	—

*One District of Columbia Gore elector abstained.

With all eyes on Florida, a number of serious irregularities surfaced. Voters in Palm Beach County were given a confusing "butterfly" ballot, resulting in more than 20,000 mismarked ballots. In other counties, registered voters were turned away at the polls because of inaccurate and incomplete voter registration lists. Some voter lists inaccurately listed eligible voters as felons. Most of these disfranchised voters were African American, who usually voted Democratic. In several largely minority counties, old voting machines that used a punch-card ballot system failed to count thousands of ballots.

For weeks after the election, the outcome was still unknown. Democrats insisted that because Bush's lead had narrowed to a few hundred votes, tallied by inaccurate voting machines, ballots in four Florida counties should be recounted by hand. Republicans pointed out that it would be unfair to recount votes in only four heavily Democratic counties, especially with no standard way of determining voter intent on punch-card ballots with ambiguous marks on them. Florida's secretary of state, Katherine Harris, a Republican who headed Florida's campaign for George W. Bush, refused to extend the deadline to allow the recounts to take place and declared Bush the winner by 537 votes out of 6 million cast statewide.

Gore contested the results, and the Florida Supreme Court ordered that the recount proceed. Bush then appealed to the U.S. Supreme Court to reverse the decision of the Florida Supreme Court. After thirty-six days of partial vote counting and court battles, in a sharply divided 5–4 decision, the U.S. Supreme Court stopped any further vote counting, with the most conservative judges voting in support of the Bush request. The four dissenting judges issued a stinging rebuke of their five colleagues responsible for the decision. In his dissenting opinion, Justice Stephen Breyer wrote that the majority ruling "can only lend confidence to the most cynical appraisal of the work of judges throughout the land."

The Aftermath

What became clear in the months after the 2000 election were the widespread flaws in the election system in Florida and elsewhere. Across the country, outdated voting machines yielded inaccurate vote counts, and long lines at polling places prevented voters from casting ballots. Low-income and minority voters were more likely to be disfranchised because they lived in precincts with faulty voting machines or overcrowded polling places. The U.S. Civil Rights Commission estimated that in Florida, black voters were nine times more likely than white voters to have had their votes rejected.

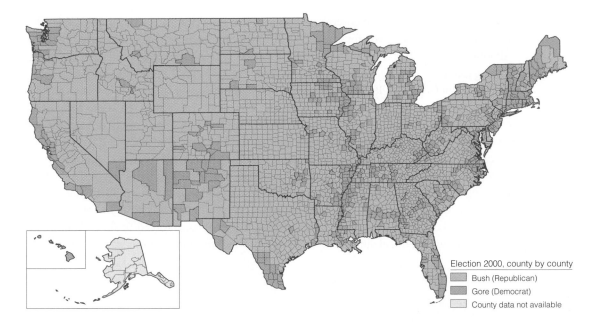

Election 2000, county by county
- Bush (Republican)
- Gore (Democrat)
- County data not available

■ **MAP 29.3**
THE CONTESTED ELECTION OF 2000   The 2000 presidential election was so close, and so fraught with problems, that it was ultimately decided by a 5–4 vote of the U.S. Supreme Court. As this map shows, Democratic votes were concentrated in the densely populated urban areas and Republican votes in the sparsely populated rural areas.

In addition to those whose votes did not count, many others were prevented from voting altogether. In Florida, "suspected felons" were removed from voter registration lists without being informed and without the opportunity to demonstrate that they were law-abiding citizens eligible to vote. An estimated 15 percent of the list was inaccurate, and more than half of those voters were African American. According to the U.S. Civil Rights Commission, "Perhaps the most dramatic undercount in Florida's election was the nonexistent ballots of countless unknown eligible voters, who were turned away, or wrongfully purged from the voter registration rolls . . . and were prevented from exercising the franchise." As a result, hundreds of African American citizens with no criminal record arrived at the polls only to discover that they had been disfranchised.

Policymakers and media moguls debated the role of the media in reporting election returns. Some argued for a blackout on early returns until all polls across the country were closed, to avoid the possibility that early results might influence voters who had not yet voted. Others proposed that only official results be announced, to avoid the problem of erroneous reporting that occurred on election night 2000. But media representatives countered that a free press should be able to report the news as it happens, although they agreed on the need to ensure accuracy.

Legacies of Election 2000

In addition to the unprecedented Supreme Court decision, the 2000 election was remarkable in other ways. For the first time, a First Lady was elected to public office: Hillary Rodham Clinton became a Democratic senator from New York. Third-party politics also critically influenced the outcome of the presidential election. Several third-party candidates had achieved national visibility during the 1990s and won elections at the state and local levels, including professional wrestler Jesse Ventura, elected governor of Minnesota in 1998 on the Reform party ticket. In 2000 Ralph Nader wreaked havoc for the Democrats with his Green party candidacy for president. Although Nader gained fewer than 3 percent of the votes, his candidacy drew off some of the left-leaning elements of the Democratic party—enough votes to cost Al Gore the election.

President George W. Bush immediately began to reverse several Clinton-era policies, including a number of environmental protections. His first major legislative success was the passage of a major tax cut. During his first year in office, the economy went from boom to bust and headed into a recession. The robust stock market of the 1990s wilted in early 2001. Nevertheless, as the new millennium dawned, the United States remained the wealthiest and most powerful nation in the world. Bush retreated from international treaties on issues ranging from global warming to nuclear test ban agreements, and he revived the Reagan-era proposal for a nuclear missile shield. But the place of the nation in the global community was yet to be defined. Soon, monumental events shattered the nation's sense of security and forced Bush to abandon his retreat from international alliances and to engage in the world in unprecedented ways.

Conclusion

In the 1990s, the role of the nation in the world shifted and a half-century of political certainties evaporated. With the Cold War now over, conflicts around the globe, many of them grounded in ancient ethnic hostilities, posed challenges for the world's most powerful nation. The United States focused on markets and trade, the nation's supply of oil, the need for political order to maintain international stability, and the danger of "rogue nations" developing nuclear arms. President Clinton tried to be a peacemaker in hot spots around the world while attempting to respond to violent episodes of international terrorism.

At home, Americans demonstrated increasing tolerance for people who looked and acted differently from themselves. Polls showed declining levels of racial, ethnic, and religious hostility and greater acceptance of homosexuality, single parenthood, and family arrangements that deviated from the nuclear family model. But episodes of racial discrimination—by police, courts, and voting officials—continued. Politics remained an arena in which culture wars flared over abortion, gun control, and welfare reform. A Democratic president faced impeachment by his Republican foes in Congress while maintaining high approval ratings from the public.

At the dawn of the new century, several crises challenged Americans' sense of security. A deeply flawed presidential election revealed profound problems in the nation's voting system. A sharp and sudden downturn in the economy shattered the optimism many middle-class people felt during the booming Clinton years and forced many of the working poor into desperate circumstances. Already reeling from these disturbing developments, the nation was soon shaken to its core by a terrorist attack that forced a new reckoning at home and abroad.

Sites to Visit

William Jefferson Clinton
www.ipl.org/div/potus/wjclinton.html
> This site contains basic information about Clinton's election and presidency and an online biography.

Distribution of Wealth and Income
www.inequality.org/facts.cfm
> This site provides facts and figures about the distribution of wealth and income in the 1990s.

American Identities
xroads.virginia.edu/~YP/ethnic.html
> This site of the American Studies program at the University of Virginia includes information and resources for studying America's multiple ethnic identities.

O. J. Simpson Trial
www.cnn.com/US/OJ/index.html
> This CNN site provides basic facts and interpretive essays, plus additional links about the O. J. Simpson trial.

Investigating the President

www.cnn.com/ALLPOLITICS/resources/1998/lewinsky/

This CNN site provides information and documents about the scandals surrounding President Clinton's impeachment.

Focus on Kosovo

www.cnn.com/SPECIALS/1998/10/kosovo/

This in-depth CNN interactive site looks at the development of turmoil in Kosovo and its resolution.

Oklahoma City Bombing

www.cnn.com/US/OKC/

This CNN interactive site has information about the domestic terrorist bombing in Oklahoma City and the trial that followed.

Why Do Campaign Polls Zigzag So Much?

www2,psych.purdue.edu/~codelab/Invalid.Polls.html

This site, created by Gerald S. Wasserman of the Psychological Sciences Department at Purdue University, examines polling data from the 1996 presidential campaign.

For Further Reading

General

Stephanie Coontz, *The Way We Really Are: Coming to Terms with America's Changing Families* (1997).

Clara E. Rodriguez, *Changing Race: Latinos, the Census and the History of Ethnicity in the United States* (2000).

Leland T. Saito and Roger Daniels, *Race and Politics: Asian Americans, Latinos, and Whites in a Los Angeles Suburb* (1998).

The Economy: Global and Domestic

Sheldon Danziger and Peter Gottschalk, *America Unequal* (1995).

Jacqueline Jones, *American Work: Four Centuries of Black and White Labor* (1998).

William A. Orme, *Understanding NAFTA: Mexico, Free Trade, and the New North America* (1996).

Tolerance and Its Limits

Jane Mayer and Jill Abramson, *Strange Justice: The Selling of Clarence Thomas* (1994).

Michael Omi and Howard Winant, *Racial Formation in the United States: From the 1960s to the 1990s* (1994).

Alan Wolfe, *One Nation, After All: What Americans Really Think About God, Country, Family, Racism, Welfare, Immigration, Homosexuality, Work, the Right, the Left and Each Other* (1998).

Violence and Danger

Joan Jacobs Brumberg, *The Body Project: An Intimate History of American Girls* (2000).

Susan Faludi, *Stiffed: The Betrayal of the American Man* (1999).

Steven Wisotsky and Thomas Szasz, *Beyond the War on Drugs: Overcoming a Failed Public Policy* (1999).

The Clinton Presidency

William C. Berman, *From the Center to the Edge: The Politics and Policies of the Clinton Presidency* (2001).

James MacGregor Burns and Georgia J. Sorenson, *Dead Center: Clinton–Gore Leadership and the Perils of Moderation* (1999).

David Maraniss, *First in His Class: A Biography of Bill Clinton* (1995).

Steven E. Schier, ed., *The Postmodern Presidency: Bill Clinton's Legacy in U.S. Politics* (2000).

The Nation and the World

John Dumbrell and David M. Barrett, *The Making of U.S. Foreign Policy* (1998).

David Halberstam, *War in a Time of Peace: Bush, Clinton, and the Generals* (2002).

Thomas H. Henriksen, *Clinton's Foreign Policy in Somalia, Bosnia, Haiti, and North Korea* (1996).

The Contested Election of 2000

E. J. Dionne and William Kristol, eds., *Bush v. Gore: The Court Cases and the Commentary* (2001).

Alexander Keyssar, *The Right to Vote: The Contested History of Democracy in the United States* (2000).

Richard A. Posner, *Breaking the Deadlock: The 2000 Election, the Constitution, and the Courts* (2001).

For quizzes and other resources on these topics, go to www.longmanamericanhistory.com.

CHAPTER 30

A Global Nation for the New Millennium

At the beginning of the third millennium, the United States was more closely connected than ever to the rest of the world. The processes of globalization—increasing trade, communication, travel, and migration—linked the nation to the rest of a world that often seemed to be torn by ethnic and religious strife. That strife from abroad impinged on Americans in a shocking new way on September 11, 2001. On a sunny Tuesday morning, 19 hijackers—four of them trained as pilots—seized control simultaneously of four large commercial jets and turned them into suicidal missiles. At 8:48 a.m., one flew into the 110-story north tower of New York City's World Trade Center, igniting an enormous fireball. Fifteen minutes later, the second plane flew into the south tower. In less than two hours, both towers collapsed, killing the thousands of people still inside. Among the dead were hundreds of firefighters, police officers, and other rescue workers who had raced into the towers to evacuate the occupants. The third plane flew into the Pentagon. The fourth was also being directed toward Washington, apparently to destroy the White House or the Capitol Building, until it crashed in a field 75 miles southeast of Pittsburgh.

The carefully coordinated assaults killed almost 3,000 people, destroyed the two tallest buildings in the country's largest city, and left a gaping hole in the headquarters of the nation's military command. Not since the Japanese assault on Pearl Harbor 60 years earlier had the United States experienced a devastating attack on its own soil. During the intervening half-century of the Cold War, the Soviet Union and other communist forces had never attempted direct aggression against the American homeland. Who was responsible for the most horrific act of terrorism against civilians in U.S. history?

The 19 perpetrators were self-styled holy warriors of a secretive, extremist Islamic organization known as Al Qaeda, organized by wealthy, charismatic Saudi Arabian expatriate Osama bin

Val McClatchey

■ Smoke rises from the crash of United Airlines Flight 93 near Shanksville, Pennsylvania. For almost all Americans, the hijackings and destruction of September 11, 2001, came indeed out of a clear blue sky. Anti-American actions of the previous decade by Islamic terrorists had created little anxiety in a powerful nation that had imagined itself safe from major attack.

Laden. Al Qaeda worked out of Afghanistan, hosted by the most repressive Islamic government on Earth, the Taliban, which rose to power in 1996 out of the chaos that followed the withdrawal of the Soviet army in 1989. The rage of bin Laden and other Islamic terrorists against the United States had been building throughout the 1990s, fueled by the presence of "infidel" American troops in Saudi Arabia since the 1991 Persian Gulf War, by American support for Israel, and by the rapid spread of secular American popular culture around the globe. At odds with moderate Islamic mainstream thought throughout the world, bin Laden announced in 1998: "To kill Americans and their allies is an individual duty of every Muslim who is able."

At the heart of American society remained a common assumption, that the United States is a democratic country. The events on United Airlines Flight 93, one of the four doomed planes on September 11, 2001, revealed the tenacity of the belief in majority rule. After the hijackers seized control and herded the passengers into the rear of the cabin, a dozen passengers and crew members were able to communicate by phone with people on the ground. They learned that two other planes had already crashed into the World Trade Center towers in New York City, and they realized that these hijackers—unlike previous ones who sought concrete gains and an escape—planned only destruction for them all. Face to face with imminent death and the certainty that many others would perish if they failed to act, the passengers discussed what to do. They made a plan to rush the hijackers, led by several large, athletic passengers, including Mark Bingham, a prominent gay businessperson and rugby player from San Francisco. Should they proceed? Quintessential Americans, they took a vote. GTE Airfone operator Lisa Jefferson heard the rest: "Are you guys ready?" asked Todd Beamer, a tall father of two from Cranbury, New Jersey. Screams and a sustained scuffle followed before the line went dead. The plane, headed for the heart of Washington, crashed in an unpopulated part of western Pennsylvania with no casualties on the ground.

> *The events on United Airlines Flight 93, one of the four doomed planes on September 11, 2001, revealed the tenacity of the belief in majority rule.*

The George W. Bush Administration

The attacks of September 11, 2001, constituted perhaps the most significant event in American life since Japan's surrender in 1945. People remember where they were when they first learned what had happened, and they recall vividly the terrible televised images of destruction. As citizens of the sole remaining superpower after the collapse of the Soviet Union in 1991, Americans had grown accustomed to unprecedented global power and influence. They had no great power rival. For most of those ten years, they had experienced rapid economic growth as well. The nation, it seemed, was wealthy and secure.

The events on September 11 changed all that. The economy, already sliding into recession, accelerated its downward course. Just seven months in office, the administration of President George W. Bush responded by leading the nation into a "war on terrorism" abroad and at home. Within two years, U.S.-led efforts succeeded in overthrowing the governments of Afghanistan and Iraq. Complicated, long-term military occupations ensued, with U.S. forces continuing to engage in bloody battles against insurgents in both countries. In an effort to prevent further terrorist attacks at home, Congress passed the "USA Patriot Act," granting greater powers to the executive branch of the federal government. Authorities detained hundreds of immigrants, primarily young men of Middle Eastern descent. These policies then faced the test of public approval in the elections of November 2004.

The President and the War on Terrorism

George W. Bush did not have an auspicious record of achievement before his election as governor of Texas in 1994 and as president of the United States six years later. He grew up primarily in Midland, Texas, the grandson of a U.S. senator from Connecticut and the eldest son of a wealthy oilman, diplomat, and eventual U.S. president, George H. W. Bush. "W.," as he was sometimes called to distinguish him from his father, attended the elite Phillips Academy in Andover, Massachusetts, and he earned degrees from Yale and Harvard Business School, though his modest academic achievements hinted at the benefits of unofficial forms of affirmative action for the scions of wealthy and powerful families. His sociability and charisma earned him many friends. He avoided going to Vietnam when he was of draft age by serving in the Air National Guard, though he apparently failed to show up for much of a year of that service in 1972.

After a mixed career in business and a strong taste for the partying life, Bush gave up drinking at age 40 and became a devout, conservative Christian. This ambitious and now more serious man made his way up in Republican political circles, benefiting from family connections as well as a warm, "regular guy" personality that appealed to many working-class Americans. Despite his father's strongly international orientation, Bush himself before his presidency had left the United States only three times to go anywhere besides Mexico. "I'm not going to play like a person who has spent hours involved with foreign policy," he admitted during the 2000 campaign. Once president, he took a unilateralist and almost isolationist stance, to the dismay of close U.S. allies abroad. The United States rejected or withdrew from international agreements limiting global warming, weapons testing, and war crime prosecutions.

George W. Bush Address to Congress (September 20, 2001)

The events of September 11 stunned all Americans and gave the president a new focus. Finding and destroying Al Qaeda and its allies was now "the purpose of this administration," Bush told his cabinet. Four weeks after the attacks on New York and Washington, U.S. planes initiated the "war on terrorism" by bombing Taliban and Al Qaeda positions in Afghanistan. By October 19, U.S. special operations forces were working on the ground with anti-Taliban Afghan insurgents. Several European nations provided troops and other military assistance. By December, the Taliban had been driven from power throughout the country, and U.S. and allied forces had killed and captured hundreds of Taliban and Al Qaeda fighters. Many of the prisoners were transferred to the U.S. naval base at Guantanamo Bay, Cuba, to be held indefinitely and interrogated as enemy combatants. Despite continued pursuit and a reward offer of $25 million, the United States was not able to find Osama bin Laden, who was assumed to be hiding in the remote, snowy mountains of the Pakistan-Afghanistan border region.

Security and Politics at Home

The war on terrorism was not only a foreign affair. Just as the onset of the Cold War in the late 1940s had incorporated a hunt for domestic traitors, the war on terrorism in the early 2000s included a search for potential Al Qaeda sympathizers at home. Like the Cold War, the war on terrorism was framed as a long-term struggle against a maniacal, evil enemy who would not be easily defeated. Also as in the Cold War, American leaders announced that some civil liberties would have to be curtailed in order to protect the nation. The USA Patriot Act of October 2001 increased the U.S. Justice Department's range of options for spying on and detaining citizens and noncitizens suspected of pro-terrorist activities. Determined to prevent another major terrorist attack, Attorney General John Ashcroft oversaw the arrest of hundreds of illegal immigrants and their imprisonment in what the Justice Department later admitted were often unduly harsh conditions—not unlike Guantanamo, observers noted. Congress created the Department of Homeland Security (DHS) in an effort to better coordinate intelligence, police, and military authorities for defending the nation from future attacks.

George W. Bush, From "National Security Strategy of the United States of America" (September 2002)

Beyond terrorism, George W. Bush sought to move the nation in the direction of what he called "compassionate conservatism." One conservative activist noted that the new administration turned out to be "more Reaganite than the Reagan administration." In the economic realm, this meant promoting the private sector and reducing federal spending on social programs for the poor. It meant reducing the government's role in regulating health and safety issues in the workplace. And it meant pushing large tax cuts through Congress in 2001 and 2003 to the disproportionate benefit of the wealthiest 1 percent of Americans. The budget surpluses of Bill Clinton's last years disappeared, as the Bush administration ran enormous annual deficits by retaining the tax cuts while sharply increasing military spending. The nation's debt grew rapidly under Bush.

> *Like the Cold War, the war on terrorism was framed as a long-term struggle against a maniacal, evil enemy who would not be easily defeated.*

Bush's conservatism did not include conserving natural resources. Bush and Vice President Dick Cheney, both former oil executives, were closely allied with corporate interests, particularly in the energy business, that sought easier access to public resources. The administration promoted oil drilling offshore and in the Arctic National Wildlife Refuge, encouraged mining and timber clear-cutting across western federal lands, and refused to regulate carbon dioxide emissions despite powerful evidence of global warming. The administration also loosened federal regulations on industrial air pollution, on water pollution by the coal industry, and on arsenic levels in drinking water.

Sexual issues remained flashpoints of political controversy. Explicit and suggestive sexuality pervaded popular culture, including two-thirds of television shows, causing particular concern among parents of young children. At the same time, Americans were increasingly accepting of homosexual couples. In *Lawrence v. Texas* (2003), the U.S. Supreme Court overturned state laws banning private homosexual behavior between consenting adults. A year later, Massachusetts legalized gay marriage. One-third of the nation's largest companies now offered employees in same-sex marriages or committed relationships the same benefits and supports, such as health care insurance, that they offered employees with traditional families. Marriage and family remained social institutions in transition, for better or worse: only 56 percent of adults were now married, compared with 75 percent 30 years earlier. And only 26 percent of American households consisted of a married couple with children.

The War in Iraq

President Bush's most momentous decision was to invade and occupy Iraq in the spring of 2003. This was a very different proposition than the attack on Afghanistan. The effort to destroy Al Qaeda and its Taliban hosts in Afghanistan had widespread support in the United States and across much of the world. By contrast, invading a sovereign nation that had not attacked or even threatened the United States divided Americans and alienated most of the rest of the world. The United Nations refused to support the invasion. America's western European allies were dismayed. Among America's major allies, only the British government of Prime Minister Tony Blair provided enthusiastic political support and a significant number of troops. Given this lack of support, why did the Bush administration invade Iraq?

Some observers pointed to personal reasons. Bush would be "finishing" the Persian Gulf War of 1991, when his father oversaw the liberation of Kuwait from Saddam Hussein's invading Iraqi forces but did not send troops to Baghdad to overthrow Saddam. Bush would also be avenging Saddam's effort to assassinate the elder Bush on a visit to Kuwait. Other observers emphasized the centrality of Iraq's oil reserves, the largest in the world after those of Saudi Arabia and Canada. The president himself claimed two primary reasons for the invasion: that Saddam possessed "weapons of mass destruction"—chemical, biological, or nuclear—and could attack the United States or its allies "on any given day," and that Iraq had ties to Al Qaeda "and was equally as bad, equally as evil and equally as destructive." But after U.S. forces occupied Iraq, these two official reasons for the war were placed in doubt. U.S. troops found no weapons of mass destruction (though Saddam had indeed used chemical weapons on dissident Iraqi civilians 15 years earlier), and Secretary of State Colin Powell admitted there was no

Behrouz Mehri, Agence France-Presse/Getty Images

■ Nothing undercut the U.S. effort to extend its influence in the Middle East more than the photographs that emerged in the spring of 2004 of U.S. troops abusing Iraqi detainees at Abu Ghraib prison outside Baghdad. Here, two of these photographs are displayed on a street in neighboring Iran. The Abu Ghraib scandal dismayed America's allies, enraged Muslims everywhere, and almost certainly enhanced Al Qaeda recruiting. One Iraqi-American observed that the Bush administration had "done a good job of occupying the land of Iraq, but a horrible job of occupying the hearts of the Iraqi people."

"smoking gun" proof of a link between Al Qaeda's religious zealots and Saddam's fiercely secular dictatorship. The bipartisan reports of both the 9/11 Commission and the Senate Intelligence Committee in 2004 found that the primary reasons the president gave for invading Iraq were not true.

A deeper reason for the U.S. invasion of Iraq appeared to be the administration's view of September 11 as an opportunity to preemptively reshape the Middle East into a region less hostile to the United States and Israel. A liberated Iraq, right in the center of the Middle East, might have a "demonstration effect" of pro-American capitalist democracy that would turn the rest of the region away from authoritarianism and Islamic revolution. Bush spoke of the overthrow of Saddam as "a watershed event in the global democratic revolution." This statement represented a highly optimistic view of how Americans might bring change to the Middle East, part of a new U.S. strategic doctrine emphasizing preemptive action against the nation's enemies. "We must take the battle to the enemy" in the war on terrorism, Bush declared in 2002, "and confront the worst threats before they emerge."

The U.S.-led offensive in Iraq that began on March 19, 2003, was a successful military action. Some 200,000 U.S. and British troops, with a few other allied forces, overran Saddam's defenses and occupied the entire nation of 25 million people within four weeks. The rapid military victory and the presence of so many U.S. troops initially stunned neighboring Iran and Syria into reducing aid to anti-Israeli terrorist groups. Most Iraqis celebrated their liberation from Saddam's brutal regime, and many seemed to welcome the American soldiers. Seven months later, U.S. soldiers captured Saddam himself.

But military occupations rarely age well, especially without sufficient troops for the task. Widespread looting ravaged Baghdad, and essential services and personal security deteriorated in the aftermath of the old government's defeat. "Baghdad," one gasoline station owner observed, "is like the Wild West now." Saddam loyalists, Iraqi nationalists of various stripes, and arriving foreign Islamic revolutionaries initiated a multi-sided insurgency against the American occupiers. The number of U.S. and Iraqi deaths shot upward, as did the number of American troops sent to Iraq. The U.S. invasion of Iraq seemed to be increasing rather than reducing the threat of terrorism to Americans and others. Indeed, some observers suggested that Osama bin Laden might be pleased to have so many U.S. troops trying to control an unhappy Muslim population for the stimulus it provided to recruiting anti-American jihadists. Sunnis and Shiites also faced off against each other in what began to look like civil war. Critics of U.S. postwar planning now included some prominent Republicans, and the commander of allied forces in Iraq, General Ricardo Sanchez, told Americans flatly "we're still at war."

The Bush administration turned over official sovereignty to a new Iraqi government on June 28, 2004, with 130,000 U.S. troops remaining in the country in an effort to provide security against insurgents. "We don't do empire," insisted Secretary of Defense Donald Rumsfeld. But two months earlier, photographs and eyewitness reports were made public of U.S. troops abusing, torturing, and sexually humiliating Iraqi detainees at the Abu Ghraib prison outside Baghdad. After a week's delay, the president finally apologized. For most Middle Easterners and for Muslims around the world, however, this was compelling evidence that Bush's rhetoric about liberating Iraq was merely a cover for what they saw as fundamental American disdain for Muslims.

The Election of 2004 and After

President Bush entered his campaign for reelection with solid support in his own party but mixed reviews from others. Many other nations considered the U.S. attack on Iraq to be unjustified and unwise. Western Europeans resented Bush's lack of interest in their concerns, making him probably the least-popular American president in Europe in 80 years. Less than three years after the attacks of September 11, 2001, Americans still tended to support him on foreign policy matters. But many voters were troubled by the growing insurgency in Iraq and by a still-weak economy, and the president's approval ratings remained below 50 percent.

The Democratic Party hoped to exploit Bush's vulnerability by nominating Senator John Kerry of Massachusetts, a decorated Vietnam War hero with a moderately liberal legislative record. Bush and Kerry had graduated from Yale within two years of each other, and both had very wealthy families. Democratic party activists hoped to blunt the appeal of the president's "war on terrorism" and emphasis on patriotism by nominating a man whose courage under fire in Vietnam contrasted with Bush's safe spot in the Texas National Guard during that war.

It did not quite work. The president prevailed in a narrow popular-vote victory. The Electoral College outcome of 2004 hinged on Ohio, where a difference of 136,000 votes put Bush over the top. Two issues predominated in the minds of the majority of voters. One was the war on terrorism, which they tended to see as the same as the war in Iraq (despite evidence to the contrary) and on which they trusted Bush's leadership more than Kerry's. The second was what voters described as "moral values," a sense that Bush—even if they sometimes did not agree with his specific policy choices—had personal integrity, a quality they were less sure of with Kerry's nuanced views of complicated policy issues. Christian conservatives were particularly important in getting Republican voters to the polls, passing initiatives in 11 states to ban gay marriage and winning four new seats in the Senate and four in the House to give the president a larger majority in Congress.

TABLE 30-1

The Election of 2004

Candidate	Political Party	Popular Vote (%)	Electoral Vote
George W. Bush	Republican	50.8	286
John Kerry	Democratic	48.3	251
Ralph Nader	Green	<1	—

The president's political fortunes declined swiftly after his reelection. The situation in Iraq continued to deteriorate in 2005, as deepening ethnic and religious divisions undermined efforts to reconstruct a stable and orderly society. At home, an ethics scandal brought down the once-powerful House majority leader, Tom DeLay of Texas, and dimmed public confidence in the Republican-run Congress. On August 29, 2005, Hurricane Katrina flooded New Orleans, causing hundreds of deaths and a massive evacuation of nearly the entire city. The Bush administration was criticized from all sides for what was widely seen as a slow and ineffectual response to an extraordinary human disaster. By May 2006 Bush's approval rating dropped to 31%, the third lowest figure (after Richard Nixon and Jimmy Carter) for any president in 50 years. In the November 2006 elections, the Republicans lost their majorities in both the House and the Senate.

The American Place in a Global Economy

While the president navigated difficult political waters, average Americans struggled to find and keep their place in a changing world economy. Mollie Brown James, for example, grew up in a small Virginia town west of Richmond. In 1950, at age nineteen, she moved to Paterson, New Jersey, joining the broad river of black Southerners who sought better economic opportunities and greater personal freedom in the North. She took a job in 1955 with the Universal Manufacturing Company in Paterson, with wages and decent treatment, unlike what had been available to her in Virginia. She stayed with Universal for thirty-four years. With union-negotiated wages, overtime work, and company-paid health insurance, she helped pull her family into the middle-class world of owning their own home and car and saving for retirement. But the peace of mind that came from a secure job vanished in 1989 when Universal closed the Paterson plant and moved its manufacturing operations to Matamoros, Mexico, just across the Rio Grande River from Brownsville, Texas.

James's job did not disappear. It moved and was inherited by twenty-year-old Balbina Duque Granados. She, too, had grown up in a small town located in an agricultural area, in the Mexican province of San Luis Potosí, and she, too, had moved 400 miles north to find better-paying work in a booming manufacturing city. She was thrilled to land the difficult, repetitive job—her "answered prayer"—at a *maquiladora*, one of the foreign-owned assembly plants along Mexico's border with the United States that wed First World engineering with Third World working conditions. Her employer was also satisfied, paying her $.65 an hour to do what James had been paid $7.91 an hour for. But Granados's job was no more secure than James's had been. The beginnings of successful worker organizing in Matamoros encouraged the company to shift many of its operations sixty miles upriver to Reynosa, where the union movement was weaker. A journalist asked whether she would move there if her job did. "And what if they were to move again?" she replied. "Maybe to Juarez or Tijuana? What then? Do I have to chase my job all over the world?"

The Logic and Technology of Globalization

Like many other workers in the United States and abroad, Mollie James and Balbina Duque Granados learned firsthand the relentlessly international logic of the economic system known as capitalism. Those who had capital—extra money—invested it in corporations, whose purpose was to produce a profit for their shareholders. A corporation's profitability depended on keeping costs—labor and materials—down and expanding into new markets. Just as the telegraph and telephone had helped create a nation unified by rapid communication in the late 1800s, the spread of personal computers and the Internet linked Americans even more closely to other nations in the late 1900s.

At the close of the twentieth century, engineering breakthroughs sped up the process of globalization. The integration of computers into every aspect of commerce and private life increased the efficiency with which businesses could operate. Computers boosted American productivity (the amount of work performed by a person in a given time period), which had declined between 1973 and 1996, and the U.S. economy enjoyed its longest-ever expansion during the presidency of Bill Clinton. Cable News Network (CNN) offered a standardized package of world news available twenty-four hours a day around the globe. CNN was so international in its aims that it banned the word *foreign* from its broadcasts.

Americans were also speeding up their daily routines as the new millennium approached. The desire for immediate gratification and efficiency that had nurtured fast food and microwave ovens encouraged the spread of cell phones, beepers, fax machines, overnight package delivery, and constant news headlines scrolling across TV screens. Computers processed more information faster on ever-smaller silicon chips. Cell phones proliferated among businesspeople, students, and drivers. As prices dropped, they even reached into poorer areas. International air travel for business and pleasure quadrupled between 1980 and 1998, and international tourism vied with oil as the world's largest industry. The spread of the Internet and the use of electronic mail (e-mail) and instant-messaging after the early 1990s epitomized the shift toward instant global communication.

Free Trade and the Global Assembly Line

The ideology of free trade underpinned the tighter meshing of Americans' lives with the world economy. Advocates of free trade argued that global markets unhindered by national tariffs benefited consumers everywhere by giving them access to the best goods at the lowest prices. America's NAFTA treaty with Canada and Mexico reflected this belief (see Chapter 29), as did the European Union with its newly unified currency, the euro. In the United States, by the start of the new millennium most leaders of both major political parties, corporate executives, bankers, and most other elites supported free trade.

But others objected to this internationalist economic ideology. Environmentalists and labor unions led the forces opposing unregulated globalization of the U.S. economy. Environmentalists warned of the pollution costs to the world's environment of U.S. factories relocating to poorer and less regulated nations, such as Mexico and China. Labor organizers decried the flight of American jobs as manufacturers sought less expensive and more compliant—often desperate—workers abroad. Human rights activists spotlighted the grim working conditions in many overseas plants, including the prevalence of child labor.

A "race to the bottom" for labor and environmental standards resulted from the development of a global assembly line. With capital able to move swiftly around the world and take its factories with it, nations and localities believed that they had little choice but to compete in offering multinational corporations the most advantageous terms possible. Such terms meant minimal government regulation, little protection for workers, nonexistent pollution standards, and local subsidies in place of corporate taxes. Corporate income taxes, which had been dropping since the 1950s, shrank by another third between 1986 and 2000. The *maquiladoras* on the Mexican border were part of a broader pattern of the corporate search for efficiency and profit, as companies, like Mollie James's Universal Manufacturing Company and RCA, took their production lines first to the American South and then abroad.

As a result, corporations and their products became less identifiable by nationality. Boeing Aircraft had long been the largest employer in the Seattle area, but was its new Boeing 777,

"On the Internet, nobody knows you're a dog."

■ **The Internet provided both immediate connections with other people around the world and the safety of personal anonymity. Internet users could not be judged by their appearance or material possessions, only by the words they typed. Americans debated whether the popularity of the Internet represented a new kind of virtual community that would strengthen their connections to each other, or merely another way for citizens to remain isolated in their own homes rather than engaged with each other in civic organizations.**

Was a Toyota made by American workers in Georgetown, Kentucky, a "foreign" car?

manufactured piece by piece in twelve different countries, an "American" airplane? Japanese companies also moved many manufacturing plants overseas, including to the United States, to be closer to important markets. Was a Toyota made by American workers in Georgetown, Kentucky, a "foreign" car?

Who Benefits from Globalization?

The increasing globalization of the U.S. economy at the end of the twentieth century created enormous wealth while sharpening class inequalities. The stock market skyrocketed. The Dow Jones average of the value of thirty top companies' stocks rose steadily from 500 in 1956, to 1,000 in 1972, to 3,000 in 1991. Then it more than tripled in value in just eight years, surpassing 10,000 in 1999. Wealthy Americans who owned the bulk of corporate stock reaped the most gains, but middle- and even working-class Americans with retirement funds invested in the market also benefited handsomely. The process of globalization and the steady expansion of the U.S. economy after 1992 also encouraged a growing belief among Americans, especially affluent ones, that markets alone offered the best solution to social problems. But markets and their strict dependence on the profit motive proved unable to preserve the quality of the environment, to pull the 37 million officially poor Americans above the poverty line ($19,200 for a family of four in 2004), or to preserve the security of the vast middle class that had stabilized American politics since World War II. Inequalities within the United States reflected growing global inequality as 20 percent of the world's people (mostly in Europe and North America) consumed 86 percent of its goods and services.

American consumers enjoyed many of the fruits of the more integrated world economy. At least in industries not dominated by monopolies, the corporate quest for lower production costs, along with fierce international competition and technological innovation, reduced prices of many goods and services. Computers, airline travel, and gasoline were all significantly less expensive in real dollars (adjusted for inflation) than they had been a generation earlier. Competition abounded in the robust retail sector of the U.S. economy, including catalog and Internet shopping. Wal-Mart represented the epitome of how the globalized economy could benefit consumers. By 2000 the discount store surpassed General Motors as the largest American company, responsible for 6 percent of all U.S. retail sales. Wal-Mart's success resulted from relentlessly cutting costs through sharp management, using cheaper imported goods and employing a nonunion workforce, and passing some of its savings along to customers in the form of lower prices.

The benefits that Americans experienced as consumers in the global economy were offset by their declining status as workers. As manufacturers moved to the Sunbelt and then overseas, high-wage, unionized jobs providing health insurance and pension benefits disappeared. Average real wages declined for more than two decades after 1973, and union membership shrank from one-third of the workforce in the early 1950s to one-tenth in 2000. Family incomes were maintained only by the addition of second and third wage earners, especially women. Americans spent more than they earned. The average household had 13 credit cards and carried $8,500 in debt on them, in addition to owing car and home mortgage payments. In 2005, the average personal savings rate dropped below zero.

Already wider in the United States than in any other industrialized nation, the distance between rich and poor continued to grow, whittling away at Americans' self-image as a middle-class society. The share of the national income going to the richest 1 percent nearly doubled in the last quarter of the twentieth century, while the share going to the bottom 80 percent shrank. Three million Americans lived in gated communities in extremely affluent suburbs, while one of five American children grew up in poverty, and 21 million citizens sought emergency food assistance each year.

The political system, which helps determine how wealth and opportunity are distributed in a society, seemed to offer little respite from the widening gap between haves and have-nots. The fraction of eligible citizens who made the effort to vote in presidential elections declined to just half in 2000 and in off-year congressional elections to a mere third, with the likelihood of voting closely correlated to a person's affluence. The fierce partisanship, personal attacks, and culture of scandal that came to dominate American politics in the past two decades alienated many.

Citizens were also disillusioned by the blatant manner in which money came to dominate the political process. With the average cost of a successful Senate campaign at $7.5 million and a House campaign approaching $1 million, few but the wealthy could campaign for Congress, and elected members spent inordinate amounts of time raising money from wealthy donors. Republican Senator John McCain of Arizona called campaign financing "an elaborate influence-peddling scheme in which both parties conspire to stay in office by selling the country to the highest bidder." The ability of business to outspend labor fifteen to one in contributing to campaigns helped ensure minimal publicity to any discussions of the gulf between rich and poor.

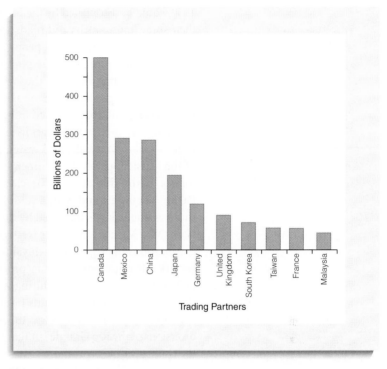

■ **FIGURE 30.1**

TOP TEN U.S. TRADING PARTNERS, 2005 (TOTAL VALUE OF IMPORTS AND EXPORTS IN BILLIONS OF DOLLARS) Americans do the most business with Canada and Mexico, followed by east Asia and then western Europe. U.S. economic vitality has always depended to some extent on foreign trade, but that dependence grew steadily in the past generation.

The Stewardship of Natural Resources

No issue was more global than the environment. Winds and waters did not respect political boundaries, nor did the materials borne on them. The condition of the natural environment affected all living creatures, yet the prevailing calculus of the market and private ownership did not apportion responsibility for its care. The free market system had no mechanism for offsetting, or even measuring, the costs of depleted natural resources. A generation ago, biologist Garrett Hardin had warned of "the tragedy of the commons": that individuals' incentives to preserve the quality of their own property did not carry over to resources held in common. Litter was an obvious example, and air, water, and ground pollution were the more serious cases. American culture had long celebrated human domination of the natural world and the benefits it brought, especially the growth in productivity that permitted living standards to rise dramatically across decades and centuries. At the same time, the rise of environmentalism and ecological understanding since 1960 offered a different way of imagining people's place on the earth.

Ecological Transformation in the Twentieth Century

Ecosystems are always dynamic, and changes in weather and Native American land use had reshaped the North American environment long before the followers of Christopher Columbus arrived on the continent. But European settlement and industrialization altered the face of the land in ways that would dumbfound a time traveler from the 1500s. Even a visitor from

1900 would be astonished by the intensity of human development of the land: vast cities with their sprawling suburbs and roads and highways everywhere. The key factor was population growth. Just as the number of people in the world quadrupled from 1.5 billion to 6 billion during the twentieth century, the population of the United States almost quadrupled from 75 million to 281 million, with the largest increase for a single decade (33 million) coming in the 1990s. Immigration and natural reproduction accounted for much of this, as did the much-longer average lifespan ushered in by antibiotics and antiviral vaccines.

The most dramatic changes in the land in the twentieth century resulted from the exploitation of wood, minerals, and water, particularly in the majority of the country lying west of the Mississippi River. Commercial logging destroyed all but 3 percent of the old-growth forests of the fifty states. The clearcuts scarring the mountainsides and hillsides of the Pacific Northwest and Alaska told the tale, as did the erosion caused by the overgrazing by cattle of public lands managed by the Interior Department's Bureau of Land Management in Utah, New Mexico, and other western states. The Mining Act of 1872 still granted to private corporations the rights to such valuable minerals as gold and copper on public land for the remarkable nineteenth-century price of $2.50 per acre. Mining companies took full advantage of the opportunity, resulting in rock and chemical wastes piled in vast slagheaps and dumped in toxic holding ponds from Arizona to Montana. In the arid but increasingly populated western states, water was the most critical resource for population growth. Increasing diversions of the Rio Grande left that now misnamed river so dry that, by 2001, it failed to reach the Gulf of Mexico, trickling to a halt 50 feet short. Groundwater pumping for agricultural irrigation in the Plains states and on the eastern slope of the Rocky Mountains was draining the vast underground Ogallala Aquifer at a rate that will empty it within a few more decades.

American prosperity came at a price. The prodigious growth of the U.S. economy in the twentieth century depended on the consumption of ever-increasing amounts of energy, most of it from coal, oil, and natural gas. Though making up less than 5 percent of the world's population, Americans accounted for a quarter of the globe's energy consumption. They depended on other countries to provide much of it for them: the United States imported 22 percent of its total energy needs and 69 percent of its oil, primarily from Saudi Arabia, Venezuela, Canada, and Mexico. Fossil fuels, such as coal and oil, could not be renewed; once burned, they were gone, and the world had a finite supply of such fuels. Americans were constructing a lifestyle that was unsustainable in the long run.

Pollution

The world's growing population was consuming five times as much fossil fuel in 2000 as in 1950, helping to stimulate a steady rise in the earth's average temperatures. Americans caused 36 percent of such carbon-based emissions, the largest contribution to the foremost environmental problem, global warming. In the summer of 2000, startled scientists found open water at the North Pole, a sight humans had never before seen. Greenhouse gases also contributed to a thinning of the ozone layer of the atmosphere, which enabled more of the sun's ultraviolet rays to reach the earth's surface and caused skin cancer rates to soar.

The internal combustion engine had long since surpassed coal burning as the leading cause of pollution. The United States produced and used more cars and trucks than any other nation. With minimal public transportation outside a handful of major cities, Americans were deeply committed to a car-dependent lifestyle. The highway infrastructure strained under the pressure of a 60 percent rise in the number of licensed drivers from 1970 to 2000 but only a 6 percent growth in total miles of roads. Negotiating traffic jams became a standard part of the daily lives of the majority of Americans who lived in the suburbs created by urban sprawl, especially around such cities as Los Angeles and Atlanta. Citizens spent three times as many hours stalled in traffic in 1999 as they had in 1982. Smog increasingly obscured such once-sublime vistas as that of Arizona's Grand Canyon.

Daily life in the United States came to depend in countless ways on the use of synthetic chemicals, production of which was 350 times greater in 1982 than in 1940. More than 50,000 known toxic waste dumps in the United States leached poisonous chemicals and heavy metals into the soil and water. Cancer rates among Americans grew sharply in the twentieth century, partly because people lived significantly longer lives (giving more time for cancers to appear) and partly because they were exposed to a much larger array of carcinogenic materials in the environment.

No synthetic product was more pervasive in the United States than plastic, a post-1945 product made from petroleum. But the most deadly and durable pollutants remained the radioactive wastes created by five decades of nuclear development. No one knew yet how to dispose safely of millions of tons of materials impregnated with plutonium and other human-made radioactive elements, 30 percent of it casually poured into dirt or stored in flimsy containers prone to leakage. The U.S. nuclear weapon complex of some 3,000 sites put its often fatal touch on the lives of millions of Americans: uranium miners, military workers, soldiers used to observe test explosions at close range, and citizens living downwind from the Nevada Test Site in Nevada and Utah. The National Academy of Sciences concluded in 2000 that many of these sites would be permanent national sacrifice zones, toxic to humans for at least tens of thousands of years.

> *No one knew yet how to dispose safely of millions of tons of materials impregnated with plutonium and other human-made radioactive elements.*

Environmentalism and Its Limitations

The ideas of most Americans about how to manage natural resources changed in the twentieth century. Environmental consciousness blossomed since the 1960s. Awareness of humans' connections with their broader ecological context led to significant reforms, such as the banning of carcinogenic pesticides and leaded gasoline, the cleaning up of polluted water in the Great Lakes, and the introduction of catalytic converters to reduce harmful emissions from automobile exhaust pipes and factory smokestacks. Recycling became common, and some dams were destroyed, freeing long-constricted rivers, such as the Penobscot in Maine. Yet issues of public land management and pollution control remained among the most controversial problems in American public life.

The relationship of Americans to their natural environment continued to be paradoxical. On the one hand, by large majorities in public opinion polls, Americans supported strong antipollution laws and the preservation of public lands from economic development. But on the other hand, in their daily lives, Americans consumed natural resources, especially gasoline, electricity, and water, at a rate unmatched by other societies. Measures that had reduced some of the nation's energy consumption since the 1970s were reversed by 2000: Congress revoked the national 55 mph speed limit in 1995, and ever-larger cars, trucks, and especially sport utility vehicles steadily reduced the average gas mileage of passenger vehicles.

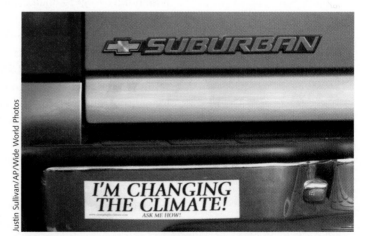

Justin Sullivan/AP/Wide World Photos

■ The oil crises of the 1970s led automobile manufacturers to improve the efficiency of gas mileage in their cars. By the early 2000s, however, gasoline was once again inexpensive and growing numbers of Americans were buying large new sport utility vehicles (SUVs) such as the Chevrolet Suburban, despite their low gas mileage. A few environmentalists placed bumper stickers on other people's SUVs to highlight the key role of auto emissions in the accelerating process of global warming.

The Expansion of American Popular Culture Abroad

Just as the U.S. economy and American environmental problems could not be separated from the outside world, the nation's cultural life grew more closely tied to that of other nations at the dawn of the new millennium. During the Cold War, from the 1940s through the 1980s, American foreign relations hinged on problems of national security and the projection of military might abroad. The dissolution of the Soviet Union in 1991 and the retreat of communism ended the bipolar division of the world and left the United States the sole remaining superpower. By 2000 American popular culture rather than armed strength had emerged as the leading edge of U.S. influence around the world. American themes and products stood out in an increasingly global society, although they were resisted by some abroad who preferred more local identities and traditions, often rooted in ethnicity or religious conviction.

A Culture of Diversity and Entertainment

Known for its informality and diversity, American culture proved powerfully attractive to peoples all over the world, partly because racial and ethnic diversity was more pronounced in the United States than in any other major power. African Americans, Latino Americans, and Asian Americans all figured prominently in the popular realms of sports, music, and films. Television was the leading medium for this culture of entertainment, beaming CNN, MTV, and "reality" around the world. From jazz to rock 'n' roll to rap, American popular music spread across the globe, as did jeans and sneakers, symbols of informality and comfort. Hollywood's movies dominated cinemas and DVD players everywhere, providing 85 percent of films screened in Europe.

The idea of individual choice pervaded American culture, backed by constitutional guarantees of freedom of expression. Freedom to choose included matters of religion, politics, and other weighty areas, which had long made the United States a beacon of liberty to people oppressed for their beliefs. But freedom of choice came increasingly by the end of the twentieth century to refer to consumer goods. The United States was the largest market in the world, and its citizens had unparalleled choices of what to buy. The premium placed on acquiring material products seemed to many foreign observers the primary American value.

> *The premium placed on acquiring material products seemed to many foreign observers the primary American value.*

Advertising grew in prominence as the central link between popular culture and the selling of goods. Sports became steadily more commercialized. Postseason college football games began in 1985 to include the names of their corporate sponsors, creating such events as the Chick-Fil-A Peach Bowl and the Weed Eater Independence Bowl. By 2000 newspapers ranked bowl games—once hallowed for their own distinctive traditions—by the simple criterion of how much money sponsors paid to participating teams. In the 1990s, "hoops" joined baseball as a popular U.S. export. National Basketball Association (NBA) games were telecast to more than 190 countries in forty-one languages. Sports also brought foreigners to the United States as professional baseball and basketball teams began recruiting Latin American, European, African, and Asian athletes.

U.S. Influence Abroad Since the Cold War

Cultural influences flowed both ways for Americans, with immigrants in particular bringing with them traditions and perspectives that refreshed the cultural mix of life in the United States. Japanese Pokémon trading cards, Thai cuisine, and Cuban salsa music helped shape daily routines for many Americans. But increased trade and communication since the end of the Cold War above all enabled the further spread of American popular culture. American-accented English straddled the globe, the language of international commerce and of 80 percent of listings on the World Wide Web. The informality and individualism of the Internet made it seem quintessentially American in style. The U.S. dollar remained the world's primary trading currency and became the de facto and even the de jure currency of many other nations.

America's most popular eatery served 20 million customers a day at its 23,000 franchises across the globe, earning half its revenues abroad. McDonald's Golden Arches appeared everywhere, from Japan and France to Russia and China. Even Mecca in Saudi Arabia, Islam's holiest site and the destination of millions of Muslim pilgrims, had a McDonald's.

Nor did only U.S. material interests spread abroad swiftly in recent years. American religious missionaries worked in poor countries around the world, combining their spiritual mission with a commitment to improving daily life in concrete ways involving health care, education, and agriculture. Pentecostalists gained millions of converts in Latin America since the 1970s, and mainstream denominations, such as Lutherans, Episcopalians, and Roman Catholics, saw their numbers rise sharply in Africa. The most fully homegrown American religion was especially active in proselytizing abroad. As a result, the Church of Jesus Christ of Latter Day Saints (Mormons), headquartered in Salt Lake City, had 5 million members in the United States and another 5 million worldwide.

The United States retained its military superiority, with a defense budget larger than that of the next ten biggest military powers combined. But the difficulties of unconventional warfare, from Vietnam in the 1960s to Somalia in 1993, combined with the apparent disappearance of a major threat to the nation's security after the demise of the Soviet Union, made U.S. policymakers and citizens reluctant to put American troops in harm's way abroad, at least until after the terrorist attacks of September 11, 2001. Instead, the expansion of American culture abroad seemed a safer and more effective way to influence other nations.

"Meritocracy worked for my grandfather, it worked for my father, and it's working for me."

■ **An important tension in American history was the conflict between the ideal of equal opportunity for all and the reality of inherited wealth and privilege. The efforts of the George W. Bush administration to eliminate the federal estate tax, which affected the inheritances of less than 1 percent of U.S. citizens, represented the latest round in the debate about the relationship between political democracy and inherited economic inequality. In a pure meritocracy, all citizens would be rewarded for their personal achievements rather than those of their parents or ancestors.**

Resistance to American Popular Culture

Like Christian, Jewish, and Hindu fundamentalists, all of whom grew prominent in the final decades of the twentieth century, Muslim fundamentalists rejected the radical egalitarianism and the unbridled pursuit of pleasure so prevalent in American popular culture. The relative equality of women and the lack of respect for traditional social and religious hierarchies seemed to them emblems of American decadence, as the Islamic rulers of Afghanistan—the Taliban—demonstrated in the 1990s in their brutal repression of women's rights. Osama bin Laden and his followers resented U.S. policies of supporting Israel and certain oil-producing Arab nations, but they also fiercely condemned the secular, egalitarian character of American society, which they considered anti-Islamic. During the 1991 Persian Gulf War, Saudi Arabian officials tried to isolate U.S. troops from Saudi citizens, fearing the effects of contact with such diverse forces as female soldiers, bawdiness, Christianity, and American music and television.

The demise of communist regimes in Russia and eastern Europe opened the gates to a flood of western influences and brought the opportunities and inequalities of a suddenly privatized economy. State-provided safety nets disappeared, class differences widened, women's economic status declined, and the old Communist parties regained some popularity among voters scared by the instabilities of American-style capitalism. Western Europeans also remained ambivalent about the spread of American values and lifestyles. Although many of them, especially among the young,

The Slow Food Movement

For many people in countries other than the United States, as for many Americans, McDonald's and other U.S.-based fast food restaurants offered an attractive dining experience. Customers everywhere appreciated the efficient and friendly service, clean surroundings, and the consistent quality of the food. Their enthusiasm explained the extraordinary international growth and profitability of such chains as Burger King and Kentucky Fried Chicken at the end of the twentieth century.

For other people, the rapid spread of fast food franchises around the globe threatened cherished values and lifestyles. The Slow Food Movement emerged in western Europe in the late 1980s as a loose-knit organization, headquartered in the northern Italian town of Bra. The movement sought to preserve and celebrate traditional cuisines and methods of food production in Europe and around the world. Slow Food's 60,000 members objected not only to the specific taste of fast food, but also to broader cultural changes symbolized by McDonald's and its competitors: the speeding up of daily life, including the loss of sociability around more leisurely meals; the gradual replacement of family farming and food production by corporate agriculture; and the erosion of distinctive local cooking and dining traditions.

Hasan Hamali/AP/Wide World

The spread of American fast food chains around the globe suggested that American culture may be a more powerful influence abroad than U.S. military might. The end of the Cold War led to McDonald's restaurants proliferating in downtown Moscow and Beijing, the capital cities of America's greatest opponents since World War II. The Golden Arches even invaded Mecca, Saudi Arabia, the holiest city of Islam.

The Slow Food Manifesto (November 9, 1989)

Our century, which began and has developed under the insignia of industrial civilization, first invented the machine and then took it as its life model.

We are enslaved by speed and have all succumbed to the same insidious virus: *Fast Life,* which disrupts our habits, pervades the privacy of our homes and forces us to eat *Fast Foods.*

To be worthy of the name, *Homo sapiens* should rid himself of speed before it reduces him to a species in danger of extinction.

A firm defense of quiet material pleasure is the only way to oppose the universal folly of *Fast Life.*

May suitable doses of guaranteed sensual pleasure and slow, long-lasting enjoyment preserve us from the contagion of the multitude who mistake frenzy for efficiency.

Our defense should begin at the table with *Slow Food.* Let us rediscover the flavors and savors of regional cooking and banish the degrading effects of *Fast Food.*

In the name of productivity, *Fast Life* has changed our way of being and threatens our environment and our landscapes. So *Slow Food* is now the only truly progressive answer.

That is what real culture is all about: developing taste rather than demeaning it. And what better way to set about this than an international exchange of experiences, knowledge, projects?

Slow Food guarantees a better future.

Slow Food is an idea that needs plenty of qualified supporters who can help turn this (slow) motion into an international movement, with the little snail as its symbol.

Slow Food operates to protect the right to pleasure, the respect of the rhythms of life and a harmonious relationship with nature. It also seeks to explore, describe and improve the culture of food, to develop a proper education of taste and smell from childhood and to safeguard and defend the agroindustrial heritage while respecting the cuisines of each single country.

The Slow Food Manifesto was ratified in Paris at the Founding Congress of the International Slow Food Movement on December 9, 1989.

Source: http://www.slowfood.com

Questions

1. What, precisely, do slow food advocates object to about fast food?

2. How important is fast food in the lives of people you know, and how does it affect their lives? ■

found American culture attractive and learned English in record numbers, traditionalists who were proud of their own national culture took a dim view of such innovations as fast food.

Other nations sometimes found the U.S. government overbearing and resented its unparalleled military power. Rapidly modernizing China, the world's most populous country, seemed a growing rival to the United States in Asia, even as the two nations became major trading partners.

Two opposing trends characterized world affairs. One consisted of the unifying forces of economic internationalism and globalization, carrying with them a tide of American-dominated cultural styles. The other was made up of the resisting forces of political and ethnic nationalism. A world more tightly integrated in economic ways was at the same time divided by ethnic conflicts. As people around the world felt themselves increasingly sucked into the vortex of a powerful global economy that they could not control, many of them responded by renewing their allegiances to older, more local traditions. Ethnic, religious, and national identities often offered more meaningful alternatives to a purely economic identity as consumers.

Identity in Contemporary America

The 2000 U.S. Census revealed a society in the midst of change. Americans have long been known as a particularly restless and mobile people, and one out of five changed residences every year. The post-1965 wave of immigrants continued to rise (and foreign adoptions rose dramatically), bringing in millions of new Americans of Asian heritage. Latino Americans came to equal African Americans in population; with 35 million people each, these groups were the nation's two largest minorities. This latest surge in immigration boosted the number of Roman Catholics and Buddhists as American society remained the most openly religious—still primarily Protestant—of the industrialized nations. Geographically, Americans lived farther south and west than earlier generations, as none of the twenty fastest-growing states were in the Northeast or Midwest. And more than half of Americans lived in suburbs.

Social Change and Abiding Discrimination

One of the most striking changes in American society over the past five decades was the desegregation of public life. Latinos and Asians became much more numerous in the United States, and African Americans emerged from the enforced separation of Jim Crow into greater prominence.

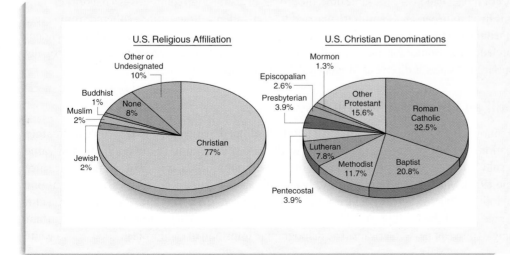

■ **FIGURE 30.2**
SELF-DESCRIBED RELIGIOUS AFFILIATION IN THE UNITED STATES, 2000   The most noticeable change of the last thirty years in American religious life has been the growth of evangelical and fundamentalist Protestant congregations (shown here as Pentecostals and "Other Protestants") and the shrinking of mainline Protestant denominations.

Roughly one-third of blacks were middle-class, and thousands won election to local, state, and national political offices. Black Americans became central in the nation's cultural life in music, literature, theater, and sports. By 2001 even a new president from the Republican party—known since 1964 for its lack of support from black voters—appointed two African Americans to direct the nation's foreign relations: Secretary of State Colin Powell and National Security Adviser Condoleezza Rice. Workplaces were racially integrated to an extent that would have been hard to imagine in 1950, and interracial marriages rose steeply in the final decades of the twentieth century.

The lives of women in the United States also changed dramatically during the last half of the twentieth century. Most worked outside the home, from jobs in the service and manufacturing sectors to careers in the professions and politics. In 2000 women made up one-third of the students in the nation's medical schools and one-half in law schools. Their presence in leading political positions ranged from local officials to more than a dozen U.S. senators, two U.S. Supreme Court justices, a U.S. attorney general, and a U.S. secretary of state. The passage of Title IX in 1972, prohibiting gender discrimination in school programs that received federal money, created a tidal wave of social change for American girls. In 1971 one in twenty-seven girls played high school sports; by 1998 the ratio was one in three. Sports programs and teams for girls comparable to those for boys nourished a new generation of American women for whom athletic competition and achievement were the norm rather than the exception.

These improvements for the majority of Americans who were not heterosexual white men jostled against abiding forms of discrimination and inequality. Violence and the threat of violence against homosexuals, people of color, and particularly women (primarily domestic violence at the hands of husbands and lovers) remained very real, but most prejudices found more subtle avenues of expression. Working women continued to average less than three-quarters the wages of working men. Many employers, police officers, store owners, bank loan officers, and others in positions of authority treated African Americans and Latino Americans with greater suspicion than they did other citizens, a practice that became known as racial profiling. Poverty and unemployment disproportionately affected black communities and families. Residential neighborhoods and public schools remained largely segregated by race, and the deeply symbolic Confederate flag still occupied a place of public honor in several southern states.

Native Americans shared this combination of improving status and continuing discrimination. Their numbers were reviving, from a mere 250,000 in 1900 to 2 million in 2000. A series of federal court decisions in the 1970s and 1980s strengthened Indians' "unique and limited" sovereignty over the tribal reservations, which constituted 2 percent of U.S. land. Starting with the Iroquois of upstate New York in 1970, several eastern Indian nations successfully sued state and federal governments for the return of parts of lands that had been illegally seized from them in the past, or for compensation. Casino revenues in the 1990s brought much-needed resources to a number of Indian nations. At the same time, the process of assimilation continued as a majority of Indians lived in urban areas and were married to non-Indians. Reservations suffered from severe unemployment rates and remained some of the poorest communities in the country, dependent on federal assistance for food and other basic necessities. Anti-Indian sentiments occasionally surfaced in states as diverse as Montana, Wisconsin, Arizona, and New York.

Still an Immigrant Society

Economic opportunity and individual liberty continued to lure millions of people from other nations to the United States at the start of the new millennium. About a million now came legally each year, and another 300,000 entered without official papers. For the first time since the 1930s, one in nine Americans had been born abroad; in New York City, the ratio was one in four. In 2004, 15 percent came from Europe, 33 percent from Asia, and 43 percent from Latin America and the Caribbean. Like Italy in 1900, Mexico in 2000 became the most important single source of new Americans. The demographic transition of California in 2000 from a white majority to a more diverse ethnic and racial mix like that of Hawaii symbolized the nation's turn to the South and West, even as the motives and work habits of the newcomers remained very much the same as those of their European predecessors.

Only the hardiest and most motivated people made the difficult, emotionally wrenching, and often dangerous move to the United States. Many fled political persecution in countries like Guatemala, Haiti, Vietnam, and Cuba. In contrast to the left-leaning and often socialist attitudes of immigrants in 1900, political refugees in 2000 were sometimes fierce anticommunists who helped pressure the U.S. government to take an even harder line toward regimes in Havana and Hanoi. Most immigrants came to stay, but some worked to save money and return home to their families, carrying with them not only money, but also bits of American culture.

Only the hardiest and most motivated people made the difficult, emotionally wrenching, and often dangerous move to the United States.

Americans responded to the wave of newcomers with an ambivalence common in previous periods of high immigration. Many in the working class feared competition from highly motivated laborers accustomed to much lower wages. Many elites worried whether cultural diversity might weaken national unity. Conservative political leaders promoted new restrictions and stronger border patrols. Some U.S. Congressmen ridiculed the idea of there being value in traveling abroad by boasting that they did not even have passports. In 1998 Republican House Majority Leader Dick Armey of Texas announced, "I've been to Europe once; I don't have to go again." Such disdain for other cultures among some American political leaders dismayed U.S. allies overseas.

Most Americans simply got used to having more immigrants around. Americans cheered for the one in four major league baseball players who were born in Latin America or had parents from there, and they became accustomed to the high number of Asian Americans in college classrooms. Many churches worked to help new arrivals adjust to life in the United States. Above all, American employers depended on immigrant workers to keep the nation's powerful economy afloat—to pick its fruits and vegetables, tend its young children, and work in its factories.

Conclusion

What held Americans together as they set off into the twenty-first century was a common loyalty to a set of ideas about economic opportunities and individual liberties. Unlike such nations as Germany and Israel, where citizenship was extended automatically only to people of a certain ethnicity, the United States awarded citizenship to all those who were born within its borders, regardless of ethnicity or race. Those born elsewhere became citizens on the basis not of their past lineage but of their future commitments—of their newly sworn loyalty to the U.S. Constitution, with its guarantees of freedom and its responsibilities of citizenship. In a vast society of multiple political and cultural beliefs, the scope of specific freedoms and the nature of individual responsibilities inevitably remained matters of ongoing tension and conflict. Nonetheless, the United States continued to address most of its problems through an orderly legal system, in contrast to the ethnic and religious strife marking so many of the world's nations.

Americans will face some basic challenges in the near future, as suggested by the four main themes of this book. First, will the currently increasing inequality in American society—in terms of income, wealth, and power—weaken the bonds that hold the nation together? Policies regarding taxes, Social Security, health care, and welfare will help determine if most Americans will continue to see themselves as middle-class members of a mostly middle-class society. The process of globalization will not make this any easier. The tighter integration of the U.S. economy and the world economy has thus far helped create great wealth, but that wealth is distributed very unevenly among Americans. Who has how much wealth and influence will remain a crucial determinant of the nation's future.

Second, the use and distribution of natural resources will almost certainly become more contentious issues. As national and world populations continue to increase, so will the demand for oil, water, and timber. How will crowding and greater competition affect the quality of American life? How long can American society remain centered on the automobile and its emphasis on individual mobility? Behind all environmental issues looms perhaps the largest issue of all: global warming and how it may reshape societies around the globe, including the United States.

Third, the expansion of American influence abroad continues to create problems as well as benefits for Americans. U.S. military, economic, political, and cultural leadership is clear. But the enormous reservoir of goodwill toward the United States that was evident around the world through much of the twentieth century has been draining rapidly in recent years. Ongoing U.S. military operations in Afghanistan and Iraq have convinced millions of peoples in those regions and elsewhere, rightly or wrongly, that the United States is an aggressive nation bent on dominating the world in general and humbling Islamic nations in particular. Whether the United States will gain more than it loses by its military engagements abroad remains an open question.

Fourth and finally, American society has always been diverse and it continues to become more so. How well will Americans hold together as a people as their ranks come to include larger numbers of immigrants, non-Christians, people of color, open homosexuals, and people of other identities not previously considered mainstream? In comparison to most other cultures, American society has been unusually inclusive of people of diverse backgrounds and beliefs. Whether it will continue to be so will shape, as much as any other factor, the future of the United States.

Sites to Visit

Smithsonian Latino Center
latino.si.edu/
This site offers an array of links to information on Latino culture and history.

How Race Is Lived in America
www.nytimes.com/library/national/race/most-recent.html
This is a collection of revealing articles from the *New York Times* in 2000 on race relations and racial identities in contemporary America.

Muslim Life in America
usinfo.state.gov/products/pubs/muslimlife/
Here, researchers can find information on Muslims in modern America and links to other sources for research.

September 11 Digital Archive
911digitalarchive.org/
Created by the Center for History and New Media and George Mason University and the American Social History Project at City University of New York Graduate Center, this site offers a large collection of stories and images from September 11, 2001, when terrorists attacked New York City and Washington, D.C.

Native Americans
www.americanwest.com/pages/indians.htm
This site contains information about American Indian history and culture, along with links to the home pages of many Indian nations.

National Security Archive at George Washington University
www.gwu.edu/~nsarchiv/
This excellent site includes the most recent declassified documents on the making of U.S. foreign policy.

Natural Resources Defense Council
www.nrdc.org/
This site contains considerable information and links about an array of current environmental issues.

For Further Reading

General

Thomas Bender, ed., *Rethinking American History in a Global Age* (2002).

Godfrey Hodgson, *More Equal Than Others: America from Nixon to the New Century* (2004).

National Commission on Terrorist Attacks, *The 9/11 Commission Report* (2004).

The George W. Bush Administration

Ivo H. Daalder and James M. Lindsay, *America Unbound: The Bush Revolution in Foreign Policy* (2003).

Thomas Frank, *What's the Matter with Kansas? How Conservatives Won the Heart of America* (2004).

George Packer, *The Assassin's Gate: America in Iraq* (2005).

Kevin Phillips, *American Theocracy: The Peril and Politics of Radical Religion, Oil, and Borrowed Money in the Twentieth Century* (2006).

The American Place in a Global Economy

Jefferson Cowie, *Capital Moves: RCA's Seventy-Year Quest for Cheap Labor* (1999).

Thomas L. Friedman, *The Lexus and the Olive Tree: Understanding Globalization* (1999).

William Greider, *One World, Ready or Not: The Manic Logic of Global Capitalism* (1997).

The Stewardship of Natural Resources

David Goodstein, *Out of Gas: The End of the Age of Oil* (2004).

Al Gore, *An Inconvenient Truth: The Planetary Emergency of Global Warming and What We Can Do about It* (2006).

J. R. McNeill, *Something New Under the Sun: An Environmental History of the Twentieth-Century World* (2000).

Worldwatch Institute, *State of the World 2005: Global Security* (2005).

The Expansion of American Popular Culture Abroad

Benjamin R. Barber, *Jihad vs. McWorld: How the Planet Is Both Falling Apart and Coming Together and What This Means for Democracy* (1995).

Chalmers Johnson, *Blowback: The Costs and Consequences of American Empire* (2000).

Richard Pells, *Not Like Us: How Europeans Have Loved, Hated, and Transformed American Culture Since World War II* (1997).

Reinhold Wagnleitner and Elaine Tyler May, eds., *"Here, There and Everywhere": The Foreign Politics of American Popular Culture* (2000).

Identity in Contemporary America

David A. Hollinger, *Postethnic America: Beyond Multiculturalism*, rev. ed. (2006).

Gary Y. Okihiro, *Common Ground: Reimagining American History* (2001).

Robert D. Putnam, *Bowling Alone: The Collapse and Revival of American Community* (2000).

Ruth Rosen, *The World Split Open: How the Modern Women's Movement Changed America* (2000).

For quizzes and other resources on these topics, go to www.longmanamericanhistory.com.

Appendix

The Declaration of Independence

In Congress, July 4, 1776

The Unanimous Declaration of the Thirteen United States of America

When, in the course of human events, it becomes necessary for one people to dissolve the political bonds which have connected them with another, and to assume, among the powers of the earth, the separate and equal station to which the laws of nature and of nature's God entitle them, a decent respect to the opinions of mankind requires that they should declare the causes which impel them to the separation.

We hold these truths to be self-evident: That all men are created equal; that they are endowed by their Creator with certain unalienable rights; that among these are life, liberty, and the pursuit of happiness; that, to secure these rights, governments are instituted among men, deriving their just powers from the consent of the governed; that whenever any form of government becomes destructive of these ends, it is the right of the people to alter or to abolish it, and to institute new government, laying its foundation on such principles, and organizing its powers in such form, as to them shall seem most likely to effect their safety and happiness. Prudence, indeed, will dictate that governments long established should not be changed for light and transient causes; and accordingly all experience hath shown that mankind are more disposed to suffer, while evils are sufferable, than to right themselves by abolishing the forms to which they are accustomed. But when a long train of abuses and usurpations, pursuing invariably the same object, evinces a design to reduce them under absolute despotism, it is their right, it is their duty, to throw off such government, and to provide new guards for their future security. Such has been the patient sufferance of these colonies; and such is now the necessity which constrains them to alter their former systems of government. The history of the present King of Great Britain is a history of repeated injuries and usurpations, all having in direct object the establishment of an absolute tyranny over these states. To prove this, let facts be submitted to a candid world.

He has refused his assent to laws, the most wholesome and necessary for the public good.

He has forbidden his governors to pass laws of immediate and pressing importance, unless suspended in their operation till his assent should be obtained; and, when so suspended, he has utterly neglected to attend to them.

He has refused to pass other laws for the accommodation of large districts of people, unless those people would relinquish the right of representation in the legislature, a right inestimable to them, and formidable to tyrants only.

He has called together legislative bodies at places unusual, uncomfortable, and distant from the depository of their public records, for the sole purpose of fatiguing them into compliance with his measures.

He has dissolved representative houses repeatedly, for opposing, with manly firmness, his invasions on the rights of the people.

He has refused for a long time, after such dissolutions, to cause others to be elected; whereby the legislative powers, incapable of annihilation, have returned to the people at large for their exercise; the state remaining, in the mean time, exposed to all the dangers of invasions from without and convulsions within.

He has endeavored to prevent the population of these states; for that purpose obstructing the laws for naturalization of foreigners; refusing to pass others to encourage their migration hither, and raising the conditions of new appropriations of lands.

He has obstructed the administration of justice, by refusing his assent to laws for establishing judiciary powers.

He has made judges dependent on his will alone, for the tenure of their offices, and the amount and payment of their salaries.

He has erected a multitude of new offices, and sent hither swarms of officers to harass our people and eat out their substance.

He has kept among us, in times of peace, standing armies, without the consent of our legislatures.

He has affected to render the military independent of, and superior to, the civil power.

He has combined with others to subject us to a jurisdiction foreign to our constitution, and unacknowledged by our laws, giving his assent to their acts of pretended legislation:

For quartering large bodies of armed troops among us;

For protecting them, by a mock trial, from punishment for any murder which they should commit on the inhabitants of these states;

For cutting off our trade with all parts of the world;

For imposing taxes on us without our consent;

For depriving us, in many cases, of the benefits of trial by jury;

For transporting us beyond seas, to be tried for pretended offenses;

For abolishing the free system of English laws in a neighboring province, establishing therein an arbitrary government, and enlarging its boundaries, so as to render it at once an example and fit instrument for introducing the same absolute rule into these colonies;

For taking away our charters, abolishing our most valuable laws, and altering fundamentally the forms of our governments;

For suspending our own legislatures, and declaring themselves invested with power to legislate for us in all cases whatsoever.

He has abdicated government here, by declaring us out of his protection and waging war against us.

He has plundered our seas, ravaged our coasts, burned our towns, and destroyed the lives of our people.

He is at this time transporting large armies of foreign mercenaries to complete the works of death, desolation, and tyranny already begun with circumstances of cruelty and perfidy scarcely paralleled in the most barbarous ages, and totally unworthy the head of a civilized nation.

He has constrained our fellow-citizens, taken captive on the high seas, to bear arms against their country, to become the executioners of their friends and brethren, or to fall themselves by their hands.

He has excited domestic insurrection among us, and has endeavored to bring on the inhabitants of our frontiers the merciless Indian savages, whose known rule of warfare is an undistinguished destruction of all ages, sexes, and conditions.

In every stage of these oppressions we have petitioned for redress in the most humble terms; our repeated petitions have been answered only by repeated injury. A prince, whose character is thus marked by every act which may define a tyrant, is unfit to be the ruler of a free people.

Nor have we been wanting in our attentions to our British brethren. We have warned them, from time to time, of attempts by their legislature to extend an unwarrantable jurisdiction over us. We have reminded them of the circumstances of our emigration and settlement here. We have appealed to their native justice and magnanimity; and we have conjured them, by the ties of our common kindred, to disavow these usurpations, which would inevitably interrupt our connections and correspondence. They, too, have been deaf to the voice of justice and of consanguinity. We must, therefore, acquiesce in the necessity which denounces our separation, and hold them, as we hold the rest of mankind, enemies in war, in peace friends.

We, therefore, the representatives of the United States of America, in General Congress assembled, appealing to the Supreme Judge of the world for the rectitude of our intentions, do, in the name and by the authority of the good people of these colonies, solemnly publish and declare, that these United Colonies are, and of right ought to be, FREE AND INDEPENDENT STATES; that they are absolved from all allegiance to the British crown, and that all political connection between them and the state of Great Britain is, and ought to be, totally dissolved; and that, as free and independent states, they have full power to levy war, conclude peace, contract alliances, establish commerce, and do all other acts and things which independent states may of right do. And for the support of this declaration, with a firm reliance on the protection of Divine Providence, we mutually pledge to each other our lives, our fortunes, and our sacred honor.

JOHN HANCOCK

New Hampshire
Josiah Bartlett
William Whipple
Matthew Thornton

Massachusetts
John Adams
Samuel Adams
Robert Treat Paine
Elbridge Gerry

New York
William Floyd
Philip Livingston
Francis Lewis
Lewis Morris

Rhode Island
Stephen Hopkins
William Ellery

New Jersey
Richard Stockton
John Witherspoon
Francis Hopkinson
John Hart
Abraham Clark

Pennsylvania
Robert Morris
Benjamin Rush
Benjamin Franklin
John Morton
George Clymer
James Smith
George Taylor
James Wilson
George Ross

Delaware
Caeser Rodney
George Read
Thomas McKean

Maryland
Samuel Chase
William Paca
Thomas Stone
Charles Carroll of Carrollton

North Carolina
William Hooper
Joseph Hewes
John Penn

Virginia
George Wythe
Richard Henry Lee
Thomas Jefferson
Benjamin Harrison
Thomas Nelson Jr.
Francis Lightfoot Lee
Carter Braxton

South Carolina
Edward Rutledge
Thomas Heyward Jr.
Thomas Lynch Jr.
Arthur Middleton

Connecticut
Roger Sherman
Samuel Huntington
William Williams
Oliver Wolcott

Georgia
Button Gwinnett
Lyman Hall
George Walton

The Articles of Confederation

Between the States of New Hampshire, Massachusetts Bay, Rhode Island and Providence Plantations, Connecticut, New York, New Jersey, Pennsylvania, Delaware, Maryland, Virginia, North Carolina, South Carolina, Georgia

Article 1

The stile of this confederacy shall be "The United States of America."

Article 2

Each State retains its sovereignty, freedom and independence, and every power, jurisdiction, and right, which is not by this confederation expressly delegated to the United States, in Congress assembled.

Article 3

The said states hereby severally enter into a firm league of friendship with each other for their common defence, the security of their liberties and their mutual and general welfare; binding themselves to assist each other against all force offered to, or attacks made upon them, or any of them, on account of religion, sovereignty, trade, or any other pretence whatever.

Article 4

The better to secure and perpetuate mutual friendship and intercourse among the people of the different states in this union, the free inhabitants of each of these states, paupers, vagabonds, and fugitives from justice excepted, shall be entitled to all privileges and immunities of free citizens in the several states; and the people of each State shall have free ingress and regress to and from any other State, and shall enjoy therein all the privileges of trade and commerce, subject to the same duties, impositions, and restrictions, as the inhabitants thereof respectively; provided, that such restrictions shall not extend so far as to prevent the removal of property, imported into any State, to any other State of which the owner is an inhabitant; provided also, that no imposition, duties, or restriction, shall be laid by any State on the property of the United States, or either of them.

If any person guilty of, or charged with treason, felony, or other high misdemeanor in any State, shall flee from justice and be found in any of the United States, he shall, upon demand of the governor or executive power of the State from which he fled, be delivered up and removed to the State having jurisdiction of his offence.

Full faith and credit shall be given in each of these states to the records, acts, and judicial proceedings of the courts and magistrates of every other State.

Article 5

For the more convenient management of the general interests of the United States, delegates shall be annually appointed, in such manner as the legislature of each State shall direct, to meet in Congress, on the 1st Monday in November in every year, with a power reserved to each State to recall its delegates, or any of them, at any time within the year, and to send others in their stead for the remainder of the year.

No State shall be represented in Congress by less than two, nor by more than seven members; and no person shall be capable of being a delegate for more than three years in any term of six years; nor shall any person, being a delegate, be capable of holding any office under the United States, for which he, or any other for his benefit, receives any salary, fees, or emolument of any kind.

Each State shall maintain its own delegates in a meeting of the states, and while they act as members of the committee of the states.

In determining questions in the United States, in Congress assembled, each State shall have one vote.

Freedom of speech and debate in Congress shall not be impeached or questioned in any court or place out of Congress: and the members of Congress shall be protected in their persons from arrests and imprisonments, during the time of their going to and from, and attendance on Congress, except for treason, felony, or breach of the peace.

Article 6

No State, without the consent of the United States, in Congress assembled, shall send any embassy to, or receive any embassy from, or enter into any conference, agreement, alliance, or treaty with any king, prince, or state; nor shall any person, holding any office of profit or trust under the United States, or any of them, accept of any present, emolument, office or title, of any kind whatever, from any king, prince, or foreign state; nor shall the United States, in Congress assembled, or any of them, grant any title of nobility.

No two or more states shall enter into any treaty, confederation, or alliance, whatever, between them, without the consent of the United States, in Congress assembled, specifying accurately the purposes for which the same is to be entered into, and how long it shall continue.

No State shall lay any imposts or duties which may interfere with any stipulations in treaties entered into by the United States, in Congress assembled, with any king, prince, or state, in pursuance of any treaties already proposed by Congress to the courts of France and Spain.

No vessels of war shall be kept up in time of peace by any State, except such number only as shall be deemed necessary by the United States, in Congress assembled, for the defence of such State or its trade; nor shall any body of forces be kept up by any State, in time of peace, except such number only as, in the judgment of the United States, in Congress assembled, shall be deemed requisite to garrison the forts necessary for the defence of such State; but every State shall always keep up a well regulated and disciplined militia, sufficiently armed and accoutred, and shall provide, and constantly have ready for use, in public stores, a due number of field pieces and tents, and a proper quantity of arms, ammunition and camp equipage.

No State shall engage in any war without the consent of the United States, in Congress assembled, unless such State be actually invaded by enemies, or shall have received certain advice of a resolution being formed by some nation of Indians to invade such State, and the danger is so imminent as not to admit of a delay till the United States, in Congress assembled, can be consulted; nor shall any State grant commissions to any ships or vessels of war, nor letters of marque or reprisal, except it be after a declaration of war by the United States, in Congress assembled, and then only against the kingdom or state, and the subjects thereof, against which war has been so declared, and under such regulations as shall be established by the United States, in Congress assembled, unless such States be infested by pirates, in which case vessels of war may be fitted out for that occasion, and kept so long as the danger shall continue, or until the United States, in Congress assembled, shall determine otherwise.

Article 7

When land forces are raised by any State for the common defence, all officers of or under the rank of colonel, shall be appointed by the legislature of each State respectively, by whom such forces shall be raised, or in such manner as such State shall direct; and all vacancies shall be filled up by the State which first made the appointment.

Article 8

All charges of war and all other expences, that shall be incurred for the common defence or general welfare, and allowed by the United States, in Congress assembled, shall be defrayed out of a common treasury, which shall be supplied by the several states, in proportion to the value of all land within each State, granted to or surveyed for any person, as such land and the buildings and improvements thereon shall be estimated according to such mode as the United States, in Congress assembled, shall, from time to time, direct and appoint.

The taxes for paying that proportion shall be laid and levied by the authority and direction of the legislatures of the several states, within the time agreed upon by the United States, in Congress assembled.

Article 9

The United States, in Congress assembled, shall have the sole and exclusive right and power of determining on peace and war, except in the cases mentioned in the 6th article; of sending and receiving ambassadors; entering into treaties and alliances, provided that no treaty of commerce shall be made, whereby the legislative power of the respective states shall be restrained from imposing such imposts and duties on foreigners as their own people are subjected to, or from prohibiting the exportation or importation of any species of goods or commodities whatsoever; of establishing rules for deciding, in all cases, what captures on land or water shall be legal, and in what manner prizes, taken by land or naval forces in the service of the United States, shall be divided or appropriated; of granting letters of marque and reprisal in times of peace; appointing courts for the trial of piracies and felonies committed on the high seas, and estab-

lishing courts for receiving and determining, finally, appeals in all cases of captures; provided, that no member of Congress shall be appointed a judge of any of the said courts.

The United States, in Congress assembled, shall also be the last resort on appeal in all disputes and differences now subsisting, or that hereafter may arise between two or more states concerning boundary, jurisdiction or any other cause whatever; which authority shall always be exercised in the manner following: whenever the legislative or executive authority, or lawful agent of any State, in controversy with another, shall present a petition to Congress, stating the matter in question, and praying for a hearing, notice thereof shall be given, by order of Congress, to the legislative or executive authority of the other State in controversy, and a day assigned for the appearance of the parties by their lawful agents, who shall then be directed to appoint, by joint consent, commissioners or judges to constitute a court for hearing and determining the matter in question; but, if they cannot agree, Congress shall name three persons out of each of the United States, and from the list of such persons each party shall alternately strike out one, in the petitioners beginning, until the number shall be reduced to thirteen; and from that number not less than seven, nor more than nine names, as Congress shall direct, shall, in the presence of Congress, be drawn out by lot; and the persons whose names shall be drawn, or any five of them, shall be commissioners or judges to hear and finally determine the controversy, so always as a major part of the judges who shall hear the cause shall agree in the determination; and if either party shall neglect to attend at the day appointed, without shewing reasons which Congress shall judge sufficient, or, being present, shall refuse to strike, the Congress shall proceed to nominate three persons out of each State, and the secretary of Congress shall strike in behalf of such party absent or refusing; and the judgment and sentence of the court to be appointed, in the manner before prescribed, shall be final and conclusive; and if any of the parties shall refuse to submit to the authority of such court, or to appear or defend their claim or cause, the court shall nevertheless proceed to pronounce sentence or judgment, which shall, in like manner, be final and decisive, the judgment or sentence and other proceedings being, in either case, transmitted to Congress, and lodged among the acts of Congress for the security of the parties concerned: provided, that every commissioner, before he sits in judgment, shall take an oath, to be administered by one of the judges of the supreme or superior court of the State where the cause shall be tried, "well and truly to hear and determine the matter in question, according to the best of his judgment, without favour, affection, or hope of reward": provided, also, that no State shall be deprived of territory for the benefit of the United States.

All controversies concerning the private right of soil, claimed under different grants of two or more states, whose jurisdictions, as they may respect such lands and the states which passed such grants, are adjusted, the said grants, or either of them, being at the same time claimed to have originated antecedent to such settlement of jurisdiction, shall, on the petition of either party to the Congress of the United States, be finally determined, as near as may be, in the same manner as is before prescribed for deciding disputes respecting territorial jurisdiction between different states.

The United States, in Congress assembled, shall also have the sole and exclusive right and power of regulating the alloy and value of coin struck by their own authority, or by that of the respective states; fixing the standard of weights and measures throughout the United States; regulating the trade and managing all affairs with the Indians not members of any of the states; provided that the legislative right of any State within its own limits be not infringed or violated; establishing and regulating post offices from one State to another throughout all the United States, and exacting such postage on the papers passing through the same as may be requisite to defray the expences of the said office; appointing all officers of the land forces in the service of the United States, excepting regimental officers; appointing all the officers of the naval forces, and commissioning all officers whatever in the service of the United States; making rules for the government and regulation of the said land and naval forces, and directing their operations.

The United States, in Congress assembled, shall have authority to appoint a committee to sit in the recess of Congress, to be denominated "a Committee of the States," and to consist of one delegate from each State, and to appoint such other committees and civil officers as may be necessary for managing the general affairs of the United States, under their direction; to appoint one of their number to preside; provided that no person be allowed to serve in the office of president more than one year in any term of three years; to ascertain the necessary sums of money to be raised for the service of the United States, and to appropriate and apply the same for defraying the public expences; to borrow money or emit bills on the credit of the United States, transmitting, every half year, to the respective states, an account of the sums of money so borrowed or emitted; to build and equip a navy; to agree upon the number of land forces, and to make requisitions from each State for its quota, in proportion to the number of white inhabitants in such State; which requisitions shall be binding; and, thereupon, the legislature of each State shall appoint the regimental officers, raise the men, and cloathe, arm, and equip them in a soldier-like manner, at the expence of the United States; and the officers and men so cloathed, armed, and equipped, shall march to the place appointed and within the time agreed on by the United States, in Congress assembled; but if the United States, in Congress assembled, shall, on consideration of circumstances, judge proper that any State should not raise men, or should raise a smaller number than its quota, and that any other State should raise a greater number of men than the quota thereof, such extra number shall be raised, officered, cloathed, armed, and equipped in the same manner as the quota of such State, unless the legislature of such State shall judge that such extra number cannot be safely spared out of the same, in which case they shall raise, officer, cloathe, arm, and equip as many of such extra number as they judge can be safely spared. And the officers and men so cloathed, armed, and equipped, shall march to the place appointed and within the time agreed on by the United States, in Congress assembled.

The United States, in Congress assembled, shall never engage in a war, nor grant letters of marque and reprisal in time of peace, nor enter into any treaties or alliances, nor coin money, nor regulate the value thereof, nor ascertain the sums and expences necessary for the defence and welfare of the United States, or any of them: nor emit bills, nor borrow money on the credit of the United States, nor appropriate money, nor agree upon the number of vessels of war to be built or purchased, or the number of land or sea forces to be raised, nor appoint a commander in chief of the army or navy, unless nine states assent to the same; nor shall a question on any other point, except for adjourning from day to day, be determined, unless by the votes of a majority of the United States, in Congress assembled.

The Congress of the United States shall have power to adjourn to any time within the year, and to any place within the United States, so that no period of adjournment be for a longer duration than the space of six months, and shall publish the journal of their proceedings monthly, except such parts thereof, relating to treaties, alliances or military operations, as, in their judgment, require secrecy; and the yeas and nays of the delegates of each State on any question shall be entered on the journal, when it is desired by any delegate; and the delegates of a State, or any of them, at his, or their request, shall be furnished with a transcript of the said journal, except such parts as are above excepted, to lay before the legislatures of the several states.

Article 10

The committee of the states, or any nine of them, shall be authorized to execute, in the recess of Congress, such of the powers of Congress as the United States, in Congress assembled, by the consent of nine states, shall, from time to time, think expedient to vest them with; provided, that no power be delegated to the said committee for the exercise of which, by the articles of confederation, the voice of nine states, in the Congress of the United States assembled, is requisite.

Article 11

Canada acceding to this confederation, and joining in the measures of the United States, shall be admitted into and entitled to all the advantages of this union; but no other colony shall be admitted into the same, unless such admission be agreed to by nine states.

Article 12

All bills of credit emitted, monies borrowed and debts contracted by, or under the authority of Congress before the assembling of the United States, in pursuance of the present confederation, shall be deemed and considered as a charge against the United States, for payment and satisfaction whereof the said United States and the public faith are hereby solemnly pledged.

Article 13

Every State shall abide by the determinations of the United States, in Congress assembled, on all questions which, by this confederation, are submitted to them. And the articles of this confederation shall be inviolably observed by every State, and the union shall be perpetual; nor shall any alteration at any time hereafter be made in any of them, unless such alteration be agreed to in a Congress of the United States, and be afterwards confirmed by the legislatures of every State.

These articles shall be proposed to the legislatures of all the United States, to be considered, and if approved of by them, they are advised to authorize their delegates to ratify the same in the Congress of the United States; which being done, the same shall become conclusive.

The Constitution of the United States of America

Preamble

We the People of the United States, in Order to form a more perfect Union, establish Justice, insure domestic Tranquility, provide for the common defence, promote the general Welfare, and secure the Blessings of Liberty to ourselves and our Posterity, do ordain and establish this Constitution for the United States of America.

Article I

Section 1

All legislative Powers herein granted shall be vested in a Congress of the United States, which shall consist of a Senate and House of Representatives.

Section 2

The House of Representatives shall be composed of Members chosen every second Year by the People of the several States, and the Electors in each State shall have the Qualifications requisite for Electors of the most numerous Branch of the State Legislature.

No Person shall be a Representative who shall not have attained to the Age of twenty five Years, and been seven Years a Citizen of the United States, and who shall not, when elected, be an inhabitant of that State in which he shall be chosen.

Representatives and direct Taxes shall be apportioned among the several States which may be included within this Union, according to their respective Numbers, *which shall be determined by adding to the whole Number of free Persons, including those bound to Service for a Term of Years, and excluding Indians not taxed, three fifths of all other Persons.** The actual Enumeration shall be made within three Years after the first Meeting of the Congress of the United States, and within every subsequent Term of ten Years, in such Manner as they shall by Law direct. The Number of Representatives shall not exceed one for every thirty Thousand, but each State shall have at Least one Representative; *and until such enumeration shall be made, the State of New Hampshire shall be entitled to chuse three, Massachusetts eight, Rhode-Island and Providence Plantations one, Connecticut five, New York six, New Jersey four, Pennsylvania eight, Delaware one, Maryland six, Virginia ten, North Carolina five, South Carolina five, and Georgia three.*

When vacancies happen in the Representation from any State, the Executive Authority thereof shall issue Writs of Election to fill such Vacancies.

The House of Representatives shall chuse their Speaker and other Officers; and shall have the sole Power of Impeachment.

---

*Passages no longer in effect are printed in italic type.

Section 3

The Senate of the United States shall be composed of two Senators from each State, *chosen by the Legislature thereof,* for six Years; and each Senator shall have one Vote.

Immediately after they shall be assembled in Consequence of the first Election, they shall be divided as equally as may be into three Classes. The Seats of the Senators of the first Class shall be vacated at the Expiration of the second Year, of the second Class at the Expiration of the fourth Year, and of the third Class at the Expiration of the sixth Year so that one third may be chosen every second Year; and if Vacancies happen by Resignation, or otherwise, during the Recess of the Legislature of any state, the Executive thereof may make temporary Appointments until the next Meeting of the Legislature, which shall then fill such Vacancies.

No Person shall be a Senator who shall not have attained to the Age of thirty Years, and been nine Years a Citizen of the United States, and who shall not, when elected, be an Inhabitant of that State for which he shall be chosen.

The Vice President of the United States shall be President of the Senate, but shall have no Vote, unless they be equally divided.

The Senate shall chuse their other Officers, and also a President *pro tempore*, in the Absence of the Vice President, or when he shall exercise the Office of President of the United States.

The Senate shall have the sole Power to try all Impeachments. When sitting for that Purpose, they shall be on Oath or Affirmation. When the President of the United States is tried the Chief Justice shall preside: And no Person shall be convicted without the Concurrence of two thirds of the Members present.

Judgment in Cases of Impeachment shall not extend further than to removal from Office, and disqualification to hold and enjoy any Office of honor, Trust or Profit under the United States: but the Party convicted shall nevertheless be liable and subject to Indictment, Trial, Judgment and Punishment, according to Law.

Section 4

The Times, Places and Manner of holding Elections for Senators and Representatives, shall be prescribed in each State by the Legislature thereof; but the Congress may at any time by Law make or alter such Regulations, except as to the Places of chusing Senators.

The Congress shall assemble at least once in every Year, *and such Meeting shall be on the first Monday in December, unless they shall by Law appoint a different Day.*

Section 5

Each House shall be the Judge of the Elections, Returns and Qualifications of its own Members, and a Majority of each shall constitute a Quorum to do Business; but a smaller Number may adjourn from day to day, and may be authorized to compel the Attendance of absent Members, in such Manner, and under such Penalties as each House may provide.

Each House may determine the Rules of its Proceedings, punish its Members for disorderly Behaviour, and, with the Concurrence of two thirds, expel a Member.

Each House shall keep a Journal of its Proceedings, and from time to time publish the same, excepting such Parts as may in their Judgment require Secrecy; and the Yeas and Nays of the Members of either House on any question shall, at the Desire of one fifth of those Present, be entered on the Journal.

Neither House, during the Session of Congress, shall, without the Consent of the other, adjourn for more than three days, nor to any other Place than that in which the two Houses shall be sitting.

Section 6

The Senators and Representatives shall receive a Compensation for their Services, to be ascertained by Law, and paid out of the Treasury of the United States. They shall in all Cases, except Treason, Felony and Breach of the Peace, be privileged from Arrest during their Attendance at the Session of their respective Houses, and in going to and returning from the same; and for any Speech or Debate in either House, they shall not be questioned in any other Place.

No Senator or Representative shall, during the Time for which he was elected, be appointed to any civil Office under the Authority of the United States, which shall have been created, or the Emoluments whereof shall have been encreased during such time, and no Person holding any Office under the United States, shall be a Member of either House during his Continuance in Office.

Section 7

All Bills for raising Revenue shall originate in the House of Representatives; but the Senate may propose or concur with Amendments as on other Bills.

Every Bill which shall have passed the House of Representatives and the Senate, shall, before it become a Law, be presented to the President of the United States; If he approve he shall sign it, but if not he shall return it, with his Objections to the House in which it shall have originated, who shall enter the Objections at large on their Journal, and proceed to reconsider it. If after such Reconsideration two thirds of that House shall agree to pass the Bill, it shall be sent, together with the Objections, to the other House, by which it shall likewise be reconsidered, and if approved by two thirds of that House, it shall become a Law. But in all such Cases the Votes of both Houses shall be determined by yeas and Nays, and the Names of the Persons voting for and against the Bill shall be entered on the Journal of each House respectively. If any Bill shall not be returned by the President within ten Days (Sundays excepted) after it shall have been presented to him, the Same shall be a Law, in like Manner as if he had signed it, unless the Congress by their Adjournment prevent its Return, in which Case it shall not be a Law.

Every Order, Resolution, or Vote to which the Concurrence of the Senate and House of Representatives may be necessary (except on a question of Adjournment) shall be presented to the President of the United States; and before the Same shall take Effect, shall be approved by him, or being disapproved by him, shall be repassed by two thirds of the Senate and House

of Representatives, according to the Rules and Limitations prescribed in the Case of a Bill.

Section 8

The Congress shall have Power To lay and collect Taxes, Duties, Imposts and Excises, to pay the Debts and provide for the common Defence and general Welfare of the United States; but all Duties, Imposts and Excises shall be uniform throughout the United States;

To borrow Money on the credit of the United States;

To regulate Commerce with foreign Nations, and among the several States, and with the Indian Tribes;

To establish an uniform Rule of Naturalization, and uniform Laws on the subject of Bankruptcies throughout the United States;

To coin Money, regulate the Value thereof, and of foreign Coin, and fix the Standard of Weights and Measures;

To provide for the Punishment of counterfeiting the Securities and current Coin of the United States;

To establish Post Offices and post Roads;

To promote the Progress of Science and useful Arts, by securing for limited Times to Authors and Inventors the exclusive Right to their respective Writings and Discoveries;

To constitute Tribunals inferior to the supreme Court;

To define and punish Piracies and Felonies committed on the high Seas, and Offences against the Law of Nations;

To declare War, grant Letters of Marque and Reprisal, and make Rules concerning Captures on Land and Water;

To raise and support Armies, but no Appropriation of Money to that Use shall be for a longer Term than two Years;

To provide and maintain a Navy;

To make Rules for the Government and Regulation of the land and naval Forces;

To provide for calling forth the Militia to execute the Laws of the Union, suppress Insurrections and repel Invasions;

To provide for organizing, arming, and disciplining, the Militia, and for governing such Part of them as may be employed in the Service of the United States, reserving to the States respectively, the Appointment of the Officers, and the Authority of training the Militia according to the discipline prescribed by Congress;

To exercise exclusive Legislation in all Cases whatsoever, over such District (not exceeding ten Miles square) as may, by Cession of particular States, and the Acceptance of Congress, become the Seat of the Government of the United States, and to exercise like Authority over all Places purchased by the Consent of the Legislature of the State in which the Same shall be, for the Erection of Forts, Magazines, Arsenals, dock-Yards, and other needful Buildings;—And

To make all Laws which shall be necessary and proper for carrying into Execution the foregoing Powers, and all other Powers vested by this Constitution in the Government of the United States, or in any Department of Officer thereof.

Section 9

The Migration or Importation of such Persons as any of the States now existing shall think proper to admit, shall not be prohibited by the Congress prior to the Year one thousand eight hundred and

eight, but a Tax or duty may be imposed on such Importation, not exceeding ten dollars for each Person.

The Privilege of the Writ of Habeas Corpus shall not be suspended, unless when in Cases of Rebellion or Invasion the public Safety may require it.

No Bill of Attainder or ex post facto Law shall be passed.

No Capitation, or other direct, Tax shall be laid, unless in Proportion to the Census or Enumeration herein before directed to be taken.

No Tax or Duty shall be laid on Articles exported from any State.

No Preference shall be given by any Regulation of Commerce or Revenue to the Ports of one State over those of another: nor shall Vessels bound to, or from, one State, be obliged to enter, clear, or pay Duties in another.

No Money shall be drawn from the Treasury, but in Consequence of Appropriations made by Law; and a regular Statement and Account of the Receipts and Expenditures of all public Money shall be published from time to time.

No Title of Nobility shall be granted by the United States: And no Person holding any Office of Profit or Trust under them, shall, without the Consent of the Congress, accept of any present, Emolument, Office, or Title, of any kind whatever, from any King, Prince, or foreign State.

Section 10

No State shall enter into any Treaty, Alliance, or Confederation; grant Letters of Marque and Reprisal; coin Money; emit Bills of Credit; make any Thing but gold and silver Coin a Tender in Payment of Debts; pass any Bill of Attainder, ex post facto Law, or Law impairing the obligation of Contracts, or grant any Title of Nobility.

No State shall, without the Consent of the Congress, lay any Imposts or Duties on Imports or Exports, except what may be absolutely necessary for executing its inspection Laws: and the net Produce of all Duties and Imposts, laid by any State on Imports or Exports, shall be for the Use of the Treasury of the United States; and all such Laws shall be subject to the Revision and Controul of the Congress.

No State shall, without the Consent of Congress, lay any Duty of Tonnage, keep Troops, or Ships of War in time of Peace, enter into any Agreement or Compact with another State, or with a foreign Power, or engage in War, unless actually invaded, or in such imminent Danger as will not admit of delay.

Article II

Section 1

The executive Power shall be vested in a President of the United States of America. He shall hold his Office during the Term of four Years, and, together with the Vice President, chosen for the same Term, be elected, as follows:

Each State shall appoint, in such Manner as the Legislature thereof may direct, a Number of Electors, equal to the whole Number of Senators and Representatives to which the State may be entitled in the Congress: but no Senator or Representative, or Person holding an Office of Trust or Profit under the United States, shall be appointed an Elector.

The Electors shall meet in their respective States, and vote by Ballot for two Persons, of whom one at least shall not be an Inhabitant of the same State with themselves. And they shall make a List of all the Persons voted for, and of the Number of Votes for each; which List they shall sign and certify, and transmit sealed to the Seat of the Government of the United States, directed to the President of the Senate. The President of the Senate shall, in the Presence of the Senate and House of Representatives, open all the Certificates, and the Votes shall then be counted. The Person having the greatest Number of Votes shall be the President, if such Number be a Majority of the whole number of Electors appointed; and if there be more than one who have such Majority, and have an equal Number of Votes, then the House of Representatives shall immediately chuse by Ballot one of them for President; and if no Person have a Majority, then from the five highest on the List the said House shall in like Manner chuse the President. But in chusing the President, the Votes shall be taken by States, the Representation from each State having one Vote; A quorum for this Purpose shall consist of a Member or Members from two thirds of the States, and a Majority of all the States shall be necessary to a Choice. In every Case, after the Choice of the President, the Person having the greatest Number of Votes of the Electors shall be the Vice President. But if there should remain two or more who have equal Votes, the Senate shall chuse from them by Ballot the Vice President.

The Congress may determine the time of chusing the Electors, and the Day on which they shall give their Votes; which Day shall be the same throughout the United States.

No person except a natural born Citizen, *or a Citizen of the United States, at the time of the Adoption of this Constitution,* shall be eligible to the Office of President; neither shall any Person be eligible to that Office who shall not have attained to the Age of thirty five Years, and been fourteen Years a Resident within the United States.

In Case of the Removal of the President from Office, or of his Death, Resignation, or Inability to discharge the Powers and Duties of the said Office, the Same shall devolve on the Vice President, and the Congress may by Law provide for the Case of Removal, Death, Resignation or Inability, both of the President and Vice President, declaring what Officer shall then act as President, and such Officer shall act accordingly, until the Disability be removed, or a President shall be elected.

The President shall, at stated Times, receive for his Services, a Compensation, which shall neither be encreased nor diminished during the Period for which he shall have been elected, and he shall not receive within that period any other Emolument from the United States, or any of them.

Before he enter on the Execution of his Office, he shall take the following Oath or Affirmation:—"I do solemnly swear (or affirm) that I will faithfully execute the Office of President of the United States, and will to the best of my Ability, preserve, protect and defend the Constitution of the United States."

Section 2

The President shall be Commander in Chief of the Army and Navy of the United States, and of the Militia of the several States, when called into the actual Service of the United States; he may require the Opinion, in writing, of the principal Officer in each of the executive Departments, upon any Subject relating to the Duties of their respective Offices, and he shall have Power to grant Reprieves and Pardons for Offences against the United States, except in Cases of Impeachment.

He shall have Power, by and with the Advice and Consent of the Senate, to make Treaties, provided two thirds of the Senators present concur; and he shall nominate, and by and with the Advice and Consent of the Senate, shall appoint Ambassadors, other public Ministers and Consuls, Judges of the supreme Court, and all other Officers of the United States, whose Appointments are not herein otherwise provided for, and which shall be established by Law: but the Congress may by Law vest the Appointment of such inferior Officers, as they think proper in the President alone, in the Courts of Law, or in the Heads of Departments.

The President shall have Power to fill up all Vacancies that may happen during the Recess of the Senate, by granting Commissions which shall expire at the End of their next Session.

Section 3

He shall from time to time give to the Congress Information of the State of the Union, and recommend to their Consideration such Measures as he shall judge necessary and expedient; he may, on extraordinary Occasions, convene both Houses, or either of them, and in Case of disagreement between them, with Respect to the Time of Adjournment, he may adjourn them to such Time as he shall think proper; he shall receive Ambassadors and other public Ministers; he shall take Care that the Laws be faithfully executed, and shall Commission all the officers of the United States.

Section 4

The President, Vice President and all civil Officers of the United States, shall be removed from Office on Impeachment for, and Conviction of, Treason, Bribery or other high Crimes and Misdemeanors.

Article III

Section 1

The judicial Power of the United States, shall be vested in one supreme Court, and in such inferior Courts as the Congress may from time to time ordain and establish. The Judges, both of the supreme and inferior Courts, shall hold their offices during good Behaviour, and shall, at stated Times, receive for their Services, a Compensation, which shall not be diminished during their Continuance in Office.

Section 2

The judicial Power shall extend to all Cases, in Law and Equity, arising under this Constitution, the Laws of the United States, and Treaties made, or which shall be made, under their Authority;—to all Cases affecting Ambassadors, other public Ministers and Consuls;—to all Cases of admiralty and maritime Jurisdiction;—to Controversies to which the United States shall be a Party;—to Controversies between two or more States;— *between a State and Citizens of another State;*—between Citizens of different States;—between Citizens of the same State claiming Lands under Grants of different States, and between a State, or the Citizens thereof, and foreign States, Citizens or Subjects.

In all Cases affecting Ambassadors, other public Ministers and Consuls, and those in which a State shall be Party, the supreme Court shall have original Jurisdiction. In all the other Cases before mentioned, the supreme Court shall have appellate Jurisdiction, both as to Law and Fact, with such Exceptions, and under such Regulations as the Congress shall make.

The Trial of all Crimes, except in Cases of Impeachment, shall be by Jury; and such Trial shall be held in the State where the said Crimes shall have been committed, but when not committed within any State, the Trial shall be at such Place or Places as the Congress may by Law have directed.

Section 3

Treason against the United States, shall consist only in levying War against them, or in adhering to their Enemies, giving them Aid and Comfort. No person shall be convicted of Treason unless on the Testimony of two Witnesses to the same overt Act, or on Confession in open Court.

The Congress shall have Power to declare the Punishment of Treason, but no Attainder of Treason shall work Corruption of Blood, or Forfeiture except during the Life of the Person attainted.

Article IV

Section 1

Full Faith and Credit shall be given in each State to the public Acts, Records, and judicial Proceedings of every other State. And the Congress may by general Laws prescribe the Manner in which such Acts, Records and Proceedings shall be proved, and the Effect thereof.

Section 2

The Citizens of each State shall be entitled to all Privileges and Immunities of Citizens in the several States.

A Person charged in any State with Treason, Felony, or other Crime, who shall flee from Justice, and be found in another State, shall on Demand of the executive Authority of the State from which he fled, be delivered up, to be removed to the State having Jurisdiction of the Crime.

No Person held to Service or Labour in one State, under the Laws thereof, escaping into another, shall, in Consequence of any Law or Regulation therein, be discharged from such Service or Labour, but shall be delivered up on Claim of the Party to whom such Service or Labour may be due.

Section 3

New States may be admitted by the Congress into this Union; but no new State shall be formed or erected within the Jurisdiction of any other State; nor any State be formed by the Junction of two or more States, or Parts of States, without the Consent of the Legislatures of the States concerned as well as of the Congress.

The Congress shall have Power to dispose of and make all needful Rules and Regulations respecting the Territory or other Property belonging to the United States; and nothing in this Constitution shall be so construed as to Prejudice any Claims of the United States, or of any particular States.

Section 4

The United States shall guarantee to every State in this Union a Republican Form of Government, and shall protect each of them against Invasion; and on Application of the Legislature, or of the Executive (when the Legislature cannot be convened) against domestic violence.

Article V

The Congress, whenever two thirds of both Houses shall deem it necessary, shall propose Amendments to this Constitution, or, on the Application of the Legislatures of two thirds of the several States, shall call a Convention for proposing Amendments, which, in either Case, shall be valid to all Intents and Purposes, as Part of this Constitution, when ratified by the Legislatures of three fourths of the several States, or by Conventions in three fourths thereof, as the one or the other Mode of Ratification may be proposed by the Congress; Provided *that no Amendment which may be made prior to the Year One thousand eight hundred and eight shall in any Manner affect the first and fourth Clauses in the Ninth Section of the first Article;* and that no State, without its Consent, shall be deprived of its equal Suffrage in the Senate.

Article VI

All Debts contracted and Engagements entered into, before the Adoption of this Constitution, shall be as valid against the United States under this Constitution, as under the Confederation.

This Constitution, and Laws of the United States which shall be made in Pursuance thereof; and all Treaties made, or which shall be made, under the Authority of the United States, shall be the supreme Law of the Land; and the Judges in every State shall be bound thereby, any Thing in the Constitution or Laws of any State to the Contrary notwithstanding.

The Senators and Representatives before mentioned, and the Members of the several State Legislatures, and all executive and Judicial Officers, both of the United States and of the several States, shall be bound by Oath or Affirmation, to support this Constitution; but no religious Test shall ever be required as a Qualification to any Office of public Trust under the United States.

Article VII

The Ratification of the Conventions of nine States, shall be sufficient for the Establishment of this Constitution between the States so ratifying the Same.

Done in Convention by the Unanimous Consent of the States present the Seventeenth Day of September in the Year of our Lord one thousand seven hundred and Eighty seven and of the Independence of the United States of America the Twelfth* IN WITNESS whereof We have hereunto subscribed our Names,

George Washington
President and Deputy from Virginia

Delaware	*South Carolina*	*New York*
George Read	John Rutledge	Alexander Hamilton
Gunning Bedford Jr.	Charles Cotesworth Pinckney	
John Dickinson	Charles Pinckney	*New Jersey*
Richard Bassett	Pierce Butler	William Livingston
Jacob Broom		David Brearley
	Georgia	William Paterson
Maryland	William Few	Jonathan Dayton
James McHenry	Abraham Baldwin	
Daniel of St. Thomas Jenifer		*Pennsylvania*
Daniel Carroll	*New Hampshire*	Benjamin Franklin
	John Langdon	Thomas Mifflin
Virginia	Nicholas Gilman	Robert Morris
John Blair		George Clymer
James Madison Jr.	*Massachusetts*	Thomas FitzSimons
	Nathaniel Gorham	Jared Ingersoll
North Carolina	Rufus King	James Wilson
William Blount		Gouverneur Morris
Richard Dobbs Spraight	*Connecticut*	
Hugh Williamson	William Samuel Johnson	
	Roger Sherman	

---

*The Constitution was submitted on September 17, 1787, by the Constitutional Convention, was ratified by conventions of the several states at various dates up to May 29, 1790, and became effective on March 4, 1789.

Amendments to the Constitution

Amendment I

Congress shall make no law respecting an establishment of religion, or prohibiting the free exercise thereof; or abridging the freedom of speech, or of the press; or the right of the people peaceably to assemble, and to petition the Government for a redress of grievances.

Amendment II

A well regulated Militia being necessary to the security of a free State, the right of the people to keep and bear Arms, shall not be infringed.

Amendment III

No Soldier shall, in time of peace be quartered in any house, without the consent of the Owner, nor in time of war, but in a manner to be prescribed by law.

Amendment IV

The right of the people to be secure in their persons, houses, papers, and effects, against unreasonable searches and seizures, shall not be violated, and no Warrants shall issue, but upon probable cause, supported by Oath or affirmation, and particularly describing the place to be searched, and the persons or things to be seized.

Amendment V

No person shall be held to answer for a capital, or otherwise infamous crime, unless on a presentment or indictment of a Grand Jury, except in cases arising in the land or naval forces, or in the Militia, when in actual service in time of War or public danger; nor shall any person be subject for the same offense to be twice put in jeopardy of life or limb; nor shall be compelled in any criminal case to be a witness against himself, nor be deprived of life, liberty, or property, without due process of law; nor shall private property be taken for public use, without just compensation.

Amendment VI

In all criminal prosecutions, the accused shall enjoy the right to a speedy and public trial, by an impartial jury of the State and district wherein the crime shall have been committed, which district shall have been previously ascertained by law, and to be informed of the nature and cause of the accusation; to be confronted with the witnesses against him; to have compulsory process for obtaining witnesses in his favor, and to have the Assistance of Counsel for his defence.

Amendment VII

In Suits at common law, where the value in controversy shall exceed twenty dollars, the right of trial by jury shall be preserved, and no fact tried by a jury, shall be otherwise reexamined in any Court of the United States, than according to the rules of the common law.

Amendment VIII

Excessive bail shall not be required, nor excessive fines imposed, nor cruel and unusual punishments inflicted.

Amendment IX

The enumeration in the Constitution, of certain rights, shall not be construed to deny or disparage others retained by the people.

Amendment X*

The powers not delegated to the United States by the Constitution, nor prohibited by it to the States, are reserved to the States respectively, or to the people.

Amendment XI
[Adopted 1798]

The Judicial power of the United States shall not be construed to extend to any suit in law or equity, commenced or prosecuted against one of the United States by Citizens of another State, or by Citizens or Subjects of any Foreign State.

Amendment XII
[Adopted 1804]

The Electors shall meet in their respective states, and vote by ballot for President and Vice President, one of whom, at least, shall not be an inhabitant of the same state with themselves; they shall name in their ballots the person voted for as President, and in distinct ballots the person voted for as Vice President, and they shall make distinct lists of all persons voted for as President, and of all persons voted for as Vice President, and of the number of votes for each, which lists they shall sign and certify, and transmit sealed to the seat of the government of the United States, directed to the President of the Senate;—The President of the Senate shall, in the presence of the Senate and House of Representatives, open all the certificates and the votes shall then be counted;—The person having the greatest number of votes for President, shall be the President, if such number be a majority of the whole number of Electors appointed; and if no person have such majority, then from the persons having the highest numbers not exceeding three on the list of those voted for as President, the House of Representatives shall choose immediately, by ballot, the President. But in choosing the President, the votes shall be taken by states, the representation from each state having one vote; a quorum for this purpose shall consist of a member or members from two-thirds of the states, and a majority of all

---

*The first ten amendments (the Bill of Rights) were ratified and their adoption was certified on December 15, 1791.

the states shall be necessary to a choice. And if the House of Representatives shall not choose a President whenever the right of choice shall devolve upon them, before *the fourth day of March* next following, then the Vice President shall act as President, as in the case of the death or other constitutional disability of the President.—The person having the greatest number of votes as Vice President, shall be the Vice President, if such number be a majority of the whole number of Electors appointed, and if no person have a majority, then from the two highest numbers on the list, the Senate shall choose the Vice President; a quorum for the purpose shall consist of two-thirds of the whole number of Senators, and a majority of the whole number shall be necessary to a choice. But no person constitutionally ineligible to the office of President shall be eligible to that of Vice President of the United States.

Amendment XIII
[Adopted 1865]

Section 1

Neither slavery nor involuntary servitude, except as a punishment for crime whereof the party shall have been duly convicted, shall exist within the United States, or any place subject to their jurisdiction.

Section 2

Congress shall have power to enforce this article by appropriate legislation.

Amendment XIV
[Adopted 1868]

Section 1

All persons born or naturalized in the United States, and subject to the jurisdiction thereof, are citizens of the United States and of the State wherein they reside. No State shall make or enforce any law which shall abridge the privileges or immunities of citizens of the United States; nor shall any State deprive any person of life, liberty, or property, without due process of law; nor deny to any person within its jurisdiction the equal protection of the laws.

Section 2

Representatives shall be apportioned among the several States according to their respective numbers, counting the whole number of persons in each State, excluding Indians not taxed. But when the right to vote at any election for the choice of electors for President and Vice President of the United States, Representatives in Congress, the Executive and Judicial officers of a State, or the members of the Legislature thereof, is denied to any of the male inhabitants of such State, being twenty-one years of age, and citizens of the United States, or in any way abridged, except for participation in rebellion, or other crime, the basis of representation therein shall be reduced in the proportion which the number of such male citizens shall bear to the whole number of male citizens twenty-one years of age in such State.

Section 3

No person shall be a Senator or Representative in Congress, or elector of President and Vice President, or hold any office, civil or military, under the United States, or under any State, who, having previously taken an oath, as a member of Congress, or as an officer of the United States, or as a member of any State legislature, or as an executive or judicial officer of any State, to support the Constitution of the United States, shall have engaged in insurrection or rebellion against the same, or given aid or comfort to the enemies thereof. But Congress may by a vote of two-thirds of each House, remove such disability.

Section 4

The validity of the public debt of the United States, authorized by law, including debts incurred for payment of pensions and bounties for services in suppressing insurrection or rebellion, shall not be questioned. But neither the United States nor any State shall assume or pay any debt or obligation incurred in aid of insurrection or rebellion against the United States, or any claim for the loss or emancipation of any slave; but all such debts, obligations and claims shall be held illegal and void.

Section 5

The Congress shall have power to enforce, by appropriate legislation, the provisions of this article.

Amendment XV
[Adopted 1870]

Section 1

The right of citizens of the United States to vote shall not be denied or abridged by the United States or by any State on account of race, color, or previous condition of servitude.

Section 2

The Congress shall have power to enforce this article by appropriate legislation.

Amendment XVI
[Adopted 1913]

The Congress shall have power to lay and collect taxes on incomes, from whatever source derived, without apportionment among the several States, and without regard to any census or enumeration.

Amendment XVII
[Adopted 1913]

The Senate of the United States shall be composed of two Senators from each State, elected by the people thereof, for six years; and each Senator shall have one vote. The electors in each State shall have the qualifications requisite for electors of the most numerous branch of the State legislatures.

When vacancies happen in the representation of any State in the Senate, the executive authority of such State shall issue writs of election to fill such vacancies: *Provided,* That the legislature of any State may empower the executive thereof to make temporary appointments until the people fill the vacancies by election as the legislature may direct.

This amendment shall not be so construed as to affect the election or term of any Senator chosen before it becomes valid as part of the Constitution.

Amendment XVIII
[Adopted 1919, repealed 1933]

Section 1

After one year from the ratification of this article the manufacture, sale, or transportation of intoxicating liquors within, the importation thereof into, or the exportation thereof from the United States and all territory subject to the jurisdiction thereof for beverage purposes is hereby prohibited.

Section 2

The Congress and the several States shall have concurrent power to enforce this article by appropriate legislation.

Section 3

This article shall be inoperative unless it shall have been ratified as an amendment to the Constitution by the legislatures of the several States, as provided in the Constitution, within seven years from the date of the submission hereof to the States by the Congress.

Amendment XIX
[Adopted 1920]

The right of citizens of the United States to vote shall not be denied or abridged by the United States or by any State on account of sex.

Congress shall have power to enforce this article by appropriate legislation.

Amendment XX
[Adopted 1933]

Section 1

The terms of the President and Vice President shall end at noon on the 20th day of January, and the terms of Senators and Representatives at noon on the 3d day of January, of the years in which such terms would have ended if this article had not been ratified and the terms of their successors shall then begin.

Section 2

The Congress shall assemble at least once in every year, and such meeting shall begin at noon on the 3d day of January, unless they shall by law appoint a different day.

Section 3

If, at the time fixed for the beginning of the term of the President, the President elect shall have died, the Vice President elect shall become President. If a President shall not have been chosen before the time fixed for the beginning of his term, or if the Pres-

ident elect shall have failed to qualify, then the Vice President elect shall act as President until a President shall have qualified; and the Congress may by law provide for the case wherein neither a President elect nor a Vice President elect shall have qualified, declaring who shall then act as President, or the manner in which one who is to act shall be selected, and such person shall act accordingly until a President or Vice President shall have qualified.

Section 4

The Congress may by law provide for the case of the death of any of the persons from whom the House of Representatives may choose a President whenever the right of choice shall have devolved upon them, and for the case of the death of any of the persons from whom the Senate may choose a Vice President whenever the right of choice shall have devolved upon them.

Section 5

Sections 1 and 2 shall take effect on the 15th day of October following the ratification of this article.

Section 6

This article shall be inoperative unless it shall have been ratified as an amendment to the Constitution by the legislatures of three fourths of the several States within seven years from the date of its submission.

Amendment XXI
[Adopted 1933]

Section 1

The eighteenth article of amendment to the Constitution of the United States is hereby repealed.

Section 2

The transportation or importation into any State, Territory, or possession of the United States for delivery or use therein of intoxicating liquors in violation of the laws thereof, is hereby prohibited.

Section 3

This article shall be inoperative unless it shall have been ratified as an amendment to the Constitution by conventions in the several States, as provided in the Constitution, within seven years from the date of the submission hereof to the States by the Congress.

Amendment XXII
[Adopted 1951]

Section 1

No person shall be elected to the office of the President more than twice, and no person who has held the office of President, or acted as President, for more than two years of a term to which some other person was elected President shall be elected to the office of the President more than once. But this Article shall not apply to any person holding the office of President when this Article was proposed by the Congress, and shall not prevent any person who may be holding the office of President, or acting as President, during the term within which this Article becomes operative from holding the office of President or acting as President during the remainder of such term.

Section 2

This article shall be inoperative unless it shall have been ratified as an amendment to the Constitution by the legislatures of three-fourths of the several States within seven years from the date of its submission to the States by the Congress.

Amendment XXIII
[Adopted 1961]
Section 1

The District constituting the seat of Government of the United States shall appoint in such manner as the Congress shall direct:

A number of electors of President and Vice President equal to the whole number of Senators and Representatives in Congress to which the District would be entitled if it were a State, but in no event more than the least populous State; they shall be in addition to those appointed by the States, but they shall be considered, for the purposes of the election of President and Vice President, to be electors appointed by a State; and they shall meet in the District and perform such duties as provided by the twelfth article of amendment.

Section 2

The Congress shall have power to enforce this article by appropriate legislation.

Amendment XXIV
[Adopted 1964]

Section 1

The right of citizens of the United States to vote in any primary or other election for President or Vice President, for electors for President or Vice President, or for Senator or Representative in Congress, shall not be denied or abridged by the United States or any state by reason of failure to pay any poll tax or other tax.

Section 2

The Congress shall have the power to enforce this article by appropriate legislation.

Amendment XXV
[Adopted 1967]

Section 1

In case of the removal of the President from office or his death or resignation, the Vice President shall become President.

Section 2

Whenever there is a vacancy in the office of the Vice President, the President shall nominate a Vice President who shall take the office upon confirmation by a majority vote of both houses of Congress.

Section 3

Whenever the President transmits to the President pro tempore of the Senate and the Speaker of the House of Representatives his written declaration that he is unable to discharge the powers and duties of his office, and until he transmits to them a written declaration to the contrary, such powers and duties shall be discharged by the Vice President as Acting President.

Section 4

Whenever the Vice President and a majority of either the principal officers of the executive departments or of such other body as Congress may by law provide, transmit to the President pro tempore of the Senate and the Speaker of the House of Representatives their written declaration that the President is unable to discharge the powers and duties of his office, the Vice President shall immediately assume the powers and duties of the office as Acting President.

Thereafter, when the President transmits to the President pro tempore of the Senate and the Speaker of the House of Representatives his written declaration that no inability exists, he shall resume the powers and duties of his office unless the Vice President and a majority of either the principal officers of the executive department or of such other body as Congress may by law provide, transmit within four days to the President pro tempore of the Senate and the Speaker of the House of Representatives their written declaration that the President is unable to discharge the powers and duties of his office. Thereupon Congress shall decide the issue, assembling within 48 hours for that purpose if not in session. If the Congress, within 21 days after receipt of the latter written declaration, or, if Congress is not in session, within 21 days after Congress is required to assemble, determines by two-thirds vote of both houses that the President is unable to discharge the powers and duties of his office, the Vice President shall continue to discharge the same as Acting President; otherwise, the President shall resume the powers and duties of his office.

Amendment XXVI
[Adopted 1971]

Section 1

The right of citizens of the United States, who are 18 years of age or older, to vote shall not be denied or abridged by the United States or any state on account of age.

Section 2

The Congress shall have the power to enforce this article by appropriate legislation.

Amendment XXVII
[Adopted 1992]

No law, varying the compensation for the services of the Senators and Representatives shall take effect, until an election of Representatives shall have intervened.

Presidential Elections

Year	Candidates	Parties	Popular Vote	Electoral Vote	Voter Participation
1789	**George Washington**		a	69	
	John Adams			34	
	Others			35	
1792	**George Washington**		a	132	
	John Adams			77	
	George Clinton			50	
	Others			5	
1796	**John Adams**	Federalist	a	71	
	Thomas Jefferson	Democratic-Republican		68	
	Thomas Pinckney	Federalist		59	
	Aaron Burr	Dem.-Rep.		30	
	Others			48	
1800	**Thomas Jefferson**	Dem.-Rep.	a	73	
	Aaron Burr	Dem.-Rep.		73	
	John Adams	Federalist		65	
	C. C. Pinckney	Federalist		64	
	John Jay	Federalist		1	
1804	**Thomas Jefferson**	Dem.-Rep.	a	162	
	C. C. Pinckney	Federalist		14	
1808	**James Madison**	Dem.-Rep.	a	122	
	C. C. Pinckney	Federalist		47	
	George Clinton	Dem.-Rep.		6	
1812	**James Madison**	Dem.-Rep.	a	128	
	De Witt Clinton	Federalist		89	
1816	**James Monroe**	Dem.-Rep.	a	183	
	Rufus King	Federalist		34	
1820	**James Monroe**	Dem.-Rep.	a	231	
	John Quincy Adams	Dem.-Rep.		1	
1824	**John Quincy Adams**	Dem.-Rep.	108,740 (30.5%)	84	26.9%
	Andrew Jackson	Dem.-Rep.	153,544 (43.1%)	99	
	William H. Crawford	Dem.-Rep.	46,618 (13.1%)	41	
	Henry Clay	Dem.-Rep.	47,136 (13.2%)	37	
1828	**Andrew Jackson**	Democratic	647,286 (56.0%)	178	57.6%
	John Quincy Adams	National Republican	508,064 (44.0%)	83	
1832	**Andrew Jackson**	Democratic	687,502 (55.0%)	219	55.4%
	Henry Clay	National Republican	530,189 (42.4%)	49	
	John Floyd	Independent		11	
	William Wirt	Anti-Mason	33,108 (2.6%)	7	
1836	**Martin Van Buren**	Democratic	765,483 (50.9%)	170	57.8%
	William Henry Harrison	Whig		73	
	Hugh L. White	Whig	739,795 (49.1%)	26	
	Daniel Webster	Whig		14	
	W. P. Magnum	Independent		11	
1840	**William Henry Harrison**	Whig	1,274,624 (53.1%)	234	80.2%
	Martin Van Buren	Democratic	1,127,781 (46.9%)	60	
	J. G. Birney	Liberty	7,069	—	

[a]Electors selected by state legislatures.

Year	Candidates	Parties	Popular Vote	Electoral Vote	Voter Participation
1844	**James K. Polk**	Democratic	1,338,464 (49.6%)	170	78.9%
	Henry Clay	Whig	1,300,097 (48.1%)	105	
	J. G. Birney	Liberty	62,300 (2.3%)	—	
1848	**Zachary Taylor**	Whig	1,360,967 (47.4%)	163	72.7%
	Lewis Cass	Democratic	1,222,342 (42.5%)	127	
	Martin Van Buren	Free-Soil	291,263 (10.1%)	—	
1852	**Franklin Pierce**	Democratic	1,601,117 (50.9%)	254	69.6%
	Winfield Scott	Whig	1,385,453 (44.1%)	42	
	John P. Hale	Free-Soil	155,825 (5.0%)	—	
1856	**James Buchanan**	Democratic	1,832,955 (45.3%)	174	78.9%
	John C. Frémont	Republican	1,339,932 (33.1%)	114	
	Millard Fillmore	American	871,731 (21.6%)	8	
1860	**Abraham Lincoln**	Republican	1,865,593 (39.8%)	180	81.2%
	Stephen A. Douglas	Democratic	1,382,713 (29.5%)	12	
	John C. Breckinridge	Democratic	848,356 (18.1%)	72	
	John Bell	Union	592,906 (12.6%)	39	
1864	**Abraham Lincoln**	Republican	2,213,655 (55.0%)	212[b]	73.8%
	George B. McClellan	Democratic	1,805,237 (45.0%)	21	
1868	**Ulysses S. Grant**	Republican	3,012,833 (52.7%)	214	78.1%
	Horatio Seymour	Democratic	2,703,249 (47.3%)	80	
1872	**Ulysses S. Grant**	Republican	3,597,132 (55.6%)	286	71.3%
	Horace Greeley	Dem.; Liberal Republican	2,834,125 (43.9%)	66[c]	
1876	**Rutherford B. Hayes**[d]	Republican	4,036,298 (48.0%)	185	81.8%
	Samuel J. Tilden	Democratic	4,300,590 (51.0%)	184	
1880	**James A. Garfield**	Republican	4,454,416 (48.5%)	214	79.4%
	Winfield S. Hancock	Democratic	4,444,952 (48.1%)	155	
1884	**Grover Cleveland**	Democratic	4,874,986 (48.5%)	219	77.5%
	James G. Blaine	Republican	4,851,981 (48.2%)	182	
1888	**Benjamin Harrison**	Republican	5,439,853 (47.9%)	233	79.3%
	Grover Cleveland	Democratic	5,540,309 (48.6%)	168	
1892	**Grover Cleveland**	Democratic	5,556,918 (46.1%)	277	74.7%
	Benjamin Harrison	Republican	5,176,108 (43.0%)	145	
	James B. Weaver	People's	1,041,028 (8.5%)	22	
1896	**William McKinley**	Republican	7,104,779 (51.1%)	271	79.3%
	William Jennings Bryan	Democratic People's	6,502,925 (47.7%)	176	
1900	**William McKinley**	Republican	7,207,923 (51.7%)	292	73.2%
	William Jennings Bryan	Dem.-Populist	6,358,133 (45.5%)	155	
1904	**Theodore Roosevelt**	Republican	7,623,486 (57.9%)	336	65.2%
	Alton B. Parker	Democratic	5,077,911 (37.6%)	140	
	Eugene V. Debs	Socialist	402,283 (3.0%)	—	
1908	**William H. Taft**	Republican	7,678,908 (51.6%)	321	65.4%
	William Jennings Bryan	Democratic	6,409,104 (43.1%)	162	
	Eugene V. Debs	Socialist	420,793 (2.8%)	—	
1912	**Woodrow Wilson**	Democratic	6,293,454 (41.9%)	435	58.8%
	Theodore Roosevelt	Progressive	4,119,538 (27.4%)	88	
	William H. Taft	Republican	3,484,980 (23.2%)	8	
	Eugene V. Debs	Socialist	900,672 (6.0%)	—	
1916	**Woodrow Wilson**	Democratic	9,129,606 (49.4%)	277	61.6%
	Charles E. Hughes	Republican	8,538,221 (46.2%)	254	
	A. L. Benson	Socialist	585,113 (3.2%)	—	
1920	**Warren G. Harding**	Republican	16,152,200 (60.4%)	404	49.2%
	James M. Cox	Democratic	9,147,353 (34.2%)	127	
	Eugene V. Debs	Socialist	919,799 (3.4%)	—	
1924	**Calvin Coolidge**	Republican	15,725,016 (54.0%)	382	48.9%
	John W. Davis	Democratic	8,386,503 (28.8%)	136	
	Robert M. La Follette	Progressive	4,822,856 (16.6%)	13	

[b]Eleven secessionist states did not participate.
[c]Greeley died before the electoral college met. His electoral votes were divided among the four minor candidates.
[d]Contested result settled by special election.

Year	Candidates	Parties	Popular Vote	Electoral Vote	Voter Participation
1928	**Herbert Hoover**	Republican	21,391,381 (58.2%)	444	56.9%
	Alfred E. Smith	Democratic	15,016,443 (40.9%)	87	
	Norman Thomas	Socialist	267,835 (0.7%)	—	
1932	**Franklin D. Roosevelt**	Democratic	22,821,857 (57.4%)	472	56.9%
	Herbert Hoover	Republican	15,761,841 (39.7%)	59	
	Norman Thomas	Socialist	881,951 (2.2%)	—	
1936	**Franklin D. Roosevelt**	Democratic	27,751,597 (60.8%)	523	61.0%
	Alfred M. Landon	Republican	16,679,583 (36.5%)	8	
	William Lemke	Union	882,479 (1.9%)	—	
1940	**Franklin D. Roosevelt**	Democratic	27,244,160 (54.8%)	449	62.5%
	Wendell L. Willkie	Republican	22,305,198 (44.8%)	82	
1944	**Franklin D. Roosevelt**	Democratic	25,602,504 (53.5%)	432	55.9%
	Thomas E. Dewey	Republican	22,006,285 (46.0%)	99	
1948	**Harry S. Truman**	Democratic	24,105,695 (49.5%)	304	53.0%
	Thomas E. Dewey	Republican	21,969,170 (45.1%)	189	
	J. Strom Thurmond	State-Rights Democratic	1,169,021 (2.4%)	38	
	Henry A. Wallace	Progressive	1,156,103 (2.4%)	—	
1952	**Dwight D. Eisenhower**	Republican	33,936,252 (55.1%)	442	63.3%
	Adlai E. Stevenson	Democratic	27,314,992 (44.4%)	89	
1956	**Dwight D. Eisenhower**	Republican	35,575,420 (57.6%)	457	60.6%
	Adlai E. Stevenson	Democratic	26,033,066 (42.1%)	73	
	Other	—	—	1	
1960	**John F. Kennedy**	Democratic	34,227,096 (49.9%)	303	62.8%
	Richard M. Nixon	Republican	34,108,546 (49.6%)	219	
	Other	—	—	15	
1964	**Lyndon B. Johnson**	Democratic	43,126,506 (61.1%)	486	61.7%
	Barry M. Goldwater	Republican	27,176,799 (38.5%)	52	
1968	**Richard M. Nixon**	Republican	31,770,237 (43.4%)	301	60.6%
	Hubert H. Humphrey	Democratic	31,270,533 (42.7%)	191	
	George Wallace	American Indep.	9,906,141 (13.5%)	46	
1972	**Richard M. Nixon**	Republican	47,169,911 (60.7%)	520	55.2%
	George S. McGovern	Democratic	29,170,383 (37.5%)	17	
	Other	—	—	1	
1976	**Jimmy Carter**	Democratic	40,828,587 (50.0%)	297	53.5%
	Gerald R. Ford	Republican	39,147,613 (47.9%)	241	
	Other	—	1,575,459 (2.1%)	—	
1980	**Ronald Reagan**	Republican	43,901,812 (50.7%)	489	52.6%
	Jimmy Carter	Democratic	35,483,820 (41.0%)	49	
	John B. Anderson	Independent	5,719,722 (6.6%)	—	
	Ed Clark	Libertarian	921,188 (1.1%)	—	
1984	**Ronald Reagan**	Republican	54,455,075 (59.0%)	525	53.3%
	Walter Mondale	Democratic	37,577,185 (41.0%)	13	
1988	**George H. W. Bush**	Republican	48,886,000 (53.4%)	426	57.4%
	Michael S. Dukakis	Democratic	41,809,000 (45.6%)	111	
1992	**William J. Clinton**	Democratic	43,728,375 (43.0%)	370	55.0%
	George H. W. Bush	Republican	38,167,416 (38.0%)	168	
	H. Ross Perot	Independent	19,237,247 (19.0%)	—	
1996	**William J. Clinton**	Democratic	45,590,703 (50.0%)	379	48.8%
	Robert Dole	Republican	37,816,307 (41.0%)	159	
	H. Ross Perot	Reform	7,866,284		
2000	**George W. Bush**	Republican	50,456,167 (47.88%)	271	51.2%
	Al Gore	Democratic	50,996,064 (48.39%)	266[e]	
	Ralph Nader	Green	2,864,810 (2.72%)	—	
	Other	—	834,774 (<1%)	—	
2004	**George W. Bush**	Republican	61,873,000 (50.8%)	286	55.3%
	John Kerry	Democratic	58,895,000 (48.3%)	251	
	Ralph Nader	Green	463,653 (<1%)	—	

[e]One District of Columbia Gore elector abstained.

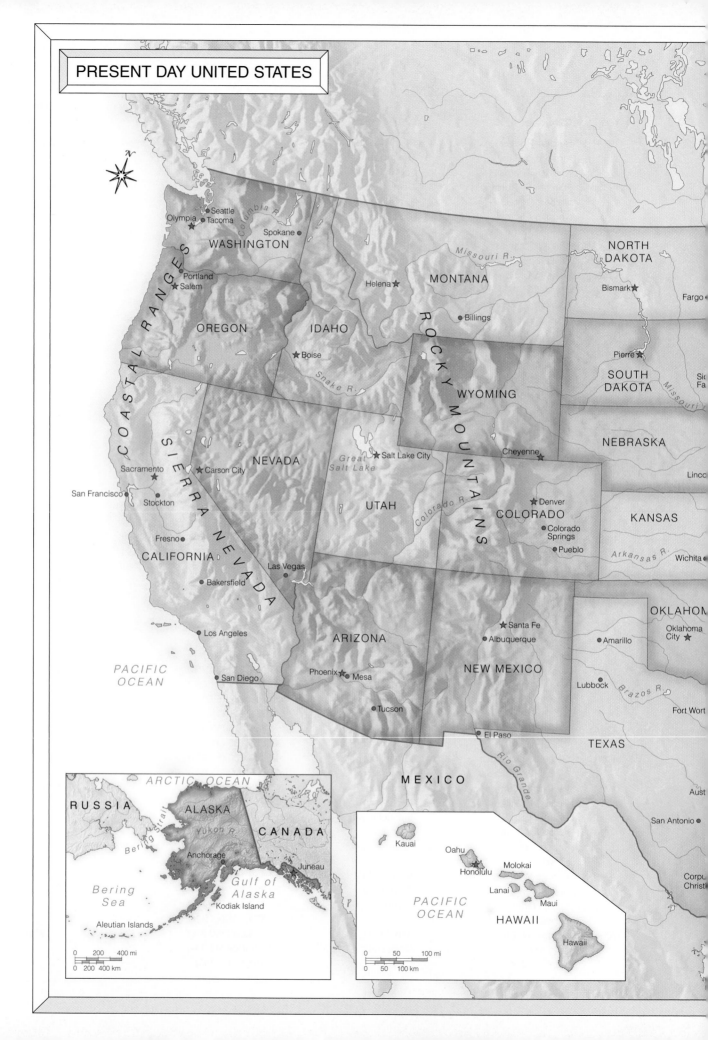

PRESENT DAY UNITED STATES

WASHINGTON
- Seattle
- Olympia ★ • Tacoma
- Spokane •
- Portland
- Salem ★

Columbia R.

OREGON

IDAHO
- Boise ★

Snake R.

MONTANA
- Helena ★
- Billings •

Missouri R.

R O C K Y

M O U N T A I N S

WYOMING

NORTH DAKOTA
- Bismark ★
- Fargo •

SOUTH DAKOTA
- Pierre ★

NEBRASKA
- Linco

C O A S T A L   R A N G E S

S I E R R A   N E V A D A

NEVADA

Great Salt Lake

- Salt Lake City ★

UTAH

Colorado R.

- Cheyenne ★

COLORADO
- Denver ★
- Colorado Springs •
- Pueblo •

KANSAS
- Wichita •

Arkansas R.

- Sacramento ★
- San Francisco •
- Stockton •
- Fresno •

CALIFORNIA

- Bakersfield •

- Las Vegas

- Los Angeles •

- San Diego •

PACIFIC OCEAN

ARIZONA
- Phoenix ★ • Mesa

- Tucson •

- Santa Fe ★
- Albuquerque •

NEW MEXICO

- Amarillo •

- Lubbock •

OKLAHOMA
- Oklahoma City ★

Brazos R.

- Fort Wort

- El Paso •

Rio Grande

TEXAS

Aust

- San Antonio •

MEXICO

- Carson City ★

Corpu
Christi

ARCTIC OCEAN

RUSSIA

ALASKA

CANADA

Yukon R.

Bering Strait

- Anchorage •
- Juneau ★

Gulf of Alaska

- Kodiak Island

Bering Sea

Aleutian Islands

| 0 | 200 | 400 mi |
| 0 | 200 | 400 km |

- Kauai

- Oahu
- Honolulu ★
- Molokai
- Lanai
- Maui

PACIFIC OCEAN

HAWAII

- Hawaii

| 0 | 50 | 100 mi |
| 0 | 50 | 100 km |

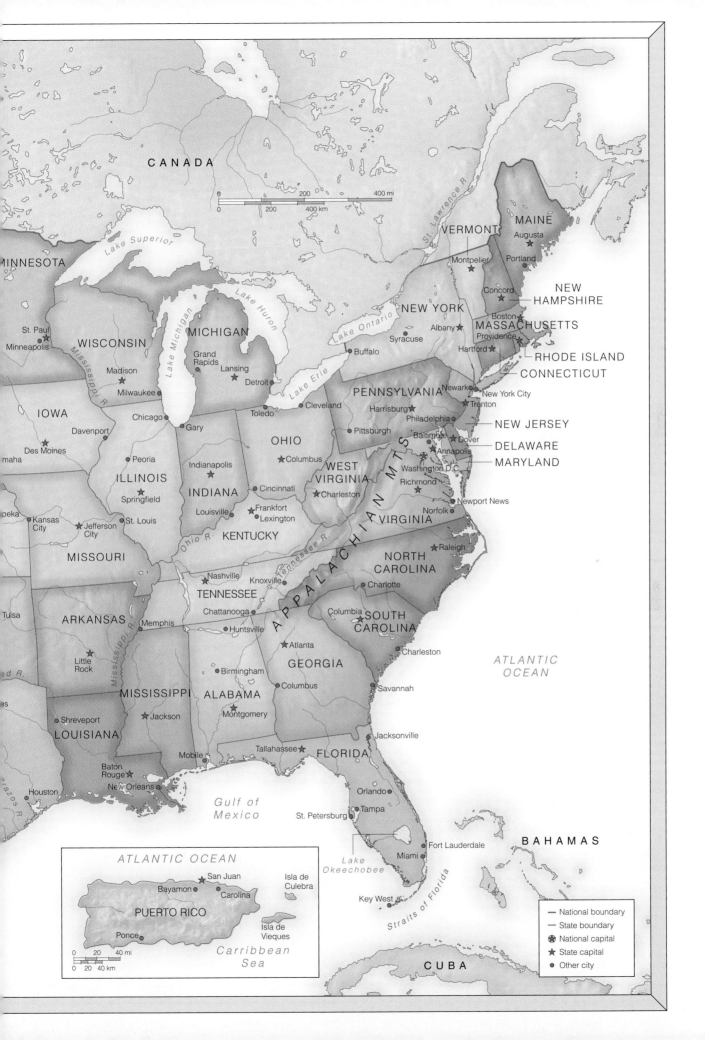

CANADA

Lake Superior

MINNESOTA

St. Paul
Minneapolis

WISCONSIN

Madison

Milwaukee

Lake Michigan

MICHIGAN

Grand Rapids

Lansing

Detroit

Lake Huron

Lake Ontario

St. Lawrence R.

VERMONT

Montpelier

MAINE

Augusta

Portland

Concord

NEW HAMPSHIRE

NEW YORK

Syracuse

Albany

Boston

MASSACHUSETTS

Providence

Hartford

RHODE ISLAND

CONNECTICUT

Buffalo

Lake Erie

PENNSYLVANIA

Newark

New York City

NEW JERSEY

Trenton

DELAWARE

MARYLAND

IOWA

Davenport

Des Moines

maha

Peoria

Chicago

Gary

Toledo

Cleveland

OHIO

Columbus

Harrisburg

Philadelphia

Pittsburgh

Baltimore

Dover

Annapolis

Washington D.C.

ILLINOIS

Springfield

Indianapolis

INDIANA

Cincinnati

WEST VIRGINIA

Charleston

APPALACHIAN MTS.

Richmond

Newport News

Norfolk

peka

Kansas City

Jefferson City

St. Louis

Louisville

Frankfort

Lexington

KENTUCKY

Ohio R.

VIRGINIA

MISSOURI

Nashville

Knoxville

Raleigh

NORTH CAROLINA

Tennessee R.

Tulsa

ARKANSAS

Memphis

TENNESSEE

Chattanooga

Huntsville

Charlotte

Columbia

SOUTH CAROLINA

Mississippi R.

Little Rock

Atlanta

Birmingham

GEORGIA

Charleston

ATLANTIC OCEAN

d R.

MISSISSIPPI

Columbus

Savannah

ALABAMA

Jackson

Montgomery

LOUISIANA

Shreveport

Mobile

Tallahassee

FLORIDA

Jacksonville

as

Baton Rouge

New Orleans

Houston

Gulf of Mexico

St. Petersburg

Orlando

Tampa

Fort Lauderdale

BAHAMAS

Miami

Lake Okeechobee

Brazos R.

ATLANTIC OCEAN

San Juan

Bayamon

Carolina

Isla de Culebra

PUERTO RICO

Ponce

Isla de Vieques

Carribean Sea

Key West

Straits of Florida

CUBA

0   20   40 mi

0   20   40 km

0   200   400 mi

0   200   400 km

National boundary

State boundary

National capital

State capital

Other city

PRESENT DAY WORLD

ARCTIC
OCEAN

GREENLAND

*Beaufort
Sea*

*Baffin
Bay*

ALASKA
(U.S.)

ICELAND

*Bering
Sea*

*Gulf of
Alaska*

CANADA

*Hudson
Bay*

*Labrador
Sea*

ATLANTIC
OCEAN

MOROCCO

UNITED STATES

WESTERN
SAHARA

*Great
Lakes*

MEXICO

*Gulf
of
Mexico*

MAURITANIA

MA

CAPE
VERDE

PACIFIC
OCEAN

BELIZE

SENEGAL

Hawaiian Is. (U.S.)

THE GAMBIA

GUINEA

BU
FA

GUATEMALA

SURINAME

GUINEA
BISSAU

SIERRA
LEONE

Kiribati

EL SALVADOR

FRENCH
GUIANA
(FR.)

LIBERIA

Tokelau

CÔTE
D'IVOIRE

French
Polynesia

Galapagos Is. (EQ.)

Samoa

Cook
Is.

ECUADOR

GHANA

Am.
Samoa

SÃO TOMÉ and
PRÍNCIPÉ

Tonga

PERU

BRAZIL

BOLIVIA

PARAGUAY

CHILE

URUGUAY

ARGENTINA

Falkland Is. (U.K.)

South Georgia (U.K.)

UNITED
STATES

0   200   400   600 mi
0   200   400   600 km

ATLANTIC
OCEAN

BAHAMAS

Turks and
Caicos Is. (U.K.)

CUBA

DOMINICAN
REPUBLIC

U.S. Virgin Is.

Cayman Is. (U.K.)

Antigua and
Barbuda

JAMAICA

HAITI

PUERTO
RICO

Guadaloupe

Dominica

Martinique

HONDURAS

St. Lucia

*Caribbean
Sea*

Barbados

NICARAGUA

St. Vincent and
the Grenadines

COSTA
RICA

Curaco

Grenada

Trinidad
and Tobago

VENEZUELA

GUYANA

*Weddell
Sea*

PANAMA   COLOMBIA

ANTARCTICA

ARCTIC
OCEAN

Svalbard Is. (NOR.)
Novaya
Zemlya
Laptev
Sea
New Siberian Is.
East
Siberian
Sea

Barents
Sea
Kara
Sea

RUSSIA

KAZAKHSTAN
Aral
Sea
Lake
Balkhash

MONGOLIA

Lake
Baikal

Sea
of
Okhotsk

Sakhalin

N. KOREA
S. KOREA
JAPAN

PEOPLE'S
REPUBLIC
OF CHINA

PACIFIC
OCEAN

TUNISIA
ISRAEL
IRAQ
IRAN
AFGHAN.
PAKISTAN
NEPAL
BHUTAN
East
China
Sea

LIBYA
JORDAN
EGYPT
BAHRAIN
QATAR
SAUDI
ARABIA
OMAN
U.A.E.
BANG.
INDIA
BURMA
(MYANMAR)
LAOS
MACAO
TAIWAN
VIETNAM
Philippine
Sea

CHAD
ERITREA
YEMEN
SUDAN
DJIBOUTI
CENT.
AFRICAN REP.
ETHIOPIA
SOMALIA
EQUA.
GUINEA
UGANDA
KENYA
DEM. REP.
OF
CONGO
RWANDA
BURUNDI
TANZANIA
Arabian
Sea
Bay of
Bengal
THAILAND
CAMBODIA
SRI
LANKA
South
China
Sea
PHILIPPINES
Northern
Mariana
Is.
Marshall
Is.

MALAYSIA
BRUNEI
SINGAPORE
PAPUA
NEW GUINEA
Nauru

ANGOLA
ZAMBIA
MALAWI
INDONESIA
Solomon Is.
Tuvalu

NAMBIA
ZIMB.
MADAGASCAR
MAURITIUS
INDIAN
OCEAN
Coral
Sea
Vanuatu
Fiji

BOTSWANA
New Caledonia (FR.)

MOZAMBIQUE
AUSTRALIA
Tasman
Sea

SOUTH
AFRICA
SWAZILAND
LESOTHO

NEW
ZEALAND

N

NORWAY
FINLAND
SWEDEN
ESTONIA
North
Sea
LATVIA
LITHUANIA
IRELAND
DENMARK
Baltic
Sea
RUSSIA
UNITED
KINGDOM
NETHERLANDS
POLAND
BELARUS
ATLANTIC
OCEAN
BELGIUM
GERMANY
LUX.
CZECH
REPUBLIC
LIECHT.
SLOVAKIA
UKRAINE
FRANCE
SWITZ.
AUSTRIA
HUNGARY
MOLDOVA
SLOVENIA
ROMANIA
Caspian
Sea
PORTUGAL
CROATIA
BOSNIA
HERZ.
SERBIA
BULGARIA
Black Sea
GEORGIA
SPAIN
ITALY
Adriatic Sea
MACEDONIA
ARMENIA
AZERBAIJAN
ALBANIA
TURKEY
MONTENEGRO
GREECE
SYRIA
IRAQ
Aegean
Sea
CYPRUS
Mediterranean
Sea
LEBANON

0   1000   2000   3000 mi
0   1000 2000 3000 km

0   200 400 600 800 mi
0 200 400 600 800 km

Glossary

Abdicate   To give up a throne or high position, to renounce sovereign power. 73

Accommodationist   A person who adapts or modifies a position to ease conflict rather than holding fast to convictions in the face of opposition. 427

Acculturate   To change the behavior of a group to conform to the behavior of the larger society. 434

Adage   A familiar saying that embodies a common observation or a wise idea. 165

Aliens   Foreign-born residents of the United States who have not been naturalized as U.S. citizens. 491

Allies   Members of an alliance, such as the military coalition led by the United States, the Soviet Union, and Great Britain during World War II. 544

Almshouse   A privately financed home for the poor; a poorhouse. 124

Amphibious landing   A military assault that begins on the water and ends on land. 305

Anarchists   Persons who reject all forms of government as inherently oppressive and undesirable. 415

Annexation   Addition of territory that had belonged to one nation into another nation. 302

Annulment   An official pronouncement nullifying a marriage, or declaring it invalid. 24

Antebellum   The extended period before a war; usually refers to the several decades immediately before the American Civil War. 257

Anthropology   The study of the origin and development of humankind. 426

Anti-Federalists   A diverse and unsuccessful coalition that opposed ratification of the Constitution and feared the increased power of the proposed central government. The Anti-Federalists were named by their opponents, the Federalists. 211

Antisemitism   Prejudice against Jews. 389

Aqueduct   An elevated conduit or channel built to transfer water flowing from a distant source, using gravity. 000

Archaic period   The second long stage of North American habitation, covering about 7,000 years, from roughly 8,000 BCE to 1000 BCE (or from 10,000 to 3,000 years ago). During this period, inhabitants adapted to diverse local environments, gathering plants and hunting smaller animals than during the previous Paleo-Indian period. 6

Archipelago   A group of islands, such as the Hawaiian archipelago. 12

Ardent   Passionate, devoted, zealous, fiery. 41

Armistice   A truce in a military conflict; a temporary halt in hostilities by agreement between the opposing sides. 439

Asiento   A contract negotiated by the Spanish crown (between 1595 and 1789) with other European powers such as Portugal, France, England, and the Netherlands to provide a fixed number of slaves annually to Spain's American colonies for a set payment. 82

Assembly line   A form of industrial production popularized by the Ford Motor Company in which workers perform one task repeatedly as the products they are jointly assembling move along a conveyor. 456

Atlatl   A weighted, handheld device that enabled early Native Americans to throw spears with added power and velocity. 7

Avid   Eager, greedy, enthusiastic. 169

Axis   A political alignment or alliance, such as the military coalition between Germany, Italy, and Japan during World War II. 532

Babel   A city described in the Old Testament where constructing a tower was made impossible by the confusion of varied languages. This term from the Book of Genesis is used to describe any scene of clamor and confusion. 110

Baby boom   The period of increased U.S. childbirths from roughly the early 1940s to the early 1960s. 575

Baby boomers   The generation of Americans born during the era from the early 1940s to the early 1960s. 665

Barracoon   An enclosure or barrack used for the confinement of slaves before their forced deportation from the African coast. 92

Bill of Rights   A set of amendments assuring basic rights, proposed by James Madison to help ensure acceptance of the newly drafted Constitution, and based on suggestions from the states. Ten of the twelve items passed by Congress were ratified by the states in 1791. Taken together, these first ten amendments to the Constitution became known as the Bill of Rights. 214

Black Codes   Southern state laws passed after the Civil War to limit the rights and actions of newly liberated African Americans. 360

Blacklist   A (figurative or real) list of persons to be denied jobs because of their alleged loyalty to a particular cause or institution. 414

Black power   The slogan used by young black nationalists in the mid- and late 1960s. 603

"Bloody shirt"   A partisan rallying cry used to stir up or revive sectional or party animosity after the American Civil War; for example, post–Civil War Republicans "waved the bloody shirt," associating some Democrats with a treasonous acceptance of secession during the war, while opponents had spilled their blood for the Union. 397

Bolsheviks   The Communist revolutionaries who overthrew the Russian czar in 1917 and established the Union of Soviet Socialist Republics (USSR). 480

Boston marriages   Unions of two women based on long-term emotional bonds in which the women live together as if married to each other. 457

Braceros   Mexican nationals working in the United States in low-wage jobs as part of a temporary work program between 1942 and 1964. (The *Bracero* program was established by an executive agreement between the presidents of Mexico and the United States, providing Mexican agricultural labor in the Southwest and the Pacific Northwest.) 578

Brunt   The principal force, shock, or stress, especially of an attack. 203

Bull Moosers   Supporters of Theodore Roosevelt in the 1912 presidential election when he broke from the Republican party and ran as a third-party candidate on the ticket of the Progressive (or Bull Moose) party. 464

Burgess   A representative elected to the popular branch of the colonial legislature in either Virginia or Maryland. 44

Cajuns   The Louisiana word for French-speaking people from Acadia (Nova Scotia) who were forced to move south in 1755 during the French and Indian War. Many of these refugees eventually moved to French Louisiana, where they have had a lasting impact on the culture. 119

Canal locks   An enclosure on a canal or other waterway equipped with gates that can be closed so that boats can be raised or lowered by adjusting the water, in order to pass from one level to another. 265

Capitalism   The now almost worldwide economic system of private ownership of property and profit-seeking corporations. 509

Capitulation   The act of formal surrender, upon specified terms. 226

Carpetbaggers   A negative term applied by Southerners to Northerners who moved to the South after the Civil War to pursue political or economic opportunities. 360

Causeway   A raised roadway crossing above open water or wet ground. 10

Cede   To surrender possession of. 312

Checks and balances   The rules controlling interactions among the executive, legislative, and judicial branches of government, making up a novel system designed to prevent any single branch from overreaching its powers, as set forth in the Constitution in 1787. 208

Civic organizations   Membership organizations that exist to further the public life and welfare of a community. 683

Coalition   An alliance of parties, factions, or nations. 279

Coffle   A procession or train of enslaved prisoners, bound together for travel (from the Arabic word for "caravan"). 92

Cold War   The conflict and competition between the United States and the Soviet Union (and their respective allies) that emerged after 1945 and lasted until 1989. 550

Colonialism   The centuries-old system of mostly European nations controlling and governing peoples and lands outside of Europe. 558

Columbian Exchange   The significant two-way interchange of plants, animals, microbes, and people that occurred once Christopher Columbus established regular contact by sea between the eastern and western hemispheres. For thousands of years before 1492, despite occasional encounters, these two separate and different "worlds" had remained isolated from each other. 17

Comfort women   Women, mostly Chinese and Korean, forced into sexual slavery by Japanese troops during World War II. 547

Commercial farming   Agricultural system producing for markets and intended to yield a profit after crops are sold. 312

Common school system   Tax-supported public education to provide elementary schooling free to young children. 297

Communism   A totalitarian form of government, grounded in the theories of German philosopher Karl Marx and the practices of V. I. Lenin in Russia, that eliminated private ownership of property in supposed pursuit of complete human equality; the system of government also featured a centrally directed economy and the absolute rule of a small group of leaders. 550

Communitarian   relating to communities practicing communitarianism, a form of cooperative living in small groups. 299

Conclave   A private meeting, secret assembly, gathering, or convention. 211

Conservationists   Advocates of conserving and protecting the natural world through the use of renewable natural resources. 462

Conspicuous consumption   A term coined by the American social theorist Thorstein Veblen to describe the behavior of wealthy persons who flaunt their status through their purchase of fine clothes, large houses, fancy cars, and other highly visible material goods. 429

Consumer Economy   An economic system in which most people work for wages, which they use to purchase manufactured goods and foodstuffs. 486

Containment   The U.S. policy during the Cold War of trying to halt the expansion of Soviet and communist influences. 556

Contraband   Goods (or, during the Civil War, slaves) seized from the enemy during war. 343

Cooperatives   Organizations that produce or market goods and that are owned collectively by people who share in their profits or benefits. 376

Coverture   French term for the dependent and legal status of a woman during marriage. Under English law, the male family head received legal rights, and his wife lost independent status, becoming, in legal terms, a *femme covert*. 68

Creoles   People born in the United States but retaining a strong cultural identification with their forebears; especially persons of mixed Spanish or French and African descent speaking a dialect of Spanish or French. 258

Czar   The monarch (king) of Russia before the 1917 revolution. 140

De facto government   A government that is exercising power as if legally constituted. 156

Détente The lessening of military or diplomatic tensions, as between the United States and the Soviet Union. 617

Diaspora The dispersion of a population abroad, whether forced or voluntary. The term is often applied to Jewish settlement outside the eastern Mediterranean region, and to the spread of Africans across the Americas, due to the Atlantic slave trade. 108

Dispossession Act of taking land or other property from a group of people. 311

Don't ask, don't tell A policy established by the Clinton administration allowing gays and lesbians to serve in the military so long as they do not disclose their sexual orientation. 667

Double V The campaign by African Americans during the Second World War to fight simultaneously for victory against fascism abroad and racial discrimination at home. 543

Dust Bowl The plains regions of Oklahoma, Texas, Colorado, and New Mexico affected by severe drought in the 1930s. 512

Ecology The web of interconnections between organisms (particularly humans) and the natural environment. 265

Electoral College An intricate system in which each state appoints electors, equal in number to its representation in Congress, to elect the president and vice president. The electoral college is a provision of the Constitution (Article II, Section 1) because the framers were unwilling to approve the direct election of president and vice president. This group, or "college," of electors still makes the selection, voting according to prior party commitments rather than individual choice. 209

Emancipation National or state-sponsored program to free slaves. 345

Embargo A government order prohibiting the entry or departure of commercial ships from a port. 245

Emigrants People who leave one place and move to another. 286

Encomienda The Spanish encomienda system, imposed in Spain's American empire, requiring Indian communities to supply labor or pay tribute to a local colonial overlord (identified as an encomendero). 63

Enfranchised citizens Persons who are entitled to vote in government elections. 251

Entente The alliance of Britain, France, and Russia, later joined by the United States, during World War I. 467

Entrepreneur A person who organizes, manages, or assumes the risks in a business venture. 255

Evangelical Protestants Christians who emphasize the importance of personal faith, as well as seeking new converts. 292

Exposé A piece of investigative journalism that exposes corruption in government, business, or other institutions. 590

Extractive enterprises Businesses that harvest or extract natural products from the land or sea (fish, timber, minerals, crops). 387

Fall line The geographical division between the Piedmont and the Atlantic coastal plain where the land slopes sharply to the sea. 315

Family wage A level of income sufficient for an individual worker, usually a man, to support a spouse and family through a single salary. 524

Fascism A form of right-wing dictatorship exalting nation and race above the individual. 348

Fatigue work Unskilled manual labor. 000

Federalists A coalition of nationalist leaders who favored creating a stronger central government to replace the Articles of Confederation; they labeled their opponents as Anti-Federalists in the late 1780s. The strongest essays endorsing their proposed new Constitution were entitled *The Federalist Papers.* 211

Federation An alliance or compact between political units that agree to surrender certain powers to a central authority while still retaining other powers. 193

Feminism The belief that women and men are of equal value and that gender roles are, to a considerable degree, created by society rather than being simply natural. 608

Fireside chats The broadcasts by President Franklin Delano Roosevelt during which he spoke directly to American families, often gathered around a radio in their living room. 517

Flappers Young women in the 1910s and 1920s who rebelled against the gender conventions of the era with respect to fashion and behavior. 486

Flotilla Any sizeable fleet of ships, or, more specifically, a naval term for a unit consisting of two or more squadrons of small warships. 134

Foreclosure A legal process of seizing private property, such as a home or farm, in order to pay off a debtor's creditors. 203

Foundling home A residence for orphaned children. 449

Free trade International economic relations characterized by multinational investment and a reduction or elimination of tariffs. 534

Free labor ideology The ideas, represented most forcefully by the antebellum Republican party, that workers should profit from their own labor and that slavery is wrong. 315

Freighter Person, vehicle, or vessel that transports goods. 317

Fusion A combination, alliance. 432

Geographic mobility The phenomenon of people moving frequently from one place to another. 433

Glacier A large body of ice that endures for centuries, advancing or receding slowly as climactic conditions change. 5

Globalization The process of integration—economic, but also cultural—of different parts of the world into a more unified system of trade and communication. 13

Grassroots democracy A political system that relies on the active participation of people at the local level. 423

Great Awakening The title that was applied, in retrospect, to the interdenominational Christian revival that swept Britain's North American colonies between the 1730s and the 1750s, inspired at first by the preaching of Jonathan Edwards and George Whitefield. (A religious revival in the early nineteenth century became known as the Second Great Awakening.) 126

Great Migration The movement of African Americans out of the South to northern cities, particularly during World War I. 474

Guerrilla war A conflict fought not on the basis of conventional warfare, but rather by mobilizing small groups of fighters who attack and harass superior forces. 288

Gun control   The legal regulation of firearms. 665

Hard currency   Coins made of precious metals such as silver, gold, or nickel, as opposed to paper bills; also called hard money or specie. 219

Harry   To torment an enemy by destructive raids or repeated small attacks. 186

Hayseeds   A derogatory term applied to rural people deemed uneducated and naive (in contrast to self-proclaimed sophisticated city dwellers). 429

Headright   Under the headright system, English colonial governments granted a fixed amount of land, usually 50 acres, to any head of household for every family member or hired hand that person brought into the colony. Sometimes fewer acres were granted for women and children on the grounds that they would clear and plant less land. 44

Hinterland   A rural area that is linked to a nearby city through trade networks. 253

Hobo   Migrant worker or poor and homeless vagrant who traveled on trains from location to location, usually in search of employment. 512

Hoovervilles   Shantytowns, named for president Hoover and occupied largely by people who lost their homes and farms during the Great Depression. 452

Humanitarian intervention   Warfare undertaken ostensibly in furtherance of humanitarian objectives. 670

Iberian   Relating to Europe's Iberian Peninsula, the location of Spain and Portugal. 32

Impressment   A policy that authorizes the seizure of persons or private property in the service of a government. 219

Indenture   A document binding one person to work for another for a given period of time. Indentured servants received food, shelter, and clothing, plus "freedom dues" when their terms of service ended to help them get started independently. 86

Injunction   A court order prohibiting a party from certain kinds of behavior—for example, barring a labor union from striking. 431

Internal improvements   Turnpikes, canals, bridges, seaports, and other projects intended to facilitate trade and transportation within the country. 251

Iroquois League   A Native American confederacy, located in central New York, originally composed of the Cayuga, Mohawk, Oneida, Onondaga, and Seneca Indians, and later including the Tuscarora as well. 38

Isthmus   A narrow strip of land connecting two larger land areas (such as the isthmus of Panama). 18

Itinerant minister   A preacher who travels from place to place without invitation, or who visits a circuit of churches on a regular basis. 129

Jim Crow   The name given to the set of legal institutions that ensured the segregation of nonwhite people in the South. 408

Juke joint   A small, inexpensive establishment where patrons could eat and drink or dance to music from a jukebox. *Juke* is a word of West African origin popularized by African Americans in the Sea Islands of South Carolina. 486

Kachina   An Indian religious system, inspired by Mexican traditions, and present in the American Southwest for more than 800 years. The kachina cult used masks for group performances associated with rain, curing, fertility, warfare, and the ancestors. Among many Pueblo and Hopi Indians, this tradition was epitomized by kachina (or katsina) dolls. 64

Kayak   A highly maneuverable, decked-in canoe used by Native Alaskans for travel and hunting. The light frame is covered with skins, and the paddle has a blade at each end. Popular modern versions of this traditional boat are made with canvas or fiberglass. 140

Kickbacks   Money paid illegally in return for favors (for example, to a politician by a person or business that has received government contracts). 367

Laissez-Faire   a belief in little or no government interference in the economy. 000

Land speculation   The act of buying land in the hope of making a profit by selling it in the future. 228

Liberalism   Originally a nineteenth-century belief in free-market capitalism; in the twentieth century, a belief in using the power of the federal government to increase opportunity and provisions for the least affluent citizens; by the twenty-first century, increasingly a belief in multicultural tolerance and inclusion. 644

Litigation   A lawsuit or legal contest. 201

Longevity   Length of life, a long duration of life. 214

Manumission   A formal emancipation from slavery; the act (by an individual owner or government authority) of granting freedom to an enslaved person or persons. 101

Market Revolution   The combined effects of transportation innovation, technological change, and economic growth, especially during the first half of the nineteenth century. 254

McCarthyism   The political campaign led by Senator Joseph McCarthy (R-Wisconsin) to blame liberals at home for setbacks to U.S. interests abroad, due to what he considered liberals' sympathies with communism. 562

Meager   Thin, sparse, scanty; lacking fullness, richness, or strength. 38

Mercantilism   A commercial policy that sought to achieve economic self-sufficency and a favorable balance of trade (often by planting colonies) in order to promote a country's prosperity, strength, and independence. Rival European imperial powers favored the strategy of mercantilism in the seventeenth and eighteenth centuries. 57

Merchant-capitalist   An entrepreneur who hires workers to perform piecework in the worker's home. 255

Mesoamerica   The transitional region between North and South America, composed of Mexico and Central America. 7

Mestizo   A person of mixed European and American Indian ancestry. 63

Middle ground   The geographical region occupied by diverse cultural groups engaged in trade. 426

Middle passage   For European slave ships, the middle passage was the second of three legs in the triangular round-trip voyage from Europe to Africa to America and back to Europe. For enslaved Africans, the middle passage came to mean not only the transatlantic journey itself, but the entire process of removal from an African homeland and ultimate sale to an American master. 91

Military-industrial complex The term given by President Dwight D. Eisenhower to the military arms industry nexus. 583

Monetary policy Government policies designed to affect the national economy through bank lending policies, interest rates, and control of the amount of money in circulation. 218

Most-favored-nation status A designation allowing countries to export their products to the United States with tariffs no greater than those levied against most other nations. 669

Muckrakers The name given to a group of investigative journalists in the early twentieth century whose exposés often challenged corporate and government power. 458

Mulatto A person of mixed European and African ancestry; the first-generation offspring of a Caucasian and a Negroid parent. 63

Muse In Greek mythology, one of the nine sister goddesses who preside over music, poetry, and the arts. 47

Mutual aid society An organization of people who voluntarily pool their resources in order to help members in times of illness or other personal crises. 284

NAACP National Association for the Advancement of Colored People, founded in 1909. 564

National security state The reorientation of the U.S. government and its budget after 1945 toward a primary focus on military and intelligence capabilities. 566

Nativists American citizens born in the United States who oppose further immigration, especially from anywhere outside northwestern Europe. 295

New Democrats Members of the Democratic party, many of them organized in the Democratic Leadership Council, who espouse center to center-right policies. 666

Nisei Japanese Americans born in the United States of Japanese immigrant parents. 535

NSC-68 The 1950 directive of the National Security Council that called for rolling back, rather than merely containing, Soviet and communist influences. 566

Nuclear family A basic family structure that has parents and their children at its center, or nucleus, but does not include grandparents, cousins, or other relatives. 284

Nullification The doctrine that a state has the right to ignore or nullify certain federal laws with which it disagrees. 272

Okies Migrants from Oklahoma who left the state during the Dust Bowl period in search of work. 513

Operative A machine tender. 624

Ordnance Cannons, artillery, and by extension general military supplies including weapons, ammunition, combat vehicles, and tools. 168

Overspeculation Buying stocks and land that turn out to be not as valuable as the investors had originally believed. 293

Pachucos Young Mexican American members of neighborhood gangs. 543

Paleo Indians The earliest human inhabitants of North America, who first migrated to the continent from Siberia more than 15,000 years ago. Faced with a warming climate and the disappearance of many large game animals roughly 10,000 years ago (8000 BCE), they learned to hunt smaller animals and adapted to varied local conditions during the Archaic Period (to c. 1000 BCE). 6

Parochial schools Schools sponsored by the Catholic Church or some other religious denomination (in contrast to public schools). 428

Patronage System that rewards political supporters with jobs and other favors. 335

Pest house In colonial times, a shelter to quarantine those possibly infected with contagious diseases (such as newcomers arriving in American ports from Africa or Europe) to prevent the spread of shipborne pestilence. 97

Placate To soothe or pacify, usually by granting concessions. 10

Planned obsolescence A concept whereby producers intend for their products to eventually become obsolete or outdated and require replacement, thus perpetuating a cycle of production and consumption. 436

Pocket veto An indirect veto of a legislative bill made when an executive (such as a president or governor) simply leaves the bill unsigned, so that it dies after the adjournment of the legislature. 358

Political machine A group that effectively exercises control over a political party, usually at the local level and organized around precincts and patronage. 490

Popular sovereignty The idea that residents of a state should be able to make decisions on crucial issues, such as whether or not to legalize slavery. 321

Postbellum Period after a war, especially after the Civil War, 1865–1877. 363

Precedent An earlier occurrence of something similar; something done or said setting an example or pattern that can justify later actions. 18

Preemptive attack A form of military aggression on the part of one country designed to thwart a perceived imminent attack from another. 438

Presidio A military garrison or fortified settlement in an area under Spanish control. 111

Privateers Ships (and their crew members) licensed to harass enemy shipping in wartime. 76

Producer economy An economic system dominated by individuals who are self-producers of manufactured goods and foodstuffs rather than employees working for wages. 486

Progressivism A notion of political reform central to the "Progressive Era" (the first two decades of the twentieth century), when urban reformers with a faith in progress sought to address local and national social problems through political and civic means. 458

Public domain Lands owned by the federal government. 424

Putting out System in which workers labor in their homes to produce goods for a merchant, who usually provides raw materials and pays them not by the hour but by each piece they finish. 255

Quitrent   A fixed rent paid annually by a tenant to a proprietor or landowner. 69

Race suicide   A fear articulated by Theodore Roosevelt and others that the low birthrate of Anglo-Saxon Americans, along with the high birthrate of immigrants from southern and eastern Europe, would result in a population in which "inferior" peoples would outnumber the "American racial stock". 454

Realignment   Change in a coalition or alliance between political parties. 308

Reconstruction   the U.S. government policies to rebuild the South after the Civil War and reintegrate it with the rest of the nation. 358

Redemption system   An eighteenth-century arrangement in which potential migrants in Europe signed up with an agent who agreed to pay for their Atlantic passage. Reaching America, the newcomer signed a pact to work for several years for an employer. In exchange for much-needed labor, the employer agreed to pay back the shipper, "redeeming" the original loan that had been made to the immigrant "redemptioner." 117

Red lining   A business practice in which lending institutions deny credit to racial or ethnic minorities who live in poor neighborhoods. 577

Redress   A remedy for a wrong; a correction or reparation. As a verb, to redress means to correct, to set right, or to remove the cause of a grievance. 149

Red Scare   Post–World War I repression of socialists, communists, and other left-wing radicals ("Reds"). 483

Regressive tax   A tax that decreases in rate as the base increases, so that someone with a large holding pays a relatively small amount. A fixed tax of $100 is regressive, since persons with $1,000 or $1 million shoulder very different relative burdens. This is the opposite of a progressive tax, where those with less pay at a lower rate. 77

Rejuvenation   To restore the youthful vigor or appearance of a thing or a person. 435

Republican mother   A wife and mother whose primary role is caring for and socializing future citizens (her children); an ideal favored by some elites after the American Revolution. 232

Requisition   To request, demand, or formally require something of someone. 36

Restitution   Giving back to the rightful owner something that has been lost or taken away. 305

Restoration   The political act of restoring monarchy to England in 1660 after the brief experiment of the Puritan Commonwealth, placing Charles II upon the throne once occupied by his Stuart father, Charles I. The following years, until the end of the Stuart family dynasty in 1688, are known in English culture and politics as the *Restoration Era*. 66

Rogue nations   A label used by the U.S. government to refer to nations it considers hostile, unpredictable, and potentially dangerous. 674

Rosie the Riveter   A heroic symbol of women workers on the homefront during World War II. 539

Sachem   Algonquin Indian term for a Native American leader or chief. 70

Scalawag   A negative term applied by southern Democrats after the Civil War to any white Southerner who allied with the Republican party. 360

Secession   Withdrawal of a state from the authority of the federal government. 250

Second New Deal   The agenda of policies and programs initiated by President Franklin Delano Roosevelt beginning in 1935 that was intended to strengthen the lot of American workers while simultaneously preserving the capitalist system. 518

Sedentary farming   Activity that requires cultivators to live in one place for extended periods of time. 228

Sedition   Acts that stir up rebellion against a government. 222

Separation of powers   The novel idea that the powers of the three branches of government—legislative, executive, and judicial—should be kept separate from one another, so that each can check and balance the powers of the other two. 208

Sharecropping   A system in which landless farmers grown crops on another person's land in exchange for a portion of the crops. 364

Sit-down strike   A strategy employed by workers agitating for better wages and working conditions in which they stop working and simply sit down, thus ceasing production and preventing strikebreakers from entering a facility to assume their jobs. 526

Sit-in   A form of civil disobedience in which activists sit down somewhere in violation of law or policy in order to challenge discriminatory practices or laws. The tactic originated during labor struggles in the 1930s and was used effectively in the civil rights movement in 1960. 581

Social Darwinism   A late-nineteenth-century variation on the theories of British naturalist Charles Darwin, promoting the idea that only the "fittest" individuals will, or deserve to, survive (i.e., the idea that society operates on principles of evolutionary biology). 397

Speakeasies   Establishments where alcohol was illegally sold during the Prohibition era. 490

Sphere of influence   An area dominated by the military, economic, and cultural power of another country. 439

Squatters   People who live on land that they do not own, without the landowner's permission. 226

Staples   Important trade items or foodstuffs. 123

Steerage   Section of a ship providing the cheapest accommodations for passengers. 000

Subsidies   Government assistance in the form of tax breaks or cash bonuses given to a person or business. 256

Subsistence homesteading   Farming to provide only for the necessities of one's family. 312

Substitute   During war, a man paid to serve in combat in another man's place. 340

Suffrage   The right to vote. 373

Sunbelt   The band of states from the Southeast to the Southwest that experienced rapid economic and population growth during and after World War II. 561

Sweatshop   A small factory where employees work long hours for low wages under poor conditions (especially in the garment industry). 659

Swords into plowshares   Turning weapons of war into productive implements, such as plows, based on the biblical passage in Isaiah 2:4. 193

Tariff   A government tax on imported goods. 218

Tejanos   Spanish-speaking residents of the Mexican (and later, U.S.) state of Texas. 266

Temperance   A social movement embracing either total opposition to alcohol consumption or support for its moderate use. 295

Tenant farmer   A farmer who raises livestock and crops on land leased from wealthier owners. 150

Tenements   Densely inhabited apartment buildings generally found in crowded and poor areas of cities where immigrants and ethnic minorities lived in unhealthy conditions. 310

Texians   The name used by U.S.-born citizens who lived in the Mexican state of Texas. 266

Theocracy   A government by officials who are regarded as divinely guided. 637

Tithe   A levy or donation (generally a tenth part) given to provide support, usually for a church. 24

Total war   The attacking of both military and civilian targets. 543

Townsend Plan   A proposal by Dr. Francis Townsend in 1934 for a 2 percent national sales tax that would fund a guaranteed pension of $200 per month for Americans older than age 60. 521

Travois   A French Canadian term for the A-frame device used by many traditional Native Americans to draw heavy loads over long distances. It consisted of two trailing poles attached to a dog or horse and supporting a platform to carry belongings. 113

Treaties   Legally binding documents ratified by nations pledging them to engage or refrain from engaging in certain actions or policies. 410

Triangular trade   The huge Atlantic slave trade that linked Europe, Africa, and the Americas from the sixteenth to the nineteenth century. Ships from Europe sailed to Africa to exchange trade goods for slaves. On their second leg (the infamous "middle passage"), these vessels transported the enslaved captives to ports in the Caribbean or on the American mainland. They completed their clockwise voyage by returning to Europe, usually carrying colonial staples produced by slaves, such as sugar, rice, or tobacco. 91

Trickle-down economics   An economic concept whereby the government aids the wealthiest strata as well as large corporations in the belief that the benefits of this aid will "trickle down" to the middle and lower classes. 489

Truman Doctrine   President Truman's March 1947 speech articulating the new policy of containment. 556

Trusts   A combination of firms or corporations created for the purpose of reducing competition and controlling prices throughout an industry. 399

Tundra   A cold and treeless plain typical of arctic and sub-arctic regions. 5

Two-party system   A system of government characterized by two major political parties that compete against each other in "winner take all" elections. 218

Unicameral legislature   A legislative body that has only one chamber, or house. 69

Utopian   Relating to communities organized to strive for ideal social and political conditions. 299

Vagrancy   The state of being unemployed and wandering from place to place. 311

Victorians   Middle-class (chiefly Protestant) people living during the reign of Queen Victoria of England (1837–1901) who identified with British culture and who professed social values such as self-control, sexual restraint, and personal ambition. 427

Vigilantes   People who seek to take the law into their own hands and punish or intimidate alleged criminals or persons who resist a certain social order (for example, white supremacy). 302

Wage slavery   The idea that wage earners are exploited by employers as harshly as slaves are exploited by their owners. 316

War chest   A fund accumulated to finance a war or earmarked to conduct some specific action or campaign. 195

War hawks   Politicians who favor specific forms of military action as a tool of U.S. foreign policy. 245

War on drugs   The global campaign spearheaded by the federal government to eliminate the production of illegal drugs and their importation into the United States, and its domestic counterpart in which drug violations are treated harshly by the legal and criminal justice system. 658

Watergate   The Washington, D.C., hotel-office complex where agents of President Nixon's reelection campaign broke into Democratic Party headquarters in 1972. Nixon helped cover up the break-in, and the subsequent political scandal was called "Watergate." 617

Welfare reform   The legislative campaign in the 1960s through the 1990s to abolish Aid to Families with Dependent Children in favor of a program that sets limits on the amount of time a poor family can receive government aid (culminating in the Temporary Aid to Needy Families Act of 1996). 635

Welfare state   A nation in which the government provides a "safety net" of entitlements and benefits for citizens unable to economically provide for themselves. 510

Wildcat banks   Small banks that make loans unsupervised by the state or other financial institutions. 267

Wobblies   Members of the Industrial Workers of the World (IWW), a radical labor union formed in 1905. 460

Yellow journalism   Newspaper articles, images, and editorials that exploit, distort, or exaggerate the news in order to inflame public opinion. 437

Yeoman   A farmer who owns a modest amount of land (but no slaves). 123

Yiddish   A language derived largely from German spoken mainly by Jews from eastern Europe. 509

Zoot suits   Distinctive clothing in the 1940s worn largely by Mexican American and African American men, characterized by flared pants, long coats, and wide-brimmed hats. 543

Credits

Index